Realities and Fantasies of German Female Leadership

Women and Gender in German Studies

Series editor:
Elisabeth Krimmer (*University of California, Davis*)

Realities and Fantasies of German Female Leadership

From Maria Antonia of Saxony to Angela Merkel

Edited by
Elisabeth Krimmer and Patricia Anne Simpson

CAMDEN HOUSE
Rochester, New York

First published 2019 by Camden House
Reprinted in paperback 2023

Camden House is an imprint of Boydell & Brewer Inc.
668 Mt. Hope Avenue, Rochester, NY 14620, USA
and of Boydell & Brewer Limited
PO Box 9, Woodbridge, Suffolk IP12 3DF, UK
www.boydellabdbrewer.com

Paperback ISBN-13: 978-1-64024-156-8
Hardcover ISBN-13: 978-1-64014-065-3

Library of Congress Cataloging-in-Publication Data

CIP data is available from the Library of Congress.

Contents

Part III. Women and Political Power in the Twentieth and Twenty-First Centuries

Acknowledgments

THE IDEA FOR THIS BOOK emerged from a combination of raised expectations and shattered hopes about women and high-profile political leadership in the second decade of the twenty-first century. Public discourse was replete with voices intent on publicly humiliating women: those in power, those aspiring to attain it, and those who accused powerful men of sexist behavior. Women across continents spoke out against systemic patterns of sexual harassment and abuse, culminating in the #MeToo movement that continues to indict the pervasiveness of gender-based discrimination and all forms of violence against women. All the while, a presumption persists that the word "leader" denotes masculinity. When women do ascend to positions of power, they often do so by birth and family or wealth and privilege. Further, assumptions about biology and leadership attributes relegate women to roles that demand behaviors that are maternal, nurturing, and conciliatory. These gendered behaviors are reinforced in echo chambers constructed by literary, historical, and media cultures. When individuals or social movements challenge them, gender stereotypes are often invoked to discredit or dismiss the rabble-rousers. While the disassociation between the words female and leadership may be widespread, the analysis of German female leaders yields insights into a national culture that both supports and undermines women with power.

Toward developing those insights, we began with a series of panels and a roundtable presented at the German Studies Association (GSA) conference in 2016. Many of the chapters in this volume emerged from that forum. We would like to express our gratitude to the contributors who undertook this collective effort with us.

This publication would not have been possible without moral and financial support from our academic homes. We are grateful for the generous support of an ENHANCE grant from the College of Arts and Sciences at the University of Nebraska–Lincoln, an institution committed to leading with research. As in previous coediting efforts, we have benefited from the insights and feedback of Jim Walker and his colleagues at Camden House. Our appreciation extends to the anonymous readers whose careful reading and constructive criticism helped advance this book toward publication.

Introduction

Elisabeth Krimmer and Patricia Anne Simpson

Dᴜʀɪɴɢ Hɪʟʟᴀʀʏ Cʟɪɴᴛᴏɴ's historical run for the presidency in 2016, anybody with even a remote interest in politics was bombarded with brutally sexist and misogynist messages and images. There was the "I Wish Hillary Had Married O.J." bumper sticker, a commercial item that appeared in 2008. In response to her campaign for the Democratic Party nomination, which she lost to Barack Obama, there was the Hillary Clinton nutcracker tchotchke and Rush Limbaugh's rhetorical question "Will this country want to actually watch a woman get older before their eyes on a daily basis?"[1] More recently, we witnessed the T-shirt that cast Trump as Perseus holding the head of the decapitated Hillary-Medusa, and the popularization of the phrase "nasty woman." While such sexism assumed a particularly virulent and violent character in the 2016 US election, it is by no means a strictly American affair, nor is it a new phenomenon. Rather, Western civilization is deeply marked by a long history of misogynist prejudices against women in positions of power. Aristophanes broached the theme of gender-based power and subversion with *Lysistrata* (411 BCE), in which female characters deploy the most important weapon, presumably, in their arsenal: withholding sex to stop a war. Similarly, *Thesmorphoriazusae* (411 BCE) expands Aristophanic comedy's repertoire, with female characters organizing to seek vengeance against contemporary male poets for their distorting representations of women. One of the comedies in the classical canon, his *Assemblywomen* (391 BCE) derives its humor from the outlandish notion that women might run the government. It is noteworthy that women who take control of their government, their bodies, and their reputations, mediated by the male imagination, provide the stuff of comedy.

While the classical canon is imbued with gender prejudice, there are counter narratives. The defender of her sex against the surge in misogynist literature in the fifteenth century, Christine de Pizan (1365–1431), modeled a mode of leadership and community; Pizan also wrote a principled defense of women. In the medieval European context, a war of words and deeds ensued, the *querelles des femmes*. The English translation of her *Le livre de la cité des dames* (1404) appeared in 1531, more than a century after Pizan's death and two decades before Mary I (Bloody Mary) and

Elizabeth I wielded real power in England. Spirited defenses and vicious attacks, in Latin and the European vernaculars, continued to unfurl for four centuries—one might say to the present. In 1558, the year the reign of Elizabeth I began, the Scottish reformer John Knox published his *First Blast of the Trumpet against the Monstrous Regiment of Women*, in which he spoke out against female monarchs: "howe abominable, odious and detestable is all such vsurped authoritie in the presence of God. . . . To promote a woman to beare rule, superioritie, dominion or empire aboue any realme, nation, or citie, is repugnant to nature."[2] The question of whether women could lead unfolded against the Renaissance background of humanist discourse about whether the female of the species could even be considered human.

The tradition of disparaging women in positions of power was carried forward into the Age of Enlightenment. G. W. F. Hegel espoused a theory of comedy in which he argues that this genre demands resolution more urgently than does tragedy, because comedic themes so topsy-turvy-ed the world. Hegel projected his fear of particularities, foremost among them gender, onto statecraft when he argued: "Stehen Frauen an der Spitze der Regierung, so ist der Staat in Gefahr, denn sie handeln nicht nach den Anforderungen der Allgemeinheit, sondern nach zufälliger Neigung und Meinung"[3] (If women are at the head of government, the state is in danger, for they do not act according to the needs of the commonwealth but according to accidental whims and opinions). Leadership, implicitly male, is destabilized when preceded with the adjective "female."

In light of this history, it is hardly surprising that even today men hold most positions of power and prestige even though women account for 52 percent of the world's population. In the Federal Republic of Germany, where women comprise 51 percent of the population, they make up 9 percent of all mayors and 18 percent of the board members of the 200 largest corporations. In contrast, 99 percent of all German receptionists are women.[4] Although women have made some progress in the last few decades, they face new hurdles as they overcome old prejudice. For example, Susan Douglas notes that women now confront a schizophrenic setup: in the fantasy world of the media, there is a glut of women in positions of power, including a plethora of female presidents, vice presidents, and prime ministers in shows such as *24*, *Commander-in-Chief*, *Veep*, *Madame Secretary*, *Homeland*, or *Borgen*. Meanwhile, in our social reality, the most popular jobs for women remain secretary, nurse, elementary and middle-school teacher, cashier, and retail salesperson.[5] Thus women are faced not only with an uphill struggle against social and political discrimination but also with an overrepresentation of female power in the media that suggests that the fight for equality has long been won and that any remaining complaints are frivolous at best or downright greedy.

Beyond and behind the representation of women in leadership positions in contemporary media, an array of manuals, guides, self-help books, and motivational literature inundates women readers with narratives and checklists geared toward clearing a route to success; cultivating strategies that shatter the glass ceiling—or rationally constructing a deeper comprehension of the complexities that account for failure. For multiple reasons, the literature that focuses on leadership is generated by a corporate business model. There is some attention to female leadership that is pertinent to the academy. Virginia Valian, author of *Why So Slow?*, relies on statistical data rather than anecdotal evidence; her research demonstrates how a "set of implicit, or nonconscious, hypotheses about sex differences plays a central role in shaping men's and women's professional lives."[6] These "gender schemas," as she calls them, call attention to the accumulation of advantage for men, and a commensurate accumulation of disadvantage for women in the course of their careers. In work about the university as an institution, Valian and coauthor Abigail J. Stewart pursue the question of diversity in leadership. In their discussion of formal leaders and their roles, they address gender-specific practices in their typology of leadership attributes. Valian and Stewart further reference a study of female college presidents that lists nine aspects of effective leadership, including "passion, reflectiveness, competence, communication ability, understanding of the role of culture, physical and emotional stamina, energy, and resilience, focus combined with forward thinking, respect and valuing of individuality and credibility."[7] Valian and Stewart observe dryly: "An academic leader could reasonably feel that this is a tall order."[8]

The substantial demands on the female leader in the "tenets" quoted above suggest that sociocultural challenges for women with power require a greater ability to thread their way through complex organizational channels—and there is no shortage of guides. Many such exhortatory volumes provide a compass for navigating corporate labyrinths. Sarah Rutherford, for example, calls attention to the interconnections between organizational cultures and women's place in society.[9] Alice E. Eagly and Linda L. Carli use the metaphor of the labyrinth because it "symbolizes the complexity of the causes of women's current situation as leaders."[10] Though leadership styles, assessed and categorized by a series of problematic but widely used metrics, such as the Myers-Briggs Type Indicator, are plural, the gender of a presumed "leader" remains singular. Eagly and Carli espouse a straightforward definition of a leader: "a person who exercises authority over other people" (*Through the Labyrinth*, 8). Why, then, do we encounter such resistance when the adjective "female" precedes the word "leader"?

The resistance, we argue in this book, is embedded in literary, cultural, and historical values that presume and preserve a fundamental opposition between the adjective "female" and the noun "leader." The synonymous relationship between "male" and "leader" allows for men to evolve, to acquire behavioral traits in response to changing environments. At certain historical junctures, social and political thinking about gender bias shifted; today, a tectonic shift reverberates across corporations and sometimes continents (as in the momentum of the #MeToo movement). With the popularization of emotional intelligence (EI) as an acquired skill in the 1990s, for example, women, perennially identified with high emotional quotients, were potentially empowered. Social scientists and researchers John D. Mayer, Peter Salovy, and David R. Caruso are specific in defining EI: "This valid conception of EI includes the ability to engage in sophisticated information processing about one's own and others' emotions and the ability to use this information as a guide to thinking and behavior."[11] A *Forbes* headline reads: "Using Emotional Intelligence Is a Woman Leader's Secret Weapon."[12] Similarly, LaRae Quy, a former FBI agent and proponent of mental toughness training, acknowledges the need for soft skills for executive success, though she remains non-committal about a correlation between gender and emotional intelligence. In our culture at large, however, the problem of seeing some behavioral traits as intrinsically gendered persists. The private/public divide exacerbates this difficulty. Rutherford writes: "This is what creates the cultural paradox of female leadership and makes it so problematic. The power of both the external gender order and the intra-psyche gender order explains women's reticence in claiming their place in the public world and men's resistance to their doing so."[13] One aim of the essays in this volume is to historicize the traits of female leadership from interdisciplinary perspectives in a collective effort to map a path through the labyrinth.

The barriers that keep women from equal access to positions of power are further complicated by the fact that feminists disagree about whether such access would even be desirable. Some feminists argue that "women in power will be corrupted by that power."[14] Consequently, they see the push for more female political leaders and CEOs not as a struggle for equal opportunities for women but as "a fight to allow women to participate equally in the oppression of the powerless and the poor."[15] Such thinkers object to a reduction of feminism to "a method of self-empowerment and self-improvement."[16] Instead, they advocate a far-reaching model of feminism that interrogates all social and political structures of oppression and inequality. As Margarete Stokowski puts it, if one asks whether "feministische Weltherrschaft eine Option ist, . . . [ist] die Antwort . . . natürlich nicht, weil Weltherrschaft generell keine Option ist . . . Ziel: Abschaffung von Herrschaft"[17] (feminist world domination is an option, . . . the answer is: of course not, because world domination is generally not an option . . . goal: abrogation of domination). To be sure, such objections are not frivolous. For example, they go some way toward explaining why women from the right end of the political spectrum, such as Margaret Thatcher, have had more success securing positions of power than women from left-leaning parties. As philosopher Kate Manne explains, "women's power will be better tolerated when it's wielded in service of patriarchal interests."[18] Finally, the issue of leadership and women's empowerment is further obfuscated by the rejection of labels. The most powerful woman in the world, German Chancellor Angela Merkel, does not identify as a feminist.

In light of the historically perceived incompatibility of women and power, women who aspired to positions of leadership had to devise strategies designed to navigate the sea of prejudices that kept them powerless. For example, in order to justify their claim to power, women have often pointed to their presumed moral superiority. Thus Jill Lepore argues convincingly that in the United States "women entered public affairs by way of an evangelical religious revival that emphasized their moral superiority, becoming temperance reformers and abolitionists."[19] Similarly, many successful female leaders have managed to marshal and redefine concepts of motherhood for political purposes. Elizabeth I of England, for example, successfully presented herself as both a Virgin Queen and a mother to her people[20] while Merkel, who is sometimes referred to with the gender-neutral pronoun "das" as in "das Merkel"—also evocative of "das Mädel" (the girl)—is often called "Mutti Merkel" (mama Merkel).[21]

In the context of German-speaking Europe, queens and empresses have rarely risen to the historical heights and political prominence of Elizabeth I. Maria Theresa (1717–80) is the only empress ever to have ruled the Hapsburg Empire. Catherine the Great of Russia (1729–96), born Sophie Friederike Auguste, Princess of Anhalt-Zerbst, came to power through a coup against her husband; she gained notoriety for her scandalous personal life, which often overshadows her survival of a dozen or so attempts to unseat her. In addition to expanding Russian territories and modernizing the country, she wrote libretti and penned a narrative exemplum for teaching the ideals of enlightenment absolutism to the children of empire, "The Tale of Fenwei" (1784).

German-speaking Europe did provide posterity with other female sovereigns who wielded power through strategic relationships to royal men. History finds a happier couple than Catherine and her emperor and a more successful married partnership in Friedrich Wilhelm III (1770–1840) and Queen Luise of Prussia (1776–1810). Her popularity added value to his ability to rule; her beauty inspired generals to deploy her in negotiations with Napoleon at Tilsit (to no avail); soldiers fought in her name, and her death triggered an outpouring of patriotic sorrow. A fierce protector of Prussia, she achieved a high profile within expanded yet still circumscribed spheres of female leadership, albeit frequently by contiguity with a royal spouse or as mother, sometimes regent, of a royal child. On a different continent, Maria Leopoldina of Austria extended Habsburg power to the Americas. Wed by proxy in 1817 to Dom Pedro (1798–1834; also Pedro I of Brazil; King Dom Pedro IV), Maria Leopoldina had acquired an education commensurate to prestige and privilege, having learned French and Latin along with music, painting, and riding. Before embarking for Brazil, she studied and learned Portuguese. Though her husband in many ways proved a disappointment, the new kingdom afforded her opportunities to share in governance as regent, advisor, and empress of Brazil. She did nothing to dismantle the system of slavery. A royal daughter and wife, she endorsed a political move for Brazilian independence from Portugal and in 1824, two years before her death, took an oath to the Brazilian constitution. Their daughter, Maria II, ascended to the Portuguese throne.[22] Still, female power was determined by relationships to male leadership and personal and political alliances predestined by hereditary bonds.

Motherhood presents a viable route to positions of power even in the twenty-first century, and this avenue to leadership has a history in German-speaking Europe that informs the essays in this volume. The intractable affiliation between motherhood and middle-class identity, with women defined by domestic citizenship, harks back to eighteenth-century manuals in the genre of *Hausmutterliteratur*. Here, ruling the household and maternal responsibilities become synonymous. Guides directed at young and inexperienced brides inculcated readers with the virtues of cleanliness and purity, but these predictable female virtues assumed a civic patina. In the 1812 edition of the *Hausmutter in allen ihren Geschäfften* (The Mother of the House in All Her Dealings), for example, Germershausen and Gericke cultivate the image of woman presiding over an immaculate household as a dutiful citizen. The middle-class woman who models cleanliness for the servants, in one articulation of praise, instills in them finer customs. Gericke writes: "Ich glaube, unser Vaterland hat schon viel dadurch gewonnen" (I believe our fatherland has already benefitted immensely from this).[23] In other words, the punctilious lady of the house, with her love of cleanliness, advances the interests of the entire nation: "Jene reinliche Hausmutter ist daher eine Patriotin, indem sie in ihrem Zirkel die Volksmenge befördert" (10; For this reason, every tidy matron is a patriot because she promotes the people within her circle). The prose stops short of describing such modeling as leadership. Another volume, attributed to Friederike Luise Löffler and which enjoyed multiple, rapid-succession editions because it was "gänzlich vergriffen" (completely sold out), maps the evolving contours of middle-class maternity, ascribing importance to this role while limiting its sphere of influence. To make the point, the author elevates maternity to a calling in the service of humanity that saturates the nineteenth century as well: "Die Mütter, denen die erste Erziehung vorzüglich obliegt, haben grosse und wichtige Pflichten, aber auch grosse, lange nicht genug erkannte Verdienste um die Menschheit" (the mothers who are primarily responsible for the early nurturing have great and important duties, but also great and insufficiently acknowledged services to humankind).[24] Motherhood, or rather, inflections of maternal roles, shift historically to reflect a synecdoche between the home and the nation, with private service subsumed ideologically into citizenship. Historian Ann Taylor Allen, in her stunning work on feminism and motherhood, observes: "At the turn of the twentieth century, when our story begins, feminist rhetoric was pervaded by the exaltation of motherhood as the woman citizen's most important right and duty."[25] Locating women's maternal role in a sociopolitical hierarchy proves complicated and demands historicization, but the conflation of female leadership with motherhood persists until today. Tellingly, a recent self-help book for aspiring female leaders by Ann Crittenden is entitled *If You've Raised Kids, You Can Manage Anything: Leadership Begins at Home.*

Once women have been successful in securing positions of power, they may choose to avoid potential conflicts between expectations inherent in the role of leader and female gender stereotypes by masculinizing themselves. Indeed, the masculinization of the female potentate is a well-worn tradition that goes back to antiquity. Gold notes that Hatshepsut, the fifth pharaoh of the Eighteenth Dynasty of Egypt "wore a false beard as part of her state costume."[26] Similarly, in her famous speech to the troops at Tilbury, Queen Elizabeth I proclaimed "I know I have the body but of a weak and feeble woman; but I have the heart and stomach of a king."[27] In more recent times, such masculinization has assumed a more inconspicuous guise, manifesting in what Classicist Mary Beard has called "the regulation trouser suits."[28] Both Democratic Presidential Candidate Hillary Clinton and German Chancellor Angela Merkel are known for their pantsuits, which have been elevated to a cultural symbol. In the 2016 election, many of Clinton's supporters wore pantsuits to the polls[29] and Merkel's pantsuits even have their own Twitter account under the moniker "@merkelsanzug."[30]

Dress codes and sartorial cultures based on binary gender identity reflect historical changes in the female body image and a proprietary relationship to it. While the confines of corsets and bulges of bustles persisted into the late nineteenth century, twentieth-century icons of fashion, such as designer Coco Chanel and actor and risk-taker Marlene Dietrich, insist that women wear the pants. The wearable signifiers of masculinity, now available to a savvy consumer and fashionista, reflect an ascent to higher status, and at least a declaration of sartorial access to human rights, for along with the dressing for the part, the attributes of power are transferred. Thus Margaret Thatcher may have shunned the trouser suit, but she too took steps to masculinize herself. Mary Beard notes that Thatcher "took voice training specifically to lower her voice."[31]

If women in positions of leadership masculinize themselves, they are responding to the fact that "our mental, cultural template for a powerful person remains resolutely male" (Beard, 53). There is a perceived incompatibility between qualities that are typically expected of a leader and those that are expected of women. Author and feminist advocate Chimamanda Ngozi Adichie, for example, points out how important it is for women to be likeable and how much the social imperative for likeability can interfere with the qualities desired in a leader: women may be expected to be modest—"We teach girls to shrink themselves, to make themselves smaller"[32]—but leaders in the political and professional arena have to sell themselves and to highlight their accomplishments.[33]

Such conflicts between role and gender expectations cannot be resolved simply by teaching women to adjust their behavior, since the standards for evaluating male and female performance in positions of power differ significantly. In other words, even if female leaders act exactly like male leaders, their behavior will be interpreted differently. Thus research indicates that women who are assertive, who insist on their accomplishments and are not afraid to speak up and introduce new ideas are likely to "pay a popularity penalty"[34] or may simply not be heard. In a series of articles about women and work, Sheryl Sandberg, author of *Lean In: Women, Work, and the Will to Lead* (2013), and Adam Grant coauthored one installment entitled: "Speaking While Female." They write: "When a woman speaks in a professional setting, she walks a tightrope. Either she's barely heard, or she's judged as too aggressive."[35] Vocal, articulate women who advocate for a political position or wear the mantle of power as comfortably as a polished pantsuit are persistently judged differently when displaying the same leadership traits as their male counterparts. In their opinion piece, Sandberg and Grant cite a study by the Yale psychologist Victoria L. Brescoli, who researches organizational behavior with a focus on relationships among gender, power, and volubility. Brescoli argues that power "has a strong, positive effect for volubility on men; no such effect exists for women." Her research further confirms the perceptions of powerful women that they can expect backlash for talking more than others.[36] This is also evidenced by a recent psychological study that concluded that "women posing as female CEOs were judged more harshly for voicing opinions too ardently while men posing as CEOs were perceived as poor leaders if they did not voice their opinions."[37] Speaking while female remains a behavior that may require hazard pay.

Clearly, the perception of leadership qualities is subject to seemingly perpetual gendering. Eagly and Carli describe a study in which participants were asked to evaluate a male and a female candidate who were alternately described as either well educated or street smart. The study showed that "the participants considered education a more important criterion of job success when he [the male candidate, EK] was well educated, and street smarts as more important when he was not" (*Through the Labyrinth*, 112). These findings are further confirmed in a study by the psychologist Madeline Heilman that provided participants with information packages about two fictional candidates, James and Andrea. In one setup, package A was attributed to James and package B to Andrea. In the second setup, the attribution of packages was reversed. Interestingly, in all scenarios in which Andrea was considered equally competent, she was also judged unlikeable, suggesting that "when women are not doubted as viable competitors for male-dominated roles, they are widely disliked and subject to social punishment" (*Down Girl*, 252). It bears mention that women are just as likely as men to offer such biased evaluations and to "engage in gendered norm enforcement behavior" (*Down Girl*, 256).

Studies such as these suggest that women do have to work harder if they want to be perceived as competent leaders. As Eagly and Carli put it, "women are held to a higher standard of leadership competence than men" (*Through the Labyrinth*, 110). If a woman decides to enter the political arena, she will be forced to hold herself to a much higher standard of personal and professional integrity than her male competitors. In their analysis of the media coverage of female senators in Berlin, social scientist Barbara Schaeffer-Hegel and her coauthors have shown that, unlike men, "es Frauen nicht möglich ist, die in der Skandalierung erfolgte Degradierung ihrer Person mit der Anrufung von Qualitäten wie Leidenschaft und Potenz zu kompensieren" (*Frauen mit Macht*, 269; it is not possible for women to compensate for the personal degradation relating to a scandal with references to qualities such as passion and potency). In discussing the initiatives of female senators, the German media registered every small mistake but hardly acknowledged political achievements (*Frauen mit Macht*, 285). It is often remarked that women suffer from a lack of confidence: they do not put themselves forward for public office if their qualifications are less than perfect. However, in light of the different standards by which their accomplishments are judged, this diffident stance appears to be a reasonable and appropriate cautionary measure.

The root cause for the differing evaluations of male and female leadership lies in men's and women's asymmetrical positions vis-à-vis power and in the nature of privilege as such. Writer and feminist scholar Sara Ahmed insightfully defines privilege as "an energy-saving device":[38] not being privileged means "having to insist on what is simply given to others; not only that, you are heard as insistent, or even, for that matter, as self-promoting."[39] Since the female gender has traditionally been excluded from positions of power, those women who now compete for such positions will, as Manne points out, "tend to be perceived as morally suspect in at least three main ways: insufficiently caring and attentive with respect to those in her orbit deemed vulnerable; illicitly trying to gain power that she is not entitled to; and morally untrustworthy" (*Down*

Girl, xiv). Moreover, because women in power are still relatively rare, they acquire a symbolic function and tend to be seen as both representative of their entire gender and as exceptional. Consequently, if a female leader fails, her failure has implications for her entire sex, suggesting that women in general are not suited to this type of work.[40] In contrast, if a male leader fails, the conclusion is simply that one should recruit a different man (*Frauen mit Macht*, 304). Conversely, if a female leader succeeds, she is no longer seen as representative of her gender, but rather perceived as one of a kind (see *Frauen mit Macht*, 174).

In her illuminating study *Women and Power*, Mary Beard concludes that "if women are not perceived to be fully within the structures of power, surely it is power that we need to redefine rather than women" (83). Beard encourages her readers to "try to pull apart the very idea of leadership" (94) and to start "thinking collaboratively about the power of followers not just of leaders . . . the ability to be effective, to make a difference in the world" (87). It has often been argued that the demands of a leadership position are incompatible with female life models, in particular, with the competing demands of work and family. But one might take this one step further and suggest that some of the qualities expected of a leader are incompatible with a life that is more fully human and with the welfare of society as such. Interestingly, in their study of the eight female senators who were part of the Berlin government in 1989, Schaeffer-Hegel and coauthors note not only that all senators were expected to be dedicated to their work 100 percent of the time ("Totalidentifikation mit der Arbeit"),[41] but also that women senators who did not prioritize the needs of their departments over the well-being of the entire city were punished for their lack of ambition and "Ressortegoismus" (*Frauen mit Macht*, 27). Clearly, such a model of leadership ultimately benefits neither individual leaders nor the communities they serve.

It would seem that a comprehensive attempt to chip away at the perceived incompatibility of women and power will seek not only to promote more women to leadership positions but also to redefine what leadership is all about. In particular, feminist theory might draw on recent studies of leadership that have begun to redefine the term in favor of qualities that are traditionally associated with women. For example, a recent book published by the Harvard Business School, *On Leadership*, lists emotional intelligence, empathy, and social skills as essential qualities of a leader: "Empathy is particularly important today as a component of leadership for at least three reasons: the increasing use of teams; the rapid pace of globalization; and the growing need to retain talent."[42] The authors of this study note further that a good leader can detect "shifts in climate and ambience; he [!] can read subtle cues and sense underlying currents of opinion" (86). They characterize outstanding leaders as selfless, claiming that they "subjugate their own needs to the greater ambition of something larger and more lasting than themselves" (134); and people-oriented, suggesting that great leaders "attended to people first, strategy second. They got the right people on the bus, moved the wrong people off" (*On Leadership*, 124). Similarly, Eagly and Carli observe a move away from command-and-control leadership in contemporary culture (*Through the Labyrinth*, 48). In this spirit of rethinking leadership, the essays in this volume seek to demonstrate the historical, cultural, literary, and political ways in which women lead, with an aim to move the needle not only on our measurements of gender identity, but also on our understanding of power as such.

Chapter Overview

The volume is divided into three sections: "The Age of Enlightened Rule?"; "Leadership as Social Activism around 1900"; and "Women and Political Power in the Twentieth and Twenty-First Centuries," with contributions organized in chronological order. Their scope and focus reflect the realities and fantasies of female leadership throughout the centuries. Although there were a number of important female sovereigns during the Age of Enlightenment, female leadership in the eighteenth century was largely confined to the realm of fantasy. Thus the first section of this collection presents analyses of literary texts that negotiate the nexus of women and power. Seth Berk opens this section with an illuminating analysis of a woman who ruled. In "Women's Political Authority in Maria Antonia Walpurgis von Sachsen's *Talestris: Königin der Amazonen* (1763)," he elaborates on an image of Maria Antonia as an aristocrat with political power who represented herself as a woman of strength. Her 1763 opera, *Talestris: Königin der Amazonen* (Talestris: Queen of the Amazons), attests to the creative legacy that expresses her engagement in the issue of female leadership. In addition to writing the music and the libretto, Maria Antonia sang the lead soprano role as Talestris before a royal audience. As Berk argues, her operatic self-staging as the leader of the Amazons lends insight into her own political machinations. Though her political power depended on that of male relatives—Maria Antonia did not successfully lay claim to the Polish crown after her husband died, primarily because of the interference of her brother-in-law—the opera presents a unique look at a powerful woman's self-representation as an Amazonian warrior queen. With its attention to the transgressions and normative portrayals of gender, Berk's analysis reveals the extent to which the opera advances a discourse about women's ability to rule. Further, Antonia's assertions of creative agency—the acts of writing and performance—emerge as a means of participating in the restricted intellectual and political debate about a female-specific relationship to wielding power.

Margaretmary Daley continues the discussion as she examines the work of a popular female writer of eighteenth-century German-speaking Europe. "Maxims of Leadership for a Silent Readership: Sophie von La Roche's *Pomona für Teutschlands Töchter* and *Mein Schreibetisch*" focuses on a learned and exemplary woman who was, Daley demonstrates, not only a prolific author and exemplary daughter, wife, and mother, but also a philosophical commentator on women's topics. In her journal *Pomona*, La Roche puts forward a prescriptive notion of exemplary women as cultural leaders; central to that notion is a woman whose intellect earns her "the approbation of Gentle Souls." Through an examination of La Roche's collective prescriptions from her journal, Daley builds a more expansive picture of eighteenth-century female leadership, allowing contemporary readers to understand La Roche's concept of power and community, the elements of which comprise sophisticated linguistic knowledge, gendered behavior, decorum, and female-centered mentoring. One of La Roche's notions of women's leadership, as Daley contends, calls for individual mentoring relationships and a female network to assess the moral worth and gender-correctness of shared ideas. La Roche's approach to women's leadership changed over time, with increasing emphasis on self-education. For evidence of this shift, Daley turns to *Mein Schreibetisch* (1799), in which she detects less endorsement of sisterhood and more desire for females she could mentor. La Roche's idea of leadership is predicated on acquiring, through the acts of reading and writing, the intellectual prowess necessary to advance literary culture and extend women's compassionate influence to society. Her own writing desk grounds the discussions of leadership qualities that focus on her exemplary female self. The arc of La Roche's concept of women's leadership has been obscured, as Daley observes, by institutional practices of literary criticism. In contrast, she sheds light on a larger corpus of women's writing around 1800, thus providing a clearer picture of the time, replete with awkward proscriptions, unsettling assumptions, and welcome prescriptions for women's success.

Almut Spalding resumes the theme of women and education in her contribution, "Marcus Aurelius, Also for Girls: Discussions on the Best Form of Government in Enlightenment Hamburg." Spalding examines writings by Elise Reimarus (1735–1805), renowned during her lifetime as a widely published educator and leader of a literary salon in German-speaking Enlightenment Europe. Specifically, the author analyzes those of Reimarus's writings that have an implicit or explicit political focus. For Reimarus, education implied education for citizenship, applicable equally to females and males. As an educator, Reimarus actively engaged in the popular eighteenth-century discourse on the best form of government, though she did so differently than did men. Rather than participating in public essay competitions on this topic, she confronted issues of fair government, power, freedom, and responsibility in writings intended especially for a young audience, those learning to become responsible citizens. These writings date from just before the Seven Years' War until after the French Revolution, with her work on the Roman emperor Marcus Aurelius falling apparently into the middle of those decades. Reimarus's works reflect the fundamental changes in political order, and to a certain extent the ideas about natural law and naturally determined gender roles, that swept across Europe and the Americas during these decades. In her earlier writings, Spalding observes, Reimarus tends to articulate her frustration with the inequality of gender and the limits placed on females participating in the governing process. In her later writings she focused more on the concept of liberty, independent of gender, and the implications of individual freedom for the state. In that sense, her portrayal of female leadership shifted over her lifetime, while her own willingness to assume a leadership role as a writer-educator remained constant. Reimarus's treatise on Marcus Aurelius Antoninus conveys her endorsement of a just government that attends to the needs of the people and advances the common good—not least, one that supports male and female education. Spalding's reading of Reimarus in the context of female leadership expands that concept to include writing, translating, and modeling citizenship in the absence of citizenship rights.

Anke Gilleir and Aude Defurne's article, entitled *"Dux Femina Facti*: Gender, Sovereignty and (Women's) Literature in Marie Antonia of Saxony's *Thalestris* and Charlotte von Stein's *Dido*," takes as its point of departure the Virgil quote: "Dux femina facti" (A woman was leader of the deed). Gilleir and Defurne argue that the figure of Dido was construed as an exemplar of a woman leader who is motivated by emotions and who prioritizes private matters over affairs of the state. Drawing on the framework of biopolitics laid out by Foucault, Agamben, and Kantorowicz, Gilleir and Defurne argue that notions of power are always inflected by issues of gender. Female sovereignty was never perceived as normal, but rather as an exceptional situation and an immanent risk precisely because the female body, conceived as both abject and prone to excess, stood in the way of state rule. Gilleir and Defurne's reading of texts by Marie Antonia of Saxony, a princess-regent, and Charlotte von Stein, lady-in-waiting of the grand duchess-regent Anna Amalie of Saxony-Weimar, demonstrates that both authors were acutely aware of the incompatibility of the female body and sovereignty but chose to present texts that invert the mythological script of the mad and raging or biologically impaired woman.

In the next article, "Crossing the Front Lines: Female Leadership, Politics, and War in *Die Familie Seldorf*," Sara Eldridge examines Therese Huber's 1795 novel about an aristocratic family at the time of the French Revolution. With a heroine who is a strong female character, the novel lends itself to interpretations ranging from a critique of patriarchy, a depiction of the ways in which the "Family Romance" of the French Revolution and its aftermath excludes women from its ideals, or an articulation of the undecidability in Huber's portrayal of both femininity and political activity as typical of women authors' "double voice" of around 1800. While acknowledging the challenge faced by women who wrote in and around the confines of prevailing gender roles, Eldridge argues that viewing *Die Familie Seldorf* in terms of female leadership offers a new way of understanding the work that Huber's novel accomplishes. Ultimately, Eldridge's reading augments our understanding of authorship as a kind of leadership. She characterizes Huber as an author who guides readers through her texts' presentations of gender roles, leading the reader through a series of experiments around gender toward the realization that gender is both shaped by experience and ultimately subject to change. This leadership that Huber provides remains relevant as women continue to struggle to navigate questions of gender identity and performance as they intersect with social training and lived experience.

The first section concludes with an article that draws parallels between eighteenth-century female sovereignty and twentieth-century female terrorists grappling with, while defying, prevailing gender roles. Inge Stephan's "Power Struggles between Women in Schiller's and Jelinek's Works" offers a comparative analysis of Schiller's *Maria Stuart* and Jelinek's *Queens' Drama*. Stephan shows that Schiller's female protagonists function as "two sides of the same coin," who, together, represent the "split image of woman" typical of male-authored literature around 1800. She points to the ideological strain inherent in the drama's attempt to transform Maria Stuart, who was rumored to have murdered her husband, into a beautiful soul. Conversely, Elisabeth is portrayed as bitter about the erotic renunciation required by her office. Thus Schiller reframes a female competition for power as an erotic rivalry and resituates his two female sovereigns safely in a more gender-appropriate sphere. In contrast, Jelinek links female power to maternity and deconstructs the notion that women derive power from motherhood. Jelinek, as Stephan notes, tears the ideological veil of Schiller's play conceptually but also through language that contrasts markedly with Schiller's elevated style. Stephan shows that Jelinek's female terrorists are both alienated from the people they seek to lead and entrapped by traditional notions of motherhood. Although Jelinek is deeply pessimistic about the possibility of social and political change, her drama does suggest that any such change would require a radical break with traditional notions of femininity.

The second section focuses on forms of female leadership in the nineteenth century that frequently revised and professionalized practices of motherhood to advance social activism and peace advocacy. To varying degrees, widespread societal ambivalence remains, not only about direct involvement in the politics of women's struggles or contemporary feminist movements, but also about the breach of boundaries between female roles in the private and public spheres. Prior to enfranchisement and attaining the full rights of citizenship, female authors and activists nonetheless made the case for a *vita activa* for women. Lauren Nossett's contribution, "Age and Purpose: Unmarried Women and Female Agency in the Works of E. Marlitt and Hedwig Dohm," confronts the persistently relevant question of age in any discussion of women and leadership. Departing from popularized and prejudicial stereotypes of older, unmarried women in the later nineteenth century, Nossett expands on the insights elaborated by historian Catherine L. Dollard. In *The Surplus Woman: Unmarried in Imperial Germany, 1871–1918*, Dollard examines the single woman not as a demographic but rather as a destabilizing force: a symptom of anxiety about contemporary social transformation that decoupled women and reproduction from the role of women as members of society. Nossett observes that unmarried women did not participate in the sexual economy and maternal agency that aligned with the ideology of the bourgeoisie, thus generating the "female surplus" that saturated the German cultural imagination. In her reading of Marlitt and Dohm, Nossett identifies a subversive quality in living the life of an older, unattached woman, acknowledging a greater potential to work and possibly participate in the public sphere. While Marlitt's protagonists discover intellectual passions that sustain them in their domestic life, Dohm's heroines discover their own value in activities of their choosing. The authors analyzed in this article, though they differ significantly in their portrayals of single women, nonetheless both challenge the notion of a surplus female existence and further dispute the validity of stereotypes. In Nossett's analysis, these fictional female figures, through different paths, assume agency, define self-worth, and discover purpose.

Lisa Fetheringill Zwicker extends and develops the changing role of maternality. In "'Heroism of the Mother': Women's Rights Pioneer Jeannette Schwerin, Motherlove, and Women's Leadership in German-Speaking Central Europe, 1890–1914," she argues that since the eighteenth century modern Western men and women have extolled the power and passion of motherlove (*Mutterliebe*). By the nineteenth century, as the historiography on maternal feminism has demonstrated, leading Central European women utilized motherlove to assert claims to playing a role in the public sphere. By the fin-de-siècle, women active outside the home as social workers, teachers, or reformers described their work in terms of *geistige Mütterlichkeit* (often translated as spiritual motherhood). Zwicker explores what this might mean in terms of the power of and possibility for women's leadership. Drawing on methods from the history of emotions, the author considers how the social construction of late nineteenth- and early twentieth-century motherlove created openings for new arguments about the power and potential of women's leadership as well as the ways that the performance of motherlove could limit women's ability to take on leadership roles. Zwicker concludes with the example of Jeanette Schwerin, who was an acknowledged leader in the German women's movement and whose early death in 1899 was a shock to women's rights advocates across Europe. Schwerin was praised for her leadership and her thoughtful decision-making, but at the same time for her personal attributes, such as her humble and polished manner. Importantly, Schwerin was openly praised for her maternal qualities. The new opportunities for women at the turn of the century enabled her to become a leader of the women's movement and a recognized expert in the new field of social work. As Zwicker concludes, ambiguity remains about the possibilities of reconciling the cultural norms of middle-class motherlove (with expectations of domestic feminine traits) and the attributes associated with becoming a leader of men.

Elisabeth Krimmer's "Strategic Optimism: Bertha von Suttner's Activism for Peace" points to a central paradox: although women are assumed to be innately inclined toward peace, they are not granted the power and authority to transform society in accordance with a pacifist vision. Drawing on theories of life writing, sovereignty, and leadership, Krimmer asks how Bertha von Suttner justified her claim to moral and political authority in her activism for peace. She parses factors that helped von Suttner become a successful political leader, such as her grounding in traditional forms of sovereignty through her aristocratic birth, her ability to define herself as a servant of a larger cause, her fantastic talent for networking and public relations, her unshakable conviction that change was possible, her profound respect for the importance of public opinion, her strategic optimism, her sense of humor, and, last but not least, her skillful navigation of gender codes. However, Krimmer also investigates the reasons for her failure to gain a wider platform, including the barrage of sexism with which von Suttner was confronted on a daily basis but also her refusal to take seriously and engage with both discourses of nationality and the realities of capitalism.

Peter Hudis's "Humanizing Socialism: The Feminist Dimension of Rosa Luxemburg's Intellectual Leadership" focuses on a leading female figure in the German Social Democratic Party (SPD), an outstanding economist, and arguably the most important female theoretician in the history of Marxism. Exploring what Luxemburg's legacy can tell us about women and leadership, Hudis argues that although her work is often discussed without reference to issues of gender, it is informed by feminist considerations. Luxemburg's refusal to separate the personal from the political anticipates an important component of contemporary feminism. Further, Hudis argues, Luxemburg considered empathy an indispensable aspect of political leadership and embraced a participatory model in which leaders seek to teach the masses to think independently. Luxemburg demonstrated intellectual leadership within the SPD in spite of opposition to female ambition and without sacrificing support for women's causes, including women's suffrage. Hudis contends that Luxemburg was neither uninterested in women's emancipation nor indifferent to sexism, but rather sought to break down the walls of sexism precisely by putting herself forth as a major Marxist theoretician.

The third section on female leadership in the twentieth and twenty-first centuries deals more directly with the nexus of gender and political power. This turbulent era has borne witness to the dissolution of empire, two world wars, the Cold War, the unification of two German states in 1990 that introduced an ostensible period of normalization of German nationhood, and the integration efforts of the European Union. Throughout these traumas, tribulations, and negotiations, women have gained and lost political power, yet always within the larger patriarchal construct of the state. The articles in this section cover a range of topics: aesthetic agency during the Third Reich, the female body in neoliberal hegemony, the changing representation of women leaders in the media, Petra Kelly and the role of gender in her legacy, far-right critique of Chancellor Angela Merkel, and finally, a comparative analysis of Hillary Clinton and, at one point, Merkel, as the most powerful woman in the world. To begin, Rachel J. Halverson's "Follow-the-Leader: Tracing Male Influence on Leni Riefenstahl's *Triumph des Willens*" sees Leni Riefenstahl as paradigmatic of the types of leadership roles available to women in Nazi Germany. On the one hand, they were subordinate to an almost exclusively male hierarchy; on the other, women were called upon to lead other women, subject to the condition that they followed the dictates of male superiors. Halverson shows that this contradiction of leading while being led is echoed in a reception history that casts Riefenstahl alternately as a pioneering filmmaker and a figure of evil. Halverson argues that neither one of these evaluations of Riefenstahl's legacy takes into account her ambivalent position that allowed for creative freedom only to the extent that her artistic vision conformed to Hitler's and Goebbels's expectations. In contrast, Halverson seeks to disrupt the notion of Riefenstahl as a solitary figure by resituating her work in the context of the cinematic vernacular of her time. For example, Halverson shows how Arnold Fanck's and Walter Ruttmann's filmic language influenced Riefenstahl's directorial agency. In so doing, Halverson asks the reader not only to think of leaders and followers as a unit but also to let go of traditional notions of cinematic auteurship that credit the director as the sole creative force while ignoring the collaborative nature of filmmaking.

Helga Druxes, in "'Leaning In': The Career Woman as Instrument of Neoliberal Critique," contends that cultural anxieties over the ageing German demographic emerge in depictions of career women of reproductive age. Her analysis of three satirical films released in 2013, 2014, and 2016—Frauke Finsterwalder's *Finsterworld*, Johannes Naber's *Zeit der Kannibalen*, and Maren Ade's *Toni Erdmann*—illuminates their trenchant critiques of neoliberalism as an exploitative and dehumanizing economic system. Druxes elaborates on how these three films transform educated female professionals and their sexuality into emblems of crisis. In *Kannibalen*, a female corporate merger consultant and in *Finsterworld* an advertising executive and a documentary filmmaker are portrayed as ruthless, strident, and needy. The female executive of Ade's *Toni Erdmann* renders this dilemma graphic. As mothers (or partners), these characters are depicted as neglectful and unfeeling, thereby endangering transgenerational reproduction. Within neoliberal doctrine, as Druxes emphasizes, crisis is embraced as strategic, but the female professional, as represented in film, responds to crisis with behavior perceived as neurotic; her body stigmatized as disorderly and malfunctioning. Druxes concludes that these films reaffirm gender stereotypes, even as they unpack the dehumanizing effects of neoliberal ideology and reinscription of female agency into a patriarchal familial system.

In "Change, Persistence, and Contradiction: The Representation of Female Political Leadership in Gendered Media," Dorothee Beck centers attention on the perception of political leaders in contemporary democracies and the media. She demonstrates the crucial importance of media coverage for women claiming power and outlines change in media representations of female political leaders over time and their impact on women's claim to political power. During the 1990s powerful women were portrayed in media according to the unspoken norm of masculinity. Beck contends that in political news media, women in top positions in the political field continue to be represented as the "other gender." There have been some detectable changes. She shows that female leadership, in the period analyzed (1994 to 2012), has been represented in contrast to the notion of a political alpha male, which has recently been subject to criticism. There have, in turn, been increasingly appreciative, yet extremely gendered, representations of female political leaders in which personal characteristics traditionally linked with the private sphere and therefore encoded as female have been enhanced. As Beck argues, this change creates a context for the appreciation of female leadership in political news media. She also shows that this linkage retains the risk of depreciation, sexualization, and re-traditionalization of women. The essay concludes with the discussion of this change as a shift in the gendered relation between the private and the public spheres.

Stephen Milder and Friederike Brühöfener focus on the cofounder of the German Green Party and leading politician during the 1980s in their contribution, "Petra Kelly: A Green Leader out of Place?" Serving as one of the party's three co-chairs from 1980 to 1982, Kelly was the Greens' lead candidate in the 1980 and 1983 Bundestag elections as well as the

1982 elections to the Bavarian Landtag. She was the only Green to serve in the Bundestag continuously from 1983 until 1990. Additionally, she was the Greens' best-known representative abroad—particularly in the United States, where she had lived in the 1960s. The authors analyze the ways that Kelly used her positions to shape the new party and the image it projected to voters, other political parties, and the international press. Kelly's use of nonviolent civil disobedience—even on the floor of the Bundestag—along with her unflinching advocacy of a peaceful Europe defined the Greens' image as a radical party that could disrupt the political status quo. Milder and Brühöfener observe that scholars have used gendered assessments to discount Kelly's ideas and mitigate her influence, such as an emphasis on the Green leader's "difficult" personality, irrationality, or ineptitude in practicing power politics. In revealing the impact of gender on Kelly's leadership, the authors offer a larger reinterpretation of the founding Greens, who were led, inspired, and brought to political significance by a woman whose approach to politics and whose thinking scholars have struggled to understand and failed to take seriously.

Patricia Anne Simpson analyzes the portrayal of Germany's first female chancellor in "'Mama Merkel' and 'Mutti-Multikulti': The Perils of Governing While Female," with a focus on aggressively misogynist critical voices. In its extremist and mainstreamed articulations, the populist far right continues to generate critiques of elected female leaders that appeal to misogyny, whether repressed or overt. Through a rhetorical and political strategy of maternalization, social protest groups, such as the Patriotic Europeans against the Islamization of the West (PEGIDA), and aligned political parties, such as the Alternative für Deutschland (AfD), rely on historically problematic gender roles to enhance their mainstream message of essentialist German-ness. In this article Simpson examines the contrasting and contradictory role of female leadership and the escalation of critical rhetoric through a series of allegories generated by far-right "feminism" and its critique of Angela Merkel as a failed mother. With regional election losses in October 2018 and sustained attacks on her policies from conservative party leaders, who responded to threats from the far right by echoing its discontent in the mainstream, Merkel announced her decision not to seek reelection at the end of her term. Through an analysis of select texts and images, the author unpacks the strategies that channel any expression of female power into the reductive image of a mother figure to practice a form of identitarian anti-politics that oppose gender equality in the public sphere.

To conclude the volume, Joyce Mushaben's "Women Leaders in Troubled Times: The Leadership Styles of Angela Merkel and Hillary Clinton" reflects the work and leadership of two women, one an experienced federal chancellor, the other a former secretary of state and US presidential candidate and senator, and their respective approaches to leadership. Mushaben observes that Angela Merkel and Hillary Clinton are each unique in terms of their personal paths to power, yet both had to reinvent themselves when pursuing national office. She further argues that both have learned a lot by observing each other over the last ten years, if only from a diplomatic distance. In this chapter Mushaben first considers their willingness (or lack thereof) to "play the gender card" during their earlier campaigns. She then addresses their respective tendencies to pursue a "transformational" model of leadership, followed by a brief analysis of their substantive overlaps with regard to the domain of foreign and security policy. Mushaben's analysis gestures at a future that acknowledges change in models of power and sovereignty, models that foreground interactive and collaboration behaviors, suggesting that the future of leadership is female.

The publication of this volume coincides with the centenary of women's suffrage in Germany during the Weimar Republic. The intervening century bore witness to a period of liberalization in strict gender roles, with ascendant women in the arts, sciences, and politics. The pathological articulation of motherhood during the Nazi era skewed any image of powerful women in leadership roles. With the rebuilding agency of the "Trümmerfrauen" (rubble women), the theoretical equality of women in socialism, the empowering women's movement of the long 1960s, and modest gains within persistently inequitable structures in the socioeconomic, private, and political spheres, gender equality remains a desideratum in German-speaking Europe. Even with the "gender-mainstreaming" policies of the European Union, we remain attentive to Virgil's narrative of 19 BCE. As Anke Gilleir and Aude Defurne write: ". . . on the other hand, 'dux femina facti' can also be read as a notice to underscore a situation so unexpected that readers need to be informed explicitly in order to grasp what is happening: a *woman* became the leader." It is our hope that this volume will advance an understanding of female leadership in a way that eradicates that sense of surprise.

Notes

[1] Cited in Rebecca Traister, *Big Girls Don't Cry: The Election That Changed Everything for American Women* (New York: Free Press, 2010), 78.

[2] John Knox, *The First Blast of the Trumpet, against the monstrous regiment of Women*, edited by Edward Arber, no. 2 (London: English Scholar's Library, 1858), 4. Project Gutenberg Ebook, http://www.gutenberg.org/files/9660/9660-h/9660-h.htm#bibliography. See also Carole Levin, *The Heart and Stomach of a King: Elizabeth I and the Politics of Sex and Power* (Philadelphia: University of Pennsylvania Press, 2013), 10.

[3] Georg Wilhelm Friedrich Hegel, *Grundlinien der Philosophie des Rechts, oder Naturrecht und Staatswissenschaft im Grundrisse, Vollständige Ausgabe.* Vol. 8, ed. Eduard Gans. 21 vols. (Berlin: Verlag von Duncker & Humblot, 1833), 231.

[4] Margarete Stokowski, *Untenrum frei* (Reinbek bei Hamburg: Rowohlt, 2016), 176.

[5] Susan J. Douglas, *Enlightened Sexism: The Seductive Message That Feminism's Work Is Done* (New York: Henry Holt, 2010), 3.

[6] Virginia Valian, *Why So Slow? The Advancement of Women* (Cambridge, MA: MIT Press, 1998), 1 and 5.

[7] Mimi Wolverton, Beverly L. Bower and Adrienne E. Hyle, *Women at the Top: What Women University and College Presidents Say about Effective Leadership* (Sterling, VA: Stylus, 2009), 159.

[8] Abigail J. Stewart and Virginia Valian, *An Inclusive Academy: Achieving Diversity and Excellence* (Cambridge, MA: MIT Press, 2018), 425–26.

[9] Sarah Rutherford, *Women's Work, Men's Cultures: Overcoming Resistance and Changing Organizational Cultures* (New York: Palgrave, 2011), 5.

[10] Alice H. Eagly and Linda L. Carli, *Through the Labyrinth: The Truth about How Women Become Leaders* (Boston: Harvard Business School Press, 2007), 8. Further references are given in the text using the short title *Through the Labyrinth.*

[11] The proliferation of scholarly and popular literature about emotional intelligence (EI) serves as an index to its widespread influence. The social scientists who laid the basis for the field published a corrective in response to overgeneralization that diluted EI as an empirical construct. See John D. Mayer, Peter Salovy, and David R. Caruso, "Emotional Intelligence: New Ability or Eclectic Traits?" *American Psychologist* 63 (2008): 503–17, here 503.

[12] LaRae Quy, "Using Emotional Intelligence Is a Woman Leader's Secret Weapon," *Forbes,* November 2, 2016, https://www.forbes.com/sites/womensmedia/2016/11/02/using-emotional-intelligence-is-a-woman-leaders-secret-weapon/.

[13] Rutherford, *Women's Work,* 26.

[14] Jane Slaughter and Robert Kern, *European Women on the Left: Socialism, Feminism, and the Problems Faced by Political Women, 1880 to the Present* (Westport, CT: Greenwood, 1981), 130.

[15] Jessa Crispin, *Why I Am Not a Feminist: A Feminist Manifesto* (Brooklyn, NY: Melville House, 2017), xiii.

[16] Crispin, *Not a Feminist,* 17.

[17] Stokowski, *Untenrum frei,* 11.

[18] Kate Manne, *Down Girl: The Logic of Misogyny* (New York: Oxford University Press, 2018), 115.

[19] Jill Lepore, "The Woman Card," in *Wolf Whistle Politics: The New Misogyny in America Today,* ed. Diane Wachtell, with an introduction by Dr. Naomi Wolf (New York: New Press, 2017), 4.

[20] Levin, *Heart and Stomach,* 3.

[21] Julia Schramm, *Fifty Shades of Merkel* (Hamburg: Hoffmann & Campe, 2016), 27.

[22] For general biographical details, see the Wikipedia article on Maria Leopoldina of Austria, last modified September 11, 2016, https://ipfs.io/ipfs/QmXoypiz jW3WknFiJnKLwHCnL72vedxjQkDDP1mXWo6uco/wiki/Maria_Leopoldina_ of_Austria.html.

[23] Friedrich Christian Germershausen and Friedrich C. Gericke, *Die Hausmutter in allen ihren Geschäfften*, 4th ed. (Hannover: Hahn, 1812), 1:10. Gericke is credited with expanding this edition.

[24] See Friederike Luise Löffler and anonymous, *Oekonomisches Handbuch für Frauenzimmer: Anweisung zu Frauenzimmer-Arbeiten zur Behandlung von Haushaltungs-Sachen und zur Körper-Schönheitspflege; Nebst einer Anleitung zur Bereitung von Speisen und Getränken für Kränke, und zur Anwendung von Haus-Mitteln*, 2 vols. 4th ed. (Stuttgart: Steinkopf, 1826), 2:780. The authorship of the *Handbuch* itself poses some authentication and attribution problems. Friederike Luise Löffler (1744–1805) of Stuttgart authored a cookbook that gained extreme popularity, such that her name became something of a franchise, variously borrowed as "Charlotte Löffler" and "A. Löfflerin." Her daughter, Henriette Huttenlocher (1780–1848), who carried on her mother's tradition, possibly penned the later forewords to subsequent editions (they are unsigned). See "Die Geschichte," *Das Virtuelle Kochbuchmuseum*, accessed April 10, 2019, http:// www.kochbuchsammler.de/geschichte.htm.

[25] Ann Taylor Allen, *Feminism and Motherhood in Western Europe, 1890–1970* (New York: Palgrave, 2005), 8.

[26] Claudia Gold, *Women Who Ruled: History's 50 Most Remarkable Women* (London: Quercus, 2015), x.

[27] Elizabeth I, Tilbury Speech, July 1588, transcribed into present-day English. British Library, *Learning Timelines: Sources from History*, accessed February 18, 2019, http://www.bl.uk/learning/timeline/item102878.html. Cited with modifications in Levin, *Heart and Stomach*, 9.

[28] Mary Beard, *Women and Power: A Manifesto* (London: Profile Books, 2017), 54.

[29] Amanda Hess, "How a Fractious Women's Movement Came to Lead the Left," in Wachtell, *Wolf Whistle Politics*, 139–53, here 144.

[30] Schramm, *Fifty Shades*, 160.

[31] Beard, *Women and Power*, 39.

[32] Chimamanda Ngozi Adichie, *We Should All Be Feminists* (New York: Anchor Books, 2012), 27.

[33] Barbara Schaeffer-Hegel et al., *Frauen mit Macht: Zum Wandel der politischen Kultur durch die Präsenz von Frauen in Führungspositionen* (Pfaffenweiler: Centaurus Verlagsgesellschaft, 1995), 57.

[34] Nancy D. O'Reilly, *Leading Women: 20 Influential Women Share Their Secrets to Leadership, Business, and Life* (New York: Adams Media, 2015), 12.

[35] Sheryl Sandberg and Adam Grant, "Speaking While Female," *New York Times*, January 12, 2015, https://www.nytimes.com/2015/01/11/opinion/sunday/speaking-while-female.html.

[36] Victoria L. Brescoli, "Who Takes the Floor and Why: Gender, Power, and Volubility in Organizations," *Administrative Science Quarterly* 56, no. 4 (2012): 622–41.

[37] O'Reilly, *Leading Women*, 28.

[38] Sarah Ahmed, *Living a Feminist Life* (Durham: Duke University Press, 2017), 125.

[39] Ahmed, *Feminist Life*, 127.

[40] See also Eagly and Carli, who note that "because leadership is usually perceived as a masculine activity, women are more vulnerable to having their successes ascribed to their hard work rather than their ability" (*Through the Labyrinth*, 79).

[41] "Struktur des modernen Parteienstaats wurde im Zuge der Aufklärung unter Ausschluß von Frauen und unter Systembedingungen geschaffen, welche die Machthabenden und um Macht Konkurrierenden—per Gesetz ausschließlich Männer—freistellte von der Verantwortung sowohl für die eigene physisch-psychische Regeneration wie auch von der Fürsorge für ihnen nahestehende Angehörige" (Schaeffer-Hegel, *Frauen mit Macht*, 13; the structure of the modern party state excluded women and was created in the course of the Enlightenment under systemic conditions that set those in power and those competing for power—exclusively men under the law—free from any responsibility for their own physical-psychic regeneration as well as from the obligation to care for their loved ones).

[42] *On Leadership* (Boston: Harvard Business Review Press, 2011), 17. Further references are given in the text using the page number alone.

Part I.

The Age of Enlightened Rule?

1: Women's Political Authority in Maria Antonia Walpurgis von Sachsen's *Talestris: Königin der Amazonen* (*Thalestris: Queen of the Amazons*, 1763)

Seth Berk

T HE ELECTRESS OF SAXONY, Maria Antonia Walpurgis Symphorosa (1724–80) was a composer, poet, singer, and artist of great merit, although she has only recently been rediscovered by scholars. Christine Fischer's *Instrumentierte Visionen weiblicher Macht* (*Orchestrated Visions of Female Power*, 2007) stands to date as the most thorough scholarly analysis of Maria Antonia's life and works.[1] Fischer combines a biography of Maria Antonia and her social context with an engaging musicological investigation of the regent's three major operas. Indeed, she emphasizes the electress's activities in almost every artistic field imaginable: as a writer of lyric and prose in both French and Italian, as a practicing musician (piano and singing), as an opera composer, and even in the visual arts, as a painter. As Fischer notes, Maria Antonia was particularly influential because of the publication and wide dissemination of her works:

> Sie machte diesen Beitrag durch Druckpublikationen von Texten und Partituren, von Stichen eigner Bilder, von Übersetzungen ihrer Texte ins Deutsche, Französische und Polnische auch in einem Maße publik und verfügbar, das aus der Perspektive ihrer Zeit und in entsprechende Relation gesetzt auch darüber hinaus als einmalig beurteilt werden muss. (*Visionen*, 7)

> [She made this contribution through printed publications of texts and sheet music, through engravings of her own paintings, and through translations of her texts into German, French, and Polish, which were also publicly disseminated to such a degree that, taken from the perspective of her time and commensurately even beyond it, can only be judged as unparalleled.][2]

Among her many works, the opera *Talestris* stands out as being particularly significant with respect to Maria Antonia von Sachsen's political ambitions as an aspiring female ruler, who sought to reshape Saxony through enlightened ideals, such as a ruler's service to the polis, and establish a vision of female leadership that transcended binary conceptions of gender and political power predicated on violence. Both Fischer and Anne Fleig rightly understand her third and final opera, *Talestris*, as her definitive self-stylization as an enlightened and capable ruler of Saxony's court.[3] This is significant because it demonstrates Maria Antonia's identification with her Amazonian protagonist. Maria Antonia's work represents one of the first literary instances of an explicit invocation of the image of the Amazon by a woman writer as a means for shaping her own identity, that is, she crafts an autofictional[4] self-staging that makes an explicit claim for her right to participate in a political arena dominated by men. Maria Antonia not only composed the music and wrote the libretto; she also performed the main role as the queen of the Amazons in the initial performance of the opera at her court. Fischer stresses that the identification between Maria Antonia and her protagonist, Talestris, is cemented through her performance of the role:

> Den Aufführungen der Werke Maria Antonias, in denen die Kurprinzessin selbst als Sängerin wirkte, muss besonderes Augenmerk gewidmet werden. Durch die direkte Verbindung von der Autorschaft zur dargestellten Figur, die sich aus der Selbstinterpretation ergibt, entstehen wichtige Bedeutungsfacetten und Interpretationsaspekte der Werke, die bisher vernachlässigt wurden: Maria Antonia verkörperte ihre Hauptfiguren im wahrsten Sinne des Wortes. Der wahrhafte Körper der Kurprinzessin verschmilzt in diesen Aufführungen mit dem imaginären Bild, das sie durch ihre Opernfiguren von sich schuf. (*Visionen*, 332)

> [Particular attention needs to be given to the performance of works by Maria Antonia in which the electoral princess herself appeared as a singer. Important facets of meaning and aspects for the interpretation of her works become apparent through the direct union of her authorship with the figure represented, which amounts to a kind of self-interpretation by the princess that has been neglected thus far: Maria Antonia embodied her protagonists in the truest sense of the word. In these performances, the actual body of the electoral princess merges with the imagined image that she created for herself through her opera figures.]

The extent to which her operatic performance merges an imagined role as the Queen of the Amazons and Maria Antonia's physical or political body remains open to discussion. But because the author did in fact embody her protagonist on the stage, her authorial situation as an educated noblewoman writing in an elite sphere of society will serve as a lens for decoding the text's transformative potential. Her work represents a historically bound autofiction performed live at the Saxon court. As such, it communicates important insights not only about the author's identity but also about her political ambitions. If one understands Maria Antonia's libretto as generating both meaning and identity, as a form of auctorial autopoiesis,[5] *Talestris* can be interpreted not only as potentially constituting her authorial identity[6] but also as enabling her to transform her authority in the social context in which the opera was written. Maria Antonia's opera can thus best be understood through a combination of historical and theoretical frameworks. Her sociopolitical situation, paired with an analysis of the semiotic significance of Amazons and Minerva in the cultural archive of the eighteenth century, will serve as the foundation for rendering a more thorough close reading of her opera, which offers us a radical vision of female leadership and, as I would like to argue, also implicitly reveals the performative malleability of gender identities.

Talestris was performed at the court of Dresden on August 24, 1763, just as the *Kurfürst* (Elector) of Saxony and King of Poland, August III (1696–1763), returned with his family and entourage from exile. The Prussian armies of Friedrich II had ravaged and occupied Saxony during the course of the Seven Years' War (1756–63), forcing August III to flee.[7] In contrast to his father, August II (1674–1733), who had pursued an aggressive foreign policy waging war against neighboring states in a fashion characteristic of absolutist rulers,[8] August III failed to maintain Saxony's military prowess. Instead, he cultivated the baroque pomp that his father had also employed to further consolidate and promote his power as an absolutist ruler, using elaborate and lavish court ceremonies to reinforce his position as the center of Saxony's political universe.[9] These included highly orchestrated masked balls, musical and theatrical performances, and the like. Maria Antonia's opera operates within this tradition, but also subtly subverts it. The military decline precipitated by August III's laissez-faire attitude toward managing his political and financial affairs was further complicated by his heir, Friedrich Christian (1722–63), whose physical frailty posed a problem for the representation of Saxony's rulers as military leaders. After an infection during his early youth permanently crippled both the prince's feet, Friedrich Christian was confined to a wheelchair, which only gave the young prince more cause to cultivate his mind.[10] However, even as an educated and enlightened monarch, Friedrich Christian's physical impairment posed a serious political problem for the court, since representations of the *Kurfürst* as an absolute (military) authority were part of a long monarchical feudal tradition. And indeed, Friedrich Christian's father had unsuccessfully tried to disinherit him, favoring instead his younger brother, Franz Xaver (1730–1806) as successor to the throne.

Into this political quagmire came the highly gifted *femme savante*, Maria Antonia Walpurgis—originally from Bavaria—who married the prince elector Friedrich Christian, her first cousin, joining the court in Dresden in 1747 and becoming Princess-Electress Maria Antonia Walpurgis Symphorosa of Saxony.[11] In the first years of their marriage, prior to the outbreak of the Seven Years' War, Maria Antonia continued to establish herself as a learned woman, particularly as a respected musical composer and librettist. In the same year as her marriage, she was welcomed into the Accademia dell'Arcadia in Rome, a learned society for artists of royal lineage to which her husband already belonged (*Visionen*, 50–64). Maria Antonia gained her pseudonym,[12] Ermelinda Talea Pastorella Arcadia (E.T.P.A.), from the Arcadian society.[13] Shortly thereafter, she composed the oratory *La conversione di Sant'Agostino* (*The Conversion of Saint Augustine*, 1750), the pastoral *Il trionfo della fedeltà* (*The Triumph of Fidelity*, 1754), and finally the dramatic opera *Talestri, regina delle amazzoni* (*Thalestris, Queen of the Amazons*, 1760). The latter can without question be considered her masterpiece, in terms of both its refined composition and its politically prescient content. Saxony's court was stable and prosperous at the time of their marriage, but the (relatively) peaceful political climate that welcomed their marriage did not last.

Maria Antonia entered into a marriage that was already marred by the specter of a power vacuum. The outbreak of the Seven Years' War had forced August III to flee from Prussian troops, and he spent the war living in "exile" at his palace in Warsaw. This absence afforded both Friedrich Christian and Maria Antonia the opportunity to govern for him *in absentia*. The pair officially handled the court's financial affairs starting in 1759, although it was Maria Antonia who largely conducted these matters.[14] Friedrich Christian officially transferred responsibility for the financial affairs of the court to Maria Antonia after the death of his father in 1763.[15] At this point, Maria Antonia was poised to assume political authority, and, as Fleig notes, had already established an influential position in Saxony, which she gained not just through marriage but through her outstanding competence as a ruler and via her husband's willing division of governing responsibilities ("'Entre souvrains,'" 45). Thus in the year when *Talestri* was first performed at the Saxon court, Maria Antonia was ready to take the reins of power and was already actively participating in the state's internal and foreign affairs. Unlike Catherine the Great's coup d'état, political change was brought about naturally through disease in Saxony, since both August III and his incompetent finance minister, Count Heinrich von Brühl, died within months of the performance of *Talestris*, in October of 1763. Sadly, Friedrich Christian joined them soon after in December, dying suddenly from a smallpox infection after having ruled a mere ten weeks.

Peint en   Pastel
par Son Altesse Royale même

Gravé par Giuseppe Canale pour sa Réception à l'Académie de Dresde 1764

Figure 1.1. A portrait of Electress Maria Antonia Walpurgis Symphorosa of Saxony next to the Polish crown, meant to signify her claim to political power. Portrait by Giuseppe Canale (1762). Dresden, Staatliche Kunstmuseum Dresden, Sax. Bildn. A 116397, SLUB / Deutsche Fotothek / Richter, Regina.

Figure 1.2. A portrait of Maria Antonia as a *femme savante*, by Pietro Rotari (ca. 1755), holding a copy of her oratoria *Il triunfo delle fedeltà* with the initials of her pseudonym, E.T.P.A. visible on the open page. Dresden, Staatliche Kunstsammlungen Dresden, Gemäldegalerie Alte Meister, SLUB / Deutsche Fotothek.

Thus, shortly after Maria Antonia had exploited the court stage for representing herself as an enlightened Amazonian queen, a political path cleared for her to assume the position of power that her opera had postulated through its imaginative praxis. For instance, she maintained a long-lasting correspondence with Saxony's former enemy, Frederick the Great, from 1763 until shortly before her death in 1780.[16] Maria Antonia began her correspondence with Frederick in the months prior to her first performance of *Talestris*. As Heinz Drewes notes, she used this opportunity to communicate with the Prussian monarch about musical affairs, and she also enclosed both her operas, *Il trionfo della fedeltà* and *Talestri, regina delle amazzoni* with her first letter on April 24, 1763.[17] But the protagonist and subject matter of *Talestris*, namely the queen of the Amazons, deals centrally with thematic questions regarding the nature of good leaders and enlightened political attitudes, particularly the legitimacy of female rule. Naturally this positions Maria Antonia's and Frederick's letters as a means to communicate about political affairs, while conveniently relying on the pretext of their shared love of music and the fine arts.[18] After the Seven Years' War, Maria Antonia actively attempted to secure the Polish crown for her son, Friedrich August (1750–1827), negotiating not only with Frederick the Great but also with the Empress of Russia, Catherine the Great. The latter certainly represents another political "Amazon" whose own political machinations contravened Maria Antonia's, resulting in the termination of their correspondence in 1772.[19] Unfortunately, Maria Antonia's political aspirations were ultimately impeded by her co-regent and the would-be heir to the throne, Franz Xaver, Friedrich Christian's younger brother.

Although Maria Antonia is generally thought to have agreed with many of the reforms proposed by Friedrich Christian, it remains an open question whether her husband was an aid or a hindrance to her political aspirations. *Talestris*, with its expression of progressive politics and enlightened ideals, stands in clear relation to the plan Maria Antonia and her husband outlined for the *rétablissement* of Saxony's court in the wake of the Seven Years' War,[20] and both lent support to Maria Antonia's claim to political power.[21] Her performance as the queen of the Amazons relates directly to her political aspirations, especially when we conceive of the opera as a means for Maria Antonia to stage herself as a potential ruler within the framework of court ceremonies. Furthermore, questions remain with regard to her willingness to go along with some of the reforms proposed by Friedrich Christian, as one of his first measures as elector was to close the court's opera, Maria Antonia's main venue for profiling herself as an aspiring female ruler (*Visionen*, 60). Although they generally saw eye-to-eye in their reforms—for example, with respect to the state support of education and the arts—this could be regarded as an exception, and even potentially as a thorn in Maria Antonia's side.

Moreover, keeping in mind the context of the Seven Years' War, which left Saxony in shambles, particular attention must be paid to the presence or absence of violence in Maria Antonia's libretto, and to what extent her Amazons conform to, subvert, or even transcend socially propagated notions of gendered political authority.

Minerva and the Amazons as Competing Symbols of Feminine Authority

While an exploration of the exact political maneuvers that Franz Xaver employed to prevent Maria Antonia from assuming a position of absolute power at Saxony's court lies outside the boundaries of this exposition, the significance that the symbols of the Amazons *and* Minerva/Pallas Athena had for female rulers in Europe during the seventeenth and eighteenth centuries must be further explicated here. *Femmes fortes*, women in positions of political power, such as Maria de Medici and Queen Christina of Sweden, positioned themselves within a patriarchal tradition of militaristic representations of feudal rulers using the tropes of Amazons and Athena. Christa Schlumbohm, for instance, notes that these visual representations served as a kind of proto-feminist propaganda against misogynist arguments that questioned women's ability to lead based on patriarchal notions about women's physical and intellectual inferiority.[22] These militant models served to underscore women's ability to rule effectively and to act as regents in the case of an underage or absent male successor. The utilization of symbols such as Minerva/Pallas Athena and the Amazons thus helped female rulers capitalize on female allegories of wisdom and courage so as to reinforce visually their equality with male rulers. The ambivalent, androgynous symbol of Minerva allowed them to transfer virtues typically reserved for men, such as wisdom (*Weisheit*), virtue (*Tugend*), courage (*Tapferkeit*), and bravery (*Mut*) to women. Both Schlumbohm and Bettina Baumgärtel, however, reject the idea that these representations of female rulers as Amazons constitute a blurring of gender distinctions, or that the utilization of the Amazon or Minerva eidolons might imply a foreign Otherness.[23] They read these images instead as representing an idealization of femininity that combines positive traits of men and women, posting a utopian kind of androgyny without negating femininity or assuming a monstrous character. Schlumbohm emphasizes that visual representations of women rulers as Amazons or as Minerva/Pallas Athena remain idealizations, and that they do not therefore threaten gender distinctions:

> Dieses Idealbild, das die italienische Renaissancekonzeption der *virago* aufnimmt, meint dabei keinesfalls die vermännlichte Frau, das

Mannweib; eine solche *femme hommasse* gilt allgemein als abschreckend. Angesetzt wird vielmehr hier eine ideale Mischung von *douceur* und *beauté* einerseits und *force* und *fierté* andererseits, von eminent weiblichen Reizen und spezifisch männlichen Eigenschaften. . . . Sie ist ein idealisierendes und ideologisches Konstrukt, dem der Replikcharakter und die Intention des Gleichwertigkeitsnachweises unschwer anzumerken sind.[24]

[This idealized image, which adopts the concept of the *virago* from the Italian Renaissance, does not in any way imply the masculinized woman, the manly woman; such a *femme hommasse* was generally held to be offensive. Rather, an ideal mixture of *douceur* and *beauté*, on the one hand, and *force* and *fierté* on the other, was joined together here from eminently feminine allures and specifically masculine character traits. . . . It is an idealizing and ideological construction, whose replicatory character and intention to prove equality are easily recognizable.]

This thesis unsatisfyingly refutes the liminality of transvestism, instead insisting that an androgynous *Mannweib* would have been considered offensive. Instead these allegorical representations merely project masculine traits onto the feminine body, which remains "beautiful" and "graceful," with the added characteristic of strength. Important for the following close reading of *Talestris*, Minerva's beauty does not stand in contrast to strength (*force*) or autonomy. The physicality, that is, the biological body of the *femme forte*, however, plays a central role in Baumgärtel's argument. Indeed, biology seems to be damning in her reading, which explicitly argues against a queen having two bodies—in the sense posited by Kantorowicz regarding the king's two bodies. Rather, she contends that a queen remains bound to her sex through her roles as mother and wife, and this motif becomes important in *Talestris* as well. Baumgärtel affirms the use of Amazonian imagery by queens, particularly by Maria de Medici, but she also contends:

Folglich dürfte die Interpretation der Amazone / Minerva, die bis heute als Beispiel für *gender crossing*, d.h. für Rollenwechsel und Vermännlichung der Frau, angeführt wird, nicht haltbar sein. Vielmehr zeigt sich, wie die Figur der Amazone / Minerva zum weiblichen Pendant des Herkules, dem männlichen Herrschersymbol nicht nur des französischen Königs, wurde und zur offiziellen, politischen Metapher für weibliche Stärke und Klugheit transzendierte. Im Falle der Regentin fand demnach keine Trennung des "politischen" Körpers vom "natürlichen" statt, sondern immer nur eine Vermischung und Überschneidung des Weiblichen mit dem Politischen.[25]

[Consequently, the interpretation of the Amazon / Minerva, which is cited even today as an example of gender crossing, that is, for the exchange of roles and the masculinization of woman, is untenable. On the contrary, it demonstrates how the figure of the Amazon / Minerva became the female counterpoint to Hercules, the masculine symbol of authority for more than just the French king, and transcended to an official, political metaphor for feminine strength and intelligence. However, in the case of the regent, no separation of the "political" body from the "natural" took place, rather only a mixing and overlapping of womanhood with politics.]

Indeed, Minerva / Pallas Athena and the Amazons found increasing popularity among numerous women in positions of power during the seventeenth century, particularly as a means for solidifying their claims to political authority through the arts and as emblems of female strength and intelligence, by visually reinforcing and legitimating claims to women's capacity to rule via patriarchally determined tropes.

Yet this trend among female rulers to identify explicitly with Minerva, who is almost always portrayed wearing armor and bearing weapons, correlated with patronage of the arts, as was the case with both Christina of Sweden and Maria de Medici. The former founded the *Accademia dell'Arcadia*, in which Maria Antonia acquired membership in 1747. Similarly, Maria de Medici commissioned Peter Paul Rubens to paint twenty-one large-format portraits of her, many of which allegorically represent her as Minerva or in the company of this or similar goddesses, such as Victoria.[26] These allegories of female authority, based on the Amazonian character traits of strength and intelligence, represented positive models for women who ruled. Portraits of female rulers as Amazons and Minerva asserted a positive image of femininity, which was also an important topic in the *querelle des femmes* in the seventeenth century, and these antique eidolons were rejuvenated through living examples of *femmes fortes* and *femmes savantes*.

Maria Antonia Walpurgis was also a contemporary of the Empress Catherine the Great of Russia (1729–96), who was famous not only as a Minerva-like protector of the arts and sciences but also for overseeing the rapid expansion of the Russian Empire, which acquired lands in what is now Poland, Lithuania, the Crimean Peninsula, Ukraine, and even Alaska.[27] While the empress also dabbled in the arts and was additionally lauded via allegorizations as Minerva,[28] her association with the Amazons gains increasing relevance with regard to Maria Antonia's claims to power and her self-staging as an Amazon. Catherine the Great was, indeed, a very real Amazon, as is evident in the famous portrait of her by Vigilius Eriksen (see fig. 1.5), where she sits atop a warhorse, not riding side-saddle in a dress, but wearing a soldier's uniform with boots and leggings.

Figure 1.3. A portrait of Marie de' Medici as a triumphant queen / as the goddess Bellone, by Peter Paul Rubens (n.d.). Paris, Department of Paintings of the Musée du Louvre, INV 1792.

Figure 1.4. Engraving of Queen Christina of Sweden as Minerva, by Jeremiasz Falck (ca. 1630–77). Braunschweig, Herzog Anton Ulrich-Museum, Alter Besitz, JFalck AB 3.26.

This Amazonian portrait famously relates to an episode from the *coup d'état* against her husband Peter III (1728–62) in July of 1762. Here Catherine stole away disguised in men's attire to give a speech to the Ismailovsky regiment, asking for its protection, after her plans for a coup had been prematurely discovered. She then had herself sworn in as regent by the Russian clergy and promptly had her husband arrested. He died under mysterious circumstances while imprisoned. Peter III had already lost a great deal of favor among his generals and the aristocracy for his admiration of Frederick the Great and consequent secession of Russian lands to the Prussian leader following the Seven Years' War. Like Friedrich Christian, Peter III also reigned only for a very brief interlude, a little over six months, before Catherine deposed him.[29]

Keeping in mind contemporaries such as Catherine the Great and the Empress Maria Theresa of Austria, Maria Antonia's choice of the Amazons as the subject matter for her third opera relates to a broader visual tradition of Amazonian and Minervan allegories actively utilized as self-stylizations by highly educated women of the nobility in seventeenth-century France. Indeed, the ideal of strong, intelligent, active, independent, and even bellicose female leaders gained a strong foundation through notions of the *femme forte* and the *femme savante*, which remained intimately connected to the eidolons of Minerva and the Amazons. At the same time,

Figure 1.5. Catherine the Great, wearing the uniform of the Preobrazhensky regiment, which supported her during her coup d'état. Portrait by Virgilius Eriksen (ca. 1762–72). Copenhagen, SMK, National Gallery of Denmark, KM 3633.

women such as Catherine the Great and Maria Theresa were also actively taking part in political affairs and governing independently as female rulers. Therefore Maria Antonia can be understood as inscribing herself into this visual tradition through her Amazonian opera.

The Court Stage as a Representative Space for Transformative Politics

As Fleig and Fischer have pointed out, Maria Antonia's poetic appropriation of the Amazon figure echoes her status as a woman occupying a position of power in Saxony's court and her identity as a *femme savante*. However, the idealization of a female leader as an Amazon does not de-potentiate the gender ambiguity bound up with the Amazons or the figure of Minerva, contrary to what Baumgärtel and Schlumbohm would have us believe. A certain ambivalence remains inherent to both archetypes; Amazons and Minerva exhibit femininity and beauty, but they also cross-dress, wearing armor and helmets, and bear weapons, often phallically connoted, which remain inherently threatening as instruments of war.[30] But Amazonian androgyny also operated within a tradition of playful performance and inversion of standard gender roles on the operatic and comedic stage, and in this sense Maria Antonia inscribes *Talestris* into a long tradition of court performances and aesthetics. These often included carnivalesque revelries that mockingly inverted social norms and hierarchies through the trope of Amazonian cross-dressing. Helen Watanabe-O'Kelly relates several reports of court festivities in German-speaking lands during the sixteenth and seventeenth centuries that usually involved men cross-dressing as cross-dressed Amazons: for instance, Johann Georg II of Saxony once dressed as Penthesilea in 1654 and set up a tournament for the women of the court.[31] Additionally, recalling her Minerva portrait, Christina of Sweden, as part of her coronation ceremonies in 1650, held an Amazonian parade in which knights appeared dressed as Amazons ("'Entre souvrains,'" 51). Indeed, cross-dressing and the Amazon thematic were endemic to the operatic stage as well—as a more specific locus of late-baroque court culture—and well over twenty operas featuring Amazons had already been written by 1700.[32] While the tradition of the *Hosenrolle* (trouser role) also has a long history on the stage,[33] the plasticity of gender is especially prominent in opera, not only because of the popularity of the Amazon mythos as a narrative subject but also because of the use of castrati to sing female parts. In these latter instances, a literal transgression against the body underwrote the imaginative representation occurring on the stage. In Maria Antonia Walpurgis's opera there are no castrati; however, since the male lead was sung by a woman, a double cross-dressing took place during the performance of

Talestris. In this regard Maria Antonia's opera, although also a celebratory performance for the birthday of August III, might be taken as a critique of social circumstances based on its suspension and inversion of norms. One thinks of Bakhtin's notion of carnivalesque laughter, which gives the opera meaning when viewed as a communicative praxis in a space of play, where gender roles are comically inverted, which implicitly subverts and reveals everyday normative behaviors as mere performances as well.

Maria Antonia Walpurgis clearly inserts herself into a long visual tradition in which female rulers stylized themselves as Amazons and Minervas. This tradition was fed by the renewed popularity of classical literature based on the revival of learning during the Renaissance, but also specifically by the ideal of the learned woman during this time and by notions of women as the stronger sex, as *femmes fortes*. Intelligent and politically astute women in positions of privilege and power recuperated notions of wisdom and heroism from men, and these women were often imagined as potentially militant Amazons. With this broader social context in mind, the performance of *Talestris* becomes particularly relevant, because Maria Antonia literally embodied the queen of the Amazons directly before the eyes of August III, king of Poland and elector of Saxony. She not only dons the helmet, armor, and weapons of the Amazons, but the title of their queen as well! Indeed, the systematic transcendence and subversion of traditional gender boundaries on the operatic stage relate to complex shifts, subversions, and constructions of gender identities in Maria Antonia's opera, particularly in the context of positing a progressive idea about female leadership at the Saxon court. Her utilization of the ambiguous Amazon imago moves beyond merely castrati singing the roles written for women, that is, soprano parts. The Amazons in *Talestris* were performed by cross-dressing women wearing "masculine" warrior costumes, which does not necessarily negate their femininity but emphasizes gender as a *performance* via meta-costumes. For instance, engravings from the partitura of *Talestris*, published by Breitkopf in 1765, show actresses playing Amazons clearly marked as Amazons through their helmets, breastplates, shields, and spears.[34] At the same time, underneath their Amazonian armor, the actresses also clearly wear the "costume" of the day: large trellised dresses that were then fashionable among ladies (see fig. 1.6). In another engraving from the 1765 partitura (see fig. 1.7), the gender of the Scythian and Amazon leads—Oronte, Talestri, Antiope, and Learco shown from left to right—is hardly discernable by their costumes. The male prisoners wear slightly smaller dresses, and the fact that Oronte was played by the Countess Mnischek further adds to the ambiguity, as her "Scythian" breastplate is actually that of an Amazon (see fig. 1.7, figure on the far left). Finally, in the engraving portraying the final confrontation between the Amazons and the Scythians (see fig. 1.8), the heteronormative fashion of the day reveals itself, with the trellised dresses

Figure 1.6. Engraving from 1765 partitura of *Talestri*, published by Breitkopf, showing Talestri on her throne. Karlsruhe, Badische Landesbibliothek, Musiksammlung, Don Mus. Dr. 2664.

Figure 1.7. Engraving from 1765 partitura of *Talestri*, published by Breitkopf, showing Oronte, Talestri, Antiope, and Learco from left to right. Karlsruhe, Badische Landesbibliothek, Musiksammlung, Don Mus. Dr. 2664.

Figure 1.8. Engraving from 1765 partitura of *Talestri*, showing the final confrontation between the Amazons and the Scythians at the opera's conclusion. Karlsruhe, Badische Landesbibliothek, Musiksammlung, Don Mus. Dr. 2664.

of the Amazons almost out-presencing their armor and weapons. While the costumes of the Amazons and Scythians largely reproduced normative fashions for men and women, the additional layer of costume placed on top throws the heteronormative dichotomy of gender into flux. The fact that traditional fashions of the day made their way onto Maria Antonia's stage connects performance to its social context.

As Christine Fischer points out, "Regarding gender, the world that Maria Antonia put on the stage was in many ways the exact reverse of that in the audience, arranged around the male monarch,"[35] since she placed herself at the center of opera, singing the most pieces and wearing the most expensive costume.[36] The *Reithalle* at the Dresden court's riding stable had been renovated into an opera house that seated 532 audience members (*Visionen*, 386), and the audience was seated in a way that mirrored the typical hierarchy of the court's social order. The auditorium was centered on the monarch, August III, and an audience member's importance was defined by how close or far they sat from the king, which was a typical practice at absolutist courts (*Visionen*, 389). As Fischer notes: "Im kleinen Theater des Reithauses wurden dabei wie üblich hierarchische Systeme kreiert und einander gegenübergestellt: eines im Zuschauerraum und eines auf der Bühne. . . . Zum andern stellte Maria Antonia damit auf der Bühne Hierarchien zur Schau, die nicht mit den im Zuschauerraum repräsentierten korrespondieren" (*Visionen*, 393; In the small theater of the riding hall, as was the normal practice, hierarchical systems were built and placed opposite from each other: one in the audience and the other on the stage. . . . Maria Antonia thus also put hierarchies on full display on the stage, which did not correspond with the one represented in the audience). Thus Maria Antonia juxtaposed her own dramatic role as the monarch of the Amazons against August III's real position of power at the court and in the seating hierarchy of the audience. Indeed, the entire operatic scenario can be understood as an inverted world, with women at the center of the action rather than the periphery.

Visions of Enlightened Amazonian Leadership: *Verdienst* versus Tradition

Interestingly, in the process of legitimating women's political authority, *Talestris* also seems to undermine polarizing gender differences between men and women, specifically through the extension of Amazonian identity to the Scythians.[37] At the opera's outset, Talestris asserts that she does not merely want to inherit her mother's throne but wants to earn the right to rule over her Amazonian sisters through service, by proving herself in battle. The head priestess of the Amazons, Tomiris, commences Maria Antonia's *opera drammatica* with a speech addressed to Talestris that emphasizes her right to rule through a matrilineal ascension to the throne:

> Komm und besteig den Thron,
> Dein mütterliches Gut und deiner Tugend Lohn.
> Komm, komm, die Zeit ist bald verflossen,
> Und um der Mutter Tod und Thränen gnug vergossen.
>
> (2r, lines 3–6)

> [Come and ascend the throne,
> Your motherly property and your virtue's reward.
> Come, come, the time is almost lost,
> And enough tears have been wept for your mother's death.]

Tomiris asserts that Talestris has indeed earned the crown with her virtue (*Tugend*), in addition to being the rightful heir, but Talestris rebels against the notion that she has a natural right to ascend the throne:

> Die unbesiegten Amazonen
> Kann ich mit nichts als Dank belohnen.
> Wenn ich bey ihren Siegen

Theil an der Ehre nahm, so fiel mir niemals ein,
Vor so viel würdigern, einst Königin zu seyn.
Mich dünckt es sollten Cronen
Mehr das Verdienst, als das Geschlecht, belohnen.
Wie sollt' ich, unerfahren,
Und in der Blüthe von den Jahren,
Ein grosses Reich mit Ruhm regieren können?
Viel lieber tragen sie die Würde einer an,
Die glücklicher, als ich, den Scepter führen kann.
Ich werde meinen Stolz blos in Gehorchen zeigen.
Nur das Verdienst soll unsern Thron besteigen.

(2r, lines 7–20)

[The undefeated Amazons
I can reward with nothing but thanks.
If, through their victories,
I took part in their honor, never would I dare to think,
To be queen before so many worthier ones.
I would wager that crowns
Should reward service
More than dynasty.
How should I, inexperienced,
And still in the bloom of youth
Be able to rule a great kingdom with glory?
Better still if they would give the honor to you,
who, happier than I, can wield the scepter forth.
I would show my pride solely in obeying.
Only merit should ascend our throne.]

In this initial translation of the original Italian libretto from 1763, blood (*sangue*) has become *Geschlecht*, which has multiple definitions: the blood of a family lineage or dynasty, or that of sex or gender, which creates a double-meaning in the context of this all-women society. Should service to the people be more important that being of noble Amazonian blood, or even being a woman? Talestris's central message—that she would rather obey (*gehorchen*) than rule and that civic service should be held as the paramount value in Amazonian society—demonstrates a commitment to her Amazonian sisters that mirrors the values of enlightened despotism. Because Talestris has not yet participated in any of the Amazons' great battles against the Scythians, she cannot claim to partake in their collective honor earned through military victories against men, which conversely points to militarism bound to absolutist rule. Her gender does not have any relation to her ability to rule, as she is operating within the norms of an Amazonian gynocracy; rather, age, talent, and commitment to service are the determining factors. For her, the humble attitude that she is merely a servant and no better than any of the other Amazons, regardless of her birth, becomes a central, egalitarian assertion. Maria Antonia's libretto pushes away from notions of divine right claimed by absolute monarchs and moves toward an enlightened notion of service (*Verdienst*). In this sense, her obedience relates to compliance with Amazonian laws and norms: only service to society and her sisters should be praised, not her matrilineal succession to the throne, which she perceives as devoid of moral validity. Inherited political power, without proof of one's own worth, implies a form of obedience that entails submission to social norms, which could be seen to extend to heteronormative social standards that call for the submission of wives to their husbands, or in the context of the court, to patriarchal primogeniture, which the opera subtly critiques from the get-go.

Central to Talestris's coronation as the queen of the Amazons, however, is a ritual oath swearing to despise all men. Amazonian society depends on this exclusion of men as monstrous Others. Talestris's sister, Antiope, is shocked by her positive stance toward their sworn archenemies, and she initially interrogates Talestris, wanting to learn who taught her such anti-Amazonian sentiments:

> Wie? hältst du das Gesetz denn nicht [für] gut,
> Auf welchem unser Glück und Freyheit ruht?
> Und sollen wir, mit neuen Plagen,
> Das alte Joch der Ungeheuer tragen?
>
> (4r, lines 3–6)

> [What? Do you not then hold the law to be best
> Upon which our happiness and freedom rests?
> And should we, with new scourges
> Wear the old yoke of those ogres?].

Talestris, in turn, holds that not all men want to subjugate and dominate women, but that many of them only want love and loyalty:

> Du irrest, wenn du alle denckst
> Als Ungeheuer zu verfluchen;
> Da tausend nichts bey uns, als Lieb und Treue, suchen.
> Ehrfurcht und Zärtlichkeit sind ihre Waffen,
> Mit denen die sich nichts, als unser Herz, verschaffen.
>
> (4r, lines 7–11)

> [You're wrong if you think all of them
> Damned as monstrous creatures;
> Where thousands seek only love and loyalty with us.
> Veneration and tenderness are their weapons,
> With which they hope to procure only our hearts.]

While "procuring hearts" is of dubious import—and may signal the objectification and control of women's sexuality through monogamous marriage (*Treue*)—a masculine (or possibly transgender) viewpoint determines Talestris's perspective on men's inherent goodness. Talestris's positive assessment of men contradicts the ideological stance that would traditionally be harbored by an Amazonian subject positioned in radical opposition to philandry. This discarded Amazonian subject position reasserts itself through the figure of Antiope, who asks: "Wer aber stösset dir so neue Lehren ein?" (5r, line 12; Who thrust such new doctrines into your mind?). The severity of Antiope's criticism reveals itself in her language. Talestris's tolerance of men results from having been penetrated (*eingestoßen*) by foreign, new "doctrines," thereby disrupting the closed society of Amazonian sisters.

It should be noted that a hybrid, androgynous subject has influenced Talestris's new tolerance for men. Talestris reveals to her sister Antiope that Orizia is actually a cross-dressing Orontes, the prince of the Scythians, who had disguised himself as an Amazon. Orontes's female persona retains an epistemological value. A programmatic interchangeability of gender evinces itself through the either-*or* inherent to the names *Or*ontes and *Or*izia, and the opera continually plays with same-sex desire and homosocial relationships that are placed into contrast with heterosexual norms that had been discarded by the Amazons. The question thus arises as to whether or not the text's poetology points toward or away from gender as having any ontological significance in terms of virtue and human dignity, and we could already ask ourselves if Amazonian sisterhood has the potential to become universal. While, from an existential perspective and according to Herodotus's account, the gynocentric Amazonian society would have had intermittently to take recourse to relations with men in order to preserve their ranks, Antiope's response to Talestris after the latter confesses that it was Orizia who taught her conveys the centricity of homosocial bonds in the Amazonian kingdom: "Die, so dein Herz mir entzog? / Wer muste sie denn seyn?" (4r, lines 14–15; Her, the one who stole your heart from me? Who could she then be?). Antiope, who is literally Talestris's sister, hereby laments the fact that Orizia had usurped a piece of Talestris's heart from her, that is, her monopoly on a homosocial, sisterly love. In asking who Orizia was, Antiope inquires not only into the identity of the woman who had stolen her sister's favor, but also posits a question regarding the significance of identity with regard to Talestris's new knowledge: how does the being/essence of Orizia—who (s)he was—determine Talestris's acquired wisdom and consequentially her identity as an Amazon.

If self-identity determines itself through knowledge gained through encounters / conflicts with (selfsame) Others, Orizia's identity becomes a central factor for the construction of Talestris's Amazonian selfhood within the text's diegesis. Talestris's relationship with Orizia / Orontes thus forms the crux of the analysis of Maria Antonia's text, whereby instances of and conflicts with Otherness serve to establish differences from the Other, which, in turn, engender contours for the stabilization of a self-identity. Yet the clear-cut differentiation between Amazons and Scythians proposed by Antiope—that all Scythian men are debased savages, wanting only to oppress and possess Amazonian women—crumbles when Talestris contends that these men are also capable of tenderness and respect and that they desire only women's love and faithfulness. Talestris's assertion can be understood as the projection of traditionally feminine character traits onto men: Talestris assumes a heteronormative gender role constructed by a male-dominated society and projects it onto the masculine Other, in terms of men's *Zärtlichkeit* and *Ehrfurcht*. Femininity encounters itself in the Other, which can again only be understood as an encounter with the selfsame, while men also project themselves onto the feminine Other by cross-dressing as Amazons. Because textual conflicts with Otherness always represent interactions with one's self, these self-projections relocate character attributes that have been (socially) repressed on an unconscious level onto the Other. The fact that the masculine perspective that Talestris internalizes was taught to her by a Scythian prince, who was cross-dressed as a cross-dressing woman (that is, in the sense that Amazons take on all traditionally all-male vocations in their society of sisters, including donning armor for battle), complicates a clear differentiation of Amazon and non-Amazon. Orontes's masquerade thus bears a revolutionary potential; nevertheless, the question remains as to what extent the opera continues to portray gender differences as masks, and to what extent gendered identities are uncloaked as social constructs and performances.

Multiple moments ensue wherein Orontes's Otherness is conflated with Amazonian selfsameness, as Talestris and Antiope are no longer able to separate his identity as a Scythian from his Amazonian alter ego, Orizia. Indeed, as later revealed through one of the many plot twists in the opera, Orontes is in fact the son of the high priestess of the Amazons, Tomiris, who was impregnated and then spurned by the king of the Scythians. While his father's crime against the Amazons further bolstered their hatred of men, Orontes's status as a hybrid figure (*Grenzgänger*), literally as a genetic mixture of both peoples, could bear an emancipatory potential, just as his cross-dressing blurs gender distinctions and calls Amazonian (and Scythian) norms into question. Yet what consequences arise from Orontes's revaluation of Amazonian morals for Amazonian sisterhood? Is Orizia / Orontes an antichrist or savior? Does this bifurcated figure portend the enslavement of the Amazons by the Scythians, as Antiope fears?

Beyond his mixed blood, which quickly recedes into the background as a non-issue, Orontes's actions determine his hybridity, and ultimately alter Talestris's perceptions about men. Yet does Talestris merely react passively to Orontes actions? Does Maria Antonia's text actually reinforce heteronormative notions about masculine aggressiveness and feminine passivity?[38] As highlighted by a background story that accompanies the 1763 edition of *Talestris*, Orontes's motivation for cross-dressing, for living "unter verstelltem Geschlechte" (n.p.; under disguised gender), rests upon tales of Talestris's beauty:

> Ihr Ruhm machte dem ungeduldigen scythischen Prinzen so viel Lust sie zu sehen, daß er einsmals, in der Hitze eines Scharmützels, den Seinigen entwischte, und sich, in Amazonen-Kleidern, unter dem Namen Orizia, in Themiscira einschlich. Die Talestris zu sehen und zu lieben, war ein Augenblick." (n.p.)

> [Her fame fostered so much desire in the impatient prince to see her that, in the midst of battle, he escaped from his compatriots and, wearing the clothing of the Amazons, infiltrated Themiscra under the name of Orizia. To see and to love Talestris took only a blink of the eye.]

In this instance, Talestris functions as a passive libidinal object for Orontes's male gaze. Talestris, like all Amazons, is a *femme fatale*, an armed woman, reminiscent of Theweleit's "phallische Frau" (phallic woman)[39] who could potentially castrate or kill Orontes, yet this danger does not negate her sexual appeal for Orontes, who, by cross-dressing as an Amazon, essentially becomes the object that he desires. He does this very successfully, to the point where "die verstellte Orizia wurde bald die Verwunderung des ganzen Reichs, und das Vergnügen der jungen Prinzessinn" (n.p.; the disguised Orizia quickly became the wonderment of the entire kingdom, and the delight of the young princess). As an Amazon, Orizia is not only socially recognized but brings joy and amusement to Talestris, which, if not containing sexual undertones, at the very least implies homosocial intimacy among the Amazonian sisterhood. Returning to the active role played by Orontes through his/her assumption of an Amazonian identity, Orontes's cross-dressing can be interpreted as explicitly marking a break from a patriarchal Scythian society and as entrance into the matrilineal realm of the Amazons. The abduction and abandonment of Orontes's mother (Tomiris) by his father epitomizes a tyrannical patriarchy, wherein little or no regard for women exists, except as sexual objects. In light of the familial history, Antiope's sentiments regarding the universal monstrosity of men seem vindicated;

nevertheless, Orontes's actions undercut such absolutes. Early in the opera, Talestris describes how Orontes infiltrated the Amazonian ranks:

> Da ihn der Vater selbst zum Feldherrn ausersehn,
> Bestürmmt' er einstens unser Lager,
> Er weicht im Streit von seinem Volck zurück,
> Tauscht Kleid und Waffen mit Geschick,
> Steht, als verstellte Amazone,
> Uns bey, und schlägt die Scythen in die Flucht.
> Er bleibt bey uns,
> Sein jugendlich sein artig Angesichte
> Macht allen Schatten von Verdacht zu nichte.
>
> (5r, lines 6–14)

> [Since his father destined him to become a field marshal,
> He one day stormed our camp,
> He retreated in battle from his own people,
> Switched his garb and weapons with skill,
> Stood, disguised as an Amazon,
> Next to us, and fought the Scythians into retreat.
> He stayed with us, His youthful and good-natured countenance
> Brought an end to any shadows of doubt.]

Orontes was chosen by his father to take over the family business: making war. Yet Maria Antonia's libretto emphasizes that Orontes fled from his father's military camp by exchanging his Scythian weapons and clothes for Amazonian equipment. Orontes joins the Amazonian horde and avoids any suspicions, primarily because he has a youthful (that is, beardless), gentle-looking face. Maria Antonia thus presents Orontes's transformation into Orizia as a process of utmost ease and gender as a highly plastic concept. The similarities between Orontes and Talestris are also quite striking. Both are attractive, and Orontes's beautiful visage endears him to the Amazons, just as Talestris's beauty arouses Orontes's desire for her and his wish to become an Amazon. Two Amazonian beauties, they are cut from the same cloth. Moreover, in addition to sharing the same dress and pulchritude, Orontes and Talestris mirror each other in terms of moral virtue.

Before revealing himself to Talestris, Orontes / Orizia successfully assumes an Amazonian identity and becomes, if only temporarily, part of the Amazonian sisterhood. Conversely, Antiope's rhetoric assumes a xenophobic character; she labels Orontes as their greatest enemy and as a traitor, and is initially astounded that a Scythian, male Other could live undetected among them. But another Scythian prince, Learch, convinces Antiope that not all men are evil, when he offers to sacrifice himself for Orontes, after the latter voluntarily surrenders to Talestris to die at her hands. When she sees that Learch loves his friend Orontes so much that he is willing to trade places with him on the gallows, Antiope has a change of heart: "Talestris hat mich nicht betrogen: / Nicht alle Männer sind doch Ungeheuer" (18r, lines 12–13; Talestris did not betray me: / Not all men are indeed monsters). As Fleig notes:

> Mit Learch und seiner Liebe zu Orontes wird das Motiv der Freundestreue eingeführt. Talestris und Antiope hegen nun umso mehr Zweifel an der Rechtmäßigkeit ihrer Gesetze. Angesichts des hohen Werts von Frauenfreundschaft in ihrer Gemeinschaft erscheint ihnen der Hass auf diese Männer erst recht fragwürdig.[40] ("'Entre souvrains,'" 48)

> [With Learch and his love for Orontes, the theme of loyal friendship is introduced. Thalestris and Antiope thus harbor more doubts about the lawfulness of their laws. In light of the high value placed on women's friendship in their community, the hatred for these men now appears very questionable.]

After Thalestris releases Learch, the entire Scythian army, thinking that Orontes had been killed by his mother Tomiris, descends on the Amazons ready to avenge their fallen prince. At this juncture, Orontes reveals himself and pleads for peace between the two warring parties:

> Stellt, endlich, schöne Kriegerinnen,
> Die alte Feindschaft ein:
> Mit Schönheit kann der Zorn nicht wohl verbunden seyn.
> Die Freundschaft sey durch Haß und Waffen nie zerrüttet.
> Es ist Orizia, (Zur Talestris.) Orontes, (Zur Tomiris.) der Geliebte,
> (Zur Talestris.) der Sohn, (Zur Tomiris,) der darum bittet.
>
> (70r, lines 8–12)

> [Beautiful warriors, abandon the age-old animosity at long last:
> Rage cannot be well allied with beauty.
> Friendship will never be overcome by hatred and arms.
> It is Orizia, (To Thalestris.) Orontes, (To Tomiris.) the beloved,
> (To Thalestris.) the son (To Tomiris.), who pleads it).]

While Orontes takes recourse to his Amazonian identity, he also posits himself as Tomiris's son, and thereby resorts to normative definitions of gender that preclude women from any kind of militancy. Thus the equality proposed by Thalestris at the opera's conclusion might need to be taken with a grain of salt:

Folgt, ihr Getreuen, folgt doch meinem Beyspiel nach
Jetzt ist die rechte Zeit. Wenn, von untreuen Männern,
Der Haß entstund, so sey, von treuen Ehegatten,
Die Freundschaft wieder hergestellt.
Wir wollen künftighinn, nicht Unterthanen, nein,
Freundinnen unsrer Nachbarn seyn.

(71r, lines 8–13)

[Comrades, come and follow my example
Now is the right time. If unfaithful men
Created our hatred, then, by loyal husbands,
Let friendship be restored again.
In the future, we no longer want to be their subjects, no,
Let us be the friends of our neighbors.]

While scholars have argued that Thalestris preserves her political authority here, refusing to allow the Amazons to become subservient to men again, it might also be argued that the very concept of the Amazons' political autonomy is undermined here, if a society of sisters becomes reintegrated with men. Thus the union of Thalestris and Orontes / Orizia and the resulting peace between the Amazons and the Scythians remains problematic. At the same time, Thalestris emphasizes that the Amazons should be the "Freundinnen" of their neighbors and not "Unterthanen," and, in this sense, one might ask if, in light of the amazing flexibility of gender roles throughout the opera, the "group of women friends" applies to the Scythian men as well. Maria Antonia's opera posits a radical transcendence of gender differences embodied by the androgynous figure of Orontes / Orizia, and gender parity also quintessentially relates to the antiwar sentiment that pervades her text, presenting a utopian vision of a universal human sisterhood and peace.

Visions of Female Leadership and the Consequences of Political Marginalization

In the context of the court performance, the final truce between Amazons and Scythians becomes politically relevant, considering that the Seven Years' War had just concluded, and that the performance of *Talestris* was intended to celebrate the return of August III to his Electoral court in Dresden. As scholars such as Matthew Head have argued "the plot intimates that reform and progress arise from Talestri's exemplary character."[41] The peace between the Amazons and the Scythians can be positively evaluated under the sign of Minerva: by choosing to represent herself as the queen of the Amazons, Maria Antonia was inserting herself into the visual tradition of *femmes savantes* and *femmes fortes* who stylized themselves as Minervas and Amazons and thus identifying herself as an intellectually gifted and competent future ruler. Thus the trope of the Amazon is not mobilized in a teratological sense, but to positively affirm women's ability to rule empowered by education and reliant on the ability to make discriminating judgments. There is a powerful subtext at work in Maria Antonia's libretto that universalizes the ideal traits for leadership and governance, regardless of gender and specifically transcending gender. The opera suggests that governance demands a keen sense of discrimination tied to notions of knowledge and reason, which connects back to Maria Antonia's self-stylization as a *femme savante*. For instance, in the opera's opening scene, Thalestris demands discrimination in rulers, and hence she initially questions her own qualifications to be queen. She then shows further discrimination when judging Orontes—always in the positive sense of making a careful evaluation in specific circumstances—and condemning Tomiris for blindly applying the Amazonian law dictating that all male prisoners be executed. Indeed, careful rational judgment that resists generalizing prejudices or blind adherence to what others determine as "normal" behavior forms the core enlightened value of the play. It does not celebrate equality in the sense that everyone is the same, but stresses and acknowledges what is individual and exceptional. Indeed, the androgyny of Orontes / Orizia ties centrally to notions of individuality, in that this hybrid figure crosses otherwise stable thresholds, including gender norms, revealing them as nothing more than prejudices, which is underscored by the fluidity of genders by cross-dressing performers on the stage.

Performing Enlightened Leadership and Transcending Gender in the Face of Political Marginalization

Because Maria Antonia played the role of Thalestris on stage, she was able to insert herself into contemporary discussions regarding women's ability to act as rulers. Scholars such as Fischer and Fleig have rightly emphasized that Thalestris remains queen of the Amazons after the peace with the Scythians, and she never explicitly renounces her authority. Fischer makes an intriguing argument when she reads both Orontes / Orizia *and* Thalestris as liminal *Grenzgänger* (border crossers). Orontes / Orizia's assumption of "feminine" Amazonian virtues has already been shown to reveal a fluidity of genders. In addition to this androgynous breaching of circumscribed behaviors, Fischer posits that Thalestris also becomes a liminal figure, when she assumes the values previously held only by men, "indem sie Tugenden annimmt, die man landläufig nur Männern zuschrieb: die Befähigung zur Leitung von Staatsgeschäften" (in that she assumes virtues that had commonly only been attributed to men: the ability to manage state affairs),[42] and she thereby emphasizes Thalestris's rise as a political ruler ("Selbststilisierung," 217). Fischer reminds us that the very first scene thematizes the succession of aristocratic power. Here, the notion of *Verdienst* bound to enlightened absolutism has been satisfied, because Thalestris's reeducation results in peace between the Amazons and Scythians, to the benefit of both peoples. Fischer astutely connects the *Frieden* at the opera's conclusion to the turbulent social context surrounding the opera's performance:

> Dem Friedensschluss zwischen den Geschlechtern in der Opernhandlung steht damit der kurz zuvor im selben Jahr 1763 erfolgte wirkliche Friedensschluss, nämlich die Beendigung des Siebenjährigen Krieges, gegenüber. Talestris Rolle als Friedensbringerin für ihr Volk korrespondiert zudem mit einem der Zuständigkeitsbereiche der Friedensgöttin Minerva. ("Selbststilisierung," 222–23)

> [The final peace between the sexes in the opera's plot is directly analogous to the actual peace agreement reached the same year, 1763, namely the end of the Seven Years' War. Thalestris's role as the bringer of peace for her people corresponds with one of the spheres of responsibility held by the goddess of peace, Minerva.]

Maria Antonia's work can be interpreted as espousing her not as a bellicose Amazon but as an enlightened potential ruler and Minerva-like bringer of peace, who supported and participated in the arts and who had already demonstrated her ability to rule in the absence of the king. The text and the performance work together to promote Maria Antonia as a qualified candidate for rule, precisely because she learns how to discriminate, make good decisions, and pass discerning judgments. Reason transcends gender on the court stage, where the performance of her opera, marked by the king's physical presence in the audience, clearly communicates that we are all representatives of *homo sapiens*.

Much could be made of the subsequent marginalization of Maria Antonia's claim to political power in the absence of a male heir of rightful age. Fleig notes that Maria Antonia made diplomatic efforts to keep Poland's crown for the electors of Saxony after August III's death, but she was confounded by another Amazon, Catherine II of Russia. Her continued correspondence with Frederick II of Prussia and Empress Maria Theresa of Austria also gives evidence of her active engagement in political affairs, but Maria Antonia lost her claim to power in Saxony with the death of her husband. Her brother-in-law, Prince Xavier, took control and even became the guardian of her children, and, as Fleig rightfully laments: "Maria Antonia brachte sieben Kinder zur Welt, von denen eines im

Kindesalter starb. Wie die rechtliche Stellung der Fürstin am Dresdener Hof aussah und warum Maria Antonia nicht selbst die Vormundschaft übernehmen konnte, ließ sich nicht zuverlässig ermitteln" ("'Entre souvrains,'" 45; Maria Antonia bore seven children, one of whom died in childhood. The legal situation of the princess at the Dresden court remained opaque, and the reasons why she was not able to assume guardianship over the state could not be conclusively ascertained). Perhaps it was in fact her gender that precluded her from attaining the political position of king, where her role as mother, like the maternal instincts that are valorized in *Talestris*, ended up determining her political exclusion, even as she transcended gender norms through the text and performance of her opera. While the performance of *Talestris* failed to effect the political change that she sought, Maria Antonia's libretto remains successful, not just as a vehicle for preserving the memory of Maria Antonia as talented *femme savante* attempting to inscribe herself into political authority via Minerva-like Amazons: her text remains relevant even today in terms of continuing questions of gender equality and transgender identities, offering a utopian vision of gender parity and an enlightened ethos based on discernment and inclusion. Maria Antonia's genius—on the stage and on the printed page—shows us the immense power women have as leaders, and *Talestris* carries precisely that message: that women rule, both politically and artistically, and that they can create a better world for us to live in, under the aegis of the Amazons.

Notes

[1] Christine Fischer, *Instrumentierte Visionen weiblicher Macht: Maria Antonia Walpurgis' Werke als Bühne politischer Selbstinszenierung* (Kassel: Bärenreiter, 2007). Further references are given in the text using the short title *Visionen*.

[2] Unless otherwise noted, all translations from the German are my own.

[3] Anne Fleig, "'Entre souvrains ce n'est pas le sexe qui décide'—Höfische Selbstinszenierung und Geschlechterrollen," in *Ordnung, Politik und Geselligkeit der Geschlechter im 18. Jahrhundert*, ed. Ulrike Weckel et al. (Göttingen: Wallstein, 1998), 41–63. Further references to this work are given in the text using the short title "'Entre souvrains.'"

[4] Martina Wagner-Egelhaaf, ed., "Was ist Auto(r)fiktion?," in *Auto(r)fiktion: Literarische Verfahren der Selbstkonstruktion* (Bielefeld: Aisthesis, 2013), 7–21.

[5] See Jacek Rzeszotnik, ed., "Einleitung," in *Schriftstellerische Autopoiesis: Beiträge zur literarischen Selbstreferenzialität* (Darmstadt: Büchner, 2011), 7–12; and Stephan Sting, "The Reading-Author as Auto-Poet," *Paragrana: Internationale Zeitschrift für Historische Anthropologie* 4, no. 2 (1995): 79–89.

[6] For a theoretical framework regarding a historical-psychoanalytical approach to textual analysis, see Karin Kelping, "Historische Mentalitätenforschung,

Literaturanthropologie und Psychohistorie," in *Frauenbilder im deutschen Barock-drama: Zur literarischen Anthropologie der Frau* (Hamburg: Kovac, 2003), 13–19.

[7] For more information regarding the Seven Years' War and its effects on Dresden and Saxony, see Hans-Peter Lühr, ed., *Sachsen und Dresden im Siebenjährigen Krieg* (Dresden: Dresdener Geschichtsverein, 2001).

[8] Karl Czok, *August der Starke und seine Zeit* (Munich: Piper, 2008).

[9] Thomas Rahn, "Psychologie des Zeremoniells: Affekttheorie und -pragmatik in der Zeremoniellwissenschaft des 18. Jahrhunderts," in *Zeremoniell als höfische Ästhetik in Spätmittelalter und Früher Neuzeit*, ed. Jörg Jochen Berns and Thomas Rahn (Tübingen: Niemeyer, 1995), 74–98.

[10] August Moritz Engelhardt, *Friedrich Christian, Churfürst von Sachsen: Ein biographischer Entwurf; Nebst Beschreibung der auf diesen Fürsten Bezug habenden und unter seiner Regierung geprägten Münzen und Medaillen* (Dresden: Wagner, 1828), 2–3.

[11] For a more thorough account of Maria Antonia of Bavaria's youth prior to her marriage with Friedrich Christian, see Carl von Weber, *Maria Antonia Walpurgis, Churfürstin zu Sachsen, geb. Kaiserliche Prinzessin in Bayern: Beiträge zu einer Lebensbeschreibung derselben*, 2 vols. (Dresden: Teubner, 1857), 1:1–29.

[12] For a detailed discussion of the relationship between anonymity and female authorship, see Susanne Kord, *Sich einen Namen machen: Anonymität und weibliche Autorschaft, 1700–1900* (Stuttgart: Metzler, 1996). Kord differentiates women authors based on class distinctions: those *femmes savantes* belonging to the nobility had less fear of reprimand or disdain for their intellectual abilities. Drawing a parallel between Catherine the Great and Maria Antonia, Kord notes: "Katharina II. und Maria Antonia Walpurgis hatten sowohl die Muße zum Schreiben als auch den nötigen finanziellen Rückhalt und brauchten außerdem keine Ächtung wegen ihrer Schriftstellerei zu fürchten" (90; Catherine II and Maria Antonia Walpurgis had both the leisure to write and also the necessary financial support, and they also had no need to fear being ostracized because of their writing).

[13] For a detailed description of the founding of the Accademia dell'Arcadia, its early history, and functionalization for the advancement of the sciences and fine arts, see the extensive entry in Johann Heinrich Zedler, ed., *Grosses vollständiges Universal-Lexicon aller Wissenschaften und Künste, Welche bißhero durch menschlichen Verstand und Witz erfunden und verbessert worden*, vol. 66 (Halle: Zedler, 1731–54), 162–70.

[14] Weber, *Maria Antonia Walpurgis*, 122–23.

[15] Weber, *Maria Antonia Walpurgis*, 138–39.

[16] See Friedrich II, King of Prussia, "Correspondance de Frédéric avec l'électrice Marie-Antoine de Saxe (24 avril 1763–28 décembre 1779)," in *Oeuvres de Frédéric le Grand*, ed. Johann D. E. Preuss (Berlin: Decker, 1854), 24:41–366.

[17] Heinz Drewes, *Maria Antonia Walpurgis als Komponistin* (Borna-Leipzig: Noscke, 1934), 16–17.

[18] Drewes, *Maria Antonia Walpurgis*, 17.

[19] Maria Theresa, Empress of Austria, and Maria Antonia Walpurgis, Electress, *Briefwechsel, 1747–1772, mit einem Anhang ergänzender Briefe*, ed. Woldemar Lippert (Leipzig: Teubner, 1908).

[20] For more on Maria Antonia and Friedrich Christian's plan for the *Rétablissement* of Saxony, see Horst Schlechte, ed., *Die Staatsreform in Kursachsen, 1762–1763: Quellen zum kursächsischen Rétablissement nach dem siebenjährigen Kriege* (Berlin: Rütten & Loening, 1958).

[21] For more on the legal legitimacy of women's political rule in the absence or death of a king during the Late Middle Ages, see Martin Kintzinger, "Die zwei Frauen des Königs: Zum politischen Handlungsspielraum von Fürstinnen im europäischen Spätmittelalter," in *Das Frauenzimmer: Die Frau bei Hofe in Spätmittelalter und früher Neuzeit*, ed. Jan Hirschbiegel and Werner Paravicini (Stuttgart: Thorbecke, 2000), 377–98.

[22] Christa Schlumbohm, "Die Glorifizierung der Barockfürstin als 'Femme Forte,'" in *Die europäische Hofkultur im 16. und 17. Jahrhundert*, ed. August Buck et al. (Hamburg: Hauswedell, 1981), 113–22, here 114–16.

[23] Bettina Baumgärtel, "Zum Bilderstreit um die Frau im 17. Jahrhundert: Inszenierungen französischer Regentinnen," in *Die europäische Querelle des Femmes: Geschlechterdebatten seit dem 15. Jahrhundert*, ed. Gisela Bock and Margarete Zimmermann (Stuttgart: Metzler, 1997), 147–82.

[24] Schlumbohm, "Die Glorifizierung,'" 114.

[25] Baumgärtel, "Zum Bilderstreit,'" 153.

[26] Silvia Neysters, "Regentinnen und Amazonen," in *Die Galerie der starken Frauen: Regentinnen, Amazonen, Salondamen*, ed. Bettina Baumgärtel and Silvia Neysters (Munich: Klinkhardt & Biermann, 1995), 98–139, here 98–103.

[27] Simon Dixon, *Catherine the Great* (London: Profile, 2009), 270–92.

[28] Ruprecht Pfeiff, *Minerva in der Sphäre des Herrscherbildes: Von der Antike bis zur Französischen Revolution* (Münster: Lit, 1990), 106–9.

[29] Dixon, *Catherine the Great*, 108–25. For more regarding gendered representations of Catherine the Great, see Ruth Dawson, "Eighteenth-Century Libertinism in a Time of Change: Representations of Catherine the Great," *Women in German Yearbook* 18 (2002): 67–88.

[30] This very ambivalence regarding gender norms and behavior is precisely what potentiates Amazons/Minerva as a symbol for women's demand for equal participation in politics and change in the status quo. See Marjorie Garber, *Vice Versa: Bisexuality and the Eroticism of Everyday Life* (London: Penguin, 1995). Indeed, the image of the cross-dressing Amazonian warrior women remained an important trope for women writers during and after the French Revolution. See Stephanie M. Hilger, *Gender and Genre: German Women Write the French Revolution* (Newark, NJ: University of Delaware Press, 2015); Julie Koser, *Armed Ambiguity: Women Warriors in German Literature and Culture in the Age of Goethe* (Evanston, IL: Northwestern University Press, 2016); and Elisabeth Krimmer, *In the Company of Men: Cross-Dressed Women around 1800* (Detroit: Wayne State University Press, 2004).

[31] Helen Watanabe-O'Kelly, "Amazonen in der sozialen und ästhetischen Praxis der deutschen Festkultur der Frühen Neuzeit," in *Soziale und ästhetische Praxis der höfischen Fest-Kult im 16. und 17. Jahrhundert*, ed. Kirsten Dickhaut, Jörg Steigerwald, and Birgit Wagner (Wiesbaden: Harrassowitz, 2009), 127–47, here 132–36.

[32] Fleig, "'Entre souvrains,'" 53–54; Daniel E. Freeman, "*La guerriera amante*: Representations of Amazons and Warrior Queens in Venetian Baroque Opera," *Musical Quarterly* 53, no. 3 (1996): 431–60.

[33] For more regarding the history of cross-dressing on the European stage, see Susanne de Ponte, *Ein Bild von einem Mann—gespielt von einer Frau: Die wechselvolle Geschichte der Hosenrolle auf dem Theater* (Munich: Edition Text + Kritik, 2013).

[34] Maria Antonia Walpurgis Symphorosa, Electress of Saxony, *Talestri, regina delle amazzoni, dramma per musica* (Leipzig: Breitkopf, 1765), n.p. Digital scans of the engravings from the 1765 partitura were provided by the Badische Landesbibliothek, Karlsruhe, Musiksammlung, Don Mus. Dr. 2664.

[35] Christine Fischer, "Self-Stylisation in a Ceremonial Context: Maria Antonia Walpurgis as *Talestri, regina delle amazzoni*," in *Italian Opera in Central Europe: Institutions and Ceremonies*, ed. Melania Bucciarelli, Borbert Dubowy, and Reinhard Strohm, vol. 1 (Berlin: BWV, 2006) 203–19, here 212.

[36] Fischer, "Self-Stylisation," 209).

[37] The following close reading makes use of the bilingual edition from 1763 and retains the German spellings of proper names. Maria Antonia Walpurgis Symphorosa, Electress of Saxony, *Talestri: Regina delle amazzoni / Talestris: Königin der Amazonen*. Dresden, 1763.

[38] Thinking here of the polarizing, heteronormative notions of gender difference wrought by Rousseau's *Emile*, which was published the same year.

[39] Klaus Theweleit, *Männerphantasien 1 und 2* (Munich: Piper, 2009), 78–98.

[40] Fleig, "'Entre souvrains,'" 48.

[41] Matthew Head, *Sovereign Feminine: Music and Gender in Eighteenth-Century Germany* (Berkeley: University of California Press, 2013), 45.

[42] Christine Fischer, "Selbststilisierungs- und Herrscherkonzepte in Maria Antonia Walpurgis' *Talestri, regina delle amazzoni*," in *Frauenstimmen, Frauenrollen in der Oper und Frauen-Selbstzeugnisse*, ed. Gabriele Busch-Salmen and Eva Rieger (Herbolzheim: Centaurus, 2000), 198–225, here 216.

2: Maxims of Leadership for a Silent Readership: Sophie von La Roche's *Pomona für Teutschlands Töchter* and *Mein Schreibetisch*

Margaretmary Daley

IN 1783, WHEN SOPHIE VON LA ROCHE introduced herself to the reading public as a journal editor, women's leadership meant being mentored and mothered simultaneously: female readers were to acquire (*erwerben*) knowledge from a female author who used her maternal voice to instruct them (*kennen lehren*):

> Ich hoffe meine Leserinnen sind mit mir zufrieden, daß ich sie vor-
> erst mit den Verdiensten unsers Geschlechts bekannt mache, weil
> ich sie dadurch ihre eigene Fähigkeiten näher kennen lehre, und
> vielleicht den edlen Ehrgeitz erwecke, auch in ihrer Art und nach
> ihren Umständen Vorzüge des Wissens und der Beschäftigungen zu
> erwerben.[1]

> [I hope that my readers are satisfied with me, in that I shall first
> make them familiar with the accomplishments of our sex, because
> through this, I can make them aware of their own capabilities, and
> perhaps arouse in them the noble ambition to acquire the advan-
> tages of knowledge and of occupation, each in her own way and
> according to her situation.]

Much of La Roche's oeuvre has been ably examined for the author's views on education and on motherhood; however, the specifics of the histori-cal articulations of female identities around 1800 are such that *Pomona für Teutschlands Töchter* (1783, Pomona for Germany's Daughters) and *Mein Schreibetisch* (1799, My Writing Desk) warrant further examination as collections of La Roche's pithy statements on women's leadership. Accordingly, we may read the excerpt below both as maternal advice and also as mentoring advice for future community leaders:

So bitte ich [. . . Gladbachs] Lesefibeln für Kinder bekannt zu machen. Sie werden dem schätzbaren Zirkel kleiner Bürgerfamilien damit viele Aufklärung, und viel gute Gesinnungen in die Seele bringen. . . . Wie leicht ist es einzusehen, daß . . . unser Familienglück, welches bey jedem guten Vater und Mutter in den Verdiensten und Wohl ihrer Kinder mehr, als in ihrem eigenen besteht, zu grossem Theil auf guter Bildung bürgerlicher Kinder ruht.[2]

[This is why I would like [. . . Gladbach's] reading primers for children to become known. They will bring invaluable enlightenment into bourgeois family circles, as well as many good inclinations into the soul. . . . It is easy to see that familial happiness, which, for every good father and mother, comes more from the accomplishments and well-being of their children than from their own, derives to a great extent from the good education of bourgeois children.]

When we collect Sophie von La Roche's prescriptions to improve women's cognitive and emotional intelligence, her theory of effective women's leadership comes into view. It is a skill set acquired through written reflections of knowledge after silent and careful reading of eclectic passages, all of which is modeled by La Roche and to be repeated by young women. It is also an eclectic skill set comprising a binary gender identity, complicity in power hierarchies, and the importance of critical reading and critical writing, and these skills are to be acquired by young women in any order and from older and wiser people, whether they are men or women. While experienced male authors have much to say, I read La Roche's prescriptions in her journal as ultimately requiring women to learn from women. In the following analysis I will detail La Roche's specific propositions for women leaders and then conclude by gesturing at the anomalies in her optimistic principles.

Pomona für Teutschlands Töchter and the Approbation of Gentle Souls

The first word of the title pays homage to the French and Latin literary traditions that La Roche admires; at the same time, as we shall see, it suits her resistance to restricting women's leadership to the rhetoric of female reproduction. Sounding like *pomme*, the French word for apple, the work's title invokes the ancient Roman goddess of the autumnal season (referencing her advanced age as a grandmother), of agriculture (sowing future seeds), and of abundance (the many followers among the daughters of Germany), thus making it clear that La Roche shapes her writing to wield a pleasant and productive female-female influence:

Pomona hingegen erscheint nur als Vorbild des stillen wahren Verdienstes eines wohldenkenden und wohlerzogenen Frauenzimmers. Man sieht sie auch in ihrem Frühling mit Blumen geschmükt, aber sie sind weiß—Farbe der Unschuld—hie und da fein geröthet, wie Sittsamkeit die Wangen eines holden Mädchens bey jeder Besorgnis für ihre Reinigkeit mit Rosenfarbe überzieht und sie schüchtern macht.[3]

[Pomona, in contrast, appears just as a model of the quiet and honest service of a well-schooled and well-bred young lady. One sees her in the springtime adorned with flowers, but they are white—the color of innocence—lightly tinged, here and there, with red as are the cheeks of a charming girl each time she is concerned for her purity and becomes timid.]

The first word of the title is indeed a synecdoche of great and repeatable productivity, emphasizing the passing of life's stages. The full title and the material within the issues make it clear that she construes her role as furthering younger women's intellectual development. She constructs a model (*Vorbild*) for the daughters of Germany (a political state that did not yet exist).

Lina! theures blühendes Mädchen! Nimm Pomona zu deinem Vorbild, . . . denke Pomona lebte auch einsam, aber ihre Tugenden wurden doch bemerkt: Sie wurde geliebt und gesucht, weil man unter der so gut gepflegten Blüthe schon die erquickende und nützliche Früchte des Herbstes voraussah.[4]

[Lina! my dear, blossoming girl! Take Pomona as your model, . . . think that although Pomona also lived alone, her virtues were nevertheless acknowledged: she was loved and sought out, because refreshing and useful autumnal fruit could be anticipated from so well-cared-for a bloom.]

Using botanical metaphors, La Roche acknowledges the alluring beauty of flowers commonly used to represent young women, but, as she explains, she explicitly passed over the goddess Flora when making her selection. La Roche states why she has chosen instead the autumnal goddess: autumn fruit is both pleasing and useful. In the full passage, moreover, it is clear that she wishes to lead women to a specific kind of figurative growth. She does not refer to the fruit of the womb—not to female fecundity from male seed—but rather to productive, possibly self-pollinating trees that represent the minds of her female readers that, when properly lead, yield a bountiful intellectual harvest.

As a concrete demonstration of the abundant influence wielded by La Roche's *Pomona*, the periodical was read widely. It was distributed over a large geographical region because Catherine the Great, whose official title was "Empress and Autocrat of all the Russians," purchased 500 subscriptions. The conditions of print culture around 1800 meant that reading material was rare, physically difficult to make and maintain, and therefore reading materials were read and reread. Compared with "Britain, France and many German states, that almost total absence of provincial newspapers in Russia [was] all the more striking";[5] yet with this and other journalistic imports, Catherine managed to bring European culture to the Russian diaspora. Indeed, with her 500 copies, the Prussian-born empress would have been able to saturate the expansive Russian Empire with this German-language journal for women.

So as to properly cultivate her readers, La Roche fills the twenty-four monthly installments of her journal with a variety of mentoring materials. When she began the journal, she presumed her readers most needed challenging materials from well-respected male authors, such as James Thomson's *The Seasons* (1726–30). She cites, translates, and elucidates a substantial section of this text in the first issue (*Pomona* 1:33–84). She gives motherly and sisterly encouragement, without a trace of sarcasm. A later excerpt shows her penning her own verse full of sisterly support: "O! gehst du, theure, Schwester!/ Eignen Ganges deine Bahn;/ Steigst, nie müde, immer vester,/ Zur Vollkommenheit hinan";[6] O do you wind along, dear Sister!/ Your own path;/ And climb, never tiring, ever more strongly/ Toward Perfection). Not unlike contemporary blogs, *Pomona* built a virtual community of like-minded readers.

A more complex example that nonetheless supports my reading of *Pomona* as advancing the theory that women ultimately provide the best support of each other can be found in the reader's letters that La Roche publishes. Such letters demonstrate the transfer of knowledge from a female leader to her female mentee. An example from one of the 1784 issues models this instructional relationship:

> Denken Sie nun, ob ich ohne ungerecht gegen mich selbst zu seyn, den Gedanken hätte unterdrücken können, um den Ihrigen zu bitten, wenn Sie mich einstens dessen würdig finden! von der Aufnahme dieses Blätgens wird nun mein Schicksal abhängen, ob ich es wagen darf, dem Ruffe meines Herzen zu folgen, Ihnen in den noch kommenden Fällen meines Lebens um Ihre gütige Belehrung zu bitten.[7]

> [Now think whether, without being unfair to myself, I could have suppressed my thought of asking for yours, if only you may find me worthy! my fate depends upon the reception this page finds, whether

I shall then dare to follow the dictates of my heart and ask you in future cases for your worthy tutelage.]

In the citation above, La Roche showcases the modesty of a female letter writer, who employs elaborate and iterative rhetorical structures when asking for advice. She is polite without undercutting her hope for a response. I suggest that she employs this tone as a strategy; she does not aim to be seen as obsequious, but rather as submissive and effective. Admittedly, submissive and effective sound incompatible today, but they are indeed paired in literature around, and especially before, 1800.[8] La Roche's demonstrations of how to give and receive female leadership presuppose politesse and tact. To an extent, today's critical readers have become uncomfortable with pathos, unable to read it without irony; however, during La Roche's career as an author the inchoate identity of the caring and intelligent mother was being limned in fiction and non-fiction with earnest portraits and didactic tracts. This is not to say that there were no female writers who used facetiousness to make their point: Luise Adelgunde Victorie Gottsched and Friederike Helene Unger both did. Yet La Roche studiously avoids quips and irony. The influence she exerts is full of empathy, the ideas are not abstruse but elevating, the effect of female-to-female instruction is neither unnatural nor detrimental, but healthy and good: it strives to achieve the approbation of noble souls. As the editor explains: "ANTWORT: Jeder Brief, welchen ich durch meine Pomona erhielt, war mir sehr willkommen . . . war mir süß . . . da ich Sie als Vorgängerin, als Vorbild Ihrer Schwestern mir dachte" (*Pomona* 3:376; Every letter that I received through *Pomona* was welcome . . . was sweet . . . in that I thought of you as my predecessor, as the paragon for your sisters). The journal captures this exchange between mentor and mentee and displays it plainly. Yet this manifest demonstration unfolds in a complex communicative situation that offers multiple levels of leadership. La Roche presents herself as the model for a young woman who is herself the exemplary model for her seven younger sisters, and all this is captured in print on the pages of *Pomona* to serve yet again as a model for the distant, silent women who read but do not send letters.

Another means through which La Roche leads is direct help. She gave Caroline von Wolzogen her first publication in *Pomona*, a travel essay, Writing from a Young Lady on her Travels through Switzerland.[9] Wolzogen later published in Friedrich Schiller's periodicals *Neue Thalia* and *Die Horen*. In this specific instance, La Roche shows leadership in a concrete way through her journal that brought women's voices to the public. Indeed, *Pomona* can be called a periodical and its form of discourse, journalism. Yet the themes and ideas contained in it destabilize this generic classification. Unfamiliar with this kind of writing, or hostile to it, critics judged these works by La Roche as a hodge-podge of recycled materials to keep her pot boiling.[10] In *Pomona*, La Roche acts both as editor and author. She contributes the majority of the written texts and develops what Helga Meise has termed a "hybrid form of writing."[11] Fascinatingly, the discourse types developed by German women around 1800 were fluid, but the definition of gender was not. La Roche is not a modern feminist, but carefully contextualized in her historical frame, it becomes evident that she championed women. Unlike today's feminists, she did not believe that men and women are equal. However, she supported woman's development, leadership, and education at the same time as her ideological compromises forced her to rank tact and diplomacy over human rights, as we shall see below in her encounter with a Black African servant. In both the journal and the writing-desk entry, many of La Roche's pretentious self-assessments echo the similarly nuanced and unappealingly ambitious position (*Ehrgeitz*) of another early German woman journalist, Luise Adelgunde Victorie Gottsched. In *Pomona* La Roche praises Gottsched for translating Addison's journal and thereby bringing the genre of the journal to Germany.[12] Like Luise Gottsched's journals, La Roche's *Pomona* provides citations of primary texts and accompanying exegetical commentary. She gives her readers necessary background information, elucidates her selection of ideas and materials, and then leads her readers to the meaning or message they should take away. La Roche's philosophical writings on gender identity and gendered ethics are not to be found in a concise treatise, but rather must be culled from the hybrid discourse of *Pomona* and *Mein Schreibetisch*.

In order for a female reader to cull and comprehend those ideas, she would have to embark on a path of cognitive and emotional education. For La Roche, as had been the case for Luise Gottsched, education of the mind began at home with one's father and then continued through marriage and beyond in interactions with literary peers. Johann Christoph Gottsched has been termed his wife's "para-academic teacher."[13] This is telling, because it simultaneously indicates the separation of his wife from public and institutional education as well as a rigorous level of knowledge being transferred via domestic mentorship. Because such knowledge transfer to *female* individuals unfolds in *private* rooms, it is nearly invisible, rendered so by the domestic aspects of the traditional exchange. La Roche's *Bildung* may begin with such a male family member as mentor; however, it insists on women continuing to educate themselves through knowledge shared in a domestic, non–institutionalized setting. Reading her journalistic texts as a serialized treatise enables us to see the extensive intellectual mentoring that La Roche offers. It is almost as if La Roche is aware of what communication theorists call interactionality (across time and distance): "Text-production and text-reception are always—even in distance-communications—interactional activities."[14] A protracted conversation, an intercommunication, occurs between the author as she represents herself on the page and the readers who are both present and distant. "The specificity of moral weeklies like the 'Reasonable Tattlers' lies not in the introduction of a fictional author figure . . . but rather in the elaboration of a fictional author-reader-communication, which has ongoing functions."[15] Subscribing to La Roche's journal may have functioned for interactional readers in the Russian Empire like enrolling in a previously recorded online course. Ultimately, it does not matter whether a reader subscribed or not, whether a reader is real or fictional. La Roche has built in a model of communication that is ongoing. Through her journal, La Roche models leadership by and for women.

In some segments, La Roche anthropomorphizes her journal and identifies with it, speaking as the voice of Pomona. In these cases, Pomona is not the eponymous goddess of ancient Roman literature but rather the maternal leader of the periodical. She is the editor, compiler, writer, narrator, and encyclopedist in one. As the voice of Pomona, La Roche praises a reader's communications to her. She reprints such epistolary communications because her educational instructions have been well followed. The participant writes of gaining "the approbation of Gentle Souls" (der Beyfall edler Seelen).[16] Still speaking as the voice of a character named Pomona, La Roche then praises this notion as the *telos*, the goal toward which all mentored readers should aspire: "Wie froh war ich, in Ihrem Schreiben so viele Liebe für alles Gute zu sehen! dieses werden die anderen nun auch nachahmen" (*Pomona*, 3:376; how happy I was to see so much love for all that is good in your writing! This the others will now imitate). In translating, I wish to capture both the linguistic sophistication and the eighteenth-century empathetic tone. While "*edel*" more specifically means "noble," I intentionally selected the less specific term "gentle," as in "gentleman" and "gentlewoman," in order to reference the larger group of the emerging middle class, the audience or readership La Roche's journal addresses. With the term "approbation" I hope to invoke many of the important aspects of her theory from tactful to testing, from gender-appropriate to fustian, and from polite to powerful.

Though her work can be read in the context of female leadership, La Roche does embrace a binary opposition between masculine and feminine categories. She defends her view of separate and unequal spheres quite frequently and includes contributions that uphold the gender dichotomy: "Muß es denn Schwäche seyn, wenn ein Weib sich lächelnd schmiegt dem Willen des Mannes? Ist's immer Schwäche, wenn die Frau sich bequemt in ihre kleine Sphäre, anerkennt die Pflicht, des Mannes Mühen zu erleichtern?" (*Pomona*, 3:379; Does it have to be weakness when a wife bends smilingly to the will of her husband? Is it always weakness if a woman makes do with her little sphere, recognizes her duty to lighten her husband's burden?). In addition, her gender ideology presupposes subordination of men to each other:

Denn wie oft geschieht es, daß ein Mann in der niedern Stelle das grössere Maas Geist und Einsicht hat? und dennoch muß er stille dem Unsinn des Obern Folge leisten. Dieß ist doch wohl der nemliche Fall, zwischen dem thörichten Mann und seiner klügern Gattin.[17]

[Then how often does it not arise that a man in a lower station has the greater portion of intelligence and perception? and nevertheless must silently carry out the nonsensical bidding of his superior. This is the same case as between a foolhardy man and his more intelligent wife.]

La Roche's social world is a hierarchical one as decreed by a Christian god and reflected in nature. She describes the art of war for her young pupil Lina as one in which thousands and thousands of men are happy to have served under a great general who has knowledge, strength, and absolute command.[18] Other readers take heart in her advocacy of education for girls and women, a privilege that existed only as an exception in prior centuries. The "dear" female readers of *Pomona* are instructed in a pleasant, sympathetic voice that shares its rich knowledge of other cultures, in particular the French, the Swiss, and the English, but also the Greek and Italian.[19] She praises sentimentally and without irony, French fashion und manners and the imposing natural Swiss landscape. The English, however, are less easily categorized: their range of knowledge reaches from weekly periodicals to ship building, from the best salesman to educational institutions such as Clare Hall in Cambridge. Again and again, she strikes the approachable tone of a mentor and offers an engaging degree of specificity in content.[20]

The central point is that La Roche constantly writes anecdotally about intercultural ideas and, on the basis of those ideas, theorizes a gender-specific acquisition of knowledge.

Ob unsere Männer Englische Pferde oder Englische Bücher zuerst nach Teutschland gebracht haben, weiß ich nicht. Von Frauenzimmer Kleidung ist gewiß, daß Englische Schnürleiber zuerst Mode wurden; ohne Zweifel, weil man dachte, die feine Leibesgestalt komme von der engen Schnürbrust her; aber es gieng damit wie mit dem feinen Englischen Rasen—die Gartenwalze und die Graß-Scheeren ließ man kommen, und gebrauchte sie, aber die natürliche Anlage des Bodens konnte nicht mitgebracht werden; und so blieben unsere Gärten ohne die grünen Sammtstücke, wie man die Brittische Graßplätze nannte, und ohne die Nymphengestalten, welche darauf spatzieren gehen sollten.[21]

I don't know whether our men first brought English horses or English books over to Germany. As concerns women's clothing, it is clear that English girdles were the first fashion; without a doubt, because one thought that the delicate shape of the body came from those tight corsets; but it was the same as with the fine English lawns—one could obtain grass clippers and a lawn-roller and make use of them, but the natural condition of the soil could not be brought over, and so our gardens remained without the velvet greens, as the British grassy plots are called, and without the nymph-like figures that were supposed to stroll around upon them.]

Admittedly, her examples may first strike us as sexist—men manage the public world and women constrain their bodies with a girdle while raising daughters in the home. However, a more careful interpretation pays heed to her focus on women as a group with an enormous, untapped potential. Let us consider how very different her themes in *Pomona* are from those of Schiller in his periodical, *Die Horen*, which he published a decade later, 1795–97, and also named after Greek goddesses. Unlike La Roche, Schiller showcases literary high culture. La Roche's *Pomona* dispenses modest wisdom. La Roche's journal narrates the potential garden of the female intellect. In doing so, she creates a figurative space, one where women comfort each other not because of broken hearts but rather to permit the educational growth of each other's minds. She employs many metaphors of vegetative growth, such as the fruit tree, to show that women's learning now will produce results later. In this reading, the publication known as *Pomona* may—perhaps must—be read as the aphoristic presentation of her ideas on a female epistemology to be absorbed by her young mentees. She continues this ambitious project throughout her oeuvre, notably also in *Mein Schreibetisch*.

Mein Schreibetisch as Maxims of Knowledge and Skills

Though her writing was trivialized for generations, La Roche's current status as a canonical author of German literature around 1800 derives from new criticism of her fiction.[22] To an extent, her non-fiction still suffers from trivialization. *Pomona* has earned a place in literary history because it can be categorized as a periodical, even though its unfamiliar tone, hybrid discourse, and length result in its being mentioned more often in passing than interpreted in depth. *Mein Schreibetisch* is even more unfamiliar, its discourse more hybrid and more loosely structured. Here is a sample of the transitions she typically uses throughout *Mein Schreibetisch*:

Abwechselnd, wie abgebrochene zufällige Sammlungen immer sind,
zeigt sich nun unter diesen Blättern eine Abschrift des Gedichts . . .
Nun sollen Sie aber etwas lesen, das sogleich dabey liegt . . .
daß ich so gerne Vergleiche aufsuche . . .
Nun ein Auszug aus dem Briefe einer geistvollen fremden Dame.[23]

[With the variety that these fragmented, haphazard collections always
have, there is among these pages a transcription of a poem . . .
Now you ought to read something that also happens to be there . . .
as I so like to draw comparisons . . .
Now an extract from a letter by a contemplative, unknown lady.]

The order of the narrative is motivated by the life of La Roche's mind
and, again, by her drive to lead others to follow her path. It is neither
pure fiction nor pure non-fiction. In tone, the prose of this publication
has some prescient journalistic qualities now common in social media.
Today's bloggers and the La Roche of the time around 1800 both
generate non-fictional narratives interwoven with a variety of genre or
media, and both depend on the celebrity of their creators. Although
Mein Schreibetisch was a print publication and its pages are numbered
sequentially, it does not have a linear narrative, as the transitional phrases
above demonstrate. *Mein Schreibetisch*, with its archaic, irksome "e" in
the middle of a familiar compound word, delivers what it advertises: an
essay in the first person about a writing desk. Sophie La Roche names the
titles of the books on her desk that she is reading, and provides titles or
descriptions of the pieces of writing she has in progress. Critics emphasize the fictional frame of the piece: Loster-Schneider and Dawson draw
attention to the epistolary device La Roche deploys in the frame.[24] The
text begins with a first-person frame, yet the overall narrative includes a
mélange of third-person commentary from others, direct second-person
address, and above all reflection and self-reflection. *Mein Schreibetisch* has
an informal narrative that interrupts itself with inserts such as book lists.
The hybridization and genre-grafting characteristics of *Pomona* continue
in *Mein Schreibetisch*. Unlike *Pomona* (and not unlike the postmodern sel-
fie), *Mein Schreibetisch* frames its content from arm's length. After publishing her first journal for Germany's daughters, La Roche continued
to employ the narrative mélange in *Schattenrisse abgeschiedener Stunden
in Offenbach, Weimar und Schönebeck* (Silhouettes of Bygone Hours in
Offenbach, Weimar, and Schönebeck), which she published in 1800.
While the style of *Schattenrisse* is similar, it is not as rich a source for wom-
en's leadership as the writing-desk essay.

Belying its title and subtitle, the overarching concerns of the writing-desk essay are as much about reading critically and thinking in maxims—which are the means to leadership for La Roche—as the serialized

journal *Pomona* was. The subtitle of the work is actually a dedication: "An Herrn G. R. P. in D." (To Mr G. R. P. in D.). It apostrophizes a man who has supposedly requested an objective, non-fictional description of the author's physical writing desk.[25] Nevertheless, the material that follows the dedication continues the work intended for Germany's daughters. We know that the male dedicatee was not purely imaginary. Secondary literature has, in fact, erred in the opposite direction, including a case of mistaken identity. Patricia Sensch has proven that the dedicatee is Johann Friedrich Christian Petersen (1788–1807) and not his brother, as earlier believed. Sensch openly criticizes extant editions of La Roche's letters and paints a Cromwellian portrait of La Roche as an important yet flawed courtly power broker in her time: "Dem komplexen Charakter der Schriftstellerin dürfte mit dem dargebotenen schlichten Antagonismus von Kopf und Herz kaum beizukommen sein. Auch die Selbsteinschätzung ist als ein von ihr arrangiertes Vexierspiel täuschender Dimensionen anzusehen"[26] (The simple binary of head and heart is hardly sufficient to shed light on the complex character of the woman writer. Even the self-assessment is to be seen as a game of deception with misleading dimensions that she set up herself). Sensch is likely correct in implying that much of the twenty-first-century research on La Roche has simplified her thought and writing techniques. Moreover, if we look to a variety of models for this type of discourse, then we can accept that *Mein Schreibetisch* has an informal tone that employs conversational structures without "erasing" La Roche as an author.[27] Even her title embodies this paradox: "my" is a first-person, possessive adjective while the writing desk is an unambiguous symbol of authorship. Yet what matters most are the pithy ideas expressed on the pages piled up on that desk. One model we can look to is the genre of the maxim popularized by Francois VI, Duc de La Rouchefoucauld in the seventeenth century; La Rouchefoucauld used an informal tone to express his pithy reflections on eclectic subjects, and La Roche was very familiar with his writing.[28] However, La Roche's maxims have an agenda uniquely her own.

As a previously published author with a known biography, the narrator of *Mein Schreibetisch* speaks poignantly of the sorrows experienced as a parent and moves nimbly to philosophical citations that lead to her own maxims or aphoristic ideas.[29] In this, La Roche's *Mein Schreibetisch* is an example of the genre of the maxim crossed with the art of the excerpt (as is, to a lesser extent, the earlier *Pomona*). The excerpt collection is an important literary genre that La Roche interweaves throughout *Mein Schreibetisch*. In her book *Lesen, Kopieren, Schreiben* Elisabeth Décultot argues that the excerpt ushered in a historical change in the epistemological practices of humanists.[30] "Beim Exzerpieren [wirkt] etwas Tieferes mit, etwas, was mit der innerlichsten Beziehung zum Gelesenen, mit der persönlichen Inbesitznahme des Buches zu tun hat" (145; When excerpting passages, something more profound occurs; something happens that has to do with one's innermost relationship to that which is read, with one's private appropriation of the book). La Roche aims to lead younger women by showing herself in action as an adept at the art of the excerpt. In this reading, *Pomona* (or at least her discussion of certain issues and certain parts of certain issues) may be seen as a primer, the first book of principles of female leadership, where La Roche lays the groundwork, while *Mein Schreibetisch* may be seen as the second contribution to women's leadership, one in which the lens has rotated 180 degrees from the direct address of the junior mentee to the practice of the seasoned expert, who has a profound relationship to that which is to be read. Starting from an intimate interior space where a personal letter may be written, the authorial perspective in *Pomona* looks out toward a garden in which the female mind ripens. The frame of *Mein Schreibetisch* directs the eye toward the author's writing materials: "eine aufrichtige Beschreibung des, auf diesem Tische und bey der Fenstermauer verbreiteten, Gemisches von Papieren und Büchern" (*Schreibetisch*, 1:6; an honest description of the mélange of papers and books spread on the table and along the window sill). Repeatedly in *Mein Schreibetisch*, La Roche shows herself to be an author who writes through the "I" and then trains the reader toward a third person, such as another writer. She thinks abstractly and imagines concrete bodies: "aus der Feder einer Person meines Geschlechts" (*Schreibetisch*, 1:103; from the quill of a person of my own gender). As a result, she highlights the relationship between women authors: "Ich liebe alles, was aus der Feder einer Person meines Geschlechts abstammt, und liebte immer vorzüglich die Briefe der Madame de Sévigné, als Model erzählender gefühl- und anmuthsvoller Briefe; war also sehr froh, auch dieses Zeugniß der Achtung, der Verdienste einer Frau zu erhalten" (*Schreibetisch*, 1:103–4; I love everything that comes from the quill of a person of my gender and I especially love the letters of Madame de Sévigné as a model of narrative letters full of feeling and of grace; I was very happy to receive this testimony of respect, of the accomplishments of a woman). La Roche goes on to name the English woman writer Lady Luxbourough, who peppers her literary products with citations from ancient Latin writers and poets. Influence by canonical works (classical and male) is meritorious. As for female writers, even though La Roche dismisses gender alone as sufficient grounds for a positive critical evaluation, the singularity of a woman author motivates particularly attentive reading.

Although she accepts a gender hierarchy I reject, La Roche's canon is patently free of the gender bias that generates an exclusively male literary canon. In her view, women's literature is more limited than men's but just as readable. Like a mother, she loves them both ("Ich liebe alles . . ."). The august academic and Protestant rector Johann Christoph

Stockhausen called the book list "the pantry of the soul."[31] La Roche amasses two bibliographical lists and inserts them in the non-fictional *Mein Schreibetisch*. These lists are titled "Verzeichniß einiger Bücher für die Handbibliothek eines Frauenzimmers von Erziehung" and "Für junge Personen beyderley Geschlechts" (Index of Some Books for the Reading Library of a Young Lady of Education and For Young People of both Genders) and both productively intermingle genres. Novels figure prominently, as they do for modern critics. Unlike contemporary lists, however, La Roche's list does not contain Goethe's *Die Leiden des jungen Werthers* (1774, The Sorrows of Young Werther) while the anonymous *Elisa*, with its paragon of woman as she ought to be, is included. It is the seventh entry in La Roche's alphabetical bibliography for educated women. La Roche recommends that women read the novel *Elisa* not only in German (the fourth edition with six new copper plates), but also in French translation alongside such purely sociohistorical tracts as "Vermischte Aufsätze zum Nachdenken und zur Unterhaltung," (Miscellaneous Essays for Thought and Entertainment), "Zur Bildung des schönen Geschlechts" (anon.; Toward the Education of the Fair Sex) and *Clariſa* (here all sixteen volumes in German translation), and *Louise or the Cottage on the Moor* (in both the English original and German translation), and no fewer than five of her own publications—one of which is "with the well-captured portrait of the author" (*Schreibetisch*, 1: n.p., follows page 384). She includes her own works and her own image, much as she makes her own writing desk a metonymy for the deliberately eclectic investigation of the principles and practices best suited to women's acquisition of the skills prerequisite to informed leadership. It starts with self-knowledge as reflected by her desktop. She herself is an exemplary female leader, and that motivates the self-portraiture. Further, her bibliography for female mentees breaks down into five anonymous and genderless works, twelve others by women (but sometimes without name, such as by the *Verfasserin* (female composer or author) of a different work), and thirteen by men, many of which are written for women, and some of which are arguably coauthored, such as T. F. Ehrmann, *Denkmahl der Freundschaft und Liebe, der verewigten Frau Mariane Ehrmann errichtet* (Memorial of Friendship and Love, Dedicated to the Immortal Mrs. Mariane Ehrmann). The percentage of women writers in La Roche's reading list exceeds the number of female-authored works a mid-twentieth-century scholar might be familiar with, even without including women who published anonymously.[32]

Many pages in *Mein Schreibetisch* illustrate La Roche's art of the excerpt and her insistence that this art is a mental skill prerequisite to knowledge. She relates one particular anecdote about herself in which all these aspects intertwine. It begins when she shuffles through her papers and sees the handwriting of another person. This reminds her of how she had met a former slave, now a domestic servant, who transcribed a poem in his handwriting. She weaves this textual encounter into the writing-desk essay by relating the words of this other person whose handwriting she has. He praises the angelic treatment he receives from his mistress, Julie Reventlaw née Schimmelmann. The anecdote tells its readers the moral to be drawn: that women are to be the model for all overseers. All estate managers and people in charge of black slaves should have the personal moral sensibilities and compassion of this one woman. The relationship between master and slave, or master and knave, or master and indentured servant, is one that La Roche explains as based on natural distinction and therefore God-given and immutable. "Du weißt, daß unsere Erdkugel unter Herrn und Knechte vertheilt ist"[33] (You know that our terrestrial sphere is divided into masters and servants). Within that God-given natural order, La Roche presumes mutual respect. Here, too, we see a parallel to her understanding of gender difference in which groups of people exist who are not equal. La Roche is uncritical of her own role. Blind to her privileges, she is content to be waited on by a servant class. The passage offers a sample of her digression-rich discourse. The first sentence of the excerpt is several lines long and begins and ends with little detours that personalize the anecdote, offer multiple possible connections to the readers, and testify to the wealth of experience the mentoring first-person speaker possesses:

> Sie, mein Freund! der weiß, was England und edle Menschen mir sind, Sie vergeben mir diese kleine Abweichung von meinem Schreibetisch, und hören noch die Geschichte von der Copie des schönen Gedichts, weil sie mir äußerst werth ist, und die Sie auch einmahl sehen müssen, da sie von einem sechzehn Jahr alten Neger gemacht wurde, welcher von den Plantagen des alten Graf Schimmelmann in die Dienste seiner Tochter kam, die ich 1779 als blühende Braut des Graf Reventlaw in Hamburg sah, 1786 in London traf, wo ihr Gemahl als dänischer Gesandte stand. (*Schreibetisch*, 1:223–24)

> [You, my Friend! who knows what England and noble people are to me, you will forgive me this minor digression from my writing desk, and listen yet to the story of the copy of the beautiful poem, because it is so extremely valuable to me, and you must some day see it yourself, because it was made by a sixteen-year-old Negro who came from the plantation of old Count Schimmelmann into the service of his daughter, whom I saw in 1779 as the blushing bride of Count Reventlaw in Hamburg, and met then in 1786 in London, where her spouse was the Danish diplomatic envoy.]

As twenty-first-century readers, we are accustomed to the complete autonomy of the text: we want fiction to be readable without thinking about its author, much less her labor to produce it. But without machines and screens, La Roche and her eighteenth-century peers were accustomed to reading handwriting. In fact, excerpting is a high-level cognitive skill she practices and preaches. "Erst durch den körperlichen, oft mühsamen Gestus des Abschreibens vollzieht sich für den Anhänger der Exzerpierkunst die Aneignung des Gelesenen"[34] (Only through the physical, often laborious gesture of writing down does the aficionado of the art of the excerpt acquire knowledge of what is read). She admires the servant and includes him in her essay because he affords the opportunity to return to her theme: exemplary leadership.

> Der junge Neger brachte mir Morgens meinen Caffe, ich fragte ihn nach seinem Vaterlande und nach seiner Erziehung, er antwortete mit der sanftesten Stimme und mit vielem Verstand auf alles. Unter andern sagte er:
> Ich bin der glücklichste von vielen tausenden meiner schwarzen Brüder, denn die Gräfin behandelt mich immer mit der Güte eines Engels.
> Wie mein Herz die edle Frau für dieses Zeugniß liebte und segnete, weiß der Himmel. Immer hatte ich mit dem Gefühl des Schmerzens an die Neger und ihr Schicksal gedacht, nun hörte ich einem sagen, daß er höchst glücklich sey, und bat Gott, allen Oberherrn seiner schwarzen Kinder einen Theil von Julie Schimmelmanns Güte zu geben. (*Schreibetisch*, 1:224–25).

> [The young Negro brought me my coffee in the morning, I asked him about his fatherland and his upbringing, he answered everything with the gentlest voice and with much understanding. Among other things, he said:
> I am the happiest of many thousands of my Black brothers, because the Countess always treats me with the goodness of an angel.
> Only Heaven knows how much my heart loved that noble woman for this testimony and blessed her. I had always thought of Negroes and their fate with a feeling of pain, yet here I heard one of them say that he was extremely happy and I prayed to God to give all overseers of his Black children some part of Julie Schimmelmann's goodness.]

La Roche is philosophic and carefully selects models of good practices for female leaders. Julie Schimmelmann von Reventlaw leads the way: the interactional virtual community of readers should follow her example. Thus the hybridized discourse of the genre-fluid *Mein Schreibetisch* furthers the project La Roche began in *Pomona*, to lead junior women to greater achievements by encouraging them to imitate her models.

Leadership as Readership and Advanced Literacy Skills

Pomona seems to some modern readers to give mixed messages.[35] As we shall see, the surest means for a woman to acquire the deep knowledge necessary to be a gentle female leader is not just to be like La Roche but to read the way she does. In the educational tract titled "Letters to Lina," La Roche models the transfer of knowledge and negotiates the thin line between learnedness that is either too masculine or too feminine. "Denn Kenntnisse sollen ihren Geist eben so gefällig zieren, als ein Blumenkranz ihre Haare, und sollen Sie eben so wenig beschweren"[36] (Because knowledge should adorn your mind just as charmingly as a wreath of flowers adorns your hair, and weigh you down just as little). La Roche makes this point repeatedly, so let us take a look at her own words and crafting of the notion.

> Wie süß werden die Stunden einer Mutter, wenn sie, während ihr Gatte seinen Berufsgeschäften abwartet, und sie die Arbeiten ihres Gesindes geordnet hat, mit ihrer Nadel sich abgiebt, und auch eine ihrer Töchter lesen läßt, die wichtige Stellen ihnen erklärt und bemerken lehrt, bey andern sie aufmuntert, dem Vater davon zu erzälen, und ihn weiter zu fragen.[37]

> [How sweet are the hours of a mother, when—while her husband is occupying his time with professional matters and she has given her domestic help its tasks—she devotes herself to her needle and has one of her daughters read to her, explains to them which passages are important, and for some other passages, encourages her to tell her father of them and to ask him further about them.]

There is much sweetness and mothering, but the crucial point is for women to read. Like Britain's soil, women in La Roche's thought are by nature beings who can and must be cultivated, which was not a universally held belief around 1800. La Roche wants her audience of young female mentees to go beyond basic literacy. To develop the more advanced faculties of a woman's heart and mind, women must be directed in their reading by more senior, smarter, and more experienced women (as well as by men who are themselves aware of the specific needs of female learners). Women should read while doing women's work, not in lieu of it, because the faculties of the mind are sexed and different (*Pomona*, 3:314). Furthermore, women should digest what they read, find salient passages, and share those insights with other women as well as with men and so follow in her method as an expert of the excerpt. In 1795 and 1797 La Roche again collected her epistolary educational essays, expanded them into a second volume, and republished them as a two-volume work: *Briefe an Lina als Mädchen* (Letters to Lina as a Girl) and *Briefe an Lina als Mutter: Ein Buch für junge Frauenzimmer die ihr Herz und ihren Verstand bilden wollen* (Letters to Lina as a Mother: A Book for Young Women Who Want to Educate Their Hearts and Minds). By putting her ideas before the public again and again, La Roche shows herself to be a leader in educating women readers.

The texts intended to be read by La Roche's female audience do not stem from an institutionally generated list of great works; yet there is a list, and its organization is intentionally eclectic, or like aleatory music. Just as La Roche frequently pairs a submissive tone with an effective one, she also often combines the diligent and the aleatory. Central to La Roche's educational theory, the idea of cultivated reading lists to inspire critical reading is present in *Pomona*, in the letters to Lina, and elsewhere: "La Roche dagegen stellt dezidiert—und damals geradezu revolutionär— das Studium der kulturellen Leistungen und der Lebensumstände von *Frauen* in den Mittelpunkt ihres Bildungskonzeptes" (La Roche, in contrast, decisively places—and this was revolutionary at the time—the study of the cultural accomplishments and living conditions of *women* in the center of her educational concept).[38] Women are coached to read like La Roche, which, as the writing-desk essay makes clear, is organized by mental arabesques and continues throughout a woman's life.

As mentioned above, *Mein Schreibetisch* offers a curated list of books for women to read in order to develop the necessary skills to become educational leaders themselves. *Mein Schreibetisch* and *Pomona* both model the kind of critical reading her readers should emulate when working their way through the reading list. Reading was a contested notion around 1800, as is evident in Christoph Martin Wieland's thoughts on the subject. Wieland, whose personal and literary relationship with La Roche stretched over her entire adult life,[39] insists that good books by authors of "talent and taste must be read aloud or half of their beauty will be lost."[40] In "Ueber das Lesen" La Roche explicitly prefers silent reading (*Pomona*, 2:845–49). She specifies that reading material on the sciences should be Christian doctrine or the history of the Bible, thus using religiously inspired reading as a springboard for gaining knowledge about the natural world, animals, plants, earth science, and then even using the Bible to appreciate the technical structure of language as used in secular poetry. Yet her ideas contradict Wieland's:

> Stille zu lesen ist das vortheilhafteste, weil man da, wie bey dem einsamen Spaziergang sich bald auf der Wiese bey Kräutern, bald

auf der Anhöhe bey der Aussicht, die uns gefällt, verweilen kan, in dem Buch auch bey diesem und jenem Stük innehält, nachdenkt, wiederholt, Auszüge schreibt, sich die Zeit, und das Land des Schriftstellers—wo diese Gesetze waren, wo diese Gewohnheit noch jetzo ist,—so dachte man damals, so denkt man jetzt: dies Gute kan ich mir eigen machen,—das kan ich anwenden, u.s.w. dieß sind die Vortheile, welche man von dem Lesen für sich hat. Höre ich aber lesen, so kan ich diese nicht so leicht thun, weil ich das Recht nicht habe, den Leser aufzuhalten, wo ich nachdenken möchte, und dann kann auch die Kunst des Vorlesers mich etwas gut finden machen, was es nicht ist, es müßte nur seyn, das ein gleichgesinnter Freund oder ein liebreicher Lehrer mir vorließt, und mich Schritt vor Schritt alles fühlen, und alles bedenken lehrt.[41]

[Silent reading is the most advantageous because, just as with solitary walks where one can tarry a while beside herbs in a meadow or on a hill to take in a pleasing view, so too can one pause here and there at passages, reflect, reread, and write out excerpts, one can imagine oneself in the time and country of the writer—where such laws were, where such customs still are—thus one thought then, thus are the current thoughts: I can acquire this good quality myself—I can apply it, etc. These are the advantages that reading for oneself has. But when I listen to reading, then I cannot so easily attend to these things, because I do not have the right to stop the reader when I want to reflect, and then the artistry of certain readers may lead me to consider something good that is not, it might just be a like-minded friend or a kind teacher is reading aloud to me, and schooling me step by step what to feel and what to think.]

She explains in great detail how to approach a book, stating that the foreword should be read in order to put oneself in the place of the author (*Schriftsteller*) and to decide whether the book merits being read. The table of contents follows, and there one should look for a section on a familiar topic. Her example is the value of friendship. Next, one should go directly to that section and read it and see if the author tells us anything new, or if he says it more beautifully or more clearly. If any of these criteria are met, one should write down excerpts and then go and read the entire text. "Auf diese Art allein kan man nützlich lesen" (*Pomona*, 2:847). She invites her readers to go back to the first issue of *Pomona* and read it this way and report back to her. The exegetical passages distinguish La Roche from a mere collector of literary *ana*. Her essay appears to have the same disorganization as her writing desk; however, the order is deliberately unpredictable. Interrupting oneself mentally to connect one idea to another is a skill.

Bringing these two publications from Sophie von La Roche into critical discourse sheds light on her influence, her innovations, her excellence, and her limitations. The second quotation cited in the beginning of this essay connects parental happiness to a good education for the middle class. It is an excerpt that is taken out of context. The larger context reveals La Roche's firm prejudices against middle- and lower-class people, servants, maids, and wet nurses, and, at the same time, her prescient apprehension of woman's fragile work-family balance:

> Denn da wir unsere Diener und Mägde aus den Familien der bürgerlichen Klasse ziehen, da sie unsere Kinder von den ersten Jahren ihres Lebens umgeben, so ist es für das Herz und Sitten unserer Kinder eben so nöthig, daß die Bürgerliche wohl erzogen werden, als es nöthig geachtet wird, eine gesunde Säugamme zu haben, so bald die Mutter ausser Stand ist, ihr Kind selbst zu stillen. Da nun würklich auch die meiste Mütter ausser Stand sind, ihre Haushaltung, und die eingeführte Lebenspflichten gegen Freund und Verwandte mit der unausgesetzten Sorge für ihre Kinder zu verbinden, so müssen sie auch Mägde bey den Kindern haben.[42]

> [Since we take our servants and maids from the families of the bourgeois class, and since they surround our children from the first years of life, it is as necessary for the heart and manners of our children that the bourgeoisie be well educated as it is necessary to have a healthy wet-nurse as soon as the mother is no longer able to nurse her child herself. Because most mothers are not able to oversee the household, handle the customary responsibilities toward friends and relatives, and also the incessant care of children, they must have maids for their children.]

In conclusion, La Roche promotes a gentle method of female leadership that is predicated on a social world in which women have less power than men. Nonetheless, female leaders develop because they are trained critical readers who know the art of the excerpt and practice it on a curated list of books—a list curated by La Roche herself. Thus La Roche advocates for widespread literacy and especially for an advanced technique of critical reading to further her own self-interest, which, paradoxically, is to serve others compassionately.

Notes

[1] Sophie von La Roche, "Ueber Engelland," in *Pomona für Teutschlands Töchter*, ed. Jürgen Vorderstemann, 4 vols. (Munich: K. G. Saur, 1987), 1:374. All citations from *Pomona* retain the original spelling and grammatical idiosyncrasies. All translations are my own. References to essays within *Pomona* are given in the notes. Other references to *Pomona* are given in the text using the title *Pomona*.

[2] La Roche, "Pomona an ihre Leserinnen," in *Pomona*, 4:860–61.

[3] La Roche, "Ueber die Gärten, ihre Göttinnen, und die Weinberge," in *Pomona*, 2:941–42.

[4] La Roche, "Ueber die Gärten, ihre Göttinnen, und die Weinberge," in *Pomona*, 2:942–43.

[5] Simon Dixon, *Catherine the Great* (Harlow, UK: Pearson, 2001), 89–90.

[6] La Roche, "Pomonens Tochter, meiner geliebtesten Schwester, Jungfrau Susanna Maria Würtzin, zum heutigen Namensfest 1784," in *Pomona*, 3:371.

[7] La Roche, "Brief," in *Pomona*, 3:374.

[8] Though beyond the scope of this research, the number of novel heroines portrayed as both submissive and effective asks for substantial analysis: Mademoiselle de Chartres in *The Princess of Cleves* (1678), Pamela in *Pamela; or, Virtue Rewarded* (1740), Sophie von Sternheim in *The History of Lady Sophie Sternheim* (17F71), Evelina in *Evelina; or, The History of a Young Lady's Entrance into the World* (1778), Elisa in *Elisa or Woman as She Ought to Be* (1795), and Dorothea in *Hermann and Dorothea* (1797).

[9] La Roche, "Schreiben einer jungen Dame, auf ihrer Reise durch die Schweiz," (1784), in *Pomona*, 3:472–87.

[10] Werner Milch, *Sophie La Roche, die Großmutter der Brentanos* (Frankfurt am Main: Societäts Verlag, 1935), 167, 177–89. Cf. Wolfgang Adam, "Die Schweizer Reisen der Sophie von la Roche," in *Helvetien und Deutschland: Kulturelle Beziehungen zwischen der Schweiz und Deutschland in der Zeit von 1770–1830*, ed. Hellmut Thomke, Martin Bircher, and Wolfgang Proß (Amsterdam: Rodopi, 1994), 33–56, here 38.

[11] On *Pomona* as nearly single-authored whereas *Iris* was collaborative, see Monika Nenon, *Aus der Fülle der Herzen: Geselligkeit, Briefkultur und Literatur um Sophie von La Roche und Friedrich Heinrich Jacobi* (Würzburg: Königshausen & Neumann, 2005), 151. On hybrid writing, see Helga Meise, "Hirnkinder: Gattungsvorgabe und hybride Schreibweise in Sophie von La Roches Pomona für Teutschlands Töchter," in *"bald zierliche Blumen—bald Nahrung des Verstands": Lektüren zu Sophie von La Roche*, ed. Monika Lippke, Matthias Luserke-Jaqui, and Nikola Roßbach (Hannover: Wehrhahn, 2008), 123–39, and Helga Meise, "'wie sehr ich die Geschichte liebe': Hybridisierung und Pfropfung in Sophie von La Roches 'Pomona für Teutschlands Töchter' am Beispiel ihres Bezuges auf die Geschichte," in *'Ich will keinem Mann nachtreten': Sophie von La Roche und Bettine von Arnim*, ed. Miriam Seidler and Mara Stuhlfauth (Frankfurt am Main: Peter Lang, 2013), 111–23; and Helga Brandes, "Die Zeitschrift 'Pomona für Teutschlands Töchter' im publizistischen Kontext des 18. Jahrhunderts," in

"Meine Freiheit, nach meinem Charakter zu leben": *Sophie von La Roche (1730–1807) Schriftstellerin der Empfindsamkeit*, ed. Jürgen Eichenauer (Weimar: VDG, 2007), 173–82.

[12] La Roche, "Ueber Engelland," in *Pomona*, 1:326–37.

[13] Nicola Kaminski dubs Johann Christoph Gottsched the "paraakademischer Lehrer" of Luise Adelgunde Victorie Gottsched: "Gottsched/in oder Umwege weiblicher Autorschaft: *Die Vernünftigen Tadlerinnen—Die Pietisterey im Fischbein-Rocke; Oder die Doctor mäßige Frau—Her Witzling*," in *Anonymität und Autorschaft: Zur Literatur- und Rechtsgeschichte der Namenlosigkeit*, ed. Stephan Pabst (Berlin: Walter De Gruyter, 2011), 89–122; here 110.

[14] Susanne Niefanger, *Schreibstrategien in Moralischen Wochenschriften: Formalstilistische, pragmatische und rhetorische Untersuchungen am Beispiel von Gottscheds 'Vernünftigen Tadlerinnen'* (Tübingen: Max Niemeyer, 1997), 96, my translation. Communication theory serves as the theoretical underpinning for Susanne Niefanger to describe the relationships of the author group constructed by Gottsched in the *Vernünftige Tadlerinnen*.

[15] Niefanger, *Schreibstrategien*, 17, 98.

[16] La Roche, "Brief," in *Pomona*, 3:374.

[17] La Roche, "Ermahnungen und Entschuldigungen," in *Pomona*, 2:832.

[18] La Roche, "Briefe an Lina," in *Pomona*, 4:1020–22.

[19] Rhetorical narratology makes a distinction that is useful here. It defines narrative as "a multidimensional purposive communication from a teller to an audience." James Phelan and Peter J. Rabinowitz, "Narrative as Rhetoric," in *Narrative Theory: Core Concepts and Critical Debates*, ed. David Herman, James Phelan, and Peter J. Rabinowitz (Columbus: Ohio State University Press, 2012), 3.

[20] On Clare Hall, see "Ueber Engelland," *Pomona* 1:331.

[21] La Roche, "Ueber Engelland," in *Pomona*, 1:336.

[22] Patricia Sensch, *Sophie von La Roches Briefe an Johann Friedrich Christian Petersen (1788–1806): Kritische Edition, Kommentare, Analyse* (Berlin: De Gruyter, 2016), 1–14.

[23] Sophie von La Roche, *Mein Schreibetisch: An Herrn G. R. P. in D.* 2 vols. (1799; rpt. Karben: Wald, 1997), 1:63–67. Further references to this work are given in the text using the short title *Schreibetisch*.

[24] Gudrun Loster-Schneider, *Sophie von La Roche: Paradoxien weiblichen Schreibens im 18. Jahrhundert* (Tübingen: Narr, 1995): "Der einleitende Entstehungsmythos inszeniert den biographisch wie literarisch gleichermaßen vertrauten Topos vom eigenen Schreiben als dem Produkt fremder, im speziellen Fall männlicher Initiative und Verantwortlichkeit" (293; The introductory myth of genesis stages the topos, which is familiar in a biographical as well as literary aspect, that one's own writing is the product of an alien and male initiative and responsibility). See also Ruth Dawson, *The Contested Quill: Literature by Women in Germany, 1770–1800* (Newark: University of Delaware Press, 2002): "In writing to a man, she needs a man's approval, and thus refers to her authorizing male reader both on the title page and throughout the book" (148).

²⁵ The piece of furniture seems to have had small interest in and of itself. See Sabine Mainberger, "Schreibtischporträts: Zu Texten von Arno Schmidt, Georges Perec, Hermann Burger und Francis Ponge," in *Möbel als Medien*, ed. Sebastien Hackenschmidt and Klaus Engelhorn (Bielefeld: transcript Verlag, 2011), 177–97, here 178.

²⁶ Sensch, *Sophie von La Roches Briefe*, 10–11.

²⁷ Dawson, *Contested Quill*, 248.

²⁸ Erdmut Jost, ed., *Sitten der schönen Pariser Welt: Sophie von La Roche und* das *Monument du Costume: Mit den 24 Stichen und dem vollständigen, erstmals ins Deutsche übertragenen Text der ersten beiden Folgen des französischen Originals* (Halle: Mitteldeutscher Verlag, 2011), 105–6.

²⁹ On La Roche's general autobiography, see Elke Ramm, *Autobiographische Schriften deutschsprachiger Autorinnen um 1800* (Hildesheim: Olms, 1998), especially 66–72, 144–46, and 177.

³⁰ Elisabeth Décultot, ed. *Lesen, Kopieren, Schreiben: Lese- und Exzerpierkunst in der europäischen Literatur des 18. Jahrhunderts*, trans. Kirsten Heininger and Elisabeth Décultot (Berlin: Ripperger & Kremers, 2014).

³¹ Johann Christoph Stockhausen, *Critischer Entwurf einer auserlesenen Bibliothek für den Liebhaber der Philosophie und schönen Wissenschaften, zum Gebrauch seiner Vorlesungen entworfen von Johann Christoph Stockhausen, der Philosophie Doctor, und des Johannei zu Lüneburg Rector, der Königl. deutschen Gesellschaft zu Göttingen und der Herzogl. zu Helmstädt Ehren-Mitgliede*, 3. ed. (Berlin: Haude & Spener, 1764), x.

³² On anonymity and women writers, see Jeannine Blackwell, "German Literary History and the Canon in the United States," in *German Studies in the United States: A Historical Handbook*, ed. Peter Uwe Hohendahl (New York: MLA, 2003), 143–73; Susanne Kord, *Sich einen Namen machen: Zur Anonymität und Pseudonymität weiblicher Autoren zwischen 1700 und 1900* (Stuttgart: Metzler, 1996), especially her distinction between intended and effective anonymity (12–13); and Stephan Pabst, ed., *Anonymität und Autorschaft: Zur Literatur- und Rechtsgeschichte der Namenlosigkeit* (Berlin: Walter De Gruyter, 2011).

³³ La Roche, "Briefe an Lina," in *Pomona*, 3:307.

³⁴ Décultot, *Lesen, Kopieren*, 145.

³⁵ Carol Strauss Sotiropoulos, *"Pomona, für Teutschlands Töchter:* Sophie von La Roche as Editor, Educator, and Narrator," *Colloquia Germanica* 33, no. 3 (2000): 213–38; "mixed messages" (215).

³⁶ La Roche, "Briefe an Lina," in *Pomona*, 2:1042.

³⁷ La Roche, "Ueber den Namen des Monats April," in *Pomona*, 3:302.

³⁸ Erdmut Jost, "Moralische Gemälde? Sophie von La Roches Kupfererklärung 'Sitten der schönen Pariser Welt,'" in *Sitten der schönen Pariser Welt: Sophie von La Roche und das* Monument du Costume; *Mit den 24 Stichen und dem vollständigen, erstmals ins Deutsche übertragenen Text der ersten beiden Folgen des französischen Originals*, ed. Erdmut Jost (Halle: Mitteldeutscher Verlag, 2011), 130–49, here 131.

[39] "Sophie von La Roches Verbindungen zu Christoph Martin Wieland, ihrem zeitweiligen Verlobten und literarischen Mentor, bestanden mit Unterbrechungen bis zu ihrem Tod." Barbara Becker-Cantarino, "Biographie," in *FrauenGestalten Weimar-Jena um 1800: Ein Bio-bibliographisches Lexikon*, ed. Stefanie Freyer, Katrin Horn, and Nicole Grochowina (Heidelberg: Universitätsverlag Winter, 2009), 221–27, here 222.

[40] "Diese Regel ist so sehr in der Natur der Sache begründet, und daher so indispensabel, daß sich mit bestem Grunde behaupten läßt, alle Dichter und überhaupt alle Schriftsteller von Talent und Geschmack müssen laut gelesen werden, wenn nicht die Hälfte ihrer Schönheiten für den Leser verloren gehen soll" (This rule is so thoroughly rooted in the nature of the matter and therefore so indispensable that it can be claimed with the best reason that all poets and indeed all writers of talent and taste must be read aloud, if half of the beauty is not to be lost to the reader.) As cited by Matthias Bickenbach, *Von den Möglichkeiten einer "inneren" Geschichte des Lesens* (Tübingen: Max Niemeyer Verlag, 1999), 21.

[41] La Roche, "Ueber das Lesen," in *Pomona*, 2:846–47.

[42] La Roche, "Pomona an ihre Leserinnen," in *Pomona*, 4:860.

3: Marcus Aurelius, Also for Girls: Discussions on the Best Form of Government in Enlightenment Hamburg

Almut Spalding

ELISE REIMARUS (1735–1805), a proud lifelong resident of the republican city state of Hamburg, consistently advocated republican government ideals that rely on the ability of its citizens to participate actively in public affairs and lead others toward the common good. This emphasis on civic participation accounts for Reimarus's insistence on an educated citizenship. In this respect she differed markedly from most contemporary educators who, for good reason, considered a curriculum with history and politics a threat to the stability of a monarchical state and wanted to limit the privilege of education to future noble rulers. Of course, even in Hamburg, citizenship did not eradicate all inequalities. Reimarus wrestled with the reality that women, relegated to domestic roles, were barred from public office and other leadership positions. In this essay I argue that Reimarus nevertheless exercised civic leadership as a writer and educator, advocating political education not only for boys but also for girls.

It was not unusual for an eighteenth-century female writer to discuss education: virtually all contemporary women writers did so.[1] But it was not at all common for a female writer explicitly to address civic education *and* to include girls in the discussion. Reimarus did just that. One of her early works is a treatise on the Roman philosopher-emperor Marcus Aurelius Antoninus (121–180 CE), aimed specifically at girls. This work reflects her understanding that effective government and civic education belong together. While the text survives only in incomplete form and was never printed, as was apparently intended, it is significant, because it shows Reimarus's use of Roman history for educating eighteenth-century girls in civic-political matters.

Her portrayal of Marcus Aurelius Antoninus conveys support for a government that promotes the well-being and happiness of the people, listens to the people and their representatives, attends to the weak and vulnerable, uses resources only for the benefit of the common good, respects laws and refrains from arbitrary revenge, and supports education, including female education. In promoting these leadership qualities across genders, based on a male model from classical Rome but intended for a female audience, Reimarus delves into a subject matter usually off-limits for women. In the following I will present Elise Reimarus as a leading female figure of the German Enlightenment and focus specifically on her interest in politics and education, comment on the manuscript and the context in which it emerged, and provide an analysis of the textual content. The treatise provides insights into Reimarus's own early engagement with political questions, her advocacy of female civic education, and her leadership in this area as a writer and educator.

Daughter of the Enlightenment

Margaretha Elisabeth ("Elise") Reimarus grew up in a family known for its dedication to the city of Hamburg and its significant contributions to the German Enlightenment. Her maternal grandfather, Johann Albert Fabricius (1668–1736), a professor of international repute at Hamburg's Akademisches Gymnasium, belonged to Hamburg's first "Patriotische Gesellschaft" (Patriotic Society), an early Enlightenment association promoting individuals' engagement for the common good. Its publication, the early moral weekly *Der Patriot* (1724–26, The Patriot), discussed topics ranging from family matters to critiques of government. Elise's father, Hermann Samuel Reimarus (1694–1768), professor at the same institution, is now most widely remembered as the author of the famed *Fragmente eines Ungenannten* (Fragments of an Unnamed Person) that Gotthold Ephraim Lessing (1729–81) published between 1774 and 1778.[2] His family ties to merchants, mayors, senators, and other city officials accorded him greater insight into government matters than was available to the average Hamburg resident. Surely this played a role when in 1765, together with friends, he founded the so-called second "Patriotische Gesellschaft" (Patriotic Society). Meeting in the Reimarus home, this organization functioned as an unofficial advisory board to the city government, recommending reforms in education, industry, trade, and other matters benefitting the city. Exposure to such discussion in her own home inspired Elise's interest in political matters at a young age.

Her brother, Johann Albert Hinrich Reimarus (1729–1814), became known to his contemporaries as a physician who introduced safer smallpox vaccinations in Hamburg and brought lightning-rod technology to the European continent. His publications range from science and philosophy to economics and trade. In the 1750s, the time most relevant for the present context, he was a university student pursuing medical studies in Göttingen, Leiden, Edinburgh, and London. He was Elise's closest lifelong confidant and supporter. As a widower, he entrusted his sister with the education of his two small children, an experience of significance for Elise's future publications. Handwriting of both Elise and her brother on surviving manuscripts indicates that they collaborated on publication projects, notably concerning civic education.

The political engagement of family and friends on behalf of Hamburg's civic life set a standard to which Elise would aspire her entire life. But for women, civic engagement was complicated. Elise expressed this in one of her "Betrachtungen"[3] (Reflections), depicting two female characters who represent opposing views. One of the characters resents the restrictions imposed on women:

> [Ein] Frauenzimmer . . . besitzt die selben Geschicklichkeiten die jene [Männer] besizen und hat daher dasselbe Vorrecht zu allen den Geschäften und Verrichtungen deren sie sich itzt allein anmasen—es gehörte dem Frauenzimmer daher so wohl wie ihnen die öffentliche Bedienungen zu bekleiden—Amter zu verwalten das Regiment zu führen: und eine ungerechte Usurpation nur habe ihm das Ruder aus den Händen gerungen welches zu führen sie mit ihnen ein gleiches Recht hatten.[4]

> [Women . . . have the same abilities as (men) and therefore have the same right to all affairs and activities that they currently claim for themselves alone. Hence women, like men, should be able to hold public office, manage agencies, lead a regiment. It was unfair abuse that pried from their hands control which they had the same right to exercise as (men).]

The other character rationalizes societal arrangements: "Ich [habe] mich einmahl gewohnt . . . mir einen jeden Stand worinn ich mich befinden soll so angenehm, und mich darinn so zufrieden zu machen als es mir immer möglich ist . . ." (I have got used . . . to accommodating myself as comfortably and happily as possible in any circumstance imposed on me). This character argues that the world would disintegrate into "entsezliche Verwirrung" (horrible chaos) if women were to enter public office. These opposing views of female roles reveal Reimarus's own inner struggle at a time when participating in civic life was still a distant dream.

Of course, some women always had political leadership roles, but they were noble women who usually filled in for a male regent, such as for a deceased husband, or a son who was not yet of age. For non-noble women, access to leadership outside religious communities came with the first profession open to females, namely that of educator.[5] In German territories this generally occurred toward the end of the eighteenth century—later than in England or France—but in the port city of Hamburg female teachers can already be documented by mid-century. How those teachers may have understood their role within the larger framework of civic-political education is difficult to say, however, because of the lack of surviving sources. Reimarus presents a rare exception. Embracing the role of writer-educator, she became prominent in contemporary German Enlightenment circles for her literary and pedagogical accomplishments, and she left writings that reveal her understanding of the role of civic education. Together with her sister-in-law, Sophie Reimarus née Hennings (1742–1817), her brother's second wife, she hosted a literary salon, the Hamburg Tea Table. It attracted as participants writers, musicians, actors, merchants, publicists, educators, and philosophers, including Jewish representatives, from near and far. Among them were Friedrich Gottlieb Klopstock (1724–1803), Johanna Elisabeth von Winthem (1747–1821), August Friedrich Hennings (1746–1828), Joachim Heinrich Campe (1746–1828) and his wife Maria Dorothea née Hiller (1741–1827), Friedrich Ludwig Schröder (1744–1816), Moses Wessely (1737–92), Sophie Becker (1754–89), Elise von der Recke (1754–1833), Sara Levy née Itzig (1761–1854), and, as long-distance members, Gotthold Ephraim Lessing (1729–81), Moses Mendelssohn (1729–86), and Friedrich Heinrich Jacobi (1743–1819). Elise Reimarus maintained an active correspondence with these and many other figures who were associated with intellectual-literary circles of the time. Today her letters can be found in the collected works of Lessing, Mendelssohn, Jacobi, and Campe.[6] Beyond the Tea Table, she was known in Hamburg for her translations of Voltaire's *Alzire* and *Zaïre* and Françoise de Graffigny's *Cénie*, which were produced on stage in 1780.[7]

In the context of this essay, her renown as an educator takes on particular importance because her long publishing record in the field of education shows connections to her study of Marcus Aurelius Antoninus. This applies especially to her writings in Campe's phenomenally successful *Kleine Kinderbibliothek* (Small Library for Children), first published in 1779. This series of readers, geared to specific age groups and field-tested for holding children's interest, quickly became a European best-seller, with at least fourteen distinct German-language editions published over a century, plus French, Polish, and Russian translations. Reimarus's characteristic dialogues can be found in all of them, depicting child protagonists, frequently girls, in life-like conversations about topics ranging from children's different social ranks to human free will.[8] Reimarus wrote these dialogues in the 1760s when she taught her brother's children, though their origins lie a decade earlier.

Reimarus's interest in politics and civic education can be traced from when she was barely eighteen to the end of her life. Unsurprisingly, most of her overtly political writings, such as her "Versuch einer Läuterung und Vereinfachung der Begriffe vom natürlichen Staatsrecht" (Explanation and Simplification of the Concepts of Natural Civil Law),[9] circulated among friends in manuscript form only. However, one text was printed during her lifetime: the pamphlet *Freiheit* (Freedom). Written in her characteristic dialogue style, it appeared anonymously during the violent 1791 Hamburg artisans' revolt.[10] By this time, shortly after the French Revolution, Reimarus addressed the topic of freedom with a different focus than in her youth, though her concern about civic matters had not changed since she had written her treatise on Marcus Aurelius Antoninus almost four decades earlier.

Elise's political writings reveal an especially close collaboration with her brother. This is evident from his occasional notes in her manuscripts, and from his own publication on civic education, *Entwurf eines allgemeinen Staats-Unterrichts für künftige Bürger* (1803; A Plan for the Universal Civic Education of Future Citizens), which draws heavily on his sister's writings. Nineteenth-century historiography erased any memory of Elise's writings with a political emphasis even more effectively than her writings for children. The present examination of her treatise on Marcus Aurelius Antoninus adds to scholarly attempts to rectify the record.

The Manuscript and Its Context

Among all of Elise Reimarus's writings known to me, the manuscript collection containing her treatise on Marcus Aurelius Antoninus posed the greatest challenge. The folder entitled "Gedanken über Erziehung" (Thoughts on Education) looks very similar to Reimarus's "Betrachtungen" (Reflections). Both folders contain a loose-leaf collection of writings dating from the author's youth, often written on recycled paper, with her father's discarded notes on the other side of the sheet. One sub-folder within "Gedanken über Erziehung" contains reflections on education, with an introduction addressed to "meine liebe Schwester" (my dear sister), Elise's younger sister Hanna Maria Reimarus (1740–1819). Other sources corroborate that once Hanna Maria's schooling with private tutors for writing, arithmetic, drawing, and languages, and at a so-called French School came to an end, a good part of her further education in the 1750s took place in the form of "mutual instruction" with her older sister Elise.[11]

The second sub-folder within "Gedanken über Erziehung" contains the treatise on Marcus Aurelius. A neatly written introduction under the heading "Philosophie" (philosophy) explains the origin of the project. But the disarray of subsequent pages, numerous marginal notes and cross references, some on inserted small pieces of paper with additional notes, and various drafts of similar content obscure the manuscript's substance to a twenty-first century reader. Clearly Marcus Aurelius Antoninus plays the role of main character, but at first I was uncertain if one could ever discern a coherent text. The only way to find out was to transcribe the text in the jumbled order in which the pages survive, then to try to piece the puzzle together. The surviving text did turn out to contain a coherent narrative, though it remains fragmentary.

Why should anyone bother to pay attention to ideas that survive only in fragments—perhaps unfinished, perhaps scattered, but definitely unpublished? This is precisely the question Angela Hunter discusses in connection with a French woman of the Enlightenment, Louise Marie-Madeleine Dupin (1706–99), whose large, unfinished feminist work *Ouvrage sur les femmes* (Treatise on Women) remains unpublished, with sections of the manuscript dispersed around the world. Hunter argues that the lack of a complete edition should not prevent us from critically examining Dupin's ideas as far as they *are* accessible to us.[12] The same applies to Elise Reimarus. While her treatise on Marcus Aurelius Antoninus survives only as a fragment, it shows females in some circles of mid-eighteenth-century Hamburg educating themselves in civic-political matters, with young Elise Reimarus leading the effort to create a girls' reader about this Roman emperor. Expressions of such thoughts by mid-eighteenth-century women who were not themselves noble regents are rare. Even a generation later, women's views on political matters often emerge only from sources that might be considered ephemeral.[13] For this reason, Reimarus's fragmentary work on Marcus Aurelius contributes a significant piece to the puzzle from which to reconstruct female participation in the political discourse on leadership in the history of German thought. The manuscript clearly dates from the mid-1750s. A draft of the introduction gives a first clue: "Was Wieland in der 20sten Note seiner moralischen Briefe von ihm [M. Aurelius Antoninus] sagt wird hier nicht am unrechten Orte stehen. 'der erste Philosoph der Kaiser war. . . .'"[14] (It won't be wrong here to repeat what Wieland says about him [M. Aurelius Antoninus] in note 20 of his moral letters. 'the first philosopher who was an emperor. . . .'). Those *Zwölf Moralische Briefe in Versen*[15] (Twelve Moral Letters in Verses) by Christoph Martin Wieland (1733–1813) appeared in 1752, which establishes the earliest possible date for Elise's treatise.

The introduction to the treatise provides further details on how this project emerged:

> Eine Gesellschaft junger Leute, die . . . eingesehen daß die bloße Leserey von Romanen u dahin gehörigen tändelhaften Schriften weder dem Geiste noch dem Herzen eine kraftvolle Nahrung gäbe, hatten sich verabredet einmal aus den Quellen des Alterthums . . . , zu schöpfen, und setzten zu diesem Zweck einen Tag in jeder Woche fest wo sie theils aus den Biographien und theils aus den Schriften berühmter Männer Vorlesungen halten wollten.

[A group of young people came to realize . . . that the mere consumption of novels and similar idle readings would not provide sus-
taining nourishment to their mind or heart. So they agreed to draw
from the sources of antiquity, . . . and for this purpose set aside one
day each week to read sometimes from famous men's biographies
and sometimes from their writings.]

The introduction then explains that these gatherings took place in a
private home, under the guidance of an older person whose presence the
young people had requested. "So begann eine Reihe von Vorlesungen die
wir unsrer jungen Leserwelt hier öffentlich mittheilen wann sie etwan auch
einmal den Versuch machen wollten diese mit ihrer gewönlichen Lectüre
abwechseln zu lassen" (Thus began a series of lectures which we hereby
publicly share with our young readers, should they also sometime try to
switch to this from their ordinary reading material.) Correspondence
corroborates that the young people mentioned here are sisters Elise and
Hanna Maria Reimarus and their close friends, sisters Anna Elisabeth
(1729–1757 or 1759) and Catharina Surland (1736–1757 or 1759). In
the spring and summer of 1753 these young women studied classical figures and history under the direction of Anna Elisabeth and Catharina's
mother, Rebecca Catharina Surland née Fürsen (d. 1767). One of the
Surland daughters must have been so witty and adept at portraying a historical event that Elise's brother suggested "sie sollte eine gute Satyre
schreiben" (she should write a good satire).[16] Johann Albert Hinrich
also complimented his sister for moving beyond reading only novels and
expressed his hope "daß Dir alle schöne u. nützliche Wissenschaften nie-
mahls mehr ekelhaft werden werden"[17] (that all fine and useful disciplines
will never again become distasteful to you). The sentiment valuing readings beyond novels is also echoed in the introduction to Elise's Marcus
Aurelius treatise. All this suggests that the manuscript itself dates from
1753 or at the latest 1754.

Rebecca Catharina Surland, who oversaw these gatherings, was the
widow of syndic Johann Julius Surland (1686–1748). Daughter and wife
of leading figures in Hamburg's city government, she most certainly had
some up-close glimpses of a republican government at work. But she was
also highly educated in her own right, especially in the area of history and
geography. Titles of books that the Reimarus siblings borrowed from or
exchanged with her attest to that expertise.[18] She would have been well
prepared to guide any group of young people in their study of classical
figures and writings.

The plan to publish the lectures from these weekly gatherings never
came to fruition. The reasons for this, and also how the now missing sections of the overall narrative were lost, remain unknown. The surviving,
incomplete text, however, stems from Elise Reimarus's pen.

Educating Rulers, Subjects, or Citizens

Reimarus's insistence on teaching history and politics at all, let alone to girls, contrasted starkly with contemporary opinions on education widely held in German territories. Her ideas about education were closer to those of the English political philosopher John Locke (1632–1704), who argued in his *Thoughts Concerning Education* (1693) that education should aim at creating citizens who could protect their own liberty. Hence even the general public needed to be literate in scientific and economic matters, as well as in law and history.[19] While the Declaration of Independence in North America bore the imprint of Locke's political thought, almost simultaneously in Berlin the Prussian minister of education, Carl Abraham von Zedlitz (1731–1793), spelled out a very different purpose of public education.

Addressing the Prussian Academy of Sciences, Zedlitz asserted in 1777 that in a monarchy, the main goal of teaching history and geography was to convince the youth of the security and protection they enjoyed under their ruler—in contrast to republics, where security depended on the whim of commoners. For Zedlitz, both the purpose and content of education were strictly tied to social class. The general populace was to be trained for obedience, and any political education must reinforce the spirit of subordination. The educated (male) elite, on the other hand, should indeed learn to think and reflect, but their history curriculum should be slanted toward the positive portrayal of imperial/monarchical governments. Portrayals of republican systems were to be de-emphasized, with a curriculum that "corrects" the impression that pupils might have of the golden age of Greece and Rome, lest they fail to grasp the difference between "Freiheit und Zügellosigkeit" (freedom and anarchy).[20] In such an environment, all teachers who demonstrated independent thinking and developed their own curriculum were deeply suspect.[21] While Zedlitz's remarks date from some twenty years *after* Elise Reimarus had written her treatise on Marcus Aurelius Antoninus, these long-held convictions about the purpose of political education illustrate all the more vividly that Reimarus pursued new directions in education.

Sources of the Treatise

Marcus Aurelius Antoninus's *Meditations Concerning Himself*—in the tradition of late Stoicism reflecting on life and death, the cultivation of the soul, a virtuous lifestyle—were part of the educational canon of the eighteenth century.[22] Indeed, Elise had probably encountered these *Meditations* in the original while learning Greek with her father. But the focus of her treatise is different. It prioritizes the emperor's actions—what he did, where he went, how he conducted himself, what he said—aspects *not* recorded in his own *Meditations*. We can conclude that Reimarus used other sources as the basis for the emperor's life account.

Probably not coincidentally, Elise began her study of Marcus Aurelius Antoninus just when her father had concluded a major project on Roman history. In 1752 he published the second volume of a splendid dual-language critical edition of the Roman History by Cassius Dio Cocceianus (ca. 155–235 CE), a project originally begun by Elise's grandfather Fabricius.[23] The work garnered considerable scholarly acclaim, which Elise and her brother followed with great interest. Almost surely Elise was familiar with the sections on Marcus Aurelius Antoninus in this work.

But the main source for her own treatise on the emperor was the first German-language translation of Marcus Aurelius Antoninus's *Meditations*, which also included an account of his life. Elise's note in December 1752 to her brother that she was reading Antoninus is revealing, not because she was reading the *Meditations* at all, but that she was reading them in German. Apparently she discovered only then that her father had had a significant role in the latest edition several years before.[24] This may have increased her interest in Roman history.

The book in question is *Des römischen Kaisers Marcus Aurelius Antoninus erbauliche Betrachtungen über sich selbst, aus dem Griechischen übersetzt, mit Anmerkungen und des Kaisers Leben erläutert* (The Roman Emperor Marcus Aurelius Antonius's Edifying Meditations on Himself, Translated from the Greek, with Notes and Comments on the Emperor's Life), by Johann Adolf Hoffmann (1676–1731), a Hamburg tutor with an interest in political matters. Elise's father must have known Hoffmann personally, owning manuscripts from his estate and numerous publications, including *Johann Adolf Hoffmanns Politische Anmerckungen über die wahre und falsche Staatskunst* (1725; Political Notes on True and False Governments).[25] Hoffmann's German-language book on Marcus Aurelius Antoninus had been immensely popular, with three reprints between 1723 and 1735. By the fourth edition in 1748, when the original author and publisher were long deceased, the new publisher asked Hermann Samuel Reimarus to review the entire work, correct errors, and update antiquated language.[26] Though the publisher must have given Hermann Samuel Reimarus at least one copy of the finished product, this title is notably absent from Reimarus's library auction catalogue—an indication that Elise kept it for her own library following her father's death. Once this main source for Elise's treatise on Marcus Aurelius Antoninus becomes clear, it also—finally—becomes possible to piece together her manuscript and recognize her editorial contributions.

Like Hoffmann's book, her treatise contains two sections—one on the emperor's life and another on his *Meditations*. However, the sequence of these two sections is reversed in Reimarus's version compared to Hoffmann's book. Reimarus drew amply but selectively from Hoffmann's work. Today this would be called plagiarism, and even then, proper attribution of ideas to original authors was expected. But other priorities often took precedence. Catherine the Great, in her *Instruction für die zu Verfertigung des Entwurfs zu dem neuen Gesetz-Buche verordnete Comißion* (1767; Instruction to the Commission Charged with Finalizing the Draft of the New Legal Code), drew so heavily on Montesquieu without naming him that she herself spoke of a "plagiat pour le bien de trente millions d'hommes" (plagiarized work for the good of thirty million people).[27] Whether Reimarus would have acknowledged her main source if her treatise had ever reached publication in print, we will never know. In any case, she never simply copied Hoffmann's book but instead condensed and omitted text, rearranged paragraphs, and sometimes offered two drafts for the same story—effectively composing a new work. (This anticipated what she would do with her German-language version of Addison's drama *Cato*.) By shaping her text about an icon of a virtuous ruler according to *her* judgment, creating her own curriculum, Reimarus engaged precisely in the type of behavior that made independently thinking teachers suspect.

Reimarus's Portrait of Marcus Aurelius Antoninus

In her portrait of Marcus Aurelius, Reimarus emphasizes the ruler with a philosophical mindset whose calm, empathetic, just, and generous treatment of his subjects inspires them also to contribute to the common good. For instance, he requires safer equipment for forced laborers in the public entertainment business: "Damit die Spiele der Klopfechter nicht zu blutig würden befahl er stat der scharfen Gewehre Rappiere zu brauchen und den Seiltanzern daß ihnen Betten u Hangematrazen untergelegt würden" (Lest the games of the fencers would become too bloody, he ordered the use of blunted daggers instead of sharp weapons, and similarly, that beds and hammocks be placed under the tightrope acrobats.). He is beloved among his troops because he cares about them: "Nach der Schlacht [gieng er] selbst auf die Wahlstadt . . . , um zu sehen, ob sich unter den Verwundeten einige fänden, deren Leben er . . . zu retten im Stande ware" (After combat he personally went to the battlefield to see if he might find some among the injured whose lives he could save). He uses resources for the common good, living modestly himself:

> Die . . . Wieder Aufbauung verschiedner Städte, die Nachlassung von Auflagen und Schulden, . . . samt den Kosten der öffentl. Schauspiele, beweisen sattsam des Kaisers . . . Freigebigkeit, die ihm zu desto größerem Ruhm gereicht, da er für sich selbst, sich der äußersten Sparsamkeit befleißigte.

[The . . . reconstruction of various cities, the cancellation of taxes and
debts, . . . and the costs of public performances, all this amply proves
the emperor's . . . generosity, which brings him all the greater fame
because for himself, he practiced the most extraordinary thriftiness.]

Marcus Aurelius respects the law and seeks arbitration with his political
enemy, the usurper Cassius:

> Wollte Cassius nur zu mir kommen: . . . Ich wollte vor dem Rath
> zu Rom mit ihm rächten; ia ich wollte ihm ohne Blutvergiessen
> das Kaiserthum abträthen; wen ihr urtheilet daß dem gemeinen
> Menschen mehr mit dem Cassius als mit Anthoninus gedient sei.

[If only Cassius came to me, . . . I would reason with him in front of
the Senate in Rome. Yes, I would relinquish the emperorship to him
without bloodshed if you judge that the common people are better
served by Cassius than by Antoninus.]

Following Cassius's death, Marcus Aurelius Antoninus even protects
Cassius's children from being penalized for their father's crimes. In
short, Reimarus draws from a variety of contexts to show what made this
emperor beloved as a leader among his subjects.

Concerning the city of Athens, Reimarus emphasizes that Marcus
Aurelius Antoninus hired teachers in various disciplines, with decent sala-
ries, and that he extended various privileges to the city. He also founded
a school for young women: "das beste war [daß er sie] auf seine Kosten
erziehen ließ" (best of all was that he assumed the cost of their education). Implying a parallel between the city of Athens and Hamburg,
Reimarus's portrayal of the emperor's support of female education suggests that Hamburg civic leaders do the same.

Twice Reimarus *added* text of her own to her portrait of the emperor.
Both instances favorably compare Marcus Aurelius Antoninus and the
contemporary Prussian king, Frederick II (1712–86, r. 1740–86). For
instance, she notes their love of philosophy and learning: "Daß Liebe
zu den Wissenschaften . . . seinen Regententugenden nur eine hohere
Weisheit geben, hat wiederum die neuere Geschichte an dem ausge-
zeichneten Beyspiel des Großen Friederichs bewiesen." (The love of
scholarship . . . adds greater wisdom to a regent's governing virtues, as
the more recent history has proven again with the outstanding example of the Great Frederick.) Had Reimarus composed her treatise a few
years later, after the Seven Years' War (1756–63), perhaps she would
not have made this comparison. Reimarus also shaped her portrayal of
Marcus Aurelius Antoninus by *omitting* details from the correspond-
ing sections in Hoffmann's book. Her treatise shows a slightly gentler

world than Hoffmann's, lacking all the gory details regarding blood, violence, torture, and other cruelties committed during battles and games for public entertainment that Hoffmann's book spells out. Also, a true Enlightenment thinker, Reimarus shows Marcus Aurelius Antoninus operating in a world free of superstition. Her treatise carefully avoids all references to miracles in critical moments of human history or divine intervention in response to human prayer. Third, Reimarus made sure that the emperor's wife, Faustina, did not appear in too negative a light. While her treatise hints at Faustina's known faults, it omits passages that show her as power hungry and selfish. Perhaps Reimarus chose this path because a self-centered Faustina would not provide a positive role model for the main audience of this treatise, young females. Additionally, this marriage between an iconic philosopher-emperor and an opportunistic woman fit neither the ideal of marriage, nor the typical, gendered power configuration of real marriages. Addressing marriage here was too complicated for young Reimarus, so she sidestepped the issue.

The second part of Reimarus's treatise on Marcus Aurelius Antoninus—her version of the emperor's own *Meditations*—confirms her relatively greater interest in his actions than his thoughts. In this section, the emperor's original meditations are reduced to about one third of the original number, and the text is significantly condensed. About one fifth of those meditations address communal or civic issues as opposed to individual virtues, which represents a higher proportion than among the original *Meditations* overall. This redaction of the emperor's own *Meditations* underscores Reimarus's appreciation of him especially for his demonstrated leadership as a ruler.

Marcus Aurelius: Intellectual Space for and Foundation of Female Civic Education

Elise Reimarus's treatise on the Roman emperor Marcus Aurelius Antoninus is significant on several levels. It demonstrates that, at a time when civic education was discouraged even for boys, there were women who educated themselves on political matters, and who used the leadership of an exemplary Roman emperor to discuss the best form of government in their own time. The treatise confirms that from a young age Reimarus promoted female civic education. Of course, she could not remove or alter the restrictions that females faced in *real* life, nor could she prevent the narrowing of gender-role ideals during the course of her lifetime, which rendered female civic leadership ever more elusive toward the end of the eighteenth century. But her work on Marcus Aurelius illustrates an important function of a writer-educator, namely that of creating an intellectual space where females could cultivate the relative freedom and the autonomy of their mind even while being excluded from positions that society values. The world women could experience in a written work represented both an escape from and compensation for the significant constraints dominating their real lives.[28] In that sense, Reimarus's work on Marcus Aurelius provided an intellectual space where girls or women could participate in discourses on the best form of government, even if they had no say in the government of the city of Hamburg. Furthermore, Reimarus's treatise on Marcus Aurelius Antoninus brings to light—by way of Hoffmann's book—the intentionality of civic education in her later writings. For example, one meditation by the emperor, pondering the purpose of beings, takes up less than five lines in Reimarus's treatise. This meditation appears in the index of Hoffmann's book under the title, "Der Mensch ist zur Arbeit geboren" (Humans Are Born for Work).[29] Curiously, though, one of Reimarus's children's dialogues bears a similar title, "Von der Arbeitsamkeit" (Of Work), and conveys the same ideas, now presented in the form of a conversation between little Louise, who prefers play over chores, and her mother.[30] These ties between Reimarus's work on Marcus Aurelius Antoninus and her later work substantiate that civic education is an intent in all her writings, especially those addressed to girls.

Finally, this study shows that examining fragmentary, unpublished manuscripts is worthwhile. Elise Reimarus's manuscript illuminates that, long before they could hold public office, women engaged with civic affairs.

Notes

[1] Annette Mohr, *Madame d'Epinays Konzeption der Mädchenerziehung im Umfeld von frauenspezifischen Erziehungstraktaten des 18. Jahrhunderts in Frankreich* (St. Ingbert: Röhrig, 1997) 15.

[2] The entire work did not appear until two centuries later: Hermann Samuel Reimarus, *Apologie oder Schutzschrift für die vernünftigen Verehrer Gottes*, ed. Gerhard Alexander, 2 vols. (Frankfurt am Main: Insel, 1972).

[3] Elise Reimarus, "Betrachtungen," in Almut Spalding, *Elise Reimarus (1735–1805), the Muse of Hamburg: A Woman of the German Enlightenment* (Würzburg: Königshausen & Neumann, 2005), appendix 1, no. 23, 328–29.

[4] Spalding, *Reimarus*, appendix 1, 329.

[5] Barbara Becker-Cantarino, *Der lange Weg zur Mündigkeit: Frauen und Literatur in Deutschland von 1500 bis 1800* (Stuttgart: Metzler, 1987), 189–90. Reprint, Munich: dtv, 1989.

[6] An edition of Elise Reimarus's correspondence is in preparation by the author.

[7] Prompt books from the Zaïre production with Friedrich Ludwig Schröder in the lead role survive. See Spalding, *Reimarus*, appendix 5, 440–98.

[8] For a list of Reimarus's contributions to various editions of Campe's *Kleine Kinderbibliothek*, see Spalding, *Reimarus*, 525–43. For example, the dialogue "Wie nöthig es ist, gehorsam zu seyn" (How Important It Is to Be Obedient) appears in at least four extant German editions, two French editions, and in Polish and Russian translations. Spalding, *Reimarus*, 540–41.

[9] Elise Reimarus, "Versuch einer Läuterung und Vereinfachung der Begriffe vom natürlichen Staatsrecht," in Spalding, *Reimarus*, appendix 7, 504–13.

[10] *Freiheit* (Hamburg: Meyn, 1791). For the case of Elise's authorship (rather than the traditional attribution to her brother), see Almut Spalding, "Siblings, Publications, and the Transmission of Memory: Johann Albert Hinrich and Elise Reimarus," in *Sibling Relations and Gender in the Early Modern World: Sisters, Brothers, and Others*, ed. Naomi J. Miller and Naomi Yavneh (Aldershot, UK: Ashgate, 2006), 216–27.

[11] Johann Albert Hinrich Reimarus (in the following abbreviated JAHR), letter (in English) to Elise Reimarus (in the following abbreviated ER), Dec. 5, 1755, London IIIr, Staatsarchiv Hamburg (in the following abbreviated StA HH), Bestand 622-1/90 Sieveking I, Neuzugang 1996. The Reimarus children's schooling is traceable in detail through the family account books. See Almut and Paul Spalding, *The Household Accounts of the Reimarus Family of Hamburg, 1728–1780: Turf and Tailors, Books and Beer*, 2 vols. (Leiden, Netherlands: Brill, 2015).

[12] Angela Hunter, "The Unfinished Work on Louise Marie-Madeleine Dupin's Unfinished *Ouvrage sur les femmes*," *Eighteenth-Century Studies* 43, no. 1 (2009): 101.

[13] For instance, Friederike Brun's outspoken political views must be gleaned from her seemingly traditional poetry, travelogues, diaries, and private correspondence. Cindy K. Renker, "The Political Voice in the Writings of Friederike Brun (1765–1835)," *Women in German Yearbook* 29 (2013): 81–96.

[14] Elise Reimarus, Gedanken über Erziehung, StA HH, Bestand 622-1/86 Reimarus, F6. All subsequent citations from the Marcus Aurelius Antoninus treatise come from this source.

[15] Only the first edition of Wieland's *Zwölf Moralische Briefe* (Frankfurt am Main: Eckebrecht, 1752) contains the cited reference in a note numbered 20 ("Erster Brief," 16); in later editions, text and note numbers are rearranged.

[16] JAHR, letter to ER, Apr 7, 1753, Göttingen XX. StA HH, Bestand 622-1/90 Sieveking I, Neuzugang 1996.

[17] JAHR, letter to ER, June 21, 1753, Göttingen XXI. StA HH, Bestand 622-1/90 Sieveking I, Neuzugang 1996.

[18] JAHR, letter to ER, June 8, 1752, Göttingen II, StA HH, Bestand 622-1/90 Sieveking I, Neuzugang 1996.

[19] Laurie M. Johnson, *Locke and Rousseau: Two Enlightenment Responses to Honor* (Lanham, MD: Lexington, 2012), 52, 54.

[20] Carl Abraham von Zedlitz, "Ueber den Patriotismus als einen Gegenstand der Erziehung in monarchischen Staaten" (trans. from French, Berlin 1777), in *Die Volksschule des Obrigkeitsstaates und ihre Kritiker: Texte zur politischen Funktion*

der Volksbildung im 18. und 19. Jahrhundert, ed. Ludwig Fertig (Darmstadt: Wissenschaftliche Buchgesellschaft, 1979), 16.

[21] Ludwig Fertig, "Einleitung: Staatsräson und Armeleutebildung," in Fertig, *Die Volksschule des Obrigkeitsstaates und ihre Kritiker: Texte zur politischen Funktion der Volksbildung im 18. und 19. Jahrhundert*, xiv.

[22] Jochen Schmidt, "Die poetologische Transformation der stoischen Euthymie: Marc Aurel und Hölderlins Ode *Dichtermut*," in *Stoizismus in der europäischen Philosophie, Literatur, Kunst und Politik: Eine Kulturgeschichte von der Antike bis zur Moderne*, ed. Barbara Neymeyr, Jochen Schmidt, and Bernhard Zimmermann (Berlin: de Gruyter, 2008), 2:951.

[23] Hermann Samuel Reimarus, ed., *Tōn Diōnos Tu Kassiu Tu Kokkōianu Rhōmaikōn Istoriōn Ta Sōzomena = Cassii Dionis Cocceiani Historiae Romanae . . .* 2 vols. (Hamburg: Herold, 1750–52).

[24] JAHR, letter (in Latin) to Hermann Samuel Reimarus, January 4, 1753, StA HH, Bestand 633-1/86 Reimarus, A22, Göttingen XXIV.

[25] *Auktionskatalog der Bibliothek von Hermann Samuel Reimarus*, redigiert von Johann Andreas Gottfried Schetelig, Hamburg 1769 und 1770 (Hamburg, 1978), entry 2802b, 219.

[26] The 1723, 1727, and 1735 editions were printed in Hamburg by Felginer, the 1748 and 1755 editions by Felginer's successor and son-in-law, Johann Carl Bohn (1712–73), a close friend of the Reimaruses. The foreword to the fourth edition does not name Reimarus, but it refers to a "skilled and famous" editor. Reimarus's identity is attested in correspondence. See also Franklin Kopitzsch, *Grundzüge einer Sozialgeschichte der Aufklärung in Hamburg und Altona*, 2nd ed. (Hamburg: Verlag Verein für Hamburgische Geschichte, 1990), 271.

[27] Catherine II, letter to d'Alembert, June 27, 1765, in *Oeuvres et correspondances inédites de D'Alembert*, ed. Charles Henry (Paris: Perrin, 1887), 239.

[28] Mohr, *Madame d'Epinays Konzeption*, 15; Becker-Cantarino, *Der lange Weg*, 193.

[29] Johann Adolph Hofmann, *Des römischen Kaisers Marcus Aurelius Antoninus erbauliche Betrachtungen über sich selbst*, 5th ed. (Hamburg: Bohn, 1755), 323. The reference is to Meditation 19 of book 8.

[30] [Elise Reimarus], "Von der Arbeitsamkeit," in *Kleine Kinderbibliothek*, ed. Joachim Heinrich Campe, 2nd ed., vol. 4 (Hamburg: Herold, 1783), 143–49. For other editions and translations, see Spalding, *Reimarus*, 525–26.

4: *Dux Femina Facti*: Gender, Sovereignty, and (Women's) Literature in Marie Antonia of Saxony's *Thalestris* and Charlotte von Stein's *Dido*

Anke Gilleir and Aude Defurne

Vergil's Dido as Political Script

"Dux femina facti" (A woman was leader of the deed): with these words Vergil's *Aeneas* concludes the narrative of misfortunes that forced a young merchant's widow named Dido to flee from her native Phoenicia to North Africa, where she founded—and became queen of—the city of Carthage. The genitive "facti' refers to the stages of her flight. Dido, shocked to learn about the killing of her husband and urgently advised to leave the country, prepares her flight with allies ("fugam Dido sociosque parabat"); available ships are seized and loaded to carry the treasures of her pursuer Pygmalion to the open sea. What remains vague in the account is the exact role Dido plays at this stage. The three-word sentence at the end, "dux femina facti," functions as a moment of investiture, underscoring that she took the lead. Yet the narrator's reticence—it is in fact the voice of the goddess Aphrodite, who recounts the history of Dido and Carthage to her son Aeneas—leaves some ambiguity as to *why* or *how* the merchant's wife became queen. On the one hand, the narrative suggests that, given the circumstances, it is only natural that Dido be the leader and hence no further explanation is needed. Yet on the other hand, "dux femina facti" can also be read as a notice to underscore a situation so unexpected that readers need to be informed explicitly in order to grasp what is happening: a *woman* became the leader.[1] In light of the prevailing expectations in Western civilization the second interpretation appears more plausible. Though ancient history and literature abound with unjust and tyrannical (male) rulers, "dux femina" signals a state of exception, a disruption in the continuation of state power.[2] In her seminal 1949 *The Second Sex*, Simone de Beauvoir concluded: "History shows that men have always had hold of all concrete power."[3] Though de Beauvoir does not focus on the history of women's relationship to political sovereignty in particular, her wry conclusion does apply to the field of political history, in which female sovereignty was never just "one rule after the other," but always appeared as an exceptional case and an immanent risk. While, as we will try to show in this article, women writers have addressed this gendered power template in different ways, Vergil's story of Dido's reign appears as a warning from ancient times.[4] The queen succumbs to a passion that makes her forsake all responsibilities as a sovereign, which is all the more troubling since her kingdom is surrounded by enemies: "on ev'ry side . . . hemm'd with warlike foes":

> Gaetulian cities here are spread around,
> And fierce Numidians there your frontiers bound;
> Here lies a barren waste of thirsty land,
> And there the Syrtes raise the moving sand;
> Barcaean troops besiege the narrow shore,
> And from the sea Pygmalion threatens more.[5]

Although Dido's sister Anna uses the precarious political situation to convince the queen to give in to her feelings for Aeneas—with him and his Trojan army the kingdom will rise—Dido's story is not about matters of state. We only learn about the stateswoman through metonyms. When Aeneas arrives in the city, he is filled with awe when he sees the buzzing activities, the works of art that testify to a high degree of civilization and eventually the queen who appears amid all this splendor. Yet her characterization as a ruling sovereign is compressed into two stanzas: "iura dabat legesque uiris, operumque laborem/partibus aequabat iustis aut sorte tahebat."[6] (She takes petitions, and dispenses laws, Hears and determines ev'ry private cause;/Their tasks in equal portions she divides,/And, where unequal, there by lots decides). In other words, queenship functions as a poetic device that enhances the magnitude of the drama, but while it is not a political script, it is nonetheless interesting in light of the history of sovereignty.

Dido's predicament transforms the *persona politica* into a wild moaning woman, whose *amour fou* annihilates political reasoning.[7] In fact, the entire fourth book deals with her despair. In the wake of feminist and queer studies, this kind of "unreasonable" emotional expression has been reinterpreted as a form of resistance to exclusion and inequality.[8] The most emblematic figure here is Sophocles's Antigone, who refuses to adopt the traditional—male—political discourse of power and opposes it with uncompromising suffering.[9] This interpretation was to some extent instigated by Hegel, who, though hardly in feminist terms, construed the conflict between Antigone and Creon as a clash between the two dimensions of humanity, represented by woman and man respectively: the (morality of the) private individual generated by and continued in the bonds of family happiness (*Familienglückseligkeit*) on the one hand and the general law (and ethics) of state and government, *das Gemeinwesen*, on the other.[10] Both Dido and Antigone are beholden to a state power that has turned against their sense of happiness. Yet Dido is not an unconditionally self-sacrificial daughter or sister. She *is* the law, the uncontested head of state, and her lapse into the private universe of feeling costs all her subjects dearly. While Antigone's suicide sets in motion a number of other suicides, it does lead to Creon's catharsis.[11] In contrast, when Dido kills herself, she not only ends her own life but drags down the entire city.[12] Antigone is a sorry case of the *conditio humanae* that Hegel called "die ewige Ironie des Gemeinwesens" (the eternal irony of the state and government).[13] Dido, on the other hand, determines the fate of the collective and effects the following scenario:

> [die Weiblichkeit] verändert durch die Intrige den allgemeinen Zweck der Regierung in einen Privatzweck, verwandelt ihre allgemeine Tätigkeit in ein Werk dieses bestimmten Individuums und verkehrt das allgemeine Eigentum des Staates zu einem Besitz und Putz der Familie.[14]

> [(Femininity), by means of intrigue, changes the general purpose of government into a private purpose, transforms its general activity into a work of this particular individual, and inverts the general possession of the state into a property and ornament of the family.]

Jeopardized State

Hegel addressed the issue of female sovereignty on several occasions. In *Phenomenology of the Spirit* (1806), it appears only marginally as part of a more general analysis of complementary gender relations in history and society. Woman, according to Hegel, is essentially rooted in the domestic sphere and family life and determined by individualism and lust. Man, as a citizen, possesses "die selbstbewusste Kraft der Allgemeinheit" (the self-aware force of generality), which enables him to be both a desiring and a free subject.[15] In his *Elements of the Philosophy of Right*, published in 1821, Hegel pursues the question of human freedom in relation to state polity in a more concrete manner and makes the categorical statement that women and public government are mutually exclusive: "Stehen Frauen an der Spitze der Regierung, so ist der Staat in Gefahr, denn sie handeln nicht nach den Anforderungen der Allgemeinheit, sondern nach zufälliger Neigung und Meinung" (When women hold the helm of government, the state is in jeopardy, because women regulate their actions not by the demands of universality but by arbitrary inclinations and opinions).[16]

Two thousand years before Hegel, Vergil's epic strikes one as a pro-lepsis of the diagnosis that women, who are always governed by partic-ular interests and in turn impose their inclinations on the state, do not qualify for sovereignty. For anyone who is familiar with women's his-tory and cultural criticism from a gender perspective, this unfailing res-onance—"varium et mutabile semper femina" (woman is ever fickle and changeable)—across a period of twenty centuries is hardly surprising. The relentless and imaginary process of producing gender differences from antiquity until today resembles a fugue: different voices resound against the backdrop of a repetitive pattern. The intellectual challenge of feminist scholarship consists in considering the diverse elements of the score in order to retrace a history of inconsistencies and similarities.[17] In taking antiquity as a point of departure and then looking at the literary remod-eling of two mythological queens by two women writers from the eigh-teenth century, in this article we want to sample some of these differences and sameness in the endlessly replayed and yet varying pattern of exclusiv-ist political theory.[18]

The eighteenth century was a period in which political moderniza-tion and the gendered premises on which it hinged began to materialize. In a world that sought a way between established monolithic rule and democratic revolutions, women became political outsiders. While phi-losophy tried to diagnose and predict, the literary archive recorded sto-ries of "subject formation and dysformation" that still await exploration today.[19] In the case of *women* writers, this is even more challenging since, as agents of (European) culture, as (non-)political subjects and (non-) artists, they were exposed to paradoxical strains of exclusion and exempli-fication.[20] If Hegel spoke apodictically of "die Weiblichkeit" (the feminin-ity) in his grand prospect of history, he could confidently rely on a gender ideology that was the precondition for the domestication of women with the dissemination of Enlightenment idea(l)s. Simply to accuse him of a misogynist grudge is missing the fact that he voiced the governing assumptions of his day. Still, there is an interesting paradox in the casu-alness of his *nota bene*: why did he need to make this remark on women and state government at all? Did the phenomenological analysis of history not make his diagnosis plausible enough? Women as political actors had disappeared with the ancien régime.[21] Scattered attempts to claim citizen-ship and political participation for women that manifested themselves in the immediate aftermath of the French Revolution had largely evaporated by the time Hegel wrote his *Phenomenology* (1806) and *Elements of the Philosophy of Law* (1820).[22] If women's access to the new collective polit-ical hegemony was not a pressing issue, then what exactly does "the state is in jeopardy" refer to? A point of reference could be the "specter" of women sovereigns from the past. For indeed European history boasts a number of women rulers who reached not only into the dark pockets of the Middle Ages or the imagination of antiquity, but also into the dawn of Hegel's era. Within the confines of the Holy Roman Empire there was, for example, Maria Theresa of Austria, who had refused to accept the title of empress but nonetheless ruled the Habsburg empire until 1780.[23] On a smaller geopolitical scale but world-famous because of her protégé Johann Wolfgang Goethe, there was Anna Amalia of Saxe-Weimar, who was at the head of her grand duchy from 1758 to 1775. In Hegel's own Prussia, Frederick II, the embodiment of "German protestant masculinity,"[24] had been a fierce opponent to women's state rule, which nevertheless his own mother desired,[25] as did his correspondent Maria Antonia, Electress of Saxony, who participated in her husband's government and after his death acted as a regent until her son's majority. And there was Catherine II of Russia, the most powerful person in the world on the eve of the revolution, who died as late as 1796 after thirty years of rule.[26] Though admired to the point of infatuation by the founding fathers of the Enlightenment Voltaire, Diderot, and d'Alembert, toward the close of the century the memory of Catherine transformed into a caricature of a voracious woman driven by lust for power and sex.[27]

Biopolitics and Gender

Though there is no direct reference in Hegel to Catherine's sovereignty, Catherine's reputation probably reinforced the idea that a woman holding power was a double anomaly in the general process of ethical progress. From a philosophical perspective one could argue that within Hegel's holistic approach toward history the categorization of women as organic and unpolitical is one of the many accidental differences he subsumed under the notion of idea. From a more down-to-earth angle, it is equally plausible to argue that Hegel's gendered taxonomy is a symptom of the biopolitical discourse of Western society. Biopolitics has been a major concept in the field of political theory for some decades. The impetus is Foucault's historical diagnosis of the process of political modernization that took place in Europe from the late seventeenth century onwards. This process consisted of the demise of absolute sovereignty (by monarchical rule), which transformed into a disciplinary administration, a "life administering power"[28] that now concerned every single subject as a living being. The absolute ruler was above the laws of his kingdom, but not above the laws of God, nature, or the law of nations and "was not expected to exercise complete control over the lives of his subjects."[29] The new mechanisms of power included the whole population as well as every individual's body. It was a system of power that "exerts a positive influence on life, that endeavors to administer, optimize, and multiply it, subjecting it to precise controls and comprehensive regulations."[30] Though Foucault speaks of a long transition period, there is consensus among contemporary political theorists that the French Revolution signified the definite turn to the regime of biopolitics. Biopolitical rule as the modern form of sovereignty has been explored extensively. Prominent is the work of Giorgio Agamben, who pursued the degeneration of the politics of life into one of death that reduced the subject to a form of "bare life" and eventually destroyed it. An interesting because more subtle voice in this analysis of modern sovereignty / biopolitics is offered by Eric Santner. Instead of focusing on the derailment of biopolitics into "thanatopolitics," Santner investigates the psychosomatic consequences of the rule of normativity on an individual scale. How does the modern subject experience his (!) body and self in a world of biopolitical pressures? How does, in other words, the symbolic order weigh upon the subject and which forms of dis-ease and disorders does it cause? Santner's example is the case of Daniel Paul Schreber (1842–1911), a German jurist who started suffering from psychosis after he was appointed judge at the High Court. As Santner argues, the appointment to this high office was the catalyst of a mental breakdown: the office turned out to be a burden on his mental well-being. Instead of generating vigorous leadership, Schreber's "investiture" led to abject experiences of self and body.[31]

This modern crisis of "the flesh" can be traced back to the theologically inspired ideology of "the king's two bodies," famously described by Ernst Kantorowicz. Kantorowicz argued that medieval political theory considered the king not only a physical creature but also, after the example of Christ, in possession of a mystical body. It was an ideology that functioned to safeguard dynastic continuity regardless of a monarch's physical state, that is, even if the emperor's clothes could not always conceal his nakedness.[32] Santner's hypothesis is that an overburdening of the subject that leads to physiological malaise is not an exclusive feature of modernity. It can already be shown to be at work in the king's body in the old order and its ideology of the Christian sovereign.[33] The process of decay of Shakespeare's Richard II, unjustly and unexpectedly invested with the highest symbolic office, is a case in point.[34]

In his fine-tuned analysis Santner pays little attention to the issue of gender. Whether they are dealing with the proto-biopolitics that are at work in the body of the king before the Revolution or with the full-scale biopolitical workings of modernity, neither Foucault, Agamben, nor Santner reflects on the situation of female rulers or subjects. Vis-à-vis such a scenario of changing sovereignty that does not gauge the situation of women, one is reminded of Joan Kelly's 1977 seminal essay "Did Women Have a Renaissance?," in which she pointed out that historical phasing, especially when it wields the rhetoric of "progress," might at times need recalibration when looked at from the point of view of women.[35] What does the history of biopolitical sovereignty look like when one takes into account sex and gender? Would an analysis of the history of women who ruled states against the backdrop of biopolitical periodization yield a different cultural-historical narrative? How did women as physiological subjects digest a symbolic investiture if the female body upon which it was bestowed was always already (*a priori*) abject?

Studies of individual cases in European history have revealed the contingencies and paradoxes that were involved when the royal mystical body was bestowed on the (physical) female body.[36] But an impression of the state of things is already revealed when one reads through the correspondence between Maria Theresa of Austria and her daughter Marie Antoinette, later queen of France.[37] The latter's life story became emblematic of the transition of sacral sovereignty into (bio)political modernity, not only because she was executed by the republic, but also because, even during her lifetime, as Lynn Hunt has revealed, a flood of scandals about her "private life" turned the representational sovereign into a female creature.[38] In the many letters to her daughter before the dawn of the Revolution, however, not only does Maria Theresa warn against frivolity, but her letters contain a leitmotif of keeping her body "in check."[39] On the one hand, this is pragmatic advice from a mother accustomed to court life; on the other it reveals the awareness of a female sovereign, who herself resented being a woman,[40] of the vulnerability of the woman ruler who must function as the "*really* existing 'general equivalent' for [the] subjects of the realm."[41] The problem of the female body invested with a symbolic office is also evident in the work of two women writers who lived during that same transition from "ancient" to modern and who moreover witnessed the reality of women in power firsthand. More than just suggesting a problem, their texts reveal how much the female body stood in the way of state rule.

Queens and Bodies: Talestris and Dido

The first is a drama, an opera in fact, written and composed in 1762 by Maria Antonia, Princess-Electress of Saxony (1724–80), *Talestri, regina delle amazzoni*, which was translated into German by Gottsched in 1766. The other is the drama *Dido*, written by Charlotte von Stein in 1794. Both writers were familiar with the reality of women and political sovereignty, the one as a princess-regent, the other as lady-in-waiting of the grand duchess-regent Anna Amalie of Saxony-Weimar. Maria Antonia was embedded in baroque court culture. During her life time she was widely renowned as a sovereign and diplomat, but her most enduring fame rests on her achievements as a versatile artist and composer. She wrote the libretto and music for the opera *Talestri* (and occasionally even sang the lead role) and her reputation as a composer still stands today.[42]

While Maria Antonia is known for her work in political governance and the arts, Charlotte von Stein's personal accomplishments are overshadowed by her association with Goethe. If her name has a familiar ring in European culture today, it is due to her historical relationship to Goethe, whose friend and confidante she was for a long time. As Arne Bohm points out, Stein's own literary work was not only neglected but met with irritation among contemporaries and later generations of literary critics. It was not printed until 1867 and even then with reluctance,[43] in particular her drama *Dido*, which was read as a (bitter) parody of the social constellation at the Weimar court. It included a caricature of Goethe in the figure of the narcissist protagonist Ogon. In recent years, however, the works of both Maria Antonia and von Stein have been detached from their immediate contexts and read as autonomous pieces of literature with political potential.[44]

Both dramas stage a mythological sovereign figure: Thalestris is queen of the Amazons, who, according to some sources, joined Alexander the Great in order to conceive his child. Dido is the famous queen of Carthage, whose image was formed by Vergil's *Aeneid*. A first striking difference between Stein's Dido and Vergil's is that Charlotte von Stein stages Dido as a *ruling* sovereign and as a widow who is dedicated to the memory of her murdered husband. There is an interesting change of roles at the outset of both stories. In Vergil it is Aeneas who describes the prosperity of Carthage when he approaches the city, and his delight stems mostly from seeing his own heroic story depicted on the city walls. In a similar vein, he happily complies with the wish of the amorous Dido that he should recount his adventures to her. Whereas the ancient Dido hangs upon her hero's words, Stein's Dido gives her own account of the state of the kingdom in her opening monologue: "Es blühet alles um mich herum, alles ist im Wohlstand, mein Volk, meine Seemacht, alle Handthierungen; es dringt keine Stimme des Mangels mehr zu meinem Ohr!"[45] (Everything that surrounds me prospers, everything is wealthy, my people, my navy, all trades; no voices of shortage reach my ear!). This is followed by a sorrowful sigh that indicates her state of profound mourning: "O mein Acerbas! Mein Gemahl! Mit dir ward mir ein Welt-All geraubt!" (*Dido*, 4; O my Acerbas! My husband! With your death I lost a whole cosmos). There is no trace of the Trojan hero in the entire drama.[46] Instead of an Aeneas who annihilates the queen's sense of sovereignty and emotional loyalty, the play stages a ruler who—literally—sacrifices herself to save her city. In doing so, Stein presents the opposite of Hegel's famous warning about women in political power and their particular interests that endanger the collective. Personal interest mingles with politics, because the sovereignty of Carthage is under threat as long as Dido refuses to marry King Jarbes, and she has sworn not to remarry. And her choice to die is presented not as a good outcome but as a sacrifice. She first contemplates a life of seclusion, but the pressing political situation makes her opt for the radical and unambiguous solution of suicide. Unlike in Vergil's story, Dido's death does not plunge Carthage into a Hobbesian warlike state of nature. It restores order and gives enduring substance to her rule, not only because she has a successor but also because the memory of her persistence will inspire the future ruler.[47]

In terms of biopolitical pressure, more precisely against the backdrop of the question how a woman (and her body) copes with the burden of the royal office, what strikes one most is the minimalist appearance of the queen as a physical person in this play. From the outset of the drama she is an almost elliptic persona, reticent in the midst of philosophers, poets, friends, and advisors who force their unsolicited advice upon her and to whom she replies in short, at times ironic, phrases. In the opening lines of the drama, Dido thanks her friend Elissa for her affection, but begs to be left alone, upon which Elissa replies that it would make her happier if the queen were to open her heart to her. Much as her bodily appearance is withheld in the whole of the drama, Dido is not given to abundant displays of her distress. There is neither lamentation nor rage, and so in both physical and linguistic terms the queen as a subject is virtually absent from the stage. Other references to her body or womanhood are also scarce. A common soldier remarks on her beauty and relates it to her position as a sovereign: "Nun, so will ich euch sagen, dass wir unsere Königin lieben, denn wer liebt nicht eine schöne Frau. Aber recht macht sie uns noch lange nicht alles" (*Dido*, 15–16; And I will tell you, that we love our queen, because who could not love a beautiful woman, but of course she does not do everything as we wish she would). However, this does not highlight the femininity of the queen but rather reveals how the *vox populi* cannot think of a female sovereign without referring to her sex. Harking back to the ideology of the king's two bodies as explored by Kantorowicz and reinterpreted by Santner, it is most of all Dido's "mythical" body, the transcendental embodiment of the sovereign, that is given expression in this drama. Various protagonists witness how the queen appears before them "als wenn ein höheres Wesen sich zu [mir] herabgelassen hatte" (as if a higher creature had descended upon [me]). The citizens wonder, "haben sie die Götter aus den Wölken gesendet?" (did the gods send her from the clouds); and the "savage" king Jarbes is warned by his general that if he should violate her, he will be blinded by the wreath of stars that adorns her head: "Der Sternenkranz, welcher das Haupt dieser irdischen Unsterblichen umwindet, wird dich verblenden oder verbrennen" (*Dido*, 77, 88, 91; The wreath of stars that encircles the head of this earthly immortal will either blind or burn you). Thus the reader is left with the mythical dimension of a sovereign who guarantees the transcendental foundation and legitimation of her powers. In other words, Stein's Dido is the opposite of the "bare life that remains of the sovereign as an abject corporeality that condenses into its flesh the abyssal dynamics of force and violence at the heart of the operations of sovereignty."[48] Though every

political discourse in history insists that female weakness raises the problem of investiture, this drama sidesteps the dilemma by transforming the
mythical lovesick queen into a mystical embodiment of sovereignty.

Marie Antonia's opera *Thalestris* also stages a female sovereign in the
midst of a political crisis, one in which she finds herself torn between
state responsibility on the one hand and personal happiness on the other.
The quandary is familiar, not only in terms of gender, but also in a more
political sense as a situation on the verge of the "state of exception" as
defined by Carl Schmitt and pursued by Agamben, when the sovereign
suspends the law because the state is endangered. While Catherine II of
Russia insisted that no reason exists that allows a sovereign to sidestep the
law, history has amply revealed that such breaches happened frequently.[49]
Thalestris opens with a young queen who succeeds her deceased mother.
She is hesitant to do so because she has fallen in love with the prince
of the Scythes and thus has broken the first law of her people, which
demands eternal hostility toward men, the Scythes in particular. Yet the
opposite of the Hegel-Dido scenario happens: she does not plunge the
state into chaos but renounces her position, since it violates the law.[50]
Thalestris does not reject sovereignty as such but the legal requirements
attendant to her investiture make it impossible for her to rule: "Nicht
eigentlich das Reich; der Eid bekümmert mich/ Den alle schuldig sind,
die hier den Thron ererben" (*Thalestris*, 5; Not the empire, but the oath
is my concern/ that has to be sworn by all those who inherit the throne).
Although the drama *Thalestris* deals with love and the all too human
desire for happiness and as such seems to merge with the mainstream concerns of the bourgeois literature of the eighteenth and nineteenth centuries, it is important to note that the dominant motive concerns political
philosophy: how can hatred that materializes in perpetual war be the legal
justification of a state? Interestingly, Maria Antonia reverses the standard
paradigm of political theory that stipulates that every state be grounded
in sacrifice, victimhood, or some other form of "original" violence. An
elegant solution of the dilemma is provided when the high priestess, who
demanded blind obedience to an unjust law, cannot summon it herself.
As a consequence the constitutional foundation of the Amazon state is
changed, and the story ends with the Scythes and Amazons celebrating
peace and future prosperity:

> Wir wollen künftig nicht der Nachbarn Unterthanen
> Nein, Freundinnen zu seyn, uns neue Wege bahnen,
> Und knüpfen von nun an, auf unbegränzte Zeit
> Das theure Liebesband, die Schwur der Einigkeit.
> Durch diese wird sich bald des Reiches Heil vermehren;
> Und jener alte Haß in Liebe sich verkehren.

(Thalestris, 118)

[In future we do not want to be the subjects of our neighbors
No, we will be friends and pave new ways
And from now on we will for the time to come tie up
the precious bond of love, swear the oaths of unity
which will soon increase the welfare of the kingdom
And the old hatred will be turned into love.]

The triumph of ethical-humanist thought over archaic laws does not converge with a female-male gender typecast that would be a prolepsis of Hegel's reading of *Antigone*. Throughout the play, men and women are staged at eye level, and both sexes use the language of prowess or sentiment indiscriminately. Instead of conforming to complementary gender patterns, the Amazon queen Thalestris and the Scythian heir-apparent Orontes form each other's mirror-image emotionally and bodily. The queen's body, lauded as "hard and strong" by her sister-counselors, is *literally* the general equivalent of all her subjects and functions as a metonymy of her (warlike) people. The script of the ailing sovereign who succumbs to the pressures of his office, even more so in urgent times, evaporates, as does the dominant duty of the queen: the need to pro-create in order to secure the continuity of rule (another issue that is not addressed in the standard theories of biopolitical sovereignty). According to the legend, the Amazon queen Thalestris called on Alexander the Great to breed children with him. Yet though Maria Antonia's drama ends with the words "bonds of love" and "increase of the welfare of the kingdom," this does not appear to be an allusion to biological procreation immedi-ately, in particular if one considers how the queen's body and those of her consorts are depicted throughout the play, that is, as hard and soldier-like.

Female Voices Versus Myth

In the first century BCE a Roman poet called Vergil wrote an epic about a hero called Aeneas, who escaped from the burning city of Troy and, by divine command, journeyed to the West in order to found the city of Rome. Both the fictional character and his Latin creator became icons in Europe's imagination, and while their story was handed down for centuries, so was that of the raving queen who ruined herself and her kingdom out of love for the hero, who failed to see that his duty transcended her singular hope of love and domestic bliss. While sys-tems of rule changed over time, and sovereignty became disentangled from myth, the legend of the inconstant queen proved fairly resistant. In fact, it crossed from ancient power structures into modern ones, not even faltering when crowds started flooding the streets, demanding rad-ical change. Vergil did not invent the scenario that women in power lead to disaster, nor did Hegel, grand narrator of universal progress, when he—nevertheless—aired his anxiety in the margins of his major thoughts. But its consistency is remarkable and worthy of critical reflection. On the verge of political modernization, Charlotte von Stein and Maria Antonia, two women writers who were each closely related to political reality, addressed the vexed gendered template of sovereignty by refiguring mythical women. Maria Antonia wrote her drama about the Amazon queen some thirty years before the French Revolution; two years after the execution of the French king and queen, Charlotte von Stein made it clear that progress on the road to modernity is irreversible. *Thalestris* still insists on the justice of innate royal sovereignty, *Dido* integrates aspects of a public voice and several mentions of the "anger of the people" that allude to the events in France.[51] Yet in spite of the changing political circumstances both dramas poignantly present cases of female sovereignty that inverse the mythological script of the mad and raging or biologically impaired and predestined woman, the fantasmatic naturalization of difference that Hegel would inscribe in his grand vision of history. In conclusion, we would like to turn one more time to Vergil's Dido, the woman who was made leader for no apparent reason. What Aeneas admires most in Carthage are the works of art that recount his own heroic story as well as the queen's invitation to rehearse that very story again and again. Tragically, Dido thus conjures up the epic that deprives her of the mythological status that her antagonist is rewarded with in times to come. It is telling, however, that the few fragments we know about Dido are related to us not by Vergil's main narrator nor by Aeneas himself, but by his mother, the goddess Aphrodite, and thus it is a woman's voice that hands down a story about a woman sovereign.

Notes

[1] It is revealing to look at different translations of this passage. Johann Heinrich Voss's 1799 rendition reads: "Es treibt ein Weib zu der That an"; John Dryden translates it as "a woman leads the way"; the latest translation into Dutch, however, "een vrouw is belast met de leiding!" (a woman has been charged with the leadership!), significantly adds an exclamation mark to indicate the exceptional nature of the situation. Vergilius, *Aeneas/Aeneis*, ed. and trans. Piet Schrijvers (Groningen, Netherlands: Historische Uitgeverij, 2011), 49.

[2] As Koschorke among others points out, women had neither voice nor status in the political discourse of Roman Antiquity. See Albrecht Koschorke et al., *Der fiktive Staat: Konstruktionen des politischen Körpers in der Geschichte Europas* (Frankfurt am Main: Fischer, 2017), 36.

[3] Simone de Beauvoir, *Das andere Geschlecht: Sitte und Sexus der Frau*, trans. Uli Aulüller and Grete Osterwald (Reinbek: Rowohlt, 2012), 190.

[4] In the introduction to his seminal 1990 work *Making Sex: Body and Gender from the Greeks to Freud*, Thomas Laqueur notes that in antiquity women, though their

bodies were not considered fundamentally different from men, were considered more vulnerable to the pleasures of the flesh. See Thomas Laqueur, *Making Sex: Body and Gender from the Greeks to Freud* (Cambridge, MA: Harvard University Press, 1990), chapter 2.

[5] Vergil, *The Aeneid*, 4, lines 39–45, trans. John Dryden, http://classics.mit.edu/Virgil/aeneid.1.i.html.

[6] Vergil, *The Aeneid*, 1, lines 507–8.

[7] In a short essay on the history of feminine interruptions of the political, Slavoj Žižek points out that Greek tragedy features two kinds of women: those who are committed to "unconditional self-sacrifice" (such as Iphigenia) and those who are transformed (by injustice or frustration) into inhuman avengers (such as Medea). Slavoj Žižek, "From Antigone to Joan of Arc," *Helios* 31, nos. 1–2 (2004): 51–62.

[8] For a summary of this reception and a new political interpretation of Antigone see Bonnie Honig, *Antigone Interrrupted* (Cambridge: Cambridge University Press, 2013), 19.

[9] Honig points out that forty years of feminist work "has interrogated again and again received depictions of women in the history of philosophy and politics." Nevertheless, the "politics of lamentation slides all too easily into the lamentation of politics" (*Antigone*, 9).

[10] In the *Phenomenology of the Spirit*, as many have remarked, the entire chapter on morality appears as a palimpsest of the Sophoclean tragedy. See Otto Pöggeler, *Schicksal und Geschichte: Antigone im Spiegel der Deutungen und Gestaltungen seit Hegel und Hölderlin* (Munich: Fink, 2004), 14, 28.

[11] At least the play indicates that Thebes will benefit from an enlightened government for the remainder of his reign.

[12] Her sister says: "extinxti te meque . . . populumque patresque/Sidonis urbemque tuam," Vergil, *The Aeneid*, 4, 684.

[13] Georg Wilhelm Friedrich Hegel, *Phänomenologie des Geistes*, vol. 3 of *Werke* (Frankfurt am Main: Suhrkamp 1970), 352.

[14] Hegel, *Phänomenologie*, 352–53. It is striking that in this passage Hegel speaks of "die ernsthafte Weisheit des reifen Alters," which almost literally resonates the closing lines of Antigone.

[15] Hegel, *Phänomenologie*, 337. On this matter see Heidemarie Bennent-Vahle, "The Female as Ethical Resource in the Philosophy of Hegel," in *Continental Philosophy in Feminist Perspective: Rereading the Canon in German*, ed. Herta Nagl-Docekal and Cornelia Klinger (University Park: Pennsylvania State University Press, 2000), 114–46.

[16] G. W. F. Hegel, *Grundlinien der Philosophie des Rechts, oder Naturrecht und Staatswissenschaft im Grundrisse* (Berlin: Nicolaische Buchhandlung, 1821) §166, 330.

[17] Judith Butler, "'Speaking Up, Talking Back': Joan Scott's Critical Feminism," in *The Question of Gender: Joan W. Scott's Critical Feminism*, ed. Judith Butler and Elizabeth Weed (Bloomington: Indiana University Press, 2011), 11–28.

[18] While Hegel pounds on family values in women's lives, the *Aeneid* makes no mention of them. If Dido reproaches Aeneas that at least he should have left her with a child, she gives voice to personal bereavement, not to her maternal instinct. Vergil, *The Aeneid*, 4, 328. Megan Cassidy-Welch and Peter Sherlock conclude their volume on gender in late medieval and early modern Europe with the statement that history reveals "massive contradictions of lived experience" in the "plurality of historical gender practice." See Megan Cassidy-Welch and Peter Sherlock, "Reflecting and Creating Gender in Late-Medieval and Early-Modern Europe," in *Practices of Gender in Late Medieval and Early Modern Europe*, ed. Megan Cassidy-Welch and Peter Sherlock (Turnhout, Belgium: Brepols, 2011), 317–26, here 320.

[19] Ortwin de Graef, "Subjects," in *Literature Now: Key Terms and Methods for Literary History*, ed. Sascha Bru, Ben de Bruyn, and Michel Delville (Edinburgh: Edinburgh University Press, 2016), 75–86, here 77.

[20] "Every female writer of the late eighteenth century was forced to grapple with the fact that the conceptualization (and realization) of female Bildung and self-determination were impeded by the contemporary construction of the female body." Elisabeth Krimmer, "German Women Writers and Classicism," in *The Literature of Weimar Classicism*, ed. Simon Richter (Rochester, NY: Camden House, 2005), 237–64, here 241.

[21] In a remarkably short period different historians, such as Joan Landes, Carole Pateman, Ute Frevert, and Lynn Hunt, convincingly demonstrated the fundamental paradox of the French Revolution: proclaiming universal civil rights while denying women access to the collective of political hegemony. See Carole Pateman, *The Sexual Contract* (Cambridge: Polity, 1988); Joan B. Landes, *Women and the Public Sphere in the Age of the French Revolution* (Ithaca, NY: Cornell University Press, 1988); Ute Frevert, ed., *Bürgerinnen und Bürger: Geschlechterverhältnisse im 19. Jahrhundert: Zwölf Beiträge* (Göttingen: Vandenhoeck & Ruprecht, 1988); Ute Frevert, *"Mann und Weib, Weib und Mann": Geschlechter-Differenzen in der Moderne* (Munich: Beck 1995); Lynn Hunt, *The Family Romance of the French Revolution* (London: Routledge, 1992).

[22] Napoleon, whom Hegel famously called "world soul" in a letter he wrote in October 1806 after finishing *The Phenomenology of the Spirit*, had eliminated women's constitutional rights as citizens. See Nicole Arnoud-Duc, "Die Widersprüche des Gesetzes," in *Geschichte der Frauen*, vol. 4, *19. Jahrhundert*, ed. Geneviève Fraisse and Michelle Perrot (Frankfurt am Main: Campus 1994), 97–140, here 116.

[23] As she had been crowned king of Hungary and Bohemia already, Maria Theresa declared famously that she did not want to change sex by being crowned *empress* of Austria. See Derek Beales, *Joseph II*, vol. 1, *In the Shadow of Maria Theresa (1741–1780)* (Cambridge: Cambridge University Press, 1987), 39.

[24] Friedrich Heer, *The Holy Roman Empire* (London: Phoenix, 1978), 255.

[25] Friedrich Heer speaks of Frederick's hate-love relationship with his "libidinous, wanton and highly intelligent mother" (*Holy Roman Empire*, 248). In her memoirs Frederick's sister, Wilhelmine, Countess of Bayreuth, who lived through the same childhood terror as her brother, mentions her mother's strategic eye on state

power during the periods of her husband's illnesses. *Mémoires de Frédérique Sophie Wilhelmine Margrave de Bareith, soeur de Fréderic le Grand, depuis l'année 1706 jusqu'à 1742, écrit de sa main* (Leipzig: Barsdorf, 1889).

[26] Joshua Sanborn and Annette Timm, *Gender, Sex, and the Shaping of Modern Europe: A History from the French Revolution to the Present Day* (Oxford: Oxford University Press, 2007).

[27] See Larry Wolff, "Die Phantasie von Katharina in der Fiktion der Aufklärung: Von Baron Münchhausen zu Marquis de Sade," in *Katharina II., Russland und Europa*, ed. Claus Scharf (Mainz: Philipp von Zabern, 2001) 307–18.

[28] Michel Foucault, *The History of Sexuality*, vol. 1, *An Introduction* (1976, repr. London: Penguin, 1990), 136.

[29] Peter Burke, *The Fabrication of Louis XIV* (New Haven, CT: Yale University Press, 1994), 40–41.

[30] Foucault, *History of Sexuality*, 137. See also Eric L. Santner, *The Royal Remains: The People's Two Bodies and the Endgames of Sovereignty* (Chicago: University of Chicago Press, 2011), 8.

[31] Eric Santner, *My Own Private Germany: Daniel Paul Schreber's Secret History of Modernity* (Princeton, NJ: Princeton University Press, 1996), 26.

[32] The fairy-tale metaphor is used by William Chester Jordan, "Introduction to the Princeton Classics Edition," in Ernst Kantorowicz, *The King's Two Bodies: A Study in Medieval Political Theology* (Princeton, NJ: Princeton University Press, 1997), ix.

[33] In other words: "there is more political theology in everyday life than we might have thought" although it may be more difficult to trace in the absence of a royal personage, Santner, *Royal Remains*, 45.

[34] Santner, *Royal Remains*, 47.

[35] Joan Kelly, "Did Women Have a Renaissance?," in Joan Kelly, *Women, History and Theory: The Essays of Joan Kelly* (London: University of Chicago Press, 1984), 19–50.

[36] See for example Bethany Aram, *Juana the Mad: Sovereignty and Dynasty in Renaissance Europe* (Baltimore: Johns Hopkins University Press, 2005); Regina Schulte, *Der Körper der Königin: Geschlecht und Herrschaft in der höfischen Welt seit 1500* (Frankfurt am Main: Campus, 2002). Theresa Earenfight rightly points out the contingencies of historical sovereignty in her article "Without the Persona of the Prince: Kings, Queens and the Idea of Monarchy in Late Medieval Europe," *Gender & History* 19, no. 1 (2007): 1–21, here 3.

[37] For a close analysis see Regina Schulte, "Madame ma chère fille—"Dearest Child": Briefe imperialer Mütter an königliche Töchter," in Schulte, *Der Körper der Königin*, 162–96.

[38] See Lynn Hunt, "The Many Bodies of Marie-Antoinette," in *Eroticism and the Body Politic*, ed. Lynn Hunt (Baltimore: Johns Hopkins University Press, 1991), 108–31. Barbara Vinken, "Marie-Antoinette oder das Ende der Zwei-Körper-Lehre," in *Das Politische: Figurenlehren des sozialen Körpers nach der Romantik*,

ed. Uwe Hebekus, Ethel Matala de Mazza, and Algrecht Koschorke (Munich: Wilhelm Fink, 2003), 86–105.

[39] Marie-Antoinette, *Correspondance secrète entre Marie-Thérèse et le Cte de Mercy-Argenteau, avec les lettres de Marie-Thérèse et de Marie-Antoinette*, ed. Alfred d'Arneth and M. A. Geffroy (Paris: Firmin-Didot, 1874–75).

[40] Beales, *Joseph II*, 1:39.

[41] Santner, *Royal Remains*, 50, my emphasis.

[42] Eva Neumayr, "Maria Antonia Walpurgis Kurfürstin von Sachsen," in *Musik und Gender im Internet: Lexikon*, 2007, http://mugi.hfmt-hamburg.de/en/Artikel/Maria_Antonia_Kurfürstin_von_Sachsen?size=1075; and Estelle Joubert, "Performing Sovereignty, Sounding Autonomy: Political Representation in the Operas of Maria Antonia of Saxony," *Music and Letters* 96, no. 3 (2015): 345.

[43] Arnd Bohm, "Charlotte von Stein's "Dido: Ein Trauerspiel," *Colloquia Germanica* 22 (1989): 39.

[44] Anne Fleig, *Handlungs-Spiel-Räume. Dramen von Autorinnen im Theater des ausgehenden 18. Jahrhunderts* (Würzburg: Königshausen & Neumann, 1999), 240–57; and Joubert, „Performing Sovereignty," 384–87.

[45] Charlotte von Stein, *Dido: Ein Trauerspiel in fünf Aufzügen*, ed. Heinrich Düntzer (Frankfurt am Main: Verlag des Freien Deutschen Hochstifts, 1867), 3–4. Further references to this work are given in the text using the short title "Dido."

[46] The sources Charlotte von Stein used have been investigated, and the fact that she borrowed so little from Vergil suggests that she probably used an older—and less well known—version of the story of Dido. Scholars have not considered that the political significance of her drama derives precisely from her play's divergence from Vergil's canonical epic. See Bohm, "Charlotte von Stein's "Dido," 38–52.

[47] In Stein's drama Dido has a brother, who fled with her from Tyrus and to whom she hands over power. Stein, *Dido*, 27.

[48] Santner, *Royal Remains*, 50.

[49] In one of the notebooks she kept to herself Catherine paraphrased d'Alembert: "It is in the interest of the state . . . the laws of which must always remain sacred to monarchs, because they last forever while subjects and rulers disappear, that men should be judged according to the law," Isabel de Madariaga, *Catherine the Great: A Short History* (New Haven, CT: Yale University Press, 1990), 4.

[50] Maria Antonia von Sachsen, *Thalestris Königinn der Amazonen: Aus dem vortrefflichen italienischen Singspiele Jhrer Königlichen Hoheit der unvergeßlichen Ermelinde Thalea in ein Deutsches Trauerspiel verwandelt / von Johann Christoph Gottscheden* (Zwickau: Stieler, 1766), 3. Further references to this work are given in the text using the short title "Thalestris."

[51] These aspects appear particularly in dialogues between Dido's confidante Elissa and her pursuer Jarbes, who tries to put her under pressure by referring to the angry mob that will take matters into its own hands (von Stein, *Dido*, 63–64).

5: Crossing the Front Lines: Female Leadership, Politics, and War in *Die Familie Seldorf*

Sarah Vandegrift Eldridge

THERESE HUBER's 1795 NOVEL *Die Familie Seldorf* has been the subject of much feminist scholarship, with varying results. Elisabeth Krimmer calls the novel "extraordinary" for the ways in which it "foils many of the expectations that we bring to eighteenth-century literature by women writers," pointing out that "Sara is a positive character in spite of all her violations of the codes of proper femininity."[1] Stephanie Hilger offers an analysis that reads Sara Seldorf's "mutilated body" as "question[ing] the ideal of wholesome femininity portrayed in bourgeois tragedy and sentimental fiction" and thereby illuminating the failure of the post-Revolutionary body politic to include women.[2] But others see Huber's critiques as insufficient: Inge Stephan argues that the novel fails to challenge prevailing models of femininity, while Wulf Köpke reads Huber as a conservative author.[3] Still others take the ambiguity of Huber's depiction of both femininity and political activity to be typical of the "double-voiced discourse" of women authors around 1800, whose work is marked by "emancipatory elements which coexist with the conventional ones."[4] These questions become further vexed when one takes into account not only Huber's use of her husband's name to publish her novels (which was not at all unusual for the period[5]) but also her far more conservative and sometimes even misogynistic comments about women writers (in correspondence and in her literary works), the importance of housekeeping, and perhaps especially her remarks about her own mother, whom she excoriated as "gar keine Hausfrau, wir wurden in Schmutz und Unordnung erzogen. . . . Sie war eine Schwärmerin, war an kein Hausgeschäft gewöhnt, liebte keine weibliche Arbeit" (not at all a housewife, we were brought up in filth and disorder . . . she was a dreamer, accustomed to absolutely no household duty, loved no feminine work).[6] Even if, as Barbara Becker-Cantarino suggests, this kind of critique is rooted at least partially in Huber's great admiration for her father, the eminent Göttingen professor Christian Gottlob Heyne, it is difficult to square with any notion of Huber as a particularly (proto-)feminist author.[7]

I want to suggest that viewing *Die Familie Seldorf* in terms of female leadership offers a new way of understanding the work that Huber's novel does without simply falling back on the further contradictions and difficulties of Huber's biography (personal and political). While female leadership is not limited necessarily to exploring questions of gender identity or performance, I view Huber's contributions to these questions in a period of shifting paradigms as especially complex and interesting. I therefore trace presentations of gender throughout *Die Familie Seldorf* to explore different facets of gender identity and the apparent contradictions both within the novel and extending into Huber's role as an author, as she utilizes the imaginative possibilities of fiction to explore potential roles beyond those presented in prescriptive advice manuals and *Hausmütterliteratur*. Although femininity is frequently connected to motherhood in Huber's novel, these connections are not straightforward, and the issues of motherhood and leadership are intertwined in complex and sometimes contradictory ways.

Ultimately, I argue that it is crucial to understand authorship *as* a kind of leadership, to conceive of Huber as an author who guides readers through her texts' presentations of gender roles. This approach is in fact consistent with aesthetic programs prior to the canonization projects of Weimar Classicism and Romanticism; proponents of reception aesthetics such as Lessing viewed literature as a school for the emotions and the imagination and the reader or viewer as receiving a kind of instruction. Huber falls historically into an interesting threshold period, in which print as a medium had already, as Michael Warner puts it in a study of early American culture, become "normally impersonal"—that is, there is no personal connection between author and reader, and thus any message must be built in to the text itself.[8] At the same time, programs of autonomy aesthetics in a Kantian and Romantic vein had not yet permeated to so-called trivial literature, as I discuss below. Finally, engagement with a literary text that views readers as being led or educated by authors via the medium of the text has also received attention in recent cognitive philosophy: in her *Deeper Than Reason: Emotion and Its Role in Literature, Music, and Art*, Jenefer Robinson recuperates the idea of literature as a "sentimental education," in which "our responses are guided and managed" by thematic, formal, and structural features of the text created by the author.[9] She views this type of sentimental education as "an important source of our pleasure in literature"; it also suggests that literature might indeed be a promising medium for working through complex problems of human life, both historical and universal.[10] Reading authorship as leadership in this way enables us to realize that Huber *uses* her novel to lead the reader through a series of experiments around gender to arrive at the notion that gender is both shaped by experience and essentially flexible. Although it is possible to assert this conclusion as a claim abstracted from the text (as indeed I have just done), it is only by following Huber through the novel itself that its full force and nuance become visible and relevant.

Women, Reading, and Writing

The decades around 1800 across which Huber's literary career unfolded were marked by a paradigm shift in gender roles from a theological to a biological model. Many scholars from the 1970s to the 1990s—most notably Claudia Honegger and Karin Hausen—argued that these biological theories, which posited sex differences as natural and therefore incontestable, ushered in an increase in the oppression of women.[11] Both Hausen and Honegger, as well as subsequent scholars such as Marion Gray, argue that the late eighteenth century saw the firm establishment of "separate spheres" for men and women, which barred women from participation in public life.[12] This narrative has been significantly nuanced in historical studies by Rebekah Habermas and Anne-Charlotte Trepp: Habermas argues that rather than dividing into spheres of male/public and female/private, the bourgeois family unit with members of both sexes placed an increased value on more intimate forms of interaction and sociability.[13] Trepp makes a similar case for the bourgeoisie of Hamburg and adds that the notion of polarization between the sexes, where it exists at all, is actually a projecting-backward of the conditions of the later nineteenth century.[14] Both of their studies attend carefully to differences and tensions between ideological statement, individual- and class-based projects of self-staging, and the lived historical reality of men and women. Helen Fronius, too, in her historical study of women authors and the literary market at the end of the eighteenth century, emphasizes the extent to which "proscriptive eighteenth-century discussions" about women were "*rhetorical* (rather than descriptive)" and investigates "how, practically, women gained access to the literary market"; Fronius thus chooses to focus on women writers' "room for manoeuvre" around the constraints of prevailing norms.[15] This is not to deny that biological-essentialist models of gender are oppressive, but they appear largely to have modernized extant forms of oppression (thus enabling them to persist for subsequent centuries) rather than initiating greater legal or material subjugation of women.

Indeed, these conditions appear to have remained relatively stable from the Protestant Reformation well into the nineteenth century: Barbara Becker-Cantarino emphasizes that under both the theological and biological models, women were subordinate to men, passed from the guardianship of their fathers to their husbands, and were represented by those fathers or husbands in the public sphere.[16] Although divorce finally became somewhat more common at the tail end of the eighteenth century, most women followed the advice of countless manuals and ped-agogical programs to conform to their husbands' wishes, because they lacked options to support themselves financially without a male provider (*Der lange Weg*, 51–58). The content of these advice manuals and edu-cation programs varied little between the sixteenth century and the eigh-teenth: women were to submit to their fathers and husbands, learn to perform household tasks without complaint, and dedicate themselves to the early education of their children (*Der lange Weg*, 149–54). In both of her studies, Becker-Cantarino makes the point that the end of the eigh-teenth century brought with it increasing literacy for women as well as men (*Der lange Weg*, 154–58). Habermas suggests that interest in the domestic sphere on the part of both men and women meant that this sphere became, at least to some extent, a place for men *and* women to educate themselves by reading (often fiction) and writing (especially let-ters).[17] Becker-Cantarino argues that a significant portion of the explosion of popularity of the genre of the novel was due to women readers, who participated in the transformation of learned Enlightenment culture into the more belletristic cultivation of Weimar Classicism and Romanticism. Fronius, in her chapter on women as readers, notes the development of several reading circles for women, numerous journals and books mar-keted toward women, and statements from multiple types of ego-docu-ments that record women's pleasure and interest in reading (as well as their need to "steal" time from other activities in order to do so) (*Women and Literature*, 94–113). Furthermore, because women were prohibited from receiving formal education, reading and discussing literature became a way in which they could guide opinions and educate each other, making encounters with literature a potential space for leadership.

Parallel to the increases in reading, more and more women were also becoming published authors. Fronius, who writes in her introduction of the "astonishing presence" of extremely prolific women writers (Huber among them) and their "undeniable literary activity," cites data collected by Helga Gallas and Anita Runge that show publications by women increasing in tandem with publication in German-speaking territories overall (*Women and Literature*, 2–3 and 137–38). Fronius disputes argu-ments that women could only become published authors if they had the support of a male mentor or advocate, arguing instead that the explana-tion for women's growing presence on the literary scene "lies partly in the history of the German book trade, and partly in women's own active pur-suit of publication" (*Women and Literature*, 139). To explore the latter factor, she analyzes large groups of women's business letters in publisher archives; in the case of the former she notes: "The decline in theology and in the use of Latin, combined with the rise of the novel, meant that women had a legitimate inspiration for their writing: their own domes-tic, social, and personal experiences. . . . Women's educational status mattered less than their ability to please the reading public" (*Women and Literature*, 144). That women writers were very much able to do so is confirmed by the increasing anxiety shown by male authors, including Goethe and Schiller, who both attempted to assert control over women's writing by acting as commenters and editors and developed an aesthetic program that denigrated the types of writing that women successfully produced.[18]

This latter point is particularly important in considering female authorship as female leadership, since that aesthetic program, which conceptualizes artworks as complete, self-contained wholes available for interpretation, continues to shape prevailing norms of literary scholarship. Jacques Rancière summarizes scholarly narratives of autonomy aesthetics neatly: "Influential histories of artistic modernity identify it with the conquest of autonomy by each art, which is expressed in exemplary works that break with the course of history, separating themselves from the art of the past and the aesthetic forms of prosaic life."[19] Although Rancière aims, in his study, to give an alternative history of artistic modernity, he does not devote attention to the aesthetic traditions that predate autonomy aesthetics. But, as Jochen Schulte-Sasse points out, artistic criteria that downplayed readers' emotional involvement with a text in favor of a distanced, critical attitude "were developed in the Age of Goethe and by Goethe and Schiller themselves in the course of coming to terms with trivial literature."[20] That is, it was in fact not the giants of Weimar Classicism or Romanticism who were succeeding most in the expanding literary market, but rather authors of so-called trivial fiction, including women. The dismissal and subsequent erasure of women from the literary canon as part of a self-perpetuating cycle of neglect dovetails with the end of aesthetic models that viewed encounters with artworks as imaginative experiences that cultivated an emotional response on the part of the reader. It is precisely this notion of reading as an imaginative experience guided by the author's formal and thematic strategies as they are presented in the artwork that I want to recover in my discussion of Huber's novel.[21]

Imagining Gender in *Die Familie Seldorf*

Investigating female leadership in a novel thus proves more complicated than simply tracing positive (or negative) portrayals of women in positions of power or authority. In my initial considerations of female leadership in *Die Familie Seldorf*, I had developed an argumentative trajectory that, I hoped, would demonstrate that Huber does indeed depict Sara Seldorf positively as a female leader. That planned argument ran something like this: after a first volume that presents views about the complementarity of the sexes that are highly typical of the era, the novel's second volume undermines those views in a series of what we might call gender experiments set among the events of the French Revolution and its aftermath. During the War in the Vendée, Huber's protagonist Sara Seldorf inhabits a masculine leadership role successfully, dressing as a man and impressing her comrades with her bravery and competence as a republican soldier—even becoming the leader of a troop of guerilla fighters. This type of war, which was new in the late eighteenth century, is crucially connected to the landscape in which it is fought, and it is in part Sara's childhood in the Vendée that enables her to fight there successfully: her leadership abilities are a product of her lived experience, and Huber offers us a model of a woman fulfilling a traditionally male role with distinction. From this I planned to demonstrate that *Die Familie Seldorf* suggests that when women are not confined to the roles historically prescribed by their gender, they can indeed be good leaders. I rehearse this argument here because it was through trying and failing to make it that I began to realize what strikes me as particularly compelling about Huber's novel: in particular, the *process* of trying on the different aspects of Huber's presentation of gender is crucial to a deeper understanding of the kind of leadership Huber demonstrates in her literary work. In the remainder of this essay, I therefore follow Huber through key scenes in the novel for the development of ideas about gender, highlighting both the arguments that initially appear to emerge from those scenes and the potential contradictions between them.

Some elements of my initial reading of female leadership provide a useful starting point: Sara Seldorf's father does serve as the mouthpiece of a gender philosophy based on the complementarity of the sexes that was becoming common in the period. In the opening scene of the novel, when Sara is disappointed that her brother seems not to care for and comfort their little sister as much as Sara does, her father explains, "Wenn du einst älter bist, wirst du lernen, daß es weibisch wäre, wenn Knaben und Männer liebten und trösteten, wie es deinem Geschlecht wohl ansteht, es zu thun" (1:7; When you are older, you will learn that it would be effeminate if boys and men loved and comforted in the way that it is appropriate for your sex to do).[22] Although Sara only understands half of what her father says at this moment, her childhood is shaped by similar lessons. Seldorf's favorite occupation, the narrator tells us shortly thereafter, "war, die Kinder eines durch das andre zu bilden" (1:25; was to form the children one by way of the other), and he tells them often: "Die Natur sezte die Vollkommenheit beider Geschlechter in der größten gegenseitigen Abhängigkeit, indem sie ihr die größte Verschiedenheit gab. Der feste, treue, eiserne Mann kann nur der sanftesten Weiblichkeit huldigen; Schwächlinge lieben Amazonen" (1:26; Nature made the perfection of both sexes in their greatest mutual dependence, in that she gave them the greatest difference. The firm, loyal, iron man can only revere the gentlest femininity; weaklings love Amazons). In this initial statement there is a slim possibility that men and women might find the appropriate partner for achieving this ideal balance individually—after all, a match between an "Amazone" and a "Schwächling" would preserve the principle of complementarity.

But Seldorf continues, focusing specifically on women:

> Damit aber das Weib diesen Zauber ihres Geschlechtes besize, muß ihr Herz kindlich bleiben, wie gebildet auch ihr Verstand sey; und unsre Achtung allein kann das Zutrauen hervorbringen, welches diese Kindlichkeit erhält. Fühlt das Weib nicht diesen Lohn seiner Liebenswürdigkeit, so sucht es sich von uns unabhängig zu machen, und dann wird es verächtlich. (1:25–26)

> [But in order for a woman to possess the magic of her sex, her heart must remain childlike, however cultivated her understanding may be; our respect alone can bring forth the trust that preserves this childishness. If a woman does not feel this reward for her lovableness, she will seek to make herself independent of us, and then she becomes contemptible.]

There is no more room for individual navigation of gender boundaries here: women who attempt to become independent are worthy only of contempt. Given that all Seldorf's pedagogical precepts "athmeten diese Grundsäze" (1:27; breathed these principles), it is unsurprising that they have a formative effect on his children. Within the first volume, Huber does not counter this philosophy explicitly, and readings of the novel as advancing a conservative model of gender roles seem, at this point, at least partly plausible.

Nonetheless, Huber also seems to undermine Seldorf's stated philosophy by portraying his utter failure as a husband and father: the pedagogical and broader life philosophies that he practices do not form his children into stable adults capable of making rational decisions. The novel opens as Seldorf and his three children are traveling to settle in Saumur (some 200 miles from Paris), and Huber's narrator offers us a brief "pre-history" of Seldorf's marriage and his wife's death. From it, we learn that Seldorf is a disappointed and bitter man, but not why he has become this way, and the narrator's hints (Huber uses foreshadowing quite masterfully here) are quickly forgotten as readers move on into the main story. The youngest child, Antoinette, dies soon after they arrive, and Sara and Theodor, deprived of nearly all outside companionship, become extremely close— Huber imbues certain scenes between them with distinct incestuous overtones. When Theodor and their sole childhood friend, Roger, assist a family in need, Sara is initially impressed by Roger's practicality, especially in contrast to Theodor's passionate but ineffective ranting. But when Roger slurps down some milk after working outdoors all day, his crude physicality disgusts Sara, and by contrast she sees her brother as an idol:

> Wie reizend lag dieser neben seinem Freund, sein schönes Gesicht auf einem Arm gestüzt, seine redenden Augen auf ihn gerichtet, seine ganze Gestalt durch die spielenden Schatten der breiten Kastanienblätter in den Strahlen der röthlichen Abendsonne, mit zauberischem Lichte umgossen! (1:79)

> [How charmingly he lay next to his friend, his beautiful face propped on his arm, his expressive eyes directed toward him, his whole figure cast by the playing shadows of the large chestnut leaves in the rays of the reddish evening sun in a magical light!]

It is specifically her brother's physical qualities that attract Sara; lest we underestimate the significance of the contrast between the two boys in Sara's mind, Huber adds "Rogers unseliger Milchnapf entschied vielleicht das Schiksal ihres Herzens!" (1:79; Roger's ill-fated milk bowl perhaps decided the fate of her heart!). Shortly thereafter the narrator remarks that "wer die jungen Leute zusammen gesehen hätte, wäre in Versuchung gewesen, Theodorn und Sara für ein Paar Liebende, und Rogern für Saras älteren Bruder zu halten" (1:95; if one had seen the young people together, one would have been tempted to take Theodor and Sara for a pair of lovers and Roger for Sara's older brother), confirming that these incestuous elements are not the anachronistic product of critical (over-) reading.

Sara's repeated rejections of Roger are complicated and, like many aspects of the novel, can be read in multiple directions: as representing Sara's inability to grow up and choose an appropriate partner *and* as a rejection of marriage and reproduction as the only possible life path for a woman. These rejections also have interesting implications for Huber's presentations of sexuality; although she knows that Roger would be an appropriate husband with whom she could form a settled household, Sara cannot overcome her physical disgust toward him. By contrast, she is immediately drawn to the charming aristocrat L***, who arrives in Saumur to spy on Roger's grandfather Berthier's political activities and is immediately struck by Sara's beauty and simplicity. Though Sara's physical feelings lead her into L***'s trap, Huber does seem to suggest that sexual attraction—or the lack thereof—is to some extent inevitable and unalterable. But at this point, Seldorf's emphasis on complementarity combined with his children's isolation has turned them inwards toward each other, and Theodor becomes Sara's model for masculinity; Sara only transfers her affections from her brother when she meets a man who strikes her as equally physically graceful and charming. Thus Seldorf's use of the two siblings to define gender roles against each other in some sense backfires: both Theodor and L*** are more effeminate than Roger, and Huber may well be playing on connotations of nobility, degeneracy, and femininity that circulated in revolutionary culture. Huber thus depicts complementarity-based models of gender difference as failing to guarantee socially stable outcomes, as Sara's early socialization with respect to her brother shapes her notions of gender complementarity in ways that her father failed to anticipate.

When Seldorf finally tells his daughter the full story of his marriage, we learn that his bitterness has both cruel and sanctimonious elements. Disillusioned with society, he believes that he has protected his children from the inherent deceitfulness and evil of the world outside, but in fact he is raising them to repeat his mistakes. Theodor, at this point in the narrative, has left home to fight on the side of the aristocracy, and Sara, lonely and naïve, has fallen in love with L***. These parallel seductions highlight the extent to which the two children are susceptible to manipulation: lacking social experience, they are immediately taken in by the romantic narrative of embattled nobility and by a stranger's attractive appearance and genteel behavior. Thus when Seldorf finally breaks his silence to tell Sara the story of his life before his children's birth—provoked into speaking by the fact that Theodor is about to marry the daughter of the very nobleman who had an affair with Seldorf's wife—his story takes on the tone of a cautionary tale that comes far too late. The disturbing details of Seldorf's story—that he married his wife only to save her reputation because the lover who had impregnated her had died; that his wife cursed him on her deathbed, saying: "Eigennuz und Herrschsucht waren die Quellen deiner Wohltaten" (1:256; selfishness and imperiousness were the source of your good deeds)—are largely lost on Sara, because she is too preoccupied with the horror of realizing that she has already broken her father's command not to attach herself to an aristocrat. Indeed, when Seldorf discovers that Sara is pregnant with L***'s child, he curses her on his deathbed, just as his wife cursed him on hers. Sara has learned nothing from her father's story, and his own inability to reflect critically on his experiences and to accept blame for his condescending and unloving treatment of his wife, as well as the inability of his children to tell when they are being deceived, certainly casts further doubt on his pedagogical principles and his gender philosophy.

The portrayals of Sara Seldorf's experiments with gender after her father's death are not straightforward, either. L*** eventually brings her and their child to Paris, but he confines them in a small apartment to wait for his visits—an exaggeration of the ideological "domestic sphere" of femininity to a veritable prison. Sara transgresses this boundary when she hears the tumult of revolutionary violence outside, and, fearing for L***'s life, she picks up her daughter and goes in search of him. In the streets, the child is accidentally shot and killed by L*** himself—Sara's very first venture into a political space results in the violent negation of her identity as a mother (the more so as the child would have survived, Huber writes, except that Sara's milk dries up after the incident). After the death of her child, and after she has discovered that L*** has been married to someone else for their entire relationship, Sara turns to revolutionary activity as a way to avenge herself, claiming: "Rache und Recht kennt und braucht auch das Weib" (2:147; Woman, too, knows and needs revenge and justice). As Sara spends more and more time in political circles, Huber depicts her as losing her identity specifically *as a woman*:

> Wie jeder Tag ihren Kopf mit neuen politischen Tollheiten füllte, so starb jeden Tag eine Faser ihres Herzens ab; selbst die Erinnerung, Tochter, Geliebte, Weib, Mutter gewesen zu seyn, äußerte sich endlich nur in heftigeren Ausbrüchen des Parteigeists auf den Tribünen der Volksgesellschaften—denn dorthin drängte sich jetzt jene Sara, deren Stimme ehemals aus mädchenhafter Scham lieblich zitterte, wenn sie einem fremden Knecht einen Auftrag ihres Vaters ausrichtete, dort stand sie jezt, und stürmte ihrer Partei wilden Beifall zu. (2:175)

> [As her head filled daily with new political follies, so daily a thread of her heart died off; even the memory of having been a daughter, lover, wife, mother expressed itself finally only in fiercer outbursts of her party spirit at the tribunals of the people's societies—for there that Sara thrust herself, she whose voice used to tremble sweetly with girlish shame when she delivered an assignment from her father to an unknown laborer, there she stood now and raved in wild approval for her party.]

The contrast between "ehemals," when Sara was "Tochter, Geliebte, Weib, Mutter" and "jetzt," when she aggressively pushes herself into public spaces and speaks out boldly and zealously, could hardly be more emphatic, and here Huber's narrator does not seem to offer any ambiguity that could mitigate the negative portrayal of Sara's "unfeminine" actions.[23] Other women who undertake political action are described as "feine, zierliche, verkehrte Geschöpfe" (fine, delicate, perverse creatures), their words as "nachplappern" (parroting) and "List der Heuchelei" (the cunning of hypocrisy) and, in comparison with Sara, as "Abarten ihres Geschlechts" (2:174–75; mutations of their sex). So the argument that Huber portrays women as successful outside of historically limited gender roles does not stand—or at least it cannot be broadly applied.

Huber also depicts an encounter with a child as reawakening Sara's humanity, thus drawing a connection between female humanity and maternal feeling. As Sara is wandering through the outskirts of the city after witnessing the king's execution, her attention is caught by children playing and by their mother holding a baby.

> Der Säugling . . . bog sich zu [Sara], . . . blikte mit heitern Kinderaugen an ihr hinauf, und legte seine kleinen Hände lächelnd an ihr Gesicht. . . . Hier zersprang die harte Rinde, die sich um Sara's Herz gebildet hat. Im Gewühl der Menschen war sie des Anbliks der Menschlichkeit entwöhnt worden: hier lachte sie ihr nun zum erstenmal wieder in ihrem reinsten, sanftesten Abdruk entgegen. (2:183)

> [The infant leaned toward [Sara], looked up at her with cheerful child's eyes, and placed its little hands, smiling, on her face. . . . Here the hard shell that had formed around Sara's heart burst. In the melee of humans she had become unaccustomed to the sight of humanity: here it laughed up at her for the first time again in its purest, gentlest stamp.]

But the children's father returns and recognizes Sara as one of the blood-thirsty women present at the king's execution, whereupon he rips the baby out of her arms. This violent denial of her role as a woman and mother causes Sara to fall into a long episode of illness and insanity—in this episode of the novel, Huber depicts dire consequences for a woman who enters the sphere of political action and abandons traditional femininity.

When Sara regains her reason, she finds herself tended by strangers. She gradually recovers, but her desire for violence and revenge have vanished. At a loss for what to do next, but feeling a vague impulse to compensate for her love affair with L*** by being a better patriot, she accompanies her caregiver Babet, who fights because she cannot bear to leave her husband, into war. They dress themselves as men and join a regiment of patriots. As Elisabeth Krimmer and others have pointed out, this has some historical basis: more women *did* fight in the conflicts following the French Revolution than in previous military conflicts.[24] It is striking, however, that Huber's depiction of Sara as a soldier is *not* marked by the same violent and wild impulses that cause Sara to lose her feminine identity in the city; instead, she remains calm and detached:

> Sie ging ruhig in den Streit, betrachtete den Tod in allen seinen Zügen, und wenn er sich ihr nahte, hatte sie ihm seine Schwäche so abgesehen, daß sie ihn wie einen verrathenen Ueberfall von sich schüttelte. (2:249)

[She went calmly into battle, observed death in all its features, and when it neared her, she had so foreseen its weakness that she shook it away from her like a betrayed ambush.]

This coolness gains her the admiration of her comrades:

> Und nun hieß Sara bald der tapfre Verrier; die schwärmenden Jünglinge verhiessen ihm Unsterblichkeit in den Jahrbüchern der Republik, und wenn er fiele, eine Stelle im Pantheon, und sie ward nach einem der blutigsten Tage, auf dem Schlachtfeld selbst, von ihren Kameraden zum Rang ihres Kapitains erhoben. (2:249–50)

> [So now Sara was soon called brave Verrier; the rhapsodizing youths promised him immortality in the annals of the Republic, and if he fell, a place in the Pantheon, and she was—after one of the bloodiest days, on the battlefield itself—raised by her comrades to the rank of their captain.]

Dressed as a man, Sara proves herself to be competent—indeed, exceptional—in fulfilling a man's role. She is brave and authoritative, but she is also compassionate and assists the starving civilians her troupe encounters in the ruined countryside.

This devastated landscape, which Huber describes in detail, shows her to be an author who, as Johannes Birgfeld puts it in his study *Krieg und Aufklärung*, "had at her disposal very precise knowledge of the characteristics of and changes in the latest art of war."[25] Here it is Huber who, not unlike her protagonist, refuses to limit her knowledge or experience to the areas viewed traditionally as appropriate for women. And this up-to-date knowledge is crucial for the novel's plot, as Sara's activity as a soldier is enabled by those changes: up until the very late eighteenth century, as Birgfeld explains, military strategy relied upon discipline and uniformity in an advancing line of soldiers.[26] Sara's slight build (which is noted by her comrades) and lack of training would have disqualified her from fighting in such an army. In the War in the Vendée, however, these techniques were countered by guerilla and scorched-earth warfare, which resulted "from the nature of the landscape and the character of the inhabitants," who would mobilize to fight battles with the anti-Republic rebels in their immediate vicinity but then return home rather than moving onward with the rebels.[27] Huber is extraordinarily aware of these developments, and she weaves them expertly into the plot of her novel. The fact that Sara is familiar with the surrounding countryside is an advantage in a war fought in a "countryside full of wooded hills and intersected by any number of brooks . . . , while the roads are deep, narrow, full of puddles, and bordered by very high quickset hedges and trees. There are no great roads or navigable rivers, the only highway being that from Mortange to Nantes, the country is, moreover covered with great rocks [and is] almost an impenetrable thicket."[28] Huber does not draw the connection between the new kind of warfare and Sara's success as a soldier explicitly, but she does remark that the landscape is, for Sara, "wohl bekannt" (2:240; well known) though much marred by the battles taking place throughout it, and Sara marks her journey by connecting it to memories from her childhood (2:230–31). It is Sara's prior lived experience that is crucial to her success as a soldier and the admiration she gains in this role. By connecting her protagonist's cross-dressing and successful career as a soldier to new developments in war strategy, Huber also emphasizes that almost every aspect of life in the late eighteenth century was in flux. Female leadership, in Sara's case, is enabled by the changing times, though these changes also come with a massive cost, as the destruction of the land around Sara's childhood home and Sara's own injured body make clear.

It is in Sara's response to this devastation and its effects on the residents of the Vendée that we see most clearly that Huber portrays Sara's femininity as intact despite her disguise, indeed, much more so than when she was still dressed as a woman:

> Wenn die hülflosen Kinder, in Sara's Mantel gehüllt, an ihrem, unter der Verkleidung, von mütterlichen Erinnerungen klopfenden Brust erwärmt, ihre kleinen Arme um ihren Hals schlugen, und bis ein schützendes Dach erreicht war, oft an ihrer Schulter einschliefen—da konnte Sara wohl zu Augenblicken ihres Schicksals vergessen, oder mit feierlicher Rührung in den Wegen selbst, die es sie zu diesem Genuß geführt hatte, einen wunderbaren und hohen Sinn ahnen. (2:267–81)

> [When the helpless children, wrapped in Sara's cloak and warmed on her breast, which pounded with motherly memories under her disguise, slung their little arms around her neck and often fell asleep before they reached a protecting roof—then Sara could forget her fate for a few moments, or intuit with solemn emotion in the very paths that had led her to this pleasure a wonderful and higher meaning.]

As in the earlier scene with the young family after the king's execution, it is encounters with children, who instinctively respond to her as a mother, that recall Sara's femininity. The difference, though, is that in this case these incidents do not provide an abrupt reawakening of a feminine side, but rather its preservation despite outward appearances. Unlike in the first volume of the novel, Sara's apparently masculine activities do not disqualify her from being a mother figure. How, then, are we to interpret this? On the one hand, it is obviously in some sense correct to say that

Huber *does* portray Sara's activities as a soldier positively, and that the persistence of her femininity underneath her man's clothing is a factor in the positivity of that portrayal: Sara can be a leader without losing her identity. Against this, however, it would be possible to argue that Huber here demonstrates a kind of disappointing gender essentialism: femininity will out, in the end, no matter what.

The ending of the novel is similarly difficult to interpret. When Sara unexpectedly finds herself fighting against her brother Theodor, she briefly loses consciousness and her sex is discovered. But even then Huber depicts her as an object of admiration, even awe, rather than ridicule. As Sara is acknowledging that Theodor must, like all the other rebels who have been captured, be sentenced to death, Huber writes:

> Sie hielt inne; über sich selbst erhaben, in reiner Begeisterung stand sie da; ihr Auge blizte, wie sie wieder anhob, war ihre Stimme fest; ihr schöner, noch halb entblößter Busen klopfte hoch, und indem er bewies, daß sie ein Weib war, löste sich der Schauder, den ihr Wesen erregte, in stiller Bewunderung auf—ihre Kriegsgefährten fühlten diesen Zauber, und traten ehrerbietig zurük. (2:284–85)

> [She paused, exalted beyond herself, in pure rapture she stood there; her eye flashed, when she lifted her voice again, it was firm; her beautiful, still-half-bared bosom heaved, and by proving that she was a woman, it dissolved the shudder that her nature provoked in silent awe—her war comrades felt this enchantment and stepped reverently back.]

Sara's career as a soldier is not portrayed as a farce or as a mistake, and, unlike her ventures into the political sphere, it does not carry dire consequences. When the troop and their prisoners return to headquarters, Sara's superior, rather than turning her over and imprisoning her for having broken the law against women serving in the army, grants her an honorable discharge (with the support of her "Waffenbrüder" [2:291; brothers-at-arms] who vouch for her "Muth" and "Ehrbarkeit" [2:292; courage and honor]) and allows her to spend the night before her brother Theodor's execution with him. It is at this point that Sara steps into her final role as an adoptive mother: the rebels with whom her brother was fighting were protecting a dying woman and her child, who turn out to be L***'s widow and their (legitimate) son. Sara takes responsibility for his care, saying: "Ja, ich folge deinem Ruf, unbegreifliches Schiksal! Hier . . . in eure Hände, meine Mitbürger, lege ich den Schwur ab: Des Knaben Tugenden sollen einst seines Vaters Verbrechen versöhnen!" (2:287; Yes, I follow your call, incomprehensible fate! Here . . . in your hands, my fellow citizens, I lay my oath: the boy's virtues shall one day compensate for his father's crimes!). Instead of continuing to fight, Sara attempts to atone for L***'s crimes by vowing to raise his son as a patriot. Motherhood thus appears not as a natural destiny but rather as a political choice. Sara refuses, however, to marry Roger, who reappears at this juncture. On one reading, this refusal of marriage and tidy resolution speaks to the possibility of female independence; on the other hand, however, one might argue that Sara is repeating her father's mistakes by raising a child in social isolation.

These ambiguous and multifaceted portrayals of and attitudes toward gender make it impossible to decide conclusively what Huber's precise views on gender are and whether we can or should understand them as primarily conservative or progressive. But this does not mean that we are forced to criticize or dismiss Huber's novel as careless, incoherent, or even hypocritical: if we instead discard the notion that the novel as literary work must offer itself to a single interpretation of its message on gender and approach it as leading us, its readers, through an imaginative *process*, several conclusions emerge. The first of these is the extent to which Huber mentions Sara's relationships to other human beings whenever she is emphasizing feminine identity (as in the passage quoted above in which Sara has forgotten that she is or has been "Tochter, Geliebte, Weib, Mutter"), whereas she highlights the absence of such connections when Sara is fulfilling masculine roles. Huber portrays this counterfactually when Sara searches for Berthier, her old neighbor and Roger's father: "Lebte Berthier, so war sie noch einmal Weib, Tochter!" (2:242; If Berthier lived, she was once again a woman, a daughter!). But as she learns that Berthier has been killed, Sara is "verwaist, ohne Schuz, ohne Zuflucht auf Erden, ohne Zukunft" (2:242; orphaned, without protection, without recourse on the earth, without a future) at which point she embarks on her career as a soldier. I want to suggest that what Huber is doing here is exploring the ways in which varying factors *combine* to create gender identity: Sara's femininity is anchored by affective connections, and when these are absent, other elements of her individuality are free to prevail. Huber depicts motherhood in multiple, complex ways, as well— Sara fails to keep her own daughter alive, but other children instinctively respond to her as a mother figure, and the novel ends with Sara choosing a role as an adoptive mother. The biological fact of having given birth is neither necessary nor sufficient for motherhood, meaning that, on the paradigm of the novel, this role is not biologically dictated but rather one that a woman can choose to inhabit.

Furthermore, this process of investigating the components of gender roles plays with the idea of gender performance and interior identity: by having her protagonist go through phases in which she is dressed as a woman but loses her femininity and, conversely, dressed as a man but with her inner femininity preserved, Huber, I suggest, is working through the idea that gender socialization begins early and continues within the context of education and family ties, but is also significantly shaped by an individual's lived experience, which may in fact run counter to training or ties. Though my terminology is certainly anachronistic, it shows how Huber *uses* her novel to lead the reader through a series of experiments around gender to arrive at the notion that gender is both shaped by experience and ultimately flexible. Nor is this a point of which she could simply inform us prescriptively or argumentatively—rather, Huber had to steer us through (in the sense of both "over the course of" and "by means of") *Die Familie Seldorf* to experience these different viewpoints. In this regard, it is she who is exhibiting female leadership, and it is leadership of a kind that remains relevant as women continue to struggle to navigate questions of gender identity and performance as they intersect with social training and lived experience.

Notes

[1] Elisabeth Krimmer, *In the Company of Men: Cross-Dressed Women around 1800* (Detroit: Wayne State University Press, 2004), 55.

[2] Stephanie M. Hilger, *Gender and Genre: German Women Write the French Revolution* (Newark: University of Delaware Press, 2015), 15.

[3] See Inge Stephan, "Revolution und Konterrevolution: Therese Hubers Roman *Die Familie Seldorf* (1795/96), in *Der deutsche Roman der Spätaufklärung: Fiktion und Wirklichkeit*, ed. Harro Zimmerman (Heidelberg: Carl Winter, 1990), 171–94. And Wulf Köpke, "Immer noch im Schatten der Männer? Therese Huber als Schriftstellerin," in *Der Weltumsegler und seine Freunde: Georg Forster als gesellschaftlicher Schriftsteller der Goethezeit*, ed. Detlef Rasmussen (Tübingen: Narr, 1988), 116–32.

[4] Anna Richards, "'Double-Voiced Discourse' and Psychological Insight in the Work of Therese Huber," *Modern Language Review* 99, no. 2 (2004): 419. Richards is one of the relatively few scholars who examine Huber's other works in addition to *Die Familie Seldorf.*

[5] See Susanne Kord, *Sich einen Namen machen: Anonymität und weibliche Autorschaft, 1700–1900* (Stuttgart: Metzler, 1996).

[6] Therese Huber, "Unsre Geschichte," in *Therese Huber—die reinste Freiheitsliebe, die reinste Männerliebe: Ein Lebensbild in Briefen und Erzählungen zwischen Aufklärung und Romantik*, ed. Andrea Hahn (Berlin: Henssel, 1989), 8. This is consistent with other remarks about her mother that Huber made in correspondence. All translations in this article, unless otherwise indicated, are my own.

[7] Barbara Becker-Cantarino, *Schriftstellerinnen der Romantik: Epoche—Werke—Wirkung* (Munich: Beck, 2000), 89–93. Simon Richter also offers a reading of Huber's work (including *Die Familie Seldorf*) in conjunction with her biography from a Lacanian perspective that understands the breast as "unruly signifier" with the potential to undermine phallic/patriarchal gender norms. Richter, *Missing the Breast: Gender, Fantasy, and the Body in the German Enlightenment* (Seattle:

University of Washington Press, 2006), 8; the chapter that treats Huber is pp. 168–215.

[8] Michael Warner, *Letters of the Republic* (Cambridge, MA: Harvard University Press, 1992), xiii.

[9] Jenefer Robinson, *Deeper Than Reason: Emotion and Its Role in Literature, Music, and Art* (Oxford: Oxford University Press, 2005), 197.

[10] Robinson, *Deeper*, 197, 207.

[11] Karin Hausen, "Die Polarisierung der 'Geschlechtercharaktere'—eine Spiegelung der Dissoziation von Erwerbs- und Familienleben," in *Sozialgeschichte der Familie in der Neuzeit Europas*, ed. Werner Conze (Stuttgart: Kletter, 1976), 363–93. Claudia Honegger, *Die Ordnung der Geschlechter: Die Wissenschaften vom Menschen und das Weib, 1750–1850* (Frankfurt am Main: Suhrkamp, 1991).

[12] Marion W. Gray, *Productive Men, Reproductive Women: The Agrarian Household and the Emergence of Separate Spheres during the German Enlightenment* (New York: Berghahn, 2000).

[13] Rebekah Habermas, *Frauen und Männer des Bürgertums: Eine Familiengeschichte (1750–1850)* (Göttingen, Vandenhoeck & Ruprecht, 2000), 325.

[14] Anne-Charlotte Trepp, *Sanfte Männlichkeit und selbstständige Weiblichkeit: Frauen und Männer im Hamburger Bürgertum zwischen 1770 und 1840* (Göttingen: Vandenhoeck & Ruprecht, 1996), 399.

[15] Helen Fronius, *Women and Literature in the Goethe Era, 1770–1820: Determined Dilettantes* (Oxford: Oxford University Press, 2007), 1. Further references to this work are given in the text using the short title *Women and Literature*.

[16] Barbara Becker-Cantarino, *Der lange Weg zur Mündigkeit: Frau und Literatur (1500–1800)* (Stuttgart: Metzler, 1987), 19–66. Becker-Cantarino rehearses these arguments in her later *Schriftstellerinnen der Romantik* (see note 7). Further references to this work are given in the text using the short title *Der lange Weg*.

[17] Habermas, *Frauen und Männer*, 316.

[18] Becker-Cantarino, *Schrifstellerinnen*, 57–58.

[19] Jacques Rancière, *Aisthesis: Scenes from the Aesthetic Regime of Art*, trans. Zakir Paul (London: Verso, 2013), xii.

[20] Jochen Schulte-Sasse, *Die Kritik an der Trivialliteratur seit der Aufklärung: Studien zur Geschichte des modernen Kitschbegriffs* (Munich: Fink, 1971), 13.

[21] I have argued elsewhere for this approach (which I cannot work out fully here in the interest of space), under the label "imaginative didacticism," as a "category with which to examine what literature . . . might be offering to its readers, both historical and universal/implied." Sarah Vandegrift Eldridge, "Imaginative Didacticism: Emotion, Individuality, and the Function of *Trivialliteratur* around 1800," *Journal of Literary Theory* 10, no. 2 (2016): 221–46, here, 236.

[22] Therese Huber, *Die Familie Seldorf*, ed. Magdalene Heuser (Hildesheim: Olms, 1989), 1:7. Further references to this novel are given in the text with volume and page number alone.

[23] Becker-Cantarino suggests that this negative portrayal does not apply to all political action on the part of women, but only the "wrong, that is, *destructive*"

political action. Becker-Cantarino, *Schriftstellerinnen*, 107. Since there is no portrayal of the "right" political action in the novel, it is impossible to say whether
this is true; all we have is the negative depiction. Hilger argues that Huber's negative depiction of Sara's political activity "highlights the paradox that [women] are
presented as furies and amazons when circumstances force them into the public
realm." Hilger, *Gender and Genre*, 25. I do not think the narrator's descriptions
allow room for such a meta-reading of these scenes; there is no ironic distanc-
ing here, especially compared with the narrator's ironic tone in, for example, the
remark about the significance of Roger's milk bowl.

[24] Krimmer, *Company of Men*, 37–41.

[25] Johannes Birgfeld, *Krieg und Aufklärung: Studien zum Kriegsdiskurs in der
deutschsprachigen Literatur des 18. Jahrhunderts* (Hannover: Wehrhahn, 2012),
2:635.

[26] Birgfeld, *Krieg und Aufklärung*, 1:65–105, esp. 100–104.

[27] Birgfeld, *Krieg und Aufklärung*, 2:648.

[28] Marquise de La Rochejaquelein, cited in Birgfeld, *Krieg und Aufklärung*, 651.

6: Power Struggles between Women in Schiller's and Jelinek's Works

Inge Stephan

T̲O̲ ̲A̲N̲Y̲O̲N̲E̲ ̲R̲E̲A̲D̲I̲N̲G̲ ̲T̲H̲E̲ ̲D̲R̲A̲M̲A̲ *Maria Stuart* (1800) by Friedrich Schiller today, more than 200 years after its Weimar premiere, the power struggle between the two queens may seem like a dusty tableau from a distant past: on the right in this picture the virginal, austere Elisabeth, queen of England, on the left her seductive and beautiful rival, Maria Stuart, queen of Scotland. And one wonders what motivated Elfriede Jelinek to choose this constellation in her play *Ulrike Maria Stuart* (2006), which bears the subtitle "Queens' drama."

I would like to formulate some theses on this topic that focus primarily on the relationship between women and power. First of all, I will offer a brief analysis of Schiller's "women's drama," which has received less attention and appreciation in traditional scholarship than his "male dramas" *Die Räuber*, *Don Carlos*, *Wallenstein* or *Wilhelm Tell*, even though its antithetic structure is considered to be particularly well executed. Moreover, on stage the tragedy of the two competing "sisters" has always stood in the shadow of the *Maid of Orleans*, which was written a little later and whose "militant femininity" has become an impetus for spectacular new productions, especially in current director-driven theater. Then I will turn to Jelinek's "Secondary Drama,"[1] which, in its reference to the "classical model," reexamines power and gender conflicts in a contemporary context. As I will show, Schiller ultimately reframes a female competition for power as an erotic rivalry and thus resituates his two female sovereigns safely in a more gender-appropriate sphere. In contrast, Jelinek links female power to maternity and deconstructs the notion that women derive power from motherhood.

Schiller

Schiller began work on *Maria Stuart* shortly after completing his Wallenstein trilogy.[2] While *Wallenstein* was about the design of a "genius of strength" (Kraftgenie) who oscillates between grandiosity and depression,[3] *Maria Stuart* is concerned with the confrontation of two female rulers who fight for power and who—despite many differences—prove similar in character, even though the contrasting arrangement of the drama leads readers to assume the opposite. In some ways, Elisabeth and Maria—much like their "royal sisters" Käthchen von Heilbronn and Penthesilea a little later in Kleist—function as "two sides of the same coin": together, they represent the "split image of woman" typical of male-authored literature around 1800.

If one understands Schiller's texts "als Ergebnisse einer produktiven Beunruhigung über den Verlauf der europäischen Zivilisation"[4] (as the results of a productive unease about the course of European civilization), one could formulate the thesis that the author—prompted by the experience of the French Revolution whose "honorary citizen" he was—parsed questions relating to the legitimacy of power, violence, and sovereignty both in the "male" model of *Wallenstein* and in the female "model" of *Maria Stuart*. Both tragedies are set in the past. *Wallenstein* transports the audience back to the turmoil of the Thirty Years' War in Germany; *Maria Stuart* is set at the English royal court in the sixteenth century, where Elisabeth I sees her claim to the throne threatened by the Scottish queen, Maria Stuart. Although both are historical dramas, they are clearly conceived as reflections about and critical commentaries on events around 1800. Both dramas were performed at the court theater in Weimar, *Wallenstein* in 1798/9, *Maria Stuart* in 1800. Unlike *Wallenstein*, which I will not discuss further here, *Maria Stuart* is especially interesting with regard to gender discourses around 1800. In presenting two competing models of "female power," Schiller engages in a debate that, in the wake of Jacobin rule in France and the so-called Amazons of the French Revolution, reached hysterical proportions in neighboring Germany. Schiller shared this horror of women who became "hyenas" with many of his contemporaries. Female regents were an accepted model of dynastic rule, as shown by such figures as Maria Theresa in Austria-Hungary, Catherine the Great in Russia, or Anna Amalia with her "Court of the Muses" (*Musenhof*) in Weimar. However, they were always seen as exceptional.

Interestingly enough, with Elisabeth and Maria, Schiller evokes the memory of two historical women rulers whose names are associated with blood and violence.[5] It is often assumed that Maria murdered her husband and we know that Elisabeth had her rival executed. Thus both are ambivalent figures, because they did not conform to common notions of gender and power, and Schiller's drama clearly strains under the effort to make these ambivalences disappear. With the focus on Maria Stuart as the "victim" of her royal sister Elisabeth and her stylization as "beautiful soul," whose "crime"—as the nurse emphasizes right at the beginning of the drama—consists of "youthful sins" that have long since been atoned for, Schiller creates, against the historical reality,[6] a figure worthy of compassion. Even so, the drama offers far more than a simple account of "victim" and "perpetrator." Maria's offenses cannot be eradicated completely—significantly, she accepts her execution as atonement for her past crimes. Moreover, tortured by fears of failure and doubts, Elisabeth too is an ambivalent figure, who tries to shirk responsibility for her opponent's death by delegating its execution to her subordinates. She sees herself as "victimized" by her role as a ruler, which demands from her the renunciation of erotic fulfillment, while she perceives Maria as a woman who has surrendered to adulterous passions, thereby violating her duties as queen.

> Der Stuart wards vergönnt,
> Die Hand nach ihrer Neigung zu verschenken,
> Die hat sich jegliches erlaubt, sie hat
> Den vollen Kelch der Freuden ausgetrunken.
> . . .
> Sie hat der Menschen Urteil nicht geachtet.
> Leicht ward es ihr zu leben, nimmer lud sie
> das Joch sich auf, dem ich mich unterwarf.
> Hätt ich doch auch Ansprüche machen können,
> Des Lebens mich, der Erde Lust zu freun,
> Doch zog ich strenge Königspflichten vor.[7]

> [The Queen of Scotland was allowed to make
> Her hand the token of her inclination;
> She hath had every freedom, and hath drunk,
> Even to the very dregs, the cup of joy.
> . . .
> She never did respect the world's opinion;
> Life was to her a sport; she never courted
> The yoke to which I bowed my willing neck.
> And yet, methinks, I had as just a claim
> As she to please myself and taste the joys
> Of life: but I preferred the rigid duties
> Which royalty imposed on me.][8]

As the quotation shows, Schiller turns political events into a "drama of the soul," in which questions of female strength and the exercise of power are transposed onto the sphere of the erotic. Thus his drama is linked to common gender norms of his time—norms that, one might add, he and his texts were instrumental in formulating. The decisive conflict of the drama—if one leaves aside the political and religious contradictions—lies in the rivalry of two women for a man. Referencing this constellation, Goethe spoke disparagingly of the quarrel between "two whores."[9] Moreover, Count Leicester, the man whom both women desire, is himself a shady figure. On the one hand he strives for power as Elisabeth's consort; on the other hand he hopes for erotic fulfillment with Maria.

Jelinek

Jelinek's choice to use the title and subtitle of Schiller's "Königinnendrama" is not her only reference to his play; rather, *Ulrike Maria Stuart* is permeated with direct quotes and ironic references to its literary predecessor. While Schiller conjures up the historic confrontation between Maria and Elisabeth in the times of the "terreur" and the "September murders," Jelinek's "Queens' drama" is set in the immediate present. The traumatic "German Autumn" and "terrorism" are among the "ghosts" that shape German cultural memory and political life even today.[10]

Of course, Jelinek's play does far more than reference Schiller: the "love triangle" between the two RAF icons Ulrike Meinhof and Gudrun Ensslin and the "bad boy" Andreas Baader develops a constellation that is already present in Schiller's play in the form of Maria and Elisabeth's rivalry for Count Leicester's love. Meinhof appears as Maria Stuart's revenant, Ensslin bears Elisabeth's features, and Baader is a grotesquely distorted copy of Count Leicester, who, of course, is already a caricature in Schiller's play. Unlike Schiller, however, Jelinek is not interested in "virginity" or "beauty of the soul." In the same brutal manner that is typical of her work, Jelinek tears apart the ideological veil that Schiller—and more so his subsequent interpreters—had laid over the events. She directs our gaze to sexuality as the actual driving force of her protagonist's thinking, feeling, and actions, which Goethe perceptively identified as the real cause of the confrontation, as I noted earlier.

The coarse language of the play is not Jelinek's but is largely taken from the secret messages of the Stammheim prisoners; it contrasts with the "elevated language" that characterizes Mary and Elisabeth's dialogue in Schiller. In her preliminary remarks on the text, Jelinek speaks of the "height" of the text that the director must necessarily "undermine":

> Ein Problem wird sein, daß die fast immer "gebundene" Sprache des Textes (Jamben, Trochäen) eine "Höhe" darstellt, die unbedingt konterkariert werden muß von der Regie. Die Figuren müssen sozusagen fast jeden Augenblick von sich selbst zurückgerissen werden, um nicht mit sich selbst ident zu werden. . . . denn diese Figuren sind ja nicht "sie selbst," sondern, nein, auch nicht einfach die berühmten, mir inzwischen längst lästigen Sprachflächen, sondern Produkte von Ideologie.[11]

> [One problem will be that almost the entire text, which is written in meter (iambs, trochees), represents a "height" that must absolutely be undermined by the director. The characters have to be torn away from themselves, so to speak, almost every moment so as not to become identical with themselves . . . because these characters are not "themselves," but rather, no, they are also not the famous

language surfaces, which meanwhile have long become annoying to me, but products of ideology.]

This "elevated language" is already disrupted in Jelinek's text, when the two protagonists unexpectedly switch from Schiller's metered language to "everyday language." I present two examples that represent many others. They show how Jelinek ironically quotes and dismantles the famous encounter between Maria and Elisabeth—which, incidentally, is not based on a historical event, but was added by Schiller. Thus "Gudrun" begins in "Elisabeth mode": "Who was it then who announced to us a downtrodden one? One still too proud we find, by no means made supple or humble by misfortune," only to then continue in "RAF-tone":

> Wir wären damals gerne effizienter gewesen, doch wir waren nicht so weit. . . . Wir sind für vieles schuldig, auch uns selber sind wir vieles schuldig noch geblieben, ich bin wohl die erste, die das zugibt, doch wir haben, und drauf bin ich stolz, das CIA-Hauptquartier und auch das Hauptquartier des 5. US-Corps angegriffen und auch das US-Hauptquartier in Heidelberg, na und, ein andres war da nicht. (73)

> [We would have liked to have been more efficient back then, but we were not ready. . . . We are guilty of a lot, we also still owe much to ourselves in many ways, I am probably the first to admit that, but we have, and I am proud of it, attacked the CIA headquarters and also the headquarters of the 5th US Corps and also the US headquarters in Heidelberg, well, and there wasn't another one.]

"Ulrike" also switches abruptly between the language of her "predecessor" and RAF language when she begins her "monologue" with the words:

> So will ich mich noch diesem unterwerfen, Schwester, auch wenn es mir recht schwerfällt, Stolz, fahr hin, ich hab ja ohnedies kein Auto mehr, keine Wohnung, keine Kinder und kein Haus, also kannst von mir aus auch du fahren, lieber Stolz. . . . Ich will vor dir mich niederwerfen, Schwester, ja, das mach ich glatt, darauf kommt es mir nicht mehr an, den Boden unter meinen Füßen habe ich längst verloren. (74)

> [Thus, I want to submit to this, sister, even if it is pretty difficult for me, pride, fly away, anyway I do not have a car anymore, no apartment, no children, and no house, so for all I care you can fly away too, dear pride. . . . I want to prostrate myself before you, sister, yes, I'll just do it, it does not matter to me anymore, I've long ago lost the ground beneath my feet.]

In light of the author's statement quoted above that her characters are not "identical," it is not surprising that "afterimage" and "prototype" are not always congruent. Thus "Ulrike" is, already in the title, oriented almost entirely toward Schiller's Maria figure. "Gudrun," however, although an Elisabeth figure, also exhibits aspects of the hated opponent in a number of passages. Just as precious jewelry and exquisite clothing are indispensable elements of Maria Stuart's feminine self-staging, "Gudrun" attaches great importance to expensive and fashionable leather jackets and cashmere pullovers, even when she is on the run—a predilection that would be fatal to her. The circumstances surrounding her arrest in a high-end boutique in Hamburg are, of course, a detail that the fashion- and capitalism-critical Jelinek savors. At the same time, the author clearly transposes her "Schiller paraphrase" into today's consumer world.

The strongest "deviation" from Schiller, however, lies in the representation of motherhood, which creates an entirely new level of conflict in Jelinek's text. Of course, this is due to the fact that Meinhof and Ensslin were both mothers—Meinhof had twin daughters, Ensslin had a son. The fact that both women left their children behind when they joined the revolutionary underground and opted for armed struggle was publicly derided, especially in the press, which took to calling them "raven mothers" and "misguided women's libbers." Of course, this topic was made for a writer like Jelinek.

However, I believe that her decision to emphasize motherhood in this context is also related to the fact that, even when she first started writing, Jelinek assigned this topic a special place in her engagement with femininity, sexuality, and power. Unlike those segments of the contemporary women's movement that considered "motherhood" and "motherliness" sources of power that could effect positive change in society, Jelinek believed that such concepts were ideological constructs designed to suppress women and deceive them about their actual powerlessness. In her texts there are no positive mother figures. Already in the early novel *Lust* (1992), a "grotesque Medea paraphrase,"[12] the protagonist Gerti kills her son, an unpleasant miniature edition of his power-loving father, with no identifiable emotion. The exclamation "Murder and Death," with which she comments on her act, recalls the slogan "liberté ou mort" of the French revolutionaries. Modified to "the RAF or death" (83), this slogan also appears in *Ulrike Maria Stuart*.

Significantly, Medea, who enjoys dubious fame as a child murderer in European literary and art history, is also cited in the Queens' Drama when "Ulrike" says:

Ach, die Medea soll ich euch jetzt geben, eure Rabenmutter! Na, dann geb ich halt auch die. Hab eh schon alles hingegeben, warum

nicht auch die Mutterschaft? Ihr seht mich selbst, Kinder, bald seht
ihr nur noch mein Bild, wie euer Vater sagt. (18)

[Oh, I should perform Medea for you now, your raven mother!
Well, then I'll perform her too. I have already given everything any-
way, why not motherhood as well? You see me myself, children, soon
you will only see my image, as your father says.]

Echoes of Euripides's *Medea* are unmistakable elsewhere as well, when the
"old man's chorus"—an ironic variant of the ancient chorus—expresses
its old-fashioned opinions on women:

Das Richterschwert, womit der Mann sich ziert, verhaßt ists in der
Frauen Hand, und grad die Frauen sind die militantesten, weil ihre
Körper viel mehr durchzustehen haben, allgemein und im speziellen,
die sind das von Geburt an ja gewöhnt, daß sie gebären müssen, und
dann sind sie dafür von uns Männern wohl verwahrt und gut ver-
wöhnt den Rest der Zeit, den sie noch haben. (11)

[The sword of the judge with which man adorns himself is hated
in the hands of women, and the women in particular are the most
militant, because their bodies have to endure much more, in general
and in particular, they are used to it from birth that they have to give
birth and then they are well kept by us men for this and well spoiled
the rest of the time that they still have.]

Addressing the "dear children" (11) who, as "princes in the tower," are
waiting impatiently for the hour of their takeover, the old men vehe-
mently advocate the death of their mother:

Nein, leben soll sie nicht, an die Gerechtigkeit des Weibes glauben
wir schon lange nicht. . . . Das Weib hat kein Gewissen, und diese,
eure Mutter, hat erst recht keins. . . . Nur die Gnade kann ihr jetzt
noch helfen, und die kriegt sie nicht, ihr lieben Kinder, ihr könnt sie
vergessen, beides, Gnade euch wie eurer Mutter, der nur ein Gott
noch gnaden kann, vergeßt sie! (11/12)

[No, she should not live, we stopped believing in the righteousness
of women a long time ago. . . . Woman has no conscience, and this
one, your mother, certainly does not have one. . . . Only mercy can
help her now, and she cannot get it, you dear children, you can forget them, both, mercy on you as well as your mother, to whom only
a god can show mercy, forget her!]

"Ulrike's" words about women have a similar tenor when she speaks about her rival "Gudrun":

> Die Frauen sind ja immer stärker als die Männer, und am stärksten sind sie wohl als Mütter. Mütter bleiben sie. Und auch als Revolutionärin sind sie stark, das ist das Gegenteil von Mutter, die aus ihrem Stolz heraustritt, wenns ums Kind geht, die sich selbst vergißt, bevor sie sich gekannt hat, komisch, hier geht das zusammen, bei der Königin geht das zusammen, . . . die kann solche Gegensätze mühelos verbinden, ich bewundere sie dafür. Diese Frauen. Mutter müssen sie ja immer sein, egal von wem. (20)

> [The women are always stronger than the men, and they are probably strongest as mothers. Mothers they remain. And as revolutionaries too, they are strong, that's the opposite of mother who sheds her pride when it is about the child, who forgets herself before she has known herself, weird, here it works together, with the queen it works together, . . . she can combine such contrasts effortlessly, I admire her for it. These women. They always have to be mothers, no matter whose.]

"Ulrike's" hatred—"ich hasse Mütter . . . obwohl ich selber eine bin" (20; I hate mothers . . . although I am one myself)—is directed specifically against the special motherhood of her opponent, who gave away her biological son and has sought and found in Andreas Baader a new "baby" (19) that belongs to her "all alone" (47). Accusingly, "Ulrike" asks her rival:

> Und was ist eigentlich mit deinem Sohn, dem leiblichen, dem echten, Blut von deinem Blut, das frag ich dich? Den hattest du doch auch und hast ihn weggeschmissen wie die leere Wursthaut, die der Mensch nicht essen mag, solang ihr Innerstes er hat zum Fressen gern. (24)

> [And what about your son, the biological, the real one, blood of your blood, I ask you? You had that one too and you threw him away like an empty sausage skin that no human likes to eat, as long as he likes to feed on what is innermost.]

The "Princes in the Tower" turn away from "Ulrike" with the words:

> Du hast nun keine Kinder mehr, Medea. Denn wir besuchen dich nicht mehr, dies allerdings auf deinen ausdrücklichen Wunsch! Du bist jetzt die Medea, die von ihren Kindern überlebt wird, recht geschieht ihr. Warum auf schlimmen Weg verfolgtest du dein Ziel,

du liebe Mami? Warum war immer abwesend die liebe Mutter, du,
wenn wir dich brauchten? Warum hast du dich nicht mehr um uns
gekümmert? Sag es uns! (24/25)

[You now no longer have any children, Medea. Because we no longer visit you, but this at your express wish! You are now the Medea
who is survived by her children, it serves her right. Why did you pursue your goal in an evil way, you dear mom? Why was dear mother
always absent, you, when we needed you? Why did not you take care
of us more? Tell us!]

In a way, "Ulrike Maria Stuart" could also be called "Ulrike Medea
Stuart": in evoking "Medea" and "Maria," Jelinek introduces—beyond
Euripides and Schiller—two powerful female figures who embody contradictory images of motherhood: on the one hand, the "blood-stained
mother," on the other, the "pure virgin"; in Western cultural history,
these two represent a "twin constellation" of ambivalent femininity.[13]
Their "power" does not correspond to any real strength: it is a product of
the imagination and of subsequent stylization.

Female Power

What is the meaning of such interpretations with respect to questions
of "female power and strength"? First of all, it is evident that Schiller's
drama is about the legitimacy of power and violence in light of the challenges posed by the 1789 Revolution in neighboring France. The historical shift and its resultant emphasis on the conflict to the rival queens
"Maria" and "Elisabeth" creates a gender discourse, which Schiller tries
to solve traditionally by stylizing and elevating the inferior queen to a
"beautiful soul," thus transforming the political question into a private
one. Jelinek approaches the topic quite differently. Her text actually
engages with the issue of "female power." Against the foil of Schiller's
drama—but located in the German present—Jelinek conceives of the two
RAF icons "Ulrike" and "Gudrun" as two figures who become political
activists, but who are, without even noticing it, entrapped by traditional
concepts of motherhood. At the same time, Jelinek explicitly interrogates
issues of power on a political level. "Ulrike" and "Gudrun" exercise violence "in the name of the people," but, like the Jacobins in the French
Revolution, they are forced to realize that "the people" do not want to
follow them.

Das Volk, zu dessen allerbesten Freunden wir uns aufgeschwungen
haben, will uns nicht, versteht uns nicht . . . das Volk will uns, doch
will es uns gefesselt und am liebsten tot und gargekocht, zur Schau

gestellt in der Vitrine eines Supermarkts. Schau selber, Schwester, ich sags dir zum letzten Mal, daß dieses Volk uns lieber tot sieht als die Feinde, die es nun tatsächlich hat, das Volk wird es noch merken, doch für uns wird's dann zu spät sein. Keiner unsrer Brüder, keine unsrer Schwestern wird die Arme öffnen und uns aufnehmen, wir halten auch kein Blutgericht ab, denn es ist ja keiner da, den wir noch töten können. (80)

[The people, whose very best friends we claim to be, do not want us, do not understand us . . . the people want us, but they want us tied and preferably dead and cooked through, put on display in the showcase of a supermarket. Look for yourself, sister, I tell you for the last time that this people would rather see us dead than the ene-mies that it actually has, the people will notice it yet, but it will be too late for us then. None of our brothers, none of our sisters will open their arms and receive us, we also do not hold a blood court, because there is no one there whom we can still kill.]

To a certain extent, "the people" already play a role in Schiller. When Elisabeth condemns her opponent to death, she complains about her putative dependence on the people: "O Sklaverei des Volksdiensts" (80; O slavery of serving the people, 80) and purports to give in only for the sake of the people: "Ihr seht, wie sich mich drängen!" (78; You see how they are pushing me!). A disillusionment of the kind experienced by the two "idealists" (46)—such is the self-perception of the two RAF women in Jelinek's work—is absent in Schiller's drama. Although in exile and prison Mary is a queen without a people, she is surrounded by men who passionately desire her. In contrast, Jelinek's characters are totally isolated. This corresponds to the real situation of the prisoners in Stammheim, but at the same time can also be understood as Jelinek's statement about the impossibility of political actions in the "German Autumn." The overwhelming power of patriarchy, which triumphs as "Germany dual fatherland" (7) about "Germany, sick mother" (60), stifles any incipi-ent revolutionary actions. Jelinek's philosophy of history could not be more pessimistic. She takes up the remark that the revolution devours its own children, attributed to Danton when he was about to be executed on the scaffold, and modifies it twice during important moments in the text. "Ulrike" alludes to it when she says: "Die Revolution frißt jetzt ein Kind, und das bin ich, ich sag dazu, wohl bekomms" (28; The revolution is feeding on a child now, and that's me, I'll say, enjoy). At a later point in the text, the "Angel Never Mind" (59) comments on the situation on earth with the following words.

Der Kapitalismus frißt die eigenen Kinder, wie die Revolution es auch tun würde, hätte sie nur dazu Gelegenheit, die kriegt sie nie, schau, wie sie sich da alle gegenseitig fressen und nicht mal nach dem Namen fragen, einer wird gar Heuschrecken sie dereinst nennen, oder etwas andres oder jemand andren, ist ja auch egal, sie fressen alles, alles fressen sie, nachdem sie alles andere auch schon aufgefressen haben! (66)

[Capitalism feeds on its own children, as the revolution would do too if it only had the opportunity, which it will never get, look how they all feed on each other and do not even ask for names, one might even call them locusts one day, or something else or someone else, does not matter, they feed on everything, everything they feed on, after they have devoured everything else already!]

This figure of the "scattered angel," which appears four times in longer passages in the text (17/18, 59–72, 87–91, 97/98), is, of course, ironically reminiscent of Walter Benjamin's "angel of history," especially when it appears in the end as "Engel in Amerika . . . wie es sich gehört, mit dem Rücken zum Publikum" (97; angel in America . . . as it should be, with its back to the audience). At the same time, however, the angel is associated with Virginia Woolf's "angel in the house." Woolf's angel referred to the traditional image of femininity that women have to "kill"[14] if they want to be artistically productive. This thesis can be extended to actions in the public sphere: to effect social change we need to break with traditional ideas of femininity.

In sum, one might claim that, on the one hand, Jelinek's text does not position women as morally superior per se, and a transfer of power to them does not automatically lead to a fairer world. On the other hand, the exclusion of women from power produces a divided, unstable, and violent society. Jelinek does not offer solutions, as Schiller did with his concept of the "beautiful soul" or Goethe with his "devilishly humane Iphigenie";[15] rather, Jelinek mercilessly criticizes the brutalization of language and of private and political relations in times of terrorism and state violence.

In conclusion, I would like to discuss briefly Nicolas Stemann's staging in Hamburg in 2006, which was analyzed in an interesting publication in the series "Theater and University in Conversation."[16] For this performance, the director, to whom we owe numerous premieres of Jelinek's plays, radically shortened the extensive drama (whose publication and distribution Jelinek had initially expressly forbidden). Stemann then made the question of "female power" more poignant by adding a provocative scene. In this scene, two women, easily identifiable as Elfriede Jelinek and Marlene Streeruwitz, appear in absurd, bright pink vagina costumes and lament the powerlessness of women on the male-dominated literary scene.[17] The textual basis for this scene is an interview with Jelinek in the magazine *Emma*. Ostensibly, Stemann broadens the question of female power and powerlessness by highlighting a feminist perspective; subliminally, however, he alludes to a possible competition between female authors in the literary field. Streeruwitz responded to this scene with a preliminary injunction, because she believed that her dignity as a woman had been injured, but her effort did not produce the desired result; Jelinek, wiser than her colleague, did not comment on this directorial decision. In fact, Stemann's vagina dialogue not only ironizes Eve Ensler's well-known vagina monologues but, in some ways, also ingeniously refers back to the dispute between the fictitious "Ulrike" and "Gudrun" in Jelinek's "Queen Drama," which had already been turned into a "pussy" competition by the historical RAF women themselves.

One might say that this takes us back full circle to Goethe, who spoke of the two whores in relation to Schiller's drama. However, it would be wrong to interpret the crude sexualization of women in Jelinek and Stemann as a fundamental defamation of women as political and cultural agents. Rather, text and staging tear up the veil of idealization that participants and interpreters alike have used to conceal the circumstances and the motives behind them—both in Schiller's "historical drama" and in the self-representation of RAF actors and their stylization by their followers.

Notes

[1] Teresa Kovacs, *Drama als Störung: Elfriede Jelineks Konzept des Sekundärdramas* (Bielefeld: transcript, 2016).

[2] Friedrich Schiller, *Marie Stuart*. Vol. 9 of *Schillers Werke: Nationalausgabe*, i.A. des Goethe und Schiller-Archivs, des Schiller-Nationalmuseums und der Deutschen Akademie, ed. Julius Petersen and Gerhard Fricke (Weimar: Hermann Böhlaus Nachfolger, 1942–2010).

[3] Dieter Borchmeyer, *Macht und Melancholie: Schillers Wallenstein*, 2nd ed. (Göttingen: Edition Mnemosyne, 2003).

[4] Michael Hofmann, *Schiller: Epoche-Werk-Wirkung* (Munich: Beck, 2003), 11. Further references are given as Hofmann, *Schiller* with the page number.

[5] See Rosalind Marshall, *Mary, Queen of Scots* (Edinburgh: National Museum of Scotland, 2013), and Jürgen Klein, *Elisabeth I. und ihre Zeit* (Munich: Beck, 2010).

[6] Peter André Alt, "Maria Stuart: Geschichtliche Quellen und ihre Entstehung," in *Schiller: Leben—Werk—Zeit; Eine Biographie*, vol. 2 (Munich: Beck, 2000), 492–509.

[7] Schiller, *Maria Stuart*, 9:75, lines 1974–84.

[8] Friedrich Schiller, *Mary Stuart: A Tragedy*, trans. Joseph Mellish, produced by Tapio Riikonen and David Widger, accessed April 10, 2019, https://www.gutenberg.org/files/6791/6791-h/6791-h.htm#link2H_4_0020.

[9] Hofmann, *Schiller*, 163.

[10] Svea Bräunert, *Gespenstergeschichten: Der linke Terrorismus der RAF und die Künste* (Berlin: Kulturverlag Kadmaos, 2015); Christina Gerhardt, *Screening the Red Army Fraction: Historical and Cultural Memory* (New York: Bloomsbury, 2018).

[11] Elfriede Jelinek, *Ulrike Maria Stuart: Königinnendrama* (Reinbek: Rowohlt Theaterverlag, n.d.), 2. Further references to this work are given in the text using page numbers alone.

[12] Inge Stephan, *Medea: Multimediale Karriere einer mythologischen Figur* (Cologne: Böhlau-Verlag, 2006), 179–81.

[13] Inge Stephan, *Musen und Medusen: Mythos und Geschlecht in der Literatur des 20. Jahrhunderts* (Cologne: Böhlau-Verlag, 1997), 147–55.

[14] Renate Berger and Inge Stephan, "Einleitung," in *Weiblichkeit und Tod in der Literatur*, ed. Renate Berger and Inge Stephan (Cologne: Böhlau-Verlag, 1987), 1–10, here 6–7.

[15] Goethe to Schiller, January 19, 1802, in Johann Wolfgang von Goethe, *Sämtliche Werke: Briefe, Tagebücher und Gespräche*, 40 vols., ed. Friedmar Apel, section 2, vol. 5:2, ed. Volker C. Dörr und Norbert Oellers (Frankurt am Main: Bibliothek deutscher Klassiker, 1999), 215.

[16] Ortrud Gutjahr, ed. *Ulrike Maria Stuart von Elfriede Jelinek* (Würzburg: Königshausen & Neumann, 2007).

[17] Katharina Plewny, "Ulrike Meinhofs Wiederkehr in Nicolaus Stemanns Inszenierung von Ulrike Maria Stuart," in *NachBilder der RAF*, ed. Inge Stephan and Alexandra Tacke (Cologne: Böhlau-Verlag, 2008), 106–20.

Part II.

Leadership as Social Activism around 1900

7: Age and Purpose: Unmarried Women and Female Agency in the Works of E. Marlitt and Hedwig Dohm

Lauren Nossett

IN THINKING ABOUT women and leadership, the question of age is paramount. After all, many of the most coveted positions of power are in the hands of older segments of the population. Specifically, old (white) men are the prime contenders for economic and political leadership positions while old women, and old unmarried women in particular, face a panoply of prejudicial notions that are designed to disempower them and keep them confined to dependent positions within the private sphere. Popular cultural stereotypes of "old maids," whose minds and hearts deteriorate in the absence of husbands and children, are rooted in the nineteenth century.[1] A subject of examination for physicians such as August Forel and Julius Weiss and sexologists such as Richard von Krafft-Ebing, the lifelong-single woman was represented as either sexually deviant, physically deficient, or both.[2] In her study of unmarried women in Imperial Germany, *The Surplus Woman*, historian Catherine L. Dollard examines the single woman as "a destabilizing force in turn-of-the-century gender norms." According to Dollard, the contemporary fears regarding a growing number of unmarried women did not reflect a demographic surfeit of unwed women but rather arose "as a consequence of the tensions and uncertainties that characterized an era of great social transformation."[3] Nevertheless, the anxiety concerning the illusory female surplus impregnated the German cultural imagination. Yet it is precisely because these women are not subordinated to a husband or limited by the duties of childcare that they are potentially available for participation in the public sphere.

What emerged in response to this prevailing unease about the role of single older women was a discourse of unique female contributions to the German state, especially in terms of what Ann Taylor Allen calls "spiritual motherhood," and, for more progressive writers, a critical reflection of a system that forced women into these dependent roles.[4] In this chapter I examine the agency of older unwed and widowed women in the works of two authors from this period: E. Marlitt (1825–87) and Hedwig Dohm

(1831–1919). Marlitt's popular novels propose a solution to the quandary about the usefulness of unmarried women and women past their repro- ductive age: unmarriageable sisters and older aunts serve as household managers, caretakers, and advisors to younger women in *Das Geheimnis der alten Mamsell* (1867, *The Old Maid's Secret,* 1871), *Die zweite Frau* (1874, *The Second Wife,* 1874), and *Die Frau mit den Karfunkelsteinen* (1885, *The Lady with the Rubies,* 1885). In *Werde, die Du bist!* (1894, *Become Who You Are,* 2006), Dohm's protagonist finds herself in a society that considers her useless: widowed, past childbearing years, and no lon- ger needed to help in childrearing, she searches for a purpose after a life devoted to the care of others. In the following, I explore the sexual and social discourse surrounding unmarried women in the nineteenth cen- tury and then turn to the representation of these women in the works of E. Marlitt and Hedwig Dohm. Although the authors vary starkly in their representations of an unmarried woman's role, their characters are not "surplus women" but rather women with passions outside the fam- ily, whose industry preserves family life, and whose prominent positions in the narratives challenge contemporary discourses of unwed and thus marginalized women. For both authors, fiction offers a realm where the many positive attributes and capabilities of older single women can be explored. Over the course of the narratives, these female characters act independently and make their own choices, displaying agency despite social pressures and customs that might otherwise limit an unmarried woman's free will. Yet neither author suggests direct participation in pub- lic leadership. Although men of the same age may occupy powerful lead- ership positions, these women are granted neither access to nor desire for such public leadership roles.

The Unmarried Woman in Nineteenth-Century Sexual and Social Discourse

The nineteenth-century physician Julius Weiss defines an "old maid" as a woman between the ages of thirty and menopause. "Die Jungfrau," he writes, "ist alt, wenn sie in das dreißigste Lebensjahr eintritt, und sie hat das Recht auf die Bezeichnung, 'alte Jungfer,' solange ihre Geschlechtsreife währt, solange sich allmonatlich reife Eichen vom Eierstocke loslösen und in die Gebärmutter wandeln, solange die monat- liche Regel vorhanden ist" (The virgin is old when she enters her thirtieth year, and she has the right to the designation "old maid," as long as her sexual maturity lasts, as long as mature little eggs detach from the ovary and migrate to the uterus every month, as long as the monthly men- struation occurs).[5] However, the tendency for "old maidenhood" could develop as early as a woman's mid-twenties, according to neurologist

Wilhelm Erb, who attributes early onset to heightened sexual desires and sexual frustration when those desires are not met.[6] A central focus of the nineteenth-century debate of woman's role in society, otherwise known as the "woman question," the surplus woman was predominantly viewed as a middle-class problem. Where single life drove the proletarian woman to satisfy carnal impulses through prostitution, according to sociologist Robert Michels, it resulted in frustrated sexual desire and bitter silence for the unmarried bourgeois woman.[7] From masturbation and homosexuality, to abnormally developed female sexual parts and deviant thoughts rejecting societal demands for marriage,[8] reasons for female abstention from marriage were the cause of much speculation at the turn of the twentieth century. In these theories, the idea that a single woman might desire a life of public, social, or individual activity outside of and beyond sexual reproduction is inconceivable.

Economic and social concerns about the alleged female surplus in Germany fueled this sexual discourse. The debate surrounding the surplus woman was "uniquely German," according to Dollard, who asserts that the surplus woman "was a cultural icon of the *Kaiserreich*" (6 and 21). The perceived overabundance of unmarried women coincided with advancements of industrialization and urbanization, which eliminated many housekeeping functions and left unmarried single women to occupy "marginal positions in the home, church, and workplace," according to Martha Vicinus (3).[9] Once suspected of witchcraft, prostitution, and other immoral acts, unmarried women in the nineteenth century were accused of a new vice: idleness (*Surplus Woman*, 24). Yet Dollard shows that the surplus woman was more a figure of the imagination than a manifestation of a real population crisis: although German marriage rates declined significantly—more than 25 percent—over the course of the 1870s, the greatest concern arose at the turn-of-the-century, when marriage rates were relatively stable (*Surplus Woman*, 71–73).[10] Therefore, Dollard argues that "while there may have been a slight increase in the female surplus among the urban middle class, the *Frauenüberschuß* of Imperial Germany was far more a rhetorical signifier of anxieties regarding social and cultural change than a verifiable demographic event" (*Surplus Woman*, 71). After all, in the absence of household chores and childrearing, single women with too much time on their hands might set their sight on public functions.

At stake in the rhetoric of "old maids" and "surplus women" is the definition of woman and her role in the German family and state. In Germany, woman, or "Frau," is synonymous with wife. "Mann" is both man and husband. To be an adult is to be married.[11] And at the turn of the century, to be a married adult was to be a productive and reproductive member of the heterosexual family. The unmarried adult, but specifically, the unmarried woman, challenged the security of the family and, by extension, the stability of the German state. In her study of colonial emigration of unmarried British women, Rita Kranidis poses a question relevant to my analysis: "If the middle-class Victorian woman's value was seen to lie in her perfect domestication, and if the unmarried working-class woman's value in her sexuality, then the middle-class emigrant spinster emerges as a hybrid: Where might her value reside?"[12] Kranidis argues that in colonial England the spinster is commodified as an export: she is a woman sent abroad for her useful labor and practical value.[13] We find similar rhetoric in the discourse of German women's associations such as the Allgemeiner Deutscher Frauenverein (General German Women's Association, ADF) and later the Bund Deutscher Frauenvereine (Federation of German Women's Associations, BDF), who frame women's aptitude for labor outside the home in terms of spiritual motherhood. In the German context, however, the unmarried woman applies these traits not abroad but at home for the betterment of the German state. Rather than demonize unmarried women as sexually deviant or idle, the doctrine of spiritual motherhood posited that the very nature of women suited them to social work that drew on "feminine" qualities of self-sacrifice, care, and nurture. Thus single women could carry out maternal duties unrealized in the family for the good of society as a whole. At the same time, the concept of spiritual motherhood kept them safely anchored in the realm of traditional female activities and thus barred these women from finding other, potentially more powerful and public, outlets for their energy. In the fiction of E. Marlitt and Hedwig Dohm, unmarried female characters possess traits of spiritual motherhood; however, as I explore below, Marlitt positions her characters primarily as caregivers and household managers, reinscribing their value within the family even as the narratives indicate these characters are capable of much more, while Dohm questions the individual cost of such a life spent in the service of others.

Industrious Old Maids: Unmarried Aunts and Sisters in E. Marlitt's Fiction

In the late nineteenth century Friederike Christiane Henriette Eugenie John, who published under the pen name "E. Marlitt," achieved international fame for her novels, which were serialized in Ernst Keil's popular German magazine *Die Gartenlaube* (The Garden Bower), published in multiple editions, translated, and disseminated to readers as far away as North America and China. Marlitt's novels, like the numerous etiquette books and pedagogical fiction from this period, are designed to indoctrinate female readers with concepts of virtue and self-sacrifice and prepare them for a life of marriage and motherhood. Her fiction, therefore, centers on young virginal heroines.[14] Yet these heroines, barely older than children themselves, are guided in their journeys to adulthood by so-called old maids, unmarried sisters, and aunts. The central roles of Tante Cordula in *Das Geheimnis der alten Mamsell*, Ulrike in *Die zweite Frau*, and Tante Sophie in *Die Frau mit den Karfunkelsteinen* within Marlitt's narratives offer alternatives to the marital trajectory of the novels and challenge the prevailing discourse surrounding older, unmarried women in two significant ways: first, these characters are not idle; they do not abstain from work, but rather are industrious, active, and pragmatic women: and second, they do not attach themselves to men, pursue romantic relationships, or become bitter and waste away from unfulfilled romantic or maternal desires. Instead, they develop intellectual passions. Although their good deeds and caregiving align with the doctrine of spiritual motherhood and largely confine them to the private realm, they discover pleasure and fulfillment in hobbies or paid work. Herself a lifelong-single woman, Marlitt proposes a compromise in her novels between contemporary social expectations of unmarried bourgeois women and the recognition of these women's abilities. On one hand, the novels value older single women and their contributions to their larger community; on the other, they locate their activities in the home and not in the public sphere.

Cordula Hellwig, Ulrike von Trachenberg, and Sophie Lamprecht are three of many unmarried female characters in Marlitt's fiction. Others include the "Seejungfer" (virgin of the lake), Susanna Hartmann, who appears in Marlitt's first published work "Die zwölf Apostel" (1865, The Twelve Apostles); the ailing Helene von Walde in *Goldelse* (1866, *Gold Elsie*, 1871), whose illness prevents her from marriage and positions her as a receiver of care, not as an active participant in the household; and the widowed Frau Hofräthin Falk in "Der Blaubart" (1866, Bluebeard), who cares for the daughter of a friend, in addition to providing charity to the poor and distressed. I have chosen to focus on the three characters named above because they are middle- to upper-class lifelong-single women who play crucial roles in their narratives.

In Marlitt's 1868 novel *Das Geheimnis der alten Mamsell*, the "old maid" Cordula Hellwig is banished to the upper stories of the house by her nephew's wife, the pious Frau Hellwig. However, she is no "madwoman in the attic."[15] Rather, she is godly without religious prejudices, generous without recognition, and skilled in healing. Only a century before she might have been considered a witch—and in fact, her grand-nephew calls her one—but she is the most honorable character in the novel. Despite living in the same house, Cordula and the young heroine Felicitas do not encounter each other until the death of the *pater familias*, Herr Hellwig. Not only are the physical similarities between nephew and aunt striking, but Cordula also takes over his tutelage of Felicitas when Frau Hellwig refuses to continue her education. She preserves German culture, extends charity to the poor, and provides Felicitas with the intellectual tools to argue for her own education and reject the class-based limitations Frau Hellwig sets for her. But Cordula, as the novel's title indicates, has a secret: she knows the Hellwig family's wealth is built on theft and deception. Marlitt endows her not only with this knowledge, but also the control of the family inheritance and the determination to see it distributed fairly after her death. As I will explore in *Die zweite Frau* and *Die Frau mit den Karfunkelsteinen*, the administration of money is crucial to Marlitt's unmarried female characters' retaining independence and influence within households where they might otherwise be viewed as financial burdens on the family resources. Additionally, in the absence of capable patriarchs, these unmarried women take on important leadership roles in their respective households.

Although still of reproductive age and not relegated to an attic, the Countess Ulrike von Trachenberg in Marlitt's 1874 novel *Die zweite Frau* is the unmarried sister and trustworthy confidante of the heroine Liane. Ugly, with stiff red hair and a broad nose, Ulrike is, in Marlitt's world, unmarriageable. After the death of her father she manages the household finances to the chagrin of her mother, who calls her "der böse Geist" (evil genius) of her household.[16] Like Cordula, Ulrike is educated and cultured, and she understands the law. And it is Ulrike to whom Liane looks for solace in her loveless marriage, to whom she and her husband turn for advice, and when Liane falls ill, it is Ulrike, "das häßliche Mädchen mit dem besonnenen, willenskräftigen Kopfe und dem Herzen voll zärtlicher, aufopfernder Mutterliebe." (the homely girl with her clear wise head and her heart full of self-sacrificing maternal love),[17] who nurtures her back to health. On one hand, Ulrike fulfills contemporary expectations of the unmarried bourgeois daughter: she selflessly arranges her life to provide support for her family. On the other, she possesses more control of the Trachenberg finances than either her childish mother or bookish brother. Like Cordula, Ulrike's financial prudence makes her a key player within a family where she otherwise would be rendered superfluous. And it is her wisdom and industry that save the familial home from the creditors.

Of all Marlitt's unmarried female characters, Tante Sophie, in the last novel published before Marlitt's death in 1887, *Die Frau mit den Karfunkelsteinen* (1885), is the most central to the novel's narrative. She cares for the children of the widowed Herr Lamprecht and manages his household. Not, in fact, an aunt, but rather a distant unmarried cousin, Sophie considers being an old maid the "klügsten Einfall ihres ganzen Lebens" (greatest piece of wisdom of her life) and keeps the Lamprecht household running despite rumors of ghosts, marital intrigue, and torrential storms that threaten to tear both family and house apart.[18] Like the Hellwig and Trachenberg families, the Lamprecht family also faces an absence of male authority. The master of the house, Herr Lamprecht, is distracted by his secret marriage. His son, who lacks paternal guidance, is greedy, petulant, and equally inept at managing the household after his father's death. Like Cordula and Ulrike, Sophie emerges to fill this gap in male leadership. She is clearly the best suited to be in charge: "in ihrem hellen Kopfe waren Familientraditionen, alte Geschäfts- und Tagebuchnotizen und die verschiedenen, oft kuriosen Nachlaßverfügungen so pünktlich registriert, wie sie kaum der Archivar einer Regentenfamilie in den Annalen sammelt" (6; in her clear head family traditions, old business announcements, and diaries, and sometimes curious testamentary dispositions, were all registered and arranged with more exactitude than is sometimes shown by the keeper of the archives of a royal family, 8). "For the reader," as Kirsten Belgum observes, "the older woman is a model of optimism, rationality, good humor, and feminine independence."[19] Not only does Sophie eradicate superstition with laughter and oversee the children's lessons, but she also possesses a house of her own and complete financial independence from the Lamprecht family.

These maternal, unmarried characters have much in common: they are educated, prudent, and wise, and also capable of so much more than they are entrusted with within the novels. Moreover, they conform to one of the three dominant *alter Jungfer* (old maid) types in the nineteenth century according to novelist and Marlitt's fellow *Gartenlaube* contributor Adelheid Weber: the hateful shrew, the helpless romantic, and the caregiving aunt. Weber frames the qualities of this aunt within her positive household role:

Unser lieber Schutzengel, zu dem wir Kinder unsere Risse und Flecken, zu dem wir jungen Mädchen unsere Herzensnöte trugen und der Bruder Studio seinen leeren Geldbeutel, und unsere Mutter ihre Haushaltungs- und Kindersorgen. Und die für uns alle Nadel und Fleckwasser, Trost und Verständnis, einen Notgroschen, guten Rat und vor allem ein liebes Wort hatte. Tante Gustchen, die das Leben so ganz überwunden hatte, daß sie es nur noch in andern lebte, die einem guten Geist so nahe war, wie nur eine ganz einsame Frau mit einem sehr großen Herzen es nach bitterem Leben werden kann.[20]

[Our dear guardian angel, to whom we children brought our cuts and bruises, to whom we young girls bore our hearts' needs, and the studying brother brought his empty pocket book, and our mother her household and child care concerns. And who had for all of us needle and stain remover, comfort and understanding, a penny in a time of need, good advice, and above all, a loving word. Aunt Gustchen, who had overcome life so entirely that she lived it only in others, who was as close to a good spirit as only a completely lonely woman with a very big heart can become after a bitter life.]

Among representations of single women, this caregiving aunt alone is "partially saved," Dollard suggests, "for through her good works she earned a place in the domestic sphere" (34). Indeed, in Marlitt's novels, unmarried women do not fear spinsterhood; rather, they desire to make themselves useful in their residences and either take up domestic employment to supplement their allowances or devote their labor and existing wealth to charity. Tante Cordula sews clothing for the poor, gives generously from her own funds, and supplements Felicitas's education with lessons. Ulrike manufactures artificial flowers, which she sells anonymously in Berlin to support her impoverished aristocratic family. Tante Sophie runs the house of Herr Lamprecht "mit fleißigen Händen, in Zucht und Ehren und weiser Sparsamkeit" (8; with busy hands, strict discipline, and a wise economy, 9) and distributes fruit from her own garden to the sick and needy. In her study of bachelors and old maids, Katrin Baumgarten observes that while the feminine virtues of devotion and warmth may belong to the young protagonists in Marlitt's novels, the charms of goodness, mildness, and sacrifice are manifest not only in marriage but also in the philanthropic foundation of these unmarried women.[21] Both Baumgarten and Belgum represent the importance of these characters largely through the assistance they offer the young heroines. But where Belgum views these figures as "truly radical feminist role models,"[22] Baumgarten does not see Marlitt's unmarried characters as having central roles in their narratives, but rather as modest, silent, and inconspicuous women,[23] a description that fails to capture the proud, piano-playing Cordula, the business-minded Ulrike, and the energetic, quick-witted Sophie. In Marlitt's world, the bourgeois family does not function without the invaluable labor, advice, and care of these women.

These characters may resemble in part the caregiving aunt Weber describes, but they are not represented as lonely women, nor are they eager to enter the state of holy matrimony. Despite claims in essays such as Schopenhauer's 1851 "Über die Weiber" ("On Women," 1872) that a woman needs a man to rule her, either a lover in her youth or a priest in her old age,[24] and pronouncements in turn-of-the-century advice books, such as Tony Schumacher's *Vom Schulmädel bis zur Grossmutter* (1900, From School Girl to Grandmother), that "kein Mädchen . . . hat nicht eine Zeit gehabt, wo es sich nicht als Braut, als Gattin und Mutter dachte" (No girl has not had a time when she did not think of herself as a bride, a wife, and a mother),[25] few Marlitt women are particularly keen to marry, nor do they attach themselves to men (neither husband nor priest). Indeed, in the examples given here, only Cordula gives any indication of a romantic drive: her love, whom she was forbidden to marry because of class differences, dies and she remains single. And yet these women do not vegetate as useless old maids,[26] but rather find enjoyment in activity and personal hobbies. Cordula's tidy, dust-free apartment with its brightly polished pianoforte brims with chirping birds and flowerbeds, busts of great composers, and ancient books, in which she takes delight. Her pleasure and purpose stem from these books: she is the keeper of knowledge and the collector of rare manuscripts and autographs of celebrated composers, including Handel, Gluck, Haydn, and Mozart. Ulrike shows no interest in marriage and instead converts the hostelry of the family estate into an extensive flower manufactory. Sophie is perhaps the most radical of these figures in that she, unlike the other characters, expressly chooses to be a lifelong-single woman.[27] Her courtyard room, like Cordula's attic apartment, is neat, homelike, and overflowing with her favorite flowers. The connection of flowers with these lifelong-single women turns the flower metaphor for female sexuality and beauty on its head: rather than Schopenhauer's vision of vegetating old maids, Marlitt's unmarried female characters are in full bloom, blossoming with life. These women are content outside of the traditional realm of marriage. They are also pragmatic and competent, with skills that should qualify them for public life, but Marlitt stops short of giving them responsibilities beyond the family.

The Active Old Woman in Hedwig Dohm's *Werde, die Du bist!*

Hedwig Dohm authored numerous polemics on women's emancipation, comedies for the theater, the novella *Werde, die Du bist!* (1894, *Become Who You Are*, 2006), and the novels *Sibilla Dalmar* (1896), *Schicksale einer Seele* (1899, Fates of a Soul), and *Christa Ruland* (1902). Her writings criticize anti-feminists, Nietzsche, and the gendered location of women. Her essays and fiction are extremely progressive for the nineteenth century and offer a contrast to Marlitt's optimistic vision of the role of an older unmarried woman in the family. Written in 1894, Dohm's novella *Werde, die Du bist!*, represents a woman's attempt to find agency and purpose after the marriages of her daughters and her husband's death. A life of self-sacrifice and subordination of personal desire has left the mid-fifties protagonist Agnes Schmidt unsure whether she has a right to live for herself or at all. Widowed, she shares two key traits with the "old maid": first, she is unmarried with no intention of remarrying; and second, she risks being deemed a dependent, surplus member of society. Yet Agnes also offers an interesting contrast to the lifelong-single women in Marlitt's fiction: the caregiving and labor that position Marlitt's unmarried figures as necessary members of the family consume Agnes's married life to such an extent that she does not develop her intellectual and spiritual passions until her widowed years. At the height of concerns about surplus and dependent women, Dohm does not highlight the domestic contributions of her heroine or insist she have any use-value at all; instead, she examines the interiority and activity of the unmarried, widowed woman.

In the short passages that frame the narrative, we observe Agnes Schmidt from the point of view of the doctors at a sanatorium, where she has lived for two years. These doctors know her as the widow of the Privy Councilor Schmidt, who prior to her husband's death was a "gute, brave, etwas beschränkte und philiströse Hausfrau . . . unwissend und völlig im Familienleben aufgehend" (good, well-mannered, somewhat limited and philistine housewife, ignorant and totally absorbed with family life).[28] Her journal, which she gives her doctor to read and which makes up the heart of the narrative, confirms this assessment of her married life. And yet, as Ruth-Ellen Boetcher Joeres and Abigail Dunn point out, Agnes's depiction of her childhood and marriage accounts for only nine pages, while her portrayal of her life after her husband's death occupies sixty-four.[29] By devoting the breadth of the novella to Agnes's widowhood, Dohm ascribes significance to her unmarried years.

Riddled with self-doubt—"Erzählenswerthes in meinem Leben? Giebt es das? Und was wäre das?" (161; Something worth telling in my life? Is there anything? And what would that be?, 9)—Agnes's writings reflect a woman learning the sound of her own voice and finding the shape of her own thoughts. She asks—seemingly for the first time—whether she lived the life she desired and even what those desires might be. At the beginning, self-censorship abounds. "Quiet!" she scolds herself when she doubts the value of her existence (161).[30] To help her imagine her identity as a single woman, she starts with the self-before-marriage, the child Agnes, and insists she was happy and led a full life. Yet even her life as a child was marked by self-sacrifice. The only joy she is allowed is reading—interestingly enough—Marlitt novels on Sundays and eating apple cake with whipped cream on holidays (163). But this love of Marlitt novels, with their contented marriages and happy endings, in no way prepares her for her own loveless marriage.

Her childhood ends with a four-year engagement, during which she sews her trousseau, learns to cook, and is groomed for her role as wife and mother. What follows is a monotonous, lonely life with a husband whom she calls a total bureaucrat (164). She describes her thirty-three-year marriage as "wolkenlos" (164; cloudless, 12), but only because she arranged her husband's life so that everything was as he wished, subordinated her desires to his demands, and bore him two healthy daughters. She anticipates a reprieve when her daughters are grown, only to become completely immersed in finding them appropriate husbands. Once her daughters marry, Agnes sets her hopes on travel. Her desire is thwarted again, this time by her husband's illness. For eight years he demands her total care, insisting his meals be prepared by her hands and becoming dissatisfied if she leaves his sickroom (167). Her devotion to this slow-dying husband is such that she does not meet her four grandchildren who were born over the course of these eight years.

When Agnes finally visits her daughters, she feels superfluous in their lives, intimidated by the women they have become, and unnerved by the insistence of her daughters and sons-in-law on calling her "Mämmchen" and "Mamachen": "als nähme man die Mutter nicht ernsthaft, nur so wie eine drollige Alte" (173; As if they didn't take their mother seriously, only as a comical, old woman, 18). Her eating habits are the subject of jokes, so that she limits her food consumption, only to become faint. During social events she is relegated to the backrooms with the children, where she is further humiliated. The children call her "Großmämmchen," tattle on her for eating cookies, and assign her the role of the enemy in their games of war. One child insists that she must not be obeyed because she is "nur eine Wittwe" (175; just a widow, 20). To which Agnes reflects: "Weises Kind. Eine Wittwe, das heißt: Dein Mann ist todt. Du bist mit ihm begraben" (175; Wise child. A widow, that means: your husband is dead. You've been buried with him, 20). This living death of an old woman is a leitmotif of the novella;[31] and in Dohm's 1903 essay, "Die alte Frau" ("The Old Woman," 2006), the state of an old woman is compared to being interred while living.[32]

The advice of the older, unmarried woman, so valuable in Marlitt's novels, is discouraged by Agnes's daughters, either as outdated or as contradicting the wishes of their husbands. Agnes's maternal knowledge on child illness is met with remonstrations: "Bitte, Mama," they say, "nur nichts Medicinisches" (176; Please, mamma, anything but medicine, 20). On education for girls: "Nur nichts über Erziehung, dann noch lieber Medicinisches" (176; Anything but education, then preferably medicine, 20–21). "Ein alter Mann," Agnes observes,

> ist er weise, kenntnißreich, gut, edelsinnig, er wird nach seinem Werth geschätzt . . . Spräche und dächte aber eine lebendige alte Frau das Weiseste und Edelste, es wäre in den Wind gesprochen. Und wer freundlich über sie urtheilt, sagt: schade, daß sie nicht jünger ist. (189)

> [An old man if he is wise, knowledgeable, good, noble-minded, is valued according to his worth. . . . However, if a living, old woman were to speak or think the wisest and noblest things, it would be spoken into the wind. And whoever judges her in a friendly way, says: too bad that she isn't younger. (30)

Given her age and experience, Agnes could offer guidance, but her knowledge and wisdom are not recognized as a resource for the family and society.

Charlotte Woodford suggests that in her marriage, Agnes Schmidt "was defined by her reproductive body" and that after the death of her husband she cannot "see any social value in her aging body."[33] I would add that Agnes was defined not only by her reproductive body but also by the labor and knowledge of her body. In Marlitt's novels the usefulness and wisdom of lifelong-single women suggest that these women are not surplus but rather integral to the prosperity of the family and society as a whole. Although Agnes's exertions as a wife and mother contribute to the success of her family, *Werde, die Du bist!* points to the rather glaring gap in this arrangement: if the family, the larger community, and even the woman herself, fail to recognize the value of these contributions, the older woman becomes superfluous.

After her husband's death, Agnes returns to the life she knows: incessant household labor. She embroiders clothes for her grandchildren, only to discover they are no longer fashionable. She gives unwanted maternal advice, overwaters plants, dusts furniture that has already been dusted, and discovers in the mirror that she has become an old woman. When she returns to the novels she once loved, she finds no pleasure in them. Her dismissal of bourgeois literature, with its restrictive ideology of femininity, can be read as a rejection of the ideology and trajectory of the bourgeoisie itself. Unlike the bourgeois novel, Dohm's novella and her protagonist's journey to self-discovery do not end with marriage but rather begin with her widowhood. Like Marlitt's characters, Agnes finds autonomy through financial independence. When she inherits ten thousand deutsche Mark from an old relative, Agnes, contrary to the wishes of her son-in-law, decides to spend the money on herself. She desires to travel and to rid herself of the "kleine Hausfrauenseele" (196; small housewife soul, 35) in favor of the *Weltseele* (world soul).

Agnes is an "alte Mignon" (172; old Mignon, 18) who dreams of Italy. The allusions to both *Wilhelm Meisters Lehrjahre* (1795–96, *Wilhelm Meister's Apprenticeship*, 1824) and her own *Italienische Reise* (1816–17, *Goethe's Travels in Italy*, 1883) establish Agnes Schmidt within a German literary tradition that harks back to Goethe. Her journey to self-discovery, her *Bildung*, happens at the ripe age of fifty-four. During her travels she has visions, feels herself alternately old and youthful, and falls in love with a young doctor. But this love, she knows, is transgressive. A seventy-year-old Goethe in love with a young woman may be admired for his "Gemüthskraft" (mental strength), but her own passions will be deemed "erotisch wahnsinnig" (230; erotically insane, 61). When the doctor, moved by the sight of her on a cliff like a great poetess, throws a bouquet of myrtles to her, she weaves them into a wreath. Yet when asked about the "Sappho" at dinner, he calls Agnes "Großmutter Psyche," a remark he instantly regrets and the unfortunate Agnes overhears (234). Although this unrequited love results in Agnes's institutionalization, the encounter, like her childhood and marriage, occupies only a few pages of her journal. The text remains focused on her self-reflection and discovery of her unmarried identity. At the end of the novella, Agnes Schmidt dies in the sanatorium wearing the myrtle crown with a drop of blood on her forehead. Despite being moved by the old woman's diary, the doctor finds no use in it for his own research. Agnes's written account of her life, like her biblically imbued death, her sacrificial labor, and maternal advice, is given no social or scientific value within this frame. Instead, Agnes's purpose exists outside societal norms, the family, and her role as a caregiver. Before giving the doctor her journal, she asks whether women who die perish like the poor thief on the cross or like Jesus, in the service of others. She answers that such women die for other women (159). In the presence of male doctors and absence of her daughters, we can only assume that her death is for her female readers. She transgresses the gender expectations of her time and, like the heroines of late eighteenth-century bourgeois tragedies, does not survive the novella. But her transgression is spiritual, not sexual. She has lived, traveled, and loved for herself and after marriage. Her death, with its heavy-handed Christian symbolism, suggests that she dies so that others might live. During her travels, Agnes writes: "Was in mir erlöst sein will, zugleich will es Andere erlösen" (209; Whatever it is in me that wants to be freed wants at the same time to free others, 45). Freedom for Agnes, as Charlotte Woodford and Anna Richards argue, lies outside of the old woman's reproductive and now aged body.[34] This emancipation from the body originates in death, according to Ruth-Ellen Boetcher Joeres.[35] However, Agnes does not have to die to escape the limitations patriarchal society sets for older women: her first taste of freedom comes when she rejects familial expectations and spends her inheritance on travel rather than giving it to her son-in-law and submitting herself to economic dependence. Freed from economic and familial constraints, Agnes discovers her *joie de vivre* once she liberates herself from the bonds of the family and her role as wife, mother, and grandmother. Her death, then, represents both a martyrdom for old women and female agency.

Dohm writes in "Die alte Frau": "War das Weib untauglich geworden zur Gebärerin Kinderpflegerin und Geliebten, so hörte ihre Existenzberechtigung auf" (204; When a woman becomes incapable of being a bearer of and caretaker of children, or a lover, then her justification for existence has ceased, 67). Superfluous in the nursery, unwelcome in the salon, and disdained by older men, the old woman is criticized for dressing too young, seen as ridiculous for riding horses, and too fearful to attend a university lecture for the scornful looks of young men. A society that measures a woman by her sexual appeal and utility grants her no use-value past her married years. Even as her contributions are rejected, she is accused of idleness. Yet despite popular assertions of laziness, the pejorative terms used to define older, single women closely align the unmarried woman with her labor: the term "spinster" is derived from a female spinner of wool.[36] And the German "Magd," like the English maid, means both "virgin" and "domestic servant." Lifelong-single women laboring within the household, Marlitt's unmarried characters are indeed "old maids." Similarly, Dohm's Agnes Schmidt does not idle away her old age and unmarried years but rather seeks purpose: first in the domestic tasks that defined her married life, and then in excursions to the theater and galleries, travel, and the search for herself. Physical and mental activity save Dohm's "old woman" from an early death. The old woman must reject social perceptions of age and discourses of use-values, old maids, and spiritual motherhood. Instead, Dohm argues, she must take her fate in her own hands. She ends her essay with a call to arms to the older woman:

> Andauerndes Schaffen, sei es mit Hand oder Kopf, wird, wie das Öl die Maschine, ihre Nerven- und Gehirnkräfte elastisch erhalten und ihr eine geistige Langlebigkeit verbürgen weit über die Jahre hinaus, die bisher für sie den Abschied vom Leben bedeuteten. Unthätigkeit ist der Schlaftrunk, den man Dir, alte Frau, reicht. Trink ihn nicht! Sei Etwas! Schaffen ist Freude. Und Freude ist fast Jugend. (224)

> [Incessant activity, be it with hand or head, will—like oil for a machine—keep the strength of her nerves and brain elastic and will guarantee her mental longevity far beyond the years that until now meant the farewell from life for her. Inactivity is the sleeping potion that you, old woman, are offered. Do not drink it! Be something! Activity is joy. And joy is almost youth. (79)]

Neither family nor society may appreciate her contributions or grant her public leadership roles, but Dohm argues that the old woman must keep active and possess agency for herself.

Conclusion: The Subversive Agency of Unmarried Women

Marlitt and Dohm's unmarried characters are not comical figures like Gotthold Ephraim Lessing's *Die alte Jungfer* (1749; *The Old Maid*, 1878), nor are they demonized and sexualized like Eduard Grisebach's Chinese widow Tien-sche in *Die treulose Witwe* (1873; The Faithless Widow). Nor do they cultivate relationships with their pets, as contemporary sexologists and physicians suggest, sink into bitterness and despair, or while away their time at the expense of the productive nuclear family. Far from idle, virgin aunts and sisters run households, cultivate knowledge, and educate young women. They are not "surplus women," but rather women integral to the family's success, whose prominent positions in these works of fiction challenge contemporary discourses of marginal unwed or widowed women. And yet, despite having much to offer, they are not appreciated by society at large and do not qualify for any of the prominent leadership roles frequently occupied by older men. At best, they are active and valued participants in the familial household; at worst, they are considered redundant once they are past reproductive age. However, they are older women with agency and desire outside or after marriage and childbearing. In this way, they are subversive figures in nineteenth-century Germany: single women who possess passion and purpose independent of husbands and children.

Notes

[1] English essayist William Rathbone Greg writes of "old maids with just enough income to live upon, but wretched and deteriorating, their minds narrowing, and their hearts withering, because they have nothing to do, and none to love, cherish, and obey," in *Why Are Women Redundant?* (London: N. Trübner, 1869), 6. First published in *National Review* 14 (1862): 434–60.

[2] In this chapter I borrow the term "lifelong singlewomen" from Maryanne Kowaleski to describe adult women who never marry and to distinguish these women from women who marry at later ages, widows, and nuns; see her essay "Singlewomen in Medieval and Early Modern Europe: The Demographic Perspective," in *Singlewomen in the European Past, 1250–1800*, ed. Judith M. Bennett and Amy M. Froide (Philadelphia: University of Pennsylvania Press, 201), 39–40.

[3] Catherine L. Dollard, *The Surplus Woman: Unmarried in Imperial Germany, 1871–1918* (New York: Berghahn Books, 2009), 7. Further references are given in the text using the short title *Surplus Woman*. For additional studies of unmarried women in the nineteenth century, see Katrin Baumgarten, *Hagestolz und Alte Jungfer: Entwicklung, Instrumentalisierung und Fortleben von Klischees und Stereotypen über Unverheiratetgebliebene* (Münster: Waxmann, 1997); Martha Vicinus, *Independent Women: Work and Community for Single Women, 1850–1920* (Chicago: University of Chicago Press, 1988); Rita S. Kranidis, *The Victorian Spinster and Colonial Emigration: Contested Subjects* (Basingstoke, UK: Macmillan, 1999); and Bärbel Kuhn, *Familienstand: Ledig; Ehelose Frauen und Männer im Bürgertum (1850–1914)* (Cologne: Böhlau, 2000).

[4] According to Allen, the argument that "woman's special talent for nurture would benefit not only her immediate family but a society which they perceived as sorely in need of the enlightened and compassionate female influence" (319) was central to the nineteenth-century German feminist argument for women's participation in the public sphere. See Ann Taylor Allen, "Spiritual Motherhood:

German Feminists and the Kindergarten Movement, 1848–1911," *History of Education Quarterly* 22, no. 3 (August 1982): 319–39.

[5] Julius Weiss, "Das Weib als alte Jungfer," in *Mann und Weib: Ihre Beziehungen zueinander und zum Kulturleben der Gegenwart*, ed. Robby Koßmann and Julius Weiss, 416–23 (Stuttgart: Union Deutsche Verlagsgesellschaft, 1908), 420. All translations in this chapter are my own except where otherwise noted.

[6] Wilhelm Erb, "Bemerkungen über die Folgen der sexuellen Abstinenz," in *Zeitschrift für Bekämpfung der Geschlechtskrankheiten*, ed. A. Blaschko, E. Lesser, and A. Neifser, 1–18 (Leipzig: Johann Ambrosius Barth, 1904), 10.

[7] Robert Michels, "Die Dirne als die 'alte Jungfer' des Proletariats und die Prostitution," in *Mutterschutz: Zeitschrift zur Reform der sexuellen Ethik*, ed. Helene Stöcker, 58–65 (Frankfurt am Main: J. D. Sauerländer, 1905), 59.

[8] See August H. Forel, *The Sexual Question: A Scientific, Psychological, Hygienic and Sociological Study for the Cultured Classes*, trans. Charles F. Marshall (London: Rebman, 1908), 226; Richard von Krafft-Ebing, *Psychopathia Sexualis: With Especial Reference to Contrary Sexual Instinct; A Medico-Legal Study*, trans. Charles G. Chaddock (Philadelphia: F. A. Davis, 1893), 429; and Weiss, "Das Weib als alte Jungfer," 418–19.

[9] Vicinus, *Independent Women*, 3.

[10] Compared with earlier centuries, the number of unmarried women in the nineteenth century is neither unique nor particularly striking. In the centuries between 1250 and 1800, for example, single women made up 10 to 20 percent of all adult women in Europe (Kowaleski, *Singlewomen*, 39). In some places, such as Zurich in the fifteenth century (1467), more than 40 percent of all adult women were single (46).

[11] Marriage, as Bennett and Froide observe, is so closely tied to adulthood that in many European languages the terms for husband and wife are also the terms for "adult male" and "adult female" (1). Indeed, the terms "Jungfrau," "Jungfer," and "Fräulein," associating female youth with virginity, were once applied to all unmarried woman. The term "alte Jungfer," designating the mature single woman, reflects a deviance from the norm.

[12] Kranidis, *Victorian Spinster*, 174.

[13] Kranidis, *Victorian Spinster*, 175.

[14] See examples of these heroines analyzed in Lauren Nossett, "Bad Mothers and Good Virgins: Gender, Identity, and Maternity in the Novels of E. Marlitt," *Women in German Yearbook* 31 (2015): 28–47.

[15] Here I refer to both the character Bertha Mason, the wife of Edward Rochester in Charlotte Brontë's *Jane Eyre* (1847), who is imprisoned by her husband in an attic apartment and described as violently insane, and Sandra M. Gilbert and Susan Gubar's book *The Madwoman in the Attic: The Woman Writer and the Nineteenth-Century Literary Imagination* (New Haven: Yale University Press, 2000), in which she examines the angel/monster dichotomy of female characters in Victorian fiction.

[16] Unless otherwise stated, all in-text references to E. Marlitt's *Die zweite Frau* refer to *Die zweite Frau: Roman in zwei Bänden; Erster Band und Zweiter Band*

(Leipzig: Ernst Keil. 1874), here 1:63. English translations are quoted from E. Marlitt, *The Second Wife: A Romance*, trans. A. L. Wister (Philadelphia: J. B. Lippincott, 1874); here, 38.

[17] Marlitt, *Die zweite Frau*, 226; Marlitt, *The Second Wife*, 298. Although A. L. Wister translates "häßliche" as "homely," "ugly" is a more accurate translation.

[18] Unless otherwise stated, all in-text references to E. Marlitt's *Die Frau mit den Karfunkelsteinen* refer to *Die Frau mit den Karfunkelsteinen* (Leipzig: Ernst Keil's Nachfolger, 1885), here 1:8. English translations are quoted from E. Marlitt, *The Lady with the Rubies*, trans. A. L. Wister (Philadelphia: J. B. Lippincott, 1885), here 10. Further references to this work are given in the text, using page numbers alone.

[19] Kirsten Belgum, "E. Marlitt: Narratives of Virtuous Desire," in *A Companion to German Realism, 1848–1900*, ed. Todd C. Kontje, 259–82 (Rochester, NY: Camden House, 2002), 272. This article owes a great deal to Belgum's article on E. Marlitt's narratives, in which she points out that these previously neglected characters are worthy of attention (272).

[20] Adelheid Weber, "Die alte Jungfer von einst und das reife Mädchen von heut," in "Die Welt der Frau," supplement, *Die Gartenlaube* 39 (1906): 610.

[21] Baumgarten, *Hagestolz*, 139.

[22] Belgum, "Narratives of Virtuous Desire," 272.

[23] Baumgarten, *Hagestolz*, 127.

[24] Arthur Schopenhauer, "Über die Weiber," in *Schopenhauer's Sämmtliche Werke, in Fünf Bänden*, vol. 5 (Leipzig: Inselverlag, 1860).

[25] Tony Schumacher, *Vom Schulmädel bis zur Grossmutter* (Stuttgart: Deutsche Verlags-Anstalt, 1900), 195.

[26] "als unnütze, alte Jungfern vegetiren" as Schopenhauer writes in "Über die Weiber" (678).

[27] Baumgarten observes that in Marlitt's narratives old maidenhood is never self-inflicted but rather a result of personal or family tragedies that make marriage impossible because the women themselves are either "grundhäßlich" or "körperlich mißgebildet" (*Hagestolz*, 127; extremely ugly or physically deformed). The former argument explains the unmarried state of Cordula, the latter that of Ulrike, but neither applies to Sophie.

[28] Unless otherwise stated, all quotes from Hedwig Dohm's *Werde, die Du bist* are taken from Hedwig Dohm, "Werde, die Du bist!" in *Wie Frauen werden: Werde, die du bist* (Breslau: Schlesische Buchdruckerei, Kunst- und Verlags-Anstalt v. S. Schottlaender, 1894), 151–236, here 151. Also available at Prose Fiction 26; https://scholarsarchive.byu.edu/sophiefiction/26. English translations are quoted from Hedwig Dohm and Elizabeth G. Ametsbichler, *Become Who You Are: With an Additional Essay, "The Old Woman"* (Albany: State University of New York Press, 2006), here 2. Further references are given in the text using page numbers alone.

[29] Ruth-Ellen Boetcher Joeres, "Die Zähmung der alten Frau: Hedwig Dohms *Werde, die Du bist*," in *Der Widerspenstigen Zähmung: Studien zur bezwungenen*

Weiblichkeit in der Literatur, ed. Sylvia Wallinger and Monica Jonas, 217–27 (Innsbruck: Inst. für Germanistik, 1986), 222. Abigail Dunn, "'Ob im Tode mein Ich geboren wird?': The Representation of the Widow in Hedwig Dohm's 'Werde, die du bist' (1894)," in *Women and Death 3: Women's Representations of Death in German Culture since 1500*, ed. Clare Bielby and Anna Richards, 88–100 (Rochester, NY: Camden House, 2010), 94.

[30] All in-text references are to the original German, unless otherwise indicated.

[31] At the beginning of her journal Agnes reflects: "Ein alter Mann, das ist ein Mensch, der nicht mehr lange lebt, dessen Tage gezählt sind, aber er lebt! Eine alte Frau aber, die arm ist und Wittwe, die ist so gut wie todt" (160; An old man—that is a person who isn't going to live much longer, whose days are numbered, but he lives! An old woman, however, who is poor and a widow, she is as good as dead, 8).

[32] Hedwig Dohm, "Die alte Frau," in *Die Mütter: Beitrag Zur Erziehungsfrage*, 201–24 (Berlin: Fischer, 1903), 204. English translations are quoted from Dohm and Ametsbichler, "The Old Woman."

[33] Charlotte Woodford, "Female Desire and the Mind-Body Binary in Fin de Siè-cle Fiction by Hedwig Dohm, Lou Andreas-Salomé and Gabriele Reuter," *German Life and Letters* 69, no. 3 (July 2016): 336–49, here 341.

[34] Woodford, "Female Desire," 341; Anna Richards, *The Wasting Heroine in German Fiction by Women, 1770–1914* (Oxford: Clarendon, 2004), 187.

[35] Boetcher Joeres, "Zähmung der alten Frau," 225.

[36] Carol Wiener, "Is a Spinster an Unmarried Woman?" *American Journal of Legal History* 20 (1976): 27–31.

8: "Heroism of the Mother": Women's Rights Pioneer Jeannette Schwerin, Motherlove, and Women's Leadership in German-Speaking Central Europe, 1890–1914

Lisa Fetheringill Zwicker

IN 1899 THE LEADERS of the women's movement organized a great memorial in the Berlin City Hall to celebrate and honor the life of Jeannette Schwerin, an activist in the new field of social work, who had died of cancer at the age of forty-seven. People from all walks of life came together to pay their respects and to express their grief at Schwerin's early death. In light of the crowds, reformers marveled that in the past only royal queens, who won public admiration as a result of their position rather than their accomplishments, had brought together so many people to mourn a woman. Twelve organizations mobilized the memorial for Schwerin's life and work, from the Bund Deutscher Frauenverein with 137 chapters and 70,000 members to the Berliner Handwerkerverein (Artisan Union), based in the capital and reform groups such as the Verein Jugendschutz (Association to Protect Youth), and Lette-Verein, which organized education and training services.[1] The memorial, the manifold newspaper obituaries, and the ways in which Schwerin was officially honored by diverse organizations testified to her importance as a leader in Berlin and in Germany as a whole.[2] And her mourning followers, as well as Schwerin herself, emphasized above all her role as a mother.

Since the eighteenth century Central European men and women have extolled the power of Mutterliebe (motherlove), even if the nature of women's roles and duties was a subject of disagreement.[3] Often such exultation served to buttress a view widely held by the middle class that women and men flourished best in separate spheres.[4] Yet in the late nineteenth century, as elite women gained access to new opportunities and as increasing numbers worked for pay outside the home, leading Central European women invoked motherlove to claim a role in the public sphere. Women active outside the home as social workers, teachers, or reformers described their work in terms of "geistige Mütterlichkeit" (spiritual motherhood).[5] Helene Lange, leader of the moderate wing of the women's movement, explained how this "geistige Mütterlichkeit" is "unabhängig von physischer Liebe und Mutterschaft," but nevertheless a force "die jede echte Frau durchdringt" (independent from physical love and motherhood [but nevertheless] permeates all true women).[6] Women's qualities of care, patience, and gentility were urgently needed for the poor of their nation. Thus a new sense of the abilities and potential of women combined with continuing beliefs in the fundamental differences between men and women helped to shape this fin-de-siècle context. The cultural construction of motherlove created opportunities for strong, diametrically opposed arguments: some employed the discourse of motherlove to stress the importance of women's work in public life; others demanded all the more vociferously that women concentrate on their children at home.

In this essay I begin by considering questions about motherlove through the contrasting examples of the melodramatic writings of Adele Crepaz and the sociological research collected by Adele Schreiber in *Mutterschaft: Ein Sammelwerk für die Probleme des Weibes als Mutter* (Motherhood: A Collection on the Problem of the Woman as Mother). These cases show how the cultural construction of late-nineteenth- and early-twentieth-century motherlove could both create openings for new arguments about the power and potential of women's leadership and closely circumscribe women's ability to take on leadership roles outside of the family. I conclude with an analysis of the leadership style of the celebrated activist and reformer Jeannette Schwerin. Her tragic early death motivated prominent politicians and women's rights advocates to describe publicly how the loss of Schwerin's leadership had dealt a blow to the women's movement in Germany. That portrait of Schwerin's character, given after her death, provides us with the perspective of the champions of the women's movement on someone who was considered a graceful motherly woman and a true leader. New opportunities for women at the turn of the century had indeed allowed Schwerin to become a leader of the women's movement and an acknowledged expert in the new field of social work. It was less clear, however, that the cultural norms that were expressed in terms of motherlove, which implied expectations of gentility, sensitivity, humility, tenderness, and devotion to others, would ever have allowed her to be a leader of men.

Motherlove

In the view of many fin-de-siècle Germans, true mothers loved ecstatically and selflessly. While commentators varied in the extravagance of their rhetoric and while ideas about motherhood were part of contested debates about the "woman question" at the turn of the century, most Germans believed that motherlove was connected to the deepest mysteries in the lives of women. Women had the potential to be infinitely giving, patient, and nurturing; they freely sacrificed themselves for their children. In this way the woman was a "Liebesengel" (angel of love).[7] The popular press describes women who woke in the morning thinking of their love for their children; this love shaped their day's activities and followed them until bedtime, and when they finally put their heads on their pillows after a long day, they closed their eyes and imagined their children as they drifted off to sleep. Poets, writers, and scholars praised motherlove for its embodiment of morality, fidelity—and pleasure. Popular journalistic accounts lovingly describe soft baby bodies and sweet kisses in stories, narratives, and poems that often focus on the body parts of mother and child. The repetition of physical imagery in poetry provides suggestive evidence for the social sanction of the deep physical connection between mother and child. The passionate ties that perhaps emerged from such physical connections were then interpreted as idealized emotional and spiritual links. In 1914 one magazine printed comments of a "langjährige Abonnentin" (longtime subscriber) "Frau Bauer" on motherlove:

> Tief in der Seele des Weibes lebt der lebendige und ewige Wunsch nach dem Kinde. Im Kind liege ihr reinstes Glück. Was ein Weib an Mutterliebe in sich birgt, das kann ein Mann nur schwach verstehen, selten aber nachempfinden. Mutterliebe ist ein Naturgesetz. Der höchste Beruf des Weibes ist Mutter zu werden!

> [Deep in the soul of the woman lives the vital and eternal wish for a child. In a child lies a woman's most pure happiness. A man can only poorly understand but seldom experience the motherlove that a woman holds inside herself. Motherlove is a natural law. The highest calling of the woman is to be a mother.][8]

Idealized motherlove of the sort that a man could "poorly understand" was nurtured in the middle class with its particularly pronounced division between men's and women's roles. The financial support from male breadwinners made it possible for wives to focus on creating a loving homelife for their children and husbands. Narratives of middle-class motherlove also assume that the families in question had enough financial stability to allow mother and child to bond without worries about the material necessities of daily life. Families in which mothers had to work for pay inside or outside of the home would face challenges in terms of their ability to follow the cultural script of idealized motherlove.[9]

In these narratives of idealized motherlove, mothers adored their children, no matter the behavior of the child. Popular publications associated with the Catholic Church, such as the journal *Monika*, particularly emphasized versions of motherhood that stressed mothers' devotion to their children. The idealized mother follows Christ's example of sacrifice and takes her place as the moral center of her society. Christian faith reinforced the values that girls learned at home from their parents. Middle-class families trained daughters from a young age to subordinate themselves to their parents and to their brothers. They were expected to cater to their brothers and to nurture their siblings. In this way, girls learned this everyday requirement of self-sacrifice from a young age. Today these fin-de-siècle expectations of middle-class motherlove seem unrealistic and perhaps even unattainable, but for people who lived at this time and for women who were disciplined to subordinate themselves to others, this ideal may well have been in reach. The social hierarchies realized in daily encounters of middle-class women with men, but also with women of lower status, such as washerwomen and servants, would have provided additional concrete examples of subordination, submission, and deference in everyday life. The sacrifice associated with the cultural script of middle-class motherlove was perhaps more possible in this period as a result of the norms of deference and subordination to those seen as superior to oneself; however, women's magazines and popular publications may have emphasized service more than it was experienced by women in day-to-day life.

This sacrifice that associated women with morality helped to cement women's status at a time when gender roles were in flux, when some women worked outside the home and some high-profile middle-class women took on university studies or professional responsibilities. The ideal of motherlove legitimated her role in the eyes of a society that otherwise seemed to attach value only to achievement, and achievement only in the economic, military, or scholarly realm. In doing so, the motherlove script functioned as a gentle critique of Germany's emerging go-ahead / get-ahead society, in which gentleness and loving-kindness were seemingly pushed to the side. Discourses of motherlove involved assumptions about both women's natural inclinations and women's duties. Observers believed that all women had the potential to develop the traits of motherliness, but that these traits needed to be cultivated, nurtured, and applauded. The new focus on intensive emotional investment in children related to demographic changes and smaller families, which allowed mothers to dedicate time to each child, as well as making the popular dissemination of information on early childhood education easier. By 1900, research in psychology and education had given new evidence of the importance of early childhood education for development. Germany led the world in the movement for rich and creative environments for young children. In the words of Hulda Maurenbrecher, this research created new responsibilities for the mother, who was not only to guide her children with infinite patience but also to educate herself to become a "wirkliche

Erzieherin" (true educator) worthy of her children.[10] Motherlove carried with it heavy responsibilities to raise moral citizens and good people; it was essential that children bring into the world with them "das Recht auf Mutterliebe" (the right to motherlove).[11]

Motherlove and Leadership

The remarkably flexible ideal of middle-class motherlove allowed for diverse, and in some cases opposite, perspectives on the connections between motherlove and leadership. Cultural norms of motherlove could confine women to the home, but they could also demand that women enter the public sphere and "perform" motherlove for the people. Adele Crepaz (1849–1919), for example, took a conservative and family-oriented approach to her understanding of motherlove. Her writings reveal an understanding of motherlove that particularly emphasizes a woman's duty to her family and children. The daughter of an Austrian civil servant, Crepaz wrote poetry, novels, dramas, political texts against women's emancipation, and a book on motherhood. Crepaz saw motherlove as a characteristic of women—a shared bond that unites all women. Her interpretation of motherlove emphasized its ecstatic and melodramatic qualities. For example, Crepaz writes here of the death of a child with particularly vivid physical descriptions:

> Von allen Schmerzen auf Erden ist der Mutterschmerz der heiligste. Kein anderes Leid kommt dem menschlichen Herzen so nahe wie dieses, kein anderes weckt das tiefsinnigste Mitgefühl im gleichen Maße wie dieses. Mutterliebe, das reinste und selbstloseste aller Gefühle, trägt das Frauenherz "himmelhoch jauchzend" zu dem höchsten Gipfel irdischer Seligkeit; des Kindes Tod stürzt es hinab in den Abgrund der allertiefsten Schmerzen. Die Muttertränen sind die heißesten, die ein Auge hienieden weint, und wenn die Zeit allen Wunden lindernden Balsam bringt—dem Mutterherzen bringt sie ihn nicht.

> [Of all the pain of the earth, the mother's pain is the holiest. No other sorrow is so near to the human heart as this one; no other wakes the deepest sympathy to same extent. Motherlove, the purest and most unselfish of all feelings, carries the woman's heart to the peaks of earthly bliss in "sky-high exultation" [quoting Goethe]; the child's death pushes [her heart] into the abyss of the very deepest pain. A mother's tears are the hottest that an eye can cry here on earth. We say that time heals all wounds—for the mother's heart there is no respite.[12]

Her description here echoes popular publications that connected the intensities of motherlove to moments of crisis, illness, death. In some cases, a son realizes the depth of his love for his mother only as she lies on her deathbed, perhaps allowing the mother-reader to imagine how she will be missed when she is gone. Stories in women's magazines of the death of a mother or a child opened a window to the depth of feelings that lay beneath the everyday hustle and bustle.

In Crepaz's passionate, all-consuming interpretation of motherlove, *all* of the mother's energy and focus is placed on the child. For Crepaz, "Das echte Mutterherz wird von dem Kinde so erfüllt und befriedigt, wie der Mann von seinem wissenschaftlichen oder künstlerischen Berufe"[13] (the true motherheart is as fulfilled and satisfied by the child as the man's [is] by his scholarly or artistic work). Apparently a mother who has not found this high level of satisfaction in life with her child in the home may well not possess a "true motherheart." With such all-encompassing romantic attachment to the child, there is little possibility of pursuing a leadership role outside the home. Even if the extravagance of her rhetoric makes Crepaz an outlier, the arguments that she makes about the satisfaction in domestic work and childcare here have a certain logic, and these arguments were available to those who criticized women's new roles outside the home.

An example of an opposing set of perspectives comes from the 800-page work *Mutterschaft: Ein Sammelwerk für die Probleme des Weibes als Mutter* (Motherhood: A Collection on the Problems of the Woman as Mother).[14] The book, edited by Adele Schreiber, includes contributions from fifty authors from German-speaking Central Europe and beyond, a majority of whom were women, including many Social Democratic, progressive, and feminist leaders, and featuring such well-known names as Lily Braun, Regine Deutsch, Hedwig Dohm, Henriette Fürth, Rosa Kempf, Ellen Key, Rosa Mayreder, Anna Plothow, Frieda Radel, Rosika Schwimmer, Hedwig Bleuler-Waser, Bertha von Suttner, and Gertrud Woker. This book makes the case, as feminists and educational reformers had argued since the mid-century, that the responsibilities and challenges of raising children required that women develop their intellectual, emotional, and physical abilities.[15] The very discourse designed to keep women "in their place" was used to advance women—and by women whose very prominence and leadership positions in the German-speaking world were themselves a silent refutation of the limiting stereotypes that the motherlove tropes might be suspected of encouraging. Thus Marie Stritt, leader of the umbrella organization for women's associations, Bund Deutscher Frauenvereine, argues for the importance of a well-rounded education in order to prepare women for motherhood. The passion of motherlove gives women the energy and determination to become their best selves for their children and for society as a whole. They do this in two ways: by raising their own children and also by applying their qualities of motherliness to the problems facing German society. Stritt further argues:

> Der kulturfördernde direkte mütterliche Einfluss der Frau auf die Gesamtheit . . . macht sich schon in verhältnismäßig kurzer Zeit bemerkbar. Er richtet sich, ureigenem mütterlichen Wesen auch hier getreu, gegen alles was krank ist am sozialen Körper. Er tritt für einen erhöhten physischen und moralischen Schutz aller Schwachen, Bedrängten, Misshandelten ein—vor allem der Kinder und der Jugendlichen, die des mütterlichen Schutzes am meisten bedürfen. Er bekämpft unerbittlich alles, was das Familienleben gefährden, er fördert was irgendwie zu seiner Erhöhung beitragen kann.

> [The direct culture-enhancing motherly influence of the woman on the whole makes itself felt even in a relatively short period. It will act, true to its innate motherly essence, against all that is sick in our social body. It advocates for the enhanced physical and moral protection of all the weak, the afflicted, the abused—above all, children and youth who need motherly protection most of all. This [motherly influence of the woman] fights inexhaustibly everything that can put family life in danger; it supports anything that can raise up family life.][16]

In another chapter in the *Mutterschaft* collection, Hedwig Bleuler-Waser, a leader in Swiss women's and temperance organizations, argues similarly that all women should be nurtured to develop their "Mütterlichkeit" (motherliness). Women who have children, as well as women who do not, can become "Menschheitsmütter" (mothers of humanity) whose "warm pulsierende Mütterlichkeit" (warm, vibrant motherliness) lead them to act in ways that will improve society for all its members. Today, however, in her view, this

> sublimierte Mütterlichkeit aber bedarf unsere Kulturwelt heute so dringend, sie ist so voller Aufgaben, die nur mit Hilfe der Frau gelößt [sic] werden können, dass wir uns nicht lange bei der Frage aufzuhalten brauchen, ob es denn richtig sei, in allen Mädchen die Mütterlichkeit zu pflegen.

> [our cultural world needs this sublimated motherliness urgently; [the world] is so full of tasks that can be solved only with the help of women that we need not be long detained by the question of whether it be right to cultivate motherliness in all girls.][17]

The 371 images—of paintings, drawings, and sculptures—in the motherhood collection reinforce, in many cases, Bleuler-Waser's point about the challenges facing German society. These images also exhibit the power and passion of women for their children, and perhaps also, women's ability to apply that intensity and determination to the problems of German-speaking Central Europe. Two of the sixty-seven chapters focus on women in caricature and the visual arts, and in those chapters, the text is a comment on the images. In general, however, the themes of these 371 images do not seem to relate to the text on the page on which the images appear. They seem to be dropped almost randomly throughout the book. Many images echo the romantic interpretation of the special and unique bond between mother and child; the images suggest that this relationship needs to be protected and nurtured, as German society was changing so swiftly. If many of the *texts* suggest that women's motherly qualities could be utilized to shape the world outside of the home and argue for women's public role in diverse spheres, many others simply revert to the static, eternal, all-encompassing bond between mother and child. Images from the medieval through rococo to nineteenth-century avant-garde art hammered home the message that motherlove was timeless and unchanging.

In fact, however, in the eighteenth and early nineteenth centuries middle-class men and women were more likely to speak of "Elternliebe" (parental love), "Kindesliebe" (filial love), or "Geschwisterliebe" (love between siblings, brotherly/sisterly love) than "Mutterliebe." In the 1836 *Conversationslexikon für das deutsche Volk* there are entries for each of these terms, but none for Mutterliebe.[18] It seems clear from the vantage point of the twenty-first century that a return to "Elternliebe" or "Kindesliebe" might well have brought feminists greater success in terms of claims to leadership than demands for new roles that emphasized women's difference from men. Feminists in the 1960s and 1970s criticized early Central European maternal feminists as conservative and less effective than their Anglo-American feminist counterparts, who concentrated on an individual's equal rights. Some twentieth-century works on the history of feminism in Germany echo these perspectives.[19] Ann Taylor Allen, however, has provided an important corrective with her arguments that historians should try to understand women of the past on their own terms. She has also effectively called into question the assumption that women's emphasis on maternal politics must link them to conservative, illiberal, authoritarian, or proto-fascist tendencies in Central Europe. At the same time, the cultural construct of motherlove did impose real limits on the possibilities for women's leadership. In the following, I focus on an example of this dynamic in turn-of-the-century Germany.

Jeannette Schwerin: Pioneer in Social Work, Loving Mother, and Women's Rights Leader

Jeannette Schwerin, whose enormous gathering to commemorate her life and death opened this chapter, was pale with dark hair and wore simple clothes. In many ways she seemed unremarkable, that is, until she would rise to the podium and speak to gathered crowds. Her friends describe how her poise, calm self-assurance, and evident knowledge and wisdom swayed her listeners and allowed her to command the attention of a whole room. She was described by her colleagues as a natural leader, one who was even predestined to rise to a leading position. The wife and daughter of doctors, Schwerin traced her roots to important Sephardic scholars and dignitaries, including Isaac ben Judah Abarbanel (1437–1508), among the most famous of medieval Sephardic Jews, a group that received new attention and admiration in the nineteenth century.[20] Her parents had long been involved in diverse organizations combating poverty and pressing for equality and social justice. But early in her marriage Schwerin also spent long hours reading and studying economic, political, and early sociological texts. Her farsighted and nuanced understanding of complicated social problems was thus due not only to the experiences of her parents but also to her detailed knowledge of the economic, historical, and cultural factors that shaped poverty and social problems in Germany.

Jeannette Schwerin did not shy away from speaking truth to powerful men. In an article about social work and service she repeatedly noted how leading figures seemed to misunderstand the contributions that women were making to improve the lives of the poor.[21] Schwerin condemned the claims of the Reichstag deputy and priest Franz Hitze, the Center Party's authority on social questions, that education and preparation for social welfare work would fundamentally alter what one [apparently a man] valued above all in a lady: her delicacy, her warmth of feelings, her good heart. Working with the poor, with the immoral, with the suffering, Hitze claimed, would reduce the lady's "Liebe zum Kleinen" (love of the little things), here the world of the home: her attention to detail, her joy in children, or perhaps even a kind of childish passion for beautiful trinkets, lovely music, or the perfectly baked cake. According to Hitze, "unsere Damen [sind uns] doch zu gut" (our ladies are too good) for work like caring for a "Trunkenbold" (drunkard).[22] Schwerin, however, insisted instead that the love, the feelings, the passions of women demanded that they serve their fellows. Why would a woman with a "guten Herzen" (good heart) turn away from those in need, especially when she knew that she could be of help? The true woman lived the ideal of loving one's neighbor; these women refused to close their eyes and turn away from the misery of the world, for that, she claimed, was a form of cowardice.

Serving others, in Schwerin's view, strengthened women. Caring for one's neighbor, in her perspective, was the responsibility of women as a matter of course. Women were *raised* to cultivate their abilities to nurture and love their family members, to support their siblings and their parents. The work of Schwerin and others in serving the poor was a logical exten-sion of these activities. If women were allowed to gain knowledge and expertise, they could more effectively help others than in their existing roles, which denied them this ability to learn and study at the highest lev-els. Women too could read dry legal or economic studies, and this work would allow them to serve others and care for others more effectively than if they did not receive this education.[23]

Schwerin had embodied these ideals in her own extensive education, her care for her family, and her commitment to associations that attempted to tackle social problems. In these decades, as women were trying to find new ways to take on leadership roles, Schwerin's particular manifestation of leadership may well have been attractive. She was a mother herself, rais-ing a son before she began to be engaged in politics at forty. In this way she enjoyed the benefits—and credibility—of having experienced moth-erhood but was no long burdened with the day-to-day responsibilities of child-nurturing. In her presentation of herself, her identity as a mother played an important role. In 1896, in fiery discussions of the conflicts between socialist and center-left middle-class women, Schwerin argued that even though the socialist women oppose them, they "werden sie nie-mals bekämpfen. Frauen gegen Frauen, Mütter gegen Mütter; dies wäre unerhört in der Geschichte der Menschheit" (would never fight them. Women against women, mothers against mothers; this would be outra-geous, unheard of in the history of humanity).[24] Schwerin's understand-ing of motherhood here suggests that it was unwomanly to fight another woman. Her statement also implies, of course, that in the act of fighting one sacrifices one's femininity. Thus Schwerin implicitly criticized socialist women for their aggressive stance against the representatives of modern and middle-class feminism. At the same time, her willingness to reach out to socialist feminists was also considered daring during this period.

Jeannette Schwerin's work across different organizations dedicated to the social question, women's rights, and the new field of social work made her a leader among progressive intellectuals in Berlin. She founded and led the Mädchen- und Frauengruppen für soziale Hilfsarbeit (Women and Girls Groups for Social Work), a precursor to Alice Salomon's first school of social work. In this way, Schwerin and Salomon helped to cre-ate social work as a profession. Her demands for the improvement of conditions and wages for garment workers, especially in the mass strikes of 1896, brought her attention from Social Democratic activists such as Clara Zetkin. Schwerin's network spread far and wide. Her prominence in a wide range of volunteer organizations helped her to build contacts with those throughout the community who cared about social work initiatives. She involved herself in diverse groups. For example, she contributed to the Verein für häusliche Gesundheitspflege (loose translation: Association for Good Health in the Home) whose members aimed to spread knowledge of best practices for promoting health and preventing disease through careful cleaning and healthy living. She assisted the Komitee für Ferienkolonien (Fresh Air Camp Committee), whose members provided opportunities for orphans and poor children to experience the pleasures of a vacation and time away from the city in the summer. Schwerin was also a founder and leader of the Berliner Verein zur Förderung der Blumenpflege in der Schule (Berlin Association to Encourage the Growing of Flowers in Schools).[25] In addition, Schwerin did important work building up the Hauspflege (household care and management) section of the Berliner Frauenverein. This organization offered assistance to women of modest means who were ill or recovering from childbirth.

Consistent with the gender ideals of the nineteenth century, teaching children the care of flowers or arranging for orphans to spend time in the country would certainly be seen as women's responsibilities. Nineteenth-century Germans associated women not only with flowers and children but also with Father Hitze's "Liebe zum Kleinen": the little tasks, the little changes, the little touches that make life comfortable and cozy. Schwerin's close friend and mentee Alice Salomon described how Schwerin considered it her duty "ihrer Familie, ihrem engsten Kreis das Heim mit dem ganzen Reichtum ihres Herzens zu erfüllen und auszugestalten, und mit ihrem feinsten Empfinden für die Bedürfnisse ihrer Umgebung in der Befriedigung jedes kleinsten, selbst unausgesprochenen Wunsches der ihrigen [zu sorgen]" (for her family, for her closest circle, to fill her home with the riches of her heart and with the finest sense for the needs of those around her and for satisfying every tiny, even unspoken wish).[26] In light of this idealized portrait of Schwerin as the nurturing mother of the home, her intensive engagement with organizations such as those that would teach children how to grow flowers would seem to be consistent with this side of her day-to-day life and work of modest, tiny acts that improved the lives of her nearest and dearest. In this part of her work, Schwerin is not leading strikes; she is not making political speeches; she is not passing legislation; she is not demanding international peace. At the same time, Schwerin's colleagues and friends believed her work for associations like these exemplified her leadership style. In her obituary, Schwerin's friends describe how these efforts gained success as a result of Schwerin's "Überzeugungskraft" (powers of persuasion): her deliberate, thoughtful, and detailed ideas, and her brilliant organizational talents: "Aus kleinen Anfängen entwickelte sich in kürzester Zeit ein lebensfähiger, in Plan und Ausführung mustergültiger Verein, der einem dringenden Bedürfnis entsprach"[27] (From small beginnings there developed in the shortest of periods a viable association, exemplary in plan and execution, that met an urgent need.)

In a striking set of images, the philosopher and ethicist Friedrich Wilhelm Foerster saw in Jeannette Schwerin's work the beginning of a new age of the "Heroismus der Mutter" (heroism of the mother). For centuries, as he vividly relates, men and women prayed to a far-away Mary, asked saints for help, and imagined queens who would provide mercy and charity. People appealed to gentlewomen in "Kirchen und Kapellen" (churches and chapels) who "mit inbrünstigen Gebeten um Fürbitte angefleht [wurden]" (were beseeched with ardent prayers for intercession). But these gentle, beautiful, noble women, described by Foerster as "mit Rosen umwunden" (bedecked with roses), were far away from the violence of the world of men. As their new day dawned, according to Foerster, women left their castles, and they showed what they could do when they acted in the world. They brought their maternal values with them, and these maternal values—of humility, care, love, peace, and stoicism—would transform the world. The example of Jeannette Schwerin, he claimed, was of the beautiful and tender queen who strode into life with her noble bearing, healing patience, forgiving gentility, and painstaking care in the smallest of details. Her self-possessed, forbearing, and tranquil presence stood in sharp contrast to, and in this way highlighted, the ugly and wild violence of men. Her loving example and her care for each individual and his or her specific needs shone a harsh light on a typically male modus operandi that was unable to move beyond administrative routines, rigid principles, and "die ganze Menschenfeindlichkeit des bureaukratischen [sic] Schemas, das selbst den reinsten Willen allmählich taub macht gegen den Aufschrei des lebendigen Lebens" (the entire misanthropy of bureaucratic procedures, which gradually make even those with the purest of intentions grow deaf to the cries of living life).[28]

Schwerin's noble bearing, her broad-based knowledge, and her delicate negotiating abilities made her a symbol of the new kind of woman who was coming into being at the turn of the century. Here at the dawn of social work as a profession, Foerster, and Schwerin herself, imagined that including women as administrators and leaders of new institutions for care of society would enable their motherliness to transform governance. Women would bring with them into government and organizations the experience of a peaceful homelife, the gentle care, anticipation of needs, and comfort of a mother's hand on a sick child. United together, the power of the state and the "heroism of the mother" would allow Germans to solve their long-debated, long-bemoaned "social question." Foerster and Schwerin believed that empowering women meant transforming the ability of the state to care for its citizens. Leadership of women such as Schwerin would make this dream a reality.[29]

But could it? Would not the "heroism of the mother," the modesty, humility, patience, sacrifice, and morality that Foerster and Schwerin envisioned make it more difficult for women to succeed at such roles as military commander, business director, grassroots politician, or university president? Concretely, Schwerin argued that women should prepare for and take on professional roles, such as factory inspector, which would seem to give them a platform to provide professional advice in a way that would be consistent with the idealized character traits that Foerster and Schwerin seemed to think that women possessed.[30] The moral expectations that Foerster and Schwerin had for women put them on a pedestal, which perhaps set them up for failure in leadership situations where living up to these high moral standards was inherently more difficult than in a home. A woman who exhibited modesty, humility, patience, sacrifice, and morality might well succeed in leading organizations when others were committed to those values. It is more difficult to imagine that a woman who embodied these idealized characteristics could successfully manage large organizations with complex budgets, competing agendas, and powerful opponents—and where followers were used to other sets of rules.

The Cultural Script of Motherlove: Broadening *and* Limiting Opportunities for Women

The focus of this essay on motherlove and leadership is part of a larger debate about women's roles and women's equality.[31] How should women, in Ann Taylor Allen's words, balance their "desire for children" and their "drive for individual self-actualization"? How could or should women combine their responsibilities and roles as mothers with work outside the home and in politics? A generation of historians has shown how the demands of women, beginning in the mid-1800s, helped to carve out a new role for women in public and break down the divide between the public and private spheres. Important political change could be initiated by women in private organizations, not just unions and political parties, and by women who still lacked political rights. This scholarship has demonstrated how women who utilized gendered discourses of women's difference could achieve reform and change. In the introduction to *Maternalism Reconsidered* Rebecca Jo Plant and Marian van der Klein argue that this scholarship has revealed how "women's quest for social justice could no longer be considered the exclusive province of 'equal rights feminism.'"[32] As early as 1992, in the introduction to their collection on maternalism and the welfare state, *Mothers of a New World*, Seth Koven and Sonya Michel argue that maternalist politics allowed for new claims for women's roles in the public sphere, new support for women and families, and for a "subversive potential" to challenge the status quo. At the same time, they also pointed to the ways that, once the welfare reforms that women had sought became institutionalized, women recipients and women reformers were often shoved aside by male political leaders.[33]

Since the 1990s, historians studying a wide range of contexts have used maternalism as an analytical tool in studies on women's education, women's activism, relations between women employers and servants, as well as on white women and women subject to European colonial powers and on welfare states more generally. The flexibility of maternalist arguments has meant that women using them have been able to argue from ideological perspectives ranging from conservative to fascist, to communist, to progressive. Thus in recent work on Latin America scholars have emphasized the ways that maternalist politics could enable progressive reforms that protected children. European scholars, on the other hand, have tended to focus on the ways that maternalist politics were utilized to promote conservative and fascist political projects.[34] Elisabeth Badinter, a Frenchwoman, has connected the emphasis on maternalist ideology across the West in the late twentieth century to a backlash against the women's movement.[35]

In this essay I have considered particular aspects of this maternalist debate, including women's aspirations to leadership and an intensely loving connection to children that is allegedly peculiar to women. What were the cultural consequences of the motherlove script? Combining maternal feminism with the cultural construction of passionate motherlove may have done quite a lot for *individual women*, in terms of elevating the role of mothers at a time when gender roles were in flux. Middle-class women could perform their motherlove as a strategy to increase their own status within their families and communities. The particularly powerful notion of motherlove helped to create a context in which women could bridge the world of public and private. Married women performed motherlove in their homes with their children; single women could perform motherlove as teachers, activists, social workers, and increasingly as doctors or factory inspectors. Women entered the public sphere; at the same time, the private sphere still remained their domain, which few wanted to relinquish. Central European feminists around 1900 could still more easily imagine the creation of communal kitchens than they could imagine sharing household duties and childcare with their husbands. Yet for the majority of women, the ubiquity and popularity of motherlove in its early twentieth-century cultural construction, when added to long-standing legal, educational, and cultural barriers to women's leadership, created obstacles for those aspiring to leadership roles in German-speaking Central Europe. For the ideal of motherlove could also support arguments proffered by the enemies of women's rights, such as the following comment by a fin-de-siècle journalist: "Die größte und schönste Macht, die wahrhaft königliche Macht ist eben doch die über die Herzen—und diese verliert die Frau, wenn sie möglichst 'Mann' sein will" (The greatest and most noble power—the truly regal power the woman possesses is precisely the power [she wields] over the heart—and the woman loses this if she wants to be a 'man').[36]

Even for those who favored women's rights, this idealized construction of motherlove would probably put barriers in the way of achieving success in other leadership roles. Marie Stritt closes her obituary for Schwerin by revealing the following:

> Immer aber, wenn wir uns ihr liebes Bild vor die Seele rufen, ist es, als ob die freundlichen klaren Augen uns Muth zusprächen, wie sie im Leben so oft gethan, und als ob die sanfte Stimme uns ermahnte, die Arbeit aufzunehmen, die sie uns hinterlassen und treu zu bleiben, wie sie es war bis zum letzten Athemzuge.

> [Whenever we call up her beloved image before our souls, it is as if her clear gracious eyes give us courage, as they so often did in life, and as if her gentle voice reminds us to take up the work that she has left behind and stay true, as she was until her last breath.][37]

Jeannette Schwerin, here with "clear gracious eyes" and "gentle voice" powerfully encourages her friends to continue their work through her presence. If one reads between the lines of the hagiography of her disciples, one can perhaps grasp the secret of Schwerin's success—not just in inspiring followers but in winning over those more powerful figures with whom she had to negotiate. Activists and established authorities alike felt able to listen, without loss of self-respect, to a woman of superior intelligence and efficiency who treated them with the kindness of an (ideal) mother, protective of their self-esteem even as she made her own case. Such a woman was a master of tact, careful not to grab the spotlight for herself, protective of the self-esteem of everyone in the room, and—in her effectiveness—providing an example that followers could look up to. Schwerin shrewdly turned her femininity and motherhood from barriers into assets. It was not a legacy, however, that every woman could adopt with equal success.

The importance of hierarchy in parts of German life and especially in institutions such as the Prussian military, the established Churches, or the civil service may have created added difficulties for more ordinary women in following a leader such as Schwerin who led through her charisma, integrity, enthusiasm, intelligence, knowledge, and loving loyalty to her fellow feminists. In the Germany of Iron Chancellor Otto von Bismarck and Emperor Wilhelm II with its glorification of the military values of hardness, strength, and pugnacity, it is difficult to see a woman like Jeannette Schwerin as a leader of *men*. Rather the example of women like Jeannette Schwerin risked hardening gender roles and boxing women into child-care and family responsibilities that would make it difficult for them to pursue work outside of the home. Schwerin herself was too smart not to have realized these risks and must have felt they were worth taking. For she not only valued her motherhood; she also believed that a motherly persona was the one best suited for making progress—for women and for the rest of society—in the world in which German women lived. Looking forward one hundred years, however, the soft skills and attributes that Schwerin embodied are now perceived to be all the more important. Schwerin's strengths in charisma, organization, responsibility, creativity, moral integrity, grit, persuasion, and, yes, love, we have realized, can create success in finishing projects—and perhaps especially, team projects—and achieving goals at least as well and often better than the qualities associated with top-down leadership. Some of the values that she and other women wanted leaders in German civic life to adopt, such as the heroism of the mother, are, one hundred years later and with a changed culture, leading to the reforms and change that they sought.

Notes

[1] Dr. Fr. W. Foerster, "Dem Andenken Jeannette Schwerin, Ansprache, gehalten bei der Gedächtnisfeier im Berliner Rathause," in *Jeannette Schwerin zum Gedächtnis* (Berlin: Max Hoffschläger, 1899), 11, 13; Dieter G. Maier and Jürgen Nürnberger, *Jeannette Schwerin durch Bildung zu Sozialreform und Emanzipation* (Berlin: Hentrich & Hentrich Verlag, 2016); Alice Salomon and Andrew Lees, *Character Is Destiny: The Autobiography of Alice Salomon* (Ann Arbor: University of Michigan Press, 2004), 30–34. Translations of German quotes are my own unless otherwise noted. For critical advice and suggestions, I am grateful to James Albisetti, Ann Taylor Allen, Margaret Lavinia Anderson, Elisabeth Krimmer, and Patricia Anne Simpson.

[2] Heidi Degethoff de Campos, "Wissen und Wollen!—Jeannette Schwerin und die Anfänge der Sozialarbeit als Frauenberuf," in *Freiburger FrauenStudien* 2 (1995): 73–83, http://nbn-resolving.de/urn:nbn:de:0168-ssoar-318341.

[3] Irmgard Roebling und Wolfram Mauser, *Mutter und Mütterlichkeit: Wandel und Wirksamkeit einer Phantasie in der deutschen Literatur* (Würzburg: Königshausen & Neumann, 1996), 12; Yvonne Schütze, "Mutterliebe—Vaterliebe: Elternrollen in der bürgerlichen Familie des 19. Jahrhunderts," in *Bürgerinnen und Bürger: Geschlechterverhältnisse im 19. Jahrhundert*," ed. Ute Frevert (Göttingen: Vandenhoeck & Ruprecht, 1988), 118–33; Yvonne Schütze, *Die gute Mutter: Zur Geschichte des normativen Musters "Mutterliebe"* (Hannover: B. Kleine Verlag, 1986); Rebecca Jo Plant, *Mom: The Transformation of Motherhood in Modern America* (Chicago: University of Chicago Press, 2010), 2; Jan Lewis, "Mother's Love: The Construction of an Emotion in Nineteenth-Century America," in *Social History and Issues in Human Consciousness: Some Interdisciplinary Connections*, ed. Andre E. Barnes and Peter N. Stearns (New York: New York University

Press, 1989), 209–29; Marga Vicedo, *The Nature and Nurture of Love: From Imprinting to Attachment in Cold War America* (Chicago: University of Chicago Press, 2013), 1–2.

⁴ Linda K. Kerber, "Separate Spheres, Female Worlds, Woman's Place: The Rhetoric of Women's History," *Journal of American History* 75, no. 1 (June 1988): 9–39; Marion W. Gray, *Productive Men, Reproductive Women: The Agrarian Household and the Emergence of Separate Spheres during the German Enlightenment* (New York: Berghahn, 2000).

⁵ Ann Taylor Allen, "Spiritual Motherhood: German Feminists and the Kindergarten Movement, 1848–1911," *History of Education Quarterly* 22, no. 3 (1982): 319–39; James C. Albisetti, *Schooling German Girls and Women* (Princeton, NJ: Princeton University Press, 2014), 97–98; Irene Stoehr, "'Organisierte Mütterlichkeit': Zur Politik der deutschen Frauenbewegung um 1900," in *Frauen suchen ihre Geschichte*, ed. Karin Hausen (Munich: C. H. Beck, 1983), 221–49; Kevin Repp, *Reformers, Critics, and the Paths of German Modernity: Anti-Politics and the Search for Alternatives, 1890–1914* (Cambridge, MA: Harvard University Press, 2000), chapter 3; and Nancy Ruth Reagin, *A German Women's Movement: Class and Gender in Hanover, 1880–1933* (Chapel Hill: University of North Carolina Press, 1995), 25–26.

⁶ Dietlinde Peters, *Mütterlichkeit im Kaiserreich* (Bielefeld: Kleine Verlag, 1984), 74, quoting Helene Lange, *Lebenserinnerungen* (Berlin: Herbig, 1921), 158; Helene Lange, "Intellektuelle Grenzlinien zwischen Mann und Frau," *Die Frau*, March 1897, 321–34; Barbara Greven-Aschoff, *Die bürgerliche Frauenbewegung in Deutschland, 1894–1933* (Göttingen: Vandenhoeck & Ruprecht, 1981), 35–43; James C. Albisetti, "Could Separate Be Equal? Helene Lange and Women's Education in Imperial Germany," *History of Education Quarterly* 22, no. 3 (1982): 301–17.

⁷ Ignotus, "Die Frau im öffentlichen Leben und die ländliche Wohlfahrtspflege," *Monika*, September 7, 1910), 422; similarly, Professor J. B. R., "Stimm- und Wahlrecht der Frauen," *Monika*, November 9, 1910, 531; Seth Koven and Sonya Michel, eds. *Mothers of a New World: Maternalist Politics and the Origins of Welfare States* (New York: Routledge, 1993).

⁸ "Die Frau gehört ins Haus?" *Thalysia*, April 1914, 84.

⁹ Emma Griffin, "The Emotions of Motherhood: Love, Culture, and Poverty in Victorian Britain," *American Historical Review* 123, no. 1 (February 1, 2018): 60–85; Reagin, *A German Women's Movement*, 3; Greven-Aschoff, *Die bürgerliche Frauenbewegung*, 40.

¹⁰ Hulda Maurenbrecher, "Die neue Auffassung von Mutterpflicht," in *Mutterschaft: Ein Sammelwerk für die Probleme des Weibes als Mutter*, ed. Adele Schreiber (Munich: Langen, 1912), 120–31, here 123.

¹¹ Laura Frost, "Mutterberuf," *Frauen-Reich*, May 14, 1910, 509.

¹² Adele Crepaz, *Mutterschaft und Mütter: Kulturgeschichtliche Studien* (Leipzig: O. Wigand, 1905), 153.

¹³ Crepaz, *Mutterschaft und Mütter*, 109.

[14] Adele Schreiber, ed. *Mutterschaft: Ein Sammelwerk für die Probleme des Weibes als Mutter* (Munich: Langen, 1912); on Schreiber, see Ann Taylor Allen, "Mothers of the New Generation: Adele Schreiber, Helene Stöcker, and the Evolution of a German Idea of Motherhood, 1900–1914," *Signs* 10, no. 3 (1985): 418–38; Ann Taylor Allen, "'The Future Is Ours': Feminists Imagine Europe in 1911," contribution to the web-feature "European History—Gender History," in *Themenportal Europäische Geschichte* (2009), http://www.europa.clio-online.de/2009/Article=415.

[15] Ann Taylor Allen, *Feminism and Motherhood in Germany, 1800–1914* (New Brunswick, NJ: Rutgers University Press, 1991), 78–80; Ann Taylor Allen, "Spiritual Motherhood," 322; Albisetti, *Schooling German Girls and Women*, 97; Stoehr, "'Organisierte Mütterlichkeit,'" 223; and Gertrud Bäumer, *Die Frau in der Kulturbewegung der Gegenwart* (Wiesbaden: J. F. Bergmann, 1904).

[16] Marie Stritt, "Die Mutter als Staatsbürgerin," in Schreiber, *Mutterschaft*, 700; Monika Simmel, *Erziehung zum Weibe: Mädchenbildung im 19. Jahrhundert* (Frankfurt am Main: Campus-Verlag, 1980).

[17] Hedwig Bleuler-Waser, "Erziehung zur Mütterlichkeit," in Schreiber, *Mutterschaft*, 70–71; Peters, *Mütterlichkeit im Kaiserreich*, 74–79; Stoehr, "'Organisierte Mütterlichkeit,'" 231.

[18] Schütze, "Mutterliebe-Vaterliebe," 119–20.

[19] Claudia Koonz, *Mothers in the Fatherland: Women, the Family, and Nazi Politics* (New York: St. Martin's, 1987), 12; Richard J. Evans, *The Feminist Movement in Germany, 1894–1933* (London: Sage, 1976), 273–74.

[20] John M. Efron, *German Jewry and the Allure of the Sephardic* (Princeton, NJ: Princeton University Press, 2016); Maier, *Jeannette Schwerin*, 7; and Irmgard Maya Fassmann, *Jüdinnen in der deutschen Frauenbewegung, 1865–1919* (Hildesheim: Georg Olms Verlag, 1996), 234–49.

[21] Jeannette Schwerin, "Dame oder Frau?" *Die Frauenbewegung*, June 1, 1896, 108.

[22] Schwerin, "Dame oder Frau?," 108.

[23] Schwerin, "Dame oder Frau?," 108.

[24] Cited in Carola Kuhlmann, *Alice Salomon und der Beginn sozialer Berufsausbildung: Eine Biographie.* (Stuttgart: ibidem Press, 2012), 35.

[25] Nine years after Schwerin's death, the Committee for Vacation-Colonies sent 4095 children from Berlin to 95 locations, costing a total of 224,253 Marks, and the Berlin Association to Encourage the Care of Flowers in Schools worked with 139 schools and sent 52,000 pots of flowers home with school children. *Die Wohlfahrtseinrichtungen von Groß-Berlin nebst einem Wegweiser für die praktische Ausübung der Armenpflege in Berlin: Ein Auskunfts- und Handbuch herausgegeben von der Zentrale für private Fürsorge vormals Auskunftstelle der Deutschen Gesellschaft für ethische Kultur* (Berlin, 1910), 114, 221.

[26] Alice Salomon, "Jeannette Schwerin: Ein Lebensbild von Alice Salomon," in *Jeannette Schwerin zum Gedächtnis* (Berlin: Max Hoffschläger, 1899), 21.

[27] Salomon, "Jeannette Schwerin," 21.

[28] Dr. Fr. W. Foerster, "Dem Andenken Jeannette Schwerin," 11, 13; Greven-Aschoff, *Die bürgerliche Frauenbewegung*, 41.

[29] Lange, *Lebenserinnerungen*, 111–12.

[30] Jeannette Schwerin, "Weibliche Fabrikinspektoren," *Jahrbuch für die Deutsche Frauenwelt* (Stuttgart: Greiner & Pfeiffer, 1899), 161–74.

[31] Ann Taylor Allen sensitively and effectively considered this "maternal dilemma" in *Feminism and Motherhood*, 241.

[32] Marian van der Klein et al., *Maternalism Reconsidered: Motherhood, Welfare and Social Policy in the Twentieth Century* (New York: Berghahn Books, 2012), 5.

[33] Koven and Michel, *Mothers of a New World*, 31; see also Seth Koven and Sonya Michel, "Womanly Duties: Maternalist Politics and the Origins of Welfare States in France, Germany, Great Britain, and the United States, 1880–1920," *American Historical Review* 95, no. 4 (1990): 1079; Karen Offen, *European Feminisms, 1700–1950: A Political History* (Stanford, CA: Stanford University Press, 1999), 236.

[34] Van der Klein et al., *Maternalism Reconsidered*, 4–5; Margaret D. Jacobs, *White Mother to a Dark Race: Settler Colonialism, Maternalism, and the Removal of Indigenous Children in the American West and Australia, 1880–1940* (Lincoln: University of Nebraska Press, 2011); Donna J. Guy, *White Slavery and Mothers Alive and Dead: The Troubled Meeting of Sex, Gender, Public Health, and Progress in Latin America* (Lincoln: University of Nebraska Press, 2000), 59.

[35] Elisabeth Badinter, *The Conflict: How Modern Motherhood Undermines the Status of Women.* (New York: Henry Holt, 2012), 29; Elisabeth Badinter, *Mother Love: Myth and Reality* (New York: Macmillan, 1981).

[36] "Die Zukunft unserer Frauen und Töchter," *Monika*, October 26, 1910, 507.

[37] Marie Stritt, "Jeannette Schwerin," *Frauen-Rundschau*, August 1, 1899, 264–67.

9: Strategic Optimism: Bertha von Suttner's Activism for Peace

Elisabeth Krimmer

T HE LIFE, WORKS, and political engagement of Bertha von Suttner (1843–1914) offer an impressive example of female leadership, but also a drastic illustration of its failure. In a twist of tragic irony, Suttner's impassioned plea for peace, her much acclaimed novel *Die Waffen nieder!* (*Lay Down Your Arms*, 1889), was published not after but before the First World War. Unlike most famous pacifist novels, including Erich Maria Remarque's *Im Westen nichts Neues* (*All Quiet on the Western Front*, 1928) and Henri Barbusse's *Le feu* (*Under Fire*, 1916), Suttner's novel was not the result of the bitter experience of the Great War but rather a sign of great prescience. And yet it so clearly lacked the power to prevent the cataclysm it warned against.

In the following, I draw on theories of life writing, sovereignty, and leadership to ask how Bertha von Suttner justified her claim to moral and political authority in her activism for peace. I am interested in factors that helped Suttner become a successful political leader, such as her grounding in traditional forms of sovereignty through her aristocratic birth, her ability to define herself as a servant of a larger cause, her fantastic talent for networking and public relations, her unshakable conviction that change is possible, her profound respect for the importance of public opinion, her strategic optimism, her sense of humor, and, last but not least, her skillful navigation of gender codes. However, I am also interested in parsing the reasons for her failure to gain a wider platform, including her refusal to take seriously and engage with discourses of nationality and with the realities of capitalism, but also, and importantly, the barrage of sexism with which she was confronted on a daily basis. By parsing the theories of authors such as Paul Julius Möbius and Otto Weininger, I want to highlight a paradox at the heart of female activism for peace: although women are assumed to be innately inclined toward peace, they are not credited with the intellectual capabilities necessary to understand society nor granted the power and authority to transform it in accordance with a pacifist vision.[1]

Effective Leadership

In seeking to understand women's access to positions of authority and leadership, it is crucial to consider the issue of social class. Without a doubt, Bertha von Suttner's privileged position as a member of the upper echelons of society contributed to her confidence in her own leadership abilities. She was born Sophia Felicita Gräfin Kinsky von Chinic und Tettau (in Prague in 1843). On her father's side, her lineage included ambassadors as well as secretaries and chancellors at the imperial court.[2] Her mother was related to Theodor Körner, but lacked the sixteen ancestors required for "Hoffähigkeit" (admission to court, *Bertha*, 43). Even so, the Suttners belonged to the highest level of the aristocracy. In her memoir, Suttner writes: "Unser Name hätte uns wohl berechtigt, in der höchsten Aristokratie zu verkehren"[3] (our name would surely have entitled us to socialize with the highest levels of the aristocracy). Suttner was used to mixing socially with the most prominent figures of her time. The "Stammbuch" of her cousin and best friend Elvira had entries by Richard Wagner, Franz Grillparzer, Ludwig I, Schiller's daughter, Justus Liebig, Giacomo Meyerbeer, Friedrich Hebbel, and Victor Hugo. When Suttner and her mother spent time in a gambling resort, Czar Alexander II casually dropped by to say hello to her friend, Yekaterina Dadiani, the widowed Princess of Mingrelia. When they vacationed in Baden-Baden, Suttner was introduced to Wilhelm I of Prussia, who then accompanied her on her morning walks. Undoubtedly, these connections with the most elite circles of society would prove invaluable during Suttner's career as a peace activist.

In trying to explain why Suttner was relatively comfortable with female authority, it is important to consider that, from an early age, she experienced women who were in charge of their own affairs. Since her father had died before she was born, she grew up in a household of women: her mother, her aunt, and her cousin Elvira. She had a male guardian, but he did not live with them and visited only rarely. In other words, Bertha von Suttner's daily life unfolded without the immediate presence of a male authority figure. To be sure, her mother's authority did not extend beyond her own household, but Suttner also had other female role models. Her extended stay of nine years in Russia provided her with several examples of female sovereignty. Since her husband's parents disapproved of the marriage, Suttner and the love of her life, Arthur Gundacar von Suttner, eloped to Mingrelia, a region in Georgia, where they initially stayed with Suttner's friend, Yekaterina Dadiani, the Princess of Mingrelia, who had fought against the Turks at the head of her army. During her years in the Caucasus, Suttner also had occasion to study the history of the region and was particularly taken with the reign of Queen Tamara in the thirteenth century, which is considered the golden age of

Georgia. In her memoir Suttner emphasized that Tamara was not only a successful queen but also a triumphant military leader. When Rokneddin, the sultan of Asia minor, was about to attack Tamara's empire, he sought to intimidate her by denigrating her gender: "Ich gebe Dir zu wissen, o Tamara, Herrscherin der Georgier, daß alle Frauen schwachen Sinnes sind" (*Memoiren*, 131; I would have you know, O Tamara, ruler of the Georgians, that all women are of weak mind). Suttner gleefully describes Tamara's response:

> Tamara las die Botschaft ohne Eile. Sie befahl ihre Truppen zu sammeln und marschierte selber an der Spitze ihrer Armee dem Feind entgegen. Selbstverständlich war der Sieg ein vollständiger; die Straßen von Tiflis wurden geschmückt und die Königin hielt ihren Einzug, strahlend wie die Sonne. (*Memoiren*, 131)

> [Tamara read the message without haste. She commanded her troops to gather and she herself marched at the head of her army toward the enemy. Of course, the victory was a complete one; the streets of Tbilisi were adorned and the queen made her entrance, bright as the sun.]

We cannot know if Suttner would have become an effective leader if her family had been less privileged, but it is likely that, had she been born into a lower- or even middle-class family, her path to a position of authority would have been more difficult. And yet Suttner's aristocratic birth alone cannot account for her success. If I had to single out those characteristics that made Suttner an effective leader and activist, I would highlight her self-perception as a servant leader, that is, as a leader who considers serving a cause her main goal; her belief that progress is possible and that one can change society for the better; her skillful handling of public relations, along with her strategic use of personal connections and relationships; and last but not least, her deft negotiation of and resistance to gender codes. In order to elucidate these qualities, I will focus on Suttner's memoir and her novel *Die Waffen nieder*, first published in 1889. She begins her memoir with a traditional *captatio benevolentiae*:

> Was mich einigermaßen berechtigt, meine Erlebnisse mitzuteilen, ist der Umstand, daß ich mit vielen interessanten und hervorragenden Zeitgenossen zusammengetroffen und daß meine Anteilnahme an einer Bewegung, die sich allmählich zu historischer Tragweite herausgewachsen hat, mir manchen Einblick in das politische Getriebe unserer Zeit gewährte und daß ich im ganzen also wirklich Mitteilenswertes zu sagen habe. (*Memoiren*, 1)

[What gives me some justification for sharing my experiences is the fact that I have met many interesting and outstanding contemporaries, and that my participation in a movement that has gradually grown to historical significance has afforded me some insight into the political mechanisms of our time, and that all in all I really have something worth sharing to say.]

Suttner apparently felt the need to preface her work with a response to possible objections to the perceived self-arrogation of writing a memoir while female. It is also notable that in justifying her presumption she refers not to her own accomplishments but to those of her friends and acquaintances and to the importance of the Peace Movement. In other words, Suttner casts herself as a medium and tool, worthy only because of the people she met and the cause she served—though, to be sure, her memoir then proceeds to relate the story of her childhood, which has nothing to do with either of the issues she just mentioned.

While Suttner's memoir does narrate aspects of her biography that are not directly relevant to her work as a peace activist, she follows through on her initial emphasis on famous contemporaries and political causes. Her memoir is conceived as an assemblage with a scrapbook-like character. She includes not only excerpts from her own diary and correspondence but also numerous letters written to her by illustrious contemporaries, citations from newspaper articles, and documents such as her birth certificate. The effect of this hybridity is complex. On the one hand, she points to these documents to downplay her own role and thus justify her memoir through references to her extended network. In essence, she positions herself as a mediator who presents the voices of illustrious men to the public. In doing so, she minimizes the importance of her own story. Indeed, while readers are presented with a vivid portrayal of her youthful self, the older Suttner disappears amid a collage of letters, information about contemporary events, and descriptions of peace conventions. One might fault Suttner for failing to construct an assertive self, but one might also conclude that she successfully crafted strategies that allowed her to circumvent the limitations of woman's proper place in the public sphere. Tellingly, in her memoir Suttner strategically selects letters that praise her and highlight her importance. For example, she includes a letter from Leo Tolstoi, who compared her to Harriett Beecher Stowe and suggested that, much as *Uncle Tom's Cabin* (1852) heralded the end of slavery, Suttner's book might signal the end of warfare (*Memoiren*, 180). Thus through these letters Suttner highlights her accomplishments while downplaying her agency and showcasing her seeming modesty and female restraint. Again and again the authors of these inserted letters praise Suttner's contributions to the cause, ask her to give talks, and invite her to attend inter-parliamentary conferences. When she gives lectures, she combats stage fright with a reminder that her public speeches are not about her. Rather, she herself is a "Nebensache" (incidental) she insists and continues, "so sprach ich völlig angstlos, mit der Sicherheit eines Boten" (*Memoiren*, 191; thus I spoke completely without fear, with the self-assurance of a messenger). Through her collage of letters and articles, Suttner not only writes the history of the peace movement but also inserts herself into that history as both a witness and an agent.

I believe that this strategy of self-assertion through self-effacement is effective in a number of ways. First, theories of leadership often state that a great leader is someone who defines himself (and it is often a himself that is at stake here) as a tool of a cause that is larger than any individual. Seen in this light, Suttner is simply doing what any great leader would do: she is putting the cause first. Second, by integrating the voices of others, Suttner is both displaying and strengthening her network. Much like the ability to see oneself as a servant of a larger cause, the power to forge connections and to communicate successfully with a large group of people is an essential quality of effective leaders. For the most part, Suttner's extended correspondence was designed to raise money and recruit casual acquaintances, intimate friends, and illustrious men for the cause of world peace. She openly acknowledged her determination to bank on the reputation of famous contemporaries—she calls this "ihre eventuelle Zustimmung zu verwerten" (*Memoiren*, 220; to utilize their potential consent)—and uses any supportive statement they send her to promote whichever cause she deems most important at the time. She also relied on strategic introductions to achieve her goals. For example, by introducing Felix Moscheles and the Marquis Beniamino Pandolfi, two key leaders in the peace movement, to each other, she was instrumental in initiating the Venetian section of the European Peace League (*Memoiren*, 162). Moreover, she understood that alliances are forged not only through intellectual agreement but also through casual gatherings, rituals and ceremonies that provide a sort of social glue: "Das zwanglose Beisammensein in gehobener Stimmung, dazu die jubelnden Rufe der Bevölkerung, das Flaggewehen, die Musikbanden: das alles bringt fast mehr die Verbrüderung und Verständigung zuwege als die vorangehen-den Verhandlungsarbeiten" (*Memoiren*, 196; An informal get-together in an elevated mood along with the cheering calls of the population, the waving of flags, the music bands: all this brings almost more fraterniza-tion and understanding than the previous negotiations). In short, one of Suttner's signal contributions to the peace movement consisted in forging social bonds and communities supportive of the common cause.

Although Suttner's strategic self-effacement furthered her goals most effectively, it also has a very clearly delineated gender component. Around 1900 (and, one might add, today), it was considered unseemly for a woman to appear ambitious and to seek power publicly and intentionally.

In portraying herself as pushed, prodded, goaded, and invited to speak and participate by the likes of Alfred Nobel and Leo Tolstoi, Suttner assumes the only female stance toward power that does not provoke an immediate sexist backlash: that of the hesitant participant who is given a seat at the table by the powerful men who really are and remain in charge.

Interestingly, Suttner's memoir also bears traces of a conversion narrative in which a frivolous young girl is transformed into a committed activist. She goes to great lengths to describe her young self as a silly teenager who thinks mostly about clothes and dalliances (*Memoiren*, 28). In describing her youth, she laments: "Ach, was war ich doch für ein oberflächliches, eitles Ding!" (*Memoiren*, 43; Oh, what a superficial, vain thing I was!),

> das ganz in geselligen Freuden aufgeht, das um die weltbewegenden Ereignisse sich nicht kümmert, dagegen an die eigene Toilette, die es bei Festgelegenheiten trug, so intensive Aufmerksamkeit wendet, daß die Erinnerung noch nach vierzig Jahren nicht erloschen ist. (*Memoiren*, 49)

> [that is completely absorbed in social pleasures, does not care about earth-shattering events, but pays such intense attention to her own get-up that she wore on festive occasions that the memory is still not extinguished after forty years.]

In describing her early years, Suttner highlights her own frivolity and emphasizes that she had no interest in politics and never read newspapers. She barely took note of the battle of Solferino of 1859, Austria and Prussia's war against Denmark in 1864, the Austrian war against Prussia of 1866, or even the Franco-Prussian war of 1870–71.

Suttner also admits that, as a young girl, she shared her culture's appreciation for all things military: "Etwas Militärfrommeres als mich gab's ja nicht" (*Memoiren*, 24; There was nobody more devoted to the military than I). Through these confessions, Suttner positions herself as traditionally female. It is as though she wants to assure her readers that she was not born an Amazon but rather conformed to gendered norms and expectations. However, in emphasizing the distance to her former self, she also introduces a sense of discontinuity into her narrative, referring to her youth as a "vages Erinnerungsbild" (*Memoiren*, 44; vague memory), and noting: "Ich kann es heute nicht begreifen, daß ich so stumpfsinnig sein konnte" (*Memoiren*, 69; I cannot understand today that I could have been so dull). Though readers may glean from this that a certain shallowness is harmless enough in one so young, Suttner clearly presents such frivolity as a stage to grow out of. Indeed, it strikes me that the most important aspect of these memories of her youth is the emphasis on change.

Throughout her memoir, Suttner conceptualizes identity itself as radically discontinuous: "Jeder Mensch, obwohl er zumeist den Wahn hegt, ein gleiches, fortgesetztes Ich mit bestimmten Charaktereigenschaften zu sein, ist ja selber eine Kette der verschiedensten Typen" (*Memoiren*, 6; Every human being, although he usually deludes himself into thinking that he is the same, continuous I with definite characteristics, is himself a chain of the most diverse types). By highlighting such discontinuities, Suttner clears the path for radical transformations. In other words, in describing her own learning process, she not only situates herself in an autobiographical tradition that goes back to Augustine's confessions, but she also offers a template for her readers that models a progression from indifference to activism.

Tellingly, Suttner's novel *Die Waffen nieder* showcases a similar conversion narrative. The novel, as Barbara Burns points out, deliberately obscures "the work's fictional base," mimicking the genre of biography.[4] Suttner's heroine, Martha Althaus, grows up in a home dedicated to military values. Her father was a general in the Austrian army and her first husband an enthusiastic soldier. Young Martha is utterly uncritical of the military: "Ich erinnere mich, daß der höchste Begriff menschlicher Größe mir in kriegerischem Heldentum verkörpert schien"[5] (I remember that the highest concept of human greatness seemed to me to be embodied in martial heroism). Thus here too, Suttner depicts a heroine who undergoes a process of growth from uncritical endorsement of warfare to outspoken opposition. Both memoir and novel offer an individual growth process as proof that mankind can learn to solve international conflicts peacefully: "Wie das Individuum (in dem vorliegenden Fall ich selber) unter dem Einfluß von Erfahrungen und Ueberlegungen ganz veränderte Anschauungen bekommen kann, so kann und wird auch die Allgemeinheit neue Einsichten gewinnen und danach handeln" (*Memoiren*, 69–70; Just as an individual (in the present case I myself) can, influenced by experience and reasoning, acquire completely changed views, so the general public can and will gain new insights and act accordingly).

I believe it is precisely this firm conviction that change is possible that accounts for Suttner's effectiveness as a leader. She believed both that people can change and that she herself was in a position to promote the critical insights that make such change possible. Perhaps the most revolutionary vision that informs her activism for peace is the conviction that there could be a world without war. Suttner's novel in particular attacks the idea that, because there have always been wars, there always will be wars (*Waffen*, 177). She draws attention to the numerous images and figures of speech that present war as inevitable, noting, for example, that wars are said to "break out," "von selber 'ausgebrochen'—ausgebrochen wie das Nervenfieber, wie das Vesuvfeuer" (*Waffen*, 38; broke out all by itself, like a nerve fever, like the Vesuvius fire). This seeming inevitability is then used to argue that pacifism is pointless—"Die Abschaffung des Krieges. Doch nein: ebensogut könnte ich sagen, man solle das Erdbeben abschaffen" (*Waffen*, 37; The abolition of war. But no, I might as well say that earthquakes should be abolished)—and that wars must be tolerated as divinely preordained: "Das von Gott gewollte . . . muß man mit Fassung und Ergebung ertragen" (*Waffen*, 23; What God wishes . . . we must bear with composure and resignation). Suttner's courage in confronting such claims of inevitability and her firm belief that change is possible account for her prominence in the contemporary peace movement and for the enduring popularity of her book.

While Suttner is best known for her novel *Die Waffen nieder*, she spent the bulk of her time giving speeches and writing political journalism. As Donath points out, she had perfected the art of the feuilleton, the political essay, and critical reportage.[6] The newspapers and magazines that published her articles include the *Neue Freie Presse, Neues Wiener Tagblatt, Neues Wiener Journal, Österreichische Rundschau, Die Zeit, Die Woche, Die Frankfurter Zeitung, Das Berliner Tageblatt*, the *New Yorker Staatszeitung, Pester Lloyd, Secolo, Courier Européen*,[7] and, of course, her own journal, *Die Waffen nieder*, which she founded in 1891 and which her colleague Alfred Fried took over as editor-in-chief in 1900 under the new title *Die Friedenswarte*; she continued to contribute her "Randglossen zur Zeitgeschichte." In addition to being published in book format, Suttner's novel was serialized in the Social Democratic journal *Vorwärts* in 1892, upon prompting by Wilhelm Liebknecht, and issued as a one-mark *Volksausgabe* in 1896. She was convinced that, as she put it, "Wir leben im Zeitalter der Reklame"[8] (We live in the age of advertising), and she left no venues untapped. She realized that an idea does not simply spread because it is reasonable or compelling, but rather gains its force through promotion: "Nicht durch eigene Kraft wirkt die Idee, sondern durch Agitation und die 'friends'"[9] (An idea does not have an impact through its own force, but rather through promotion and "friends"). Because she believed that nothing can oppose "die unwiderstehliche Gewalt einer hinreichend unterrichteten und energisch organisierten öffentlichen Meinung" (*Memoiren*, 147; the irresistible power of sufficiently informed and energetically organized public opinion), she did all she could to educate the masses, and she did so knowing full well what a difficult challenge she was facing. Although Suttner was often called naïve, she knew that the task of enlightening the public is an arduous and often futile endeavor. Albeit optimistic in her public statements, in her letters she at times expressed her frustration with "die kompakte Masse" whose "Dummheit ist wie ein Abgrund von Schlamm"[10] (stupidity is like an abyss of mud).[11]

The conviction that one must work tirelessly to promote new insights and to help spread the idea of peace also informs Suttner's memoir. Here

she pursues her self-declared goal of educating the public by acknowledging and discussing opinions that are different from her own.[12]
Throughout, she introduces the perspectives of her opponents and thus
initiates a discourse that is designed to reach out to readers with different
backgrounds and ideologies. Again, it is through the integration of other
voices that she not only legitimizes her own presence in the public sphere
but creates a dialogue that is designed to draw her readers to her side.

Just as Suttner was aware of the challenges attendant to educating
the masses, she was also acutely aware of gender stereotypes. Even so, her
public statements rarely dwelled on the discrimination she experienced. In
her memoir she does occasionally mention belittling comments motivated
by her gender, but she uses the experience to showcase her final triumph.
Thus she notes that she published her book *Das Maschinenzeitalter:
Zukunftsvorlesungen über unsere Zeit* (*The Machine Age: Future Lectures
about Our Times*, 1899) under a pseudonym because she was afraid that

> das Buch diejenigen Leser, die ich mir wünschte, nicht erreichen
> würde, wenn es mit einem Frauennamen gezeichnet wäre, denn
> in wissenschaftlichen Kreisen herrscht so viel Vorurteil gegen
> die Denkfähigkeit der Frauen, daß das mit einem Frauennamen
> gezeichnete Buch von solchen einfach ungelesen geblieben wäre.
> (*Memoiren*, 140)

> [the book would not reach those readers whom I wished for if it
> were signed with a female name, for in scientific circles there is so
> much prejudice against the ability of women to think that a book by
> a woman would simply have remained unread.][13]

Tellingly, this concession to contemporary prejudice is not the endpoint
of this particular episode. Rather, Suttner uses this opportunity to cite
from numerous positive reviews of her book and humorously remembers
a dinner conversation during which, after hearing much praise for the
book and its anonymous author, she expressed a desire to buy it and was
told that "das ist kein Buch für Damen" (*Memoiren*, 149; that is no book
for ladies).

Finally, to me, the most admirable and perhaps most important character trait that distinguishes Suttner from many of her contemporaries
and that goes a long way toward explaining her untiring commitment
to the promotion of world peace is her unbreakable optimism and her
great capacity for hope. She has often been accused of naivety, but she
herself insisted repeatedly that her optimism did not stem from ignorance
or blindness to the obstacles in her way: "Nicht als ob wir die Hindernisse
des Weges nicht gesehen hätten. Wir waren uns derselben schmerzlich
bewußt" (*Memoiren*, 288; Not that we did not see the obstacles on the

way. We were painfully aware of them). This statement is borne out by her letters and diary entries, which are far less optimistic than her public statements. Thus Suttner records her resignation and disappointment in her diary, stating that she is "über die Friedenssache pessimistisch"[14] (pessimistic about the cause of peace). Similarly, although she continued to lobby the rich, famous, and powerful for her cause, she also admits in a letter: "Nun weiß man, was es bedeutet, wenn hohe Herren sagen: Ich werde sehen, was sich tun läßt. Da tut sich gewöhnlich gar nichts"[15] (Now we know what it means when gentlemen say: I'll see what I can do. Usually absolutely nothing happens). In comparing Suttner's public and private statements, it becomes evident that her optimism is often strategic. Far from being the result of ignorance and naivety, it is rooted in hard work and conviction. Suttner knows that nothing will change if we stop believing in change. Consequently, in all her public statements, she insists that, although progress is not linear but unfolds as a complicated dance of forward movement and regression, the future will ultimately be better. She declares that the peace movement gets stronger every day and, to prove her point, she cites the example of a lone violet in a field of snow. Although such a delicate flower may appear fragile and isolated, it is a sign of spring and future victory (*Memoiren*, 242–43).

Failure of Leadership?

In identifying reasons that kept Suttner from connecting with her readers and listeners, I believe we must first highlight and analyze the barrage of sexism with which she was confronted on a daily basis. Misogynist stereotypes pervade not only the responses of her contemporaries but also the scholarly literature to this day. In light of Suttner's outstanding accomplishments, it is easy to forget that she lived in a society in which women could not attend political assemblies, vote, run for office, or attend university. While Suttner was celebrated by some, more often than not she was ridiculed and treated with disrespect.[16] In the following, I will parse the theories of the most prominent contemporary purveyors of misogynist philosophy, including Paul Julius Möbius and Otto Weininger. I believe that analyzing their works is all the more important because Möbius and Weininger are frequently evoked but rarely read. And yet their thoughts shaped the political and social atmosphere in which female activists such as Suttner sought to advocate for peace.

Among the charges most frequently leveled at Suttner was that of naivety.[17] Carl von Ossietzky, for example, himself a pacifist and the recipient of the 1935 Nobel Peace Prize, accused Suttner of sentimentality and "Weltfremdheit" (cluelessness).[18] Ossietzky believed that women did not have the same firm grasp of reality and depth of thought that men possess. Consequently, they cannot form realistic plans that one could actually implement. Ossietzky writes,

> sie fand für die Idee keine stärkere Ausdrucksform als die Wehleidigkeit. Sie kämpfte mit Weihwasser gegen Kanonen. . . . Wie so viele Frauen, die aus reiner Weiberseele für die Verwirklichung eines Gedankens kämpfen, der männliche Spannkraft und unge-trübten Tatsachenblick erfordert, glitt sie ins Chimärische.[19]

> [she found no stronger expression for the idea than self-pity. She fought cannons with holy water . . . Like so many women who, from their pure female soul, fight for the realization of a thought that demands male vigor and an untroubled factual gaze, she slipped into chimera.]

In noting that women are incapable of deep thinking, Ossietzky was merely repeating a conviction that was pervasive in contemporary gender discourses. Eduard Reich, for example, author of *Studien über die Frauen* (*Studies about Women*, 1875), declared that female thinking is more suited to skimming surfaces than probing depths, more "für die Oberfläche als für die Tiefe" (for the surface rather than the depth).[20] Suttner was familiar with Reich's work as well as with Paul Julius Möbius's *Über den physiologischen Schwachsinn des Weibes* (*About the Physiological Idiocy of Woman*, 1903), which expounded the author's theories about women's natural intellectual inferiority and warned against the dire consequences of educating women: "Alle intellektuellen Weiber, die bisher gelebt haben, haben nicht so viel geleistet wie ein einziger grosser Mann, und doch sind sie fast alle geschädigt worden. . . . Der schlimmste Schade ist natürlich die Unfruchtbarkeit"[21] (All the intellectual women who have lived so far have not done as much as one great man, and yet almost all of them have been damaged. . . . Of course, the worst damage is infertility). It strikes me as crucial that Möbius not only denigrates women's intellect but also rejects out of hand the notion that any form of development or improvement could be possible: "so wenig, wie wir die Entwicklung des Menschen zu einem Uebermenschen zu erwarten haben, ebensowenig ist eine Aenderung der einmal festgelegten Geschlechtscharaktere wahrscheinlich"[22] (just as we cannot expect the development of man into a superhuman, we must consider a change of established sexual characters unlikely).[23] To top it off, Möbius warns against the horrors that would unfold if women had power: "In den Zeiten politischer Unsicherheit hat man mit Schrecken die Ungerechtigkeit und Grausamkeit der Weiber kennen gelernt, ebenso an den Weibern, die unglücklicherweise zur Herrschaft gekommen sind" (*Schwachsinn*, 18; In times of political insecurity we have become acquainted with the injustice and cruelty of women, and similarly in the case of women who have unfortunately come to power).

Much like Möbius, who argued that women feel but cannot think or analyze (38), Otto Weininger's infamous *Geschlecht und Charakter: Eine prinzipielle Untersuchung* (*Gender and Character: An Investigation of Fundamental Principles*, 1908) suggests that, for women, feeling and thinking are one and the same.[24] Unlike Möbius, however, Weiniger theorizes the possibility of intermediate sexual stages, of manly women and feminine men. At first glance this may appear to be forward thinking. However, in Weininger's hands it is an integral element of a deeply misogynist theory. Although Weininger grants that there are some select women who produce cultural and intellectual works of some significance, he insists that these exceptional beings are psychologically and intellectually male: "Alle mit einem gewissen Recht berühmten und geistig irgendwie hervorragenden Frauen weisen stets zahlreiche männliche Züge auf"[25] (all women who have some right to fame, and women who stand out mentally in some form, always have many masculine traits). Consequently, any female accomplishment offers further proof of male genius so that "die Personen auf der weiblichen Liste, genau besehen, auch nur wieder für die Männlichkeit des Genies Zeugnis ablegen würden"[26] (the individuals on the female list, upon close inspection, again would bear witness only to the masculinity of genius).[27] Since Weininger's opus magnum clocks in at some 600 pages, one could continue this list of thoroughly sexist statements ad infinitum.[28]

While Möbius and Weininger considered themselves disinterested scientists, their theories served as powerful ammunition in ideological and political wars. One should never underestimate the extent to which pernicious gender stereotypes can be summoned to destroy political opponents. Moreover, in Suttner's case such public sexist attacks were manifested not only in the form of commentary; rather, Suttner was also "a frequent target of cartoons and general lampooning."[29] Indeed, the contemporary press brims with attempts to ridicule and degrade her, variously calling her "Gschaftelhuberin" (busybody), "Friedensbertha" (peace Bertha), and "Judenbertha" (Jew Bertha) because of her friendship with Theodor Herzl and her commitment to fighting anti-Semitism. All too often, political attacks on pacifism took the form of personal attacks on Suttner and her gender: "Ich erhalte jetzt öfters anonyme Schmähbriefe. Gewöhnlich von antisemitischem Geist durchwehte. . . . Und daneben immer den freundlichen Hinweis auf Kochlöffel und Strickstrumpf" (cited in *Bertha*, 211; I now often receive anonymous insulting letters. Usually an anti-Semitic spirit wafts through them. . . . And alongside, always the friendly reference to cooking spoon and knitted stocking). In calling Suttner blue-eyed, vapid, and clueless, her attackers dispensed with the need to respond to her arguments and instead denied her the right to speak altogether.[30] Consider Felix Dahn's little ditty "Die Waffen hoch! Das Schwert ist Mannes eigen, / Wo Männer fechten, hat das Weib zu schweigen, / Doch freilich, Männer gibt's in diesen Tagen, / Die sollten lieber Unterröcke tragen"[31] (Arms up! The sword belongs to man. Wherever men fight, the woman has to be silent. But, of course, there are men these days who should wear petticoats).

While the misogyny of a Möbius, Weininger, or Dahn does not surprise, it is somewhat more frustrating that some of these prejudices have informed secondary literature to this day. In addition to attacks on her personality, Suttner's talents are frequently belittled. Thus Häntzschel has pointed out that *Die Waffen nieder* is a best-seller that was "von der Germanistik totgeschwiegen" (ignored by German Studies).[32] In an article from 1957, Leitich pokes fun at Suttner's supposed lack of talent when she notes that Suttner, to whom she refers by first name, received expensive instruction in singing with little success and then expands her comment into a wholesale demolition of Suttner's accomplishments by adding a telling "auch" (also): "Doch *auch hier* [author's emphasis] schien Bertha mehr geplätschert als gelernt zu haben"[33] (But here too Bertha seemed to have dabbled more than learned). Leitich also recycles the notion of Suttner's much proclaimed naivety, noting that it is the kind of naivety "wie sie vielleicht nur einer Frau gegeben ist, die gar nicht alle Schwierigkeiten sieht"[34] (as it may only be given to a woman who does not even see all the difficulties).[35] Similarly, Donath compliments Suttner for her extensive journalistic work, all the more remarkable since she "nicht alle Zusammenhänge der Weltpolitik richtig verstand"[36] (did not properly understand all the interrelations of world politics). And Lughofer points out that, contrary to her own claims, Suttner was not instrumental in the creation of the Nobel Prize for Peace and blames her for being "zu rechthaberisch und fordernd" (too self-righteous and demanding) in her interaction with the Nobel Prize Committee.[37] Lughofer argues that the credit for both the conception and funding of the Nobel Peace Prize should go to Alfred Nobel alone, a rather surprising claim since, unlike Suttner, who believed in the efficacy and necessity of international cooperation and regulations, arbitration, peace congresses, and multilateral negotiations, Nobel was convinced that war could only be prevented by manufacturing ever more powerful weapons. Judged by this principle, there was no need for a prize; Nobel's dynamite factories would have done plenty to promote peace.[38]

Clearly, sexism hampered Suttner's ability to participate in public life in the most drastic way and allowed many to ridicule her and her message. But I believe that in seeking to account for the futility of her antiwar efforts, we must dig deeper. In the following, I want to consider two issues: Suttner's stance toward capitalism and toward nationalism. The issue of capitalism is raised by Marlene Streeruwitz, who locates the failure of Suttner's novel to effect change in her lack of attention to social and economic factors: "Das Projekt ist gescheitert, weil die Auslassung der Außenwelt etwa in Form ökonomischer Zwänge und staatlicher Voraussetzungen die kapitalistische Politik einer Wirklichkeit in diesem Roman bewusst verleugnet"[39] (The project has failed because the omission of the outside world, in the form of economic constraints and conditions of the state, for example, deliberately denies the capitalist politics of a reality in this novel). To be sure, in *Die Waffen nieder*, pacifism is front and center, while economic and social issues are sidelined. And yet, although Suttner was born to privilege, it would be wrong to think of her as a lady born with a silver spoon in her mouth who was blind to the economic deprivation of others. During her self-imposed exile in Russia she experienced dire poverty and even hunger. Throughout her life, she had to deal with financial difficulties. And while her fight did not focus on social justice, she was not blind to it either, and the nickname "red Bertha" (*Bertha*, 419) was not entirely undeserved. Suttner drew attention to the link between huge military expenditures and impoverishment (*Bertha*, 471) and proposed a definition of happiness based on social equality, declaring that she did not want the kind of happiness "welches aus Glanz, aus Rang- und Reichtumsgenuß besteht, denn von diesem muß jeder instinktiv fühlen, daß es nur auf Kosten der Armut und der Niedrigkeit der anderen bestehen kann; solches Glück ist allen Verbesserungsideen und Reformplänen und überhaupt Änderungen abhold" (cited in *Bertha*, 90; that consists of splendor, of the enjoyment of rank and wealth, for everyone must instinctively feel that this can exist only at the expense of the poverty and lowliness of others; such luck is averse to all ideas for improvement and plans for reform, and in general to all change).[40] Since she was theoretically aware of the link between mass poverty and rampant militarism, one might be tempted to attribute her lack of attention to social issues to the immense demands made on her time by her peace activism. Hamann comments on Suttner's colossal workload, ranging from intellectual to secretarial work: "eine riesige Korrespondenz und alle anfallenden praktischen Dinge bis zu der Beschaffung von ermäßigten Bahnkarten für die Frauen und Töchter, die die Abgeordneten mit nach Rom nehmen wollten" (*Bertha*, 155; an enormous amount of correspondence and all the practical things that came up, including obtaining tickets for the women and daughters whom the delegates wanted to take to Rome). But one might also wonder if the sidelining of economic factors was in itself a political decision, necessitated by her strategy of recruiting the rich and famous for her fight. Tellingly, Suttner turned a blind eye to some rather problematic aspects of her famous friends, including the invention and production of dynamite by Alfred Nobel or the exploitation of peasants by Ekaterina.

Apart from the question of the sidelining of economic issues, I wonder if Suttner's disinterest in nationalism made it difficult for her to connect with large groups of readers and listeners. Although she greatly valued the notion of "Heimat" (*Memoiren*, 140; homeland), she considered nationalism a movement of the past (*Memoiren*, 6).[41] In her memoirs she argues forcefully that the well-being of mankind as such trumps that of any individual nation: "Jedenfalls steht das Interesse der Menschheit, steht das absolute Recht immer höher als die Spezialvorteile eines Landes" (*Memoiren*, 428; In any case, the interest of mankind, the absolute law is always higher than the special advantages of a country). Similarly, her novel *Die Waffen nieder* promotes the interests of mankind over those of the nation: "Lass nur einmal einen höheren Begriff als den der Nation, nämlich den der Menschheit und der Menschlichkeit, als gemeinsames Ideal aufgefasst werden" (*Waffen*, 359; For once let a higher notion than that of the nation, namely that of humanity and humaneness, be understood as a common ideal). Unlike her memoir, which does not fully engage with the question of nationalism, her novel seeks to make a case for globalism. She begins by admitting that nationalism holds some appeal— "Das Nationalitätsprinzip war vielleicht doch etwas, das mit elementarer Kraft Betätigung erheischte" (*Waffen*, 120; The nationality principle was perhaps something that demanded activity with elemental force)—but then mounts a case against it by drawing our attention to the fact that the notion of what or who constitutes a nation is ever-shifting. Thus she notes that the former allies Prussia and Austria were quick to turn against each other and even go to war in 1866, the so-called Brothers War. Furthermore, Suttner's protagonist represents nationalism as ill-befitting Austrians who live in a multiethnic empire: "überhaupt paßt dieses ganze Prinzip nicht für Österreich; Böhmen, Ungarn, Deutsche, Kroaten—wo ist da das Nationalitätsband" (*Waffen*, 123; in general, this whole principle does not suit Austria; Bohemians, Hungarians, Germans, Croats— where is the bond of nationality). Thus she highlights the hybridity that underlies the presumption of unity and uniformity. While I find these arguments compelling, I believe that they address only very few aspects of the rather complex question of nationalism. Suttner's novel carefully parses all aspects of warfare, but it fails to address the paradox that her own proposed solution of international cooperation and treaties relies, at its most basic level, on the existence of functional and sovereign nation states. She had indeed, as she writes, "verlernt, den Krieg vom nationalen Standpunkt aus zu betrachten" (*Waffen*, 341; unlearned how to look at war from a national point of view). Suttner tends to draw a straight line from individuals to nations and thus fails to account for the fundamentally different dynamics of groups. Tellingly, in the statutes of the Austrian Peace Association nations are quite literally defined simply as groups of individuals.[42] Along the same lines, Suttner believed that the norms of individual behavior can be transferred directly to the interactions of larger entities: "Schon Manchen war es klar, daß zwischen Nationen dasselbe Verhältnis Platz greifen könne und solle, welches zwischen Individuen durch Gesetz und Sitte vorgeschrieben war: nämlich die Beschränkung der Selbstsucht durch Rücksichtnahme auf die Interessen der Anderen";[43] It was already clear to some that the same relation could and should take place between nations that was prescribed between individuals by law and custom: namely, the limitation of selfishness by a consideration of the interests of others). In light of these assumptions, it is hardly surprising that the gap between the fervent nationalism of the prewar period and Suttner's rational concept of nationhood remained unbridgeable.

The Measure of Success

Although I have investigated the reasons for what I have provocatively called Suttner's failure to reach a wider platform, I am acutely aware that the term failure is relative. One might argue with Susanne Jalka that the very fact that we talk and think about peace as much as we do owes a great deal to Bertha's von Suttner's life work (see Lechner and Stohl). But my point is of a different nature. If we want to clear space for female moral and political leadership, it is important to think carefully about the strategies women use, but it is equally important to think about and shine a light on responses to these strategies. As Bertha von Suttner used to say: "Wenn in einem Raume ein Ton stark erklingt, so beweist das nicht so sehr die Fülle des Tones als die Güte der in dem betreffenden Raume herrschenden Akustik" (*Memoiren*, 151; When a sound resonates powerfully in a room, it does not so much prove the richness of the sound as the quality of the acoustics prevailing in the room in question). In other words, it is not enough to theorize female leadership. For a leader to be effective, we need to improve the societal conditions in which leadership unfolds and to educate the followers on whom every leader depends.

Notes

[1] For an overview of women and the peace movement see Ruth Roach Pierson, ed., *Women and Peace: Theoretical, Historical and Practical Perspectives* (London: Croom Helm, 1987).

[2] Brigitte Hamann, *Bertha von Suttner: Ein Leben für den Frieden* (Munich: Piper, 1991), 12. Further references are given in the text using the short title *Bertha*.

[3] Bertha von Suttner, *Memoiren* (Altenmünster, Loschberg: Jazzybee Verlag, 2016), 43. Further references are given in the text using the title, *Memoiren*.

[4] Barbara Burns, "Bertha von Suttner's *Die Waffen nieder!* The Roots and Reception of a Pacifist Manifesto," in *Fontane and Cultural Mediation: Translation and*

Reception in Nineteenth-Century German Literature; Essays in Honor of Helen Chambers, ed. Ritchie Robertson and Michael White, 158–69 (Leeds: Maney, 2015), 160.

[5] Bertha von Suttner, *Die Waffen nieder!* (Berlin: Deutsche Literaturgesellschaft Europa Center, 2008), 8. Further references to this work are given in the text using the short title *Waffen.*

[6] Adolf A. Donath, "Bertha von Suttner und die kleine Form," *Acta Universitatis Wratislaviensis Germanica Wratislaviensia* 20 (1974): 83–95, here 89.

[7] See Anja Shepela, "Bertha von Suttner: Eine Frau steht ihren Mann," in *Patentlösung oder Zankapfel: German Studies für den internationalen Bereich als Alternative zur Germanistik—Beispiele aus Amerika,* ed. Peter Pabisch (Bern: Peter Lang, 2005), 227–50, here 234.

[8] Shepela, "Bertha von Suttner, 235.

[9] Cited in Donath, "kleine Form," 90. Taken from Suttner's diary.

[10] Gisela Brinker-Gabler, ed. *Kämpferin für den Frieden, Bertha von Suttner: Lebenserinnerungen, Reden und Schriften; Eine Auswahl* (Frankfurt am Main: Fischer Taschenbuch, 1982), 136.

[11] See also "Die Lüge, der Schimpf, die Gemeinheit: Das sind die Waffen, mit welchen jene kämpfen—und das dumme, dumme, dumme (im Katechismus zwar genügend unterrichtete) Volk tut mit" (cited in Hamann, *Bertha,* 204).

[12] As a side note, it bears mention that while Suttner engages with opinions that are different from her own, her memoir does not tackle the tangled question of memory and indeed short-circuits the issue altogether by presenting a collage of documents. In so doing, Suttner skirts the question of truth that plagues all memoirs and avoids the "irresolvable conflict between the capabilities of memory and the demands of narrative. The latter demands specifics; the former is really bad at them," Ben Yagoda, *Memoir: A History* (New York: Riverhead Books, 2009), 109. It would appear that plumbing the depths of an unreliable memory does not go with the activist agenda Suttner promotes.

[13] Suttner's decision to publish anonymously or under a pseudonym was motivateded by sexism. She believed that a pseudonym would guarantee that "die Leute das Buch ernster nehmen, denn das Vorurteil gegen die Frauen haben wir zwei—und auch Bebel—noch lange nicht todtgemacht" (people take the book more seriously because the two of us—and also Bebel—have not eradicated the prejudice against women by a long shot). Cited in Edelgard Biedermann, "Eine Genossin des leibhaftigen Gottseibeiuns? Zu Bertha von Suttners Briefwechsel mit Irma von Troll-Borostyani. 1886–1890," in *Österreich in Geschichte und Literatur mit Geographie* 45, no. 2b-3 (2001): 134–52, here 140. See also Suttner's foreword to *Maschinenzeitalter*: "Wenn ich diesmal anonym vor das Publikum trete, so geschieht es, weil mein Name, wenn genannt, gerade solche Kreise meinem Buche verschließen könnte, für die es hauptsächlich bestimmt ist" (If I step before the public anonymously this time, then it is because my name, if it were mentioned, could block access to my book for the people for whom it is meant most of all). Bertha von Suttner, *Das Maschinenzeitalter: Zukunftsvorlesungen über unsere Zeit* (Zurich: Verlagsmagazin, 1889), no page number.

[14] Bertha von Suttner, "Tagebuchaufzeichnungen," in *Kämpferin für den Frieden, Bertha von Suttner*, ed. Gisela Brinker-Gabler (Frankfurt am Main: Fischer, 1982), 117–140, here 127.

[15] Bertha von Suttner, "Reise nach Amerika: Begegnung mit Präsident Roosevelt," in Brinker-Gabler, *Kämpferin für den Frieden* (Frankfurt am Main: Fischer, 1982), 105–7, here 106.

[16] Lughofer notes that "at the Berlin Conference of 1908, though already a Nobel Prize winner and prominent supporter of the Union, she was given no place of honor and had to hunt for a seat in the audience among the other visitors." Johann Georg Lughofer, "Bertha von Suttner: A Prototypical European Writer," *Letter: Journal for Linguistics and Literary Studies* 9 (2011): 186–209, here 204.

[17] See Shepela, "Bertha von Suttner," 227.

[18] Karl von Ossietzky, *Rechenschaft*, accessed Feb. 15, 2019; http://gutenberg.spiegel.de/buch/rechenschaft-1947/12.

[19] Ossietzky, *Rechenschaft*.

[20] Eduard Reich, *Studien über die Frauen* (Jena: Hermann Costenoble, 1875), 226. Suttner cites Reich in *Maschinenzeitalter*: "Der Verstand der Frauen ist . . . mehr für die Oberfläche als für die Tiefe, mehr für die Form als für die Substanz" (91; Women's understanding is . . . more superficial than deep, more for form than for substance). She was also familiar with Möbius's work; see her comment that "nicht ein einziger nur auf die Idee kam, daß 'Jemand' dem 'schwachsinnigen Geschlechte' angehören könnte" (*Memoiren*, 147; not one person thought that "somebody" belonged to the "feebleminded" sex). On the claim that women are incapable of concentrated thinking, see Biedermann, "Eine Genossin," 149.

[21] Paul Julius Möbius, *Über den physiologischen Schwachsinn des Weibes* (1903; repr. San Bernadino, CA: The Perfect Library, 2017), 7.

[22] Möbius, *Schwachsinn*, 6.

[23] Möbius considered women a "Mittelding zwischen Kind und Mann" (15; a middle thing between child and man) and believed that "Cultur ein Mörder ist" (8; culture is a murderer) first because "Uebermässige Gehirntätigkeit macht das Weib nicht nur verkehrt, sondern auch krank" (excessive brain activity makes a woman not only perverse but also ill), but also because it leads women away from their one true calling, motherhood, even though "jeder andere weibliche Beruf als der der Mutter ein kümmerlicher Notbehelf ist" (11; every female profession other than motherhood is a pitiful substitute). Möbius also claims that, as they age, women lose what little intellect they have faster than men (26).

[24] Otto Weininger, *Geschlecht und Charakter: Eine prinzipielle Untersuchung* (Vienna: Wilhelm Braumüller, 1908), 128. See also "Ihr mangelt das intellektuelle Gewissen. Man könnte bei ihr von 'logical insanity' sprechen" (192; She lacks an intellectual conscience: one might speak of 'logical insanity.').

[25] Weininger, *Geschlecht und Charakter*, 80.

[26] Weininger, *Geschlecht und Charakter*, 88.

[27] See also "Ein weiblicher Genius ist demnach eine contradiction in adjecto" (Weininger, *Geschlecht und Charakter*, 242).

[28] Weininger argues that women have a rather loose grasp on reality (which, he notes, is why they often believe themselves to be victims of sexual attacks, 251); that they have no interest in science; cannot be evil, only amoral (254); that they have no dignity (260), only to conclude: "der tiefstehende Mann steht also noch unendlich hoch über dem höchststehenden Weibe, so hoch, daß Vergleich und Rangordnung hier kaum mehr statthaft scheinen" (345; the low-ranking man is thus still infinitely superior to the highest ranking woman, so superior that comparison and order of rank hardly seem appropriate here). In summation, Weininger notes that women have no soul and therefore wonders: "Ist es [das Weib] also noch Mensch? Oder ist es Tier? Oder Pflanze?" (394; Is it [the woman] still human? Or is it animal? Or plant?).

[29] Isabella Ackerl, "Lay Down Your Arms," *Austria Today* 3 (1993): 48–50, here 50.

[30] See Streeruwitz, who speaks of the "Diskriminierung dieses Texts über die Verunglimpfung der Schreiberin als sentimental oder blauäugig" (discrimination against this text by means of disparaging the writer as sentimental or blue-eyed). Marlene Streeruwitz, *Autorinnen feiern Autorinnen: Marlene Streeruwitz über Bertha von Suttner* (Vienna: Mandelbaum Verlag, 2014), 59. In her excellent essay Streeruwitz also compares the Wikipedia entries on Picasso and Bertha von Suttner and concludes: "Was in der Biografie Picassos zum Werk gerinnt, bestimmt bei Bertha von Suttner das Leben, aus dem das Werk abgeleitet werden soll" (27; what solidifies as work in the biography of Picasso is in Bertha von Suttner's case seen to determine a life from which her work derives). She notes further: "Genau mit solchen Versuchen, die in einem phantasierten Schulaufsatzstandardstil gehobener Sprache verfasst werden, wird Ideologie festgeschrieben" (29; it is precisely through such attempts that are composed in a fantasized school essay style of elevated language that ideology is reinscribed).

[31] Felix Dahn, *Gedichte*, accessed February 15, 2009; http://gutenberg.spiegel.de/buch/gedichte-87/86.

[32] Günter Häntzschel, "*Die Waffen nieder.* Bertha von Suttners Antikriegsroman; Zur Poetik und Ideologie der Frauenliteratur," in *Poetik und Geschichte: Viktor Zmegac zum 60. Geburtstag*, ed. Dieter Borchmeyer (Tübingen: Niemeyer, 1998), 102–17, here 102. Interestingly, Zelewitz links literary reputation to politics when he points out that Ebner-Eschenbach, who is seen as apolitical, is much appreciated, while Suttner's work is called trivial. See Klaus Zelewitz, "Die Waffen nieder und der explizite bzw. implizite Vorwurf der Trivilität," *Studia Austriaca: An International Journal devoted to the Study of Austrian Culture and Literature* 16 (2008): 9–22, here 13. However, even Tolstoi, who approved of her politics, called Suttner untalented: "Gut formuliert. Man spürt die tiefere Überzeugung, aber unbegabt" (cited in Zelewitz, "Waffen nieder," 11).

[33] Ann Tizia Leitich, "Bertha Suttner (1843–1914)," *Neue österreichische Biographie ab 1815: Große Österreicher Band 1* (Vienna: Amalthea Verlag, 1957), 66–75, here 67.

[34] Leitich, "Bertha Suttner," 66.

[35] See also Leitich's comment that Suttner's husband "hatte das etwas passive Temperament der Männer, die mit älteren Frauen glücklich werden" (69; had the somewhat passive temperament of men who become happy with older women).

[36] Donath, "kleine Form," 93.

[37] Johann Georg Lughofer, "Erinnerungskultur in Österreich: Eine Annäherung anhand des Fallbeispiels Bertha von Suttner 2005," *Acta Neophilologica* 40, nos. 1–2 (2007): 155–65, here 159; see also Hamann, *Bertha von Suttner*, 352.

[38] See the following statement by Nobel: "An dem Tag, da zwei Armeekorps sich gegenseitig in einer Sekunde werden vernichten können, werden wohl alle zivilisierten Nationen zurückschaudern und ihre Truppen verabschieden" (cited in Suttner, *Memoiren*, 234; The day that two army corps have the capacity to destroy each other in one second, all civilized nations will most likely draw back in horror and dismiss their troops). See also Frieling, who points out that Nobel believed that "die Vervollkommnung der Vernichtungsmittel bei der Kriegsführung größere Aussicht haben würde, die Kriege zu beenden, als alle Friedenskongresse" (the perfection of weapons of destruction in wars would have a greater chance of ending wars than all peace conferences). Simone Frieling, "Alfred Nobel: Der erfolgreiche Erfinder des Dynamits, der gescheiterte Dichter und seine vergebliche Liebe zur Pazifistin Bertha von Suttner," literaturkritik.de.

In this, Nobel was the norm, not the exception. Consider the following verses by Rilke: "Nun merket wohl: Es gibt kein Waffen nieder, / Weil's keinen Frieden ohne Waffen gibt" (Now note well: there is no down weapons / because there is no peace without weapons), Rainer Maria Rilke, *Sämtliche Werke*, ed. Ernst Zinn and Ruth Sieber-Rilke (Frankfurt am Main: Insel, 1992), 3:415–16.

[39] Streeruwitz, *Autorinnen feiern Autorinnen*, 56;

[40] "Die soziale Frage ist es, welche, indem sie alle anderen Angelegenheiten durchdringt, auch die Krieg- und Friedensfrage zur Lösung bringen wird" (cited in Hamann, *Bertha von Suttner*, 137; It is the social question that will bring about a solution to the question of war and peace because it penetrates all other matters).

[41] In *Maschinenzeitalter*, Suttner declares that in the society of the future "von der Nation . . . unfehlbar jede Spur verschwunden sein wird" (21; without fail, every trace of the nation will have disappeared).

[42] See Brinker-Gabler, *Kämpferin für den Frieden*, 52.

[43] Suttner, *Maschinenzeitalter*, 9.

10: Humanizing Socialism: The Feminist Dimension of Rosa Luxemburg's Intellectual Leadership

Peter Hudis

> *There is nothing more changeable than human psychology. That's especially because the psyche of the masses, like Thalatta, the eternal sea, always bears within it every latent possibility: deathly stillness and raging storm, the basest cowardice and the wildest heroism. The masses are always what they* must *be according to the circumstances of the times, and they are always on the verge of becoming something totally different from what they seem to be. My dear little girl, "disappointment with the masses" is always the most reprehensible quality to be found in a political leader. A leader with the quality of greatness applies tactics, not according to the momentary mood of the masses, but according to higher laws of development, and sticks firmly to those tactics despite all disappointments and, for the rest, calmly allows history to bring its work to fruition.*
>
> —Rosa Luxemburg[1]

ROSA LUXEMBURG PENNED these words while imprisoned in the notorious Wronke Fortress during the First World War, as part of an effort to come to terms with one of the darkest moments of modern history. At the time all hope for radical social transformation seemed to have evaporated in the face of statist militarism and the capitulation of most of the socialist movement to it. We do not face the same conditions today, but in many respects her words reach out beyond the break between the generations. The crisis facing us may even be more serious, since it has become hard to pin hopes for human emancipation on the forward progress of history when existing society seems to be marching headlong toward global planetary destruction—while descending into a depth of racism, misogyny, and political degeneracy not seen in decades. Nevertheless, Luxemburg's comment speaks to us in important ways, since it is hard to envision any alternative to our present predicament that does not acknowledge the capacity of masses of people to awaken, change, and ultimately *fulfill* the historical mission to realize their human potential.

Luxemburg was no accidental bystander to the traumas of her time, and it is to be expected that her life and work would tell us much about female leadership. She was both a leading figure in the German Social Democratic Party (SPD)—one of the largest socialist parties ever to have existed—and the most outstanding woman theoretician in the history of Marxism. Even if we were to put aside her specific political commitments (something she would no doubt strongly decry), she can rightly be considered among the greatest female economists of the twentieth century.[2] In light of her many contributions, it stands to reason that she would be seen as an exemplar of the effort to break through the barriers and preconceptions that have often stood in the way of women's participation in politics. Largely for this reason, her stature has only grown with the passage of time—something that cannot be said of many of the leading figures in the Marxist tradition that she subjected to ruthless criticism, such as Karl Kautsky, V. I. Lenin, and Leon Trotsky.

At the same time, a persistent duality appears to have characterized responses to her work. For a long time it was widely assumed by many of her admirers as well as critics within the socialist movement that she was not interested in feminism or women's struggles, since she wrote little about them and never directly involved herself in the feminist movements of her time. Often her theoretical work is today discussed without considering issues of gender and sexuality—as if they have little bearing on her intellectual contribution. This extends to the relative lack of discussion of her work on the part of contemporary feminist theorists, who likewise tend to presume that she had little or nothing to say about women. More recently, however, a different appraisal of her work has emerged. A growing number of feminist thinkers and activists view Luxemburg's refusal to separate the personal from the political—most emphatically expressed in her voluminous correspondence—as an anticipation of the concerns of contemporary feminism.[3] As Vivian Gornick put it in her review of *The Letters of Rosa Luxemburg*,

> From earliest times, Luxemburg had felt existentially homeless. She believed that "home" was to be found in a cause great enough to make world and self come together in a common effort to renew the human race. That effort, of course, was socialism. At the same time, she understood—really understood—that socialism had to be made, on a daily basis, from the inside out, through the internal struggle of people to humanize (that is, "socialize") themselves, even as they worked for radical change. She knew instinctively that if socialists closed down inside, they'd become the kind of people who, devoid of fellow feeling, would make police-state socialism. This was Luxemburg's single most important insight—*that socialists must remain empathic beings throughout their revolutionary lives.* Otherwise, she asked, what kind of world would they be making?[4]

206 ◆ Peter Hudis

This astutely captures Luxemburg's contribution to questions of revolutionary leadership. She never doubted that leaders were needed (the claim that she dismissed organization in favor of spontaneity is a myth). But she did not define her role, as well as that of others, as being an instrument of power that imposes its will upon mass struggles. Leadership, in her eyes, centered on eliciting from the masses their capacity to think for themselves, feel for themselves, and chart a path to liberation for themselves. A leader, she held, is one who opens the mind of the oppressed to their yet-to-be-discovered human possibilities. But how can anyone achieve that if they shield themselves from their emotional, mental, and affective dimensions? No one who knew Luxemburg would ever accuse her of sentimentalism. But no one could accuse her of insensitivity to the subjective dimension of human experience either. Thus Luxemburg's model of leadership incorporated distinctly feminist ideals, even if she did not label them as such.

While Luxemburg may have *anticipated* what can happen when efforts to change the world fail to rethink, redefine, and reshape what it means to be human, today we are living through the ultimate *consequences* of the failure to do so. A hundred years of botched and unfinished revolutions oppresses the living like a dead weight, making it all the harder to envision an alternative to capitalism—at the very moment when creating such an alternative has never been more urgent. We surely need to move forward by directly targeting the economic and political structures of capitalism, but in a way that is distinguished from the self-limited approaches to social transformation that has characterized so much of the past. Exploring Luxemburg's legacy in light of the *connection* between her political and economic theory and her emphasis on personal growth and transformation is, I believe, the best way to come to terms with what her legacy tells us about the challenges facing female leadership.

A Key Turning Point in Luxemburg's Development

The critical turning point in Rosa Luxemburg's life is 1898, when the 27-year-old graduate of the University of Zurich (she was the first woman in Europe to earn a doctorate in Public Law and Economic Affairs) moved to Berlin to become active in the German socialist movement. She became a revolutionary activist in Russian-occupied Poland as a teenager and by 1896 the leader of a Marxist political party, the Social Democracy of the Kingdom of Poland (SDKP). But she had much higher ambitions than serving as a Polish adjutant to the SPD (although she initially served in this role by campaigning for SPD candidates in Polish-speaking parts of Germany, such as Silesia). She wanted to become part of the *leadership* of the *German* party, and in turn, an influential *theoretical* voice in the Second International, in which the SPD played the leading role.

This was a lofty aspiration for a young, relatively unknown Jewish woman from "backward" Poland—especially given the rather staid and hierarchical structure of the SPD. Moreover, Luxemburg was seeking to make her mark on a party that had been around for many years and was by now the largest working-class political organization known to history. It was not at all clear (including to herself, initially) that she would be able to find a place for herself within it—especially given the widespread barriers to accepting women as theoreticians.

This by no means suggests that the SPD was indifferent to women's liberation. The opposite was in fact the case. Among the two best-selling books in the history of the SPD was Frederick Engels's *Origin of the Family, Private Property, and the State* (1884) and August Bebel's *Women under Socialism* (1879). More workers undoubtedly read these books than Marx's *Capital*. There was a serious and abiding theoretical interest within the SPD and Second International as a whole in the origins of women's oppression and how it would be overcome in a socialist society. Moreover, the SPD had a powerful women's section comprising tens of thousands of members that agitated for women's suffrage and equal rights, anchored by the bimonthly women's publication *Gleichheit* (Equality, edited by Clara Zetkin, who became one of Luxemburg's closest friends).[5]

It therefore comes as no surprise that upon her arrival several SPD leaders urged her to become active in the women's branch of the party. But she adamantly refused. The standard explanation is that she did so because she was not interested in feminism and considered it a diversion from the more pressing demands of the proletarian class struggle. The matter is not so straightforward, however, given the many instances in which she gladly participated in women's affairs. The decisive factor was her insistence on not being sidelined from participating in the central task of the party leadership—developing the *theoretical* perspectives that male SPD members viewed as their preserve. Indeed, as of 1898 no women served in leading bodies in the party, and few did so even a decade later.[6] The photos of party leaders gathered for party congresses are of an exclusively male group—until Luxemburg enters the picture. Support for women's rights did not necessarily translate into cultivating women leaders.

What proved decisive in breaking through such barriers was Luxemburg's critique of Eduard Bernstein's call to revise Marxism along reformist lines, issued just as she arrived in Germany. Bernstein was not just one of the main leaders of the SPD; Engels himself had anointed him literary executor of Marx's archives. Undeterred by his popularity and status in the International, Luxemburg issued a systematic refutation of his position in *Reform or Revolution*. She demonstrated on the basis of empirical evidence that Bernstein was wrong to claim that Marx's advocacy of revolutionary transformation had become obsolete. She demonstrated on the basis of her training in mathematical economics that his adoption of marginal utility theory obscured the dynamics by which labor is dominated by capital. And she demonstrated on the basis of her knowledge of Marxist theory that his effort to "remove the dialectical scaffolding of Marx's thought" represented "an attempt to shatter the intellectual arm with the aid of which the proletariat . . . is yet enabled to triumph over the bourgeoisie."[7] Although her critique of Bernstein rested on thoroughly materialist premises, she did not claim that the objective contradictions of capital would automatically lead to a post-capitalist society. Instead, as she was to do for the rest of her life, she held that an essential precondition for the emancipation of the working class is its *mental and spiritual* development. For this reason, she reserved her sharpest comments for Bernstein's claim that "the movement is everything, the goal is nothing." Failure to articulate the ultimate goal of the struggle, she insisted, not only cuts off access to the future—it also makes it impossible to adequately comprehend the present. She wrote, "The secret of Marx's theory of value, of his analysis of money, his theory of capital, his theory of the rate of profit, and consequently of the whole existing economic system is . . . the final goal, socialism. And precisely because, *a priori*, Marx looked at capitalism from the socialist's viewpoint, that is, from the historical viewpoint, he was enabled to decipher the hieroglyphics of capitalist economy," (*Reader*, 150–51). Luxemburg's critique of revisionism made a deep impression on both party leaders and rank-and-file activists. Yet although the leaders of the party applauded Luxemburg's abilities and worked with her to keep Bernstein's revisionism at bay, it soon enough became clear that they shared some of his illusions about the ability to seize power through purely parliamentary means. Luxemburg made no secret of her irritation at trade union officials as well as such leading figures of the SPD as August Bebel, which was one of many reflections of her independent spirit. Hence, although Luxemburg became a major figure in the party and gained a prominent place for herself in the Second International, tensions between her and her closest colleagues repeatedly came to the surface. Nowhere was that more true than when it came to her response to the 1905 Russian Revolution.

The Impact of the 1905 Russian Revolution

The 1905 revolution was the first nationwide revolution in which the working class played a leading role. That it occurred unexpectedly in "backward" Russia instead of "advanced" Western Europe made it all the more impressive. Luxemburg devoted an enormous amount of time and energy to analyzing it—and ultimately participating in it by going to Warsaw (and subsequently St. Petersburg and Finland) at the end of 1905.

In 1905 she composed dozens of articles and essays on the events, some of which represent a veritable *daily* account of an unfolding revolution.[8] Many appeared in *Vorwärts*, the daily newspaper of the SPD executive, which appointed her chief editor in October 1905.[9] She also published many pieces in the Polish revolutionary press, such as *Czerwony Sztandar* (issued by her party, the Social Democracy of the Kingdom of Poland and Lithuania [SDKPiL]). These writings served as the raw material from which she developed a distinctive concept of revolutionary transformation.

Luxemburg had a keen eye for how the Russian masses created new forms of democratically organized grassroots committees, clubs, unions, and parties to advance the revolution. The *spontaneous* actions of the working class, she held, showed that it was instinctively democratic as well as socialist in orientation. She wrote in March 1905:

> The first wave of general strike and workers' uprising, which flowed from Petersburg through the entire empire, including through our country, was to a large extent spontaneous. Not in the sense that the workers rose up blindly, without any understanding of what was going on. On the contrary, the slogans and ideas of the struggle, which were circulated widely by Social Democracy, were so much "in the air," were such a natural expression of the workers' needs and had so much entered into the flesh and blood of the proletariat, that the only thing needed was an initial nudge for the entire mass of workers instinctively to rise up to do battle in response to the news from Petersburg.[10]

Here (as elsewhere) she does not counterpoise spontaneity to organization, as if one substitutes for the other. While political parties and leaders cannot *create* revolutionary upsurges from whole cloth, they nevertheless play a crucial role in developing *ideas* that can inspire the masses to rise up against existing conditions. Luxemburg adhered to the need for political organization and "vanguard" parties no less than Bebel, Kautsky, Lenin, or anyone else who emerged from the Second International.[11] As she put it, "The more effectively and vigorously the revolutionary core succeeds now in building a road for the *party organization* to reach the masses, the quicker the victory and the fewer the casualties we will suffer in the next confrontation with absolutism."[12] The *form* of the relation between spontaneity and organization, not one versus the other, was central to her concept of revolution.[13] And the proper form of leadership, she held, was to *enlighten* the masses rather lecturing them like a schoolmaster.

During and after 1905, Luxemburg sought to enlighten the German and West European workers about the Revolution by urging them to adopt the *mass strike* as the central vehicle of class struggle. She believed that her task, as political leader, was to get the German workers to "speak Russian." This hardly resonated, however, with the leaders of the German Trade Unions, who were offended at the thought that the Russian working class had something to teach the "organized" Germans. At one conference the debate got intense when she was accused of stepping outside of her gender role:

> Comrade Schmidt, in his personal remarks about me, starts out by reproaching me for a lack of kindliness—that is, a courteous, friendly, comradely tone. I feel deeply touched and very contrite. Fortunately I know a way to correct this lack, and to raise myself to a level of true and proper kindliness. (Laughter.)

> Proof of this is given in an article that Comrade Hué recently published in the German mineworkers' paper [which states]:[14] "For those who show such an excess of 'revolutionary' energy as do our systematic promoters of the general strike—it is time for them to take a practical part in the Russian fight for freedom instead of pushing along the general strike discussion from their summer vacation resorts." And so off you go, you "theoreticians of the class struggle"—off to the fight for freedom in Russia! In other words, Comrade Hué invites us in the most kindly and comradely fashion to go to that place where very recently the public prosecutor assisted my close party comrade, Marcin Kasprzak, to achieve the highest honor that can be rendered to any Social Democrat [that is, being executed].[15]

Matters were hardly better, however, when it came to relations with SPD leaders who had earlier rallied to her side during the revisionism controversy. They now began to pull back from her insistence on promoting radical demands, fearing that it would compromise their parliamentary representation and electoral support. By the time she published her 1906 pamphlet *The Mass Strike, the Political Party, and the Trade Unions*, she was much closer to Lenin and the Bolsheviks than to most of her SPD colleagues. And in 1910, when Kautsky argued that the time had come to close down the discussion of the mass strike in order to protect the party's prospects in upcoming parliamentary elections, she broke from him and denounced him in the sharpest of terms.

The feud took on sexist dimensions, with Victor Adler writing to Bebel, "The poisonous bitch will yet do a lot of damage, all the more because she is as clever as a monkey, while on the other hand her sense of responsibility is totally lacking and her only motive is an almost perverse desire for self-justification."[16] Bebel replied by referring to "the wretched female's squirts of poison." He later wrote to Kautsky, "It is an odd thing about women. If their partialities of passions or vanities come anywhere into question . . . even the most intelligent of them flies off the handle . . . a regulating reason does not exist."[17]

Luxemburg's Relationship to the European Women's Movements

Luxemburg probably did not know of the above comments, but she was aware by 1910 that the depth of opposition to her within the party had a lot to do with the fact that she was a woman. Yet she chose not to fight on that level, choosing instead to show she could defeat the party leaders on their turf—their claims to being the bearers of Marxist theoretical orthodoxy.[18]

This did not mean, however, that she distanced herself from public support for and involvement in the women's movement. As early as 1902 she sharply critiqued the Belgian Socialist Party for dropping its demand for women's suffrage in exchange for forming an electoral coalition with the Liberals.[19] As Nancy Holmstrom has argued, her criticisms of family life in this period "were actually in advance of the bourgeois women's organizations of the time."[20] And in 1902 Luxemburg wrote an article for *Gleichheit* on Russian women, stating:

> Today the number of female proletarians who want to construct "heaven here on earth" for themselves and their class is growing day by day. A profound and exhilarating desire for education shows itself in the ranks of the women workers as the socialist idea of emancipation is awakened. The revolutionary movement relates to these women as a bearer of culture, in the broadest sense of that word. Not only does it enlighten them socially and politically, not only does it steel their character by enjoining in them the principles of solidarity and self-sacrifice, but it also teaches them the most basic skills of reading, writing, arithmetic, etc. The living conditions of the female Russian proletarian sensitize her to the truths of socialist salvation.[21]

Luxemburg actively participated in the movement for women's suffrage, and to a greater degree than often appreciated—especially as seen from her 1912 essay "Women's Suffrage and Class Struggle." It strongly argued for women's right to vote even as she emphasized the advantages of the working-class women's movement over bourgeois women's movements that limit themselves to demanding the political rather than *social* emancipation of women. Her essay also raised a subject that is central to many ongoing debates in contemporary feminist theory—the relationship between productive and unproductive labor. She argued:

> As long as capitalism and the wage system rule, only that kind of work is productive which produces surplus value, which creates capitalist profit. From this point of view, the music-hall dancer whose legs sweep profit into her employer's pocket is a productive worker, whereas all the toil of the women and mothers of the proletariat within the four walls of the home is considered unproductive work. This sounds crude and crazy, but it is an accurate expression of the crudeness and craziness of today's capitalist economic order. (*Reader*, 241)

Luxemburg emphasized that labor that produces surplus value (often by the male worker in the factory) is not "better" or more prone to "revolutionary consciousness" than labor that does not produce surplus value (such as the unpaid domestic labor performed by women in the home). Rather, from the *capitalist* point of view the only kind of labor that is "valued" is that which augments surplus value—which is why women's labor is so often denigrated and considered not worthy of compensation. Far from endorsing this state of affairs, Luxemburg argued that this is further evidence of capitalism's *irrationality*. The implication is that women's labor will finally be acknowledged for its affirmative social role only once the capitalist system of value production is abolished.

Luxemburg's relation to the women's movements evolved over time, in that she accorded it greater importance as the years wore on. This may have been due, in part, to her repeated incarcerations, which led her to form deep bonds with her fellow women prisoners. She wrote to Clara Zetkin on November 9, 1916: "It would have been a heart-felt joy for you to see these women." She goes on to report that the women greeted her by saying they "missed [her] so much because she always spoke a sharp word directly to the party leaders, and because she [was] the kind of person that the people higher up in the party would rather see going *into* prison than coming out of it" (*Letters*, 355–56). Two years later, shortly after her release from jail, in a letter of November 24, 1918, she urged Zetkin to immediately get to work creating a women's branch of her organization, the Spartakusbund: "A women's paper must be produced by us here in Berlin, either as an independent weekly or biweekly or as a daily supplement to *Rote Fahne*. . . . And it is such an urgent matter! Every day lost is a sin (*Letters* 481).

The Personal *Is* Political

What most of all reveals Luxemburg's feminist dimension is her correspondence with her longtime comrade and lover, Leo Jogiches. His reputation has suffered major blows over the years, not all of them justified. To be sure, he was a somewhat cold, calculating figure who had great trouble expressing his emotions—something that Luxemburg chided him for repeatedly. And he treated Luxemburg very poorly at times, especially when their love affair ended in 1907. However, Luxemburg always held him in the highest regard (she worked closely with him long after the end of their romantic relationship; indeed, right to the end of her life), and for good reason.[22] He was a brilliant organizer who was totally devoted to the revolutionary cause and would bear any risk to bring to justice those in positions of power and privilege (he lost his life trying to track down those who murdered Luxemburg in 1919). A proper account of his life has yet to be published—it is no small feat to write one, since he rarely wrote and most of what he did write has not survived.[23]

Luxemburg's letters to Jogiches reflect a persistent effort on her part to connect the personal and political, as she pushed back against any fixation on revolutionary politics at the expense of exploring the "inner world" of human feelings, emotions, and affections. "The only thing that causes me agony and makes me feel dreary," she writes on March 25, 1894, in a letter to him, "is the *Sprawa* [the Cause]." She adds: "That would all be fine if at least *in addition to that, alongside of that*, there was a bit of the human person, the soul, the individual to be seen. But from you there's nothing, absolutely nothing"(*Letters*, 10). In another letter to him, written on July 3, 1900, she states: "One must constantly carry out anew an inner review, or inventory, of oneself, in order to reestablish order and harmony" (*Letters*, 138). This plea for self-examination largely fell on deaf ears; she wrote on July 16, 1897: "My dear one, my love, I am not complaining, I am not asking for anything, all I want is that you not interpret any weeping on my part as 'just the scenes that women put on'" (*Letters*, 35). The problem was not just that Jogiches seemed to view her insistence on exploring the inner life of the individual as female sentimentalism, but rather that as she grew in political and theoretical stature, their relationship became more tense and distant on political matters as well.

The experience of the 1905 revolution dramatically altered their relationship. Prior to that point Luxemburg took little interest in the day-to-day details of running an organization, leaving that to Jogiches. But upon arriving in Russian-occupied Poland at the end of 1905 and plunging directly into the revolution, she was now actively organizing the underground resistance and participating in building up her revolutionary party. This led to profound tensions in their relationship, as Luxemburg increasingly felt she could fly on her own without him. Raya Dunayevskaya, who was one of the first to reclaim Luxemburg for modern feminism, is one of the few commentators who sought to unravel the factors that led to their breakup in 1907: "In a word, it was not only intellectually, as a pamphleteer, that she was reaching new heights, but organizationally. No doubt, she no longer considered Jogiches's organizational expertise as sacrosanct. . . . What we do know is that the tensions led to a breakup of their intimacy, without any way breaking up their revolutionary political activity."[24] In this interpretation, the experience of an actual revolution so dramatically impacted Luxemburg as to compel her to no longer put up with Jogiches's indiscretions—which by 1907 were numerous. Since revolution was the central focus of her life and work, it is only to be expected that experiencing one would leave a deep personal impact. In any case, she stated shortly after the breakup, "I am I, once more, since I have become free of Leo."[25]

The Role of Revolutionary Reason in Luxemburg's Politics

In light of what I have outlined above, Luxemburg's decision not to devote herself mainly to women's struggles or respond directly to sexist attacks upon her does not indicate that she was either uninterested in women's emancipation or indifferent to sexism. It can be argued, of course, that her decision to establish herself as a major Marxist theoretician and political leader instead of focusing on the women's movement was an opportunistic move on her part, designed to bolster her chances of winning a more prestigious position in the Second International. After all, none of the other leaders of the socialist women's movement, including Zetkin, became part of the inner circle that dominated the SPD and the Second International. And yet, while Luxemburg was surely ambitious, she was also extremely principled, and it seems out of character for her to adopt a course of action based purely on a quest for personal fame. And in light of her renowned tendency to fall out with an assortment of colleagues from across the political spectrum, it is especially hard to argue that her political stance was dictated by a desire to seek accommodation with leading lights of the socialist movement. A far more coherent claim, it seems to me, is that Luxemburg did more to break down the walls of sexism and male chauvinism by putting herself forth as major Marxist theoretician than if she had decided not to do so. By refusing to be marginalized or "pigeon-holed" to "the woman question," she felt she had a better chance of leaving a lasting imprint on the radical movement.

Luxemburg understood (as the most creative Marxists always have) that the hallmark of class society is the division between mental and manual labor. And she understood that this division of labor is the basis of women's oppression. As she argues in her *Introduction to Political Economy*, mental labor—such as planning, organizing, and theorizing—was long ago monopolized by men, who prevented women from sharing in it. Women were instead largely relegated to the domestic sphere, and independent intellectual activity—at least insofar as it impacts the political development of society—was reserved for males. As she put it in her notes on ancient Greece and Rome,

> Within slavery, total separation of mental and manual labor likewise took place. . . . The exclusion of slaves from mental life led of course to the rulers creating laws that benefitted their own interests. . . . It is not much different today. There were laws and a dominant class that did not take part in the production process. Those who created all the assets had to submit to them. In socialist society knowledge will be the common property of everyone. All working people will have knowledge.[26]

Luxemburg held that the task facing the workers' movement was to break from the separation of mental and manual labor by encouraging the downtrodden to think for themselves and develop their capacity for independent action. This defined, for her, the role of a revolutionary organization. She was aware that reason and rationalism—including Enlightenment Rationalism—was often used as a tool of domination and oppression. But the problem with the Enlightenment, she held, was not its rationalism but that it was restricted to a particular class—the bourgeoisie. With the destruction of class society, enlightenment reason would "be the common property of everyone."

Although Luxemburg herself never did so, we can interpret such statements as a challenge to the very basis of sexism. Luxemburg did not question the importance of the affective dimension, as especially seen from her correspondence. But just as she refused to accept Jogiches's resistance to expressing his inner, emotional life, she refused to accept the idea that systematic thought is reserved for men. To be sure, as Jacqueline Rose notes, she did not restrict "thought" (*Denkweise*) to systematic or original thinking—but the totality of her work indicates that she placed the greatest emphasis upon it.[27] Her standpoint challenges those who would denigrate reason and rationality as inherently regressive forces that inevitably serve the purposes of male domination. As Alhelí de María Alvarado-Díaz argues,

> Rosa Luxemburg was in no way indifferent to the situation of women in her time. It may not have been the headline issue in her militant agenda, but her concern over gender standards was clearly present throughout her lifespan. Coherent with her campaign against opportunism, Rosa's refusal to depict herself as a victim of

gender inequality gives her greater stature as a woman who chose not to invest time in useless discussions with men [who] she knew were incapable of transforming their own viewpoints on the question. Rosa chose to make her political career an example for other women to follow, showing that it was possible to be a woman, a revolutionary, and a thinker, regardless of the social prejudices of the times.[28]

This judgment is confirmed by the considerable number of women who became inspired by her example to become involved in radical politics—and to assert themselves, in doing so, as leaders in their own right.

Democracy and Socialism

Another crucial dimension of Luxemburg's contribution to political leadership was her understanding of the relation between democracy and socialism. It is a theme that defines virtually all of her work, and reaches beyond the historical context of her times in addressing challenges facing anti-capitalist movements in the twenty-first century.[29]

Democracy, for Luxemburg, was inseparable from socialism, since socialism, she insisted, represents the abolition of the rule of the few by the rule of the many—the producers. A non-democratic socialism is a contradiction in terms. At the same time, she problematized the question of democracy by pointing to the limitations of *bourgeois*, parliamentary democracy that leaves the economic foundations of capitalism untouched. Socialism cannot exist without *economic* democracy, she held, since it requires freely associated producers controlling the process of production and distribution of the social product. But economic democracy cannot be actualized without *political* democracy—without the unfettered freedom to think, criticize, and express oneself. She was never one to propose grafting a system of economic democracy through coops, workers' councils, or similar forms upon a system that denies citizens their basic political rights.

Luxemburg's view that there can be no democracy without socialism and no socialism without democracy was at the heart of the many heated arguments she carried on with fellow socialists throughout her career. It was central to her relation to German Social Democracy—and no less so toward revolutionary socialists such as Lenin. Shortly before the 1905 Revolution, in 1904, she took issue with Lenin on the grounds that his organizational concepts are "imbued, not with a positive creative spirit, but with the sterile spirit of the night-watchman state,"[30] which reduces the rank-and-file to docile, unthinking recipients of commands from above. And in 1905, in response to the split within the Russian Social Democratic Labor Party (RSDLP), she took issue with the Bolsheviks for their sectarianism, referring to "the so-called Lenin faction's . . . somewhat 'Cossack' way of resolving a party dispute."[31] These criticisms became more intense in the following years (especially from 1912 onward), when Lenin moved to purge the RSDLP of many Mensheviks and others opposed to his political agenda.

Nevertheless, these organizational disputes—important as they were—did not stop them from continuing to work together. What drove them further apart was not the issue of organization as much as that of revolution, specifically, the Bolsheviks' actions following their seizure of power in 1917. Luxemburg supported the October Revolution on the grounds that only the Bolsheviks dared to push the revolution in a needed socialist direction. However, in 1918 she sharply critiqued them for proceeding as if democratic governance by the working class was dispensable. In *The Russian Revolution* she famously castigates Lenin and Trotsky for shutting down freedom of expression, establishing the CHEKA, and moving toward a single-party state. She wrote to Julian Marchlewski on September 14, 1918:

> It is clear that, under such conditions, i.e., being caught in the pincers of the imperialist powers from all sides, neither socialism nor the dictatorship of the proletariat can become a reality [in Russia], but at the most a caricature of both. I'm afraid that this situation is clear only for you, for me, and for a few others. . . . This notion of [Karl] Radek's, for example, of "slaughtering the bourgeoisie" or even just threatening along those lines, is indeed idiocy *summo grado*; [it] only discredits socialism, and nothing more. (*Letters*, 473–74)

"The basic error of the Lenin-Trotsky theory," she held, "is that they too, just like Kautsky, oppose dictatorship to democracy." In contrast, she stated in *The Russian Revolution*, what is needed is "a dictatorship of the *class*, not of a party or of a clique." This requires "the broadest public forum on the basis of the most active, unlimited participation of the mass of the people, of unlimited democracy" (*Reader*, 307–8). This is because "socialism will not and cannot be created by any government, however socialistic. Socialism must be created by the masses, by every proletarian. Only that is socialism, and only thus can socialism be created."[32]

There is a parallel between Luxemburg's view of democracy and her embrace of enlightenment reason. She criticized the latter, not for its rationalism, but for its being viewed as the property of the "educated" classes. She instead wanted it to extend to *everyone*. Likewise, she criticized bourgeois democracy, not because it is democratic, but because it is limited to the bourgeoisie. It too must be extended to everyone—on the economic and political level. Their integrality is the only way to *get to* socialism.

Luxemburg's life project can be summed up as she wrote in a letter to Matilde Wurm on December 28, 1918:

> See that you remain a *human being*. To be a human being is the main thing, above all else. And that means: to be firm and clear and *cheerful*, yes, cheerful in spite of everything and anything, because howling is the business of the weak. To be a human being means to joyfully toss your entire life "on the giant scales of fate" if it must be so, and at the same time to rejoice in the brightness of every day and the beauty of every cloud. Oh, I don't know any recipe that can be written down on how to be a human being, I only know when a person *is* one. (*Letters*, 363)

This passage, like so many others penned by Luxemburg, shows that she did not view revolution as a mere means for securing political power and obtaining economic growth and development. For her, revolution was about *transforming the human personality*—that is, uprooting the conditions that compel human relations to take on a *dehumanized* form. This, for her, was both a political and *personal* project. Political, in that the social structures that maintain and reproduce dehumanized social relations need to be thoroughly uprooted; personal, in that such a goal cannot be achieved unless individuals subjected to dehumanized social relations find ways to reclaim their humanity in the very course of the struggle. She understood that even the most repressive and alienated system or regime is incapable of stifling the urge to grasp and fulfill our human potential. This perspective "put the stamp on everything she did and ever hoped to make real. And it created so totally different a direction for women's liberation that it makes it possible for our age to first understand it fully—in a great measure more fully than she, herself, was conscious of."[33]

Luxemburg suffered many setbacks and tragedies, but she understood that it is not possible to "joyfully toss your entire life on the giant scales of fate" unless we believe that our efforts will be redeemed by a successful outcome. That does not mean there *will* be a successful outcome. But without the belief in a better future, the present becomes all the more impoverished.

Notes

[1] *Epigraph*: Rosa Luxemburg, *The Letters of Rosa Luxemburg*, ed. Georg Adler, Peter Hudis, and Annelies Laschitza (London: Verso Books, 2011), 374. Further references are given in the text using the short title *Letters*.

[2] Luxemburg's four book-length works all deal with Marxian economics—*The Industrial Development of Poland; The Accumulation of Capital; The Accumulation of Capital, or What the Epigones Have Made Out of Marx's Theory—An*

Anti-Critique; and *Introduction to Political Economy*. These can be found, newly translated, in Rosa Luxemburg, *The Complete Works of Rosa Luxemburg*, Vol. I: Economic Writings 1, ed. Peter Hudis (London: Verso, 2013), and Vol. II: Economic Writings 2, ed. Peter Hudis and Paul Le Blanc (London: Verso, 2015).

[3] See especially Jacqueline Rose, *Women in Dark Times* (London: Bloomsbury, 2014); Frigga Haug, *Beyond Female Masochism: Memory-Work and Politics* (London: Verso, 1992); Frigga Haug, *Rosa Luxemburg und die Kunst der Politik* (Hamburg: Argument, 2007); Andrea Nye, *Philosophia: The Thought of Rosa Luxemburg, Simone Weil, and Hannah Arendt* (New York: Routledge, 1994); and Raya Dunayevskaya, *Rosa Luxemburg, Women's Liberation and Marx's Philosophy of Revolution* (Chicago: Illinois University Press, 1991).

[4] Vivian Gornick, "History and Heartbreak: The Letters of Rosa Luxemburg," *Nation*. April 13, 2011.

[5] *Gleichheit* began publication in Stuttgart in 1891; it bore the subhead *Zeitschrift für die Interessen der Arbeiterinnen* (Journal Published in the Interests of Working Women).

[6] It was not until 1908 that a woman, Luise Zietz, was appointed to the executive committee of the SPD. For Luxemburg's evaluation of her politics, see Luxemburg, letter to Clara Zetkin, March 9, 1916, *Letters*, 356.

[7] Rosa Luxemburg, "Social Reform or Revolution," in *The Rosa Luxemburg Reader*, ed. Peter Hudis and Kevin B. Anderson (New York: Monthly Review Books, 2004), here 162. Further references to this work are given in the text using the short title *Reader*.

[8] Luxemburg's writings on the 1905 revolution will appear as the third volume of *The Complete Works of Rosa Luxemburg* in 2018. All references to her writings on 1905 in this chapter are to the original articles and essays.

[9] See her letter to Jogiches of November 1, 1905: "You see, since yesterday I've been involved with *Vorwärts* on a daily basis, having to start from 4 in the afternoon." Luxemburg, letter to Leo Jogiches, November 1, 1905, in *Gesammelte Briefe*, vol. 2, ed. Annelies Laschitza (Berlin: Dietz, 1999), 228.

[10] Rosa Luxemburg, "Pod znakiem Socjaldemocracji," *Czerwony Sztandar*, March 24, 1905, 3.

[11] The notion that Lenin invented the concept of a centralized "vanguard party" is a myth; it derives instead from German Social Democracy. Lenin simply sought to apply it to Russian conditions—in a form that Luxemburg disagreed with. For more on this, see Peter Hudis, "Lenin and Luxemburg," in *The Palgrave Handbook of Leninist Political Philosophy*, ed. Tom Rockmore and Norman Levine (Basingstoke, UK: Palgrave Macmillan, 2017).

[12] Luxemburg, "Pod," 3.

[13] Nevertheless, Luxemburg's adherence to the traditional concept of a vanguard party often led her, unfortunately, to pursue centralist policies in the SDKP and SDKPiL that parallel, in some respects, Lenin's organizational practices. This is documented in Hudis, "Lenin."

[14] This paper was the *Deutsche Bergarbeiter-Zeitung*.

[15] Rosa Luxemburg, "Remarks at Jena Congress on Relations between the Party and the Trade Unions, with Reference to the 1905 Revolution in Russia," in *Protokoll über die Verhandlungen des Parteitages der Sozialdemokratischen Partei Deutschlands: Abgehalten zu Jena vom 17. bis 23. September 1905* (Berlin: Vorwärts, 1905), 599. Kasprzak, a close colleague of Luxemburg's from the time they were teenagers, was hanged by the tsarist government in Warsaw on September 9, 1905, shortly before the congress was held.

[16] Friedrich Adler, ed. *Briefwechsel mit August Bebel und Karl Kautsky* (Vienna: Wiener Volksbuchhandlung, 1954), 510.

[17] Quoted in Karen Honeycutt, "Clara Zetkin: A Left-Wing Socialist and Feminist in Wilhelmian Germany" (PhD diss., Columbia University, 1975), m 241.

[18] There is a parallel here to Luxemburg's refusal to openly respond to repeated anti-Semitic attacks on her from party members. For Luxemburg's attitude towards anti-Semitism and her Jewish identity, see Kevin B. Anderson and Peter Hudis, "Rosa Luxemburg (1871–1919): Universalism and Particularism," in *Makers of Jewish Modernity*, ed. Jacques Picard et al. (Princeton, NJ: Princeton University Press, 2016), 159–72; and Rory Castle, "A Study of the Identity, Family, and Background of Rosa Luxemburg (1871–1919)" (PhD diss., Swansea University, 2016), 285–313.

[19] Luxemburg, "A Tactical Question." In Luxemburg, *Reader*, 235.

[20] Nancy Holmstrom, "Rosa Luxemburg: A Legacy for Feminists?," in *Rosa Remix*, ed. Stefanie Ehmsen and Albert Scharenberg (New York: Rosa Luxemburg Stiftung, 2017), 32–36, here 33.

[21] Rosa Luxemburg, "Russische Arbeiterinnen im Kampfe," *Die Gleichheit*, April 23, 1902, 3.

[22] Luxemburg's closest friends, who knew Jogiches well, had an overwhelmingly positive view of him. Clara Zetkin said of Jogiches: "He was one of those very masculine personalities—an extremely rare phenomenon these days—who can tolerate a great female personality"; quoted in Paul Frölich, *Rosa Luxemburg: Her Life and Work* (New York: Monthly Review Press, 1972), 14.

[23] While we have Luxemburg's letters to Jogiches, until very recently almost none of his letters to her had surfaced and it was assumed they were destroyed after his death. In January 2019 it was announced that 5,000 of his letters had been discovered in an archive in Moscow. These have yet to be made available and it is unclear how many were to Luxemburg. Wladyslaw Feinstein-Leder, a leader of the SDKPiL who was briefly Luxemburg's lover after her breakup with Jogiches in 1907, wrote a short biography (in Polish) of Jogiches in 1929, but Stalin prevented its publication (Feinstein-Leder was killed during the Great Purge of 1938). It was published in the Polish original in 1976 by the great Polish labor historian Feliks Tych, who labored for 20 years on a comprehensive biography of Jogiches, but the book was left unfinished at his death in 2016.

[24] Dunayevskaya, *Rosa Luxemburg*, 91–92.

[25] Quoted in Nettl, *Rosa Luxemburg* (London: Verso Books 2019), 383.

[26] Luxemburg, "Slavery," in *Works*, 1:312.

[27] See Rose, *Women in Dark Times*, 48.

[28] Alhelí de María Alvarado-Díaz, "Heroine of the Revolution," in *Rosa Remix*, ed. Stefanie Ehmsen and Albert Scharenberg (New York: Rosa Luxemburg Stiftung, 2017), 43–50, here 47.

[29] For more on this, see Peter Hudis, *Marx's Concept of the Alternative to Capitalism* (Chicago: Haymarket, 2013).

[30] Luxemburg, "Organizational Questions of Russian Social Democracy," Luxemburg, *Reader*, 256.

[31] Rosa Luxemburg, "Russische Parteistreitigkeiten," June 23, 1905, in *Gesammelte Werke*, vol. 1.2, ed. Annelies Laschitza et al. (Berlin: Dietz Verlag, 2000), 593.

[32] Luxemburg, "Our Program and the Political Situation," in *Reader*, 368.

[33] Dunayevskaya, *Rosa Luxemburg*, 83–84.

Part III.

Women and Political Power in the Twentieth and Twenty-First Centuries

11: Follow-the-Leader: Tracing Male Influence on Leni Riefenstahl's *Triumph des Willens*

Rachel J. Halverson

Historian Claudia Koontz paints a striking portrait of women and female leadership in Nazi Germany in her seminal *Mothers in the Fatherland: Women, the Family, and Nazi Politics* (1987): "No one woman conformed to either the passive-docile or the heartless-brutish model. Few vapid Eva Brauns or cruel Irma Grieses. Instead, troops of Leni Riefenstahls—ambitious, determined, opportunistic—marched along, caught up in the Nazi tide."[1] With these words Koontz has bestowed no small honor on Leni Riefenstahl; for Koontz, Riefenstahl embodies the prototype of the leadership role women came to play in Nazi Germany. "Marching along" to the dictates of male Nazi leaders, women were relegated to leadership roles subordinate to the regime's patriarchal hierarchy (*Mothers*, 6). In Riefenstahl's case, this created a tension between following the leader and being a leader in her own right; specifically, her brand of female leadership on the set, behind the camera, and in the editing room entailed dutiful subordination to male power. Subject to Hitler's and Goebbel's demands, yet leading her crew to realize her desired cinematic aesthetic, Riefenstahl made *Triumph des Willens* (Triumph of the Will, 1935), a film that remains to this day the pinnacle of her cinematic achievements. As Riefenstahl biographer Jürgen Trimborn so emphatically states:

> *Triumph des Willens* ist wahrscheinlich das meistzitierte Werk der Filmgeschichte. Keine Dokumentation über den Nationalsozialismus kommt heute ohne Bilder aus diesem Film aus, kein anderer Film hat unsere visuelle Vorstellung, was Nationalsozialismus war, so tief geprägt wie er. Der Film wurde zum Dreh- und Angelpunkt in Riefenstahls Biographie, festigte ihre Position im Dritten Reich und verlieh ihr, solange das NS-Regime existierte, einen nahezu unantastbaren Status. Daß es gerade eine Frau war, die die faschistische Männerwelt auf Zelluloid bannte, sorgte, damals vielleicht noch stärker als heute, für Aufsehen, das die ehrgeizige Regisseurin sichtlich genoß.[2]

[*Triumph des Willens* is probably the most cited work of film history. No documentation on National Socialism today neglects to include images from *Triumph des Willens*, and no other film created a more profound visual impression of the movement. *Triumph des Willens* became the pivotal point of Riefenstahl's biography, establishing her position in the Third Reich and conferring upon her a near invincibility that would last for as long as the Nazi regime existed. And the fact that it was a woman who captured the male world of fascism on film created a sensation—at that time perhaps more so than it would today—that the ambitious director visibly enjoyed.[3]]

Trimborn's designation of Riefenstahl as an "ehrgeizige Regisseurin" (ambitious female director)[4] in the male-dominated world of Nazi Germany read in conjunction with Koontz's characterization of German women willing to conform to gender roles to achieve a "short-term advantage" (*Mothers*, 12) paves the way for a reexamination of Riefenstahl as a follower and leader in Nazi Germany. The tension between subordination to ideology and ascension to a place of power and leadership characterizes the fraught position of Leni Riefenstahl. In the following, I analyze eulogies published after Riefenstahl's death and representations of Riefenstahl in recent film histories, and highlight the influence of two major male filmmakers—Arnold Fanck and Walter Ruttmann—on Riefenstahl and the making of *Triumph des Willens*. Through these analyses it will become clear that we cannot separate Riefenstahl's leadership from her subordination to Nazi politics.

As time has passed, Riefenstahl's persona, reception of her work, and her international stature have blurred attempts to characterize and classify her. The response to Riefenstahl's death at the age of 101 on September 8, 2003, exposed a tellingly split verdict on the filmmaker and her legacy. Announcement of her passing triggered a swift response from the German press. Articles and obituaries published immediately after her death portray her as a creative talent in isolation, vigilantly dismissing criticism of the films she made for Hitler, and reveal an underlying tension between her persona and the reception of her work that shapes perceptions of Riefenstahl to this day.[5] Several tributes cast her as one of the "umstrittensten Persönlichkeiten des Jahrhunderts"[6] (most controversial personages of the century) while another article places her and actor and director Gustaf Gründgens in the same category of "das wohl prominenteste Beispiel für die Verführbarkeit des Künstlers durch die politische Macht in Deutschland"[7] (probably the most prominent example of the seducibility of artists by the political powers in Germany). In eulogizing Riefenstahl's accomplishments, biographical highlights consistently include references to Hitler and to her two major films made during the Nazi period, *Triumph des Willens* and *Olympia: Fest der Völker* and *Fest der Schönheit* (Olympia Part 1: Festival of Nations and Olympia; Part 2: Festival of Beauty, 1938), in addition to her photography of the Nuba in the 1970s in Africa and her underwater photography in the years leading up to her death. Other aspects, however, are mentioned more selectively, most notably the filmmakers and cinematographers who played a significant role in her life and career. Articles in the *Frankfurter Allgemeine Zeitung* and the *Süddeutsche Zeitung*, for example, reference Arnold Fanck, the esteemed director who cast Riefenstahl in her first cinematic role.[8] Similarly, Reiner Rother notes the undying loyalty that cameramen like Hans Ertl, Walter Frentz, and Heinz von Jaworsky had for her. Regardless of differences in specific details, these obituaries share an almost singular focus on Riefenstahl, and their frequent use of superlatives in describing both her person and her accomplishments implicitly elevates her to the leading ranks of German filmmakers in the twentieth century.

Riefenstahl began her career as a leading lady and is remembered, both positively and negatively, as an actress and filmmaker. This succinct summation of Riefenstahl's biography echoes the portrait painted of her life and work in *The Wonderful, Horrible Life of Leni Riefenstahl*, made in 1993 when she was in her nineties, still diving and actively pursuing underwater filmmaking.[9] This documentary by Ray Müller opens with a polarized view of Riefenstahl as either "a feminist pioneer or a woman of evil" (00.03.05–00.03.09) and the unequivocal statement that Riefenstahl "is still the most famous female film director in the world" (00:03:50–00:03:55). These mutually exclusive articulations of Riefenstahl's legacy demand that her films be seen as the singular, autonomous achievements of a creative force that is either good or evil, but not both. Yet within the context of Nazi Germany Riefenstahl's leadership role was not as unshackled as these black-and-white classifications insinuate. As Koontz underscores, for a female leader in Nazi Germany, "Autonomy existed only in relationship to women within her sphere and did not translate into bargaining power in male administrations. Women felt free only as long as their wishes were congruent with Nazi demands" (*Mothers*, 15). Thus, the independence and creative license Riefenstahl exerted in the shooting and editing of *Triumph des Willens* ultimately had to conform to the parameters of Hitler's and Goebbel's expectations, expectations that were shaped by the work of major male filmmakers of the time. Ultimately, Riefenstahl's work itself was a collaborative endeavor from start to finish.

Recent scholarly publications document that film experts continue to designate Riefenstahl as *the* representative woman filmmaker in the history of German cinema. Sabine Hake characterizes her as an innovator, one of very few directors to "develop a unique filmic style in full accordance with Nazi ideology"[10] and as a contributor to the "extensive visual archive" from which Hollywood draws images of evil.[11] Thomas Doherty casts her as "the Valkyrie goddess of Third Reich Cinema, the lone shining star in a constellation of dim hacks"[12] and devotes an entire chapter of his book *Hollywood and Hitler* to her. Recent German film histories, such as Maggie Hoffgen's *Studying German Film* (2009), Stephan Brockmann's *A Critical History of German Film* (2010), and Jennifer Kapczynski and Michael D. Richardson's *A New History of German Film* (2012), all dedicate entire chapters to Riefenstahl's *Triumph des Willens*.[13] The chapter on *Triumph des Willens* in Hoffgen's *Studying German Film* is the only one of the book's fourteen that covers the work of a female director. In Brockmann's *A Critical History of German Film* (2010), only two of the thirty-four chapters examine films by female directors: Riefenstahl's *Triumph des Willens* and Margarethe von Trotta's *Die bleierne Zeit*. In Kapczynski and Richardson's 600-plus-page tome, female film directors fare similarly, with one chapter devoted to the premiere of *Triumph des Willens* and one to Ulrike Ottinger's documentary *Prater*. Indeed, Riefenstahl and *Triumph des Willens* have become the token female contribution consistently highlighted in narratives of twentieth-century German cinema. Again, Riefenstahl emerges as a singular cinematic force almost by default, because of her gender, her directorial achievements, and her career under the Nazi dictatorship.

The question thus becomes how Riefenstahl's behavior played out in both cinematic and political circles and what implications this has for the leadership role in which Riefenstahl as a woman and director has been placed. Fundamental to approaching Riefenstahl's work from this angle is recognizing that she did not make her films in creative isolation, nor did she make them by herself. Contemporary films and fellow filmmakers all shaped her work as a director. Moreover, as in all major productions, Riefenstahl relied on sizeable camera crews and numerous assistants during the production of both *Triumph des Willens* and *Olympia*.[14] More importantly, Riefenstahl herself never claimed sole credit for her work, but instead publicly acknowledged the influence of fellow directors and their films, as well as the excellence and importance of her film production team to each project. Despite this, her image as a lone leading directorial force continues to hold sway, an image that I hope to correct in my reexamination of Riefenstahl and her seminal documentary of the 1934 National Socialist party convention in Nuremberg. Reading *Triumph des Willens* through the lens of female leadership helps us understand more fully the implications her opportunism has for her legacy as a filmmaker.

Analysis of Riefenstahl's references to the people and films influential in the making of *Triumph des Willens*, specifically her tutelage under Arnold Fanck, the founder of the film genre *Bergfilme* (mountain films),[15] and her roles in these films, as well as her statements on her limited collaboration with Walter Ruttmann and her familiarity with his documentary *Berlin: Sinfonie der Großstadt* (Berlin: Symphony of a Great City, 1927), establish Riefenstahl as a director acutely aware of and receptive to major innovators in the field. On this foundation of recognition, I trace overlaps in personnel and compare the mise-en-scène, shots, and editing in Riefenstahl's *Triumph des Willens* with six of Fanck's *Bergfilme* in which Riefenstahl starred, and with Ruttmann's *Berlin: Sinfonie der Großstadt*. This analysis ultimately will delineate the degree to which Riefenstahl was following in Fanck's and Ruttmann's footsteps and the extent to which she was blazing her own path in filmmaking. Although her vision for *Triumph des Willens* is undeniably the driving force around which her production team rallied, Riefenstahl's acknowledgment of the importance of her crew in making the film demands that it too share the responsibility for making a film that glorified Hitler and his followers.

Intersections and Collaborations

Sources indicate that Riefenstahl had a crew of approximately 120 people working with her in Nuremberg during the filming of *Triumph des Willens*.[16] The credits page in her *Behind the Scenes of the National Party Convention Film* (1935) lists eighteen cameramen, including the highly skilled Sepp Allgeier as Director of Photography.[17] In fact, Allgeier had worked extensively with Fanck before filming for Riefenstahl, first on her *Der Sieg des Glaubens* (The Victory of Faith, 1933) and then on *Triumph des Willens*. After *Triumph des Willens*, he continued to work with Fanck on *Die weiße Hölle vom Piz Palü* (White Hell of Pitz Palu, 1935), *Training zum Skifilmen* (Training for Filming Skiing, 1935), and *Ein Robinson: Das Tagebuch eines Matrosen* (Robinson: Diary of a Sailor, 1939/40).[18] In total, Allgeier was the cameraman for thirteen of Fanck's films as well as for *Der Kampf ums Matterhorn* (Fight for the Matterhorn, 1928), for which Fanck wrote the script, and *Die weiße Kunst* (White Art, 1924/25), which Allgeier filmed and directed and Fanck edited. Of particular note are *Das Wunder des Schneeschuhs* (The Miracle of the Snowshoe), part 1 (1919/20) and part 2 (1921/22), and the documentary *Im Kampf mit dem Berge* (In the Fight with the Mountain, 1921) all directed by Fanck and filmed by both Fanck and Allgeier.[19]

Table 11.1, which follows, documents Allgeier's extensive work with Fanck, including *Das weiße Stadion* (*The White Stadium*, 1927/28) on which Fanck and Ruttmann collaborated, and establishes him as the strongest creative conduit between the two directors, aside from the connection to Riefenstahl herself. Given Fanck and Allgeier's extensive collaboration, it would be difficult to deny their synergy behind the camera. Thus Allgeier's subsequent work with Riefenstahl serves as an additional channel of influence between Fanck and Riefenstahl.

In front of the camera, Riefenstahl quickly became one of Fanck's leading ladies. She starred in six of his *Bergfilme*: *Der heilige Berg* (The Holy Mountain, 1925/26), *Der große Sprung* (The Big Leap, 1927),

Table 11.1. Personnel overlap between Fanck's films
and Riefenstahl's *Triumph des Willens*

Fanck Films	Crew Overlap
Das Wunder des Schneeschuhs, 1. Teil (1919/20)	Sepp Allgeier (camera; cast member)
Im Kampf mit dem Berge	Sepp Allgeier (camera)
Das Wunder des Schneeschuhs, 2. Teil (1919/20)	Sepp Allgeier (camera; cast member)
Pömperlis Kampf mit dem Schneeschuh (1922)	Sepp Allgeier (codirector of photography)
Der Berg des Schicksals (1923/24)	Sepp Allgeier (camera)
*Die weiße Kunst*** (1924/25) edited by Fanck	Sepp Allgeier (director, camera); Fanck (editor)
*Der heilige Berg** (1925/26)	Sepp Allgeier (camera)
*Der große Sprung** (1927)	Sepp Allgeier (camera)
Das weiße Stadion (1927/28)	Sepp Allgeier (camera); Fanck and Walter Ruttmann (coeditors)
*Der Kampf ums Matterhorn*** (1928)	Sepp Allgeier (camera); Fanck and Nunzio Malasomma (cowriters)
*9990m mani padme hum*** (1928)	Paul Lieberenz (camera); Fanck and Willy Rath (coeditors)
*Die weiße Hölle von Piz Palü** (1929)	Sepp Allgeier (camera)
*Stürme über dem Montblanc** (1930)	Sepp Allgeier (camera)
*Der weiße Rausch: Neue Wunder des Schneeschuhs** (1930/31)	Hans Karl Gottschalk (camera), Walter Riml (cast member)
*S.O.S. Iceberg** (1932/33)	Walter Riml (cast member)

* Indicates films in which Riefenstahl was a cast member.
** Indicates films that Fanck did not direct.

Die weiße Hölle von Piz Palü, Stürme über dem Montblanc (Storm over Mont Blanc, 1930), *Der weiße Rausch* (White Ecstasy, 1930/31), and *SOS Eisberg* (S.O.S. Iceberg, 1932/33). Undoubtedly, this extensive work with one director would be a formative experience for any actress. In Riefenstahl's case, it also proved formative for her own future work as a director.[20] In *The Wonderful, Horrible Life of Leni Riefenstahl*, for example, Fanck is cited as her "great mentor,"[21] and Doherty refers to Fanck as Riefenstahl's "first motion picture mentor."[22] As both her director and mentor, Fanck essentially taught Riefenstahl how to make films. Specifically, he conveyed to her the crucial importance of editing.[23] In her *Memoiren*, Riefenstahl recalls that while editing the footage for *Triumph des Willens*, she used "ein kleines Lytaxgerät, womit auch Fanck seine Filme, solange sie Stummfilme waren, geschnitten hatte"[24] (a small Lytax instrument, like the one Fanck had used to cut his films—at least the silent ones).[25] Tellingly, images, editing, characters, storyline, and scene composition characteristic of Fanck's *Bergfilme* can be found throughout *Triumph des Willens*.

Riefenstahl's first film with Fanck, *Der heilige Berg*, in which she starred in a role Fanck wrote specifically for her,[26] establishes the mold for her future roles in his films. Fanck's usage of dramatic images and editing tell the compelling love story of the beautiful dancer Diotima (Riefenstahl) and a lone mountain climber. The film's prelude opens with stunning shots of the German Alps interspliced with shots of Diotima dancing, first on the beach and then against a backdrop of the mountain face. Expansive shots of the sky are dominated by towering cumulous clouds, an image Riefenstahl would employ in the opening sequence of *Triumph des Willens*, where cloud formations preface and accompany Hitler's arrival in the city by plane. Next, the film moves to interior shots of Diotima performing onstage for an adoring audience. This dance sequence[27] echoes the prelude to a certain degree, yet here shots of Diotima dancing are intercut with head shots of the enraptured young skier and the eremitic mountain climber who watch from the theater loge seating. As her performance ends, the audience storms to the front of the theater, reaching their arms out to her on stage. Here the editing is reminiscent of silent films and is used to communicate messages to the audience without written or spoken lines, in this case how the skier and climber are fascinated by, and the audience enthusiastic about, the dance they have just witnessed. Riefenstahl relies heavily on this technique in *Triumph des Willens* where—with the exception of the prologue, the identification of key persons with text frames, and the inclusion of speeches—music provides the only auditory commentary on the images projected. In the sequence showing Hitler's arrival at the airport and travel by motorcade into the city center, for example, close-ups of the faces of individual bystanders alternate with pans of the masses, arms outstretched in the Hitler salute to communicate unified support for the Führer. No intertitles or voiceovers verbalize that the assembled masses welcome Hitler to their city. Taken from behind Hitler standing in his motorcade car, panning shots capture old and young, women and men, civilians and men in uniform as they greet Hitler en masse with the Nazi salute. A five-second close-up of the beaming faces of individual children (00:07:45–00:07:50) confirms the unequivocal message of adoration and support for the leader of the Third Reich.

Similarly, Fanck's second film starring Riefenstahl, *Die weiße Hölle von Piz Palü*, exhibits aesthetic components that also appear in *Triumph des Willens*. Shots of snow-covered mountains in the two-minute opening sequence establish these geological features as breathtakingly beautiful yet formidable members of the film's cast. Shots of the mountains through the windows of a cabin architecturally frame the mountains in the background and visually juxtapose the safe and secure interior world of the inhabitants of the cabin with the raw unconquered nature of the mountain peaks. In *Triumph des Willens*, Riefenstahl employed a similar framing technique. Here, building arches frame the military processional through the streets of Nuremberg. In *Die weiße Hölle* nature reappears in cloud segments intercut with shots of Dr. Johannes Krafft, Hans Brandt, and Maria Marjoni, played by Riefenstahl, sleeping in the mountain cabin; these shots foreshadow a storm on the mountain that they will soon have to confront. Fanck's influence on Riefenstahl is undeniable in the images, shots, and editing techniques that Riefenstahl transferred to her own work.

Extensive climbing sequences in challenging weather and avalanche conditions, characteristic of the genre, comprise a significant amount of the action in Fanck's *Bergfilme*.[28] Since almost all his films are set in the Alps or, in the case of *SOS Eisberg*, on the massive glaciers on the coast of Greenland, a strikingly vertical aesthetic prevails. Furthermore, shots of mountains, trees, and cabins from both a worm's eye and a bird's eye perspective continually reinforce the strong vertical orientation in the films' *mise*-en-scènes. This is reflected in the filming of the human subjects as well: low-angle or high-angle long shots capture characters ascending or descending the mountain or perched precariously on a mountain ledge, buffeted by wind and snow. Even more notably, frequent low-angle head shots of the main characters literally and figuratively ask viewers to look up to these mountaineering leaders as they traverse treacherous grades and face challenging weather conditions on their way to the summit. Such shots emphasize the gravity and singularity of their efforts to conquer the mountain and set them apart from the groups of nameless villagers or skiers who populate the alpine landscapes; these main characters are ultimately cast as leaders in the struggle between man and nature. The appearance of female characters in scenes shot in such extreme conditions indicates a loosening of gender roles that paves the way for Riefenstahl to position herself in a domain previously reserved for men.

In underscoring this leadership dynamic, the standard constellation of characters in Fanck's *Bergfilme* provides a template for filming leaders and their followers, clearly an essential component in Riefenstahl's depiction of the party elite in *Triumph des Willens*. Furthermore, the gender dynamics in Fanck's work foreshadow the professional environment Riefenstahl herself would experience as a director mentored by and collaborating with male colleagues. Central to the narrative of each of Fanck's *Bergfilme* is a core group consisting of two male leads and one female, played by Riefenstahl. Often an older woman or man plays a supporting role, such as Karl's mother in *Der heilige Berg* and Hella Armstrong's father in *Stürme über Mont Blanc*. Groups of skiers, villagers, or townspeople complete the cast. Head shots emphasize facial expressions at key points and thus serve as an emotional commentary on the unfolding story. Frequent use of low-angle head shots of the main characters communicates not only their role in the film's narrative but also their leadership in the effort to summit the mountain or conquer the challenges of a glacial landscape. This technique transferred well to *Triumph des Willens*, where Riefenstahl utilized it to introduce a vertical orientation into her filming of the party convention to underscore the hierarchical relationship between party leaders, SA troops, and the adoring masses. Thus Riefenstahl was able to highlight leadership roles played by key party figures visually. Moreover, she innovatively adapted this technique further to achieve an even more stunning effect. By placing the camera on a small track laid around Hitler during several of his speeches, she captured 360-degree low-angle shots of the Führer; this spatial dimension underscores his supreme leadership. Hitler literally becomes the human embodiment of a mountain that rises above the masses and intimidates all who would attempt to challenge him.

The roles Riefenstahl plays in Fanck's *Bergfilme* also foreshadow the leadership position she eventually assumed behind the camera. As the dancer Diotima in *Der heilige Berg*, as the recently engaged Maria Marjoni in *Die weiße Hölle vom Piz Palü*, as the astronomer's daughter Hella Armstrong in *Stürme über dem Mont Blanc*, and as Professor Dr. Karl Lorenz's wife, Hella Lorenz, in *SOS Eisberg*, Riefenstahl played women who pushed the boundaries of traditional gender roles; their professional and athletic prowess transgressed the conventional female roles of sex object, girlfriend, fiancée, and wife. Diotima is a dancer, a star in her own right. Maria Marjoni joins her fiancé Hans Brandt and Dr. Johannes Krafft in scaling the mountain and endures the same physical demands, frigid temperatures, gusting winds, and pelting snow. Hella Armstrong is shown to be mesmerized as she looks through her father's telescope and Hannes's microscope. Indeed, her father comments that she would make a poor housewife, given her fascination with science and skiing, an observation that does not deter her from these pursuits. Like Maria, she keeps pace with Hannes while skiing and climbing the mountain. Similarly, Hella Lorenz leaves the comfort of her warm European apartment to join the search-and-rescue mission for her long-lost husband off the coast of Greenland. Her skill as a pilot even garners compliments from her fellow airmen. After crash landing her seaplane in icy waters, she, like the men on the expedition, meets the elements head-on, albeit sustained by her prospective reunion with her husband. Clearly, each of Riefenstahl's characters is a leading lady who embraces the new opportunities open

to women in 1920s Germany. Although they are clearly exploring the
frontier of emancipation, they follow men whose paths up the mountain
or the glacier determine their paths, too. It is a form of female leadership that Riefenstahl will become all too familiar with in the course of
her career as a director: women serve in a leadership capacity, but in an
environment controlled by men. When she stepped behind the camera,
Riefenstahl remained to a great degree in a role she had established as a
leading lady who followed the path chosen by her male counterparts.

Relationships and Reputations

In recounting her professional journey, Riefenstahl interweaves her relationships to directors and cinematographers and their work into the personal narrative of her professional journey. In fact, her *Memoiren* (1987) is
a name-dropping tour de force, and the one name that surfaces repeatedly
in her account of the preparations to make *Triumph des Willens* is that
of Ruttmann.[29] She relates that in 1933, following her return to Berlin,
Goebbels summoned her to his official residence (*Dienstwohnung*) and
proposed that she make a feature film with him—*Die siebte Großmacht*
(*Memoiren*, 202–3). However, Riefenstahl suggests immediately that
Ruttmann would be better suited for the job:

> Ich unterbrach ihn: Von diesem Gebiet habe ich keine Ahnung,
> da würde ich Sie schwer enttäuschen. Das wäre eine interessante
> Aufgabe für Walter Ruttmann, der den hervorragenden Dokumen-
> tarfilm "Berlin, Sinfonie einer Großstadt" gemacht hat."
>   Goebbels winkte ab: "Ruttmann ist Kommunist, der kommt
> dafür nicht in Frage."
>   "Aber begabt ist er," widersprach ich. (*Memoiren*, 203)

> [I broke in. "I know nothing about that area: you'd be greatly dis-
> appointed in me. It would be an interesting assignment for Walter
> Ruttmann, who made that outstanding documentary *Berlin,
> Symphony of a Great City.*"
>   Goebbels shook his head: "Ruttmann is a Communist; we can't
> possibly consider him."
>   "But he *is* talented," I retorted. (*A Memoir*, 142)]

Here Riefenstahl's response reveals three key points: she is not schooled
in the making of documentary films; she is familiar with Ruttmann's film;
and she classifies the proposed project as a documentary. This underscores
how she stages herself as someone who thinks in artistic, not political
terms. To her, Ruttmann is suitable for the job because of his directorial experience, a matter separate from his political orientation. Trimborn

refutes Riefenstahl's recollection that Ruttmann should be contracted to make the entire film, underscoring that he was at no point responsible for anything more than the prologue.[30] In a subsequent conversation with Hitler, she refuses his invitation to film the party convention, this time arguing that she has never even seen a party convention and repeating that she has no experience in making documentary films (*Memoiren*, 205). In yet another conversation with Hitler, she insists that she cannot make the film, because she cannot even distinguish the SA from the SS (*Memoiren*, 222). Thus, in her recollection, Riefenstahl does not cast herself in a leadership role; rather, she downplays her abilities as a filmmaker and instead defers to the expertise of a well-established male director.

Eventually, casting herself as a powerless victim in her narrative, she can resist Hitler's demands no longer and is contracted to make the film about the 1934 party convention. She claims that she acquiesced because "Ich sah ein, daß ich Hitlers Widerstand nicht brechen konnte. Nun wollte ich wenigstens versuchen, möglichst gute Arbeitsbedingungen zu erreichen" (*Memoiren*, 222; I realized I could not break Hitler's resolve. Now at least I had to try and obtain the best possible working conditions, *A Memoir*, 158). She is given a budget of 300,000 Reichsmark and appoints Ruttmann as the film's codirector (*Dietrich & Riefenstahl*, 311), a match that would prove not to be made in heaven, according to Riefenstahl:

> Ich stellte mir den Film nur aus Dokumentar-Aufnahmen vor. Ruttmann hatte aber eine ganz andere Auffassung. Er sagte, es wäre unmöglich, nur aus Reden und Aufmärschen einen abendfüllenden interessanten Film zu machen. Er sah die Aufnahmen vom Parteitag nur als letztes Drittel des Films, während der Hauptteil den Aufstieg der NSDAP zeigen sollte, das heißt, wie aus sieben Mann in wenigen Jahren eine so große Partei wie die NSDAP entstand. (*Memoiren*, 217)

> [I thought of the Party rally film purely in terms of documentary shots, but Ruttmann had a very different conception. He said it would be impossible to turn speeches and parades into an interesting full-length movie, and suggested that the parades should fill only the last third, while the main portion should show the rise of the Nazi Party; that is, the process by which seven men grew into a party of tremendous power within such a short time. (*A Memoir*, 154)]

In retrospect, Riefenstahl and Ruttmann's collaboration was doomed from the outset. Ruttmann's initial footage for the project confirmed Riefenstahl's concerns: "Ein Wirrwarr von Aufnahmen—auf der Straße flatternde Zeitungen, aus deren Titelseiten der Aufstieg der NSDAP sichtbar gemacht werden sollte. Wie konnte Ruttmann nur eine solche

Arbeit vorzeigen!" (*Memoiren*, 221; It was a jumble of shots of news-papers fluttering along a street, their front pages tracing the rise of the Nazi Party. I didn't understand how Ruttmann could present such work, *A Memoir*, 157). Confronted with concrete evidence of their artistic differences, Riefenstahl decided to remove Ruttmann from the project and become its sole director (*Memoiren*, 221; *Dietrich & Riefenstahl*, 314). Clemens Zimmermann offers an alternative explanation, citing competition ("aus Konkurrenzgründen") between Riefenstahl and Ruttmann as the reason for his removal.[31] The film's prologue[32] is all that physically remains of Ruttmann's work (*Dietrich & Riefenstahl*, 319). However, Riefenstahl's film itself contains a number of striking similarities to Ruttmann's documentary and thus casts his dismissal in a different light. Moreover, creating the "best possible working conditions" translated into assembling a crew with cameramen, several of whom had worked extensively with Fanck.

Both *Berlin: Sinfonie der Großstadt* and *Triumph des Willens* portray cities from dawn to the dark of night, marked by the circadian rhythm of human activities. Ruttmann captures a day in the life of Berlin, explicitly marking the passage of time with shots of clock towers and clock faces—5 a.m., 8 a.m., and 12 noon.[33] Riefenstahl compresses the six-day party convention in Nuremberg into three days, using convention activities, daylight, and darkness to mark the event's temporal progression.[34] Riefenstahl, like Ruttmann, inserts brief segments of blank black frames to divide one segment of the film from the next. Ruttmann, however, pairs these segments with text to state the ending of one act and the beginning of the next explicitly. In doing so, he demarcates individual movements in his cinematic symphony. The absence of such intertitles in Riefenstahl's film downplays the explicit orchestration of shots and film footage that underlie the film's composition and underscores the illusion that events portrayed on the screen unfolded as seamlessly as they appear on the screen.

Perhaps the most obvious point of connection between the two films is the shared focus on urban landscapes. Both films open with aerial views that introduce viewers to their respective cities and that are reminiscent of the establishing aerial shots of formidable mountain peaks and glaciers that open Fanck's *Bergfilme*. It has not escaped scholars that Riefenstahl followed Ruttmann's lead, opening with shots of airplanes filmed from airplanes.[35] In fact, Trimborn cites Ruttmann's original plans for the prologue published in *Die Licht-Bühne* after the party convention, which included Hitler's arrival by plane.[36] In other words, the dramatic opening aerial sequence in *Triumph des Willens* should perhaps be credited to Ruttmann, not Riefenstahl. The extended aerial shots in both films include major architectural landmarks that dominate the scene's composition: the Berlin Cathedral, the largest church in Berlin, and the *Burg* (fortress) in Nuremberg, a monument to Germany's feudal past. In *Triumph des Willens*, viewers meet the city before Hitler enters the picture. This acknowledges the historic and symbolic significance of Nuremberg as a party stronghold of the National Socialist dictatorship and as the center of the medieval German Reich[37] and thus implicitly establishes its suitability as the stage for the party convention. It is, however, important to note that Riefenstahl's opening shots of the Nuremberg city center differ slightly from those of Ruttmann's Berlin. While the dimmer lighting in *Sinfonie der Großstadt* places the sequence clearly at dawn, Riefenstahl's Nuremberg emerges from an early morning shroud of clouds, lending the city an almost mythical quality and contributing to the sense that subsequent events will be magical and mystical,[38] an aspect of the film Hake terms a "convergence of modernity and myth."[39] Allowing viewers a glimpse of the technology that made these aerial views possible, both directors include shots from a plane of other planes in flight to showcase the aeronautical advancements that allowed them to capture Berlin and Nuremberg from above. Of course, Riefenstahl's footage has the added bonus of presenting the airplane that is ferrying Hitler to his destination.

Although it is obvious that Berlin and Nuremberg are the subject and object of the respective films, their role is far more multifaceted. In both *Sinfonie der Großstadt* and *Triumph des Willens*, the cities' physical structures function at times as extensions of the camera, a type of "architectural lens" that circumscribes a shot within a shot, a technique also used by Fanck in his *Bergfilme*. For example, a shot taken from a train exiting a tunnel in Ruttmann's film[40] outlines a unique view of the city from the train trestle, a novel perspective not found on postcards and accessible only to those riding in the locomotive. Like Ruttmann, Riefenstahl uses architecturally framed shots to invite viewers to see Nürnberg through unique cinematic windows and to showcase the military spectacle portrayed in her film. For example, a shot through two arches frames the troops that participate in the "Grand Review" through the city[41] and thus visually interweaves the city, its citizens, and troops in a manner that suggests that they shared permanence, splendor, and solidity.

Given the circadian organization of both films, it is not surprising that they contain similar scene compositions. Both films, for example, include communal bathing segments: men washing up after work in *Berlin: Sinfonie der Großstadt*,[42] members of the SA washing up in an encampment at dawn in *Triumph des Willens*.[43] Both segments feature strikingly similar close-up shots that are dominated by the men themselves and capture various stages of grooming—washing faces and hands, shaving, and combing hair. Displayed in this manner, cleanliness becomes a shared cultural value integral to daily life and pursued joyously, whether concluding a day's work or preparing to participate in a day of important events. The underlying insinuation of homosocial bonding in both films suggests that the worlds of work and military service are uncontested realms of male social interaction. Given Riefenstahl's familiarity with Ruttmann's film, her inclusion of this almost identically shot scene proves that his impact on her directorial work extends beyond mere admiration; by mirroring this scene, Riefenstahl chose to embrace aspects of Ruttmann's cinematic vernacular.

Riefenstahl and the Responsibilities of Leadership

Riefenstahl's leadership role in Nazi Germany unfolded in decidedly gender-defined parameters: her leadership was possible only within prescribed spheres of influence, subordinate to male control and command. Myra Marx Ferree drew attention to the "outsider" role of women in Nazi Germany in her *Varieties of Feminism: German Gender Politics in Global Perspective*: "The Nazi regime further affirmed the self-pronounced maleness of the Imperial German state epitomized in its bureaucracy, its universities, and its military, so women's political outsiderness was unchallenged."[44] The predominance of patriarchal power structures in Nazi Germany thus defined the framework in which Riefenstahl worked and to which she had to subjugate herself in order to fulfill her contractual agreement and complete *Triumph des Willens*. This, in fact, corroborates her own narrative of making the film: she simply could not say no to the Führer's request that she document the party convention cinematically. Implicit in her version of the story is her freedom from all reproach; her work was artistically valid in and of itself, since she was uninterested in and powerless against the moral corruptness of the larger political sphere in which she was operating.

However, Riefenstahl's claim of complete impotence and insignificance vis-à-vis the hierarchy to which she was wed does not ring true. In *Mothers in the Fatherland* (1987), Koontz articulates the contradictions inherent in Riefenstahl's self-justification:

> The separation of masculine and feminine spheres, which followed logically and psychologically from Nazi leaders' misogyny, relegated women to their own space—both beneath and beyond the dominant world of men. The Nazi system rested on a female hierarchy as well as a male chain of command. . . . Far from remaining untouched by Nazi evil, women operated at its very center. (*Mothers*, 6)

For Koontz, women in Nazi Germany were not passive, powerless bystanders swept up in the movement's momentum, but rather complicit participants: "Autonomy existed only in relationship to women within her sphere and did not translate into bargaining power in male administrations. Women felt free only as long as their wishes were congruent with Nazi demands" (*Mothers*, 15). Even in her self-circumscribed world of moviemaking and commitment to higher aesthetic ideals, Riefenstahl nevertheless was operating in support of the Nazi regime. The point she makes in her defense—that she was never a member of the Nazi party— remains unimpressive given the fact that women composed less than 5 percent of party membership.[45] Unlike other women who served the Nazi regime, though, she was essentially a lone figure leading a cadre of male colleagues. This, however, is neither new nor surprising. Yet coupled with Riefenstahl's subordinate relationship to Fanck and Ruttmann and the strong influence of their films on Riefenstahl's *Triumph des Willens*, a different assessment of Riefenstahl as a female leader emerges.

Underlying the classification of Riefenstahl as a cinematic savant or propagator of fascist aesthetics is the tradition of auteurship, which credits the director as the dominant creative force and leaves all other contributors in the shadows. This asks that Riefenstahl must either be credited for her cinematic brilliance or damned for her collusion with Hitler and the National Socialists, but ignores the collaborative nature of filmmaking itself. And yet, as I have shown in my analysis, the creative triangle between Fanck, Ruttmann, and Riefenstahl was a powerful force. As early as 1927 critics viewed Ruttmann's *Sinfonie der Großstadt* and Fanck's *Bergfilme* as "wesensverwandt" (*Dietrich & Riefenstahl*, 312; similar in character). Riefenstahl herself was at the vortex of this creative synergy, working in concentric circles of power in the Third Reich and the world of moviemaking; and in each circle, she was following the leader. In this respect, she joined the ranks of German women whom Koontz terms "missionaries" (*Mothers*, 12) for the Nazi party. Hitler and Goebbels ruled the larger circle in which she was tasked with making *Triumph des Willens*, while Fanck's and Ruttmann's fame and influence set the standards for cinematic creativity. Most histories of twentieth-century German cinema relegate Riefenstahl to the role of *the* path-breaking female director who made cinematic history with her innovative use of tracking shots. Undeniably, she was an innovator—building a track for the camera to move around Hitler as he gave speeches at the party convention, for example, was ingenious—but she also filmed in the cinematic vernacular of the time, a vernacular articulated by major male directors, such as Fanck and his *Bergfilme* and Ruttmann and his *Berlin: Sinfonie der Großstadt*. Ultimately, Riefenstahl and *Triumph des Willens* are products of both a fascist regime's patriarchal limitation of women's influence and the male-dominated world of early twentieth-century cinema. As a filmmaker, Riefenstahl should be remembered for what she was—an "ambitious, determined, opportunistic" woman following the leaders for her own personal and professional gain. Contrary to her own narrative, she is not a victim of the times and circumstances in which she made movies, but rather she shares the responsibility with all others who contributed to Hitler's rise to power and the evil propagated under his dictatorship.

Notes

[1] Claudia Koontz, *Mothers in the Fatherland: Women, the Family, and Nazi Politics* (New York: St. Martin's, 1987), 12. Further references are given in the text using the short title *Mothers*.

[2] Jürgen Trimborn, *Riefenstahl: Eine Karriere; Biographie*, 3rd ed. (Berlin: Aufbauverlag, 2007), 199–200.

[3] Jürgen Trimborn, *Leni Riefenstahl: A Life*, trans. Edna McCown (New York: Faber & Faber, 2007), 106.

[4] Unless otherwise noted, all translations are my own.

[5] Jodie Foster has explored making a film about Riefenstahl for this very reason: see Rainer Rother, "Die Regisseurin Leni Riefenstahl ist im Alter von 101 Jahren gestorben—ein Nachruf: Die Unberührbare," *Berliner Zeitung*, September 10, 2003, http://www.berliner-zeitung.de/die-regisseurin-leni-riefenstahl-ist-im-alter-von-101-jahren-gestorben---ein-nachruf-die-unberuehrbare-16029982. More recently, Steven Soderbergh considered the possibility of a Riefenstahl biopic as well; see Kevin Jagernauth, "Soderbergh Says Abandoned Leni Riefenstahl Biopic Would Focus on Director Battling the Studio System," *Indie Wire*, September 23, 2013, http://www.indiewire.com/2013/09/soderbergh-says-abandoned-leni-riefenstahl-biopic-would-focus-on-director-battling-the-studio-system-93359/.

[6] See "Die Ästhetin des absolut Schönen," *Süddeutsche.de Kultur*, May 19, 2010, http://www.sueddeutsche.de/kultur/leni-riefenstahl-tot-die-aesthetin-des-absolut-schoenen-1.895416. Wilfried Wiegand, "Die Traumtänzerin," *Frankfurter Allgemeine Zeitung*, September 9, 2003, http://www.faz.net/aktuell/feuilleton/leni-riefenstahl-die-traumtaenzerin-1120259.html.

[7] "Leni Riefenstahl 101-jährig gestorben," *Stern*, September 9, 2003, http://www.stern.de/fotografie/trauer-leni-riefenstahl-101-jaehrig-gestorben-3514808.html.

[8] See "Die Ästhetin des absolut Schönen" and Wiegand, "Traumtänzerin."

[9] Ray Müller, dir., *The Wonderful, Horrible Life of Leni Riefenstahl*, 1993.

[10] Sabine Hake, *German National Cinema*, 2nd ed. (London: Routledge, 2008), 85.

[11] Sabine Hake, *Screen Nazis: Cinema, History and Democracy* (Madison: University of Wisconsin Press, 2012), 34.

[12] Thomas Doherty, *Hollywood and Hitler: 1933–1939* (New York: Columbia University Press, 2013), 293.

[13] See Maggie Hoffgen, *Studying German Film* (Leighton Buzzard, UK: Auteur, 2009), 45–59; Stephan Brockmann, *A Critical History of German Film* (Rochester, NY: Camden House, 2010), 151–65; Jennifer Kapczynski and Michael D. Richardson, eds., *A New History of German Film* (Rochester, NY: Camden House, 2012), 255–61.

[14] Anton Kaes, for example, notes a similarity between the mass scenes in Riefenstahl's *Triumph des Willens* and the mass scenes in Fritz Lang's *Metropolis* (1927). Anton Kaes, "*Metropolis* (1927): City, Cinema, Modernity," in *Weimar Cinema:*

An Essential Guide to Classic Films of the Era, ed. Noah Isenburg (New York: Columbia University Press, 2009), 176.

[15] Stefanie Weinsheimer, "Bergfilm," in *Reclams Sachlexikon des Films*, ed. Thomas Koebner (Stuttgart: Philipp Reclam, 2002), 62.

[16] Karin Wieland, *Dietrich & Riefenstahl: Der Traum der neuen Frau* (Munich: Carl Hanser Verlag, 2011), 317. Further references are given in the text using the short title *Dietrich & Riefenstahl*.

[17] Leni Riefenstahl, *Behind the Scenes of the National Party Convention Film*, trans. David Culbert (Chicago, IL: International Historic Films, 2010), 8.

[18] Unless otherwise indicated, the filmographies for the cinematographers listed for *Triumph des Willens* were accessed on http://www.filmportal.de, an online database of the Deutsches Filminstitut sponsored by the Beauftragte der Bundesregierung für Kultur und Medien, the Bundesministerium für Wirtschaft und Technologie, the Initiative für Kultur und Kreativwirtschaft der Bundesregierung, the Filmförderungsanstalt, the Hessisches Ministerium für Wirtschaft und Kunst, and the Murnau Stiftung.

[19] Some of the cameramen for *Triumph des Willens* also worked together on other films prior to working for Riefenstahl on *Triumph des Willens*. Allgeier also worked with Siegfried Weinmann on Karl Hartl and Luis Trenker's *Berge in Flammen* (1931). Arthur von Schwertführer worked with Walter Bohne on Louis Ralph's *Unsere Emden* (1926) and with Walter Bohne and Franz Koch on Ralph's *Kreuzer Emden* (1932), with Karl Attenberger on Willy Reiber's *Klettermaxe* (1926/1927), and with Hans Karl Gottschalk on *Die Liebe der Bajadere* (1925). Hans Karl Gottschalk teamed with Karl Attenberger for the filming of *Die abenteuerliche Hochzeit* (1925). Attenberger and Franz Koch worked together on Phil Jutzi and Karl Lutz's *Kindertragödie* (1927). Paul Lieberenz and Karl Vass were both on the camera crew for Carl Froelich's *Volldampf voraus!* (1933/34). Walter Riml took still shots for *Das blaue Licht* (1931/32), Riefenstahl's debut film, which she directed, edited, and also starred in, and *Triumph des Willens* was the first film he worked on as a cinematographer.

[20] Hoffgen, *Studying German Film*, 49.

[21] *The Wonderful, Horrible Life of Leni Riefenstahl*, 01:41:37.

[22] Doherty, *Hollywood and Hitler*, 294.

[23] See Birgit Haustedt, *Die wilden Jahre in Berlin: Eine Klatsch- und Kulturgeschichte der Frauen* (Dortmund: Edition Ebersbach, 1999), 180; Doherty, *Hollywood and Hitler*, 294.

[24] Leni Riefenstahl, *Memoiren* (Munich: Albrecht Knaus Verlag, 1987), 230. Further references are given in the text using the title *Memoiren*.

[25] Leni Riefenstahl, *Leni Riefenstahl: A Memoir* (New York: Picador, 1992), 165. Further references are given in the text using the short title *A Memoir*.

[26] Leni Riefenstahl, "How I Came to Film . . . ," trans. Jon Cho-Polizzi, in *The Promise of Cinema: German Film Theory 1907–1933*, ed. Anton Kaes, Nicholas Baer, and Michael Cowan (Oakland: University of California Press, 2016), 135.

[27] Arnold Fanck, dir., *Der heilige Berg*, 1926, 00:10:44–00:15:50.

[28] Weinsheimer, "Bergfilm," 62.

[29] Riefenstahl's memoirs are not unproblematic. As Susan Sontag so clearly illustrates in her 1974 essay "Fascinating Fascism," In *Under the Sign of Saturn*, 71–105, First Vintage Books Edition (New York: Vintage Books, 1981). Riefenstahl is a master of reinvention. In addition, her narrative of the making of *Triumph des Willens* in her memoir is intertwined with her parallel narrative of Goebbels's increasingly aggressive romantic advances.

[30] Trimborn, *Leni Riefenstahl: A Life*, 204.

[31] Clemens Zimmermann, "Die politischen Dokumentarfilme von Leni Riefenstahl: *Sieg des Glaubens* (1933)—*Triumph des Willens* (1935)—*Tag der Freiheit: Unsere Wehrmacht* (1935)," in *Kunst und Ästhetik im Werk Leni Riefenstahls*, ed. Markwart Herzog and Mario Leis. edition text + kritik (Munich: Richard Boorberg Verlag, 2011), 66.

[32] "Am 5. September 1934/20 Jahren nach dem Ausbruch des Weltkrieges/16 Jahre nach dem Anfang deutschen Leidens/19 Monate nach dem Beginn der deutschen Wiedergeburt/flog Adolf Hitler wieder nach Nürnberg um Heerschau abzuhalten über seine Getreuen."

[33] Walter Ruttmann, dir., *Berlin: Sinfonie der Großstadt*, 1927, 00:04:16, 00:17:04, and 00:35:59.

[34] Daniel Knopp, *NS-Filmpropaganda: Wunschbild und Feindbild in Leni Riefenstahls "Triumph des Willens" und Veit Harlens "Jud Süß"* (Marburg: Tectum Verlag, 2004), 35–36.

[35] Zimmermann, "Dokumentarfilme," 67; Stefanie Grote, "Objekt' Mensch: Körper als Ikon und Ideologem in den cineastischen Werken Leni Riefenstahls; Ästhetisierter Despotismus oder die Reziprozität von Auftragskunst und Politik im Dritten Reich" (PhD diss., Viadrina European University, 2004), 93. https://opus4.kobv.de/opus4-euv/frontdoor/index/index/docId/40.

[36] Trimborn, *Leni Riefenstahl: A Life*, 205.

[37] Jackson J. Spielvogel, *Hitler and Nazi Germany: A History*, 3rd ed. (Upper Saddle River, NJ: Prentice Hall, 1996), 48.

[38] Riefenstahl uses this same technique again in her *Olympia: Fest der Völker*, enveloping the Greek statues in swaths of fog/mist as they transition to actual athletes, and in *Olympia: Fest der Schönheit* as German athletes emerge from early morning mist on their training run through the forest.

[39] Hake, *Screen Nazis*, 74.

[40] Ruttmann, *Berlin: Sinfonie der Großstadt*, 00:35:35.

[41] Riefenstahl, *Triumph des Willens*, 1935, 01:30:01.

[42] Ruttmann, *Berlin: Sinfonie der Großstadt*, 00:48:14.

[43] Riefenstahl, *Triumph des Willens*, 00:17:02.

[44] Myra Marx Ferree, *Varieties of Feminism: German Gender Politics in Global Perspective* (Stanford, CA: Stanford University Press, 2012), 43.

[45] Claudia Koontz, "The Fascist Solution to the Woman Question in Italy and Germany," in *Becoming Visible: Women in European History*, 2nd ed., ed. Renate Bridenthal, Claudia Koontz, and Susan Stuard (Boston: Houghton Mifflin, 1987), 504.

12: "Leaning In": The Career Woman as Instrument of Neoliberal Critique

Helga Druxes

POLITICAL SCIENTISTS David Chandler and Julian Reid discuss the neo-liberal subject as a frantic maker of choices. They argue that such an anxious quest for control through an individualized form of decisionism presents the only weapon against uncertainty and risk. In the following, I show that, in three recent comedic treatments, female executives in corporate leadership roles are portrayed as dangerously vulnerable, in the sense that they expose the conceptual flaws of neoliberal self-referentiality. I define neoliberal self-referentiality as the solipsistic worldview of actors engaged 24/7 in a system where everything is marketized. According to the corporate data portal Statista, for 2016, the overall percentage of German women in leadership positions falls between 12.5 and 16.9 percent, with companies with 101–550 employees occupying the lower end of the spectrum and those with more than 10,000 employees showing the somewhat higher percentage of women in management. Since Germany boasts a predominance of small and mid-size companies, companies with fewer women in leadership positions, that is between 12.9 and 14.1 percent, are more common than larger corporations with their somewhat higher percentages. These figures indicate that women lag significantly behind in leadership positions in the German business workplace.[1] Female managerial positions involve control over budgets and authority over subordinates, but are often subject to review by superiors as well. The power of female managers to implement their own decisions is often relative. In the neoliberal marketplace, female middle managers continue to be under pressure to self-optimize by combining their business acumen with so-called "soft skills" for employee management, all the while monitoring their bodies for slimness and youthful attractiveness. If they boldly state an economic decision at a business meeting, they may receive criticism for being too strident or unethical.[2] Performance reviews may describe women with emotive clichés as supportive rather than aggressive, implicitly denying them leadership potential. At the same time, the business world is the only arena where there is a sustained engagement with the concept of female leadership, as there is a constant feedback loop of job performance surveys and profitability.

Traditionally, women are taught to self-monitor their bodies and their conduct to a much greater extent than men. Therefore, as the Germanists Hester Baer, Carrie Smith-Prei, and Maria Stehle have argued, "neoliberalism constructs women as its ideal subjects."[3] Their willing embrace of the neoliberal credo of self-optimization along with their consumerism and their work ethic are exaggerated to the point of caricature in recent satirical German feature films. While these works expose the dehumanizing effects of corporate neoliberalism in a global-ized system, they fall short by deflecting some of the blame onto "shrew-ish" females in leadership roles. The filmmakers betray their reflexive conservatism when they wonder if a woman in a position of corporate authority can also be a good mother. Focusing on women through the lens of motherhood re-emotionalizes contemporary filmic discourse and may express an antifeminist point of view. Whether female directors of satire (a genre that by definition thrives on distortion) are less prone to these gendered political regressions is one of the questions that I seek to address here.

What cultural anxieties over the ageing German demographic emerge in depictions of career women of reproductive age? How do these anxiet-ies fit into a globalized neoliberal paradigm? Three satirical films, Frauke Finsterwalder's and cowriter Christian Kracht's *Finsterworld* (Darkworld; 2013), Johannes Naber's *Zeit der Kannibalen* (Time of the Cannibals; 2014), and Maren Ade's *Toni Erdmann* (2016), provide trenchant cri-tiques of neoliberalism as a sinister economic system that exploits and dehumanizes.[4] Yet in all three films educated female professionals and their sexuality are transformed into emblems of crisis. In *Kannibalen*, corporate merger consultant Bianca and in *Finsterworld*, the advertising executive Frau Sandberg and the documentary filmmaker Franziska are portrayed as ruthless, strident, or needy. The consultant Ines Conradi of Ade's *Toni Erdmann* graphically embodies the exploitative nature of neoliberalism in an internationally mobile body that scarcely ever gets a chance to rest or luxuriate. All of these female characters are portrayed as difficult, overly self-disciplined, and/or unduly regimenting men to whom they are close.

How would females who strive ceaselessly to be seen as entrepre-neurial firebrands, worthy of promotion and esteem from their male col-leagues, find time for a personal life, let alone a family? The question of social reproduction across generations hinges on motherhood, not only on individual labor. While the mothers we encounter in *Kannibalen* and *Finsterworld* are demonized as "bad" mothers, younger entrepreneurial women of prime childbearing age are vilified for their pronounced lack of interest in taking on the additional labor of motherhood. Bianca in

Kannibalen mocks her colleague Öllers for his deficient parenting skills and presents herself as a seemingly asexual predatory strategist in the boardroom. Franziska in *Finsterworld* fails to achieve an artistic vision as an independent filmmaker, even as she is deluded about the value of her project, and behaves in an egotistical, even emasculating manner toward her boyfriend. When two boys attack a smaller girl right in front of her, she ignores them in favor of dictating a dinner shopping list over her cell phone to her boyfriend. Franziska is stereotyped as too self-involved to act in a maternal manner. Frau Sandberg, an advertising executive, is always on the road and neglects her teenage son both for her work and her overly symbiotic relationship with her husband. Ines is a single woman of childbearing age in her late twenties to early thirties who is alienated from her family; at work, she presents as scarily efficient and rigid. In these films, the corporate woman's lack of compliance with conventional gender roles undermines her credibility and opens her to critique. Women bear a disproportionate burden in humanizing the neoliberal workplace, while the critical focus on their failings obfuscates both the actual underrepresentation of women in positions of authority, and the incompetence or lack of professionalism on the part of their male colleagues.

As mothers (or partners), these corporate career women are depicted as neglectful and unfeeling to the point that they drive their male offspring to monstrous behavior against a young woman who might be a future romantic partner, and to criminal scapegoating of the one character coded as ethnically "other." Transgenerational reproduction is thus endangered, reflecting cultural anxiety over delayed childbirth in contemporary Germany. The first two films then shift to the African subcontinent, where some kind of climax is reached. The third film uses the Balkans as a stage for ludic improvisation and reinvention. These shifts indicate that neoliberalism creates a deterritorialized sense of identity, allowing the central characters to avoid moral responsibility for the business failures they actively bring about. They may become disoriented as to what country they are in, which contributes to the downfall of the executives in *Kannibalen*. Or they revert to either a colonialist disdain for or a nostalgic idealization of foreign locales. They gain no realistic insight into the workings or social context of a specific place.

Within neoliberal doctrine, crisis is embraced as creative, as a stimulant for flexibility and innovation. However, when the female professional responds to crisis, her behavior is seen as neurotic, and her body stigmatized as disorderly and malfunctioning. Thus these comedies reaffirm gender stereotypes, even as they unpack the dehumanizing effects of neoliberal ideology. Even when the female executive produces mock crises for the sake of self-parody, the camera exposes her partially undressed or nude body to voyeuristic scrutiny. Filmic critiques of neoliberalism, even those

246 ♦ HELGA DRUXES

by feminist directors like Maren Ade, are executed on the undressed or ridiculous female body, vacillating between body shaming and viewer titillation. The young female executives Ines, Bianca, and Franziska are childless and partnered with males they ignore or treat dismissively; this shared attitude toward heteronormative relationships is portrayed as problematic, even though their male colleagues act in much the same ways. The only older female executive presented, Frau Sandberg from *Finsterworld*, neglects her son. In coding competitive and careerist behavior as unfeminine, *Kannibalen* and *Finsterworld* attempt to voice concerns about Germany's ageing demographic, playing up an obsession with the low birthrate of highly educated women. These characters embody anxieties about shifting demographics. Their bodies become metonymies for the crisis of the ideology of free choice.

In contemporary Germany, roughly a third of all residents remain single. Women with a university degree tend to postpone childbearing, although a 2011 study indicated more births compared with the low rate of 1.5 children in 2008. The rate increased for the years 2015 to 2016, especially in cities. The 2016 rate was 3.2 percent higher than the previous year. In a 2016 survey, however, more respondents argued that children are too expensive (63 percent, up from 58 percent five years before), or that having children would negatively impact their personal freedom (61 percent), or their career (55 percent).[5] These numbers may suggest how insidious the neoliberal mantra of constant self-improvement has become, but conversely they may show that full-time work and career advancement are important values for women who have invested significant time and effort in their education.[6]

The films present such women through a stereotypical lens, as the "disorderly virago," who makes a spectacle of herself and is in need of public censure. In contrast, a feminist perspective might explore the potential of female executives as agents of systemic change. Despite their hard work and intelligent maneuverings in a neoliberal world of predators, Ines and Bianca are presented as grotesque in the final scenes of each film. While Ines learns to poke fun at herself and her work environment, the last take of *Toni Erdmann* shows her in her business suit, trying on her deceased grandmother's frumpy hat, a beret-like oval topper made of woven straw. Even though she learned to clown around with verbal and physical levity in prior scenes, in this final image, the lingering camera gaze invites us to read Ines as grotesque spinster—old and young at the same time, and most importantly, alone. Her sober gaze might indicate resignation toward her future, as she is stuck in a pose of waiting. I contend that Ade ultimately posits Ines as a sad, somewhat inscrutable paradox—in direct contrast to the opening of the film, where she introduces Ines's father as a likeable, effervescent madcap joker.

Cannibals in Hotel World

The unsympathetic portrayal of a female executive serves to de-politi-cize the critique of neoliberal global predatory capitalism. The character Bianca operates according to a secret agenda, which fuses her boss's long-term planning with her personal goals: to surveil her colleagues and climb the career ladder at their expense. By making viewers privy to a denoue-ment in which all the "cannibals," even the smart woman, are outwitted, the film creates an illusion of control in a globalized market governed by rampant aggression.

Kannibalen presents Bianca as an ambitious, highly skilled junior business consultant, whose credentials include a medical degree and expe-rience working for an NGO. Approximately in her thirties, she is not only younger and more intelligent, but more flexible than the two senior males on her team, Öllers and Nederländer. All three are characterized as neoliberal predators employed by a company in Hamburg that advises businesses in India and Nigeria how to merge, refinance, and maximize production in the global marketplace. While the men routinely address each other by their last names, Bianca is referred to by her first name as soon as she joins the team. This singles her out as a subaltern in the neo-liberal pecking order, since the only other characters referred to in this way are the hotel workers.

We soon learn that Bianca was given a covert mission by her boss: to observe her team-mates and report on which one has more leadership potential and should be promoted after a vacancy arises. Bianca is pre-sented as a slender woman with a severe hairstyle who wears glasses and monochromatic business suits. After work, she reads guidebooks and sug-gests several times to her coworkers that she would like to explore the old town, or that they might all go out to an ethnic restaurant, although typ-ically one that serves something other than the local cuisine. Marooned in global chain hotels that only vary their décor in a nod to the coun-tries where they are located, she clumsily attempts to engage her veiled African room cleaner in conversation about women's appearance or musi-cal tastes, saying she herself opposes cosmetic surgery for older women, or that she likes Afrobeat. These overtures fall flat, as Bianca's interest is patently self-centered. She does not get to know the locals as individuals any more than her male colleagues do, and is only slightly more aware that doing so might be worthwhile. Bianca never does get outside: ultimately, she is a willing captive of a neoliberal machine that relentlessly harnesses workers to self-optimization despite its valorized systemic unpredictabil-ity, such as sudden changes in the work environment or company struc-ture. While Öllers has a young son at home with an itchy skin condition, Bianca has no personal attachments, which are portrayed as burdensome and expensive.

In comparison to the men in *Kannibalen,* Bianca appears to be an ideal neoliberal operative. Nederländer is a slimy careerist obsessed with personal fitness and preparedness for crisis, such as fire breaking out at the hotel. He is hampered by his anxious egocentric routines, alternating with choleric outbursts toward staff and business partners. He even snoops in Öllers's email and Bianca's Facebook contacts to discern their weaknesses. Despite her superior professional and human qualifications, Bianca is nonetheless typecast as a single career woman and feminist of the stern schoolmarm variety. If anything, the stressed father figure Öllers, whose name is a play on the northern German dialect word for old and who soldiers on for the company despite his disillusionment, is offered up as an identificatory character. This audience manipulation reaffirms conservative gender stereotypes about salaried men versus bluestockings that go back to the 1950s in the Federal Republic, when the so-called Würmeling law was passed to force professional women back into the home in favor of male war veterans and returning POWs. Married women had to cede their place in the work sphere, while single women were allowed to stay employed, as they had to support themselves. This law reinstated a binary between women idealized as mothers and homemakers versus single women who found personal fulfillment in the workplace, but who were treated with condescension.

Misogynistic attitudes mix with racism when neoliberalism is exported from the Global North to the Global South. These crosscutting factors of gender, race, and capitalist profiteering are alluded to, but not to empower those individuals targeted by them. Rather, the empowerment of the revolutionaries unfolds off camera, which further heightens the viewers' sense of foreboding and doom. The company plunges local businesses into crisis by advising that they suddenly move production out of the country (from India to Pakistan) at the bidding of a global investor, or by randomly withdrawing from a small African family business that expanded abroad by borrowing heavily. Even though these neoliberal practices are overtly critiqued as arbitrary and inhumane, the film also unashamedly revives colonialist attitudes toward African women. Hotel workers are willing to prostitute themselves for money, or sell drugs, even abase themselves in front of the German bosses for a chance to leave their country: "I beg you, take me with you. I have a Master Degree in Economics. I am fluent in four languages . . . I am not married. I am a virgin. I don't have AIDS. Take me with you."[7] As the female Nigerian office assistant who speaks these words tries to strip for the men in a somewhat desultory way, Bianca struggles with her, trying to force her to keep her clothes on. Bianca tries to soothe the employee with the words: "I am your friend," but is angrily rebuffed: "No, you are not my friend" and pushed aside. The Nigerian woman continues to undress and cry out to the men "please, I beg you, take me with you."

Bianca then pleads with her colleagues: "Please, show some initiative!" (Bitte, unternehmt doch mal was!), paralleling the African woman's pleas, but her feminist intervention fails. By focusing on the tussle between the two women, the camera reinscribes stereotypes about women competing with each other over male attention. Eventually, Öllers calls hotel security to remove the Nigerian woman. Thus men are portrayed as "executives" who invoke a hierarchical chain of command and delegate messy jobs to specialists, while women's attempts to restore order are ineffectual and devolve into catfights. As we see in subsequent scenes, Bianca's pale face is scratched from this incident. She covers these blemishes with makeup and pulls down her hair to hide them, whereas the men show no physical signs of wear and tear. The film argues that women cannot defuse a crisis with soft skills; aggressive law enforcement wins the day. *Kannibalen* thus reinscribes aggressive behavior as masculine, legitimating masculinity by denigrating women as impulsive or ineffectual, as triggers for crisis rather than solvers.

The Nigerian professional's degradation is meant to be comedic, but its voyeuristic display reassures viewers that she is not a threatening competitor in the global marketplace despite all her qualifications. For viewers, this scene implies that Nigeria exists only as a foil to a global North caught up in asserting white dominance over the South. In the end, reified gender roles are reinstated by neoliberal globalism, as Bianca is similarly degraded when her drunk German CEO demands in a Skype meeting that she strip for him and masturbate for his benefit. While the Nigerian woman rejects her gesture of female solidarity across racial difference, the camera and the male hierarchy put both women into the same category.

Two similarly offensive scenes occur in Nederländer's abusive and infantilizing treatment of male room-service workers. He threatens them for imaginary infractions, twists their ears, and kicks them in the behind, shouting: "Your job will soon be done by a robot." Even as viewer anxieties about precariousness and international competition are stimulated, a fantasy of white dominance is alternately ridiculed and reinforced. The men are often physically violent and smash furniture or insult employees without perceptible negative consequences. They behave like rock stars on tour, simply because they are abroad in poorer countries. Both men dismiss Africans and Indians as uncivilized, religious fundamentalists. The only global competitors whose dominance they fear are the Chinese. As Bianca ironically states during a drink after work: "Keiner hat mehr Spaß am Kapitalismus außer die Chinesen" (Nobody enjoys capitalism any more, except for the Chinese). Once more, foreigners as a group are depicted as naïve and childlike, reflecting a German colonialist attitude. The Germans are viewed as fixated on their work ethic. From the perspective of an overarching critique of neoliberalism, the German characters are equally culpable—intersectional identities shift according to perspective, with male subjects homogenizing all women; and global perspectives homogenizing all Germans and Nigerians.

As Sheryl Sandberg recommends in her simplistic advice book for professional women, Bianca certainly "leans in" for her "seat at the table."[8] She demands respect for her credentials and often works late into the night to impress in meetings. In the end, however, she is caught in the same trap as her male coworkers. Their company is sold to an American entrepreneur, who quite suddenly offers them all a highly desirable promotion to partner. This offer turns out to be a ruse to implicate them as codefendants in a global lawsuit against the new owner. While the clever Bianca is less blinded by greed and does not sign, she does not manage to extricate herself from the next crisis. The rapidity with which these crises unfold mimics the globalized neoliberal marketplace, in which uncertainty is the order of the day. Focused on business affairs and profoundly incurious about real-life conditions in the host countries, the German executives ignore the persistent ominous sounds of shooting outside the hotel. Thus they are caught unaware when the Taliban attack and civil war breaks out. The terrorists invade the hotel and shoot everyone. The final shot zooms in on the room door where Bianca and the men cower. Even though Bianca barricaded the room as best she could, the door is being shot at and hacked open with an axe. Viewers see the three formerly high-handed executives reduced to terrified crybabies, the men far more so than Bianca, who watches wide-eyed. Then the screen abruptly cuts to black.

The corporate "cannibals" of the title are just bit players whose power to transact business evaporates as soon as their credit cards are blocked. Their cowering defeat forces them to confront who they were all along—feminized cogs in a neoliberal network whose sudden reversals they cannot outmaneuver. After the team had closed on its first deal together and they all got drunk in the hotel bar, Öllers made a sarcastic toast to the company: "In der Company zu arbeiten ist *ganz* toll! Egal wo du bist, du bist sofort vernetzt, du hast zu jedem gleich 'nen Draht wie in 'ner großen Familie—auf die Company!" (Working for the company is so awesome! No matter where you are, you are networked right away, you have an instant connection to everyone just like in a big family—here's to the company!). The film exploits Germans' anxieties of losing their national identity in a global marketplace of competing interests guided solely by the profit motive. Not only is the company not like a "big family," there is no more solidarity to be found in the upwardly mobile family unit itself. Öllers has constant fights over the phone with his wife, Sophie, who promptly divorces him when he fails to make partner. She is coded as selfish, as she wants a big villa and resentfully mothers their toddler son Anton, who is beset by severe allergies and is still in diapers at the age of three and a half. The film wants us to assume that Sophie is a bad mother, just as Öllers is an unreliable father, whose frequent phone calls mimic neoliberal cycles of unpredictable stimulus followed by abrupt disengagement. The "rapacious" Bianca merely copies a pessimistic neoliberalism that Öllers embodies. However, by sharing only Öllers's point of view throughout the film, viewers are encouraged to identify with a traditional male-breadwinner perspective reliant on a strict division of domestic sphere and work sphere. Öllers gleefully lies to his wife about where he is, or what is preventing him from listening to her tirades. Viewers become complicit as they listen in on a disembodied screeching female voice at the other end of the line. This perspective fits with the misogynistic representation of Bianca's body, shown after drunken sex with Öllers reclining on the bed wearing nude knee-highs that bisect her legs and make her appear distinctly middle-aged and matronly.

Bianca's attempt to protect a stranger reminds us that caring for others is a liability in a neoliberal environment. Her selfless gesture is incompatible with the imperative of propulsive self-reinvention that David Chandler and Julian Reid identify "as the fundamental property that people and individuals worldwide must possess in order to . . . make the 'right choices' in the development of sustainable responses to threats and dangers posed by [their] environment."[9] *Kannibalen* satirizes that premise, showing the humiliation of Bianca's intellect by her own body's reflexes: she throws up repeatedly and becomes stalemated after her attempt to flee the hotel fails. Overall, the film posits that neoliberalism is inhumane and cynically exploitive, but still places the imperative to be resilient to danger squarely on Bianca, thereby turning her into a symbol of neoliberal faux feminism.

Termagants of the Dark World

The 2014 satire *Finsterworld* offers a parallel to the characters of Bianca and Sophie Öllers in the figure of Frau Sandberg, a negligent mother of a teenager and rapacious businesswoman. Like Öllers, Herr Sandberg is also portrayed as a bad father and son. However, he is not demonized to the same extent as his wife. He neglects to call their son Maximilian regularly when he travels on business with her; he also forgets to visit his mother, whom he has placed in an old folks' home. Like her American namesake Sheryl Sandberg, the demanding Frau Sandberg gets results. However, while her resilience strategy is understood to be effective, it is coded as unfeminine and harsh. Unforeseeable dangers and frustrations lurk in new environments, yet the Sandbergs believe in insulating themselves in the comforting beige interior of a luxury rental car: "Es ist richtig nett jetzt . . . in der Blase, so abgeschottet, alles Störende bleibt draußen" (it is really pleasant right now . . . in the bubble, away from bothersome things, everything disturbing stays out). A wistful nostalgia for a life in harmony with nature is invoked as a remedy against the evils of neoliberal consumerism; it becomes the only cultural construct that the film does not debunk, even though the nature scenes are imbued with an unreal fairy-tale beauty and saturated colors.

The sublime hill panorama of Tanzania provides the conclusion for the third storyline and for the film as a whole, in which Africa becomes the antidote to the narcissism of the other central female character of child-bearing age, documentary filmmaker Franziska. She is intent on making a "neorealist" documentary, as she explains to her boss: "'n trauriger Film, mit 'n bisschen Hoffnung natürlich auch . . . na, also, Hoffnung, auf 'ne bessere Zukunft, und äh äh . . . und Veränderung, so raus aus der Starre" (a sad film with a bit of hope also of course, well, I mean hope for a better future, and um um, change, like getting beyond paralysis). Finsterwalder and her husband and coauthor Kracht posit that a return to nature, or exotic travel would reinvigorate a jaded German subjectivity, an assumption that revives a romantic fallacy. The German homeland is spoilt by violence against animals, and by men or women who are willing, but bored captives of consumer society. The film illustrates this in the conversations heterosexual couples have, in which they complain about how ugly Germany is, how rude and surly people are, how frustrating their work-life is and on and on, without realizing that they themselves could decide to make changes. Their inability to discern the true causes of their anhedonia and aggression is produced by the rigorous modeling of the neoliberal subject as someone who shies away from truly autonomous decisions in favor of self-optimization.

Finsterwalder focuses her critique on women within heterosexual couples, thus giving voice to a backlash against feminism. Her gender politics can be reduced to the trite conceit that the world would be redeemed if women were more nurturing. According to this logic, Frau Sandberg is a neglectful mother whose educational failure caused her son Maximilian to become a cynical manipulator: "Habt ihr mich jemals in den Arm genommen? Ich kann mich an keinen einzigen Tag erinnern, an dem du mal was für mich gekocht hast. Andere können sagen, hier schmeckt es wie zu Hause, und ich hab' keine *fucking* Ahnung, wie das schmeckt. . . . Was bist du bloß für 'ne Mutter?" (Did you ever hug me? I can't remember a single day where you cooked something for me. Others can say, here, this tastes like home, and I haven't got a fucking clue what that tastes like. . . . What kind of a mother are you?). Similarly, Franziska does not intervene to protect a young girl who is being attacked by several boys in the playground right in front of her, because she is too busy making a banal phone call. This demonization of inattentive mother figures echoes recent right-wing populist advocacy for a return to traditional gender roles, spearheaded by, among others, New Right publicist Ellen Kositza and former ARD-newscaster–turned-Alternative-for-Germany (AfD) spokesperson Eva Herman.[10]

Men of the Earth

In comparison with the two films discussed above, the 2016 comedy hit *Toni Erdmann* sharpens the rebelliousness of the female executive toward male authority figures. We first encounter Ines during a brief visit to her family in Germany before she flies back to work in Romania, where her German consulting team is tasked with plans to modernize the local oil industry. This means recommending job cuts and streamlining the production process to make local plants internationally competitive. Ines is so focused on her mission that she has become a slave to texting and is constantly at the beck and call of her German boss, a demanding but indecisive older male. Ines's father, Winfried, by contrast, is presented as playful and spontaneous with a strong ethic of caring—in other words, anathema to the neoliberal mindset. Winfried is a divorced music teacher at a middle school in Aachen, who also takes care of his grumpy elderly mother and the ancient family dog. His own politics appear to be left-liberal: we see him carrying his belongings in a small cloth shoulder bag, which codes him as an eco-friendly liberal, and he lives in a modest row house. But is Winfried an emancipatory feminist or a traditional father figure? Ines, unlike her parents, enjoys a swanky jet-setting lifestyle. She is a social climber who joined a globalized upper class that almost exclusively speaks English at work, and is deployed to "emerging" regions where global corporations see a chance for development and profit. Ines's women friends are two Americans: an event planner and the wife of an architect. Ines does not have any Romanian friends, despite having worked there for some time. Her managerial standing is indicated by the expensive designer clothes she wears and her towering high heels (her footwear makes it hard for her to walk and she is shown relying on a driver).

When Winfried realizes that his daughter has forgotten how to be humane in her interactions, not just with him, but with others in general, and is actually unhappy in her new life of constant availability to her company, he decides to stage an intervention. Winfried flies to Bucharest for an unannounced visit, further prompted by his loneliness after the death of the family dog. His first attempt to reconnect goes badly, as Ines resents her father's presence and does not make time to show him around or introduce him to her coworkers and friends. In a second attempt to subvert Ines's routines, Winfried resurfaces as the maverick life coach "Toni Erdmann." Erdmann sports a shaggy brown wig reminiscent of Mick Jagger's hairstyle and a set of protruding Neanderthal-like false teeth. His get-up is a grotesque caricature of business attire. Toni appears irrepressibly at Ines's work meetings, where he makes fun of her boss, her work routines, and her friends. Ines simply cannot shake him off. Irritated at first, Ines cannot fail to be amused by Erdmann's persistence, chutzpah, and humor. She begins to play a supporting role as his occasional sidekick, while still struggling to maintain her businesslike demeanor. Erdmann's ludic attitude to life and business brings to mind the German-South Korean philosopher Byung-Chul Han's discussion of the "emancipatory potential of play" as a counter-strategy against the neoliberal mindset: "Das Spiel macht einen ganz anderen Gebrauch der Dinge möglich, der diese von der Theologie und Teleologie des Kapitals befreit" (Play enables a totally different usage of things, which frees them from the theology and teleology of capital).[11] Han goes on to describe "Profanierung" (profanation) as "die Dinge, die den Göttern gehörten . . . wieder dem freien Gebrauch der Menschen zurückzugeben" (returning those things that were reserved for the Gods to humans' free use). We can think of Toni's parodic play with neoliberal rituals as a profanation that opens up a new way of seeing for Ines.

It becomes evident to the viewer that prior to Toni's arrival Ines was utterly incurious about Romanian culture and the relative poverty of this newcomer country to the European Union (EU). She is trapped by her own utilitarianism toward her environment. Every day, Ines takes a car service between her luxury condo, the office tower where she works, a shopping mall, and various high-end restaurants—in social geographer Paul Virilio's terms, these are all "urban non-places" typical of postmodern globalized capitalism.[12] In Toni's company, by contrast, she experiences an unscripted visit to a Romanian middle-class home; they also drive far out into the countryside to the oil fields. There they meet some of the local workers, as well as miners whom her company, and specifically Ines as the lead consultant, plan to lay off. Winfried/Toni questions this strategy because it would only increase poverty in this rural backwater. For the first time, he and his daughter have a real debate over a concrete political and ethical issue, and we see Winfried's empathy shining through Toni's clownish mask. In contrast, Ines maintains that modernization is unstoppable, and that it is impossible to avoid its negative effects. If she does not lay these workers off, somebody else will. Even Toni becomes implicated in the abrupt firing of a worker when he points out the man's oil-blackened hands. The local boss decides to terminate this employee for a safety infraction, in an effort to appear decisive and masculine before his outside evaluators Ines and Toni. Ade thus suggests that individuals cannot reverse the neoliberal system, and while Ines eventually rebels, she does not truly opt out of it in the end.

Up to this point in the film, Ines had interacted with subalterns only in a distant, authoritarian manner. She ignores, for instance, the fact that her P. A. Anca put a great deal of effort into securing the apartment she occupies. In a humiliating scene at work, Ines forces Anca to swop blouses in the bathroom after Ines stained her own shirt with blood. Ade shows Ines's harshness as a kind of self-mutilation, exemplified by Ines's painful tugging out of a damaged toenail so that she can teeter around on her high heels that, to her mind, complete her office look.

Toni ridicules his daughter's attention to a perfect exterior by wearing increasingly hideous sets of false teeth, behaving in a disinhibited manner around food and drink, and inserting himself into business conversations with outrageous tall tales. Ines's coworkers cannot come close to Toni's playfulness, even when they take drugs, drink to excess, or engage in kinky sex. A main reason for their inability to play is their deep insecurity. They cannot be sure whether Toni is a clown and a fraud, or whether he might have the fabulous connections of which he boasts. Even Ines's boss, Henneberg, does not know how to read Toni. And yet, though he is flummoxed by him, Henneberg accepts Toni into his inner circle, while he orders Ines to spend her weekend taking his wife shopping. This behavior stands in evidence of corporate sexism: "uppity" career women can be quickly "put in their place" by insisting they run private errands for the boss and his family.

The more Ines witnesses Toni ridiculing her lifestyle and coworkers, the more she enjoys his irrepressible wit and improvisational charm. She begins to imitate him. At the private Easter celebration of a Romanian family, she grudgingly learns to decorate an egg with a traditional wax-painting technique. Toni pretends to be the German Ambassador and claims that Ines is his assistant, a "Miss Schnuck." As Miss Schnuck, Ines is given license to improvise. At her father's urging (and with his musical accompaniment on the keyboard), she launches into a spirited, if embarrassed, impromptu rendition of the Whitney Houston song "The Greatest Love of All." For the first time in a long time, she is not afraid to perform for the sheer joy of improvisation. There is no profit motive. The Romanian family is a bit mystified by this odd couple. They tolerate Ines's weirdness and Toni's patent lies, without asking for anything in exchange. They even let Toni borrow a Bulgarian folk costume after Ines leaves, just because he is intrigued by it. Their behavior is a counter-model to neo-liberal business practices: they are not socializing to increase their profit or make connections. However, the family's cultural difference is also romanticized as intriguingly "other."

And yet the father-daughter relationship that we see here can suspend neoliberal hierarchies only temporarily. Emboldened by her father's jokey disruptiveness, in evidence throughout his performance as Toni, Ines decides to throw herself a birthday party at her home, inviting her coworkers and girlfriends. Initially, Ines's corporate superego takes charge: she orders a lavish buffet of catered food and asks a party service to redecorate her living room with potted plants and grasses to give it an exotic air. She dresses up in an expensive, very short and tight designer outfit, but forgets to remove the price tag. Now her id takes over: feeling constricted in the skin-tight dress, she pokes at her back with a fork to snag the price tag. Then she decides it is stupid to wear something so tight that she cannot even bend down to put on her high heels. She frantically struggles out of the constricting dress—the symbol of the neoliberal carapace that she is shedding. The doorbell rings. Ines spontaneously answers the door dressed only in her underpants. She improvises, claiming that she is naked because her party has a nude theme. It is a trust-building exercise, she avers, so all her guests should get naked, too. All but one comply, even though they feel shame and confusion. They respect Ines's assertive manner so much that they will do her bidding no matter what. Several coworkers assemble uneasily, shielding their private parts with gift bags, their shoes, or their hands. The gifts they bring Ines are small and impersonal, like the pocket calculator Anca gives Ines, because, as she says, "you always take mine." Surprisingly, Anca's comment makes Ines tear up, because she regrets how mercenary she has been in all her interactions with Anca and others. Ines now begins to question the ideology that was the lynchpin of her managerial style. She allows herself to be suffused with a variety of visible emotions, ranging from shame to compassion, from self-pity to filial love. Ade suggests that collectively stripping naked is a guarantor of more genuine social relations, a sloughing off of neoliberalism's corset. Unlike the spurned Nigerian employee in *Kannibalen*, who strips naked in an act of self-prostitution, Ines's stripping is an act of parodic iconoclasm and daring, as she demands that others follow her lead, which allows her to establish dominance.

Then a monstrously large hairy creature with no face enters the apartment. This is Winfried/Toni in his most outrageous incarnation yet, dressed as a Kukeri figure. In Bulgaria, this ancient folk figure visits houses to dispel evil ghosts and introduce spring. The Kukeri is traditionally impersonated by an old man to "teach" young men how to claim a mate and impregnate her, so that the natural cycle may continue. Toni-Kukeri scares Ines's superior Gerald by laying his paw on his shoulder. Then he reaches out for Ines and presents her with some asters that he clearly tore out of the garden beds outside the condo development. They have a large chunk of soil clinging to them. This detail is relevant because Toni's last name "Erdmann" also links him to soil, and his function in the film is to remind Ines of her homeland and her roots. However, Ines does not partner up with a mate to have children, as the Bulgarian ritual tradition commands. She follows the Kukeri outside into a public park, observes him interacting with a couple of locals and a little girl, and then she, too, runs after him and calls out to him: "Papa!" (Daddy, 2:18:03) and hugs him tight.

This climactic scene references the first encounter between Franziska and her boyfriend dressed as a furry creature in *Finsterworld*, in which Sandra Hüller, the actress who plays Ines, played the role of Franziska. While Franziska is horrified by the furry creature and has a panic attack,

Ines acts intrigued and follows it. The fact that it leads her outside into the natural world suggests a radical change for Ines, one that Franziska was not willing to entertain at that point in her trajectory away from neoliberal utilitarianism, but one that she, too, ultimately embraces. Ines also walks barefoot. dressed only in a robe, in public among strangers, a break in decorum meant to signify a revolution in her thinking. Such behavior is the stuff of nightmares for conformist characters like Franziska, Frau Sandberg, or Bianca. None of them learn to play. For Bianca, presenting a disheveled physical appearance signals her decline and even foreshadows her violent end. Ines's disheveled exterior merely signals a productive crisis but does not necessarily indicate a deep internal rejection of what Byung-Chul Han calls "neoliberal psychopolitics."[13] The very next scene fast-forwards to Ines dressed in her business suit once more, after a year has elapsed. Ade hints that Ines's transformation may not have left a lasting mark on her corporate sense of self.

The occasion is her grandmother's funeral in Germany. While some of the relatives squabble over mementos, Ines takes nothing. She and her father go to the basement, where the grandmother kept a closet full of hats. They each wear one and clown around. It becomes evident that Ines's inheritance is not monetized as the neoliberal system would stipulate, but consists of her emotional license to reinvent herself, to proudly display her eccentricity. Nonetheless, Ines is still working in the corporate sector at a more prestigious firm in China. The final long take presents her standing immobile in the backyard, wearing an odd hat, as she waits for her father to return with the camera. She eventually removes the set of false teeth she had borrowed from her father. We leave her facing the garden, with a quizzical look on her face.

Ade postulates that the younger working–age cohort of trained professionals never completely escape neoliberalism, even though they may resent it or poke fun at it. With her "highly political film"[14] Ade sensitizes viewers to the class pretensions and illiberal authoritarianism ingrained within the neoliberal straightjacket. According to actor Peter Simonischek who plays Toni, Toni rather than Ines is the director's real hero, his performance creates a space in which "der Bürger für Momente mutiert zum richtigen Pophelden" (2:30; the citizen transforms for a few instants into a genuine pop hero). Winfried/Toni is able to be such a playfully anarchic force, not least because of his age and liberal politics. Much of his role playing involves scaring his audience by pretending to be a dangerous oddball—Ade's ironic comment on most Germans' all too obedient adherence to norms and rules, which may produce violent tendencies in some. Winfried is of retirement age and may opt out, while Ines still has decades of work ahead of her.

Ade asks what makes work fulfilling, and what is ethical in our relation to ourselves and to others. Female leaders such as Ines learn to temper their drive to succeed as they begin to understand that eccentricity can generate creativity, and that divergent views are not to be dismissed out of hand. Even so, the last shot lingers on Ines as a solitary figure in a garden, looking sober. Her costume suggests the spinster rather than a woman at the peak of her sexual reproductivity. With this haunting final image, Ade participates in the demonization of educated females as a social problem, framing their frustration as a driver for the restlessness of neoliberal economic practice.

In *Finsterworld*, Franziska takes her boyfriend's advice to expose herself to something unknown and wild in Africa. While the catastrophic climax of *Kannibalen* portrays Africa as a haven for terrorists, in *Finsterworld* it is idealized as a sublime landscape that can inspire newly attentive ways of interacting with native people. As Franziska gazes at a distant mountain, a Kikuyu woman dressed in a vibrant red cloak and wearing jangling silver earrings walks up to her, silently shares the view, and then asks for a cigarette. Franziska herself is dressed in monochromatic ochers and yellows rather than her previous bright red skirt, suggesting that she is learning to blend in with nature. Her nostalgic costuming in a long safari skirt reanimates a Hollywood fantasy of iconic white women explorers and chroniclers à la Isak Dinesen or Beryl Markham in films such as *Out of Africa* (1985) and *World without Walls* (1986). Personal transformation requires, so Finsterwalder implies, an awareness of one's own situatedness versus a historical past. While Finsterwalder references the German commemoration of the Holocaust as disingenuous in a subplot centered on a school excursion to a concentration camp, she ultimately reverts to the stereotype of the timeless African nomad as a panacea for German disenchantment. Escape into a subculture that emphasizes roleplay is seen as merely one way out of the stultifying demands of an adult neoliberal identity. Such disinhibition is shown to have local rather than systemic effects.

Reinscribing Gender Stereotypes

All three films suggest that "leaning in" at the table of corporate power necessarily involves an opting out of family and intimacy. To their credit, the films acknowledge the pound of flesh that neoliberalism demands from all its employees. While *Kannibalen* is a morality tale about globalized corporate greed, *Finsterworld* participates in a grumpy "culture of complaint" that has long been prevalent in German society. Finsterwalder's characters lack human fellow feeling and have become too functionalistic. Tellingly, those who present an eccentric subversion of daily routines are male rather than female: a chiropodist, a policeman, and a student. Mothers such as the younger Frau Sandberg or career women such as Franziska are shown as selfish promoters of a work fixation to the detriment of nurturing qualities. These women have become too masculine, while feminized men are rewarded as long as they find a subculture niche. The underlying gender stereotypes are reaffirmed by these maneuverings. Among these films, only *Toni Erdmann* acknowledges the emotional cost of self-abnegation in the pursuit of career advancement.

Neither "leaning in" nor "opting out" dismantles power relations within the neoliberal collective, an arena in urgent need of critical discussion that these films either strive to avoid, or, as does *Toni Erdmann*, present with a madcap comedic touch. Ade revives female stereotypes from American comedy films of the 1930s and 1940s, which characterized women as unpredictable, childlike, or spoilt "dizzy dames."[15] The goal of *Toni Erdmann* is to reinsert Ines into the family paradigm even if she herself refuses to procreate. Despite being close to retirement and irrelevance in the German workplace, Winfried reinvents a crucial role for himself as his daughter's life coach. This move casts him as a moral authority at the center of neocolonial business transactions in Eastern Europe. Even though Winfried is ageing, he still has relevance and his behavior commands attention. The German nuclear family and the father figure are reasserted as powerful, constituting a conservative move to reassure cultural anxieties over Germany's ageing demographics and the imminent introduction of quotas for German women professionals in upper management.[16] A final fear factor is the threat to the economic predominance of locally owned small and mid-size companies. These entities still form the backbone of the German economy, while foreign-owned companies of this size do more international trade and reap higher profits. The three films catastrophize those gradual transformations into a subsumption of German companies by international investors, and scapegoat female business leaders by presenting them as agents of destructive change.

Notes

[1] See Statista, "Frauenanteil in Führungspositionen in Deutschland nach Anzahl der Mitarbeiter in Unternehmen," June 30, 2016, https://de.statista.com/statistik/daten/studie/182510/umfrage/frauenanteil-in-fuehrungsposi tionen-nach-unternehmensgroesse/. See also Statistisches Bundesamt, "61% der tätigen Personen arbeiten in kleinen und mittleren Unternehmen," statistics for 2014, https://www.destatis.de/DE/ZahlenFakten/GesamtwirtschaftUmwelt/UnternehmenHandwerk/KleineMittlereUnternehmenMittelstand/Aktuell.html.

[2] J. M. Kidwell, R. E. Stevens, and A. L. Bethke, "Differences in Ethical Perceptions between Male and Female Managers: Myth or Reality?" *Journal of Business Ethics* 6, no. 6 (August 1987): 489–93.

[3] Hester Baer, Carrie Smith-Prei, and Maria Stehle, "Digital Feminisms and the Impasse: Time, Disappearance, and Delay in Neoliberalism," *Studies in 20th*

and 21st Century Literature 40, no. 2 (2016): 3, http:dx.doi.org/10.4148/2334-4415.1881.

[4] Frauke Finsterwalder, dir., *Finsterworld* (2013): *Filmportal.de*, http://www.filmportal.de/; Johannes Naber, dir., *Zeit der Kannibalen* (Berlin: Studio TV Film, 2014); and Maren Ade, *Toni Erdmann* (Berlin: Komplizen Film, 2016). All translations in this chapter, unless otherwise noted, are my own.

[5] "Können sich Paare in Deutschland wirklich keine Kinder leisten?," *T-online News*, October 13, 2016, http://www.t-online.de/leben/familie/id_79247010/kinderlosigkeit-warum-die-deutschen-so-wenig-kinder-bekommen.html. See also Statistisches Bundesamt, "Immer mehr Frauen bleiben kinderlos," *Der Spiegel*, November 7, 2013, http://www.spiegel.de/politik/deutschland/statistisches-bundesamt-immer-mehr-frauen-bleiben-kinderlos-a-932324.html. In states and city states of the former West Germany, between 22 percent and 30 percent of university-educated women remained childless in 2016.

[6] For an overview of the entanglement of nation with changing family configurations in postwar Germany, see Patricia Anne Simpson, "Introduction," *Reimagining the European Family* (New York: Palgrave Macmillan, 2013), 6–10.

[7] *Kannibalen*, 55:10.

[8] Sheryl Sandberg and Nell Scovell, *Lean In: Women, Work, and the Will to Lead* (New York: Knopf Doubleday, 2013), 27.

[9] David Chandler and Julian Reid, *The Neoliberal Subject: Resilience, Adaptation and Vulnerability* (London: Rowman & Littlefield, 2016), 1.

[10] See Ellen Kositza, *Gender ohne Ende oder Was vom Manne übrigblieb* (Schnellroda: Antaios, 2013); Eva Herman, *Das Eva-Prinzip: Für eine neue Weiblichkeit* (Munich: Pendo, 2006).

[11] Byung-Chul Han, *Psychopolitik: Neoliberalismus und die neuen Machttechniken* (Frankfurt am Main: Fischer, 2015, 2016), 73.

[12] Trevor Boddy, "Underground and Overhead: Building the Analogous City," in *Variations on a Theme Park*, ed. Michael Sorkin (New York: Noonday, 1992), 123–53.

[13] Han, *Psychopolitik*, 30: "Das Disziplinarregime organisiert sich Deleuze zufolge wie 'Körper.' Es ist ein biopolitisches Regime. Das neoliberale Regime verhält sich wie 'Seele.' So ist die Psychopolitik seine Regierungsform. . . . Motivation, Projekt, Wettbewerb, Optimierung und Initiative gehören in die psychopolitische Herrschaftstechnik des neoliberalen Regimes" (The disciplinary regime according to Deleuze organizes itself like a body. It is a biopolitical regime. The neoliberal regime behaves like a soul. Its form of government is psychopolitics. . . . Motivation, project, competition, optimization, and initiative are instruments of power for the neoliberal regime).

[14] Peter Simonischek, Interview, in *Extras*, Maren Ade, *Toni Erdmann*, DVD, 2017 (2:30).

[15] Cf. Howard Hawks, *Bringing Up Baby* (1938), Frank Capra, *It Happened One Night* 1934), Gregory La Cava, *My Man Godfrey* (1936).

[16] Julia Löhr, "Frauen in der Führung—viel Gerede, wenig Veränderung," *Frankfurter Allgemeine Zeitung*, January 7, 2016, http://www.faz. net/aktuell/wirtschaft/wirtschaftspolitik/frauenanteil-in-fuehrungsposi tionen-hat-sich-kaum-veraendert-14001753.html. See also René Söllner, "Der deutsche Mittelstand im Zeichen der Globalisierung," Statistisches Bundesamt, https://www.destatis.de/DE/Publikationen/WirtschaftStatistik/2016/02/ DeutscherMittelstand_022016.pdf?__blob=publicationFile. Söllner's analysis shows that the percentage of foreign-owned small and mid-size companies is rising. Most of the parent companies are located in other European countries, with only 10 percent in the United States and 4 percent in Japan. On average, they produce more profit than locally owned ones.

13: Change, Persistence, and Contradiction: The Representation of Female Political Leadership in Gendered Media

Dorothee Beck

Angela Merkel is the first female German chancellor, but she is not the first female head of government. Louise Schroeder preceded her when she became the first female lord mayor of Greater Berlin from 1947 to 1948. It took another forty-five years for the first female prime minister, Heide Simonis, to come into office in Schleswig-Holstein in 1993 when her male predecessor resigned in the aftermath of a scandal. Since then there have been five more female heads of government at the state level in Germany. Almost all of them took office as a successor to a male politician during an election period or, as in the case of Christine Lieberknecht in Thuringia in 2009, when the top male candidate und then premier was not accepted in the post-electoral coalition of Christian Democrats (CDU) and Social Democrats (SPD). The only exception was the Social Democrat and then opposition leader Hannelore Kraft in North Rhine-Westphalia (NRW), who gained office as prime minister in 2010 in the course of the general election.

In contemporary democracies people tend to perceive political leaders mainly through the media. Thus for women claiming power, media coverage is crucial. In the present chapter I seek to outline changes in media representations of female political leaders over the last two decades and the impact these representations have on women's claim to political power. I will draw on the findings of my earlier study about the media coverage of female top candidates running for the prime ministry in election campaigns at the state level.[1] I will focus on the first female prime minister in Germany, Heide Simonis (1993–2005 in Schleswig-Holstein), as well as Andrea Ypsilanti, who failed to form a red and green minority coalition, that is, a coalition of the Social Democrats and the Green Party, in Hesse in 2008, and Hannelore Kraft, prime minister in NRW from 2010 to 2017. All of them were Social Democrats. This is due to the fact, that the SPD, within the time frame of the study, was the only party with more than one female candidate for prime ministry at the state level. Further reflections about media representations of Angela Merkel (CDU), as well as Gesine Schwan (SPD), who ran for the federal presidency in 2004 and 2009, and the Secretary of Defense, Ursula von der Leyen (CDU), are included.[2]

As masculinity was (and partly still is) the unspoken norm in the political field, media coverage in the 1990s obviously did not generate gender-specific narratives for powerful women and instead portrayed them within masculine-coded terms. I argue that, even today, political news media represent women in top positions in the political field as the "other gender." But there has been a change, albeit inconsistent, from general depreciation to more differentiated representations linked to specific contexts.

I show that female leadership, over the period analyzed (from 1994 to 2012), is conceived in opposition to the notion of a political alpha male. In elections up to the early years of 2000, this alpha male was seen as a thoroughbred political leader. More recently this image has come under criticism. Still, in Germany there is a wider range of figures of speech used for male politicians, such as man of action, the intellectual, the workers' leader, the paper shuffler, and the *Landesvater* (the state's father). In contrast, for female political leadership, there is only one dominant metaphor, the *Landesmutter* (the state's mother).[3]

The concept of the *Landesmutter* transfers formerly private attributes of care to the public sphere, which gives rise to notable contradictions. This shift is accompanied by increasingly positive, yet extremely gendered, representations of female political leaders, all of which highlight characteristics that are typically attributed to women who, from a classical perspective, are linked to the private sphere. Moreover, this shift forms a context in which an appreciation of female leadership in political news media becomes possible. Yet I will also show that this specific linkage holds the risk of depreciation, sexualization, and re-traditionalization of women.

In this essay I will analyze specific examples and contexts of both appreciation and denigration in the media of female German politicians. I conclude with a discussion of this phenomenon as a shift in the relation between the private and the public spheres. In classical conceptualizations the two spheres are polar opposites. Feminist theories have argued that this polarity implies a gendered hierarchy. Skills and attributes that are associated with and valued in the public sphere, such as soberness, objectivity and reason, are considered masculine, while those that are linked to the private sphere, such as empathy, care, and emotion, are seen as feminine.[4] This dichotomy places women who claim political leadership in a double bind.[5] They can either be "real" women or "true" political leaders, but not both. In the following, I argue that in recent media coverage this double bind is subject to a fundamental change.

Media Representation and Reality in the Political Field: A Research Gap

Numerous studies by Hoecker and Hoecker and Fuchs have evaluated the participation of women in local, federal, and European politics in quantitative terms.[6] Similarly, several studies have assessed the effects of the gender quota in the political parties.[7] In the 1990s empirically informed studies concluded that women in politics often felt like strangers,[8] they lacked professional skills,[9] and they felt compelled to deny or hide their gender.[10] I argue that these findings no longer describe the situation of female politicians today. This shift has gone undetected because, with few exceptions,[11] there has been a lack of qualitative research in political science in Germany that focuses on female political participation from a gender perspective over the last two decades.

In related disciplines such as media sociology and communication studies, analyses of media representations of female political leaders tend to focus exclusively on Angela Merkel's chancellorship from 2005 on. In the wake of the 2005 general election, Scholz buried the narcissistic political alpha male, identified with the "Media Chancellor" Gerhard Schröder, and replaced him with Merkel's style of leadership, widely depicted as composed, sober, and unpretentious.[12] Furthermore, Lünenborg and Meier describe a change in notions of political masculinity in the news media: as masculinity was no longer conceived as the unspoken norm in the political field, the male gender became visible and subject to discussion.[13] This coincides with the previously mentioned shift of attributes regarding care from the private to the political public sphere.

Academic discourse that focuses specifically on Merkel's media coverage has raised the question: Is there a "Merkel factor," that is, is Merkel an exception amid a plethora of derogatory representations of female politicians?[14] Or are there factors and contexts that favor positive representations of female political leaders in general? This view is advanced in comparisons of media representations of Merkel and the former socialist candidate for the French presidency, Ségolène Royal.[15]

Although there are numerous references to media representations of female leadership, very few relate to actual political situations. There is very little recent research on the relation between media representations and social reality. In the present study I focus on media representations of female top candidates at the state level in Germany in order to begin to fill the gap in the research on the impact of media representations on female leaders' claims to power.

The First Female Prime Minister:
The Boss and the Eccentric Woman

"Frauen werden immer dann etwas, wenn Männer aus der Kurve flie-gen" (women only ever have a chance when men spin out of control).[16] This quote, ascribed to Heide Simonis, the first female prime minister in Germany (Schleswig-Holstein, 1993 to 2005), suggests that a wom-an's political career is linked to political scandal provoked by men, as it was in her own case. Seen as an alternative to scandal-ridden male politi-cians, women find themselves in the position of *Trümmerfrauen* ("rub-ble women"). This metaphor, widely used in the German media, implies that women sort out the mess that men have left behind. It refers to the women who cleared away the debris, especially in Berlin, after the Second World War. In this metaphor, female political leaders are not "normal" politicians in their own right, but are represented as "others," that is, as placeholders in the case of male failure.

When Simonis's career took off, the media positioned her alongside well-known and respected male Social Democrats, who acknowledged her political talent. But once she was in office, the media referenced private contexts and body practices to construct a gender hierarchy that con-trasted Simonis with political alpha males. On the one hand, the media referred to the mutual political dependence of Simonis and Chancellor Gerhard Schröder. On the other hand, the news articles featured tradi-tional gestures, such as the gentleman Schröder holding the door open for Simonis or embracing her publically, "auch wenn das manchmal zu dem Eindruck führt, die Frau verschwinde hinter dem Mann (even if this sometimes creates the impression that the woman disappears behind the man).[17]

In the 2000 election Simonis's CDU opponent was the former Federal Secretary of Defense Volker Rühe, who was considered the likely winner. But shortly before the election a scandal concerning political donations of dubious origin destroyed his prospects. The media con-structed a corporeal and intellectual contrast between the slight woman and the giant soldierly man. At first Simonis was portrayed as a mousy person afraid of her blustering rival. Later she relied on clever tactics to deflate her alpha male opponent. At the same time, the media highlighted the collection of snow globes and wooden ducks in her office, thus deval-uing her anew.[18]

These contradictory approaches imply an ongoing uncertainty about how to represent a powerful woman. When Simonis assumed office in 1993, the German media, for the first time, had to cover a female polit-ical leader's skills and management style. At first the media seized this opportunity for an illustrative contrast: the pragmatic woman with a uni-versity degree in economics, also experienced in budgetary policies as a

Secretary of Finance, was compared to her predecessor Björn Engholm, who was depicted as a handsome intellectual high-flyer. At the same time, the media did not know how to report on Simonis. For the first time the metaphor *Landesmutter* referred to the governor herself, not to the governor's wife. The media came to use *Landesmutter* as a synonym for prime minister, but also to capture Simonis's unpretentious relation to her *Landeskinder* and her friendly relations with her kitchen cabinet. However, when she exercised power, for example to make her (male) cabinet members carry out her decisions, she was portrayed with masculine-coded attributes, such as "der Boss," a word that connotes the masculine gender, as in "bossman."[19]

The media also presented a feminine and nonpolitical picture of Heide Simonis: the chatterbox and eccentric woman who wears fancy hats and collects hundreds of teapots and cushions at flea markets. With such references the media trivialized Simonis's personal life. Paradoxically, the eccentric woman coexisted without challenging the image of the boss. One explanation for this seeming contradiction could be that although the media had to acknowledge Simonis's unquestionable leadership skills, they could not reconcile her power with her gender. Thus they used masculine descriptors when referring to her as a leader and trivializing descriptors when referring to her as a woman.

During Simonis's tenure in government, her media image changed: the pragmatic economic and financial expert became a prime minister without a message. The SPD began to sell her as "our Heide." Election posters featured nothing but the denominative mark "HE!DE." In the 2000 election campaign, a group of supporters, who wore red hats, were called "Heide hat's." This is a play on words that associates "Heide's (fancy) hats" with the German expression "Heide hat es," (Heide has that certain something). Subsequently, the media accused Simonis and her party of "personality cult." They suggested that the likeable and unpretentious prime minister was being pushed to the fore to make people forget the government's lack of accomplishments and political vision for the state of Schleswig-Holstein.

In the 2005 election the SPD—again with Simonis as top candidate—lost votes. Yet Simonis succeeded in forming a red and green minority coalition, which would be supported by the party of the Danish minority.[20] However, during the parliamentary election of the prime minister—in Germany, prime ministers at the state level are not elected by popular vote, but by parliament—she lost by one vote in four different ballots. This abrupt, and undeserved, end to her career gave rise to a backlash in the media: she was referred to as an old woman who needs help to walk upstairs, who clings to power and does not know when to step back. Some journalists even suggested that now all that is left for her is bickering with her husband. And even worse, much like other women, she would not know how to park her car (*Griff zur Macht*, 194–95).

In sum, the media were unable to find narratives that adequately represented the first female political leader in Germany. When she exercised power, Simonis was coded masculine. And yet at the same time she was trivialized as an eccentric woman. Finally, her failure to garner the necessary votes gave rise to a gender backlash in the media.

Andrea Ypsilanti: Joan of Arc's Rise and Fall

Another top candidate at the state level in Germany was Social Democrat Andrea Ypsilanti in Hesse. In 2008 Ypsilanti failed to form a red and green minority coalition tolerated by the left-wing party, *Die Linke*. In 2007 Roland Koch, one of the leading Christian Democrats, was the uncontested prime minister in Hesse. It was widely predicted that the SPD stood no chance of winning the election in January 2008. In a crucial party vote, the left-wing Andrea Ypsilanti, who was the party's chairperson in Hesse at that time, prevailed over the chairman of the parliamentary group and right-wing representative, Jürgen Walter. At first, media coverage was disparaging: no political and management skills, lack of self-confidence, poor speaker, poor self-presentation, and inability to connect with the people.

Such negative coverage notwithstanding, shortly before the election the campaign turned into a race to catch up. Koch made major political mistakes and Ypsilanti gained profile. The media spoke of the amazing triumph of an underestimated feminine woman over a political alpha male. "Er bekam seine Bronchitis nicht kuriert, sie blühte auf. Seine Sympathiewerte sanken, ihre kletterten nach oben. Er wirkte aggressiv und angespannt, sie euphorisch und erleichtert[21] (He could not shake his bronchitis, she blossomed. His popularity fell, hers climbed. He appeared aggressive and stressed, she euphoric and at ease). Now she was portrayed as "links, weich, weiblich"[22] (left-wing, soft, feminine). Femininity enhanced her political profile and offered a contrast to the alpha male. On one side there was the down-to-earth woman, daughter of a worker, and a social climber who acquired a university degree, mother of a twelve-year-old son, and one who knows everyday life and struggles; on the other side there was the privileged son of a minister, a lawyer who climbed straight to the top, and an ice-cold power broker.

At the same time, the media raised doubts about Ypsilanti's credibility through references to private contexts. Her political profile was defined through discussions of her rise on the social ladder. Some referred to the reform of public education in Germany in the sixties and seventies imple-mented by the Social Democrats. Because of these reforms Ypsilanti was able to attain a high-school qualification. During her campaign she prom-ised more school reforms, but her own son attended a private school. Although she explained that this was due to a lack of public full-time schools nearby, it raised doubts about the sincerity of her political beliefs. Moreover, although she was represented as a positive alternative to the alpha male, political relevance continued to be defined in masculine terms. The media emphasized that former party rivals from ex-chancellor Schröder's staff supported Ypsilanti, who was now willing to heed their advice. The *Frankfurter Allgemeine Zeitung* even noted that Ypsilanti had adopted Schröder's favorite "V for victory" sign, "das auch als Ypsilon durchgehen könnte"[23] (that could also pass as a Y).

As a result of the January 2008 election, the SPD lagged behind the CDU by only 0.1 percent. None of the political camps had a majority to form a government. The only options were a coalition of CDU and SPD ("große Koalition") or a collaboration of the Social Democrats with both the Green Party and *Die Linke*, which, for the first time, moved into the parliament of Hesse. In the election campaign Ypsilanti had rejected a coalition with either the CDU or *Die Linke*. After weeks of discussions and exploratory talks, she proposed a red and green minority coalition tolerated by *Die Linke*. Since this had been taboo in the SPD, the media now spoke of a broken promise.

In the weeks following the election, Ypsilanti's media image under-went drastic changes. Now she was seen as impervious to (male) advice, dishonest, unreliable, an egomaniac obsessed with power. Before, the steadiness she had shown in political conflicts was seen as proof of politi-cal competence. Now it was ironized with religious metaphors, including references to Joan of Arc.[24]

Instead of focusing on the political consequences of this new coa-lition, media coverage was characterized by a backlash. Female political ambition was seen as "abnormal," much like in the elections of the 1990s (*Griff zur Macht*, 160). Now reporters claimed that Ypsilanti was too emotional for reasonable decisions, for example, about the budget or economic subsidies, while, intellectually, she would have to depend on her (male) kitchen cabinet.

The sharp public criticism made Ypsilanti fair game. *Spiegel Online*, the web service of the news magazine *Der Spiegel*, published a fabricated commentary that insinuated that female politicians like Ypsilanti would soon end up performing a striptease in public.[25] In the end, Ypsilanti had to give up her plan to form a minority cabinet when four members of parliament of her own party refused to support it.

The media coverage of Ypsilanti's rise and fall allows insight into both the changes and the staying power of stereotypes of political femininity. In the 1990s there was widespread consensus in the news media that male politicians are capable of leadership whereas female politicians lack leadership skills.[26] Then the narrative shifted as the media began to report on the unexpected rise of an underestimated woman. This shows that in today's news media political leadership and femininity are not necessarily seen as incompatible.[27] But public discourses on female political leaders reference private contexts and highlight contrasts between political masculinity and femininity. Moreover, the case of Heide Simonis shows that political failure opens the door to re-traditionalization. Thus in terms of media images Ypsilanti, unlike Simonis, was a victim of sexism.

Hannelore Kraft: Prototyping the *Landesmutter*

When Hannelore Kraft first ran for the SPD top candidacy in NRW in 2010, she was a classic *Trümmerfrau*. Five years before, the Social Democrats had lost the election and, as a consequence, were no longer the governing party in a state that had traditionally gone to the Social Democrats. Almost all the SPD leaders had left to take jobs in the federal government in Berlin or in the economy. Thus Kraft became party chairman and opposition leader, "ohne sich noch gegen männliche Konkurrenz durchsetzen zu müssen" without having to prevail over male competitors)," a claim that implies that only male competitors are real competitors.[28]

Media coverage of Kraft resembled that of Andrea Ypsilanti to a striking degree. Like Ypsilanti, Kraft was considered incapable of governing a state. Even so, the election campaign was portrayed as a game of catch-up. An underestimated woman chasing an incumbent who made mistakes and was involved in a scandal. She was portrayed as a woman from humble beginnings, who rose through the ranks because of a good education. She was also portrayed as "die Frau, die sich nicht traut"[29] (the woman who lacks self-confidence). *Der Spiegel* detected a typically female oscillation between "I want to" and "I don't dare"[30] (Pendeln zwischen "ich will" und "ich trau' mich nicht"). Although Kraft was the first in her family to go beyond a high-school education, the media commented that she did not immediately find the courage to get a college education but instead started an apprenticeship in a bank. Similarly, although she did attend university later on, it was pointed out that she was not too far away from her family. Because of students' high failure rate, she did not study law, as she had wanted, but economics. In the end she returned to her hometown and took a secure job in a state-run consultancy firm for small enterprises.

The media image of the "woman who doesn't trust herself" was advanced most forcefully in the post-election period. As in Hesse, no political party had a clear majority. Kraft expended considerable time and effort on exploratory talks and, because of Ypsilanti's experience in Hesse, shied away from forming a red and green minority cabinet. In the end the Green Party forced a public commitment. Unlike Ypsilanti in Hesse, she relied on changing majorities and did not want her government to depend on toleration by any other party.

Two years later, in 2012, the minority coalition failed to pass the budget in parliament. The next election was scheduled for the same year. Now Kraft was set to become *the Landesmutter*: sympathetic and emotional, caring for her *Landeskinder*, accessible, down-to-earth, and direct. According to *Der Spiegel* she was perceived as accessible, available to all her constituents for a chat and a cup of coffee anytime they wanted to.[31] *Der Spiegel* attributed the success of her minority cabinet, which functioned far longer than anybody expected, to her empathy.

Much like reports on Simonis and Ypsilanti, media coverage of Kraft referenced the private realm, particularly different characteristics associated with motherhood: self-sacrifice, which manifests as sleep deprivation; the rigorous and exacting mother, when Kraft scolded photographers for taking photos of her putting on makeup. The media noted that she preferred a quiet entrance during campaign events—she was simply there—rather than marching in like a matador with music and rhythmical clapping. This can be interpreted as a mother who is always there without putting herself in the spotlight.

The *Süddeutsche Zeitung* commented that these qualities allowed her to please not only her son but also her party and her voters.[32] Furthermore, she was portrayed in sharp contrast to her Christian Democratic rivals—first, the prime minister of 2010, Jürgen Rüttgers, who was depicted as cold and wooden, and subsequently, in 2012, the then Federal Secretary of the Environment Norbert Röttgen, whose image was that of an intellectual high-flyer from Berlin.

But the image of the *Landesmutter* also had a downside: from the perspective of the media, Kraft was incapable of cutting spending and reducing the deficit. Instead, in blind motherly love, she threw money down the drain to solve every single problem of her *Landeskinder*: programs to help degree holders find apprenticeships, programs for young delinquents, and programs for pregnant women who faced trying times.[33] Here some media adopted the opposition's nickname for Hannelore Kraft, *Schuldenkönigin* (queen of debts). As with Heide Simonis, the SPD was accused of using the *Landesmutter* to hide their lack of political vision.

In the 2012 election the red and green coalition was confirmed in office with a majority. Because of her success *Spiegel Online* declared that Kraft, and thus a woman, was now the SPD's new star and a model for the three male politicians of her party who were all competing for candidacy as chancellor at the federal level. Kraft had shown the three how to win an election and was now more popular than any of them. But she did not want to throw her hat in the ring. "So wird jeder andere Kandidat mit dem Manko leben müssen, für viele Parteimitglieder zweite Wahl zu sein."[34] (In that case any other candidate will have to live with the drawback of being second choice for many party members). In the media, Kraft was seen as a highly qualified candidate for chancellor. At the same time her refusal to run for office was accentuated. This media image of her reluctance can be interpreted as that of a mother staying at home with the kids and not following a career of her own.

The notion of Hannelore Kraft as *Landesmutter* shows that attributes of motherly care have shifted to the political public sphere. These qualities are no longer employed exclusively to exclude women from the political field, as they were in earlier decades.[35] They also reference a highly gendered notion of female political leadership. Yet these representations are ambiguous and can continue to restrict women's agency in the public sphere. The notion of "blind motherly love," for example, is used to devalue women.

Mothers of the Nation and the Squadron: Female Political Leaders at the Federal Level

When Angela Merkel first took office as German chancellor, the media positively contrasted her with her predecessor, the "Media Chancellor" Gerhard Schröder. She was widely characterized as calm, sober, and unpretentious.[36] At the same time, she was considered a cool and reserved physicist, her profession before she became a politician. Initially, Merkel declared her gender politically irrelevant,[37] a decision that, some critics believed, had cost votes in the 2005 general election.[38] In the following years her image became warmer and references to motherhood more frequent.

In fact, although she had no children of her own, the media represented Merkel as a mother in three different ways. The first was *Mutti Merkel* (Mommy Merkel), referring to an incident when Merkel scolded one of her cabinet members for not wearing a coat on a cold winter day. *Mutti* became the name for the only woman allowed to call to order the gang of little rascals in Merkel's cabinet. Seen in this light, *Mutti* can be interpreted as a warm feminine-coded nickname for the uncontested boss. In earlier media reports, she was depicted as a "black widow" ready to kill any and all rivals in her own party. In contrast, the term *Mutti* reduced her alpha-male colleagues to pubescent scalawags.

The second version of Merkel's motherly image casts her as the *Mutter der Nation* (mother of the nation), more or less the *Landesmutter* at the national level. The nation's mother performs a female presidential habitus, elevated above everyone, especially above the parties, and bestows upon the Germans national identification. In the media this image is best captured by her famous statement when Germany faced a refugee crisis in the summer of 2015: "Wir schaffen das!" (We'll make it!).

The nation's mother is closely connected to the *schwäbische Hausfrau* (Swabian housewife).[39] Untiring, the Swabian housewife cares for her children. She economizes and does not live on credit. This nickname connects neoliberal and austerity policies to everyday experience. Consequently, at the European level, the Swabian housewife turns into the Iron Lady who imposes crippling austerity programs on other countries.

For Merkel, motherly characteristics did not bear the risk of re-traditionalization and denigration. Her power was uncontested. On the contrary, these nicknames softened and gendered the public image of a successful but reserved female leader. Dülcke and Futh concluded that the media accentuated this aspect of her image as a cornerstone of her popularity.[40] Yet in the aftermath of the 2017 general election, when it took almost six months to form a government, doubts arose about Merkel's remaining power. Now motherly images seem to vanish. It would be interesting to investigate this further.

Merkel's 2013 cabinet included the surprise appointment of Ursula von der Leyen as Secretary of Defense. In her career at the federal level, the mother of seven had first served as Secretary of Family Affairs, then Secretary of Labor and Social Affairs. Von der Leyen was the first German female Secretary of Defense, one of the masculine core departments in the federal government. The media nicknamed her *Mutter der Kompanie* (mother of the squadron). Historically this was a nickname for the first sergeant, who was considered the soldiers' fatherly confidant. Today this nickname designates a person who leads an undisciplined lot with empathy and strength.

"Mother of the squadron" forms the framework within which media discourses about von der Leyen's first actions as defense secretary unfolded. One of von der Leyen's first initiatives concerned work/life balance in the army, a balance that, she believed, had to be improved. Even though the soldiers' families agreed with her, the media tied this issue to von der Leyen's gender. Similarly, media comments on von der Leyen's decisions referenced the realms of family and household. For example, the media referred to the dismissal of an undersecretary of state as "spring-cleaning."[41]

In her previous career, von der Leyen had integrated her seven children into her self-representation. Because of this, her public image as a politician was closely linked to her familial role. I would argue that in von der Leyen's case, unlike in Merkel's, references to traditionally feminine qualities and spheres of activity served to denigrate her and question her leadership skills.

In 2004 and 2009 Gesine Schwan, then president of the European University Viadrina in Frankfurt an der Oder, served as the SPD candidate for the federal presidency. When Chancellor Gerhard Schröder first presented her in 2004, hardly anybody knew who she was. According to the myth surrounding her nomination, Schröder surprised her on the phone while she was on a lecture tour in the United States. The subsequent media coverage portrayed her as a successful, assertive, and cheerful intellectual, but it was clear that no one thought that she had a realistic chance of winning the election.[42] The media portrayed Schwan with female-coded attributes, such as "caring" and "peace-loving," but without political power. In contrast, Horst Köhler, her Christian Democratic competitor, was assessed as "presidential" in numerous reports.[43] Nevertheless, in 2004 the election was close, and Köhler won by only fifteen votes.

Five years later, public discourse preceding the election was drastically different. Now Köhler was the president, the Social Democrats had entered a coalition with the Christian Democrats, and Schwan was no longer a little known, albeit cheerful professor. In the SPD there was infighting about the best strategy for the next presidential election: Should the SPD support the incumbent, or should they seize the chance to enhance their profile for the upcoming parliamentary election by running a candidate of their own? The latter position won out, and Schwan agreed to a second attempt. But the media clearly did not appreciate the fact that she was competing against a respected incumbent. Schwan was now portrayed as abnormally ambitious, ruthless, and vain. Media coverage of her candidacy did not discuss her main platform, the erosion of democracy. Instead, numerous reports found fault with the fact that she depended on the votes of the left-wing party, *Die Linke*, in a manner that is reminiscent of Andrea Ypsilanti's earlier failure in Hesse.

Gesine Schwan's two candidacies show that the media consider the career of a female politician legitimate when it is approved by a powerful man. If a female candidate is ambitious in her own right, she is judged abnormal, ruthless, and vain. And her political profile and program are irrelevant in the media coverage when she is considered to be powerless or to have no prospect of winning. This has not changed much since the nineties (*Griff zur Macht*, 226–27, 229).

Political Public and Private Spheres:
From Dichotomous to Complementary

The examples analyzed above show that media coverage that presents female political leaders in a derogatory or appreciative light is context-specific. Apart from Louise Schröder, Prime Minister Heide Simonis, who governed Schleswig-Holstein from 1993 to 2005, was the first female head of government in Germany. The media failed to find a narrative fit for a woman in power and instead oscillated between portraying her as a masculine-coded boss and an eccentric woman.

And yet Andrea Ypsilanti's and Hannelore Kraft's candidacies at the state level in 2008, 2010, and 2012, as well as Gesine Schwan's first candidacy for the presidency at the federal level in 2004, suggest that major changes have been taking place. Femininity and political leadership are no longer defined as polar opposites. Rather, the media now marshal specific contexts and narratives that have come to be associated with powerful women. At the beginning of this development, the trope of the *Trümmerfrau* implied that women did not have the requisite skillset for political leadership. Later—and additionally—the trope of the underestimated woman who triumphs over a lost alpha male arose. Finally, there was the figure of the little known but talented woman who is discovered and promoted by a powerful man.

Female political leaders' capabilities and credibility are brought into play in an extremely gendered manner. The media construct the political leadership skills of female politicians in contrast to the proverbial alpha male. Credibility is assessed through references to private contexts. In both scenarios references to motherly qualities and care abound. However, for female political leaders (or women who seek a political career), this framework can result in different outcomes. Thus the three versions of motherhood ascribed to Angela Merkel soften the reserved image of the first female German chancellor and optimize her public image. But when the motherly political profile derives from a female politician's actual role in the family, as in the case of Secretary of Defense Ursula von der Leyen, there is a tendency to denigrate and belittle. Thus, attributing maternal qualities to female political leaders can produce both positive and negative results, as evidenced by the media coverage of Hannelore Kraft, the likeable down-to-earth prime minister of NRW, who was seen as a welcome alternative to alpha males. Furthermore, when the image of blind motherly love is applied to deficit spending, it serves to belittle not only the politician but also her political program.

My analysis shows that derogatory media coverage of female political leaders is context-specific. A female politician who follows her own ambition is considered abnormal, ruthless, and vain. In contrast, ambition is an indispensable character trait for a male political alpha male, such as the young Gerhard Schröder, who is said to have rattled the fence outside the chancellor's office shouting, "Ich will hier rein" (Let me in!). Undoubtedly, ambition is coded masculine. Even today, ambition marks the rift between political leadership and femininity. It also shows that political relevance and meaning are still coded masculine.

In the context of failure and defeat, media coverage also constructs female leadership in a derogatory manner. In the examples provided above this is particularly evident in the media coverage of Heide Simonis's failed election to prime minister in 2005 and of Andrea Ypsilanti's failure to form a red and green minority cabinet tolerated by *Die Linke* in Hesse in 2008. Simonis was characterized as a scolding old woman clinging to power. And in Hesse, Ypsilanti became a victim of sexist coverage, while her attempt to move beyond political taboos was of no interest to the media.

In sum, media coverage of the competence, credibility, and political profile of female political leaders is defined by a gendered contrast to the political alpha male and often linked to maternal qualities. When failure and defeat come into play, gendered coverage means belittlement, trivialization and re-traditionalization.

I argue that my analysis of the media coverage of female political leaders shows a shift in the relation between the private and the political spheres. Up to and including the tenure of Prime Minister Simonis, media coverage constructed the private and public spheres as polar opposites defined by a gender hierarchy that situated men in the political public sphere while women were seen as caregivers in the private familial context. Seen in this light, women were either poor politicians or no politicians at all.

In the first decade of the twenty-first-century a major shift can be observed, possibly catalyzed by Angela Merkel's election to chancellor in 2005. Descriptors that were formerly linked to the private sphere are now employed to cast female politicians as alternatives to the model of the thoroughbred male political leader. In this context, female politicians are being valued. Still the notion of essentially gendered attributions lingers. But now the "female" qualities are regarded as assets and are no longer merely "private." In this respect, the private sphere takes over a function that was previously reserved for the public sphere. Frequently, media reports about a female political leader reference the private sphere when they evaluate her political program, credibility, and capability. When it comes to news media, the relation between the public and private spheres is no longer (only) dichotomous. Instead, the private sphere takes on a complementary function to the political public sphere, at least in respect to female political leaders. With this concept I transfer Watzlawick's definition of complementary relations in communication to the political public sphere.[44] In contrast to symmetric relations, complementary relations are characterized by difference, which nonetheless is often hierarchic. Future studies should analyze whether there is a similar change relating to men.

A dichotomous concept of the relation between the political public and the private spheres implies a double bind for women, as described by Jamieson:

> A double bind is a rhetorical construct that posits two and only two alternatives, one or both penalizing the person being offered them. In the history of humans, such choices have been constructed to deny women access to power and, where individuals manage to slip past their constraints, to undermine their exercise of whatever power they achieve. The strategy defines something "fundamental" to women as incompatible with something the woman seeks—be it education, the ballot, or access to the workplace.[45]

The shift in relation between the two spheres entails a fundamental change of this double bind. In the new model, the two alternatives offered to women do not exclude one another. Instead, in media coverage, they have to be performed in perfect harmony. As the media draw on private contexts, attributes, and narratives to characterize a female political leader, discrepancies between the private and the public person have punitive consequences, such as a lack of credibility. Although the expectations for a politician and for a woman are now more compatible, the double bind persists, as female political leaders are still linked to both spheres. Unlike men, who, as the unspoken norm in the political field, have always had agency in the public sphere, women have to perform both in their traditional role in the family and in the political function they seek to achieve. Consequently, if women fail or incur criticism, they can be denied the status of a political personality. Thus female political leaders who are subject to coverage by the media still have to consider the effects of gendered expectations.

Notes

Special thanks to Prof. Michaela R. Winchatz for discussing intercultural differences and possible misunderstandings, and for proofreading.

[1] Dorothee Beck, *Politikerinnen und ihr Griff zur Macht: Mediale Repräsentationen von SPD-Spitzenkandidatinnen bei Landtagswahlen* (Bielefeld: transcript, 2016), further references are given in the text using the short title *Griff zur Macht*. The sample included six top candidates in eleven campaigns: Renate Schmidt in Bavaria in 1994 and 1998; Ingrid Stahmer in Berlin in 1995; Heide Simonis in Schleswig-Holstein in 1996, 2000, and 2005; Ute Vogt in Baden-Württemberg in 2001 and 2006; Andrea Ypsilanti in Hesse in 2008; and Hannelore Kraft in North Rhine-Westphalia in 2010 and 2012, all of them Social Democrats. The database consisted of some 400 articles published in leading news media during

the height of the election campaigns (about four weeks before the election) plus another 50 articles published during three efforts to constitute red and green minority governments. The method applied was a qualitative content analysis. See Philipp Mayring, *Qualitative Inhaltsanalyse: Grundlagen und Techniken*, 11th rev. ed. (Weinheim: Beltz, 2010), and Margrit Schreier, "Varianten qualitativer Inhaltsanalyse: Ein Wegweiser im Dickicht der Begrifflichkeiten," *Forum: Qualitative Sozialforschung* 15, no. 1, Art. 18 (2014), http://www.qualitative-research. net/index.php/fqs/article/view/2043/3635. For an additional exemplary hermeneutic analysis of some of the articles, see Frank Kleemann, Uwe Krähnke, and Ingo Matuschek, *Interpretative Sozialforschung: Eine Einführung in die Praxis des Interpretierens*, 2nd ed. (Wiesbaden: Springer VS, 2013), http://nbn-resolving. de/urn:nbn:de:1111-20130725424; Jo Reichertz, *Gemeinsam interpretieren: Die Gruppeninterpretation als kommunikativer Prozess* (Wiesbaden: Springer VS, 2013); Jo Reichertz and Hans-Georg Soeffner, "Hans-Georg Soeffner: Expanding the Action Repertoire of Societies; Hans-Georg Soeffner im Gespräch mit Jo Reichertz," *Forum: Qualitative Sozialforschung* 5, no. 3, Art. 29 (2004), http:// www.qualitative-research.net/index.php/fqs/article/view/561/1215; Andreas Wernet, *Einführung in die Interpretationstechnik der objektiven Hermeneutik*, 3rd ed., Qualitative Sozialforschung (Wiesbaden: VS, 2009).

[2] Dorothee Beck, "Mutti ist die beste: Die Mutter-Metapher als politische Kategorie in den Medien," In *O mother, where art thou?—(Queer-)Feministische Perspektiven auf Mutterschaft und Mütterlichkeit*, ed. Maya Dolderer et al. (Münster: Westfälisches Dampfboot, 2016); Elke Grittmann and Tanja Maier, "Der Präsident und die Herausforderin—Geschlechterkonstruktionen von Spitzenkräften in der Politik aus medienethischer Perspektive," in *Gender im medienethischen Diskurs*, ed. Petra Grimm and Oliver Zöllner, 153–68 (Stuttgart: Franz Steiner, 2014); Thomas Koch, "Immer nur die Frisur? Angela Merkel in den Medien," in *Warum nicht gleich?*, ed. Christina Holtz-Bacha and Nina König-Reiling, 146–66 (Wiesbaden: VS, 2007), http://link.springer.com/ chapter/10.1007/978-3-531-90540-2_10; Sylka Scholz, ed., *"Kann die das?" Angela Merkels Kampf um die Macht* (Berlin: Dietz, 2007). While it would be interesting to investigate the impact of the relation between the respective politician's party affiliation (CDU, SPD) and the political stance of different media and their coverage, such an investigation goes beyond the scope of this chapter.

[3] The metaphors *Landesmutter* and *Landesvater* derive from the scattered regionalism in German history. With the notion *Landesvater*, paternalistic characteristics were attributed to a sovereign. His wife, the *Landesmutter*, took care of her *Landeskinder* in a charitable commitment. Nowadays these metaphors represent male as well as female prime ministers at the state level in Germany.

[4] Karin Hausen, "Die Polarisierung der 'Geschlechtscharaktere'—Eine Spiegelung der Dissoziation von Erwerbs- und Familienleben," in *Sozialgeschichte der Familie in der Neuzeit Europas*, ed. Werner Conze, 363–93 (Stuttgart: Klett, 1976).

[5] Kathleen Hall Jamieson, *Beyond the Double Bind: Women and Leadership* (New York: Oxford University Press, 1995), 13–14.

[6] Beate Hoecker, *Frauen und das institutionelle Europa: Politische Partizipation und Repräsentation im Geschlechtervergleich* (Wiesbaden: Springer VS, 2013); Beate Hoecker and Gesine Fuchs, eds., *Handbuch politische Partizipation von*

Frauen in Europa (Wiesbaden: VS, 1998); Beate Hoecker and Gesine Fuchs, *Ohne Frauen nur eine halbe Demokratie: Politische Partizipation von Frauen in den osteuropäischen Beitrittsstaaten*, Eurokolleg 49 (Bonn: Friedrich-Ebert-Stiftung, Internationale Politikanalyse, 2004).

[7] See, for example, Louise K. Davidson-Schmich, *Gender Quotas and Democratic Participation: Recruiting Candidates for Elective Offices in Germany* (Ann Arbor: University of Michigan Press, 2016), http://www.press.umich.edu/8137405; Louise K. Davidson-Schmich and Isabelle Kürschner, "Stößt die Frauenquote an ihre Grenzen? Eine Untersuchung der Bundestagswahl 2009," *Zeitschrift für Parlamentsfragen* 42, no. 1 (2011): 25–34; Katharina Inhetveen, *Institutionelle Innovation in politischen Parteien: Geschlechterquoten in Deutschland und Norwegen*, Studien zur Sozialwissenschaft (Wiesbaden: Westdeutscher Verlag, 2002); Amalia Sdroulia, *Frauen in der Politik: Spielregeln des politischen Geschäfts; Eine Untersuchung am Beispiel von Politikerinnen der Fraktion "Bündnis 90/Die Grünen" im Niedersächsischen Landtag* (Marburg: Tectum, 2007).

[8] Bärbel Schöler-Macher, *Die Fremdheit der Politik: Erfahrungen von Frauen in Parteien und Parlamenten* (Weinheim: Deutscher Studien-Verlag, 1994).

[9] Helga Foster, Helga Lukoschat, and Barbara Schaeffer-Hegel, eds., *Die ganze Demokratie: Zur Professionalisierung von Frauen für die Politik*, Feministische Theorie und Politik 12 (Pfaffenweiler: Centaurus, 1998).

[10] Birgit Meyer, *Frauen im Männerbund: Politikerinnen in Führungspositionen von der Nachkriegszeit bis heute* (Frankfurt am Main: Campus, 1997).

[11] Most notably Isabelle Kürschner, *Den Männern überlassen wir's nicht! Erfolgreiche Frauen in der CSU* (Baden-Baden: Nomos, 2009); and Bettina Munimus, *Heide Simonis: Aufstieg und Fall der ersten Ministerpräsidentin Deutschlands* (Stuttgart: Ibidem, 2010).

[12] Scholz, *"Kann die das?"*; Christina Holtz-Bacha, "Frauen, Politik, Medien: Ist die Macht nun weiblich?," in *Frauen, Politik und Medien*, ed. Christina Holtz-Bacha (Wiesbaden: VS, 2008), 3–24; Christina Holtz-Bacha, "Mit den Waffen einer Frau? Politikerinnen im Wahlkampf," in *Warum nicht gleich?*, ed. Christina Holtz-Bacha and Nina König-Reiling (Wiesbaden: VS, 2007), 79–104, http://link.springer.com/book/10.1007/978-3-531-90540-2.

[13] Margreth Lünenborg and Tanja Maier, "'Kann der das überhaupt?' Eine qualitative Textanalyse zum Wandel medialer Geschlechterrepräsentationen," in *Ungleich mächtig: Das Gendering von Führungspersonen aus Politik, Wirtschaft und Wissenschaft in der Medienkommunikation*, ed. Margret Lünenborg and Jutta Röser (Bielefeld: Transcript, 2012), 65–126.

[14] See Koch, "Immer nur die Frisur?"

[15] Florence Absolu, *Les femmes politiques dans la presse: Mythèmes, biographèmes et archétype; Les représentations genrées de Ségolène Royal et Angela Merkel dans la presse française et allemande pendant leurs campagnes électorales / Politikerinnen in der Presse: Mytheme, Biographeme und Archetyp; Die gender-betonte Darstellung von Angela Merkel und Ségolène Royal in den deutschen und französischen Printmedien während ihrer Wahlkampagnen* (Würzburg: Königshausen & Neumann, 2014); Mareike Kutt, *Auf dem Weg zur Macht: Politische Kommunikation*

in Deutschland und Frankreich; Die Darstellung von Angela Merkel und Ségolène Royal in der Wahlkampfberichterstattung überregionaler Tageszeitungen (Duisburg: WiKu, 2010).

[16] *Süddeutsche Zeitung,* February 15, 2005, 3 All translations of media quotations are my own.

[17] *Frankfurter Allgemeine,* February 5, 2005, 3;

[18] *Der Spiegel,* January 31, 2000, 40).

[19] *Süddeutsche Zeitung,* February 21, 2000, 3.

[20] Referred to as "toleration," this model implies that a party supports the government in specific issues instead of entering a coalition. Quite common in Scandinavian countries, it offers a way out in parliaments with unclear majorities.

[21] *Spiegel Online,* January 27, 2008.

[22] *Spiegel Online,* January 17, 2008.

[23] *Frankfurter Allgemeine Zeitung,* January 22, 2008, 3.

[24] *Der Spiegel,* September 1, 2008, 33.

[25] *Spiegel Online,* September 2, 2008.

[26] Barbara Schaeffer-Hegel and Silke Ude, "Anke Martiny und die Presse," in *Frauen mit Macht: Zum Wandel der politischen Kultur durch die Präsenz von Frauen in Führungspositionen,* ed. Barbara Schaeffer-Hegel et al., 2nd ed. (Pfaffenweiler: Centaurus, 1998), 243–64.

[27] Jamieson, *Beyond the Double Bind,* 16,

[28] *Frankfurter Allgemeine,* May 11, 2012, 3.

[29] *Süddeutsche Zeitung,* June 16, 2010, 4.

[30] *Der Spiegel,* April 30, 2012, 29.

[31] *Der Spiegel,* April 30, 2012, 30.

[32] *Süddeutsche Zeitung,* May 11, 2012, 6.

[33] *Der Spiegel,* April 30, 2012, 31.

[34] *Spiegel Online,* May 13, 2012.

[35] Charlotte Gnändiger, *Politikerinnen in deutschen Printmedien: Vorurteile und Klischees in der Berichterstattung* (Saarbrücken: VDM, 2007), 137; Mervi Pantti, "Portraying Politics: Gender, Politik und Medien," in Holtz-Bacha and König-Reiling, *Warum nicht gleich?,* 17–51, here 39.

[36] Carsten Brosda, "Wenn der Rahmen nicht zum Bild passt . . . Politische und mediale Deutungsangebote im Wahlkampf," in *Macht ohne Verantwortung: Medien im Wahlkampf 2013; Erfahrungs-Wissen und Kontext-Analysen aus Praxis und Forschung* (Berlin: Heinrich Böll Stiftung, 2013), 59–71, here 69.

[37] Doreen Fantke, Olga Schmidt, and Anett Zeidler, "'Nur weil sie eine Frau ist?' Merkel und die Geschlechterfrage," in Scholz, *"Kann die das?,"* 81–96.

[38] Holtz-Bacha, "Frauen, Politik," 13; Holtz-Bacha, "Waffen einer Frau," 93–94.

[39] The Swabians in southwest Germany are said to be not only thrifty but stingy. And they would work tirelessly.

[40] Dana Dülcke and Sascha K. Futh, "Die 'Mutter der Nation' gegen den 'Panzer-kandidaten'—Geschlechterbilder in der Berichterstattung der Printmedien zum Bundestagswahlkampf 2013," in *Die Massenmedien im Wahlkampf: Die Bundestagswahl 2013*, ed. Christina Holtz-Bacha, 249–73 (Wiesbaden: Springer VS, 2015), 269.

[41] "Ursula von der Leyen—Die Putzfrau der Bundeswehr," *Start Thinking Now*, accessed June 29, 2017, https://startthinkingnow.wordpress.com/gender-in-den-medien/presse/ursula-von-der-leyen-die-putzfrau-der-bundeswehr.

[42] In Germany the federal president is not elected by popular vote. Instead, a federal election assembly is formed by the federal members of parliament plus the same number of representatives from the sixteen states.

[43] Dorothee Beck, "Die Kategorie Geschlecht im Kampf um politische Macht: Erfolg und Scheitern von SPD-Spitzenpolitikerinnen," in *Progressive Mehrheiten mit der SPD? Für eine linke Politik jenseits der Neuen Mitte*, ed. Max Reinhardt, Stefan Stache, and Stephan Meise, 387–424 (Berlin: LIT, 2014), 410–13; Nancy Drinkmann and Claudio Caballero, "Eine Frau ist eine Frau ist eine Frau? Die Berichterstattung über die Kandidaten der Bundespräsidentenwahl 2004," in Holtz-Bacha and König-Reiling, *Warum nicht gleich?*, 167–203, here 182, 197–98, http://link.springer.com/chapter/10.1007/978-3-531-90540-2_11. See also Grittmann und Maier, "Der Präsident und die Herausforderin."

[44] Paul Watzlawick, Janet Beavin Bavelas, and Don D. Jackson, *Menschliche Kommunikation: Formen, Störungen, Paradoxien*, 10th ed. (Bern: Huber, 2000), 68–70.

[45] Jamieson, *Beyond the Double Bind*, 13.

14: Petra Kelly: A Green Leader out of Place?

Stephen Milder and Friederike Brühöfener

HAVING SERVED AS party cochair and lead candidate in four elections, Petra Karin Kelly became the first spokesperson of the Green Party's delegation to West Germany's federal parliament, the Bundestag, in 1983. Kelly was, by that time, known internationally as the Greens' leader and renowned for her role in the peace movement. She was named "Woman of the Year" by the Philadelphia-based group Women Strike for Peace in 1983, and awarded the Right Livelihood Foundation's "Alternative Nobel Prize" for her activism in 1982. At her acceptance speech in Stockholm, Kelly argued that the formation of "a nonviolent, ecological, and non-exploitative republic," required that "women must change their consciousness, break from the patriarchal circle, and free themselves from such ill-suited ideals as those of the masculine, patriarchal, and nuclear society."[1] The leadership positions she held, the accolades she received, and her outspoken views all drew attention to Petra Kelly. But it was ultimately her gender that defined the way she was seen by her contemporaries. She was described by fellow Green politicians such as Wilhelm Knabe and scholars such as Dieter Rucht as a modern-day "Joan of Arc."[2] The image stuck. In an August 2017 segment on the emergence of the Green Party, which aired throughout Germany as part of the history and science program *Planet Wissen*, Kelly was referred to as the "Joan of Arc of the atomic age."[3]

In the early 1980s Kelly was famous, female, and outspoken, but why has she consistently been compared to a French patriot of the fifteenth century? For Knabe, the comparison was intended to show that Kelly "embodied the new emancipatory self-understanding of the [Green] Party." His statement can be interpreted as a reference to both Joan of Arc's legacy as an exceptional and emancipated woman who led an army of men into battle and her role in liberating France from British rule. *Planet Wissen* explained that Kelly resembled Joan in that she was "just as idealistic as she was uncompromising." For Rucht and his coauthor Roose, the comparison with the Maid of Orleans was intended to reflect the idea that, unlike other political leaders, Kelly was merely a standard bearer, who played "no strategically important function" in her party.[4] All in all, the comparisons suggest that Kelly stood far outside of West German mainstream politics. She seemed to have more in common with an exceptional young woman who, more than 500 years ago, had led the French military to victories in the Hundred Years' War than with her counterparts in the Bundestag—more than 90 percent of whom were male and traditional career politicians.

Perhaps it was necessary to search far and wide for appropriate comparisons for Kelly because there were so few women in the Bundestag in the 1980s, let alone women with leadership roles in German politics. At the time Kelly was elected, women comprised a mere 8.5 percent of the federal parliament. And while Chancellors Schmidt and Kohl had each appointed one token woman minister to their cabinets, no woman had ever served as chair of her party's delegation to the federal parliament.[5] Nonetheless, imagining a woman in power did not require thinking back to the fifteenth century. When Kelly entered the Bundestag, Margaret Thatcher had already been prime minister of the United Kingdom for four years and Simone Veil had just completed a three-year term as president of the European Parliament. But the comparison with the Maid of Orleans—as opposed to the Iron Lady—was made for a reason. Petra Kelly represented and embodied a type of femininity very different from that of Margaret Thatcher. In the context of West German mainstream politics, Kelly did not represent an accepted ideal of femininity. She was seen as overly idealistic, irrational, and emotional—attributes traditionally gendered feminine. And yet her ideas and practices also differed considerably from those of Other Green party politicians and leading feminists, who did not always agree with her penchant for direct-action politics or her emphasis on the idea that women would not be emancipated by gaining equal rights if that meant earning the right to "stand beside men in the various national armies" or "learn[ing] to operate a nuclear reactor."[6] She was an outsider in West German political culture and seemed ill-suited to be a political leader during the confrontational "second Cold War."[7] She certainly did not fit the traditional norms and customs of the Bundestag, which was dominated by men who claimed to practice rational and pragmatic—attributes traditionally gendered masculine—Realpolitik. And yet Kelly was widely viewed as the single most important leader of the Green Party in the early 1980s. Her paradoxical status as both outsider and leader is the premise of this chapter.

We seek to resolve this paradox by studying Kelly within her environment. We show how Kelly's political convictions and the way she acted in parliament—but more importantly, her sex and her gender—were perceived as "different" in the 1980s Bundestag and we seek to explain why this was the case. We find that the fact that Kelly was a woman who acted differently than other parliamentarians—both male and female—and that she promoted a vision of women's emancipation that transcended simple equality, motivated descriptions of Kelly as a latter-day Joan of Arc. These differences between Kelly and her colleagues, in other words, underpinned the widespread understanding of her position in the Bundestag as that of an "idealistic lone warrior."[8] And yet, casting Kelly as a starry-eyed loner normalizes the male-dominated Bundestag of the 1980s, implicitly reinforcing the idea that an outspoken woman did not and could not belong there. In contrast, we argue that the Bundestag itself represented a particular narrow strand of the German public, not German society as a whole. Its particularities meant that the Bundestag was alien to the new approaches to politics that became increasingly important to West Germans during the "Euro-Missiles" crisis of the early 1980s. Consequently, Kelly and her fellow "founding Greens'"[9] challenged the political establishment by representing previously unrepresented groups and ideas in parliament. Specifically, Kelly helped initiate significant changes that enabled erstwhile outsiders to find a foothold within the political establishment by purposely accentuating her differences, not just from other parliamentarians, but more importantly from parliamentary culture. In so doing, she made parliament more representative of German society as a whole.

In the following we make our case in three steps. First, we briefly introduce Kelly, showing how she developed a different approach to politics than even many of her Green colleagues because she lived outside the Federal Republic of Germany (FRG) from the time she turned twelve until she entered parliament at the age of thirty-five in 1983. Using Kelly's own speeches and writings, as well as details from several biographies, we show how her experiences abroad helped her to think outside the box of West German politics, but also familiarized her with mainstream politics and taught her to work effectively within the political establishment, for example, in the European Economic Communities (EEC) in Brussels. Second, we look at Kelly's career in the Bundestag. We describe how her fellow parliamentarians found her approach to parliamentary politics—even her manner of speaking—unfamiliar and exceptional. On the basis of data on the history and composition of the Bundestag, however, we show here that Kelly was perceived as an outsider in parliament during the 1980s primarily because the parliament itself represented only a certain stratum of the German population. Finally, in the conclusion we offer some thoughts as to how Kelly's accentuation of her difference—especially her gender—in parliament helped lead the way toward important changes in the Bundestag that made the German political establishment more reflective of German society as a whole.

"In contrast to most of us, she came from far away": The Transnational Politicization of Petra Kelly

Ruth Bevan, one of the first scholars to write about Petra Kelly, titled her article, "The *Other* Green."[10] For Bevan, Kelly's "'otherness' consisted of her attempt to link the issues of peace, environmentalism, and feminism under the rubric of the Greens, and her rejection of *national* political objectives."[11] But Kelly was not the *Other* Green just because she insisted on interlinking issues widely considered the lynchpins of Green politics or because she believed those matters transcended West Germany—such ideas, after all, were shared by many of her Green colleagues.[12] Rather, her "otherness" was rooted in her politicization, which differed fundamentally from that of the other founding Green Party members. Kelly's political coming of age in Washington, DC, during the late 1960s and her career at the European Commission in Brussels during the 1970s made her exceptional within her party. According to her Green Party colleague Antje Vollmer, Kelly's experiences in Washington and Brussels gave her "methods, familiarity with the media, this moral emphasis, and new topics."[13] Kelly, in other words, was both more used to the establishment than her fellow Greens and more comfortable with morally driven politics that relied on new methods.

Kelly's alternative approach to politics had its beginnings in her transnational biography.[14] Petra Karin Lehmann was born in November 1947 in Günzburg, but her family did not remain in the provincial Bavarian town for long. Her father, who had come to Günzburg as a refugee from the East, walked out on the family when Petra was six; she never saw him again. When her mother married the American serviceman John Edward Kelly in 1958, young Petra took on her stepfather's last name. In 1960, the Kelly family left Germany for the United States, where Petra attended high school in the southeastern states of Georgia and Virginia before enrolling at American University (AU) in Washington, DC. Though her family remained in the United States, Kelly chose to return to Europe after graduating from AU in May 1970. She received her MA in European Integration at the University of Amsterdam in May 1971 and began working at the European Commission, first as an intern, and then as a staffer on the Economic and Social Committee, in October 1971. It was only after she was elected to the Bundestag in 1983 that she returned permanently to the FRG.[15]

The year 1968 played an important part in the development of Kelly's political consciousness, as it did for many of her fellow founding Green Party members; however, in Kelly's case, 1968 was important for very different reasons. As a German studying in the United States, Kelly struggled to identify with either the German or the American student movements. She felt that the "student revolutionaries" at AU lacked discipline, but considered their German counterparts too "scientific" and thus lacking in the "love, community, [and] human warmth" that she considered necessary to effect change.[16] Though she personally experienced both the riots in Washington, DC, after the assassination of Martin Luther King, Jr. on April 4, 1968, and the entrance of Warsaw Pact tanks into Prague that August (where she happened to be on vacation with her grandmother), she did not take part in any street protests during those tumultuous months. But this is not to say that Kelly was politically ignorant or uninterested. On the contrary, she spent April 1968 running for AU's student senate. Her campaign posters showed her posing with a motorcycle and bore the slogan "vote for a strong woman."[17] She also organized the university's "International Week" and excelled as a student volunteer coordinator for the presidential campaigns of Robert F. Kennedy and then Hubert Humphrey.[18] Instead of taking politics to the streets, Kelly's political activities in 1968 followed a more traditional path. A self-described "strong woman," she unflinchingly asserted herself within the male-dominated political establishment. As she later wrote, "women must be willing to be powerful."[19]

Kelly's decision to return to Europe was made in part because of her disappointment in Humphrey's loss to Republican Richard Nixon in the 1968 Presidential election.[20] But even if that experience cooled her desire to become a US citizen, it did not cause her to lose her conviction that meaningful change could be made within establishment structures. She chose to study European Integration at the University of Amsterdam and then moved to Brussels to work for the European Commission, thus gaining an insider's understanding of the EEC that was unique among her Green Party colleagues. Following an internship at the European Commission's Secretariat-General, she became an administrative trainee at its Economic and Social Committee. Kelly was a supporter of European integration, as evidenced by her decision to study the subject in Amsterdam and to make a career as a Brussels "Eurocrat." But she was also interested in efforts to reform an institution that she referred to as the "profit-addicted EEC," becoming active in groups such as the Young European Federalists and the West European Socialists.[21] She was particularly interested in fostering Europe-wide democracy. In a 1973 article for the United Nation's *Vista* magazine, she heaped praise on Commission President Sicco Mansholt's efforts to "get the people involved [in Europe] at every local level."[22] She also gave speeches on the future of Europe. At the University of Coleraine in Northern Ireland in May 1975, she advocated direct elections to the European Parliament.[23] An essay Kelly later wrote on "Women and Power" helps to explain her complicated relationship with the institutions of the political establishment. Though she did not want to "loyally adapt" herself to the "male value of hierarchy" that underpinned such institutions, she was not averse to seeking political power in order to put her "own ideas of an emancipatory society into practice."[24]

After visiting the village of Wyhl in rural South Baden over Easter in 1975, Kelly became an outspoken advocate of a new model of an emancipatory society that she believed could be used to transform establishment politics in Europe. Her visit to the village was prompted by local people's protests against a proposed nuclear reactor, which had culminated in the occupation of the construction site. Though Kelly was not herself active in the struggle, she saw it as a model for the sort of action that was necessary to create a more open and more democratic Europe. Wrangling her way onto the podium at a mass demonstration held on the occupied construction site, she told grassroots antinuclear protesters: "[In Brussels] we are waiting for Wyhl."[25] After returning to Brussels, she wrote a three-page memo proposing that her comrades in the West European Socialists visit places like Wyhl in order to conduct "action research, [establish] contact with various grassroots groups, [and become familiar with] 'spectacular actions'" like the Wyhl occupation. In the long run, the group could adopt the reactor opponents' model and use "GRASSROOTS RESISTANCE!!!!!" to transform Europe.[26]

Yet even as she became a committed advocate of grassroots resistance and spectacular bottom-up actions, Kelly did not lose sight of establishment politics. She continued to advocate for direct elections to the European Parliament, as a means of increasing the representation of ordinary Europeans in Brussels.[27] When a number of newly formed local and regional green parties and candidates' lists began exploring the possibility of participating in the first direct elections to the European Parliament, which were finally scheduled for June 1979, Kelly joined them enthusiastically. But she did not conceive of the European elections as a means of contesting power in the traditional sense. While other organizers of the group that decided to name itself Alternative Political Association— The Greens (Sonstige Politische Vereinigung [SPV]—Die Grünen) were focused on building a national political party first and foremost, Kelly emphasized collaboration with friends and fellow activists across Europe.[28] She was interested in developing the Greens as an organization, but she had—as Bevan later argued—little time for "national" goals. She wanted the nascent German Green Party to cooperate closely with counterparts in other EEC countries, and to foster a "decentralized, non/nuclear, non/military [sic] and gentle Europe—a Europe of the Regions and of the People."[29] Though she understood the workings and the importance of establishment political organizations, Kelly saw them as means to an end. She was interested in using the apparatus of the EEC and the workings of German electoral politics to foster a wholly new Europe, ostensibly from the bottom up. That approach matched her understanding of how women could assert themselves in male-dominated political institutions in order to redefine power in a way that not only reflected women's values and women's experience but also emphasized environmental protection and peaceful international relations. As a feminist, environmentalist, and peace activist, Petra Kelly was gauging new ways to do politics.

Out of Place in the Bundestag

Petra Kelly sought to assert herself in Europe's political arena by taking a leading role in a string of Green Party electoral campaigns. As a result, the otherwise unknown EEC employee began to establish herself as a leader of the environmental and peace movements. In 1979, she was chosen as SPV Die Grünen's lead candidate in the campaign for the European Parliament.[30] Campaigning all over West Germany, and in several other EEC countries besides, Kelly proved herself an "electrifying" public speaker capable of drawing big audiences and building excitement about the campaign.[31] She also handled the media well, becoming internationally known on account of impressive television interviews (*Aktivistin*, 261–63). Though SPV Die Grünen failed to win seats in the European Parliament, Kelly's strong performance established her standing as one of the most famous Green Party members and earned her a repeat spot as lead candidate in two further failed Green electoral campaigns: the 1980 Bundestag election and the 1982 election to the Bavarian parliament. At the same time, she became a regular speaker at the massive demonstrations against NATO plans to station new nuclear missiles in West Germany. Finally, in the 1983 Bundestag election, with Kelly once again serving as lead candidate, the Greens scored 5.6 percent of the vote and won twenty-seven seats in the federal parliament.[32] In essence, then, her status as a grassroots activist was solidified by her experience representing a nationally organized political party in its electoral campaigns and speaking at mass rallies. For Kelly, there was no contradiction here. Because of her experiences in Washington and Brussels, she saw the political establishment as an ideal site for the sort of insurgent politics pioneered at the local level by activists in the peace and environmental movements.

Kelly used an analogy from the world of soccer to explain how she thought the Green parliamentary delegation could practice movement-style politics in parliament: if the peace and ecology movement outside of parliament were the "standing leg" (*Standbein*) of Green politics, the parliamentarians were the "kicking leg" (*Spielbein*). In other words, the Greens in the Bundestag were a national mouthpiece for grassroots activists, doing their work on a far grander scale. "Parliaments are a place like the market square . . . where we can speak, introduce our standpoints and depart with information . . . parliament is not a goal but part of a strategy," she explained. Though she concluded her thoughts on the subject with the claim that the "most important thing is to work on the grassroots, to change at the grassroots," it was clear that Kelly attributed particular importance to activist-parliamentarians like herself, who could lead by bringing grassroots issues to the national stage.[33] This idea epitomized her approach to leadership: by introducing new issues and new methods to parliament, Kelly led by example.

Kelly's first days in the Bundestag revealed how her approach to parliamentary work was shaped by her notion of grassroots activism and her wish to represent extra-parliamentary movements in Bonn. On the day of the Bundestag's constitutive session, the Greens used the language of street protest to give voice to the concerns of the movements in parliament. The new Green MPs organized a "ritual procession" to the *Bundeshaus* and carried with them "a huge rubber globe and a branch of a tree that was dying from pollution in the Black Forest." They were accompanied by "representatives from various citizens' movements and from other countries."[34] In her maiden speech in parliament, which she gave a few weeks later on May 4, 1983, Kelly made the Greens' role vis-à-vis the movements explicit. Proclaiming herself a parliamentary spokesperson for the "peace and ecology movement," she warned her Bonn colleagues that it was time for "civil disobedience on many levels" and that "the Greens in the Bundestag would not risk any less than our allies in the extra-parliamentary movements."[35] To be sure, she followed through on her threat. Earlier that same day, Kelly and her Green Party colleague Gaby Gottwald had interrupted a speech by Chancellor Helmut Kohl by unfurling a banner protesting German involvement in Nicaragua on the floor of the Bundestag. Kelly also used her status as a member of parliament to participate in numerous other acts of civil disobedience and high-profile protests, for example, at the German embassy in Pretoria, South Africa, and at Alexanderplatz in East Berlin, without incurring any of the serious consequences that activists without her special status as an MP would likely have faced. Relying on both words and deeds, Kelly seemed determined to turn parliament into a public forum for the nation, dominated by unruly activism and free speech.

Yet the Bundestag, which was quite unlike any market square in Germany, would not tolerate her behavior. In her biography of Petra Kelly, Saskia Richter argues that Kelly struggled because she did not have a firm "footing in the Bundestag" (*ohne Boden im Bundestag*). According to Richter, Kelly was out of place in the Bundestag, because the plenary hall did not lend itself to street demonstration of like-minded sweater-wearing peace activists, environmentalists, and ecofeminists. Instead, it was occupied by "Petra Kelly's opponents, the shapers of economic and defense policy. They did not applaud when Petra Kelly spoke of the atomic threat" (*Aktivistin*, 286). But even if her fellow parliamentarians' insults bothered Kelly, her vast experience working within the political establishment, from the Humphrey campaign to the EEC's Economic and

Social Committee, suggests that she had some idea what to expect in the Bundestag's plenary hall. If Kelly was without footing in the Bundestag, it was not simply because of frequent disagreement with her colleagues. The problem was that her fellow parliamentarians refused even to accept her as an MP because of her political convictions, her way of "doing politics," and especially her gender.

When Kelly entered the Bundestag, the plenary hall was structurally and visibly dominated by men wearing suits and ties.[36] The men of the Green Party—"these guys" (*Typen*) as Interior Minister Friedrich Zimmermann complained[37]—did not fit the gender image and habitus of the West German male politician because of their woolen sweaters, sneakers, and long beards. Female Green Party politicians such as Kelly or her colleague Waltraud Schoppe, whose "full red curls, deep voice, and flowing dresses" caught the attention of parliamentarians and the press, stood out not only because of the way they dressed or styled their hair but also simply because they were women. As the Green Party parliamentarian Hubert Kleinert later remembered, the mere presence of women such as Kelly and Schoppe was in and of itself "for many from the establishment parties a provocation." The Bundestag, he recalled, was dominated by a "fraternity-like atmosphere full of hooting and knee-slapping."[38]

In the 1980s, women members of parliament were in a space that had long excluded women, one that continued to be gendered masculine. Historical research on the eighteenth- and nineteenth centuries shows that concepts such as *Volk*, nation, or citizenship were gendered masculine when they first emerged in Central Europe. Political rights were seen as men's natural prerogative. Women could not join German political parties and organizations until 1908, when the Prussian *Vereinsgesetz* was changed. Since they did not gain the right to vote or stand for election until after the November 1918 revolution, women did not enjoy political influence as voters or elected politicians in the German Empire.[39] Nonetheless, when women finally did gain the right to vote, they came to the polls in high numbers and elected forty-one female politicians to the Constituent National Assembly of the Weimar Republic—incidentally, forty-one is also the number of women who served in the Bundestag in 1982, the year before Kelly and her Green colleagues first entered parliament.[40]

The lack of growth in women's representation might come as a surprise, since the democratization of the Federal Republic has been a central narrative of German mainstream history. Yet scholars of German women's history have long questioned this account and offered explanations for the exclusion of women from traditional parliamentary politics. Some argue that the lack of female delegates, parliamentarians, and political leaders may have been due in part to the legacy of the Nazi regime. Since the Nazi state was fashioned as a men's state (*Männerstaat*), women were excluded from political leadership positions and lost their right to stand for election. After 1945, West Germany's early postwar reconstruction was defined by a return to "normalcy," which included the reestablishment of traditional gender norms and roles. While women were once again relegated to the roles of mother, housewife, and domestic caretaker, the roles of producer, provider, and protector were ascribed to men.[41] At the same time, the realm of politics "was to remain a male preserve."[42] Although West German women, like their Weimar predecessors, came out to vote in high numbers, they were underrepresented in all of the political parties and in every type of parliament, especially in party leadership or government positions. Women constituted only 7 percent of the members of the first Bundestag in 1949 and made up for only 15 percent of party membership in the 1950s (Heineman 139).

This model of male breadwinner/female homemaker, which undoubtedly influenced women's political participation, remained dominant in West Germany for decades to come.[43] Women continued to be excluded from West German politics, and especially the Bundestag, in ways that resembled their exclusion from earlier German politics and parliaments. For instance, between 1962 and 1985 female membership in the Social Democratic Party of Germany (Sozialdemokratische Partei Deutschlands, SPD) rose from 19 to 25 percent and in the Christian Democratic Union of Germany (Christlich Demokratische Union Deutschlands, CDU) from 15 to 22 percent.[44] This minimal growth did not translate into increased female participation in any of the parties' national boards. Women's membership in the Bundestag was sobering as well. Between the Bundestag's first (1949–53) and ninth legislative period (1980–83), the number of female parliamentarians fluctuated between 6.8 percent and 8.5 percent.[45]

When the Greens first entered parliament at the beginning of the tenth legislative period (1983–87), 51 women were elected to the parliament, which then comprised 520 seats. The minuscule 28-member Green delegation, however, included ten women. Moreover, Petra Kelly and Marieluise Beck-Oberdorf served alongside Otto Schily as the Green delegation's first chairs or "spokespeople." Since the Green delegation comprised hardly 5 percent of parliament but nearly 20 percent of its female members, and since it was the only delegation chaired by women, it is clear that Kelly and the other female members of the Green Party represented a tiny minority that was "out of place" in the male-dominated parliament.

Though Kelly's gender was the most important reason why she was out of place in parliament, she was excluded for other reasons as well. In particular, the vast majority of the 469 men and most of the fifty-one women sitting in parliament did not support Petra Kelly's political positions. Rather, the plenary hall was filled with advocates of precisely those policies that Kelly had protested against for years. The Greens entered the Bundestag only four years after NATO's 1979 Dual-Track Decision, which simultaneously offered arms reduction negotiations to the USSR and called for the stationing of new mid-range "Euro-missiles" throughout Western Europe. The Social Democrat Helmut Schmidt, who enthusiastically supported the Dual-Track Decision as chancellor, was also one of West Germany's staunchest supporters of nuclear power and critical of "eco-radicals" such as the Greens. In the early eighties, national and international politics were defined by men who were willing to adhere to the logic of the Dual-Track Decision. Initially, Ronald Reagan, who became US president in January 1981, pursued a "zero option" that aimed at the destruction and dismantling of all nuclear weaponry on both sides of the Iron Curtain. But he soon changed his agenda and called for the modernization of US weaponry. The Christian Democrat Helmut Kohl, who became West German chancellor following a vote of no confidence against Schmidt in October 1982, welcomed Reagan's willingness to expand America's nuclear arsenal. Kohl and his foreign minister, Hans Dietrich Genscher of the Free Democratic Party (Freie Demokratische Partei, FDP), assured Reagan that their government would uphold the principles of the Dual-Track Decision. Despite widespread opposition among the German public, the stationing of Pershing II rockets on West German soil commenced in December 1983 following a parliamentary vote in November. Since the leaders of all other parliamentary parties supported the Dual-Track Decision, and American journalists even worried that Green Party opposition to Euro-missiles would somehow push Germany out of NATO, it is hardly surprising that Bundestag members did not applaud Petra Kelly when she spoke of the atomic threat.[46]

The exasperation of her male colleagues might have been exacerbated by the topics Kelly chose to work on in parliament. She became a member of the prestigious parliamentary Committee on Foreign Affairs. Like the committees that focused on economics and finances, internal affairs, and defense, the Committee on Foreign Affairs was dominated by male parliamentarians. Throughout the 1970s, female membership in these committees never comprised more than 6.7 percent. In contrast, between 15.6 and 18.8 percent of the members in the committees for Education, Research, Technology Assessment, and Family Affairs, Senior Citizens, Women, and Youth were women.[47] Overall, then, women were underrepresented in committees that addressed policy fields closely associated with men and masculinity and over-represented (at least in comparison to their miniscule total representation in parliament) in committees that dealt with issues that were seen as the natural and common domain of women.[48] In this context it is hardly surprising that Petra Kelly's approach to foreign policy was criticized by other parliamentarians, including even her then-Green-Party-colleague Otto Schily, who claimed that Kelly "did world politics without any sort of logistics."[49] Schily's comment, made shortly after Kelly's death, may not have been meant as a put-down, but it nonetheless implied that Kelly's improvisational approach to world politics was quite different from the careful work of the Committee on Foreign Affairs.

Yet seeing herself as part and instrument of grassroots peace and ecology movements, Kelly identified with and embraced not only the movements' goals but also their philosophies and self-image. She did not see the need for the sort of "logistics" that Schily assumed were essential to foreign policy. Instead, when it came to preventing war, she put her faith in the "political techniques of nonviolence—noncooperation, civil disobedience, grassroots organizing, fasting, and so forth." Certainly, such actions required planning and coordination, but Kelly emphasized their "integrity and self-sacrifice," which would "awaken our opponent's conscience and bring about a change of heart."[50] Though Kelly attributed that approach to her readings of Gandhi and Martin Luther King, it could easily be conceived as a "soft," feminine alternative to 1980s male Realpolitik, for neither of these two leaders fit hegemonic concepts of Cold War political masculinity. And such approaches shaped Kelly's work and image as an activist and politician, since she embraced the movements' appreciation of subjectivity and emotions. Fear of the "nuclear apocalypse" became central to the self-image and political message of the peace activists who opposed NATO's Dual-Track Decision.[51] In this, the movements differed from the general political culture of the 1950s and 1960s where "angst about the prospect of nuclear annihilation" did not feature prominently.[52] Such angst was equally unacceptable in the Bundestag in 1983. Nonetheless, in the 1970s and 1980s, West German peace activists began to harness the emotional energy of fear as a useful method to counter the cold rationalities of the government and the military.[53] This appreciation of subjectivity and emotions was visible in both Petra Kelly's writings and her approach to work in parliament. Embracing a "self-image as sensitive, nurturing, caring for life and for the world's ills,"[54] she argued that doing green politics meant "being affectionate while at the same time subversive." Kelly hoped for a gentle and nonviolent form of politics and warned her fellow Greens that the party's growing power could result in the loss of "tenderness" (*Zärtlichkeit*).[55] Likewise, when the party lost its seats in parliament after the 1990 election, Kelly claimed that the Green Party's "smugness" and its decision to abandon "spirituality and ecofeminism" in favor of "Realpolitik" were to blame.[56]

Despite Kelly's emphasis on peaceful, affectionate, and even spiritual politics, her strong, self-assured, and highly critical style of speaking was perceived as jarring by the Bundestag establishment. As self-appointed spokeswoman of the grassroots peace and ecology movements, Kelly used movement activists' language in parliament and frequently recounted her own experiences as a protester. In her fiery response to Defense Minister Dr. Manfred Wörner's September 1983 parliamentary address on the Dual-Track Decision, for example, she informed Wörner that he was "breaking international law and behaving in a criminal fashion." She then asked the minister bluntly: "Would you rather be dead or a mass murderer, Mr. Wörner?" Kelly also explicitly linked her speeches in parliament with her actions in the public sphere, calling out the government for saying nothing after "the police . . . deployed water cannons and dogs against us—also against MPs, who were protesting nonviolently" at a missile deployment site.[57] A few months later, in a June 1984 debate on European integration, she spoke disparagingly of Chancellor Kohl's "pathetic" announcement of a "Europe of Citizens" despite high unemployment throughout the EEC, and also criticized the "trigger happy" European vision of former Chancellor Schmidt. But she did note that new European border policies would benefit "us all . . . even the demonstrators, the Greens, and the entire European ecology and peace movement . . . who will no longer be stopped at the border" en route to demonstrations in neighboring countries.[58]

Many contemporaries perceived Kelly's speeches to be a weaponized volley of words that did not leave any room for counter arguments (*Aktivistin*, 286). Following her first speech in the Bundestag, in which Kelly criticized the "many men" in parliament for their "campaigns of defamation against the peace movement" and told Chancellor Kohl that he was incapable of "acting in accordance with moral categories," the FDP politician Schäfer argued that her performance contradicted the movements she sought to represent. Schäfer perceived Kelly's speech as hateful and militant and not at all conforming to the nonviolent ideals of the peace movement.[59] Kelly often received such responses from speakers who followed her to the rostrum; the Social Democrat Scheer, for example, claimed that Kelly's denunciation of the SPD "had neither enriched nor fertilized debates on the politics of peace."[60]

Interjections during her first speeches in the Bundestag also targeted her tempo: "Not so fast, Madam Colleague" or "Please be considerate of the stenographers" (*Aktivistin*, 286). Moreover, the irritation with her pace was not limited to her early days in the Bundestag. "Why do you actually talk so crazily fast?" asked the host of a German talk show in 1990. "Maybe," Kelly answered, "it's because women have 2,000 years to catch up on" (*Aktivistin*, 366). Interestingly, Saskia Richter, who comments on this interview in her biography of Kelly, states that Kelly responded "smiling, her head tilted, forcefully," and that she kept trying to get a word in, because she perceived herself to be at a constant disadvantage. However, Kelly's conversational and rhetorical behavior can also be interpreted in a different way. Her way of speaking could signal that she wanted to "lean in"—to use a modern-day phrase—and be part of the conversation, but it may also have been a preventive measure to ensure that her political opponents did not interrupt her. Indeed, the well-known German feminist Alice Schwarzer believed that "top candidate Kelly" "tried to capitalize on feminist anger by presenting herself as a woman of peace at the same time as she fought a battle of position with the men."[61]

Although Kelly was a self-proclaimed "ecofeminist," her position vis-à-vis the women's movement compounded her difficulties in parliament. She routinely embraced positions that were at odds not only with the male establishment of the Bundestag but also with those of leading feminists. Schwarzer, for example, agreed with the male parliamentarians' criticisms of Kelly. She denounced the Green Party activist for appealing to airy "mysticism" and for her "avoidance of mentioning the basic reality." Kelly, she complained, never tackled issues real women dealt with on a daily basis, such as "the question of power between the sexes . . . sexual violence, the ideology of love, or critiques of femininity." Somewhat perversely, Schwarzer considered Kelly's murder at the hand of her lover, the retired Bundeswehr General Gert Bastian, the final piece of evidence of her avoidance of reality. Kelly's advocacy for sensuality and love, Schwarzer concluded, offered no defense when she was confronted by a man armed with a Derringer .38 pistol.[62] For Schwarzer and for her critics in the Bundestag, then, Kelly's central failing was her idealism, her failure to take cold, hard facts seriously.

From Outsider to Insider?

As the frequent comparisons to Joan of Arc attest, assessments of Petra Kelly's career and her legacy have been dominated by the perception that, though she was an important inspiration for Green politics, she was out of place in the Bundestag and thus contributed little to the realization of Green Party political goals. Such conclusions hinge on the idea that there was something wrong with Kelly, not with the parliament in which she served. These arguments imply that Kelly failed to understand the male-dominated Realpolitik of the Bundestag or, more simply put, the actual material workings of politics. These sorts of interpretations wrongly accept traditional politics as the benchmark for all "others" who do not fit the characteristics of male career politicians. Thus they sell short the career of a woman who had worked extensively in establishment politics, and proven herself quite capable during an American Presidential campaign and in the corridors of power in Brussels. Instead, Kelly's purposeful accentuation of difference—from her different approach to politics, to her different sex and gender—ought to be seen as the essence of her contribution to the transformation of German politics.

After all, regardless of Kelly's experience and her skill as a purveyor of Green ideas, there is no doubt that she was an outsider in the Bundestag and in the West German political establishment more generally. Women were not welcome in the Bundestag of the early 1980s. Kelly's unconventional political practices defied gender norms and did not conform to the habitual style of debate in parliament. And yet it was precisely in these areas that Kelly and her Green Party colleagues effected the most significant change in parliament. After the arrival of the Greens, the West German parliament saw a tremendous increase in women's participation. In 1998, just fifteen years after the Greens were first seated in the Bundestag, women comprised a full 30 percent of the parliament.

Andrei Markovits, one of the leading scholars of the Green Party, promotes the idea that the Greens' greatest achievements concern a transformation of political culture, or the "wider discourse and demeanor of German public life." Here Kelly's influence is readily apparent. In a 2015 assessment of the Greens' influence thirty years after they first entered parliament, Markovits argues that the Green Party succeeded in effectively aligning "the norm in the quotidian *habitus* of contemporary Germany" with values that are typically identified with the "countercultural ghetto." Thus German capitalism became more "ecological, peaceful, inclusive, moderate, and considerate . . . a capitalism with a human touch and face."[63] Such language is reminiscent of Kelly's mode of speaking in the 1980s—when almost everything about her was considered alien to Germany's political mainstream. It follows, then, that perhaps the Greens' seminal contributions to German politics and society stems from precisely the challenge Kelly brought to the Bundestag in 1983. Even if the transformation of German politics has fallen far short of what might have satisfied Kelly herself, she contributed significantly to changes that made the German political establishment far more reflective of the German people as a whole.

Notes

[1] Petra Kelly, "Acceptance speech—Petra Kelly," *The Right Livelihood Award* (December 31, 1982), http://www.rightlivelihoodaward.org/speech/acceptance -speech-petra-kelly/. All translations, unless otherwise noted, are our own.

[2] Wilhelm Knabe, quoted in Saskia Richter, *Die Aktivistin: Das Leben der Petra Kelly* (Munich: Deutsche Verlags-Anstalt, 2010), 236. Further references to this work are given in the text using the short title *Aktivistin*. Dieter Rucht and Jochen Roose, "Von der Platzbesetzung zum Verhandlungstisch? Zum Wandel von Aktionen und Struktur der Ökologiebewegung," in *Protest in der Bundesrepublik: Strukturen und Entwicklungen*, ed. Rucht (Frankfurt am Main: Campus, 2001), 173–210.

[3] "Entstehung der Grünen: Petra Kelly," *Planet Wissen*, August 3, 2017. https:// www.planet-wissen.de/geschichte/deutsche_geschichte/entstehung_der_ gruenen/pwiepetrakelly100.html.

[4] They referred to arguments that Joan of Arc never fought against the British on the battlefield but accompanied the troops holding the banner. See Rucht and Roose, "Platzbesetzung," 201.

[5] It was only in 2002, with the appointment of Angela Merkel as chairperson of the CDU/CSU Bundestag delegation, that a woman chaired the delegation of one of Germany's two national people's parties.

[6] Petra Kelly, "Acceptance speech—Petra Kelly," *The Right Livelihood Award.*

[7] On the idea of the 1980s as a "second Cold War," see Eckart Conze, Martin Klimke, and Jeremy Varon, "Introduction: Between Accidental Armageddons and Winnable Wars; Nuclear Threats and Nuclear Fears in the 1980s," in *Nuclear Threats, Nuclear Fear, and the Cold War of the 1980s,* edited by Eckart Conze, Martin Klimke, and Jeremy Varon (Cambridge: Cambridge University Press, 2017): 1–24, here 1.

[8] See entries for the year 1985 in Petra Kelly's biography at *Lebendiges Museum Online,* last accessed January 20, 2018; https://www.hdg.de/lemo/biografie/petra-kelly.html.

[9] The term "founding Greens" (*Gründungsgrüne*) was coined by Silke Mende in her important study of the Greens' emergence. Silke Mende, *"Nicht rechts, nicht links, sondern vorn": Eine Geschichte der Gründungsgrünen* (Munich: Oldenbourg, 2011).

[10] Quotation in subheading cited from Antje Vollmer, *Eingewandert ins eigene Land: Was von Rot-Grün bleibt* (Munich: Pantheon, 2006), 26.

[11] Ruth Bevan, "Petra Kelly: The *Other* Green," *New Political Science* 23, no. 2 (2001): 181–202, here 182. Emphasis in the original.

[12] On the importance of the peace, environmental, and women's movements for the founding of the Greens, see Andrei Markovits and Philip Gorski, *The German Left: Red, Green, and Beyond* (Oxford: Oxford University Press, 1993), esp. chapter 4.

[13] Vollmer, *Eingewandert ins eigene Land,* 26.

[14] This argument is made more fully in Stephen Milder, "Thinking Globally, Acting (Trans)locally: Petra Kelly and the Transnational Roots of German Green Politics," *Central European History* 43, no. 2 (2010): 301–26.

[15] On Kelly's early life, see Richter, *Die Aktivistin;* Sara Parkin, *The Life and Death of Petra Kelly* (London: Harper Collins, 1994); and Monika Sperr, *Petra Kelly: Politikerin aus Betroffenheit* (Munich: Bertelsmann, 1984).

[16] Petra Kelly, "To A.U.'s revolutionaries" (poem, Brussels, n.d. [possibly May 1972]), PKA 530,23; Petra Kelly, Untitled (seminar paper, American University, Spring Semester 1970), 10–12, PKA 530,1.

[17] Parkin, *Life and Death,* 53.

[18] Kelly showed such talent as a student organizer that she was called in her dorm room by Vice President Humphrey and flown to Minneapolis for the campaign's concluding rally on election night.

[19] Petra Kelly, *Thinking Green! Essays on Environmentalism, Feminism, and Nonviolence* (Berkeley: Parallax, 1994), 12.

[20] A November 7, 1968, article in the *Minneapolis Tribune* recounted Kelly's discussions with recently defeated candidate Humphrey over whether or not to become an American citizen in the wake of his loss. The article is quoted extensively in Parkin, *Life and Death*, 46–47.

[21] Petra Kelly, Untitled, speech, Wyhl, March 31, 1975, PKA 3166.

[22] Petra Kelly, "Mister New Europe," *Vista*, April 1973, 19, PKA 531,14. Kelly and Mansholt were lovers at the time that Kelly wrote this highly flattering piece about Mansholt.

[23] Petra Kelly, "Europe . . . It is a little mainland off the coast of Northern Ireland," speech at the University of Coleraine, Northern Ireland, May 7, 1975, PKA 533,4.

[24] Kelly, *Thinking Green!*, 13.

[25] Petra Kelly, Untitled. (Speech, Wyhl, March 31, 1975). PKA 3166.

[26] Petra Kelly, "WAS TUN?？？ Einige Aktionsmöglichkeiten für die Westeuropäischen Sozialisten!" (November 1975), PKA 534,2. Emphasis in the original.

[27] Petra Kelly and Roland Vogt, "Ökologie und Frieden: Der Kampf gegen Atomkraftwerke aus der Sicht von Hiroshima," *Forum Europa*, January/February 1977: 18, PKA 534,4.

[28] Stephen Milder, "'Eine [grenzüberschreitende] Entscheidungsschlacht gegen Atomkraftwerke': Die grüne Wahlkampagne(n) für das europäische Parlament in Westdeutschland und Frankreich in 1979," in *Die Ökologie im linken und rechten Spektrum: Konvergenzen und Divergenzen zwischen Deutschland und Frankreich von 1970 bis heute*, edited by Birgit Metzger, Annette Lensing, and Olivier Hanse (Hamburg: Peter Lang, 2018), 209–27.

[29] Petra Kelly, "My dear Friends and Comrades," letter, Brussels, March 24, 1979), PKA 540,6.

[30] Kelly was elected SPV Die Grünen's lead candidate by those in attendance in March 1979 in Frankfurt. Lukas Beckmann, who met Kelly for the first time at the meeting, recalled that she was chosen as lead candidate because "her vivacity, her knowledge, and her commitment impressed everyone." Quoted in Parkin, *Life and Death*, 88–89.

[31] Vollmer, *Eingewandert*, 34.

[32] Including a non-voting seat for West Berlin, there were twenty-eight members in the Greens' delegation.

[33] Cited in Markovits and Gorski, *The German Left*, 121, from Petra Kelly, "Wir müssen die Etablierten entblössen wo wir können," in *Die Grünen: Regierungspartner von morgen?* ed. Jörg Mettke (Reinbeck bei Hamburg, 1982), 26–35, here 31.

[34] Charlene Spretnak and Fritjof Capra, *Green Politics: The Global Promise* (New York: Dutton, 1984), xiii.

[35] German Bundestag, Plenary Protocol, 10th Legislative Period, 4th meeting, May 4, 1983: 128.

298 ◆ Stephen Milder and Friederike Brühöfener

[36] For the "male body" as the norm in modern politics, see Mechthild Cordes, *Frauenpolitik: Gleichstellung oder Gesellschaftsveränderung* (Wiesbaden: VS Verlag für Sozialwissenschaften, 1996), 73–74.

[37] "Muntere Zeiten," *Der Spiegel*, March 14, 1983, 29–33.

[38] Mariam Lau, "Orgasmus im Bundestag," *Die Zeit*, March 27, 2013.

[39] Ute Frevert, "'Unser Staat ist männlichen Geschlechts': Zur politischen Topographie der Geschlechter vom 18. bis frühen 20. Jahrhundert," in *Mann und Weib, und Weib und Mann: Geschlechter-Differenzen in der Moderne*, edited by Ute Frevert, 61–132 (Munich: Beck, 1995), 109.

[40] Julia Sneeringer, *Winning Women's Votes: Propaganda and Politics in Weimar Germany* (Chapel Hill: University of North Carolina Press, 2002).

[41] On West Germany's reconstruction, see Robert G. Moeller, *Protecting Motherhood: Women and the Family in the Politics of Postwar West Germany* (Berkeley: University of California Press, 1996); Frank Biess, *Homecomings: Returning POWs and the Legacies of Defeat in Postwar Germany* (Princeton, NJ: Princeton University Press, 2006); Mark E. Spicka, *Selling the Economic Miracle: Economic Reconstruction and Politics in West Germany, 1949–1957* (New York: Berghahn Books, 2007).

[42] Elizabeth Heineman, *What Difference Does a Husband Make: Women and Marital Status in Nazi and Postwar Germany* (Berkeley: University of California Press, 1999), 139.

[43] Karen Hagemann, Konrad Jarausch, and Cristina Allemann-Gironda, "Children, Families, and States: Time Policies of Childcare and Schooling in a Comparative Historical Perspective," in *Children, Families, and States: Time Policies of Childcare, Preschool, and Primary Education in Europe*, ed. Cristina Allemann-Ghionda, Karen Hagemann, and Konrad H. Jarausch (New York: Berghahn Books, 2011), 3–50.

[44] Oskar Niedermeyer, "Die soziale Zusammensetzung der Parteimitgliederschaften," Bundeszentrale für politische Bildung, July 12, 2017, www.bpb.de/politik/grundfragen/parteien-in-deutschland/zahlen-und-fakten/140358/soziale-zusammensetzung. See also Beate Hoecker, *Politische Partizipation von Frauen: Kontinuität und Wandel des Geschlechterverhältnisses in der Politik* (Opladen: Leske + Budrich, 1995); Karen Hagemann and Donna Harsch, "Entanglements of Gender, Politics, and Protest in the Historiography on the Two Post-1945 Germanys," in *Gendering Post-1945 German History: Entanglements*, ed. Karen Hagemann, Donna Harsch, and Friederike Brühöfener (New York: Berghahn Books, 2019), 21–44.

[45] It was only during German unification that the number of female parliamentarians rose above 10 percent. See Brigitte Geißel and Virginia Penrose, "Dynamiken der politischen Partizipation und Partizipationsforschung: Politische Partizipation von Frauen und Männern September 2003," *Gender Politik Online*, 10, http://www.fu-berlin.de/sites/gpo/pol_sys/partizipation/Dynamiken_der_politischen_Partizipation/index.html.

[46] Robert Hager, "What Shake-Up in West Germany Means to U.S.," *US News and World Report*, October 4, 1982.

[47] Hilde Coffé and Katia Schnellecke, "Female Representation in German Parliamentary Committees: 1972–2009," presentation at the ECPR General Conference, Bordeaux, September 5–7, 2013. https://ecpr.eu/filestore/paper-proposal/24876915-576b-42af-a5e8-55630fb57038.pdf.

[48] See Sybille Küster, "Inklusion und Exklusion: Nationsbildung und Geschlecht in Deutschland," in *Geschichte als Experiment: Studien zu Politik, Kultur und Alltag im 19. und 20. Jahrhundert*, ed. Daniela Münkel and Jutta Schwarzkopf (Frankfurt am Main: Campus Verlag, 2004), 207–16; Elisabeth Zellmer, "Der lange Weg zur Kanzlerin: Frauen und Politik im Spiegel deutscher Zeitgeschichte," in *Gesichter der Demokratie: Porträts zur deutschen Zeitgeschichte*, ed. Bastian Hein, Manfred Kittel, and Horst Möller (Munich: DeGruyter, 2015), 361–74.

[49] "Der alte Mann und das Mädchen," *Der Spiegel*, October 26, 1992.

[50] Kelly, *Thinking Green!*, 62.

[51] See, for example, Susanne Schregel, *Der Atomkrieg vor der Wohnungstür: Eine Politikgeschichte der neuen Friedensbewegung in der Bundesrepublik, 1970–1985* (Frankfurt am Main: Campus, 2011); Judith Michel, "'Richtige' und 'falsche' Angst in der Debatte um den Nato-Doppelbeschluss," in *Angst in den Internationalen Beziehungen*, ed. Patrick Bormann, Thomas Freiberger, and Judith Michel (Göttingen: V & R unipress, 2010), 251–72; Albrecht Weisker, "Powered by Emotion? Affektive Aspekte in der westdeutschen Kernenergiedebatte zwischen Technikvertrauen und Apokalypseangst," in *Natur- und Umweltschutz nach 1945: Konzepte, Konflikte, Kompetenzen*, ed. Franz-Josef Brüggemeier and Jens Ivo Engels (Frankfurt am Main: Campus, 2005), 202–21; Frank Biess, "Die Sensibilisierung des Subjekts: Angst und 'Neue Subjektivität' in den 1970er Jahren," *Werkstatt Geschichte* 49 (2008): 51–71.

[52] Benjamin Ziemann, "German Angst? Debating Cold War Anxieties in West Germany," in *Understanding the Imaginary War: Culture, Thought and Nuclear Conflict, 1945–1990*, ed. Matthew Grant and Benjamin Ziemann (Manchester, UK: Manchester University Press, 2016), 116–39, here 126.

[53] Susanne Schregel, "Konjunktur der Angst: 'Politik der Subjektivität' und 'neue Friedensbewegung,' 1979–1983," in *Angst im Kalten Krieg*, ed. Bernd Greiner, Christian Th. Müller, and Dirk Walter (Hamburg: Hamburger Edition, 2009), 495–520, here 508–15.

[54] Belinda Davis, "The Gender of War and Peace: Rhetoric in the West German Peace Movement of the Early 1980s," *Mitteilungsblatt des Instituts für soziale Bewegungen* 32 (2004): 99–130, here 123.

[55] Petra Kelly, "Zärtlichkeit in der Politik (1984)," in *Mit dem Herzen denken: Texte für eine glaubwürdige Politik* (Munich: Beck, 1990), 18–22.

[56] Petra Kelly, "Beyond the Greens," *Ms.* November/December 1991: 70–72, here 70.

[57] Deutscher Bundestag, Stenographischer Bericht, 23. Sitzung (September 16, 1983), 1614–1615.

[58] Deutscher Bundestag, Stenographischer Bericht, 77. Sitzung (June 28, 1984), 5607–5608.

59 Deutscher Bundestag, Stenographischer Bericht, 4. Sitzung (May 4, 1983), 131.

60 Deutscher Bundestag, Stenographsicher Bericht, 23. Sitzung (September 16, 1983), 1616.

61 Alice Schwarzer, *Eine tödliche Liebe: Petra Kelly und Gert Bastian* (Cologne: Kiepenheuer & Witsch, 1993), 116.

62 Schwarzer, *Eine tödliche Liebe*, 116–19.

63 Andrei Markovits and Joseph Klaver, "Alive and Well in the Fourth Decade of Their Bundestag Presence: A Tally of the Greens' Impact on the Federal Republic of Germany's Political Life and Public Culture," *German Politics and Society* 33, no. 4 (Winter 2015): 112–40, here 113–14, 116. Emphasis in the original.

15: "Mama Merkel" and "Mutti-Multikulti": The Perils of Governing While Female

Patricia Anne Simpson

THE SEISMIC IMPACT of Western election cycles in 2016 fractured the image of women as world leaders and citizens. The US presidential race morphed into a face-off between liberal and conservative ideologies that succeeded in polarizing oppositional politics and dividing the nation along attributes of intersectional identities, not least gender lines. While the 2017 federal elections in the Federal Republic of Germany confirmed Chancellor Angela Merkel for another term at the helm of the most powerful country in the European Union (EU), she has faced significant challenges in building the coalition necessary for effective national and transnational leadership. Tepid endorsements of the election results proclaimed it "inconclusive," and the media rapidly turned the EU spotlight on Emmanuel Macron, "France's energetic young president."[1] With successful elections seemingly transcending race and gender differences, many were quick to proclaim that ours is a post-racial, post-gender, and post-national world. Yet the election results of 2016 and subsequent surges in gender-specific protest, against systemic sexual harassment, for example, point to the persistence of patriarchal structures in personal and professional realms. Contemporary democracies are undergoing a radical shift in the negotiation of gender politics that empower a largely white male demographic to repossess power, privilege, and entitlement allegedly disrupted by the rise of "political correctness" and images of gendered and racialized otherness. In this essay I examine the contrasting and often contradictory projections of female leadership and the escalation of critical rhetoric through a series of allegories generated by far-right antifeminism and the critique of Merkel as a failed and multicultural mother. In other words, I inventory the perils of governing while female through an analysis of select texts and images, including the portrayal of Merkel as "Frau Europa"; the "enigmatic," mysterious, and inscrutable Mona Lisa of the European Union; the gender-neutral portrayals that acknowledge her power and rationality; and the maternalizing depictions of her as

"Mama Merkel" and "Mutti-Multikulti" in response to her handling of the refugee crisis.

Merkel herself is the subject of continued scholarly and popular analysis. Political scientists, cultural critics, and comparative gender-studies scholars focused attention on her leadership style, her memory politics,[2] and her policies.[3] Scholarly attention culminates in the publication of Joyce Marie Mushaben's *Becoming Madam Chancellor: Angela Merkel and the Berlin Republic.*[4] In this first study of its kind, Mushaben charts Merkel's course toward becoming the "world's most powerful woman." In her work, Mushaben reaffirms that gender still matters, and examines specifically how one woman uses power "to improve the human condition" (6). In addition, Mushaben claims boldly that "this chancellor has done more to advance gender equality in united Germany than all of her predecessors combined" (308), even though Merkel deemphasizes her gender in the political realm. Traditionally and persistently masculinized, leadership traits associated with "charisma" and "vision" are not tools in her toolkit. It is also the case that Merkel's leadership skills have evolved in office.[5] Dorothee Beck's examination of female political leadership and gendered media coverage follows changes in the way women are portrayed, though masculinity as the unarticulated political norm persists.[6] Recognizing the dominant metaphor of the *Landesmutter*, Beck parses its meaning when applied to Merkel, not always in a depreciative way (Mutti Merkel, Mutter der Nation, schwäbische Hausfrau).[7]

By contrast, other scholars highlight the derogatory public projections of feminized leadership traits, such as a lack of decisiveness. In her article "Angela Merkel's Discourse about the Past," Yoder writes: "During the early years of her leadership, she was criticized for her cautious style and her indecision, eventually inspiring a new German verb, *merkeln*, or to dither" (2). In examining fifty-eight speeches delivered since 2006, Yoder further observes that 38 percent of Merkel's speeches address the traumas to twentieth-century German history (5). She concludes that Merkel references German collective memory, integrating German-German history and evoking "dominant memory discourse about WWII and the Holocaust as a guide to action" (7). This analysis situates Merkel's contemporary humanitarianism in a discourse embedded in historical knowledge and collective memory (9). In her fourth and final term, Merkel's commitment to the nation is in question. The chancellor's decision to open Germany to refugees, judged by the electorate, the popular press, and social media, was interpreted as a humanitarian act, but one that has been gendered by her vocal critics. If she is a Landesmutter, fraught and problematic as that designation is—the semantics deteriorate when the "Mutter" embraces "Kinder" from beyond the borders of the "Land," and the resulting critique amounts to an accusation of miscegenation as a betrayal of the nation. The private maternal is then excluded from politics of the public sphere, destabilizing a female claim to political power.

Increasingly, the image or specter of an unapologetically nationalist leader appeals to an increasingly nationalist electorate. In many corners, circles, and corridors of European political architectures, Merkel is seen to have overspent any credibility capital she may have accrued when she overrode the Dublin accords and opened Germany's borders to refugees fleeing war and privation: the levels of pushback and backlash render any humanitarian impulse a punishable offense. The decision, however, is cast in ethical, rather than political terms. According to James Traub, "only two countries, Germany and Sweden, took their moral obligations seriously enough to accept the political risk of throwing open their doors to refugees. Both lived to rue their impulsive generosity and to block new avenues of arrival."[8] Attributes associated with exercising political power, agglomerated in self-help sections as "leadership skills," frequently enter into alignment with gendered identities. In this case, the longevity of a mindset that treats the feminine synonymously with the morally ideal—a public version of the Victorian "angel in the house"—explicates Merkel's decision. Editor of the special issue of *German Politics* on the first *Bundeskanzlerin*, Louise K. Davidson-Schmich writes: "Although most countries' populations are at least half female, the executive branch of government has historically been dominated by men virtually everywhere on earth; for this reason, national-level executive offices are highly 'masculinised.'"[9] As is often the case, gendered attributes are transferable: moral male leaders can be portrayed as feminized and therefore weak; data-driven, pragmatic, and unemotional women in positions of power are often masculinized and critiqued on that basis. Cosmopolitan humanitarianism itself is gendered.

In the mid-2010 incarnation of the Newer World Order, former binaries of capitalist and communist, West and East, industrialized and developing, have been subsumed into an opposition between globalism, even with its problematic neoliberal patina, and aggressive nationalisms associated with right-wing populism, xenophobia, and beleaguered ethnocentrism. In popular terms, Europeans tend to perceive themselves as the "losers" of globalization, attributing victory to rising economies beyond their borders. Thomas B. Edsall analyzes the reliance of conservative parties on white voters in Europe and the United States in these terms, with nationalism encompassing "resistance to open borders and to third-world immigration" and globalization defined as "receptivity to open borders, the expansion of local and nationalistic perspectives, and for support for a less rigid social order and for liberal, cultural, immigration and trade policies."[10] These political positions confer and clash within national boundaries, not least in Germany, where a chorus of voices from across the political spectrum have made closed borders a refrain. In general, those who endorse an inclusive and integrated worldview also support cultural globalization, with liberal immigration policies, multiculturalism, and secular tolerance; those who identify with the victims of globalization broadcast their anxieties about "cultural take over" and feeling "foreign in their own country."[11] Feeling foreign in Germany correlates with the perception of unbridled Islamization. With liberal or left-centrist governments facing hard times in several of its European neighbors, Germany's center, too, is shifting its weight to accommodate the rise of right-wing nationalism gaining momentum and political ground by instrumentalizing Muslim immigration and the presumed dilution of German identity. Both in its extremist and now mainstreamed articulations, the populist far right is generating critiques of female leaders that appeal to a repressed and unleashed misogyny, which, in turn, is deeply rooted in identitarian, nativist ideologies. With varying degrees of success, far-right critiques of female leadership display a contempt for powerful women who depart from their retro model of the feminine and a nostalgia for the family. One strategy adopted by critics of policy, positioned from the far right, formulates a reassertion of German "authenticity" by straining a particular mixture of feminism through a problematic, conservative sieve. In response to "Gender Mainstreaming," a program advanced by the European Union to achieve gender equity according to a specific timeline, with metrics and scores to assess progress, conservative women raise their voices and wield their pens in protest, joining the chorus of PEGIDA protesters, among others who insist on "traditional" female roles in the family and society. Curiously, the definition of gender mainstreaming seems innocuous: it "involves the integration of a gender perspective into the preparation, design, implementation, monitoring and evaluation of policies, regulatory measures and spending programmes, with a view to promoting equality between women and men, and combating discrimination."[12]

Yet this declaration elicits impassioned critique from the far right, accompanied by selective and sometimes distorting acknowledgments of German-German histories.

While the demographics typical of such right-wing populist movements are predominantly male, the Patriotische Europäer gegen die Islamisierung des Abendlandes (Patriotic Europeans against the Islamization of the West, PEGIDA) and the Alternative für Deutschland (Alternative for Germany, AfD) have ostensibly lifted the glass ceiling for women within their own ranks by deploying women members as "Frontfrauen" to project a commitment to female leadership. At the same time, however, their views espouse and underwrite a neoliberal "feminism" that in fact reiterates traditionally ancillary female attributes. The interplay among right-wing movements, widespread use of social media, and public demonstrations across the Federal Republic of Germany constructs and consolidates a sense of persecuted community, united in the effort to recuperate a fractured or forgotten national identity. The strategy of deploying women as leaders to recover their role as political ancillaries to strong men can best be described as cynical.

Antifeminism at Work

Motivating such decisions is the recoding of antifeminism and a new semantics of feminine agency to elect subordination; simultaneously, this brand of antifeminism advocates an ideal of national maternity through a critique of political correctness and a purportedly patriotic commitment to reverse a declining German birthrate and protect the nation from un-German otherness. With disturbing regularity, as I contend, Merkel's critics project an image of failed maternity onto the head of state. Despite the occasional ascent of women to powerful political positions, Western democracies have failed to foster a positive model of female leadership, beyond the genealogically bequeathed and residual role of queen.

The strategies employed by her detractors—and more than a few of her erstwhile supporters and CDU colleagues—beckon a somewhat unlikely comparison from the annals of literary theory. In his signature essay, "The Resistance to Theory," Paul de Man responds to a request from the Committee on Research Activities of the Modern Language Association (MLA) for a contribution on literary theory for a volume on scholarship in modern languages and literatures. De Man thematizes the quandary prompted by the solicitation; the resulting essay on teaching, literature, and literary theory in the American academy does not fit tidily into a pedagogical model for literary instruction; instead, he offers a commentary on contemporary resistance to theory. In unpacking the anxieties and occasional paroxysms triggered by the reception of "foreign, mostly but not always continental influences," de Man elaborates on his interpretation of a widespread rhetorical and psychological strategy:

> It is a recurrent strategy of any anxiety to defuse what it considers threatening by magnification or minimization, by attributing to it claims of power of which it is bound to fall short. If a cat is called a tiger it can easily be dismissed as a paper tiger; the question remains however why one was so scared of the cat in the first place. The same tactic works in reverse: calling the cat a mouse and then deriding it for its pretense to be mighty.[13]

This primarily rhetorical and theoretical insight can be extended to the political anxieties played out in the public sphere. After a poor showing in the federal elections and speaking out against a call for new elections, Merkel fielded criticism from CDU opposition. Delegate Wolfgang Grieger, demanding her resignation, lashed out at her energy, defense, social, and family policies; he compared her manner of ruling to that of a squire (*Gutsherrnart*): "'Heute ist der Tag, an dem wir sagen müssen: Die Kaiserin hat keine Kleider an—sie ist nackt.' Noch nie sei ein Kanzler so 'machtgeil und unpatriotisch' gewesen, sagte Grieger" ("Today is the day when we must say: the empress is wearing no clothes—she is naked." Never has a chancellor been so "horny for power and unpatriotic").[14] According to reports, other delegates reacted with disapproval of Grieger's extreme formulations, which nonetheless corroborate the patterned response to anxiety. He dismisses twelve years of her leadership; crowns her an empress, strips her verbally, accuses her of being inordinately obsessed with power, in sexualized terms with the vernacular use of *geil*, and subsumes this sexual prurience into the ultimate slap of failed German patriotism.

The peculiar compensatory relationship between male-dominated right-wing movements and the prominence of female leadership in these movements complicates the anti-politics that undermine a democratic and cosmopolitan public sphere. Repeatedly, PEGIDA and AfD have installed women in the ranks of their leadership. Appearance matters. The foregrounding of female innocence, Christian faith, and family values resurrects maternal primacy in contemporary German female iconographies of citizenship.

Politically, far-right social movements and parties oppose Muslim immigration, a volatile topic exacerbated by the welcoming politics of Chancellor Angela Merkel, who repeatedly and publicly defends the fundamental humanity of the decision. With its own past haunted by the specter of pathological nationalism and anti-Semitism, the Federal Republic of Germany briefly garnered accolades for the acceptance of more than one million refugees. The racism, xenophobia, misogyny, and nationalism explicit in the far right's platform, although still abnegated by many of its supporters, continue to propel the politics of PEGIDA into the mainstream. PEGIDA's politics of negation illustrate a widespread strategy of the far right toward naturalizing and nationalizing extremist views, reclaiming the nation, and unraveling the social fabric of equality. More generally, anti-globalization proponents successfully mobilize the language of natural catastrophe to characterize the relentless "flood" of asylum seekers and migrants. However, the anti-immigration stance engages other oppositional vocabularies that reveal much about German identitarian politics. The antifeminist rhetorical strategies that shape the far right's anti-politics also have a wider impact through dissemination in the mainstream and social media.

The marginalization of a particular construction of German masculinity, economically destabilized by the decline of the male-breadwinner model and ascent of the professional and political woman, have fueled vitriolic attacks on "gender mainstreaming," defined as the rather uncontroversial, if not bland, presumption of equality between men and women. The reassertion of an entitled German-ness naturalizes a totalizing relationship between ethnicity and the territory of the nation state—effectively homogenizing the rhetoric of anti-immigration and attacks on political and economic anti-equality. The political leadership of a female chancellor becomes a target for a range of projections that combine to foster an especially virulent culture of misogyny.

Gender Mainstreaming

The fear of trespass or breach motors PEGIDA's anti-politics. PEGIDA's Facebook page, which self-identifies the Patriotic Europeans as a "community organization," demands that borders be closed immediately—"borders save lives"—in order to defend the unitary Fortress Europe. Further, PEGIDA proudly proclaims: "We are not politically correct." The rhetorical strategy of populist excitable speech patterns and far-flung, fact-free argument has a new label, "Themenhopping" (topic hopping).[15] There is, I would argue, a more motivated relationship between racism and misogyny that challenges the seeming randomness explicit in that term. The seventeenth point of PEGIDA's manifesto states: "Pegida ist gegen dieses wahnwitzige Gender-Mainstreaming, auch oft Genderisierung genannt, die nahezu schon zwanghafte, politisch korrekte Geschlechtsneutralisierung unserer Sprache" (PEGIDA is against the crazy "gender mainstreaming" also often called "genderizing," the almost compulsory politically correct gender neutralization of our language).[16] In the updated Facebook page, the "about" section no longer publicizes Pegida's 19-point position paper. The hysteria over "Genderismus, "Genderwahn," even "Gender-Terror"[17] may seem to have subsided. A further click on the Notes section, dated May 2015, leads to the Dresden Theses that represent PEGIDA's ostensibly more moderate and mature demands: PEGIDA 2.0. Thesis 1 demands the preservation of German-ness, back-pedaling from the more vehement demand for the preservation of the Judeo-Christian world (from the 19-point position paper): "Schutz, Erhalt und respektvoller Umgang mit unserer Kultur und Sprache" (Protection, preservation, and respectful interaction with our culture and language)[18] while the diatribe against politically correct "gender insanity" has been subsumed into a demand for political reform:

> Reformation der Familienpolitik sowie des Bildungs-, Renten- und Steuersystems. Besonders die Förderung einer nachhaltigen Familienpolitik muss Priorität erhalten, um einen Stopp oder sogar die Umkehr des demographischen Wandels zu erreichen. Der Kinderwunsch darf nicht aufgrund von wirtschaftlichen Ängsten unterdrückt werden.[19]

[Reformation of family policy, as well as the education, pension, and tax system. In particular, the promotion of a sustainable family policy must be given priority in order to stop or even reverse demographic change. The desire to have children must not be suppressed because of economic fears.]

The language of PEGIDA at its most inflammatory is forged in the realm of the irrational and emotional, but it resonates nonetheless. Here PEGIDA intersects with publicists on the far right, for example, with Ellen Kositza, wife of Götz Kubitschek, a German publisher, journalist, and right-wing activist associated with identitarian movements. Her claims about advancing female identities in resistance to "gender mainstreaming" and with contempt for "political correctness" have led some to wonder about the possibility of a "nationalist feminism."[20] There are clearly theoretical contradictions between the transnational nature of feminism and supremacist overtones of nationalism. Kositza contributes to an understanding of these contradictions in ways that help us locate the repudiation of feminism and reversion to nationalism on the far right. Kositza's antifeminist manifesto *Gender ohne Ende* (Gender without End) discusses the intimate link between political and sexual correctness: "Gemeint ist die wirkungsmächtige Schnittmenge zwischen Feminismus und politischer Korrektheit. Kurz gesagt: sc [sexual correctness] ist das Mittel, Feminsmus der Zweck" (What is meant is the effective intersection between feminism and political correctness. In short, sc is the means, feminism is the end).[21] The idea of "sexual correctness" has not enjoyed the widespread usage of its intended antecedent, PC. In her role as conservative intellectual everywoman, Kositza appears to advocate for a type of sexual empowerment for women to contradict the normative effects of PC cultures that implicitly disempower men and ostensibly contribute to worse sex for all. This rhetorical move obviates the need to examine critically the subordination of women in the public sphere while proclaiming their emancipation in the realm of the private and sovereignty over the body. This type of argument has become a trope of the Right. They espouse alliances across a spectrum of questionable practices, underwritten by diatribes about the evils of the EU, threats against Russia from the West, the purportedly uncontainable and intolerable influx of refugees and asylum seekers, whom they blame for terrorist attacks,[22] deteriorating family values, the loss of national German identity, and not least, the anti-democratic politics of Chancellor Angela Merkel.

The far-right, ultra-conservative "feminist" critique of Merkel warrants an examination of the influence of gender on policy. Particularly important are examinations of Merkel's family policies and assumptions about women in power. In analyzing Merkel's first term in office, political scientist Angelika von Wahl advances and supports three hypotheses about female leadership: Merkel demonstrably improved reconciliation and anti-discrimination policies; she exercised caution in appearing "too supportive" of female appointees, for example, Ursula von der Leyen; finally, von Wahl concludes:

> In contradiction to the literature, Merkel *did* risk alienating core constituents with the reforms in family policy, particularly the "daddy-month." This risk was, however, limited to a smaller and today demographically less central group of constituents (conservative older males), while promising an influx of a new generation of centrist and younger voters. Merkel and her Minister did not extend these vigorous reform efforts for women's equality from family policy to anti-discrimination. Powerful business interests and the church have systematically rejected such measures. These constituents are taken very seriously as they continue to be extremely relevant for the CDU.[23]

Von Wahl further arrives at conclusions that directly refute the far right's claim that family policy is in free-fall; she summarizes her findings in asserting that Merkel's gender-specific policies vary:

> Social rights in the family seem to be strengthened and actively transformed under Merkel, while the implementation of civil rights in employment is only grudgingly supported. Considering that Chancellor Merkel and Minister von der Leyen have the power to represent women in employment, a core concern in modern economies, Merkel's initial hostility ("absolute job-killer") to anti-discrimination is quite remarkable. It is also significant insofar as Merkel hails originally from a state with an extremely high participation of women in the labour market.[24]

In her examination of intersectionality in Merkel's female leadership, von Wahl suggests that East German identity trumps gender in some decisions. From a data-driven perspective, she analyzes the chancellor's decisions and their impact on family policy and employment. With considerable explanatory force, she contextualizes the relationship between Merkel and von der Leyen with attention to the intersectional aspects of the chancellor's identity.

The historically determined definition of male and female gender roles infuses antifeminism's insistence on claims of East German authenticity and the strength and superiority of its women. To return to this recoding of independent women as anti-feminists of the New East, concerns about gender and regional identity resurface in inconsistent and sometimes disingenuous ways. Kositza, for example, is East German by choice (she herself hails from the former West). She has consciously chosen, according to her terms, the better Germany for freedom in gendered identity. Thus Kositza praises the "Ostfrau" as emancipated, avant-garde, and accomplished, because of the range of working-class jobs practiced by women in the GDR and the theoretical equality of women. Further, she embraces their resistance to superficiality: they do not feel compelled to purchase makeup.[25] This valorization glosses over the historical conditions that disproportionately affected Eastern women in unified Germany. Mushaben observes: "Eastern women were hit hard by unemployment and the elimination of socialist benefits, and were less likely to be rehired by Western employers" (*Becoming Madam Chancellor*, 69). With her own investment in place and her personal choice clear, Kositza endorses the superiority of the East German woman perhaps at the expense of their reality.

With a cadre of self-credentializing[26] "publicists" and politicians, PEGIDA leaders, relying on mobilized stereotypes of German femininity, exploit historical moments and meanings to make connections with a broad spectrum of supporters. An examination of the organization's and affiliates' deployment of female images, gendered language, and maternal myths, demonstrates the ways PEGIDA's implicit conjunction of anti-immigration and pro-family politics reclaims German national identity via a new-right misogyny.

Public Mothers

Albeit a predominantly male political movement, typical of such right-wing constellations, PEGIDA has lifted the glass ceiling for women. For example, Tatjana Festerling functions as the "Frontfrau" of PEGIDA. Less visible affiliates include Eva Herman, who advocates a neoliberal return to conventional gender roles through choosing submission. An advocate of traditional gender roles and mythologized motherhood, Eva Herman, author of *Das Eva-Prinzip: Für eine neue Weiblichkeit* (The Eva Principle: For a New Femininity, 2006), was fired from her job at the ARD television network in 2007 for praising Hitler's policies to boost the German birth rate.[27] In her work on far-right media strategies and their move into the mainstream, Helga Druxes counts Herman among the formerly credentialed conservative German journalists who, discredited by articulating extremist views, now espouse "right populist esoteric views" and use web-based news broadcasts to ply their trade.[28] Among these views is the recoding of anti-feminism through a critique of political correctness and a declining German birthrate.

The peculiar compensatory relationship between male-dominated right-wing movements and the prominence of female leadership complicates the anti-politics that undermine the public sphere. Sociologist Karl-Heinz Reuband attributes the overrepresentation of men in right-wing movements in part to their potentially martial appearance, also to their social stance.[29] And yet, PEGIDA and AfD have repeatedly installed women in the ranks of their leadership. Appearance matters. Druxes calls attention to strategies familiar from white nationalism in the United States and to the gender dynamic within PEGIDA that associates German white femininity with the need for protection:

> Pegida's co-founder, Kathrin Oertel, a housewife from Dresden, was placed front-and-center at marches with her flowing blonde hair, dressed in a white parka—the very picture of endangered female innocence, and the opposite of a career politician. Posters proclaimed "Für die Zukunft unserer Kinder," "Keine Glaubenskriege auf deutschem Boden," "Multi-kulti stoppen: Meine Heimat bleibt deutsch" ("For our children's future," "No religious wars on German soil, "Stop multiculturalism: my homeland will stay German").[30]

The foregrounding of female innocence, Christian faith, and family values resurrects maternal primacy in contemporary German female iconography. The alignment between far-right nationalist and identitarian parties, such as Marine Le Pen's National Front (FN) in France, and a politics that opposes gender equality in the public sphere is ultimately consistent with social narratives that resonate with white nationalism, identitarian and nativist ideologies, retrograde gender roles, and preservationist stratagems designed to avert the extinction of "diverse" European genes, with Germans purported to be swimming at the deep end of the pool.

The idea of Europe issues from a familiar myth: the inaugural rape that situates Europe on a promontory of Asia recapitulates divine desire, betrayal, violence, and trespass. With uncanny tenacity, images of female agency are interwoven with European border transgressions. The contrast of female leadership and escalating critical rhetoric, articulated and illustrated through a series of allegories, underwrites the argument that the greater the superlatives of praise, the more emphatic the expletives in response. The 2010 *Time* cover depicts Angela Merkel as "Frau Europa," the most powerful woman in the European Union. Anxiety about how she will wield that power is explicit. Three years later, she becomes "enigmatic," mysterious and inscrutable—other artists depict her as the Mona Lisa with that uninterpretable semi-smile. The *Time* 2015 "Person of the Year" portrait renders her features as a nearly gender-neutral composition of planes and angles, beige and blue with a pop of red. Mushaben notes that Merkel is the first woman to be featured in three decades (*Becoming Madam Chancellor*, 122).[31] Her personhood as a leader trumps gendered identity because of her policies. With an attempt to preserve the main accomplishment of the EU, namely open(-ish) borders, the chancellor presides over a territory of cosmopolitanism: She handled the refugee crisis in Germany as well as the serious economic problems in the European economy: "Merkel's legacy—her bold, fraught, immensely empathetic act of leadership—challenges more than the comfort of European life. It also challenges the comfort of assumptions about any group, including, if it works out, Germans."[32] The expectation that Merkel will fulfill particular roles plagues her chancellorship and propels her image from one female allegory to another.

Before Merkel's decision to open borders, a prelude of sorts took place in 2015 when, at a public appearance at a school in Rostock, a young and sobbing Palestinian teenager, Reem Sahwil, speaking perfect German, explained the threat of deportation and asked why she faced it. After a moment of apparent speechlessness, Merkel "comforted" her with the explanation that the teenager was one of "thousands and thousands" that Germany could not help. She said: "politics is sometimes hard. You're right in front of me now and you're an extremely nice person. But you also know in the Palestinian refugee camps in Lebanon are thousands and thousands and if we were to say you can all come . . . we just can't manage it."[33] The encounter went viral.

That assertion gave way to the much praised and equally ridiculed: "Wir schaffen das" (we can do it). The anxieties and fears unleashed by the influx of more than one million refugees into Germany heightened the tensions, especially when terrorist attacks, some perpetrated by men who had entered the country as refugees, led to confirmation bias on a national scale. Vociferous critiques of Merkel from the far right appeared in headlines decrying her as "Queen of the smugglers" (*Schlepperkönigin*), or issuing the command "arrest Merkel,"[34] thus demonizing and criminalizing her political agency. In the immediate aftermath of the terrorist attack in Berlin (December 19, 2016), AfD leader Marcus Pretzell tweeted: "These are Merkel's dead." The attribution of agency to Merkel, as a mother who can give life and as an instrument of death responsible for terrorism, negates her political identity and maternalizes her power.

This metamorphosis is consistent with processes of desexualization projected onto female leaders, as noted by Margarete Stokowski in her book about contemporary feminism and sexuality, *Unterrum frei*. Critics, bent on dismantling her power rhetorically, resort to gendering language: "Sie ist dann entweder 'das Merkel,' das geschlechtslose Wesen, oder 'Mutti,' die Urform des Weiblichen" (Either she is 'little Merkel,' the sexless being, or 'Mommy,' the primal form of the feminine).[35] The disparaging tone of the discourse heightens the conflict between local detractors who feel betrayed by neoliberalism and the cosmopolitics implicit in German *Willkommenskultur*. The process by which the "leader of a free Europe" and the formerly heralded humanitarian Merkel transformed into the allegory of a bad mother illuminates the rhetorical and social politics of negation that extend the trope of Europa as female fragility and simultaneously create a maternal monster.

The most extreme articulation of this transformation from maternal leader to criminal caricature is legible in the work of publicist Jürgen Elsässer. A journalist formerly known for leftist leanings, he gleefully and frequently engages in Merkel-bashing, beyond a critique of her politics or policies. Erstwhile left-wing activist, and the founder and editor of the right-wing populist magazine *Compact*, Elsässer once repudiated German identity but counts himself now among its staunchest advocates. Equally impassioned is his sustained diatribe against Merkel. With photoshopped, sensationalist covers of Merkel behind bars ("Merkel verhaften?" [arrest Merkel?], December 2015), or the chancellor in a headscarf ("Mutti Multikulti" [Mama multiculti], August 2015), *Compact*'s editor and contributors vilify the chancellor, frequently in gendered terms. In one broadcast episode Elsässer sits in a triangular constellation with two of his contributors. The three men flip to the Merkel article and comment on the cover, emphasizing the creases and deep lines around her mouth, as if collagen shifting were a political liability. In some ways, however, the inability to conform to a particular idea/l of female beauty have become (cheek)bones of contention. Mushaben, with the rhetorical force of *enumeratio*, catalogues the artifacts and images that replicate or miniaturize Merkel's persona: "No other leader qualifying for various 'most-powerful' lists has encountered so many questionable tributes; in addition to the Merkel 'Barbie Doll,' she has witnessed a never-ending stream of before/after hairdo montages, paper-doll sets, a comic book, animated 'dance' videos, a 'Blazer Watch,' and the inevitable pantsuit jokes" (*Becoming Madam Chancellor*, 23). The miniatures and look-alikes have the effect of making Merkel absurd, undermining the gravitas of her political power, but none are ultimately as arch or potent as the far-right critique of the chancellor for her decision to open the nation to refugees. This vitriol is attributed to her role as pro-Muslim public mother, legible in the photoshopped visage.

Merkel herself bears some responsibility for the resistance to integrate German society. Throughout the 1990s, debates about multiculturalism and diversity ebbed and flowed around escalating attacks against visible minorities in the relatively new Federal Republic, united since 1990; and counter-demonstrations, which took the form of candle-lit silent vigils. Even sympathizers noted that the silence that prevailed at the demonstrations of solidarity exposed the absence of a debate or even a vocabulary about racism in postwar and post-Wall Germany. The toxic cocktail of Muslimizing Merkel's appearance, then maternalizing her leadership role, not only negate the power of her decisions and trivialize her status as the last standing leader of the free world, but also speak volumes about the underlying anxieties about plural societies and intersectional identities.

In her work on multiculturalism in the Federal Republic, Martina Wasmer, a researcher affiliated with the Center for Survey Research and Methodology (GESIS, formerly ZUMA) in Mannheim, notes Merkel's 2010 declaration "that all attempts to build a multicultural society had 'utterly failed.'"[36] She locates this assertion in the context of European discussions about the commitment to multiculturalism, its definitions, and its societal implementations. With quantitative research gleaned from public-opinion surveys, Wasmer analyzes the precarious status of diversity in Germany. She observes: "Although current usage of 'multicultural' or *multikulti* signals the problems that Germany's multiculturalism is faced with, the term is seldom explicitly at the centre of public debates over relevant issues" (170). The dismissive connotations of the term *multikulti*, more familiar from the 1990s, resurfaced in the polemics surrounding the acceptance of refugees in 2015, referencing a derogatory valence. The conditions that stabilize its signification have changed. Until the humanitarian decision to open borders and keep them porous despite criticism that would eventually inform her decision to step down from a leadership position after severe losses in regional elections (October 2018), Merkel had no convincing or coherent agenda of diversity or multiculturalism. Wasmer concludes the essay, which predates the refugee crisis, on an upbeat note: "On the other hand, the fact that Germany—in contrast to most of its neighbors—has no right-wing populist party with significant success at the polls gives reason to hope."[37] That was then.

Analyses of German public opinion need frequent updating, particularly when examining the rise of right-wing populism. The decibel level of far-right populist critiques of Merkel becomes shriller in response to the visibility of her decisions. Projecting parenthood onto political decisions that are perceived to originate in humanitarian feelings seems exclusive to the critics of female leaders. When President Barack Obama advocated for immigration reform, no one was tempted to dub him "Papa Obama." But in the case of Merkel, the human has been subsumed into the category of the maternal. However, the impulse to maternalize Merkel is not confined to the self-credentializing far right. *Newsweek*, too, attaches the label to suggest a necessary and naturalized relationship between the highly controversial acceptance of Syrian refugees and the mantle of motherhood. The hyper-masculinity of the far right and proponents of Islamophobia, such as PEGIDA practitioners, creates a gendered opposition to tip the balance against a female leader. In Freud's essay on negation, intergenerational gender politics revolve around the form and content of a therapeutic dialogue between patient and male analyst. "'Die Mutter ist es *nicht'*" (It is not the mother).[38] The insistent negation serves to determine the source of the patient's neurosis: his female parent. This utterance ultimately confirms Freud's knowledge that the core of the problem is indeed the mother. Freudian theory may seem an imperfect tool, but the process of negation that exposes the overdetermined maternalizaton of all personal and public malaise disassembles the mythopoeic narrative subtext of the far right's project and platform of anti-politics, which metamorphose the rape of Europa into the end of the European Union.

Notes

[1] Steven Erlanger, "At E.U. Meeting, a Hobbled Merkel and a Stalled Agenda," *New York Times*, December 15, 2017, https://www.nytimes.com/2017/12/15/world/europe/eu-angela-merkel-emmanuel-macron.html?rref=collection%2Ftimestopic%2FMerkel%2C%20Angela&action=click&contentCollection=timestopics&region=stream&module=stream_unit&version=latest&contentPlacement=6&pgtype=collection.

[2] Jennifer A. Yoder, "Angela Merkel's Discourse about the Past: Implications for the Construction of Collective Memory in Germany," *Memory Studies* (August 2017): 1–17. http://journals.sagepub.com/doi/abs/10.1177/1750698017727807.

[3] See for example Louise K. Davidson-Schmich, ed., *German Politics* 20, no. 3 (September 2011). This special issue provides both a cogent overview and in-depth case studies of Merkel's chancellorship through a lens of gender and intersectionality. Davidson-Schmich, along with other contributors, acknowledges the impact and influence of Merkel's origins; she is a Protestant and trained scientist who grew up in the former German Democratic Republic. The volume focuses on Merkel's first term in office.

[4] Joyce Marie Mushaben, *Becoming Madam Chancellor: Angela Merkel and the Berlin Republic* (Cambridge: Cambridge University Press, 2017). Further references to this work are given in the text using the short title *Becoming Madam Chancellor*.

[5] See also Joyce Marie Mushaben, "Women Leaders in Troubled Times: The Leadership Styles of Angela Merkel and Hillary Clinton," chapter 16 in this volume.

[6] Dorothee Beck, "Change, Persistence, and Contradiction: The Representation of Female Political Leadership in Gendered Media," chapter 13 in this volume.

[7] See also Mushaben, *Becoming Madam Chancellor*, 70.

[8] James Traub, "Angela Merkel's Great Escape," *Foreign Policy* (September 2017): 2. http://foreignpolicy.com/2017/09/21/angela-merkels-great-escape/#.

[9] Louise K. Davidson-Schmich, "Gender, Intersectionality, and the Executive Branch: The Case of Angela Merkel," *German Politics* 20, no. 3 (September 2011): 325–41, here 325.

[10] Thomas B. Edsall, "The End of the Left and the Right as We Knew Them," *New York Times*, June 22, 2017, https://www.nytimes.com/2017/06/22/opinion/nationalism-globalism-edsall.html. See also Paul W. James, *Globalism, Nationalism, Tribalism: Bringing Theory Back In* (London: Sage, 2006), for a reading of the tensions and historical framework of these forces.

[11] This expression characterizes the self-definition of voters not only in Germany but in the United States as well. See Arlie Russell Hochschild, *Strangers in Their*

Own Land: Anger and Mourning on the American Right (New York: New Press, 2016). From the perspective of a sociologist of emotions, Hochschild's work examines, not without empathy, the factors that influence seemingly contradictory support for Trump in Louisiana. The politics of emotion certainly play a role in the voting patterns of the German far right.

[12] European Institute for Gender Equity (EIGE), accessed June 8, 2018, http://eige.europa.eu/gender-mainstreaming/what-is-gender-mainstreaming. See also Mushaben, *Becoming Madam Chancellor*, 70.

[13] Paul de Man, "The Resistance to Theory," in *The Resistance to Theory* (Minneapolis: University of Minnesota Press, 1986), 3–20, here 5.

[14] "Delegierter greift Merkel an—'machtgeil und unpatriotisch.'" *Die Welt*, November 25, 2017, https://www.welt.de/politik/deutschland/article170960258/Delegierter-greift-Merkel-an-machtgeil-und-unpatriotisch.html.

[15] Simone Rafael, "Die Mitte und der 'Genderwahn,'" in *Wut, Verachtung, Abwertung: Rechtspopulismus in Deutschland*, ed. Andreas Zick and Beate Küpper (Bonn: Dietz, 2015), 78–94, here 94.

[16] "Positionspapier der PEGIDA," Menschen in Dresden website, accessed April 9, 2019, https://www.facebook.com/pegidaevofficial/.

[17] Rafael, "Die Mitte und der 'Genderwahn,'" 78.

[18] PEGIDA Facebook page, accessed January 3, 2017, https://www.facebook.com/pg/pegidaevofficial/notes/?ref=page_internal.

[19] PEGIDA Facebook page, accessed January 3, 2017, https://www.facebook.com/pg/pegidaevofficial/notes/?ref=page_internal.

[20] Mariam Lau, "Ellen Kositza: 'Nebenbei: knallrechts,'" *Zeit Online*, January 30, 2018. She writes: "Sieht so ein nationalistischer Feminismus aus?" (Is this what nationalist feminism looks like?).

[21] Ellen Kositza, *Gender ohne Ende* (Schnellroda: Edition Antaios, 2008), 54–55.

[22] "Europe's far right blames migration crisis for Paris attacks," *Deutsche Welle*, November 17, 2015. Björn Höcke, in a political address uploaded to his Facebook page, July 2015, asserts: "Terroristische Schläfer in Thüringen. Das ist die Realität im Jahre 2015" (Terrorist sleeper cells in Thuringia. That is the reality in the year 2015). https://www.facebook.com/Bjoern.Hoecke.AfD/videos/1589628774611736/, page no longer available.

[23] Angelika von Wahl, "A 'Women's Revolution from Above'? Female Leadership, Intersectionality, and Public Policy under the Merkel Government," *German Politics* 20, no. 3 (2011): 392–409, here 405.

[24] Von Wahl, "A 'Women's Revolution,'" 405.

[25] Kositza, *Gender ohne Ende*, esp. 35, 53–62, and 75. It should be noted that Kositza is essentially self-published.

[26] On "self-credentializing" Internet use by Aleksandr Dugin and Kevin MacDonald, see Alexandar Mihailovic, "Hijacking Authority: Academic Neo-Aryanism and Internet Expertise," in *Digital Media Strategies of the Far Right in Europe and the United States*, ed. Patricia Anne Simpson and Helga Druxes (Lanham, MD: Lexington Books, 2015), 83–102, esp. 84. There Mihailovic writes that

both neo-Aryanism and internet expertise "are intent upon the construction of self-validating scholarly subcultures that have a strong diegetic component with specific appeal to non-rationalist modes of discourse, while intersecting with larger communities of political action." These strategies, perhaps given the close association between German and Russian far-right proponents, overlap with those of PEGIDA, Quer-Denken's Vogt, and *Compact*'s Elsässer.

[27] Helga Druxes, "Manipulating the Media: The German New Right's Virtual and Violent Identities," in Simpson and Druxes, *Digital Media Strategies of the Far Right in Europe and the United States*, 123–39, here 125.

[28] Druxes, "Manipulating the Media," 125.

[29] Karl-Heinz Reuband, "Außenseiter oder Repräsentation der Mehrheit? Selbst- und Fremdwahrnehmung der Teilnehmer von PEGIDA-Kundgebungen," in *PEGIDA: Rechtspopulismus zwischen Fremdenangst und "Wende"-Enttäuschung: Analysen im Überblick*, ed. Karl-Siegbert Rehberg, Franziska Kunz, and Tino Schlinzig (Bielefeld: transcript Verlag, 2016), 165–87, here 170: "Je abweichender die Position, die man in der Gesellschaft kraft Zugehörigkeit und Verhalten einnimmt und je größer das Risiko, desto größer der Männeranteil" (the more divergent the position that you assume in society according to membership and behavior and the greater the risk, the greater the proportion of men).

[30] Helga Druxes, "'MONTAG IST WIEDER PEGIDA-TAG!' Pegida's Community Building and Discursive Strategies," *German Politics and Society* 34, no. 4 (Winter 2016): 17–33, here 23.

[31] In 1989 *Time* named Corazon Aquino, first female president of the Philippines, person of the year. See Radhika Jones, "Here's Why It's Been 29 Years Since a Woman Was Person of the Year," *Time*, December 9, 2015, http://time.com/4141766/time-person-of-the-year-angela-merkel-women/.

[32] Nancy Gibbs, "Chancellor of the Free World," *Time* online (December 2016); available at http://time.com/time-person-of-the-year-2015-angela-merkel-choice/?iid=toc, accessed October 22, 2016.

[33] Quoted in Kate Connolly, "Angela Merkel Comforts Sobbing Refugee but Says Germany Can't Help Everyone," *Guardian*, July 16, 2015, https://www.theguardian.com/world/2015/jul/16/angela-merkel-comforts-teenage-palestinian-asylum-seeker-germany. See also Mushaben, *Becoming Madam Chancellor*, 279.

[34] Foremost among the critical voices is Jürgen Elsässer in his magazine *Compact*.

[35] Margarete Stokowski, *Untenrum frei* (Reinbek bei Hamburg: Rowohlt, 2016), 76.

[36] Martina Wasmer, "Public Debates and Public Opinion on Multiculturalism in Germany," in *Challenging Multiculturalism: European Models of Diversity*, ed. Raymond Taras (Edinburgh: Edinburgh University Press, 2013), 163–89, here 163.

[37] Wasmer, "Public Debates," 184.

[38] Sigmund Freud, "Die Verneinung," accessed June 8, 2018, http://gutenberg.spiegel.de/buch/die-verneinung-915/1. The essay, originally published in 1925, focuses on the content of the utterance, rather than its form.

16: Women Leaders in Troubled Times: The Leadership Styles of Angela Merkel and Hillary Clinton

Joyce Marie Mushaben

> *Man is the hidden reference in language and culture;*
> *women can only aspire to be as good as a man;*
> *there is no point in trying to be as good as a woman.*
>
> —Dale Spender (1984)[1]

OVER THE LAST THREE DECADES scholars have generated a plethora of organizational studies, laboratory experiments, public-opinion polls, and even mega-analyses trying to determine whether or not women and men "lead differently." Because men have dominated most public domains for centuries, it is understandable that citizens worldwide have a tendency to view "exercising leadership" as something inherently male, as something men can and should do. Elites and followers likewise conflate the ways in which men *behave* with what really "works" when it comes to serving as a leader.

Most broad empirical studies regarding leadership stem from the business administration and organizational psychology domains, given the ability of those scholars to draw on the large populations needed to ensure a "representative" sample—even if women are only minimally present at higher managerial levels.[2] According to various mega-studies, most of the empirically tested gender differences turn out to be quite small, or not even statistically significant. As Alice H. Eagly and Mary C. Johannesen-Schmidt stress, however, "small differences, when repeated over individuals and occasions, can produce large consequences."[3] Ironically, participants are more inclined to assign stereotypical gender traits and role expectations to male and female leaders in experimental or laboratory settings than do raters or subordinates in real-world, organization-specific studies. Sex differences tend to disappear when men and women occupy the same positions and are charged with managing concrete tasks, allowing researchers to control for differences that usually stem from the societal context, institutional imperatives, or special situational factors.

We need not dwell for long on the stereotypical traits and behaviors attributed to women and men across regional and national boundaries, assessed by way of various "inventories" and "scales."[4] We are all familiar with the characterizations of women as accommodating, community-minded, cooperative, demure, emotional, gentle, helpful, kind, nurturing, participatory, quiet, relationship-oriented, risk-averse, sensitive, subordinate, supportive, sympathetic, and warm—although none of these traits seemed to apply to the (first) Iron Lady, Margaret Thatcher, for instance. Men are described as aggressive, ambitious, assertive, competitive, controlling, daring, dominant, forceful, independent, loud, rational, rule-oriented, and self-confident—many traits that do appear to describe Donald Trump. Unfortunately, focusing on "traits" often impels researchers to conflate personality and style with qualifications and substance.[5] "Projecting gravitas" is a far cry from being able to marshal controversial policies through complex legislative processes, no matter how essential they may be to the national interest.[6] Very few of the studies assessing *descriptive* versus *substantive representation*, generated by a rapidly expanding feminist-theoretical complex, offer detailed treatments of women's real-world performance as leaders across multiple terms in office, if only because there have been so few of them.

Historically rooted gender stereotypes nonetheless shape the ways in which voters and pundits *perceive* individual women who are lucky or privileged enough to secure powerful positions in business or government. Stereotyping can and does produce its own institutional, social, and economic realities.[7] Female leaders often find themselves wedged between the proverbial rock and hard place. Across the 1970s, 1980s and 1990s, women who conformed to ascribed gender profiles (or even "looked feminine") were judged incapable of meeting the rigors and requirements associated with a particular office: how could a caring mother participate in parliamentary debates lasting until 2 a.m., or fly off to a three-day global summit? The Green *Feminat* of the 1980s proved that an all-woman executive could accomplish all its tasks during normal working hours ("9 to 5"); one could ask, why do men need longer to accomplish the same things?[8] Or does the United States Congress vote on its own salary increases well after midnight in the hope that hardworking taxpayers will not notice that their own real wages, by contrast, have been declining in value since the 1960s?

Alternatively, if women did engage in male-normed behaviors by acting in strong, assertive, and decisive ways, it was construed as proof that they were neglecting or violating their natural (or "god-given") roles, for which they would also be negatively sanctioned.[9] Less than ten years ago German critics from the Right and the Left claimed that Angela Merkel, a childless female chancellor (publicly admonished by Gerhard Schröder's *fourth* wife) was incapable of producing good family policies. First Lady

Hillary Clinton was likewise pilloried for trying to introduce a national health-care system in 1993, rather than "just staying home to bake cookies."[10] Men enjoy access to a much wider range of "gender-appropriate" behaviors. Even when women make equivalent investments in their own human capital, they still derive substantially smaller gains, as our ongoing debates over pay inequality prove. It takes a lot more than a Harvard degree and a bit of "leaning in" to rise to the top: while the number of female Harvard MBAs has risen from eight out of 684 in 1965 (just over 1 percent), to 25 percent in 1985, to 40 percent among the 2014 graduates, Wall Street remains a male bastion.[11]

Ironically, women can also benefit from such stereotypes: they may be perceived as *more* effective, either because their evaluators did not expect much from them in the first place, or because they had to meet higher standards initially in order to secure managerial jobs, then have to continue outperforming others on a daily basis just to keep their positions.[12] If women do not exhibit the "same" leadership skills as men, it is probably because they faced subtle, or not-so-subtle, forms of discrimination all the way up the career ladder. Existing training, recruitment, and promotion regimes have long denied women access to mentors, internships, contracts, bonuses, and corner offices with a view. Recognizing the value of symbolic politics, First Lady Hillary Clinton immediately found herself a basement office in the West Wing, realizing that a nicer place in the East Wing would exclude her from the "inner circle" of presidential advisors. Rather than assuming that each sex is ordained by nature to fulfill certain roles, perhaps we can learn from the globalizing LGBT** movement that few, if any human behaviors are genetically anchored in either an XX or an XY chromosome set.

In order to assess the effectiveness of women as policy makers, we need to generate many more detailed studies as to *how* they lead, the purpose of qualitative case studies. A few years ago I undertook a comparison of the leadership styles evinced by Kurt Georg Kiesinger and Angela Merkel, both of whom headed Grand Coalitions in postwar Germany. I attributed significant overlaps in their respective political styles and decision-making modes to the special institutional imperatives imposed by (what used to be) an exceptional set of party-political constraints. To the extent that "gender mattered," it was the forceful Minister-President from Baden-Württemberg who had to adapt his behavior to manage the strong personalities from opposing parties comprising his national cabinet. Kiesinger displayed allegedly female leadership skills between 1966 and 1969, combining "mediating," "listening" and other "informal" management techniques.[13] Ironically, my article was rejected by two oft cited US-feminist journals: one reviewer specifically objected because I had not presented a "counter-factual" case, impossible to do with a statistical sample consisting of only two Grand Coalition leaders separated by four decades.

The study I present here is also statistically "unrepresentative" by definition. My reflections involve two women—one a veteran federal chancellor, the other a former secretary of state and US presidential candidate—and their respective approaches to leadership. Angela Merkel and Hillary Rodham Clinton are both unique in terms of their personal paths to power, yet both had to reinvent themselves in pursuit of national office. I would argue further that both learned a lot by observing each other over a ten-year period, if only from a diplomatic distance. I first consider their willingness (or lack thereof) to "play the gender card" during their earlier campaigns. Next I address their respective tendencies to pursue a "transformational" model of leadership, and follow this with a brief analysis of their substantive overlaps with regard to one traditionally male-normed issue arena: foreign and security policy.

"To Play or Not to Play, That Is the Question": The Gender Card

Although she was not the first woman to seek the Democratic presidential nomination in US history, Pat Schroeder was the first to be scrutinized morning, noon, and night by the male-dominated media, looking for something else to sensationalize once they caught the leading contender, Gary Hart, having an extramarital affair. When asked point blank by one reporter, "Are you running as a woman?," Schroeder responded: "Do I have a choice?"[14]

Once it became clear that Angela Merkel would serve as the 2005 CDU chancellor candidate, she was immediately subjected to a physical makeover, having been mocked for years regarding her hair, her clothes, and her so-called "Jesus sandals."[15] She had already declared during her years as Helmut Kohl's Minister of Women and Youth (1991–94) that she did not identify with "feminism"; it was therefore not surprising that she assiduously avoided discussions of so-called women's issues during her first campaign. Shortly after she was elected, *Die Zeit* featured a front-page photo of her walking across a stage at a party gathering, to be introduced by an earlier rival for power, Edmund Stoiber. The fact that she appeared in a black pantsuit led me to comment at a German Studies Association conference one week later that conservative hardliners had probably rallied to support Merkel because they were able to imagine her as "an honorary man," that is, as a temporary CDU placeholder, until they could find a *real man* to replace all of the "Andes Pact" rivals she had already knocked out of the picture.[16]

It is worth recalling that the first time Lenelotte von Bothmer (SPD, mother of six) addressed her fellow Bundestag members wearing a pant-suit on October 14, 1970, the *BILD Zeitung* featured her on page one with the headline, "No way, Madam Representative." The *Hannoversche Alllgemeine* headline proclaimed, "You are a dishonorable dame" (Sie sind ein würdeloses Weib).[17] The seventeen men from Bavaria who showed up in "greasy" *Lederhosen* in 1949 did not make the headlines, although men would eventually be ordered to wear belts in place of sus-penders in the 1950s. Die *Macht der Hosenanzüge* (the power of pant-suits, a term used by *Der Spiegel*) would acquire new political weight by the late 1990s. The chancellor kept the makeup and the hairdo, but she has been beleaguered in recent years by running commentaries on her modestly priced but very colorful blazer collection.[18] While subsequent reports on high-level meetings between the FRG chancellor and US Secretary of State Hillary Clinton stressed their necklaces, black slacks, practical shoes, and compatible colors ("Merkel in lilac, Hillary in corn-flower-blue"), their descriptions of each other emphasize intelligence, determination, and honesty.[19]

Having consciously refused to play the gender card the first time around, it was natural that Merkel's second election campaign was also devoid of references to "women's" issues. Her most effective campaign poster in 2009 nonetheless consisted of a larger-than-life image of a smiling chancellor, underscored with the motto, *Wir haben die Kraft* (We have the strength). One could read the "we" to mean not the party in general but rather the CDU women in particular, such as Ursula von der Leyen, Annette Schavan, Beate Baumann, Hildegard Müller, and Maria Böhmer. Since 2005 Angela Merkel has been named "the World's Most Powerful Woman" eleven times over; although she only came in fourth in 2010 (behind Michele Obama, business executive Irene Rosenfeld, and celebrity Oprah Winfrey), she continues to hold the global record for this title. Merkel still publicly eschews the feminist label, yet she has already done more to directly advance the equality of German women and men than all her predecessors combined.[20] She has impelled lawmakers to introduce guaranteed infant and child care, pater-nal leave, and corporate quotas, funded special programs for women in STEM (known in Germany as MINT) fields,[21] and even appointed the nation's first female defense minister, Ursula von der Leyen, the mother of seven children. In addition to drawing on her socialization under an East German gender regime that took female labor market participa-tion for granted, she has effectively leveraged EU mandates, a looming demographic deficit, and the support of powerful female media moguls. The women who advise her are collectively derided as Girls' Camp, although her inner circle also includes discreet men.

Lacking the political capital that her German counterpart had accrued as CDU General Secretary, as *Fraktionsführerin* (parliamentary caucus leader) and opposition leader, yet openly proud of her feminist credentials, Hillary Rodham Clinton was forced to walk a very different gender tightrope during her first run for the US presidency. For starters, her decision to "stand by her man" during husband Bill's impeachment proceedings (over the Monica Lewinski scandal and Paula Jones's harassment claims) angered many would-be feminist supporters. Although finally having a woman in charge of the White House would have rendered her, literally, the embodiment of progressive political change, Clinton unexpectedly found herself competing against a charismatic black male candidate—a former "caring" community organizer named Barack Obama—in wooing antiestablishment voters. She had to simultaneously underscore her rational-choice "experience" as a world-traveling First Lady and as a tough-on-defense Senator from New York in an effort to win over moderates and less "hawkish" independents. Opting *not* to play the gender card in 2008 did not spare Clinton some very hostile, degrading, and outright misogynistic media treatments: one McCain supporter yelled out "Kill the bitch" at a campaign rally, but the Republican candidate merely chuckled. Had equivalent racial slurs been used against Obama, we would have witnessed massive public outrage and multiple libel lawsuits against the Fox TV channel and various talk-show radio hosts.[22] Instead, the Supreme Court's 2010 *Citizens United* verdict (involving a privately funded video personally vilifying Hillary) virtually eliminated fact-checking, candidate-responsibility, and limits on secret campaign financing, which subsequently rendered the 2016 Clinton-Trump presidential campaign one of the dirtiest ever.

Having added four years of foreign experience as secretary of state in the first Obama cabinet, Hillary Clinton transcended two of those earlier hurdles, only to face a new world of hateful social-media pundits and "know-nothing" voters, who were egged on by an openly misogynist, antiestablishment contender rejected by many elites *within* the Republican party itself. Donald Trump publicly excoriated Clinton for "playing the gender card," but rather than ask "do I have a choice?," Hillary built her campaign on commitments to women, families, equal opportunity for minorities, and shoring up an eroding middle class. The strongest attacks on her "ties" to Wall Street, defense-hawks, and other establishment forces were launched, paradoxically, by a 74-year-old white male socialist running as a Democrat who opposed gun registration and had first been sent to Congress by the tiny rural state of Vermont twenty-six years earlier: Bernie Sanders.

Gender and Style: Transformational versus Transactional Leadership

Perhaps because we still constitute an underrepresented group in the real world of politics, finance, academia, and defense, women of my generation have spent a lot of time "theorizing" about power, and what we would do with it, should we ever reach a state of gender parity. Based on current projections, US females will not occupy an equitable number of seats in Congress until 2121, despite accounting for 51 percent of 321 million citizens.[23] Time and space constraints preclude an extensive review of the literature describing the male-normed nature of most political, religious, financial, and scientific institutions, no matter what country or region we consider.[24] It is only fair to note that the dominant paradigms describing the leadership styles of men and women arose prior to our scholarly "discovery" of *intersectionality*. It is easy to grasp that women and men differ in many ways, even if we cannot agree on the relative impact of nature versus nurture, but we still have trouble finding balanced male/female leadership samples large enough to ensure "methodologically robust" analysis. The concept of *intersectionality* reminds us that differences *among* women, rooted in race/ethnicity, class, age, religion, or sexual orientation may be just as significant as those between the sexes. Men, too, have "gender," overlapping with other sources of human diversity, but one does not find many mainstream political scientists researching male differences.

Americans find it easy to label someone a "real leader," while Germans rarely stress qualities inhering in a single person. As a result of historical experiences, the latter avoid using the term *Führer*; modern political discourse focuses on power (*Macht*), competencies, and party goals rather than on personal agendas or "visions." Max Weber identified three sources of *legitimate rule*—rooted in charismatic, traditional, and legal (rational) authority, respectively, but the German sociologist's classic, qualitative reflections would not be judged empirically or methodologically rigorous enough in the fields that generate most of today's "leadership" literature.[25] The limited publications found on this subject in Germany tend to draw on English-language sources, although the structural constraints imposed by that country's federalized parliamentary system differ significantly from both the US separation of powers, and the anti-regulation orientation shaping management practices among American businesses. Conventional wisdom offers two ideal types that conveniently align with the traits, roles, and behaviors stereotypically attributed to men and women who exercise power.

The male-normed version, *transactional leadership*, foresees a leader who "rewards or disciplines followers with regards to performance." This type stresses (presumably consistent) performance standards, designated assignments and task-specific goals, along with a tendency "to focus on task completion and employee compliance." The effective manager is expected to depend "quite heavily on organizational rewards and punishments to influence employee performance."[26] The general style is that of "command and control," which relies on hierarchical structures, organizational loyalty, narrowly delineated objectives, clear lines of authority (suggesting accountability), and a hands-off approach ("long periods" of non-involvement), until a crisis triggers some kind of heroic, personalized decision-making (*Chef-Sache*, a matter for the boss).

Modern studies suggest that male managers pay close attention to employees' mistakes but evince little concern for personal circumstances or workplace conditions (for example, sexual harassment) that might hinder their effective performance. The tendency to focus on "the bottom line," at the expense of monitoring, providing feedback, or communicating with lower-level employees, goes a long way in explaining the collapse of the subprime housing market and the "toxic asset" meltdown that hit the banking sector in 2008. Should anyone ask me to identify a modern manager who seems to embody this transactional leadership caricature, I would immediately respond, Donald Trump, with his signature reality-TV line: "You're fired."

Generically, if not genetically ascribed to women, *transformational leadership* "occurs when the leader stimulates the interest among colleagues and followers to view their work from a new perspective."[27] This type of individual "generates an awareness of the mission or vision of the organization, and develops colleagues and followers to higher levels of ability and potential . . . to look beyond their own interests toward interests that will benefit the group."[28] Instead of drawing clear lines between superiors and subordinates, this leader cultivates stakeholders by displaying empathy and fostering a participatory environment ("team-work") to garner trust and respect. Commands are replaced by discussion and "plain speaking," control yields to partnership, and authority defined in terms of rungs on a power-ladder matters less than shared principles and pragmatism.

Emotional intelligence is another quintessential trait: "the ability to monitor one's own and others' feelings and emotions, to discriminate among them and to use this information to guide one's own thinking and actions."[29] Far from being "touchy-feely," emotional intelligence rests on self-control, self-confidence, the ability to handle conflict, and tolerance for stress.[30] In a rapidly changing global environment, "IQ and technical skills are probably baseline requirements for executive roles, but without emotional intelligence the best-trained manager won't make a great leader."[31] Recent studies suggest that even in the corporate world, boards with growing numbers of women are not only better at managing change but are also proving to be more "profitable."[32]

Angela Merkel's calm demeanor and principled responses to the Fukushima meltdown, the Euro-crisis, Putin's annexation of the Crimea, and the refugee crisis lead me to classify her as a transformational leader. While the pundits routinely described Hillary as cold, impersonal, and emotionally detached, she was usually being measured against the histrionics of Trump, "unfiltered" talk-show hosts, and a media landscape that is still very male-dominated, male-normed, and male-owned. The people who work with these women describe both of them as thick-skinned, humorous, and quite "personable."

Leadership Substance: Playing Bridge instead of Poker

Although Merkel and Clinton were exposed to diametrically opposed political systems and gender regimes during their formative years, these two women not only overlap with regard to their contemporary fashion preferences (pantsuits!) and leadership styles.[33] They also tend to overlap in terms of their approaches to foreign and defense policy, two governance structures that have displayed little historical tolerance for cracks in their respective glass ceilings. In this case, I argue that Merkel was able to follow a trajectory established by Adenauer in the wake of Nazi atrocities and unconditional surrender, in an effort to re-embed Germany in a peaceful, democratic community of nations. Clinton, by contrast, came to embrace new "national security" content by way of international learning experiences to which she was initially exposed as a "powerless" First Lady, followed by her eight years as a US senator. While the chancellor has continued to build on the German tradition now known as "civilian power," the former secretary of state put a good deal of effort into cultivating what she calls "smart power."

During her four terms as chancellor, Angela Merkel sought to balance an unwavering commitment to the Atlantic Alliance with a *Realpolitik*-effort to keep Russia engaged in international dialogue, ever since she delivered her first speech at the Munich Security Conference in 2003. Hanns Maull was among the first to use the term *civilian power* in specifying the long-standing parameters of FRG foreign and security policy, beginning with a recognition of its special historical responsibility for advancing European integration.[34] The German approach to foreign-policy making is primarily normative, emphasizing peace, freedom, democracy, justice, the rule of law (national and international), and human rights. Despite a greater willingness to reference "national interests" since unification, Merkel has adhered to multilateralism, cooperation, and a preference for action via international institutions. She shares a broader historical skepticism regarding the utility of military force that nonetheless accepts the centrality of NATO and the complementary role of the EU's Common Foreign, Security and Defense Policy. Her embrace of the FRG's "culture of restraint" has not precluded a willingness to deploy the Bundeswehr abroad, particularly in response to humanitarian crises.

Merkel recognized further that, given its restored sovereignty, unified Germany would have to assume greater international responsibility—for example, in the global war on terrorism. That has not prevented her, or her cabinet members, from regularly referring to her country's limited financial resources. She has displayed an inordinate amount of emotional intelligence and self-confidence, and has demonstrated a high level of tolerance for conflict and stress meted out by members of her own party, as well as by the CSU. Having digested Russian economist Nikolai Kondriatiev's lessons regarding long-term waves and super-cycles, Merkel rarely responds spontaneously or aggressively to a crisis, preferring bridge-building and the politics of small steps.[35] While she played to "national interests" in relation to the Euro-crisis, her stance on the subsequent refugee crisis can be construed as "leading by example." But even the decision to suspend the EU Dublin accords and open Germany to 1.3 million refugees in 2015 had its roots in her reflections on thirty-five years of GDR life, devoid of human rights, coupled with concerns over a future demographic deficit.

Clinton voted in favor of George W. Bush's disastrous war in Iraq and displayed certain hawkish tendencies while serving on the Senate Armed Services Committee; influenced, perhaps, by her husband's inaction regarding Rwanda but subsequent use of NATO firepower to stop "ethnic cleansing" in Kosovo, she was not inclined to "shoot first, ask questions later." By contrast, Trump's aggressive rhetoric against North Korea and Iran suggests that he would "bomb first" and then ignore the questions. During her 2009 State Department confirmation hearings, Clinton quoted the Roman poet Publius Terentius (known as Terence), who began life as a slave but later became a well-loved playwright: "In every endeavor the seemly course for wise men is to try persuasion first." She added: "The same truth binds wise women as well."[36]

In a 2014 interview, and later in a book describing her global encounters as America's top diplomat, Clinton defined *smart power* as "another way of talking about American engagement, other than unilateralism and the so-called boots on the ground."[37] The Bush administration saw saber-rattling and military might as the primary tool for addressing conflict abroad, having largely ignored the terrorist threat prior to 9/11 (a transactional trait). Like Putin's quick seizure of the Crimea, Bush's lightning strikes on Afghanistan and Iraq were equivalent to a game of high-stakes poker, with little reflection on what might follow. Obama's tendency to wait *too long* (also transactional) to assist Syrian rebels, however, may have allowed ISIS to gather momentum—and high-powered weapons of its own.[38]

The First Lady's travels following the 1995 UN Beijing Conference ("women's rights are human rights, and human rights are women's rights") triggered her gradual embrace of a normative, holistic orientation rarely seen among her predecessors. Like Merkel (whom she first met in 1994), Clinton generally preferred pragmatic over ideological options in selecting "the right combination of tools" tailored to each situation. As she opined in relation to her *Hard Choices*:

> Beyond the traditional work of negotiating treaties and attending diplomatic conferences, we had to—among other tasks—engage activists on social media, help determine energy pipeline routes, limit carbon emissions, encourage marginalized groups to participate in politics, stand up for universal human rights, and defend common economic rules of the road. Our ability to do these things would be crucial measures of our national power.[39]

Exposed to the Pentagon's Quadrennial Reviews through her work on the Senate Armed Services Committee, Madam Secretary institutionalized the Quadrennial Diplomacy and Development Review for the State Department, to map out concrete steps for turning smart power into "twenty-first-century statecraft" practice, by "harnessing new technologies, public-private partnerships, diaspora networks, and other new tools . . . [to carry] us into fields beyond traditional diplomacy, especially energy and economics."[40] As one advisor observed, that may sound "like a bunch of bureaucratic mumbo jumbo," but for a ministerial domain long recognized as "an organization that's risk adverse and conservative, [with] a culture that doesn't reward planning and discourages change, this kind of coordination and strategizing [was] monumental."[41] The Trump administration subsequently gutted these reforms, by refusing to fill roughly 30 percent of all prior positions at the State Department and eliminating all of Clinton's global "gender equality" initiatives.

Conclusion: Leadership and the Race to the Future

Although she opposed quotas in the 1990s and avoided the "gender card" during her first two campaigns, Merkel began admitting during her third term that she had experienced disadvantages as a woman in politics. In addition to revealing a few "personal things" in her 2013 public-forum interview with *Brigitte Magazine* moderators, she subsequently introduced policies that have already helped to level the playing field for women across significant domains (for example, in corporations, STEM fields, and the military). Mocked again for refusing to label herself a feminist at the women's summit she hosted while presiding over the 2017 G-20 meeting in Berlin, Merkel nonetheless became the first world leader to incorporate the concluding Communiqué of the "W20-Dialog Process" into the official G20 Final Communiqué, based on a wide array of UN, OECD (Organisation for Economic Co-operation and Development), ILO (International Labour Organization, IMF (International Money Fund), and World Bank statistical reports. She moreover called for the "mainstreaming" of W20 initiatives into ongoing G20 negotiation tracks and "Sherpa meetings."[42]

As described by Valerie Hudson and Patricia Leidl, Hillary Clinton quickly came to see women's rights as germane to US national security, requiring a multifaceted, multilateral approach.[43] The Hillary Doctrine holds: "Women's equality is not just a moral issue, it's not just a humanitarian issue, it's not just a fairness issue. It is a security issue, it is a prosperity issue, and it is a peace issue." Clinton declared further that "the subjugation of women is a direct threat to the common security of the world and to the national security of [the United States]"—a position completely discounted by the two Trump appointees who have thus far replaced her at the State Department.[44]

UN Security Council Resolution 1325, unanimously adopted in 2000, also recognized that "a democracy without the full participation of women is a contradiction in terms."[45] This did not stop the old guard from complaining that "Clinton was devaluing the office of secretary of state by meeting with so many, well, women."[46] Charles Bowdon went so far as to ask: "Isn't focusing on women just like putting a gas mask on the canary, when you really should be fixing the coal mine?" Constituting 51 percent of the world's population, women are hardly equivalent to a single canary; as Hudson and Leidl note, gender relations *are* the coal mine![47] Countries in which women possess few rights, which also are marked by high levels of gender-based violence, are the most inclined to engage in sectarian strife and hybrid warfare. As Dale Spender elaborates further:

> Feminism has fought no wars. It has killed no opponents. It has set up no concentration camps, starved no enemies, practiced no cruelties. Its battles have been for education, for the vote, for better working conditions, for safety in the streets, for child care, for social welfare, for rape crisis centers, for women's refuges, reforms in the law. If someone says, "oh, I'm not a feminist," I ask, "Why? What's your problem?"[48]

Since the 1980s the European Union has come to adopt a system of decision-making that entails a "pooling of sovereignty." In short, a distinctive mode of supranational authority that feminists would characterize as "power with" has replaced the conventional, male-normed mode of decision-making involving "power over."[49] The latter was defined by Max Weber (then borrowed by Robert Dahl), as "A's ability to make B do what B would not necessarily do." Efforts to return to intergovernmentalism, or in the UK case, "national sovereignty" by way of the Brexit vote, will do little to resolve complex, border-transcending problems such as migration, terrorism, and climate change. The old motivational tools invoked by "transactional" leaders are also losing their mystical powers and effectiveness, as Trump's failed efforts to impose all of his legislative preferences on a Republican-dominated Congress showed through 2018; his use of "firepower" vis-à-vis his own Executive Office and cabinet appointees has only made the White House more dysfunctional.

"Command and control" mechanisms are being replaced by interactive, collaborative behaviors even in the corporate domain—for example, at Google and Microsoft. The "competition for the best brains" is rooted in a global economy that increasingly favors mental power over military might. As early as 2000, *Business Week* determined that "after years of analyzing what makes leaders most effective and figuring out who's got the Right Stuff, management gurus now know how to boost the odds of getting a great executive: Hire a female."[50] In other words: *Die Zukunft, auf gut deutsch gesagt, ist weiblich*—the future of leadership is female.[51]

Notes

[1] *Epigraph*: Dale Spender, *Time and Tide Wait for No Man* (London: Pandora, 1984), 201.

[2] For examples, see the classic, Rosabeth Moss Kantor, *Men and Women of the Corporation* (New York: Basic Books, 1977); also, Cristina Trinidad and Anthony H. Normore, "Leadership and Gender: A Dangerous Liaison?," *Leadership & Organization Development Journal* 26, no. 7 (2005): 574–90; Alice H. Eagly and Linda L. Carli, "The Female Leadership Advantage: An Evaluation of the Evidence," *Leadership Quarterly* 14 (2003): 807–34; Barbara Moran, "Gender Differences in Leadership," *Library Trends* 40, no. 3 (1992): 475–91; Sally A. Carless, "Gender Differences in Transformational Leadership: An Examination of Superior, Leader and Subordinate Perspectives," *Sex Roles* 39, nos. 11/12 (1998): 887–902; Thomas W. Kent et al., "Gender Differences and Transformational Leadership Behavior: Do Both German Men and Women Lead in the Same Way?" *International Journal of Leadership Studies* 6, no. 1 (2010): 52–66; and Paul L. Koopman et al., "National Culture and Leadership Profiles in Europe: Some Results from the GLOBE Study," *European Journal of Work and Organizational Psychology* 8 no. 4 (1999): 503–20.

[3] Alice H. Eagly and Mary C. Johannesen-Schmidt, "The Leadership Styles of Women and Men," *Journal of Social Issues* 57, no. 4 (2001): 781–97, here 795.

[4] A few examples include the Multifactor Leadership Questionnaire; the Leadership Behavior Inventory; the Global Transformational Leadership Scale; the

Positive Organizational Behavior Model; and the Ethical Leadership Scale. For mega-study evidence, see Eagly and Carli, "The Female Advantage"; see also Koopman et al., "National Culture."

[5] European politicians usually work their way up the party ladder by concentrating on particular policy fields, in contrast to US politicians who use the "revolving door," entering politics as "business men," and later assuming positions as high-paid lobbyists.

[6] Citing one-time Democratic primary contender Patricia Schroeder, "And please call me Ms. President," *New York Times*, February 22, 1999, A17.

[7] Eagly and Carli, "The Female Leadership Advantage, 821.

[8] In 1984 six women, including Antje Vollmer (a single mother and Protestant pastor), were elected to head the Green Party executive board. See "Wir wollten nicht die Männer entmachten: die Grünen Christa Nickels, Antje Vollmer und Annemarie Borgmann über das neue Bonner Feminat," *Der Spiegel*, April 23, 1984.

[9] In the late 1800s Myra Bradwell (Illinois) was denied the right to practice law, while Virginia Happersett (Missouri) was denied the right to vote; in both cases, Supreme Court justices referred to sex roles ordained by God, thus violating the separation of Church and state foreseen by the First Amendment to the United States Constitution.

[10] "Gerhard Schröder und Doris Schröder-Köpf trennen sich," *Der Tagesspiegel*, March 27, 2015. Curiously, no one challenged her non-mother status when Kohl, heading a party that still adhered to *Kinder-Küche-Kirche* thinking, placed Merkel in charge of women and youth policies. Nor did anyone attack Chancellor Schröder, heading a Red-Green government, for refusing to expand child-care options, despite an existing EU mandate. The Clinton quote, which caused a stir among those favoring stay-at-home housewives, was reported in an *ABC Nightline* show, "Making Hillary an Issue," on March 26, 1992.

[11] Carmen Nobel, "HBS Cases: Women MBAs at Harvard Business School," *Working Knowledge* (HBS), March 6, 2013.

[12] The double standard is alive and well: men may still be judged effective even when they perform poorly. Major Wall Street firms continued to pay out multi-million dollar bonuses after the 2008 meltdown, "to keep the best people"—the same men who brought down the system in the first place!

[13] Joyce Marie Mushaben, "The Best of Times, the Worst of Times: Angela Merkel, the Grand Coalition and 'Majority Rule' in Germany," *German Politics* 34, no. 1 (2016): 1–25.

[14] "And please call me Ms. President," *New York Times*, February 22, 1999.

[15] Joyce Marie Mushaben, *Becoming Madam Chancellor: Angela Merkel and the Berlin Republic* (Cambridge: Cambridge University Press, 2017).

[16] Having imbibed a lot of Chevas Regal on a flight to Santiago, Chile, a group of young, aspiring CDU politicians agreed never to compete directly with each other for key party positions; they later ganged up against Merkel's first effort to become the chancellor candidate, but she managed to beat out all her rivals, one by one, by 2005.

[17] "Sie sind ein würdeloses Weib," *Hannoversche Allgemeine,* October 15, 1970.

[18] See Julia Schramm, *Fifty Shades of Merkel* (Hamburg: Hoffmann & Campe, 2016).

[19] See "Merkel und Clinton: Im Hosenanzug der Macht," *Der Spiegel* on-line, April 14, 2011.

[20] Joyce Marie Mushaben, "The Reluctant Feminist: Angela Merkel and Gender Equality Policy in Germany," *Femina Politica* 27, no. 2 (2018): 83–95.

[21] Science, technology, engineering, and mathematics.

[22] Susan J. Carroll, "Reflections on Gender and Hillary Clinton's Presidential Campaign: The Good, the Bad, and the Misogynic," *Politics & Gender* 5, no. 1 (2009): 1–20; also, http://signsjournal.org/ask-a-feminist-carroll-walters/.

[23] Institute for Women's Policy Research, *Women's Share of Seats in Congress, 1960–2013, with Projection for Political Parity in 2121* (Washington, DC, 2013).

[24] For evidence, see Koopman et al., "National Culture."

[25] Max Weber, "Die drei reinen Typen der legitimen Herrschaft," *Preussische Jahrbücher* 187, nos. 1–2 (1922).

[26] James Macgregor Burns, *Leadership* (New York: Harper & Row, 1978), cited in Barbara Mandell and Shilpa Pherwani, "Relationship between Emotional Intelligence and Transformational Leadership Style: A Gender Comparison," *Journal of Business and Psychology* 17, no. 3 (2003): 387–404, here 390.

[27] Burns, *Leadership,* cited in Mandell and Pherwani, "Relationship between Emotional Intelligence and Transformational Leadership Style," 390.

[28] Burns, *Leadership,* cited in Mandell and Pherwani, "Relationship between Emotional Intelligence and Transformational Leadership Style," 390.

[29] P. Salovey and J. D, Mayer, "Emotional Intelligence," *Imagination, Cognition and Personality* 9, no. 3 (1990): 185–211; here 189, cited in Mandell and Pherwani, "Relationship between Emotional Intelligence and Transformational Leadership Style," 390.

[30] Salovey and Mayer, "Emotional Intelligence," 189, cited in Mandell and Pherwani, "Relationship between Emotional Intelligence and Transformational Leadership Style," 391.

[31] Salovey and Mayer, "Emotional Intelligence," cited in Mandell and Pherwani, "Relationship between Emotional Intelligence and Transformational Leadership Style," 398.

[32] "Companies with More Women Board Directors Experience Higher Financial Performance, according to Latest Catalyst Bottom Line Report," *Catalyst.org,* January 15, 2004, http://www.catalyst.org/media/companies-more-women-board-directors-experience-higher-financial-performance-according-latest.

[33] Merkel presented Clinton with a framed copy of a *Frankfurter Allgemeine Zeitung,* showing them both in pantsuits (heads missing), with their hands in front (in the chancellor's now famous rectangular gesture, or *Raute*) asking readers to guess who was the real Merkel. The photo (#50) also appears in Clinton's book, *Hard Choices* (New York: Simon & Schuster, 2014).

34 See Sebastian Harnisch and Hanns W. Maull, eds., *Germany as a Civilian Power? The Foreign Policy of the Berlin Republic* (Manchester, UK: Manchester University Press, 2001).

35 Kondriatiev maintained that technological innovations resulted in K-waves, understood as 40–60 year cycles of high and low growth, a thesis that did not find favor with Stalin; he was sent to the gulag and executed in 1938.

36 Hillary Rodham Clinton, Senate Nomination Hearings, downloaded from www.state.gov, transcript from January 13, 2009.

37 Clinton, *Hard Choices*, 51.

38 Jeffrey Goldberg, "Hillary Clinton: 'Failure' to Help Syrian Rebels Led to the Rise of ISIS," *Atlantic*, August 10, 2014.

39 Clinton, *Hard Choices*, 33.

40 Clinton, Hard Choices, 551.

41 Aaron David Miller, cited in Adriene Klasa "Debating Hillary," *Foreign Policy*, June 20, 2012.

42 See "Women20 Germany 2017 Communiqué," April 26, 2017, http://www.w20-germany.org/fileadmin/user_upload/documents/W20_Communique_Final.pdf.

43 Valerie M. Hudson and Patricia Leidl, *The Hillary Doctrine: Sex and American Foreign Policy* (New York: Columbia University Press, 2015).

44 Hudson and Leidl, *The Hillary Doctrine*, xiv.

45 Hudson and Leidl, *The Hillary Doctrine*, 21.

46 Cited in Hudson and Leidl, *The Hillary Doctrine*, 59; see also Isobel Coleman, "A Powerful Voice for Women around the World," *New York Times*, May 12, 2013.

47 Hudson and Leidl, *The Hillary Doctrine*, 73.

48 Dale Spender, *Man Made Language* (London: Routledge & Kegan Paul, 1980).

49 See Gabriele Abels and Joyce Marie Mushaben, *Gendering the European Union: New Approaches to Old Democratic Deficits* (Basingstoke UK: Palgrave Macmillan, 2012).

50 Cited in Eagly and Johannesen-Schmidt, *Leadership Styles*, 795.

51 As in other European languages, German articles are curiously denoted by gender; *der*, *die* and *das* all translate into *the* for masculine, feminine, and neuter nouns, rendering this German phrase a play on words.

Bibliography

Abels, Gabriele, and Joyce Marie Mushaben. *Gendering the European Union: New Approaches to Old Democratic Deficits.* Basingstoke, UK: Palgrave Macmillan, 2012.

Absolu, Florence. *Les femmes politiques dans la presse: Mythèmes, biographèmes et archétype; Les représentations genrées de Ségolène Royal et Angela Merkel dans la presse française et allemande pendant leurs campagnes électorales / Politikerinnen in der Presse: Mytheme, Biographeme und Archetyp; Die gender-betonte Darstellung von Angela Merkel und Ségolène Royal in den deutschen und französischen Printmedien während ihrer Wahlkampagnen.* Würzburg: Königshausen & Neumann, 2014.

Ackerl, Isabella. "Lay Down Your Arms." *Austria Today* 3 (1993): 48–50.

Adam, Wolfgang. "Die Schweizer Reisen der Sophie von la Roche." In *Helvetien und Deutschland: Kulturelle Beziehungen zwischen der Schweiz und Deutschland in der Zeit von 1770–1830*, edited by Hellmut Thomke, Martin Bircher, and Wolfgang Proß, 33–56. Amsterdam: Rodopi, 1994.

Ade, Maren, dir. *Toni Erdmann.* Berlin: Komplizen Film, 2016.

Adichie, Chimamanda Ngozi. *We Should All Be Feminists.* New York: Anchor Books, 2012.

Adler, Friedrich, ed. *Briefwechsel mit August Bebel und Karl Kautsky.* Vienna: Wiener Volksbuchhandlung, 1954.

Ahmed, Sara. *Living a Feminist Life.* Durham, NC: Duke University Press, 2017.

Albisetti, James C. "Could Separate Be Equal? Helene Lange and Women's Education in Imperial Germany." *History of Education Quarterly* 22, no. 3 (1982): 301–17.

———. *Schooling German Girls and Women.* Princeton, NJ: Princeton University Press, 2014.

Allen, Ann Taylor. *Feminism and Motherhood in Germany, 1801–1914.* New Brunswick, NJ: Rutgers University Press, 1991.

———. *Feminism and Motherhood in Western Europe, 1890–1970.* New York: Palgrave, 2005.

———. "'The Future Is Ours': Feminists Imagine Europe in 1911." Contribution to the web feature "European History—Gender History." Accessed March 1, 2019. In *Themenportal Europäische Geschichte* (2009). http://www.europa.clio-online.de/2009/Article=415.

———. "Mothers of the New Generation: Adele Schreiber, Helene Stöcker, and the Evolution of a German Idea of Motherhood, 1900–1914." *Signs* 10, no. 3 (1985): 418–38.

———. "Spiritual Motherhood: German Feminists and the Kindergarten Movement, 1848–1911." *History of Education Quarterly* 22, no. 3 (1982): 319–39.

Alt, Peter André. "Maria Stuart: Geschichtliche Quellen und ihre Entstehung." In *Schiller: Leben—Werk—Zeit; Eine Biographie*, 2:492–509. Munich: Beck, 2000.

"Der alte Mann und das Mädchen." *Der Spiegel*, October 26, 1992.

Alvarado-Díaz, Alhelí de María. "Heroine of the Revolution." In *Rosa Remix*, edited by Stefanie Ehmsen and Albert Scharenberg, 43–50. New York: Rosa Luxemburg Stiftung, 2017.

Anderson, Kevin B., and Peter Hudis. "Rosa Luxemburg (1871–1919): Universalism and Particularism." In *Makers of Jewish Modernity*, edited by Jacques Picard, Jacques Revel, Michael P. Steinberg, and Idith Zertal, 159–72. Princeton, NJ: Princeton University Press, 2016.

Aram, Bethany. *Juana the Mad: Sovereignty and Dynasty in Renaissance Europe*. Baltimore: Johns Hopkins University Press, 2005.

Arnoud-Duc, Nicole. "Die Widersprüche des Gesetzes." In *Geschichte der Frauen*, vol. 4, *19. Jahrhundert*, edited by Geneviève Fraisse and Michelle Perrot, 97–140. Frankfurt am Main: Campus, 1994; Paris: Maison des Sciences de l'homme, 1991.

"Die Ästhetin des absolut Schönen." *Süddeutsche.de Kultur*, May 19, 2010. http://www.sueddeutsche.de/kultur/leni-riefenstahl-tot-die-aesthetin -des-absolut-schoenen-1.895416.

Badinter, Elisabeth. *The Conflict: How Modern Motherhood Undermines the Status of Women*. New York: Henry Holt, 2012.

———. *Mother Love: Myth and Reality*. New York: Macmillan, 1981.

Baer, Hester, Carrie Smith-Prei, and Maria Stehle. "Digital Feminisms and the Impasse: Time, Disappearance, and Delay in Neoliberalism." *Studies in 20th and 21st Century Literature* 40, no. 2 (2016): 3.

Bäumer, Gertrud. *Die Frau in der Kulturbewegung der Gegenwart*. Wiesbaden: J. F. Bergmann, 1904.

Baumgärtel, Bettina. "Zum Bilderstreit um die Frau im 17. Jahrhundert: Inszenierungen französischer Regentinnen." In *Die europäische Querelle des Femmes: Geschlechterdebatten seit dem 15. Jahrhundert*, edited by Gisela Bock and Margarete Zimmermann, 147–82. Stuttgart: Metzler, 1997.

Baumgarten, Katrin. *Hagestolz und Alte Jungfer: Entwicklung, Instrumentalisierung und Fortleben von Klischees und Stereotypen über Unverheiratetgebliebene*. Münster: Waxmann, 1997.

Beales, Derek. *Joseph II*. Vol. 1, *In the Shadow of Maria Theresa (1741–1780)*. Cambridge: Cambridge University Press, 1987.

Beard, Mary. *Women and Power: A Manifesto*. London: Profile Books, 2017.

Beaumont, Jeanne-Marie Leprince de. *Auszug aus der alten Geschichte, zur Unterweisung der Kinder*. 3 vols. Translated from the French and with a foreword by Johann Adolf Schlegel. Leipzig: Weidmann & Reich, 1766.

Beck, Dorothee. "Die Kategorie Geschlecht im Kampf um politische Macht: Erfolg und Scheitern von SPD-Spitzenpolitikerinnen." In *Progressive Mehrheiten mit der SPD? Für eine linke Politik jenseits der Neuen Mitte*, edited by Max Reinhardt, Stefan Stache, and Stephan Meise, 387–424. Berlin: LIT, 2014.

———. "Mutti ist die beste: Die Mutter-Metapher als politische Kategorie in den Medien." In *O Mother, Where Art Thou?—(Queer-)Feministische Perspektiven auf Mutterschaft und Mütterlichkeit*, edited by Maya Dolderer, Hannah Holme, Claudia Jerzak, and Madeleine Tietke, 71–83. Münster: Westfälisches Dampfboot, 2016.

———. *Politikerinnen und ihr Griff zur Macht: Mediale Repräsentationen von SPD-Spitzenkandidatinnen bei Landtagswahlen*. 1st ed. Bielefeld: transcript, 2016.

Becker-Cantarino, Barbara. "Biographie." In *FrauenGestalten Weimar-Jena um 1800: Ein Bio-bibliographisches Lexikon*, edited by Stefanie Freyer, Katrin Horn, and Nicole Grochowina, 221–27. Heidelberg: Universitätsverlag Winter, 2009.

———. *Der lange Weg zur Mündigkeit: Frau und Literatur (1500–1800)*. Stuttgart: Metzler, 1987, 189–90. Reprint, Munich: dtv, 1989.

———. *Schriftstellerinnen der Romantik: Epoche—Werke—Wirkung*. Munich: Beck, 2000.

Belentschikow, V. "Bertha von Suttner and Lev N. Tolstoj." *Zeitschrift für Slawistik* 28 (1983): 284–301.

Belgum, Kirsten. "E. Marlitt: Narratives of Virtuous Desire." In *A Companion to German Realism, 1848–1900*, edited by Todd C. Kontje, 259–82. Rochester, NY: Camden House, 2002.

Beljentschikov, Walentin. "Bertha von Suttner in Rußland." *Literatur und Kritik* 103 (1976): 140–52.

Bennett, Judith M., and Amy M. Froide, eds. *Singlewomen in the European Past, 1250–1800*. Philadelphia: University of Pennsylvania Press, 2013.

Bennent-Vahle, Heidemarie. "The Female as Ethical Resource in the Philosophy of Hegel." In *Continental Philosophy in Feminist Perspective: Rereading the Canon in German*, edited by Herta Nagl-Docekal and Cornelia Klinger, 114–46. University Park: Pennsylvania State University Press, 2000.

Berger, Renate, and Inge Stephan, "Einleitung." In *Weiblichkeit und Tod in der Literatur*, edited by Renate Berger and Inge Stephan, 1–10. Cologne: Böhlau-Verlag, 1987.

Beßlich, Barbara. "Cato als Repräsentant stoisch formierten Republikanertums von der Antike bis zur Französischen Revolution." In *Stoizismus in der europäischen Philosophie, Literatur, Kunst und Politik: Eine Kulturgeschichte von der Antike bis zur Moderne*, edited by Barbara Neymeyr, Jochen Schmidt, and Bernhard Zimmermann, 1:365–92. Berlin: De Gruyter, 2008.

Bevan, Ruth A. "Petra Kelly: The *Other* Green." *New Political Science* 23, no. 2 (200): 181–202.

Bickenbach, Matthias. *Von den Möglichkeiten einer "inneren" Geschichte des Lesens.* Tübingen: Max Niemeyer, 1999.

Biedermann, Edelgard. "Eine Genossin des leibhaftigen Gottseibeiuns? Zu Bertha von Suttners Briefwechsel mit Irma von Troll-Borostyani, 1886–1890." *Österreich in Geschichte und Literatur mit Geographie* 45, no. 2b–3 (2001): 134–52.

Biess, Frank. *Homecomings: Returning POWs and the Legacies of Defeat in Postwar Germany.* Princeton, NJ: Princeton University Press, 2006.

———. "Die Sensibilisierung des Subjekts: Angst und 'Neue Subjektivität' in den 1970er Jahren." *Werkstatt Geschichte* 49 (2008): 51–71; and 23 (2014): 615–37.

Birgfeld, Johannes. *Krieg und Aufklärung: Studien zum Kriegsdiskurs in der deutschsprachigen Literatur des 18. Jahrhunderts.* Hannover: Wehrhahn, 2012.

Blackwell, Jeannine. "German Literary History and the Canon in the United States." In *German Studies in the United States: A Historical Handbook,* edited by Peter Uwe Hohendahl, 143–73. New York: MLA, 2003.

Bleuler-Waser, Hedwig. "Erziehung zur Mütterlichkeit." In Schreiber, *Mutterschaft: Ein Sammelwerk für die Probleme des Weibes als Mutter,* 70–71.

Boddy, Trevor. "Underground and Overhead: Building the Analogous City." In *Variations on a Theme Park,* edited by Michael Sorkin, 123–53. New York: Noonday, 1992.

Bohm, Arnd. "Charlotte von Stein's "Dido: Ein Trauerspiel." *Colloquia Germanica* 22 (1989): 38–52.

Borchmeyer, Dieter. *Macht und Melancholie: Schillers Wallenstein.* 2nd ed. Göttingen: Edition Mnemosyne, 2003.

Bordieu, Pierre. *The Logic of Practice.* Cambridge: Cambridge University Press, 1990.

Braker, Regina. "Bertha von Suttner on the Dreyfus Affair: A Pacifist Commentary." *Selecta: Journal of the Pacific Northwest Council on Foreign Languages* 17 (1996): 29–32.

———. *Weapons of Women Writers: Bertha von Suttner's "Die Waffen nieder" as Political Literature in the Tradition of Harriet Beecher Stowe's "Uncle Tom's Cabin."* New York: Peter Lang, 1995.

Brandes, Helga. "Die Zeitschrift 'Pomona für Teutschlands Töchter' im publizistischen Kontext des 18. Jahrhunderts." In *"Meine Freiheit nach meinem Charakter zu leben": Sophie von La Roche (1730–1807), Schriftstellerin der Empfindsamkeit,* edited by Jürgen Eichenauer, 173–82. Weimar: Th. Müntzer, 2007.

Bräunert, Svea. *Gespenstergeschichten: Der linke Terrorismus der RAF und die Künste.* Berlin: Kulturverlag Kadmaos, 2015.

Brescoli, Victoria L. "Who Takes the Floor and Why: Gender, Power, and Volubility in Organizations." *Administrative Science Quarterly* 56, no. 4 (2012): 622–41. First published February 29, 2012.

Brinker-Gabler, Gisela, ed. *Kämpferin für den Frieden, Bertha von Suttner: Lebenserinnerungen, Reden und Schriften; Eine Auswahl.* Frankfurt am Main: Fischer Taschenbuch, 1982.

Broad, Jacqueline, and Karen Green. *History of Women's Political Thought in Europe, 1400–1700.* New York: Cambridge University Press, 2009.

———, eds. *Virtue, Liberty, and Toleration: Political Ideas of European Women, 1400–1800.* The New Synthese Historical Library 63. Doordrecht, Netherlands: Springer, 2007.

Brockmann, Stephen. *A Critical History of German Film.* Rochester, NY: Camden House, 2010.

Brosda, Carsten. "Wenn der Rahmen nicht zum Bild passt . . . Politische und mediale Deutungsangebote im Wahlkampf." In *Macht ohne Verantwortung: Medien im Wahlkampf 2013; Erfahrungs-Wissen und Kontext-Analysen aus Praxis und Forschung,* 59–71. Berlin: Heinrich Böll Stiftung, 2013.

Burke, Peter. *The Fabrication of Louis XIV.* New Haven, CT: Yale University Press, 1994.

Burns, Barbara. "Bertha von Suttner's *Die Waffen nieder!* The Roots and Reception of a Pacifist Manifesto." In *Fontane and Cultural Mediation: Translation and Reception in Nineteenth-Century German Literature; Essays in Honor of Helen Chambers,* edited by Ritchie Robertson and Michael White, 158–69. Leeds: Maney, 2015.

Burns, James Macgregor. *Leadership.* New York: Harper & Row, 1978.

Butler, Judith. "'Speaking Up, Talking Back.' Joan Scott's Critical Feminism." In *The Question of Gender: Joan W. Scott's Critical Feminism,* edited by Judith Butler and Elizabeth Weed, 11–28. Bloomington: Indiana University Press, 2011.

Campe, Joachim Heinrich. "Ueber einige verkannte wenigstens ungenützte Mittel zur Beförderung der Indüstrie, der Bevölkerung und des öffentlichen Wohlstandes." Wolfenbüttel, 1786. In Fertig, *Die Volksschule des Obrigkeitsstaates und ihre Kritiker,* 30–37.

Capra, Frank, dir. *It Happened One Night.* Columbia Pictures, 1934.

Carless, Sally A. "Gender Differences in Transformational Leadership: An Examination of Superior, Leader and Subordinate Perspectives." *Sex Roles* 39, nos. 11/12 (1998): 887–902.

"Carolina Michaëlis, deutsche Frau und Gelehrte." In *Die Frau,* August 1894, 718–22.

Carroll, Susan J. "Reflections on Gender and Hillary Clinton's Presidential Campaign: The Good, the Bad, and the Misogynic." *Politics & Gender* 5, no. 1 (2009): 1–20. http://signsjournal.org/ask-a-feminist -carroll-walters/.

Cassidy-Welch, Megan, and Peter Sherlock. "Reflecting and Creating Gender in Late-Medieval and Early-Modern Europe." In *Practices of Gender in Late Medieval and Early Modern Europe,* edited by Megan Cassidy-Welch and Peter Sherlock, 317–26. Turnhout, Belgium: Brepols, 2011.

Castle, Rory. "A Study of the Identity, Family, and Background of Rosa Luxemburg (1871–1919)." PhD diss., Swansea University, 2016.

Chamberlain, Lesley. "Quietism and Polemic: A Dialectical Story." *Common Knowledge* 15, no. 2 (2009): 181–96.

Chandler, David, and Julian Reid, *The Neoliberal Subject: Resilience, Adaptation and Vulnerability.* London: Rowman & Littlefield, 2016.

Clinton, Hillary Rodham. *Hard Choices.* New York: Simon & Schuster, 2014.

———. Senate Nomination Hearings, transcript from January 13, 2009. www.state.gov.

Coffé, Hilde, and Katia Schnellecke. "Female Representation in German Parliamentary Committees: 1972–2009." Presentation at the ECPR General Conference, Bordeaux, September 5–7, 2013. https://ecpr.eu/filestore/paperproposal/24876915-576b-42af-a5e8-55630fb57038.pdf.

Coleman, Isobel. "A Powerful Voice for Women around the World." *New York Times,* May 12, 2013.

"Companies with More Women Board Directors Experience Higher Financial Performance, According to Latest Catalyst Bottom Line Report." *Catalyst.org,* January 15, 2004. http://www.catalyst.org/media/companies-more-women-board-directors-experience-higher-financial-performance-according-latest.

Connolly, Kate. "Angela Merkel Comforts Sobbing Refugee but Says Germany Can't Help Everyone." *Guardian,* July 16, 2015. https://www.theguardian.com/world/2015/jul/16/angela-merkel-comforts-teenage-palestinian-asylum-seeker-germany.

Conze, Eckart, Martin Klimke, and Jeremy Varon, eds. "Introduction: Between Accidental Armageddons and Winnable Wars; Nuclear Threats and Nuclear Fears in the 1980s." In *Nuclear Threats, Nuclear Fear, and the Cold War of the 1980s,* edited by Eckart Conze, Martin Klimke, and Jeremy Varon, 1–24. Cambridge: Cambridge University Press, 2017.

Cordes, Mechthild, *Frauenpolitik: Gleichstellung oder Gesellschaftsveränderung.* Wiesbaden: VS Verlag, 1996.

Crepaz, Adele. *Mutterschaft und Mütter: Kulturgeschichtliche Studien.* Leipzig: O. Wigand, 1905.

Crispin, Jessa. *Why I Am Not a Feminist: A Feminist Manifesto.* Brooklyn, NY: Melville House, 2017.

Curtis-Wendlandt, Lisa. "Legality and Morality in the Political Thought of Elise Reimarus and Immanuel Kant." In Curtis-Wendlandt, Gibbard, and Green *Political Ideas of Enlightenment Women,* 91–107.

———. "No Right to Resist? Elise Reimarus' Freedom as a Kantian Response to the Problem of Violent Revolt." *Hypathia* 27, no. 3 (November 2012): 755–73.

Curtis-Wendlandt, Lisa, Paul Gibbard and Karen Green. "Introduction." In Wendlandt, Gibbard, and Green, *Political Ideas of Enlightenment Women,* 1–13.

————, eds. *Political Ideas of Enlightenment Women: Virtue and Citizenship.* Aldershot, UK: Ashgate, 2013.

Czok, Karl. *August der Starke und seine Zeit.* Munich: Piper, 2008.

Dahn, Felix. *Gedichte.* Accessed February 15, 2009. http://gutenberg. spiegel.de/buch/gedichte-87/86.

Davidson-Schmich, Louise. "Gender, Intersectionality, and the Executive Branch: The Case of Angela Merkel," *German Politics* 20, no. 3 (September 2011): 325–41.

————. *Gender Quotas and Democratic Participation: Recruiting Candidates for Elective Offices in Germany.* Ann Arbor: University of Michigan Press, 2016. http://www.press.umich.edu/8137405.

————, ed. *German Politics* 20, no. 3 (September 2011).

Davidson-Schmich, Louise K., and Isabelle Kürschner. "Stößt die Frauenquote an ihre Grenzen? Eine Untersuchung der Bundestagswahl 2009." *Zeitschrift für Parlamentsfragen* 42 (2011): 25–34.

Davis, Belinda. "The Gender of War and Peace: Rhetoric in the West German Peace Movement of the Early 1980s." *Mitteilungsblatt des Instituts für soziale Bewegungen* 32 (2004): 99–130.

Dawson, Ruth. *The Contested Quill: Literature by Women in Germany, 1770–1800.* Newark: University of Delaware Press, 2002.

————. "Eighteenth-Century Libertinism in a Time of Change: Representations of Catherine the Great." *Women in German Yearbook* 18 (2002): 67–88.

De Graef, Ortwin. "Subjects." In *Literature Now: Key Terms and Methods for Literary History*, edited by Sascha Bru, Ben de Bruyn, and Michel Delville, 75–86. Edinburgh: Edinburgh University Press, 2016.

de Madariaga, Isabel. *Catherine the Great: A Short History.* New Haven, CT: Yale University Press, 1990.

de Man, Paul. "The Resistance to Theory." In *The Resistance to Theory*, 3–20. Minneapolis: University of Minnesota Press, 1986.

Décultot, Elisabeth, ed. *Lesen, Kopieren, Schreiben: Lese- und Exzerpierkunst in der europäischen Literatur des 18. Jahrhunderts.* Translated by Kirsten Heininger and Elisabeth Décultot. Berlin: Ripperger & Kremers, 2014.

Degethoff de Campos, Heidi. "Wissen und Wollen!—Jeannette Schwerin und die Anfänge der Sozialarbeit als Frauenberuf." *Freiburger FrauenStudien* 2 (1995): 73–83. http://nbn-resolving.de/urn:nbn:de:0168-ssoar-318341.

Deutscher Bundestag, Stenographischer Bericht, 4. Sitzung (May 4, 1983).

Deutscher Bundestag, Stenographischer Bericht, 23. Sitzung (September 16, 1983).

Deutscher Bundestag, Stenographischer Bericht, 77. Sitzung (June 28, 1984).

Dixon, Simon. *Catherine the Great.* London: Profile, 2009; also Harlow, UK: Pearson, 2001.

Doherty, Thomas. *Hollywood and Hitler, 1933–1939.* New York: Columbia University Press, 2013.

Dohm, Hedwig. "Werde, die Du bist!" In Dohm and Ametsbichler, *Wie Frauen werden: Werde, die du bist*, 151–236.

Dohm, Hedwig, and Elizabeth G. Ametsbichler. "Die alte Dame." In Dohm and Ametsbichler, *Die Mütter: Beitrag zur Erziehungsfrage*, 201–24. Berlin: Fischer, 1903.

———. *Become Who You Are: With an Additional Essay, "The Old Woman."* Albany: State University of New York Press, 2006.

———. *Wie Frauen werden: Werde, die du bist*. Breslau: Schlesische Buchdruckerei, Kunst- und Verlags-Anstalt v. S. Schottlaender, 1894.

Dolan, Julie, Melissa M. Deckman, and Michele L. Swers. *Women and Politics: Paths to Power and Political Influence*. Lanham, MD: Rowman & Littlefield, 2018.

Dollard, Catherine L. *The Surplus Woman: Unmarried in Imperial Germany, 1871–1918*. New York: Berghahn Books, 2009.

Donath, Adolf A. "Bertha von Suttner und die kleine Form." *Acta Universitatis Wratislaviensis Germanica Wratislaviensia* 20 (1974): 83–95.

———. "Bertha von Suttner und die Polen." *Lenau-Forum für Vergleichende Literaturforschung* 3, nos. 3–4 (1971): 79–96.

Douglas, Susan J. *Enlightened Sexism: The Seductive Message That Feminism's Work Is Done*. New York: Henry Holt, 2010.

Drewes, Heinz. *Maria Antonia Walpurgis als Komponistin*. Borna-Leipzig: Noscke, 1934.

Drinkmann, Nancy, and Claudio Caballero. "Eine Frau ist eine Frau ist eine Frau? Die Berichterstattung über die Kandidaten der Bundespräsidentenwahl 2004." In *Warum nicht gleich?*, edited by Christina Holtz-Bacha and Nina König-Reiling, 167–203. Wiesbaden: VS Verlag, 2007. http://link.springer.com/chapter/10.1007/978-3-531-90540-2_11.

Druxes, Helga. "Manipulating the Media: The German New Right's Virtual and Violent Identities." In Simpson and Druxes, *Digital Media Strategies of the Far Right in Europe and the United States*, 123–39.

———. "'MONTAG IST WIEDER PEGIDA-TAG!' Pegida's Community Building and Discursive Strategies." *German Politics and Society* 34, no. 4 (Winter 2016): 17–33.

Dülcke, Dana, and Sascha K. Futh. "Die 'Mutter der Nation' gegen den 'Panzerkandidaten'—Geschlechterbilder in der Berichterstattung der Printmedien zum Bundestagswahlkampf 2013." In *Die Massenmedien im Wahlkampf: Die Bundestagswahl 2013*, edited by Christina Holtz-Bacha, 249–73. Wiesbaden: Springer VS Verlag, 2015.

Dunayevskaya, Raya. *Rosa Luxemburg, Women's Liberation and Marx's Philosophy of Revolution*. Chicago: Illinois University Press, 1991.

Dunn, Abigail. "'Ob im Tode mein Ich geboren wird?': The Representation of the Widow in Hedwig Dohm's 'Werde, die du bist' (1894)." In *Women and Death 3: Women's Representations of Death in German Culture since 1500*, edited by Clare Bielby and Anna Richards, 88–100. Rochester, NY: Camden House, 2010.

Eagly, Alice H., and Linda L. Carli, "The Female Leadership Advantage: An Evaluation of the Evidence," *Leadership Quarterly* 14 (2003): 807–34.

———. *Through the Labyrinth: The Truth about How Women Become Leaders.* Boston: Harvard Business School Press, 2007.

Eagly, Alice H., and Mary C. Johannesen-Schmidt, "The Leadership Styles of Women and Men," *Journal of Social Issues* 57, no. 4 (2001), 781–97.

Earenfight, Theresa. "Without the Persona of the Prince: Kings, Queens and the Idea of Monarchy in Late Medieval Europe." *Gender & History* 19, no. 1 (2007): 1–21.

Edsall, Thomas B. "The End of the Left and the Right as We Knew Them." *New York Times,* June 22, 2017. https://www.nytimes.com/2017/06/22/opinion/nationalism-globalism-edsall.html.

Efron, John M. *German Jewry and the Allure of the Sephardic.* Princeton, NJ: Princeton University Press, 2016.

Ehmsen, Stefanie, and Albert Scharenberg, eds. *Rosa Remix.* New York: Rosa Luxemburg Stiftung, 2017.

Eldridge, Sarah Vandegrift. "Imaginative Didacticism: Emotion, Individuality, and the Function of *Trivialliteratur* around 1800." *Journal of Literary Theory* 10, no. 2 (2016): 221–46.

Elizabeth I. Tilbury Speech, July 1588, transcribed into present-day English. British Library: Learning Timelines: Sources from History. Accessed February 18, 2019. http://www.bl.uk/learning/timeline/item102878.html.

Engelhardt, August Moritz. *Friedrich Christian, Churfürst von Sachsen: Ein biographischer Entwurf; Nebst Beschreibung der auf diesen Fürsten Bezug habenden und unter seiner Regierung geprägten Münzen und Medaillen.* Dresden: Wagner, 1828.

Engell-Gunther, J. "Die Mutter." In *Schweizer Frauenheim,* October 27, 1894.

"Entstehung der Grünen: Petra Kelly." *Planet Wissen,* August 3, 2017. https://www.planet-wissen.de/geschichte/deutsche_geschichte/entstehung_der_gruenen/pwiepetrakelly100.html.

Erb, Wilhelm. "Bemerkungen über die Folgen der sexuellen Abstinenz." In *Zeitschrift für Bekämpfung der Geschlechtskrankheiten,* edited by A. Blaschko, E. Lesser, and A. Neifser, 1–18. Leipzig: Johann Ambrosius Barth, 1904.

Erlanger, Steven. "At E.U. Meeting, a Hobbled Merkel and a Stalled Agenda." *New York Times,* December 15, 2017. https://www.nytimes.com/2017/12/15/world/europe/eu-angela-merkel-emmanuel-macron.html?rref=collection%2Ftimestopic%2FMerkel%2C%20Angela&action=click&contentCollection=timestopics&region=stream&module=stream_unit&version=latest&contentPlacement=6&pgtype=collection.

"Europe's Far Right Blames Migration Crisis for Paris Attacks." *Deutsche Welle,* November 17, 2015.

Evans, Richard J. *The Feminist Movement in Germany, 1894–1933*. London: Sage, 1976.

Fanck, Arnold, dir. *Der große Sprung*. Movie, UFA, 1927.

———. *Der heilige Berg*. Movie, UFA, 1925/26.

———. *S.O.S. Iceberg*. Movie, Universal, 1932/33.

———. *Stürme über dem Montblanc*. Movie, Aafa Film AG, 1930.

———. *Die weiße Hölle von Piz Palü*. Movie, H. R. Sokal Film GmbH, 1929.

———. *Der weiße Rausch*. Movie, H. R. Sokal Film GmbH, 1930/31.

Fantke, Doreen, Olga Schmidt, and Anett Zeidler. "'Nur weil sie eine Frau ist?' Merkel und die Geschlechterfrage." In Scholz, *"Kann die das?" Angela Merkels Kampf um die Macht*, 81–96.

Fassmann, Irmgard Maya. *Jüdinnen in der deutschen Frauenbewegung, 1865–1919*. Hildesheim: Georg Olms Verlag, 1996.

Fertig, Ludwig. *Campes politische Erziehung*. Impulse der Forschung 27. Darmstadt: Wissenschaftliche Buchgesellschaft, 1977.

———. "Einleitung: Staatsräson und Armeleutebildung." In Fertig, *Die Volksschule des Obrigkeitsstaates und ihre Kritiker*, vii–xlii.

———, ed. *Die Volksschule des Obrigkeitsstaates und ihre Kritiker: Texte zur politischen Funktion der Volksbildung im 18. und 19. Jahrhundert*. Texte zur Forschung 30. Darmstadt: Wissenschaftliche Buchgesellschaft, 1979.

Finsterwalder, Frauke, dir. *Finsterworld* (2013): *Filmportal.de*. http://www.filmportal.de/.

Fischer, Christine. *Instrumentierte Visionen weiblicher Macht: Maria Antonia Walpurgis' Werke als Bühne politischer Selbstinszenierung*. Kassel: Bärenreiter, 2007.

———. "Selbststilisierungs- und Herrscherkonzepte in Maria Antonia Walpurgis' *Talestri, regina delle amazzoni*." In *Frauenstimmen, Frauenrollen in der Oper und Frauen-Selbstzeugnisse*, edited by Gabriele Busch-Salmen and Eva Rieger, 198–224. Herbolzheim: Centaurus, 2000.

———. "Self-Stylisation in a Ceremonial Context: Maria Antonia Walpurgis as *Talestri, regina delle amazzoni*." In *Italian Opera in Central Europe*, vol. 1, *Institutions and Ceremonies*, edited by Melania Bucciarelli, Borbert Dubowy, and Reinhard Strohm, 203–19. Berlin: BWV, 2006.

Fleig, Anne. "'Entre souvrains ce n'est pas le sexe qui décide'—Höfische Selbstinszenierung und Geschlechterrollen." In *Ordnung, Politik und Geselligkeit der Geschlechter im 18. Jahrhundert*, edited by Ulrike Weckel, Claudia Opitz, Olivia Hochstrasser, and Birgitt Tolkemitt, 41–63. Göttingen: Wallstein, 1998.

———. *Handlungs-Spiel-Räume: Dramen von Autorinnen im Theater des ausgehenden 18. Jahrhunderts*. Würzburg: Königshausen & Neumann, 1999.

Foerster, Dr. Fr. W. "Dem Andenken Jeannette Schwerin, Ansprache, gehalten bei der Gedächtnisfeier im Berliner Rathause." In *Jeannette Schwerin zum Gedächtnis*. Berlin: Max Hoffschläger, 1899.

Föllinger, Sabine. "Der Einfluß der stoischen Philosophie auf die Grundlagen der modernen Wirtschaftstheorie bei Adam Smith." In *Stoizismus in der europäischen Philosophie, Literatur, Kunst und Politik: Eine Kultur-geschichte von der Antike bis zur Moderne*, edited by Barbara Neymeyr, Jochen Schmidt, and Bernhard Zimmermann, 2:1063–79. 2 vols. Berlin: De Gruyter, 2008.

Forel, August. H. *The Sexual Question: A Scientific, Psychological, Hygienic and Sociological Study for the Cultured Classes*. Translated by Charles F. Marshall. London: Rebman, 1908.

Foster, Helga, Helga Lukoschat, and Barbara Schaeffer-Hegel. *Die ganze Demokratie: Zur Professionalisierung von Frauen für die Politik*. Feministische Theorie und Politik 12. Pfaffenweiler: Centaurus, 1998.

Foucault, Michel. *The History of Sexuality*, vol. 1, *An Introduction*. Translated from the French by Robert Hurley. 1976. Reprint, London: Penguin, 1990.

"Die Frau gehört ins Haus?" *Thalysia*. April, 1914.

"Frauenanteil in Führungspositionen in Deutschland nach Anzahl der Mitarbeiter in Unternehmen." *Statista*, June 30, 2016. https://de.statista.com/statistik/daten/studie/182510/umfrage/frauenanteil-in-fuehrungspositionen-nach-unternehmensgroesse/.

Frédérique Sophie Wilhelmine, Margravine. *Mémoires de Frédérique Sophie Wilhelmine Margrave der Bareith, soeur de Fréderic le Grand, depuis l'année 1706 jusqu'à 1742, écrit de sa main*. Leipzig: Barsdorf, 1889.

Freeman, Daniel E. "*La guerriera amante*: Representations of Amazons and Warrior Queens in Venetian Baroque Opera." *Musical Quarterly* 53, no. 3 (1996): 431–60.

Freud, Sigmund. "Die Verneinung" (1925). Accessed June 8, 2018. http://gutenberg.spiegel.de/buch/die-verneinung-915/1.

Frevert, Ute, ed. *Bürgerinnen und Bürger: Geschlechterverhältnisse im 19. Jahrhundert: Zwölf Beiträge*. Göttingen: Vandenhoeck & Ruprecht, 1988.

———. *"Mann und Weib, Weib und Mann": Geschlechter-Differenzen in der Moderne*. Munich: Beck 1995.

———. "'Unser Staat ist männlichen Geschlechts': Zur politischen Topographie der Geschlechter vom 18. bis frühen 20. Jahrhundert." In Frevert, *"Mann und Weib, und Weib und Mann,"* 61–132.

Freyer, Stefanie, Katrin Horn, and Nicole Grochowina, eds. *FrauenGestalten Weimar-Jena um 1800: Ein Bio-bibliographisches Lexikon*. Heidelberg: Universitätsverlag Winter, 2009.

Friedrich II, King of Prussia. "Correspondance de Frédéric avec l'électrice Marie-Antoine de Saxe (24 avril 1763–28 décembre 1779)." In *Oeuvres de Frédéric le Grand*, edited by Johann D. E. Preuss, 24:41–366. 30 vols. Berlin: Decker, 1854.

Frieling, Simone. "Alfred Nobel: Der erfolgreiche Erfinder des Dynamits, der gescheiterte Dichter und seine vergebliche Liebe zur Pazifistin Bertha von Suttner." Accessed March 6, 2019. literaturkritik.de.

Frölich, Paul. *Rosa Luxemburg: Her Life and Work*. New York: Monthly Review Press, 1972.

Fronius, Helen. *Women and Literature in the Goethe Era, 1770–1820: Determined Dilettantes*. Oxford: Oxford University Press, 2007.

Frost, Laura. "Mutterberuf." *Frauen-Reich*, May 14, 1910, 509.

Garber, Marjorie. *Vice Versa: Bisexuality and the Eroticism of Everyday Life*. London: Penguin, 1995.

Gay Levy, Darline, and Harriet B. Applewhite. "A Political Revolution for Women? The Case of Paris." In *Becoming Visible: Women in European History*, edited by Renate Bridenthal, Susan Mosher Stuard, and Merry E. Wiesner, 264–92. Boston: Houghton Mifflin, 1998.

Gebauer, George Christian. *Grund-Riß zu einer Umständlichen Historie der vornehmsten Europäischen Reiche und Staaten, mit einer Vorrede von dem mannigfaltigen Nutzen der Historischen Wissenschaft und nöthigen Registern versehen*. 3rd ed. Leipzig: Fritsch, 1749.

Geißel, Brigitte, and Virginia Penrose. "Dynamiken der politischen Partizipation und Partizipationsforschung: Politische Partizipation von Frauen und Männern," August 2003. https://www.fu-berlin.de/sites/gpo/pol_sys/partizipation/Dynamiken_der_politischen_Partizipation/index.html.

Gerhardt, Christina. *Screening the Red Army Fraction: Historical and Cultural Memory*. New York: Bloomsbury, 2018.

German Bundestag, Plenary Protocol, 10th Legislative Period, 4th meeting, May 4, 1983.

Germershausen, Friedrich Christian, and Friedrich C. Gericke. *Die Hausmutter in allen ihren Geschäfften*. Vol. 1 of 5. 4th ed. Hannover: Hahn, 1812.

Gibbs, Nancy. "Chancellor of the Free World," *Time* online (December 2016). http://time.com/time-person-of-the-year-2015-angela-merkel-choice/?iid=toc.

Gilbert, Sandra M., and Susan Gubar. *The Madwoman in the Attic: The Woman Writer and the Nineteenth-Century Literary Imagination*. New Haven: Yale University Press, 2000.

Gnändiger, Charlotte, *Politikerinnen in deutschen Printmedien: Vorurteile und Klischees in der Berichterstattung*. Saarbrücken: VDM, 2007.

Goethe, Johann Wolfgang von. *Sämtliche Werke: Briefe, Tagebücher und Gespräche*. 40 vols. Edited by Friedmar Apel. Vol. 5, sect. 2., edited by Volker C. Dörr und Norbert Oellers. Frankfurt am Main: Bibliothek deutscher Klassiker, 1999.

Gold, Claudia. *Women Who Ruled: History's 50 Most Remarkable Women*. London: Quercus, 2015.

Goldberg, Jeffrey. "Hillary Clinton: 'Failure' to Help Syrian Rebels Led to the Rise of ISIS." *Atlantic*, August 10, 2014.

Goodman, Dena. "Woman and the Enlightenment." In Bridenthal, Stuard, and Wiesner, *Becoming Visible: Women in European History*, 232–62.

Gornick, Vivian. "History and Heartbreak: The Letters of Rosa Luxemburg." *Nation*, April 13, 2011.

Gray, Marion W. *Productive Men, Reproductive Women: The Agrarian Household and the Emergence of Separate Spheres during the German Enlightenment*. New York: Berghahn, 2000.

Green, Karen. *The Woman of Reason: Feminism, Humanism and Political Thought*. New York: Continuum, 1995.

Greg, William Rathbone. *Why Are Women Redundant?* London: N. Trübner, 1869. First published in *National Review* 14 (1862): 434–60.

Greven-Aschoff, Barbara. *Die bürgerliche Frauenbewegung in Deutschland, 1894–1933*. Göttingen: Vandenhoeck & Ruprecht, 1981.

Griffin, Emma. "The Emotions of Motherhood: Love, Culture, and Poverty in Victorian Britain." *American Historical Review* 123, no. 1 (February 1, 2018): 60–85.

Grittmann, Elke, and Tanja Maier. "Der Präsident und die Herausforderin—Geschlechterkonstruktionen von Spitzenkräften in der Politik aus medienethischer Perspektive." In *Gender im medienethischen Diskurs*, edited by Petra Grimm und Oliver Zöllner, 153–68. Stuttgart: Franz Steiner, 2014.

Groetsch, Ulrich. "Reimarus, the Cardinal, and the Remaking of Cassius Dio's *Roman History*." In *Between Philology and Radical Enlightenment: Hermann Samuel Reimarus (1694–1768)*, edited by Martin Mulsow, 103–32. Leiden: Brill, 2011.

Grote, Stefanie. "'Objekt' Mensch: Körper als Ikon und Ideologem in den cineastischen Werken Leni Riefenstahls; Ästhetisierter Despotismus oder die Reziprozität von Auftragskunst und Politik im Dritten Reich." PhD diss., Viadrina European University, 2004. https://opus4.kobv.de/opus4-euv/frontdoor/index/index/docId/40.

Gutjahr, Ortrud, ed. *Ulrike Maria Stuart von Elfriede Jelinek*. Würzburg: Königshausen & Neumann, 2007.

Guy, Donna J. *White Slavery and Mothers Alive and Dead: The Troubled Meeting of Sex, Gender, Public Health, and Progress in Latin America*. Lincoln: University of Nebraska Press, 2000.

Habermas, Rebekah. *Frauen und Männer des Bürgertums: Eine Familiengeschichte (1750–1850)*. Göttingen: Vandenhoeck & Ruprecht, 2000.

Hagemann, Karen, and Donna Harsch, "Entanglements of Gender, Politics, and Protest in the Historiography on the Two Post-1945 Germanys." In *Gendering Post-1945 German History: Entanglements*, edited by Karen Hagemann, Donna Harsch, and Friederike Brühöfener, 21–44. New York: Berghahn Books, 2019.

Hagemann, Karen, Konrad Jarausch, and Cristina Allemann-Ghionda. "Children, Families, and States: Time Policies of Childcare and Schooling in a Comparative Historical Perspective." In *Children, Families, and States: Time Policies of Childcare, Preschool, and Primary Education in Europe*, edited by Cristina Allemann-Ghionda, Karen Hagemann, and Konrad H. Jarausch, 3–50. New York: Berghahn Books, 2011.

Hager, Robert. "What Shake-Up in West Germany Means to U.S." *US News and World Report*, October 4, 1982.

Hake, Sabine. *German National Cinema*. 2nd ed. London: Routledge, 2008.

———. *Screen Nazis: Cinema, History and Democracy*. Madison: University of Wisconsin Press, 2012.

Hamann, Brigitte. *Bertha von Suttner: Ein Leben für den Frieden*. Munich: Piper, 1991.

Han, Byung-Chul. *Psychopolitik: Neoliberalismus und die neuen Machttechniken*. Frankfurt am Main: Fischer, 2015.

Häntzschel, Günter. *"Die Waffen nieder: Bertha von Suttners Antikriegsroman; Zur Poetik und Ideologie der Frauenliteratur."* In *Poetik und Geschichte: Viktor Zmegac zum 60. Geburtstag*, edited by Dieter Borchmeyer, 102–17. Tübingen: Niemeyer, 1998.

Harnisch, Sebastian, and Hanns W. Maull, eds., *Germany as a Civilian Power? The Foreign Policy of the Berlin Republic*. Manchester, UK: Manchester University Press, 2001.

Haug, Frigga. *Beyond Female Masochism: Memory-Work and Politics*. London: Verso, 1992.

———. *Rosa Luxemburg und die Kunst der Politik*. Hamburg: Argument, 2007.

Hausen, Karin. "Die Polarisierung der 'Geschlechtscharaktere'—Eine Spiegelung der Dissoziation von Erwerbs- und Familienleben." In *Sozialgeschichte der Familie in der Neuzeit Europas*, edited by Werner Conze, 363–93. Stuttgart: Klett, 1976.

Haustedt, Birgit. *Die wilden Jahre in Berlin: Eine Klatsch- und Kulturgeschichte der Frauen*. Dortmund: Edition Ebersbach, 1999.

Hawks, Howard. *Bringing Up Baby*, 1938.

Head, Matthew. *Sovereign Feminine: Music and Gender in Eighteenth-Century Germany*. Berkeley: University of California Press, 2013.

Heer, Friedrich. *The Holy Roman Empire*. London: Phoenix, 1978.

Hegel, Georg Wilhlem Friedrich. *Grundlinien der Philosophie des Rechts, oder Naturrecht und Staatswissenschaft im Grundrisse*. Berlin: Nicolaische Buchhandlung, 1821.

———. *Grundlinien der Philosophie des Rechts, oder Naturrecht und Staatswissenschaft im Grundrisse, Vollständige Ausgabe*. Vol. 8, ed. Eduard Gans. 21 vols. Berlin: Verlag von Duncker & Humblot, 1833.

———. *Phänomenologie des Geistes*. Vol. 3 of *Werke*. Frankfurt am Main: Suhrkamp, 1970.

Heineman, Elizabeth. *What Difference Does a Husband Make: Women and Marital Status in Nazi and Postwar Germany*. Berkeley: University of California Press, 1999.

Herbst, Ada. "Was Mutterliebe vermag." *Schwäbische Frauenzeitung*, October 17, 1897.

Herman, David, James Phelan, Peter J. Rabinowitz, Brian Richardson, and Robyn Warhol. *Narrative Theory: Core Concepts and Critical Debates*. Columbus: Ohio State University Press, 2012.

Herman, Eva. *Das Eva-Prinzip: Für eine neue Weiblichkeit*. Munich: Pendo, 2006.

Hess, Amanda. "How a Fractious Women's Movement Came to Lead the Left." In Wachtell, *Wolf Whistle Politics: The New Misogyny in America Today*, 139–53.

Hilger, Stephanie M. *Gender and Genre: German Women Write the French Revolution*. Newark: University of Delaware Press, 2015.

Hochschild, Arlie Russell. *Strangers in Their Own Land: Anger and Mourning on the American Right*. New York: New Press, 2016.

Hoecker, Beate. *Frauen und das institutionelle Europa: Politische Partizipation und Repräsentation im Geschlechtervergleich*. Wiesbaden: Springer VS Verlag, 2013.

———. *Politische Partizipation von Frauen: Kontinuität und Wandel des Geschlechterverhältnisses in der Politik*. Opladen: Leske + Budrich, 1995.

Hoecker, Beate, and Gesine Fuchs. *Handbuch politische Partizipation von Frauen in Europa*. Wiesbaden: Springer VS Verlag, 1998.

———. *Ohne Frauen nur eine halbe Demokratie: Politische Partizipation von Frauen in den osteuropäischen Beitrittsstaaten*. Eurokolleg 49. Bonn: Friedrich-Ebert-Stiftung, Internationale Politikanalyse, 2004.

Hoffgen, Maggie. *Studying German Film*. Leighton Buzzard, UK: Auteur, 2009.

Hofmann [*sic*], Johann Adolph. *Des römischen Kaisers Marcus Aurelius Antonius erbauliche Betrachtungen über sich selbst, aus dem Griechischen übersetzt, mit Anmerkungen und des Kaisers Leben erläutert*. 5th ed. Hamburg: Bohn, 1755.

Hofmann, Michael. *Schiller: Epoche-Werk-Wirkung*. Munich: Beck, 2003.

Holmstrom, Nancy. "Rosa Luxemburg: A Legacy for Feminists?" In Ehmsen and Scharenberg, *Rosa Remix*, 32–36.

Holtz-Bacha, Christina. "Frauen, Politik, Medien: Ist die Macht nun weiblich?" In Holtz-Bacha, *Frauen, Politik und Medien*, 3–24.

———, ed. *Frauen, Politik und Medien*. Wiesbaden: VS Verlag, 2008.

———. "Mit den Waffen einer Frau? Politikerinnen im Wahlkampf." In Holtz-Bacha and König-Reiling, *Warum nicht gleich?*, 79–104. http://link.springer.com/chapter/10.1007/978-3-531-90540-2_5.

Holtz-Bacha, Christina, and Thomas Koch. "Der Merkel-Faktor—Die Berichterstattung der Printmedien über Merkel und Schröder im Bundestagswahlkampf 2005." In Holtz-Bacha, *Frauen, Politik und Medien*, 49–70.

Holtz-Bacha, Christina, and Nina König-Reiling, eds. *Warum nicht gleich?* Wiesbaden: VS Verlag, 2007. http://link.springer.com/chapter/10.1007/978-3-531-90540-2_5.

Honegger, Claudia. *Die Ordnung der Geschlechter: Die Wissenschaften vom Menschen und das Weib, 1750–1850*. Frankfurt am Main: Suhrkamp, 1991.

Honeycutt, Karen. "Clara Zetkin: A Left-Wing Socialist and Feminist in Wilhelmian Germany." PhD diss. Columbia University, 1975.

Honig, Bonnie. *Antigone Interrrupted*. Cambridge: Cambridge University Press, 2013.

Huber, Therese. *Die Familie Seldorf.* Edited by Magdalene Heuser. Hildesheim: Olms, 1989.

———. *Therese Huber—die reinste Freiheitsliebe, die reinste Männerliebe: Ein Lebensbild in Briefen und Erzählungen zwischen Aufklärung und Romantik.* Edited by Andrea Hahn. Berlin: Henssel, 1989.

———. "Unsre Geschichte." In *Therese Huber—Die reinste Freiheitsliebe, die reinste Männerliebe,* 7–12.

Hudis, Peter. "Lenin and Luxemburg." In *The Palgrave Handbook of Leninist Political Philosophy,* edited by Tom Rockmore and Norman Levine, 201–9. Basingstoke, UK: Palgrave Macmillan, 2017.

———. *Marx's Concept of the Alternative to Capitalism.* Chicago: Haymarket, 2013.

Hudson, Valerie M., and Patricia Leidl. *The Hillary Doctrine: Sex and American Foreign Policy.* New York: Columbia University Press, 2015.

Humphries, Michael L. "Michel Foucault on Writing and the Self in the *Meditations* of Marcus Aurelius and *Confessions* of St. Augustine." *Arethusa* 30, no. 1 (1997): 125–38.

Hunt, Lynn. *The Family Romance of the French Revolution.* London: Routledge, 1992.

———. "The Many Bodies of Marie-Antoinette." In *Eroticism and the Body Politic,* edited by Lynn Hunt, 108–31. Baltimore: Johns Hopkins University Press, 1991.

Hunter, Angela. "The Unfinished Work on Louise Marie-Madeleine Dupin's Unfinished *Ouvrage sur les femmes." Eighteenth-Century Studies* 43, no. 1 (2009): 95–111.

Hutton, Sarah. "Virtue, God, and Stoicism in the Thought of Elizabeth Carter and Catharine Macaulay." In *Virtue, Liberty, and Toleration: Political Ideas of European Women, 1400–1800,* edited by Jacqueline Broad and Karen Green, 137–48. The New Synthese Historical Library 63. Doordrecht, Netherlands: Springer, 2007.

Ignotus. "Die Frau im öffentlichen Leben und die ländliche Wohlfahrtspflege." In *Monika,* September 7, 1910.

Inhetveen, Katharina. *Institutionelle Innovation in politischen Parteien: Geschlechterquoten in Deutschland und Norwegen.* Studien zur Sozialwissenschaft. Wiesbaden: Westdeutscher Verlag, 2002.

Institute for Women's Policy Research. *Women's Share of Seats in Congress, 1960–2013 with Projection for Political Parity in 2121.* Washington, DC: Institute for Women's Policy Research, 2013.

Jacobs, Margaret D. *White Mother to a Dark Race: Settler Colonialism, Maternalism, and the Removal of Indigenous Children in the American West and Australia, 1880–1940.* Lincoln: University of Nebraska Press, 2011.

Jagernauth, Kevin. "Soderbergh Says Abandoned Leni Riefenstahl Biopic Would Focus on Director Battling the Studio System." *Indie Wire,* September 23, 2013. http://www.indiewire.com/2013/09/soderbergh-says-abandoned-leni-riefenstahl-biopic-would-focus-on-director-battling-the-studio-system-93359/.

James, Paul W. *Globalism, Nationalism, Tribalism: Bringing Theory Back In.* London: Sage, 2006.

Jamieson, Kathleen Hall. *Beyond the Double Bind: Women and Leadership.* New York: Oxford University Press, 1995.

J. B. R., Professor. "Stimm- und Wahlrecht der Frauen." In *Monika*, November 9, 1910.

Jelinek, Elfriede. *Ulrike Maria Stuart: Königinnendrama.* Reinbek: Rowohlt Theaterverlag, n.d.

Joeres, Ruth-Ellen Boetcher. "Die Zähmung der alten Frau: Hedwig Dohms *Werde, die Du bist.*" In *Der Widerspenstigen Zähmung: Studien zur bezwungenen Weiblichkeit in der Literatur*, edited by Sylvia Wallinger and Monica Jonas, 217–27. Innsbruck: Institut für Germanistik, 1986.

Johnson, Laurie M. *Locke and Rousseau: Two Enlightenment Responses to Honor.* Lanham, MD: Lexington, 2012.

Jones, Radhika. "Here's Why It's Been 29 Years since a Woman Was Person of the Year," *Time*, December 9, 2015. http://time.com/4141766/time-person-of-the-year-angela-merkel-women/.

Jordan, William Chester. "Introduction to the Princeton Classics Edition." In *The King's Two Bodies: A Study in Medieval Political Theology*, edited by Ernst Kantorowicz, ix–xxiv. Princeton, NJ: Princeton University Press, 1997.

Jost, Erdmut. "Moralische Gemälde? Sophie von La Roches Kupfererklärung 'Sitten der schönen Pariser Welt.'" In Jost, *Sitten der schönen Pariser Welt*, 130–49.

———, ed. *Sitten der schönen Pariser Welt: Sophie von La Roche und* das Monument du Costume; *Mit den 24 Stichen und dem vollständigen, erstmals ins Deutsche übertragenen Text der ersten beiden Folgen des französischen Originals.* Halle: Mitteldeutscher Verlag, 2011.

Joubert, Estelle. "Performing Sovereignty, Sounding Autonomy: Political Representation in the Operas of Maria Antonia of Saxony." *Music and Letters* 96, no. 3 (2015): 344–89.

Kaes, Anton. "*Metropolis* (1927): City, Cinema, Modernity." In *Weimar Cinema: An Essential Guide to Classic Films of the Era*, edited by Noah Isenburg, 173–91. New York: Columbia University Press, 2009.

Kaminski, Nicola. "Gottsched/in oder Umwege weiblicher Autorschaft: *Die Vernünftigen Tadlerinnen—Die Pietisterey im Fischbein-Rocke; Oder die Doctormäßige Frau—Her Witzling.*" In *Anonymität und Autorschaft: Zur Literatur- und Rechtsgeschichte der Namenlosigkeit*, edited by Stephan Pabst, 89–122. Berlin: Walter de Gruyter, 2011.

Kapczynski, Jennifer, and Michael D. Richardson, eds. *A New History of German Film.* Rochester, NY: Camden House, 2012.

Karr, Mary. *The Art of Memoir.* New York: Harper Perennial, 2015.

Kelly, Joan. "Did Women Have a Renaissance?" In Joan Kelly, *Women, History and Theory: The Essays of Joan Kelly*, 19–50. London: University of Chicago Press, 1984.

Kelly, Petra. "Beyond the Greens." *Ms. Magazine*, November/December 1991, 70.

———. "Europe . . . It is a little mainland off the coast of Northern Ireland." Speech at the University of Coleraine, Northern Ireland, May 7, 1975. PKA 533,4.

———. "Mister New Europe." *Vista*, April 1973. PKA 531,14.

———. "My dear Friends and Comrades." Letter, Brussels, March 24, 1979. PKA 540,6.

———. *Thinking Green! Essays on Environmentalism, Feminism, and Nonviolence*. Berkeley: Parallax, 1994.

———. "To A.U.'s revolutionaries." Poem, Brussels, n.d. (possibly May 1972). PKA 530,23.

———. Untitled. Seminar paper, American University, Spring Semester 1970, 10–12, PKA 530,1.

———. Untitled. Speech, Wyhl, March 31, 1975. PKA 3166.

———. "WAS TUN???? Einige Aktionsmöglichkeiten für die Westeuropäischen Sozialisten!" November 1975. PKA 534,2.

———. Zärtlichkeit in der Politik (1984). In *Mit dem Herzen denken: Texte für eine glaubwürdige Politik*, 18–22. Munich: Beck, 1990.

Kelly, Petra, and Roland Vogt, "Ökologie und Frieden: Der Kampf gegen Atomkraftwerke aus der Sicht von Hiroshima." *Forum Europa*, January/February 1977. PKA 534,4.

Kelping, Karin. "Historische Mentalitätenforschung, Literaturanthropologie und Psychohistorie." In *Frauenbilder im deutschen Barockdrama: Zur literarischen Anthropologie der Frau*, 13–19. Hamburg: Kovac, 2003.

Kent, Thomas W., Carrie A. Blair, Howard F. Rudd, and Ulrich Schuele. "Gender Differences and Transformational Leadership Behavior: Do Both German Men and Women Lead in the Same Way?" *International Journal of Leadership Studies* 6, no. 1 (2010): 52–66.

Kerber, Linda K. "Separate Spheres, Female Worlds, Woman's Place: The Rhetoric of Women's History." *Journal of American History* 75, no. 1 (June 1988): 9–39.

Key, Ellen. "Mütterlichkeit." In *Mutterschaft: Ein Sammelwerk für die Probleme des Weibes als Mutter*, edited by Adele Schreiber, 591. Munich: Langen, 1912.

Kidwell, J. M., R. E. Stevens, and A. L. Bethke. "Differences in Ethical Perceptions between Male and Female Managers: Myth or Reality?" *Journal of Business Ethics* 6, no. 6 (August 1987): 489–93.

King, Kathryn R. "Patriot or Opportunist? Eliza Haywood and the Politics of The Female Spectator." In Wright and Newman, *Fair Philosopher: Eliza Haywood and The Female Spectator*, 104–21.

Kintzinger, Martin. "Die zwei Frauen des Königs: Zum politischen Handlungsspielraum von Fürstinnen im europäischen Spätmittelalter." In *Das Frauenzimmer: Die Frau bei Hofe in Spätmittelalter und früher Neuzeit*, edited by Jan Hirschbiegel and Werner Paravicini, 377–98. Stuttgart: Thorbecke, 2000.

Kleemann, Frank, Uwe Krähnke, and Ingo Matuschek. *Interpretative Sozialforschung: Eine Einführung in die Praxis des Interpretierens.* 2nd ed. Wiesbaden: Springer VS Verlag, 2013. http://nbn-resolving.de/urn:nbn:de:1111-20130725424.

Klein, Jürgen. *Elisabeth I und ihre Zeit.* Munich: Beck, 2010.

Knopp, Daniel. *NS-Filmpropaganda: Wunschbild und Feindbild in Leni Riefenstahls "Triumph des Willens" und Veit Harlens "Jud Süß."* Marburg: Tectum Verlag, 2004.

Knox, John. *The First Blast of the Trumpet against the Monstrous Regiment of Women.* Edited by Edward Arber. London: English Scholar's Library, 1858. Project Gutenberg Ebook. http://www.gutenberg.org/files/9660/9660-h/9660-h.htm#bibliography.

Koch, Thomas. "Immer nur die Frisur? Angela Merkel in den Medien." In Holtz-Bacha and König-Reiling, *Warum nicht gleich?*, 146–66.

"Können sich Paare in Deutschland wirklich keine Kinder leisten?" *T-online News*, October 13, 2016. http://www.t-online.de/leben/familie/id_79247010/kinderlosigkeit-warum-die-deutschen-so-wenig-kinder-bekommen.html.

Koontz, Claudia. "The Fascist Solution to the Woman Question in Italy and Germany." In *Becoming Visible: Women in European History*, 2nd ed., edited by Renate Bridenthal. Claudia Koontz, and Susan Stuard, 499–534. Boston: Houghton Mifflin, 1987.

———. *Mothers in the Fatherland: Women, the Family, and Nazi Politics.* New York: St. Martin's, 1987.

Koopman, Paul L., Deanne N. Den Hartog, Edvard Konrad, M. Bodur, S. Booth, D. Bourantas, and N. Boyacigill. "National Culture and Leadership Profiles in Europe: Some Results From the GLOBE Study," *European Journal of Work and Organizational Psychology* 8, no. 4 (1999): 503–20.

Kopitzsch, Franklin. *Grundzüge einer Sozialgeschichte der Aufklärung in Hamburg und Altona.* 2nd ed. Hamburg: Verlag Verein für Hamburgische Geschichte, 1990.

Köpke, Wulf. "Immer noch im Schatten der Männer? Therese Huber als Schrifstellerin." In *Der Weltumsegler und seine Freunde: Georg Forster als gesellschaftlicher Schriftsteller der Goethezeit*, edited by Detlef Rasmussen, 116–32. Tübingen: Narr, 1988.

Kord, Susanne. *Sich einen Namen machen: Zur Anonymität und Pseudonymität weiblicher Autoren zwischen 1700 und 1900.* Stuttgart: Metzler, 1996.

Koschorke, Albrecht, Thomas Frank, Ethel Matela de Mazza, and Susanna Lüdemann. *Der fiktive Staat: Konstruktionen des politischen Körpers in der Geschichte Europas.* Frankfurt am Main: Fischer, 2017.

Koser, Julie. *Armed Ambiguity: Women Warriors in German Literature and Culture in the Age of Goethe.* Evanston, IL: Northwestern University Press, 2016.

Kositza, Ellen. *Gender ohne Ende oder Was vom Manne übrigblieb.* Schnellroda: Antaios, 2008.

Kovacs, Teresa. *Drama als Störung: Elfriede Jelineks Konzept des Sekundärdramas.* Bielefeld: transcript, 2016.

Koven, Seth, and Sonya Michel, eds. *Mothers of a New World: Maternalist Politics and the Origins of Welfare States.* New York: Routledge, 1993.

———. "Womanly Duties: Maternalist Politics and the Origins of Welfare States in France, Germany, Great Britain, and the United States, 1880–1920." *American Historical Review* 95, no. 4 (1990): 1076–108.

Kowaleski, Maryanne. "Singlewomen in Medieval and Early Modern Europe: The Demographic Perspective." In *Singlewomen in the European Past, 1250–1800,* edited by Judith M. Bennett and Amy M. Froide, 38–81. University of Pennsylvania Press, 1999.

Krafft-Ebing, Richard von. *Psychopathia Sexualis: With Especial Reference to Contrary Sexual Instinct; A Medico-Legal Study.* Translated by Charles G. Chaddock. Philadelphia: F. A. Davis, 1893.

Kranidis, Rita S. *The Victorian Spinster and Colonial Emigration: Contested Subjects.* Basingstoke, UK: Macmillan, 1999.

Krimmer, Elisabeth. "German Women Writers and Classicism." In *The Literature of Weimar Classicism,* edited by Simon Richter, 237–64. Rochester, NY: Camden House 2005.

———. *In the Company of Men: Cross-Dressed Women around 1800.* Detroit: Wayne State University Press, 2004.

Kuhlmann, Carola. *Alice Salomon und der Beginn sozialer Berufsausbildung: Eine Biographie.* Stuttgart: ibidem Press, 2012.

Kuhn, Barbel. *Familienstand: Ledig; Ehelose Frauen und Männer im Bürgertum (1850–1914).* Cologne: Böhlau, 2000.

Kürschner, Isabelle. *Den Männern überlassen wir's nicht! Erfolgreiche Frauen in der CSU.* Baden-Baden: Nomos, 2009.

Küster, Sybille. "Inklusion und Exklusion: Nationsbildung und Geschlecht in Deutschland." In *Geschichte als Experiment: Studien zu Politik, Kultur und Alltag im 19. und 20. Jahrhundert,* edited by Daniela Münkel and Jutta Schwarzkopf, 207–16. Frankfurt am Main: Campus Verlag, 2004.

Kutt, Mareike. *Auf dem Weg zur Macht: Politische Kommunikation in Deutschland und Frankreich; Die Darstellung von Angela Merkel und Ségolène Royal in der Wahlkampfberichterstattung überregionaler Tageszeitungen.* Duisburg: WiKu, 2010.

La Cava, Gregory. *My Man Godfrey.* Film. 1936.

La Roche, Sophie von. *Mein Schreibetisch: An Herrn G. R. P. in D.* 2 vols. 1799. Reprint, Karben: Wald, 1997.

———. *Pomona für Teutschlands Töchter.* 4 vols. Edited by Jürgen Vorderstemann. Munich: K. G. Saur, 1987.

Landes, Joan B. *Women and the Public Sphere in the Age of the French Revolution.* Ithaca, NY: Cornell University Press, 1988.

Lange, Helene. "Intellektuelle Grenzlinien zwischen Mann und Frau." *Die Frau,* March 1897, 321–34.

———. *Lebenserinnerungen.* Berlin: Herbig Verlag, 1921 and 1928.

Laqueur, Thomas. *Making Sex: Body and Gender from the Greeks to Freud.* Cambridge, MA: Harvard University Press, 1990.

Lau, Mariam. "Ellen Kositza, 'Nebenbei: knallrechts.'" *Zeit Online*, January 30, 2018.

———. "Orgasmus im Bundestag." *Die Zeit*, March 27, 2013.

Lechner, Isabella, and Edith Stohl. "Manchmal dachte ich, ich wäre sie: Regisseurin Edith Stohl im Interview über ihre erste eigene Fernseh-dokumentation zur Friedensnobelpreisträgerin Bertha von Suttner. Accessed December 11, 2017. http://derstandard.at/2256802/Manchmal-dachte-ich-ich-waere-sie.

Leitich, Ann Tizia. "Bertha Suttner (1843–1914)." In *Neue österreichische Biographie ab 1815: Große Österreicher Band 1*, 66–75. Vienna: Amalthea Verlag, 1957.

"Leni Riefenstahl 101-jährig gestorben." *Stern*, September 9, 2003. http://www.stern.de/fotografie/trauer-leni-riefenstahl-101-jaehrig-gestorben3514808.html.

Lepore, Jill. "The Woman Card." In Wachtell, *Wolf Whistle Politics*, 3–15.

Levin, Carole. *The Heart and Stomach of a King: Elizabeth I and the Politics of Sex and Power.* 2nd ed. Philadelphia: University of Pennsylvania Press, 2013.

Lewis, Jan. "Mother's Love: The Construction of an Emotion in Nine-teenth-Century America." In *Social History and Issues in Human Con-sciousness: Some Interdisciplinary Connections*, edited by Andre E. Barnes and Peter N. Stearns, 209–22. New York: New York University Press, 1989.

Löffler, Friederike Luise. *Oekonomisches Handbuch fuer Frauenzimmer: Anweisung zu Frauenzimmer-Arbeiten zur Behandlung von Haushal-tungs-Sachen und zur Körper-Schönheitspflege; Nebst einer Anleitung zur Bereitung von Speisen und Getränken für Kränke, und zur Anwendung von Haus-Mitteln.* 2 vols. 4th ed. Stuttgart: Steinkopf, 1826.

Löhr, Julia. "Frauen in der Führung—viel Gerede, wenig Veränderung," *Frankfurter Allgemeine Zeitung*, January 7, 2016. http://www.faz.net/aktuell/wirtschaft/wirtschaftspolitik/frauenanteil-in-fuehrungsposi-tionen-hat-sich-kaum-veraendert-14001753.html.

Loster-Schneider, Gudrun. *Sophie von La Roche: Paradoxien weiblichen Schrei-bens im 18. Jahrhundert.* Tübingen: Narr, 1995.

Lughofer, Johann Georg. "Bertha von Suttner: A Prototypical European Writer." *Letter: Journal for Linguistics and Literary Studies* 9 (2011): 186–209.

———. "Erinnerungskultur in Österreich: Eine Annäherung anhand des Fallbeispiels Bertha von Suttner 2005." *Acta Neophilologica* 40, nos. 1–2 (2007): 155–65.

Lühr, Hans-Peter, ed. *Sachsen und Dresden im Siebenjährigen Krieg.* Dres-den: Dresdener Geschichtsverein, 2001.

Lünenborg, Margreth, and Tanja Maier. "'Kann der das überhaupt?' Eine qual-itative Textanalyse zum Wandel medialer Geschlechterrepräsentationen."

In *Ungleich mächtig: Das Gendering von Führungspersonen aus Politik, Wirtschaft und Wissenschaft in der Medienkommunikation*, edited by Margret Lünenborg and Jutta Röser, 65–126. Bielefeld: Transcript, 2012.

Luxemburg, Rosa. *The Complete Works of Rosa Luxemburg*. Vol. 1, *Economic Writings 1*, edited by Peter Hudis. London: Verso, 2013.

———. *The Complete Works of Rosa Luxemburg*. Vol. 2, *Economic Writings 2*, edited by Peter Hudis and Paul Le Blanc. London: Verso, 2015.

———. *Gesammelte Briefe*. Vol. 2. Edited by Annelies Laschitza. Berlin: Dietz Verlag, 1999.

———. *Gesammelte Werke*. Vol. 1.2. Edited by Annelies Laschitza and Eckhard Müller, et al. Berlin: Dietz Verlag, 2000.

———. *The Letters of Rosa Luxemburg*. Edited by Georg Adler, Peter Hudis, and Annelies Laschitza. London: Verso Books, 2011.

———. "Pod znakiem Socjaldemocracji." *Czerwony Sztandar*, March 24, 1905.

———. "Remarks at Jena Congress on Relations between the Party and the Trade Unions, with Reference to the 1905 Revolution in Russia." In *Protokoll über die Verhandlungen des Parteitages der Sozialdemokratischen Partei Deutschlands, abgehalten zu Jena vom 17. bis 23. September 1905*. Berlin: Vorwärts, 1905.

———. *The Rosa Luxemburg Reader*. Edited by Peter Hudis and Kevin B. Anderson. New York: Monthly Review Books, 2004.

———. "Russische Arbeiterinnen im Kampfe." *Die Gleichheit*, April 23, 1902.

Maier, Dieter G., and Jürgen Nürnberger. *Jeannette Schwerin: Durch Bildung zu Sozialreform und Emanzipation*. Berlin: Hentrich & Hentrich Verlag, 2016.

Mainberger, Sabine. "Schreibtischporträts: Zu Texten von Arno Schmidt, Georges Perec, Hermann Burger und Francis Ponge." In *Möbel als Medien*, edited by Sebastian Hackenschmidt and Klaus Engelhorn, 177–97. Bielefeld: transcript Verlag, 2011.

"Making Hillary an Issue." *ABC Nightline*, aired March 26, 1992.

Mandell, Barbara, and Shilpa Pherwani. "Relationship between Emotional Intelligence and Transformational Leadership Style: A Gender Comparison." *Journal of Business and Psychology* 17, no.3 (2003): 387–404.

Manne, Kate. *Down Girl: The Logic of Misogyny*. New York: Oxford University Press, 2018.

Maria Antonia von Sachsen. *Thalestris Königinn der Amazonen: Aus dem vortrefflichen italienischen Singspiele Jhrer Königlichen Hoheit der unvergeßlichen Ermelinde Thalea in ein Deutsches Trauerspiel verwandelt, von Johann Christoph Gottscheden*. Zwickau: Stieler, 1766.

Maria Antonia Walpurgis Symphorosa, Electress of Saxony. *Talestri, regina delle amazzoni, dramma per musica*. Leipzig: Breitkopf, 1765, n.p.

———. *Talestri: Regina delle amazzoni / Talestris: Königin der Amazonen*. Dresden, 1763.

Maria Theresa, Empress of Austria, and Maria Antonia Walpurgis, Electress. *Briefwechsel, 1747–1772, mit einem Anhang ergänzender Briefe.* Edited by Woldemar Lippert. Leipzig: Teubner, 1908.

Marie-Antoinette. *Correspondance secrète entre Marie-Thérèse et le Cte de Mercy-Argenteau, avec les lettres de Marie-Thérèse et de Marie-Antoinette.* Edited by Alfred d'Arneth and M. A. Geffroy. Paris: Firmin-Didot, 1874–75.

Markovits, Andrei, and Philip Gorski, *The German Left: Red, Green, and Beyond.* Oxford: Oxford University Press, 1993.

Markovits, Andrei, and Joseph Klaver. "Alive and Well in the Fourth Decade of Their Bundestag Presence: A Tally of the Greens' Impact on the Federal Republic of Germany's Political Life and Public Culture." *German Politics and Society* 33, no. 4 (Winter 2015): 112–40.

Marlitt, E. *Die Frau mit den Karfunkelsteinen.* Leipzig: Ernst Keil's Nachfolger, 1885.

———. *Das Geheimnis der alten Mamsell.* Vol. 1. Leipzig: Ernst Keil, 1874.

———. *Das Geheimnis der alten Mamsell.* Vol. 2. Leipzig: Ernst Keil, 1874.

———. *The Lady with the Rubies.* Translated by A. L. Wister. Philadelphia: J. B. Lippincott, 1885.

———. *The Old Maid's Secret.* Translated by H. J. G. London: Trahan, 1871.

———. *The Second Wife: A Romance.* Translated by A. L. Wister. Philadelphia: J. B. Lippincott, 1874.

———. *Die zweite Frau: Roman in zwei Bänden; Erster und Zweiter Band.* Leipzig: Ernst Keil, 1874.

Martin, Dieter. "Wielands Auseinandersetzung mit dem Stoizismus aus dem Geist skeptischer Aufklärung." In *Stoizismus in der europäischen Philosophie, Literatur, Kunst und Politik: Eine Kulturgeschichte von der Antike bis zur Moderne,* edited by Barbara Neymeyr, Jochen Schmidt, and Bernhard Zimmermann, 2:857–73. Berlin: De Gruyter, 2008.

Marx Ferree, Myra. *Varieties of Feminism: German Gender Politics in Global Perspective.* Stanford, CA: Stanford University Press, 2012.

Maurenbrecher, Hulda. "Die neue Auffassung von Mutterpflicht." In Schreiber, *Mutterschaft: Ein Sammelwerk für die Probleme des Weibes als Mutter,* 120–31.

Mayer, John D., Peter Salovy, and David R. Caruso. "Emotional Intelligence: New Ability or Eclectic Traits?" *American Psychologist* 63 (2008): 503–17. DOI: 10.1037/0003-005x.63.6.503.

Mayring, Philipp. *Qualitative Inhaltsanalyse: Grundlagen und Techniken.* 2nd rev. ed. Weinheim: Beltz, 2010.

McNamara, Jo Ann. "Matres Patriae/Matres Ecclesiae: Women of Rome." In *Becoming Visible: Women in European History,* 3rd ed., edited by Renate Bridenthal, Susan Mosher Stuard, and Merry E. Wiesner, 77–103. Boston: Houghton Mifflin, 1998.

Meise, Helga. "Hirnkinder: Gattungsvorgabe und hybride Schreibweise in Sophie von La Roches 'Pomona für Teutschlands Töchter.'" In *"bald zierliche Blumen—bald Nahrung des Verstands": Lektüren zu Sophie von*

La Roche, edited by Monika Lippke, Matthias Luserke-Jaqui, and Nikola Roßbach, 123–39. Hannover: Wehrhahn, 2008.

———. 'wie sehr ich die Geschichte liebe': Hybridisierung und Pfropfung in Sophie von La Roches 'Pomona für Teutschlands Töchter' am Beispiel ihres Bezuges auf die Geschichte." In *"Ich will keinem Mann nachtreten": Sophie von La Roche und Bettine von Arnim*, edited by Miriam Seidler and Mara Stuhlfauth, 111–23. Frankfurt am Main: Peter Lang, 2013.

Mende, Silke. *"Nicht rechts, nicht links, sondern vorn": Eine Geschichte der Gründungsgrünen*. Munich: Oldenbourg, 2011.

"Merkel und Clinton: Im Hosenanzug der Macht." *Der Spiegel Online*, April 14, 2011.

Meyer, Birgit. *Frauen im Männerbund: Politikerinnen in Führungspositionen von der Nachkriegszeit bis heute*. Frankfurt am Main: Campus, 1997.

Michel, Judith. "'Richtige' und 'falsche' Angst in der Debatte um den Nato-Doppelbeschluss." In *Angst in den Internationalen Beziehungen*, edited by Patrick Bormann, Thomas Freiberger, and Judith Michel, 251–72. Göttingen: V&R unipress, 2010.

Michels, Robert. "Die Dirne als die 'alte Jungfer' des Proletariats und die Prostitution." In *Mutterschutz: Zeitschrift zur Reform der sexuellen Ethik*, edited by Helene Stöcker, 58–65. Frankfurt am Main: J. D. Sauerländer, 1905.

Mihailovic, Alexandar. "Hijacking Authority: Academic Neo-Aryanism and Internet Expertise." In Simpson and Druxes, *Digital Media Strategies of the Far Right in Europe and the United States*, 83–102.

Milch, Werner. *Sophie La Roche, die Großmutter der Brentanos*. Frankfurt am Main: Societäts Verlag, 1935.

Milder, Stephen. "'Eine [grenzüberschreitende] Entscheidungsschlacht gegen Atomkraftwerke': Die grüne Wahlkampagne(n) für das europäische Parlament in Westdeutschland und Frankreich in 1979." In *Die Ökologie im linken und rechten Spektrum: Konvergenzen und Divergenzen zwischen Deutschland und Frankreich von 1970 bis heute*, edited by Birgit Metzger, Annette Lensing, and Olivier Hanse. Hamburg: Peter Lang, 2018.

———. "Thinking Globally, Acting (Trans)locally: Petra Kelly and the Transnational Roots of German Green Politics." *Central European History* 43, no. 2 (2010): 301–26.

Möbius, Paul Julius. *Über den physiologischen Schwachsinn des Weibes*. 1903. Reprint San Bernadino, CA: 2017.

Moeller, Robert G. *Protecting Motherhood: Women and the Family in the Politics of Postwar West Germany*. Berkeley: University of California Press, 1996.

Mohr, Annette. *Madame d'Epinays Konzeption der Mädchenerziehung im Umfeld von frauenspezifischen Erziehungstraktaten des 18. Jahrhunderts in Frankreich*. St. Ingbert: Röhrig, 1997.

Moran, Barbara. "Gender Differences in Leadership." *Library Trends* 40, no. 3 (1992): 475–91.

Morris-Keitel, Helen G. "(R)Evolution: From Edelleute to Edelmenschen— Bertha von Suttner's Pathway to Peace." *Seminar: A Journal of Germanic Studies* 50, no. 1 (2014): 34–50.

———. "Der wissende Mensch: Das Bildungskonzept Bertha von Suttners." *Sinn und Form: Beiträge zur Literatur* 59, no. 3 (2007): 378–92.

Moss Kantor, Rosabeth. *Men and Women of the Corporation*. New York: Basic Books, 1977.

Müller, Ray, dir. *The Wonderful, Horrible Life of Leni Riefenstahl*. Film. 1993 (DVD 1998).

Munimus, Bettina. *Heide Simonis: Aufstieg und Fall der ersten Ministerpräsidentin Deutschlands*. Stuttgart: Ibidem, 2010.

"Muntere Zeiten." *Der Spiegel*, March 14, 1983, 29–33.

Mushaben, Joyce Marie. *Becoming Madam Chancellor: Angela Merkel and the Berlin Republic*. Cambridge: Cambridge University Press, 2017.

———. "The Best of Times, the Worst of Times: Angela Merkel, the Grand Coalition and 'Majority Rule' in Germany." *German Politics* 34, no. 1 (2016): 1–25.

———. "The Reluctant Feminist: Angela Merkel and Gender Equality Policy in Germany." *Femina Politica* 2 (2018): 83–95.

Naber, Johannes, dir. *Zeit der Kannibalen*. Berlin: Studio TV Film, 2014.

Nenon, Monika. *Aus der Fülle der Herzen: Geselligkeit, Briefkultur und Literatur um Sophie von La Roche und Friedrich Heinrich Jacobi*, Würzburg: Königshausen & Neumann, 2005.

Nettl, J. P. *Rosa Luxemburg*. Oxford: Oxford University Press, 1966.

Neumayr, Eva. "Maria Antonia Walpurgis Kurfürstin von Sachsen." In *Musik und Gender im Internet: Lexikon*, 2007. http://mugi.hfmt-hamburg.de/en/Artikel/Maria_Antonia_Kurfürstin_von_Sachsen?size=1075.

Neymeyr, Barbara, Jochen Schmidt, and Bernhard Zimmermann, eds. *Stoizismus in der europäischen Philosophie, Literatur, Kunst und Politik: Eine Kulturgeschichte von der Antike bis zur Moderne*. 2 vols. Berlin: De Gruyter, 2008.

Neysters, Silvia. "Regentinnen und Amazonen." In *Die Galerie der starken Frauen: Regentinnen, Amazonen, Salondamen*, edited by Bettina Baumgärtel and Silvia Neysters, 98–139. Munich: Klinkhardt & Biermann, 1995.

Niedermeyer, Oskar. "Die soziale Zusammensetzung der Parteimitgliederschaften." Bundeszentrale für politische Bildung. July 12, 2017. www.bpb.de/politik/grundfragen/parteien-in-deutschland/zahlenund-fakten/140358/soziale-zusammensetzung.

Niefanger, Susanne. *Vernünftige Tadlerinnen: Schreibstrategien in Moralischen Wochenschriften: Formalstilistische, pragmatische und rhetorische Untersuchungen am Beispiel von Gottscheds "Vernünftigen Tadlerinnen."* Tübingen: Max Niemeyer, 1997.

Nobel, Carmen. "HBS Cases: Women MBAs at Harvard Business School." *Working Knowledge* (HBS), March 6, 2013.

Nossett, Lauren. "Bad Mothers and Good Virgins: Gender, Identity, and Maternity in the Novels of E. Marlitt." *Women in German Yearbook* 31 (2015): 28–47.

Nye, Andrea. *Philosophia: The Thought of Rosa Luxemburg, Simone Weil, and Hannah Arendt.* New York: Routledge, 1994.

Offen, Karen. *European Feminisms, 1700–1950: A Political History.* Stanford, CA: Stanford University Press, 1999.

On Leadership. Boston: Harvard Business Review Press, 2011.

O'Reilly, Nancy D. *Leading Women: 20 Influential Women Share Their Secrets to Leadership, Business, and Life.* New York: Adams Media, 2015.

Ossietzky, Karl von. *Rechenschaft.* Accessed February 15, 2019. http://gutenberg.spiegel.de/buch/rechenschaft-1947/12.

Pabst, Stephan, ed. *Anonymität und Autorschaft: Zur Literatur- und Rechtsgeschichte der Namenlosigkeit.* Berlin: Walter de Gruyter, 2011.

Pantti, Mervi. "Portraying Politics: Gender, Politik und Medien." In Holtz-Bacha and König-Reiling, *Warum nicht gleich?*, 17–51.

Parkin, Sara. *The Life and Death of Petra Kelly.* London: Harper Collins, 1994.

Pateman, Carole. *The Sexual Contract.* Cambridge: Polity, 1988.

Penny, Laurie. *Meat Market: Female Flesh under Capitalism.* Winchester, UK: zero books, 2010.

Peters, Dietlinde. *Mütterlichkeit im Kaiserreich.* Bielefeld: Kleine Verlag, 1984.

Pfeiff, Ruprecht. *Minerva in der Sphäre des Herrscherbildes: Von der Antike bis zur Französischen Revolution.* Münster: Lit, 1990.

Phelan, James, and Peter J. Rabinowitz. "Narrative as Rhetoric." In *Narrative Theory: Core Concepts and Critical Debates*, edited by David Herman, James Phelan, and Peter J. Rabinowitz, 3–8. Columbus: Ohio State University Press, 2012.

Pierson, Ruth Roach, ed. *Women and Peace: Theoretical, Historical and Practical Perspectives.* London: Croom Helm, 1987.

Plant, Rebecca Jo. *Mom: The Transformation of Motherhood in Modern America.* Chicago: Chicago University Press, 2010.

Plewny, Katharina. "Ulrike Meinhofs Wiederkehr in Nicolaus Stemanns Inszenierung von Ulrike Maria Stuart." In *NachBilder der RAF*, edited by Inge Stephan und Alexandra Tacke, 106–20. Cologne: Böhlau-Verlag, 2008.

Pöggeler, Otto. *Schicksal und Geschichte: Antigone im Spiegel der Deutungen und Gestaltungen seit Hegel und Hölderlin.* Munich: Fink 2004.

Ponte, Susanne de. *Ein Bild von einem Mann—gespielt von einer Frau: Die wechselvolle Geschichte der Hosenrolle auf dem Theater.* Munich: Edition Text + Kritik, 2013.

Quy, LaRae. "Using Emotional Intelligence Is a Woman Leader's Secret Weapon." *Forbes*, November 2, 2016. https://www.forbes.com/sites/womensmedia/2016/11/02/using-emotional-intelligence-is-a-woman-leaders-secret-weapon/.

Rafael, Simone. "Die Mitte und der 'Genderwahn.'" In *Wut, Verachtung, Abwertung: Rechtspopulismus in Deutschland*, edited by Andreas Zick and Beate Küpper, 78–94. Bonn: Dietz, 2015.

Rahn, Thomas. "Psychologie des Zeremoniells: Affekttheorie und -pragmatik in der Zeremoniellwissenschaft des 18. Jahrhunderts." In *Zeremoniell als höfische Ästhetik in Spätmittelalter und Früher Neuzeit*, edited by Jörg Jochen Berns and Thomas Rahn, 74–98. Tübingen: Niemeyer, 1995.

Ramm, Elke. *Autobiographische Schriften deutschsprachiger Autorinnen um 1800*. Hildesheim: Olms, 1998.

Rancière, Jacques. *Aisthesis: Scenes from the Aesthetic Regime of Art*. Translated by Zakir Paul. London: Verso, 2013.

Reagin, Nancy Ruth. *A German Women's Movement: Class and Gender in Hanover, 1880–1933*. Chapel Hill: University of North Carolina Press, 1995.

Reich, Eduard. *Studien über die Frauen*. Jena: Hermann Costenoble, 1875.

Reichertz, Jo. *Gemeinsam interpretieren: Die Gruppeninterpretation als kommunikativer Prozess*. Wiesbaden: Springer VS Verlag, 2013.

Reichertz, Jo, and Hans-Georg Soeffner. "Hans-Georg Soeffner: Expanding the Action Repertoire of Societies; Hans-Georg Soeffner im Gespräch mit Jo Reichertz." *Forum: Qualitative Sozialforschung* 5 (3 Art. 29), 2004. http://www.qualitative-research.net/index.php/fqs/article/view/561/1215.

Reimarus, Elise. "Betrachtungen." In *Elise Reimarus (1735–1805), the Muse of Hamburg: A Woman of the German Enlightenment*, by Almut Spalding, appendix 1, no. 23, 328–29. Würzburg: Königshausen & Neumann, 2005.

———. *Freiheit*. Hamburg: Meyn, 1791.

———."Versuch einer Läuterung und Vereinfachung der Begriffe vom natürlichen Staatsrecht." In Spalding, *Reimarus*, appendix 7, 504–13.

———. "Von der Arbeitsamkeit." In *Kleine Kinderbibliothek*, edited by Joachim Heinrich Campe, 4:143–49. 2nd ed. Hamburg: Herold, 1783.

Reimarus, Hermann Samuel. *Apologie oder Schutzschrift für die vernünftigen Verehrer Gottes*. Edited by Gerhard Alexander. 2 vols. Frankfurt am Main: Insel, 1972.

———, ed. *Tōn Diōnos Tu Kassiu Tu Kokkōianu Rhōmaikōn Istoriōn Ta Sōzomena = Cassii Dionis Cocceiani Historiae Romanae . . .* 2 vols. Hamburg: Herold, 1750–52.

Renker, Cindy K. "The Political Voice in the Writings of Friederike Brun (1765–1835)." *Women in German Yearbook* 29 (2013): 81–96.

Repp, Kevin. *Reformers, Critics, and the Paths of German Modernity: Anti-Politics and the Search for Alternatives, 1890–1914*. Cambridge, MA: Harvard University Press, 2000.

Reuband, Karl-Heinz. "Außenseiter oder Repräsentation der Mehrheit? Selbst- und Fremdwahrnehmung der Teilnehmer von PEGIDA-Kundgebungen." In *PEGIDA: Rechtspopulismus zwischen Fremdenangst und "Wende"-Enttäuschung; Analysen im Überblick*, edited by Karl-Siegbert

Rehberg, Franziska Kunz, and Tino Schlinzig, 165–87. Bielefeld: transcript Verlag, 2016.

Richards, Anna. "'Double-Voiced Discourse' and Psychological Insight in the Work of Therese Huber." *Modern Language Review* 99, no. 2 (2004): 416–29.

———. *The Wasting Heroine in German Fiction by Women, 1770–1914*. Oxford: Clarendon, 2004.

Richter, Saskia. *Die Aktivistin: Das Leben der Petra Kelly*. Munich: Deutsche Verlags-Anstalt, 2010.

Richter, Simon. *Missing the Breast: Gender, Fantasy, and the Body in the German Enlightenment*. Seattle: University of Washington Press, 2006.

Riefenstahl, Leni. *Behind the Scenes of the National Party Convention Film*. Translated by David Culbert. Chicago, IL: International Historic Films, 2010.

———. "How I Came to Film . . ." Translated by Jon Cho-Polizzi. In *The Promise of Cinema: German Film Theory, 1907–1933*, edited by Anton Kaes, Nicholas Baer, and Michael Cowan, 134–35. Berkeley: University of California Press, 2016.

———. *Leni Riefenstahl: A Memoir*. New York: Picador, 1992.

———. *Memoiren*. Munich: Albrecht Knaus Verlag, 1987.

———, dir. *Olympia: Fest der Völker* und *Fest der Schönheit*. Film. Olympia Film GmbH, 1936–1938.

———, dir. *Triumph des Willens*. Film. Leni Riefenstahl Produktion, 1935.

Rilke, Rainer Maria. *Sämtliche Werke*. Edited by Ernst Zinn and Ruth Sieber-Rilke. Frankfurt am Main: Insel, 1992.

Robinson, Jenefer. *Deeper Than Reason: Emotion and Its Role in Literature, Music, and Art*. Oxford: Oxford University Press, 2005.

Roebling, Irmgard, and Wolfram Mauser. *Mutter und Mütterlichkeit: Wandel und Wirksamkeit einer Phantasie in der deutschen Literatur*. Würzburg: Königshausen & Neumann, 1996.

Roelofs, H. Mark. "The Confessional Vocation: The Ancient Origins of Modern Individualism's Vital Core." *European Legacy* 7, no. 4 (2002): 429–43.

Rose, Jacqueline. *Women in Dark Times*. London: Bloomsbury, 2014.

Rother, Rainer. "Die Regisseurin Leni Riefenstahl ist im Alter von 101 Jahren gestorben—ein Nachruf: Die Unberührbare." *Berliner Zeitung*, September 10, 2003. http://www.berliner-zeitung.de/die-regisseurin-leni-riefenstahl-ist-im-alter-von-101-jahren-gestorben---ein-nachruf-die-unberuehrbare-16029982.

Rucht, Dieter, ed. *Protest in der Bundesrepublik: Strukturen und Entwicklungen*. Frankfurt am Main: Campus, 2001.

Rucht, Dieter, and Jochen Roose. "Von der Platzbesetzung zum Verhandlungstisch? Zum Wandel von Aktionen und Struktur der Ökologiebewegung." In Rucht, *Protest in der Bundesrepublik: Strukturen und Entwicklungen*, 173–210.

Rutherford, Sarah. *Women's Work, Men's Cultures: Overcoming Resistance and Changing Organizational Cultures.* New York: Palgrave, 2011.

Ruttmann, Walter, dir. *Berlin: Sinfonie der Großstadt.* Film. 1927.

Rzeszotnik, Jacek, ed. "Einleitung." In *Schriftstellerische Autopoiesis: Beiträge zur literarischen Selbstreferenzialität,* 7–12. Darmstadt: Büchner, 2011.

Salomon, Alice. "Jeannette Schwerin: Ein Lebensbild von Alice Salomon." In *Jeannette Schwerin zum Gedächtnis.* Berlin: Max Hoffschläger, 1899.

Salomon, Alice, and Andrew Lees. *Character Is Destiny: The Autobiography of Alice Salomon.* Ann Arbor: University of Michigan Press, 2004.

Sanborn, Joshua, and Annette Timm. *Gender, Sex, and the Shaping of Modern Europe: A History from the French Revolution to the Present Day.* Oxford: Oxford University Press, 2007.

Sandberg, Sheryl, and Nell Scovell, *Lean In: Women, Work, and the Will to Lead.* New York: Knopf Doubleday, 2013.

Sandberg, Sheryl, and Adam Grant, "Speaking While Female." *New York Times,* January 12, 2015.

Santner, Eric L. *My Own Private Germany: Daniel Paul Schreber's Secret History of Modernity.* Princeton, NJ: Princeton University Press, 1996.

———. *The Royal Remains: The People's Two Bodies and the Endgames of Sovereignty.* Chicago: University of Chicago Press, 2011.

Schaeffer-Hegel, Barbara, with Helga Foster, Helga Lukoschat, Rita Mersmann, Silke Ude, and Ulla Weber. *Frauen mit Macht: Zum Wandel der politischen Kultur durch die Präsenz von Frauen in Führungspositionen.* Pfaffenweiler: Centaurus Verlagsgesellschaft, 1995.

Schaeffer-Hegel, Barbara, and Silke Ude. "Anke Martiny und die Presse." In Schaeffer-Hegel, Foster, Lukoschat, Mersmann, Ude, and Weber, *Frauen mit Macht,* 243–64.

Schiller, Friedrich. *Maria Stuart.* Vol. 9.1 of *Schillers Werke: Nationalausgabe,* i.A. des Goethe und Schiller-Archivs, des Schiller-Nationalmuseums und der Deutschen Akademie, edited by Nikolas Immer. Neuauflage. Weimar: Hermann Böhlaus Nachfolger, 2010.

———. *Mary Stuart: A Tragedy.* Translated by Joseph Mellish. Project Gutenberg Ebook #6791, produced by Tapio Riikonen and David Widger.

Schlechte, Horst, ed. *Die Staatsreform in Kursachsen, 1762–1763: Quellen zum kursächsischen Rétablissement nach dem siebenjährigen Kriege.* Berlin: Rütten & Loening, 1958.

Schlumbohm, Christa. "Die Glorifizierung der Barockfürstin als 'Femme Forte.'" In *Die europäische Hofkultur im 16. und 17. Jahrhundert,* edited by August Buck, 113–22. Hamburg: Hauswedell, 1981.

Schmidt, Jochen. "Grundlagen, Kontinuität und geschichtlicher Wandel des Stoizismus." In Neymeyr, Schmidt, and Zimmermann, *Stoizismus in der europäischen Philosophie, Literatur, Kunst und Politik,* 1:3–133.

———. "Die poetologische Transformation der stoischen Euthymie: Marc Aurel und Hölderlins Ode *Dichtermut.*" In Neymeyr, Schmidt, and

Zimmermann, *Stoizismus in der europäischen Philosophie, Literatur, Kunst und Politik*, 2:951–62.

Schöler-Macher, Bärbel. *Die Fremdheit der Politik: Erfahrungen von Frauen in Parteien und Parlamenten*. Weinheim: Deutscher Studien-Verlag, 1994.

Scholz, Sylka. *"Kann die das?" Angela Merkels Kampf um die Macht*. Berlin: Dietz, 2007.

Schopenhauer, Arthur. *Schopenhauer's Sämmtliche Werke, in fünf Bänden*. Vol. 5. Leipzig: Inselverlag, 1860.

———. *Studies in Pessimism: A Series of Essays*. Translated by T. Bailey Saunders. London: Swan Sonnenschein, 1872.

Schramm, Julia. *Fifty Shades of Merkel*. Hamburg: Hoffmann & Campe, 2016.

Schregel, Susanne. *Der Atomkrieg vor der Wohnungstür: Eine Politikgeschichte der neuen Friedensbewegung in der Bundesrepublik, 1970–1985*. Frankfurt am Main: Campus, 2011.

———. "Konjunktur der Angst: 'Politik der Subjektivität' und 'neue Friedensbewegung,' 1979–1983." In *Angst im Kalten Krieg*, edited by Bern Greiner, Christian Th. Müller, and Dierk Walter, 495–520. Hamburg: Hamburger Edition, 2009.

Schreiber, Adele, ed. *Mutterschaft: Ein Sammelwerk für die Probleme des Weibes als Mutter*. Munich: Langen, 1912.

Schreier, Margrit. "Varianten qualitativer Inhaltsanalyse: Ein Wegweiser im Dickicht der Begrifflichkeiten." *Forum: Qualitative Sozialforschung* 15 (1 Art. 18), 2014. http://www.qualitative-research.net/index.php/fqs/article/view/2043/3635.

Schroeder, Patricia. "And Please Call Me Ms. President," *New York Times*, February 22, 1999, A17.

Schulte, Regina. *Der Körper der Königin: Geschlecht und Herrschaft in der höfischen Welt seit 1500*. Frankfurt am Main: Campus, 2002.

———. "Madame ma chère fille"—"Dearest Child": Briefe imperialer Mütter an königliche Töchter." In Schulte, *Der Körper der Königin*, 162–96.

Schulte-Sasse, Jochen. *Die Kritik an der Trivialliteratur seit der Aufklärung: Studien zur Geschichte des modernen Kitschbegriffs*. Munich: Fink, 1971.

Schumacher, Tony. *Vom Schulmädel bis zur Grossmutter*. Stuttgart: Deutsche Verlags-Anstalt, 1900.

Schütze, Yvonne. *Die gute Mutter: Zur Geschichte des normativen Musters "Mutterliebe."* Hannover: B. Kleine Verlag, 1986.

———. "Mutterliebe—Vaterliebe: Elternrollen in der bürgerlichen Familie des 19. Jahrhunderts." In *Bürgerinnen und Bürger: Geschlechterverhältnisse im 19. Jahrhundert*, edited by Ute Frevert, 118–33. Göttingen: Vandenhoeck & Ruprecht, 1988.

Schwarzer, Alice. *Eine tödliche Liebe: Petra Kelly und Gert Bastian*. Cologne: Kiepenheuer & Witsch, 1993.

Schwerin, Jeannette. "Dame oder Frau?" *Die Frauenbewegung*, June 1, 1896, 108.

———. "Weibliche Fabrikinspektoren." In *Jahrbuch für die Deutsche Frauen-welt*, 161–74. Stuttgart: Greiner & Pfeiffer, 1899.

Sdroulia, Amalia. *Frauen in der Politik: Spielregeln des politischen Geschäfts; Eine Untersuchung am Beispiel von Politikerinnen der Fraktion "Bündnis 90/Die Grünen" im Niedersächsischen Landtag.* Marburg: Tectum, 2007.

Sensch, Patricia. *Sophie von La Roches Briefe an Johann Friedrich Christian Petersen (1788–1806): Kritische Edition, Kommentare, Analyse.* Berlin: De Gruyter, 2016.

Shepela, Anja. "Bertha von Suttner: Eine Frau steht ihren Mann." In *Patentlösung oder Zankapfel: German Studies für den internationalen Bereich als Alternative zur Germanistik—Beispiele aus Amerika*, edited by Peter Pabisch, 227–50. Bern: Peter Lang, 2005.

Simmel, Monika. *Erziehung zum Weibe: Mädchenbildung im 19. Jahrhundert.* Frankfurt am Main: Campus-Verlag, 1980.

Simonischek, Peter. "Interview," in *Extras*, Maren Ade, *Toni Erdmann.* DVD, 2017.

Simpson, Patricia Anne. *Reimagining the European Family.* New York: Palgrave Macmillan, 2013.

Simpson, Patricia Anne, and Helga Druxes, eds. *Digital Media Strategies of the Far Right in Europe and the United States.* Lanham, MD: Lexington Books, 2015.

Slaughter, Jane, and Robert Kern. *European Women on the Left: Socialism, Feminism, and the Problems Faced by Political Women, 1880 to the Present.* Westport, CT: Greenwood, 1981.

Smith, Sidonie. *A Poetics of Women's Autobiography: Marginality and the Fictions of Self-Representation.* Bloomington: Indiana University Press, 1987.

Smith, Sidonie, and Julia Watson. *Reading Autobiography: A Guide for Interpreting Life Narratives.* Minneapolis: University of Minnesota Press, 2010.

Sneeringer, Julia. *Winning Women's Votes: Propaganda and Politics in Weimar Germany.* Chapel Hill: University of North Carolina Press, 2002.

Söllner, René. "Der deutsche Mittelstand im Zeichen der Globalisierung," *Statistisches Bundesamt*, 2016. https://www.destatis.de/DE/Publika tionen/WirtschaftStatistik/2016/02/DeutscherMittelstand_022016. pdf?__blob=publicationFile.

Solnit, Rebecca. *The Mother of All Questions.* Chicago: Haymarket Books, 2017.

Sontag, Susan. "Fascinating Fascism." In *Under the Sign of Saturn*, First Vintage Books Edition, 71–105. New York: Vintage Books, 1981. First published in 1974.

Spalding, Almut. *Elise Reimarus (1735–1805), the Muse of Hamburg: A Woman of the German Enlightenment.* Würzburg: Königshausen & Neumann, 2005.

———. "Siblings, Publications, and the Transmission of Memory: Johann Albert Hinrich and Elise Reimarus." In *Sibling Relations and Gender in* the Early Modern World: Sisters, Brothers, and Others, edited by Naomi J. Miller and Naomi Yavneh, 216–27. Aldershot, UK: Ashgate, 2006.

Spalding, Almut, and Paul Spalding. The Household Accounts of the Reimarus Family of Hamburg, 1728–1780: Turf and Tailors, Books and Beer. 2 vols. Leiden, Netherlands: Brill, 2015.

Spedding, Patrick. "Measuring the Success of Haywood's Female Spectator (1744–46)." In Wright and Newman, Fair Philosopher: Eliza Haywood and The Female Spectator, 193–211.

Spender, Dale. Man Made Language. London: Routledge & Kegan Paul, 1980.

———. Time and Tide Wait for No Man. London: Pandora, 1984.

Sperr, Monika. Petra Kelly: Politikerin aus Betroffenheit. Munich: Bertelsmann, 1984.

Spicka, Mark E. Selling the Economic Miracle: Economic Reconstruction and Politics in West Germany, 1949–1957. New York: Berghahn Books, 2007.

Spielvogel, Jackson J. Hitler and Nazi Germany: A History. 3rd ed. Upper Saddle River, NJ: Prentice Hall, 1996.

Spretnak, Charlene, and Fritjof Capra. Green Politics: The Global Promise. New York: Dutton, 1984.

Spurlock, John C., and Cynthia Magistro. New and Improved: The Transformation of American Women's Emotional Culture. New York: New York University Press, 1998.

Statista. "Frauenanteil in Führungspositionen in Deutschland nach Anzahl der Mitarbeiter in Unternehmen," June 30, 2016. https://de.statista.com/statistik/daten/studie/182510/umfrage/frauenanteil-in-fuehrungspositionen-nach-unternehmensgroesse/.

Statistisches Bundesamt. "61% der tätigen Personen arbeiten in kleinen und mittleren Unternehmen." https://www.destatis.de/DE/ZahlenFakten/GesamtwirtschaftUmwelt/UnternehmenHandwerk/KleineMittlereUnternehmenMittelstand/Aktuell_.html.

———. "Immer mehr Frauen bleiben kinderlos," Der Spiegel, November 7, 2013. http://www.spiegel.de/politik/deutschland/statistisches-bundesamt-immer-mehr-frauen-bleiben-kinderlos-a-932324.html.

Stein, Charlotte von. Dido: Ein Trauerspiel in fünf Aufzügen. Edited by Heinrich Düntzer. Frankfurt am Main: Verlag des Freien Deutschen Hochstifts, 1867.

Stephan, Inge. Medea: Multimediale Karriere einer mythologischen Figur. Cologne: Böhlau-Verlag, 2006.

———. Musen und Medusen: Mythos und Geschlecht in der Literatur des 20. Jahrhunderts. Cologne: Böhlau-Verlag, 1997.

———. "Revolution und Konterrevolution: Therese Hubers Roman Die Familie Seldorf (1795/96)." In Der deutsche Roman der Spätaufklärung: Fiktion und Wirklichkeit, edited by Harro Zimmerman, 171–94. Heidelberg: Carl Winter, 1990.

Stewart, Abigail J., and Virginia Valian. An Inclusive Academy: Achieving Diversity and Excellence. Cambridge, MA: MIT Press, 2018.

Still, Judith. "Isabelle de Charrière's Three Women—Adopting and Adapting Hospitality after Kant." *German Life and Letters* 64, no. 1 (January 2011): 19–30.

Sting, Stephan. "The Reading-Author as Auto-Poet." *Paragrana: Internationale Zeitschrift für Historische Anthropologie* 4, no. 2 (1995): 79–89.

Stockhausen, Johann Christoph. *Critischer Entwurf einer auserlesenen Bibliothek für den Liebhaber der Philosophie und schönen Wissenschaften, zum Gebrauch seiner Vorlesungen entworfen von Johann Christoph Stockhausen, der Philosophie Doctor, und des Johannei zu Lüneburg Rector, der Königl. deutschen Gesellschaft zu Göttingen und der Herzogl. zu Helmstädt Ehren-Mitgliede.* 3rd ed. Berlin: Haude & Spener, 1764.

Stockwell, Rebecca. "Bertha von Suttner and Rosika Schwimmer: Pacifists from the Dual Monarchy." In *Seven Studies in Medieval English History and Other Historical Essays*, edited by Richard H. Bowers, 141–201. Jackson: University Press of Mississippi, 1983.

Stoehr, Irene. "'Organisierte Mütterlichkeit.' Zur Politik der deutschen Frauenbewegung um 1900." In *Frauen suchen ihre Geschichte*, edited by Karin Hausen, 221–49. Munich: C. H. Beck, 1983.

Stokowski, Margarete. *Untenrum frei*. Reinbek bei Hamburg: Rowohlt, 2016.

Strauss Sotiropoulos, Carol. *"Pomona, für Teutschlands Töchter*: Sophie von La Roche as Editor, Educator, and Narrator." *Colloquia Germanica* 33, no. 3 (2000): 213–38.

Streeruwitz, Marlene. *Autorinnen feiern Autorinnen: Marlene Streeruwitz über Bertha von Suttner*. Vienna: Mandelbaum Verlag, 2014.

Stritt, Marie. "Jeannette Schwerin." *Frauen-Rundschau*, August 1, 1899, 264–67.

———. "Die Mutter als Staatsbürgerin." In Schreiber, *Mutterschaft: Ein Sammelwerk für die Probleme des Weibes als Mutter*, 700.

Stuve, Johann. "Von Armenschulen." In Fertig, *Die Volksschule des Obrigkeitsstaates und ihre Kritiker*, 38–50. First published in "Gelehrte Beiträge" of *Braunschweigische Anzeigen*, 1787.

Suttner, Bertha von. *Das Maschinenzeitalter: Zukunftsvorlesungen über unsere Zeit*. Zurich: Verlagsmagazin, 1889.

———. *Memoiren*. Altenmünster: Jazzybee Verlag, 2016.

———. *Die Waffen nieder!* Berlin: Deutsche Literaturgesellschaft Europa Center, 2008.

Theriot, Nancy M. *Mothers and Daughters in Nineteenth Century America: The Biosocial Construction of Femininity*. Lexington: University Press of Kentucky, 1996.

Theweleit, Klaus. *Männerphantasien 1 und 2*. Munich: Piper, 2009. First published 1977 by Verlag Roter Stern.

Tomhave Blauvelt, Martha. "The Work of the Heart: Emotion in the 1805–35 Diary of Sarah Connell Ayer." *Journal of Social History* 35, no. 3. (2002): 577–92.

Traister, Rebecca. *Big Girls Don't Cry: The Election That Changed Everything for American Women.* New York: Free Press, 2010.

Traub, James. "Angela Merkel's Great Escape." *Foreign Policy,* September 2017. http://foreignpolicy.com/2017/09/21/angela-merkels-great-escape/#.

Trepp, Anne-Charlotte. *Sanfte Männlichkeit und selbstständige Weiblichkeit: Frauen und Männer im Hamburger Bürgertum zwischen 1770 und 1840.* Göttingen: Vandenhoeck & Ruprecht, 1996.

Trimborn, Jürgen. *Leni Riefenstahl: A Life.* Translated by Edna McCown. New York: Faber & Faber, 2007.

———. *Riefenstahl: Eine Karriere; Biographie.* 3rd ed. Berlin: Aufbauverlag, 2007.

Trinidad, Cristina, and Anthony H. Normore. "Leadership and Gender: A Dangerous Liaison?" *Leadership & Organization Development Journal* 26, no. 7 (2005): 574–90.

Uehlein, Friedrich A. "'Stoisch, wahrhaft sokratisch': Epiktet und Marc Aurel in der Philosophie Shaftesburys." In Neymeyr, Schmidt, and Zimmermann, *Stoizismus in der europäischen Philosophie, Literatur, Kunst und Politik,* 2:1047–62.

Valian, Virginia. *Why So Slow? The Advancement of Women.* Cambridge, MA: MIT Press, 1998.

van der Klein, Marian, Rebecca Jo Plant, Nichole Sanders, and Lori R. Weintrob. *Maternalism Reconsidered: Motherhood, Welfare and Social Policy in the Twentieth Century.* New York: Berghahn Books, 2012.

Vergil, *The Aeneid.* Translated by John Dryden. http://classics.mit.edu/Virgil/aeneid.1.i.html.

Vergilius, *Aeneas/Aeneis.* Edited and translated by Piet Schrijvers. Groningen, Netherlands: Historische Uitgeverij, 2011.

Vicedo, Marga. *The Nature and Nurture of Love: From Imprinting to Attachment in Cold War America.* Chicago: University of Chicago Press, 2013.

Vicinus, Martha. *Independent Women: Work and Community for Single Women, 1850–1920.* Chicago: University of Chicago Press, 1988.

Vinken, Barbara. "Marie-Antoinette oder das Ende der Zwei-Körper-Lehre." In *Das Politische: Figurenlehren des sozialen Körpers nach der Romantik,* edited by Uwe Hebekus, Ethel Matala de Mazza, and Albrecht Koschorke, 86–105. Munich: Wilhelm Fink, 2003.

Vollmer, Antje. *Eingewandert ins eigene Land: Was von Rot-Grün bleibt.* Munich: Pantheon, 2006.

von Wahl, Angelika. "A 'Women's Revolution from Above'? Female Leadership, Intersectionality, and Public Policy under the Merkel Government." *German Politics* 20, no. 3 (2011): 392–409.

Wachtell, Diane. *Wolf Whistle Politics: The New Misogyny in America Today.* With an introduction by Dr. Naomi Wolf. New York: New Press, 2017.

Wagner-Egelhaaf, Martina, ed. "Was ist Auto(r)fiktion?" In *Auto(r)fiktion: Literarische Verfahren der Selbstkonstruktion,* 7–21. Bielefeld: Aisthesis, 2013.

Warner, Michael. *Letters of the Republic.* Cambridge, MA: Harvard University Press, 1992.

Wasmer, Martina. "Public Debates and Public Opinion on Multiculturalism in Germany." In *Challenging Multiculturalism: European Models of Diversity*, edited by Raymond Taras, 163–89. Edinburgh: Edinburgh University Press, 2013.

Watanabe-O'Kelly, Helen. "Amazonen in der sozialen und ästhetischen Praxis der deutschen Festkultur der Frühen Neuzeit." In *Soziale und ästhetische Praxis der höfischen Fest-Kult im 16. und 17. Jahrhundert*, edited by Kirsten Dickhaut, Jörg Steigerwald, and Birgit Wagner, 127–47. Wiesbaden: Harrassowitz, 2009.

Watzlawick, Paul, Janet Beavin Bavelas, and Don D. Jackson. *Menschliche Kommunikation: Formen, Störungen, Paradoxien.* 10th ed. Bern: Huber, 2000.

Weber, Adelheid. "Die alte Jungfer von einst und das reife Mädchen von heut." *Die Gartenlaube* 39, supplement *Die Welt der Frau* (1906): 609–10.

Weber, Carl von. *Maria Antonia Walpurgis, Churfürstin zu Sachsen, geb. Kaiserliche Prinzessin in Bayern: Beiträge zu einer Lebensbeschreibung derselben.* Vol. 1. Dresden: Teubner, 1857.

Weber, Max. "Die drei reinen Typen der legitimen Herrschaft." *Preussische Jahrbücher* 187, nos. 1–2 (1922): 1–12.

Weininger, Otto. *Geschlecht und Charakter: Eine prinzipielle Untersuchung.* Vienna: Wilhelm Braumüller, 1908.

Weinsheimer, Stefanie. "Bergfilm." In *Reclams Sachlexikon des Films*, edited by Thomas Koebner, 62–64. Stuttgart: Philipp Reclam, 2002.

Weisker, Albrecht. "Powered by Emotion? Affektive Aspekte in der Westdeutschen Kernenergiedebatte zwischen Technikvertrauen und Apokalypseangst." In *Natur- und Umweltschutz nach 1945: Konzepte, Konflikte, Kompetenzen*, edited by Franz-Josef Brüggemeier and Jens Ivo Engels, 203–21. Frankfurt am Main: Campus, 2005.

Weiss, Julius. "Das Weib als alte Jungfer." In *Mann und Weib: Ihre Beziehungen zueinander und zum Kulturleben der Gegenwart*, edited by Robby Koßmann and Julius Weiss, 1:416–23. Stuttgart: Union Deutsche Verlagsgesellschaft, 1908.

Wernet, Andreas. *Einführung in die Interpretationstechnik der objektiven Hermeneutik.* 3rd ed. Qualitative Sozialforschung. Wiesbaden: VS Verlag, 2009.

Wiegand, Wilfried. "Die Traumtänzerin." *Frankfurter Allgemeine Zeitung*, September 9, 2003. http://www.faz.net/aktuell/feuilleton/leni-riefenstahl-die-traumtaenzerin-1120259.html.

Wieland, Karin. *Dietrich & Riefenstahl: Der Traum der neuen Frau.* Munich: Carl Hanser Verlag, 2011.

Wiener, Carol. "Is a Spinster an Unmarried Woman?" *American Journal of Legal History* 20 (1976): 27–31.

Wiener, P. B. "Bertha von Suttner and the Political Novel." In *Essays in German Language, Culture and Society*, edited by Siegbert S. Prawer, R. Hinton Thomas, and Leonard Forster, 160–76. London: University of London, 1969.

Wilhelmine, Countess of Bayreuth. *Mémoires de Frédérique Sophie Wilhelmine Margrave de Bareith, soeur de Fréderic le Grand, depuis l'année 1706 jusqu'à 1742, écrit de sa main.* Leipzig: Barsdorf, 1889.

Wilputte, Earla A. "'Too Ticklish to Meddle With': The Silencing of The Female Spectator's Political Correspondents." In Wright and Newman, *Fair Philosopher: Eliza Haywood and The Female Spectator*, 122–40.

"Wir wollten nicht die Männer entmachten: Die Grünen Christa Nickels, Antje Vollmer und Annemarie Borgmann über das neue Bonner Feminat." *Der Spiegel*, April 23, 1984.

Die Wohlfahrtseinrichtungen von Groß-Berlin nebst einem Wegweiser für die praktische Ausübung der Armenpflege in Berlin: Ein Auskunfts- und Handbuch herausgeben von der Zentrale für private Fürsorge vormals Auskunftstelle der Deutschen Gesellschaft für ethische Kultur. Berlin, 1910.

Wolff, Larry. "Die Phantasie von Katharina in der Fiktion der Aufklärung: Von Baron Münchhausen zu Marquis de Sade." In *Katharina II., Russland und Europa*, edited by Claus Scharf, 307–18. Mainz: Philipp von Zabern, 2001.

Wolverton, Mimi, Beverly L. Bower and Adrienne E. Hyle. *Women at the Top: What Women University and College Presidents Say About Effective Leadership.* Sterling, VA: Stylus, 2009.

Woodford, Charlotte. "Bertha von Suttner's *Die Waffen nieder!* and Gabriele Reuter's *Aus guter Familie*: Sentimentality and Social Criticism." In *The German Bestseller in the Late Nineteenth Century*, edited by Charlotte Woodford and Benedict Schofield, 206–23. Rochester, NY: Camden House, 2012.

———. "Female Desire and the Mind-Body Binary in Fin de Siècle Fiction by Hedwig Dohm, Lou Andreas-Salomé and Gabriele Reuter." *German Life and Letters* 69, no. 3 (July 2016): 336–49.

Wright, Lynn Marie, and Donald J. Newman. *Fair Philosopher: Eliza Haywood and The Female Spectator.* Bucknell Studies in Eighteenth Century Literature and Culture. Lewisburg, PA: Bucknell University Press, 2006.

———. "Introduction." In Wright and Newman, *Fair Philosopher: Eliza Haywood and The Female Spectator*, 13–41.

Yagoda, Ben. *Memoir: A History.* New York: Riverhead Books, 2009.

Yoder, Jennifer A. "Angela Merkel's Discourse about the Past: Implications for the Construction of Collective Memory in Germany." *Memory Studies* (August 2017): 1–17.

Yolton, Jean S. *John Locke: A Descriptive Bibliography.* Dulles, VA: Thoemmes, 1998.

Zedler, Johann Heinrich, ed. *Grosses vollständiges Universal-Lexicon aller Wissenschaften und Künste, Welche hitzhero durch menschlichen Verstand und Witz erfunden und verbessert worden.* Halle: Zedler, 1731–54.

Zedlitz, Carl Abraham von. "Ueber den Patriotismus als einen Gegenstand der Erziehung in monarchischen Staaten." Translated from the French, Berlin 1777. In Fertig, *Die Volksschule des Obrigkeitsstaates und ihre Kritiker*, 3–18.

Zelewitz, Klaus. "Die Waffen nieder und der explizite bzw. implizite Vorwurf der Trivilität." *Studia Austriaca: An International Journal devoted to the Study of Austrian Culture and Literature* 16 (2008): 9–22.

Zellmer, Elisabeth. "Der lange Weg zur Kanzlerin: Frauen und Politik im Spiegel deutscher Zeitgeschichte." In *Gesichter der Demokratie: Porträts zur deutschen Zeitgeschichte*, edited by Bastian Hein, Manfred Kittel, and Horst Möller, 361–74. Munich: De Gruyter, 2015.

Ziemann, Benjamin. "German Angst: Debating Cold War Anxieties in West Germany." In *Understanding the Imaginary War: Culture, Thought and Nuclear Conflict, 1945–1990*, edited by Matthew Grant and Benjamin Ziemann, 116–39. Manchester: Manchester University Press, 2016.

Zimmermann, Clemens. "Die politischen Dokumentarfilme von Leni Riefenstahl: *Sieg des Glaubens* (1933)—*Triumph des Willens* (1935)—*Tag der Freiheit: Unsere Wehrmacht* (1935)." In *Kunst und Ästhetik im Werk Leni Riefenstahls*, edited by Markwart Herzog and Mario Leis, 59–92. edition text + kritik. Munich: Richard Boorberg, 2011.

Žižek, Slavoj. "From Antigone to Joan of Arc." *Helios* 31, nos. 1–2 (2004): 51–62.

"Die Zukunft unserer Frauen und Töchter." *Monika*, October 26, 1910.

Contributors

DOROTHEE BECK is an independent scholar and founder of the media agency Medienberatung (https://www.dorothee-beck.de).

SETH BERK is a visiting lecturer in German at the University of Pittsburgh.

FRIEDERIKE BRÜHÖFENER is an assistant professor of history at the University of Texas, Rio Grande Valley.

MARGARETMARY DALEY is an associate professor of German and comparative literature at Case Western Reserve University.

AUDE DEFURNE is a PhD candidate in German at KU Leuven, Belgium.

HELGA DRUXES is a professor of German and the chair of German and Russian at Williams College.

SARAH VANDEGRIFT ELDRIDGE is an associate professor of German at the University of Tennessee–Knoxville.

ANKE GILLEIR is a professor of German at KU Leuven, Belgium.

RACHEL J. HALVERSON is a professor of German and chair of the Department of Modern Languages at the University of Idaho.

PETER HUDIS is a professor of humanities and philosophy at Oakton Community College.

ELISABETH KRIMMER is professor of German at the University of California, Davis.

STEPHEN MILDER is an assistant professor of politics and society at the University of Groningen, Netherlands.

JOYCE MARIE MUSHABEN is a Curators' Professor of Comparative Politics at the University of Missouri–St. Louis.

LAUREN NOSSETT is a visiting assistant professor of German at Randolph-Macon College.

Patricia Anne Simpson is chair of the Department of Modern Languages and Literatures and a professor of German at the University of Nebraska–Lincoln.

Almut Spalding is director of global programming and a professor of world languages and cultures at Illinois College, Jacksonville.

Inge Stephan is an emerita professor of German at Humboldt University of Berlin.

Lisa Fetheringill Zwicker is an associate professor of history at Indiana University, South Bend.

Index

body shaming, 246
Britain: Joan of Arc and, 281, 296n4;
La Roche's intercultural ideals,
66–67; the role of unmarried
Victorian women, 150
Bundestag: challenging the gendered
space, 288–90; Greens' electoral
victory, 287; Kelly as "other,"
290–93, 294–95; Kelly's acts of
civil disobedience, 288–89; Kelly's
grassroots political approach, 287–
88; Kelly's leadership role, 281–82;
Kelly's rhetorical style and behavior,
292–94; women's exclusion from
party chairs, 296n5
Bush (George W.) administration,
327–28

capitalism: contemporary relevance
of Luxemburg's work, 205–6;
Luxemburg's view of democracy
and socialism, 216–17; Suttner's
stance on, 196–97. *See also*
neoliberal self-referentiality
castrati, 40–41
Catherine the Great, 5, 39 (fig.),
54, 112n49; as Amazon, 36, 39;
gendered image of, 101; Maria
Antonia's political ambitions,
33; plagiarized work, 91; social
acceptability of her writing,
56n12; supporting La Roche's
Pomona, 62
Chandler, David, 243, 251
children: Berlin Association to
Encourage the Care of Flowers
in Schools, 175, 182n25;
Dohm's novella on married life,
156–58; film satirization of career
women as mothers, 244–45;
idealized motherlove, 167–68;
motherlove and the death of,
169–70; Schwerin's social activism
and advocacy for, 175; von der
Leyen's media image, 273; women
balancing self-actualization with
maternal desire, 177–78

Christian Democrats (CDU), 262,
267–68, 273
Christina of Sweden, 36, 38 (fig.), 40
church-state separation (US), 331n9
cinema. *See* films; Riefenstahl, Leni
cinematographic technique,
Riefenstahl's, 231–33, 236–38
civic participation, 82–83
civic service, inherited power and,
44–46, 54
civilian power, 326
Clinton, Bill, 323
Clinton, Hillary Rodham, 332n33;
expectation of "gender-
appropriate" behavior, 319–20;
foreign and defense policy,
327–28; gendering the presidential
campaigns, 323; leadership style,
19–20; pantsuits, 7; transactional
leadership style, 326–28; women's
rights doctrine, 329
clothing and makeup. *See* fashion
coalition governments, 262–63, 269–
71, 275
colonial life, the role of unmarried
Victorian women, 150
Compact magazine, 313
complementary of the sexes in *Die
Familie Seldorf*, 118–21
complementary relations, 275–76
*Conversationslexikon für das deutsche
Volk*, 172
corporate domain. *See* neoliberal
self-referentiality
coup by Catherine the Great, 39
Crepaz, Adele, 166, 169
critical reading and critical writing, 60,
63, 68–69, 74–77
cross-dressing women: Catherine the
Great's coup, 39; in *Die Familie
Seldorf*, 118, 124; gender role
inversion in *Talestris*, 40–44;
political potentiation of women,
48, 57n30; in *Talestris*, 49–50
cultural construction of motherlove,
166–69

death, degeneration of politics as, 102